# Counseling Theories and Techniques for Rehabilitation and Mental Health Professionals

**Fong Chan, PhD, CRC,** received his PhD in rehabilitation counseling psychology from the University of Wisconsin–Madison in 1983. He is a full professor and director of clinical training (PhD Rehabilitation Psychology Program) in the Department of Rehabilitation Psychology and Special Education, University of Wisconsin–Madison. He is also the codirector of the Rehabilitation Research and Training Center on Evidence-Based Vocational Rehabilitation Practices. Before joining the faculty at University of Wisconsin–Madison in 1992, he was on the faculty in the Department of Psychology at the Illinois Institute of Technology for 4 years and the Department of Rehabilitation Counseling Psychology at the University of Texas Southwestern Medical Center for 5 years. He is a certified rehabilitation counselor, a licensed psychologist, and a fellow in the American Psychological Association. Dr. Chan has more than 30 years of experience conducting applied rehabilitation research in the topical areas of psychosocial interventions, demand-side employment, transition and postsecondary education, evidence-based practice, and research methodologies. Dr. Chan has published over 250 refereed journal articles and book chapters. In addition, he is the editor of four textbooks: *Case Management for Rehabilitation Health Professionals; Counseling Theories and Techniques for Rehabilitation Health Professionals; Understanding Psychosocial Adjustment to Chronic Illness and Disability: A Handbook for Evidence-Based Practitioners in Rehabilitation;* and *Certified Rehabilitation Counselor Examination Preparation: A Concise Guide to the Foundations of Rehabilitation Counseling.* He also served as the co-chair for the U.S. Department of Education Rehabilitation Services Administration's 33rd Institute for Rehabilitation Issues on Evidence-Based Practice.

**Norman L. Berven, PhD,** is professor emeritus in the Department of Rehabilitation Psychology and Special Education, University of Wisconsin–Madison, having served on the faculty since 1976, and he has chaired the rehabilitation psychology program for more than 20 years. He previously held positions as a rehabilitation counselor at the San Mateo County Mental Health Service in California (now the San Mateo County Behavioral Health and Recovery Services), as a research associate at the ICD Rehabilitation and Research Center (now the Institute for Career Development) in New York City, and as an assistant professor at Seton Hall University. He is licensed as a psychologist and as a professional counselor by the state of Wisconsin and also holds the certified rehabilitation counselor credential. He is a fellow in the American Psychological Association and is a member of several professional associations in counseling, rehabilitation counseling, assessment, and counselor education. He has published more than 80 journal articles and book chapters on topics related to rehabilitation counseling, assessment, and counselor education and training. He has received the James F. Garrett Award for a Distinguished Career in Rehabilitation Research from the American Rehabilitation Counseling Association (ARCA), the ARCA Distinguished Professional Award, the American Counseling Association (ACA) Research Award, and 10 ARCA Research Awards. He has also received distinguished alumni awards from the Graduate Programs in Rehabilitation at the University of Iowa and from the rehabilitation psychology program at the University of Wisconsin–Madison.

**Kenneth R. Thomas, DEd,** received his undergraduate and graduate education at Penn State University and his psychoanalytic education at the Center for Psychoanalytic Study in Chicago. Prior to receiving his doctoral degree, Dr. Thomas worked as a rehabilitation counselor for the Pennsylvania Bureau of Vocational Rehabilitation at the Pennsylvania Rehabilitation Center in Johnstown. Following a 1-year academic appointment in the counselor education program at Penn State, he joined the faculty at the University of Wisconsin–Madison. At Wisconsin, he held several administrative positions, including chair of the Department of Rehabilitation Psychology and Special Education, chair of the Department of Therapeutic Science, and director of the Educational and Psychological Training Center within the School of Education. He was awarded professor emeritus status at the university in 2002. He has published three books and more than 125 refereed journal articles and book chapters in the areas of counseling, rehabilitation, disability, and psychoanalysis. He is a past president of the American Rehabilitation Counseling Association (ARCA), a fellow in three divisions of the American Psychological Association, and a recipient of the James Garrett Award for a Distinguished Career in Rehabilitation Research from the ARCA. He has also received the University of Wisconsin School of Education Distinguished Faculty Achievement Award, and he holds Alumni Fellow status at Penn State University.

# Counseling Theories and Techniques for Rehabilitation and Mental Health Professionals

## Second Edition

**Fong Chan, PhD, CRC**
**Norman L. Berven, PhD**
**Kenneth R. Thomas, DEd**

*Editors*

SPRINGER PUBLISHING COMPANY

NEW YORK

Springer Publishing Company, LLC
11 West 42nd Street
New York, NY 10036
www.springerpub.com

*Acquisitions Editor*: Sheri W. Sussman
*Composition*: Exeter Premedia Services Private Ltd.

*ISBN*: 978-0-8261-9867-9
*e-book ISBN*: 978-0-8261-9868-6
*Instructor's Manual ISBN*: 978-0-8261-2287-2
*Instructor's PowerPoint Slides ISBN*: 978-0-8261-2289-6

**Instructor's Materials: Instructors may request supplements by e-mailing textbook@springerpub .com**

15 16 17 / 5 4 3 2 1

The author and the publisher of this Work have made every effort to use sources believed to be reliable to provide information that is accurate and compatible with the standards generally accepted at the time of publication. The author and publisher shall not be liable for any special, consequential, or exemplary damages resulting, in whole or in part, from the readers' use of, or reliance on, the information contained in this book. The publisher has no responsibility for the persistence or accuracy of URLs for external or third-party Internet websites referred to in this publication and does not guarantee that any content on such websites is, or will remain, accurate or appropriate.

**Library of Congress Cataloging-in-Publication Data**
Counseling theories and techniques for rehabilitation and mental health professionals / [edited by] Fong Chan, PhD, CRC, Norman L. Berven, PhD, and Kenneth R. Thomas, DEd.—Second edition.
    p. ; cm
    ISBN 978-0-8261-9867-9
    1. People with disabilities—Rehabilitation.    2. Rehabilitation counseling.
    I. Chan, Fong.
    HV1568.C65 2015
    362.17′86—dc23
                                                                        2014039784

Printed in the United States of America by McNaughton & Gunn.

*This book is dedicated to the authors of the individual chapters,
a highly competent and dedicated group of colleagues, including a
number of former doctoral students in rehabilitation counseling/
psychology at the University of Wisconsin–Madison. We sincerely
appreciate their contributions to this book and their patience and
support in the long process of bringing this project to fruition.*

# Contents

## PART V: PROFESSIONAL ISSUES

# Contributors

**Abigail Akande, MS**   Doctoral Candidate, Department of Disability and Psychoeducational Studies, University of Arizona, Tucson, Arizona

**Norman L. Berven, PhD**   Professor Emeritus, Department of Rehabilitation Psychology and Special Education, University of Wisconsin–Madison, Madison, Wisconsin

**Jill L. Bezyak, PhD**   Associate Professor, Department of Human Rehabilitative Services, University of Northern Colorado, Greeley, Colorado

**Malachy Bishop, PhD, CRC**   Professor and Coordinator of the Doctoral Program, Department of Early Childhood, Special Education, and Rehabilitation Counseling, University of Kentucky, Lexington, Kentucky

**John Blake, PhD**   Assistant Professor, Department of Counseling, Rehabilitation Counseling, and Counseling Psychology, West Virginia University, Morgantown, West Virginia

**Elizabeth A. Boland, PhD, CRC**   Associate Professor and Director, Graduate Program in Rehabilitation Counseling, Western Washington University, Everett, Washington

**Jessica Brooks, PhD, CRC**   Assistant Professor, Department of Disability and Addiction Rehabilitation, University of North Texas, Denton, Texas

**Tierra A. Caldwell**   Doctoral Student, Department of Educational Psychology, Counseling, and Special Education, Penn State University, University Park, Pennsylvania

**Elizabeth da Silva Cardoso, PhD**   Professor and Director of the Mental Health Counseling and Rehabilitation Counseling Programs, Hunter College, City University of New York, New York, New York

**Fong Chan, PhD, CRC**   Professor, Department of Rehabilitation Psychology and Special Education, University of Wisconsin–Madison, Madison, Wisconsin

**Julie A. Chronister, PhD**   Associate Professor and Director of the Rehabilitation Counseling Program, Department of Counseling, San Francisco State University, San Francisco, California

**Patrick Corrigan, PsyD**   Distinguished Professor of Psychology, Illinois Institute of Technology, Chicago, Illinois

**Maria-Cristina Cruza-Guet, PhD**   Lecturer, Department of Psychiatry, Program for Recovery & Community Health, Yale School of Medicine, New Haven, Connecticut

**Charles Edmund Degeneffe, PhD**   Professor and Coordinator of the Rehabilitation Counseling Program, Interwork Institute, San Diego State University, San Diego, California

**Nicole Ditchman, PhD, CRC, LCPC**   Assistant Professor, Department of Psychology, Illinois Institute of Technology, Chicago, Illinois

**Mary O'Connor Drout, PhD**   Program Director, Rehabilitation Counseling Program, Adler University, Chicago, Illinois

**Allison R. Fleming, PhD**   Assistant Professor, Department of Early Childhood, Special Education, and Rehabilitation, University of Kentucky, Lexington, Kentucky

**Rochelle V. Habeck, PhD**   Research Consultant, Habeck and Associates, Kalamazoo, Michigan

**Debra A. Harley, PhD**   Provost's Distinguished Professor, Department of Early Childhood, Special Education, and Rehabilitation, University of Kentucky, Lexington, Kentucky

**Linda E. Hedenblad, MSE**   Linda Hedenblad Consulting, Madison, Wisconsin

**James T. Herbert, PhD, CRC, LPC**   Professor and Program Coordinator, Rehabilitation and Human Services, Department of Educational Psychology, Counseling, and Special Education, Penn State University, University Park, Pennsylvania

**Garrett Huck, MS**   Doctoral Candidate, Department of Rehabilitation Psychology and Special Education, University of Wisconsin–Madison, Madison, Wisconsin

**Ruth A. Huebner, PhD**    Child Welfare Researcher, Kentucky Department of Community-Based Services, Frankfort, Kentucky

**Ebonee T. Johnson, PhD, CRC**    Assistant Professor, Department of Rehabilitation and Disability Studies, Southern University–Baton Rouge, Baton Rouge, Louisiana

**Nev Jones, PhD**    Postdoctoral Fellow, Medical Anthropology, Stanford University, Stanford, California

**Brian Kamnetz, PhD**    Assistant Professor, Department of Speech, Hearing, and Rehabilitation Services, Mankato State University, Mankato, Minnesota

**John F. Kosciulek, PhD**    Professor, Office of Rehabilitation and Disability Studies, Department of Counseling, Educational Psychology and Special Education, Michigan State University, East Lansing, Michigan

**Eun-Jeong Lee, PhD, CRC, LCPC**    Associate Professor, Department of Psychology, Illinois Institute of Technology, Chicago, Illinois

**Hanoch Livneh, PhD, CRC**    Emeritus Professor, Department of Counselor Education, Portland State University, Portland, Oregon

**Michelle C. Lizotte, MS**    Doctoral Student, Office of Rehabilitation and Disability Studies, Department of Counseling, Educational Psychology and Special Education, Michigan State University, East Lansing, Michigan

**Ruth Torkelson Lynch, PhD**    Emeritus Professor, Department of Rehabilitation Psychology and Special Education, University of Wisconsin–Madison, Madison, Wisconsin

**Michele Mahr, MS**    Doctoral Candidate, Department of Rehabilitation Psychology and Special Education, University of Wisconsin–Madison, Madison, Wisconsin

**Trevor J. Manthey, MSW**    Doctoral Candidate, University of Kansas, and Principal, Manthey Consulting, Lawrence, Kansas

**Erin Martz, PhD, CRC**    Researcher, Veterans Administration Portland Healthcare System; Rehabilitation Counselor, Rehability; Vocational Consultant, Social Security Administration, Portland, Oregon

**Erin Moser, MS**    Doctoral Candidate, Department of Rehabilitation Psychology and Special Education, University of Wisconsin–Madison, Madison, Wisconsin

**Elias Mpofu, PhD**    Professor and Head, Rehabilitation Counseling Discipline, Faculty of Health Sciences, The University of Sydney, New South Wales, Australia

**Deirdre O'Sullivan, PhD** Assistant Professor, Department of Educational Psychology, Counseling, and Special Education, Penn State University, University Park, Pennsylvania

**Brian N. Phillips, PhD** Assistant Professor, Department of Rehabilitation Psychology and Special Education, University of Wisconsin–Madison, Madison, Wisconsin

**Warren R. Rule, PhD** (Deceased) Professor Emeritus, Department of Rehabilitation Counseling, Virginia Commonwealth University, Richmond, Virginia

**John See, PhD** Professor Emeritus, Department of Rehabilitation and Counseling, University of Wisconsin–Stout, Menomonie, Wisconsin

**Linda R. Shaw, PhD** Professor and Department Head, Department of Disability and Psychoeducational Studies, University of Arizona, Tucson, Arizona

**Jerome Siller, PhD** Professor Emeritus, Department of Psychology, New York University, New York, New York

**Susan Miller Smedema, PhD** Assistant Professor, Department of Rehabilitation Psychology and Special Education, University of Wisconsin–Madison, Madison, Wisconsin

**Jennifer L. Stoll, PhD** Clinical Neuropsychologist, Mercy Institute of Neuroscience, Mercy Health System, Janesville, Wisconsin

**David R. Strauser, PhD** Professor, Department of Kinesiology and Community Health, University of Illinois at Urbana–Champaign, Champaign, Illinois

**Timothy N. Tansey, PhD, CRC** Assistant Professor, Department of Rehabilitation Psychology and Special Education, University of Wisconsin–Madison, Madison, Wisconsin

**Kenneth R. Thomas, DEd** Professor Emeritus, Department of Rehabilitation Psychology and Special Education, University of Wisconsin–Madison, Madison, Wisconsin

**Robert A. Williams, PhD** Associate Professor, Department of Counseling, San Francisco State University, San Francisco, California

**Arnold Wolf, PhD** Professor, Department of Counseling, Hunter College, City University of New York, New York, New York

**Jodi Wolff, MSSW** Director of Clinical Services, Muscular Dystrophy Association; Doctoral Student, Department of Disability and Psychoeducational Studies, University of Arizona, Tucson, Arizona

# Preface

The purpose of the second edition of this book is to provide state-of-the-art treatment relevant to the dominant theories and techniques of counseling and psychotherapy from a rehabilitation and mental health counseling perspective. In all cases, the chapters were contributed by rehabilitation health professionals and scholars who have special, if not extraordinary, expertise and national visibility in the content areas addressed. The book is intended for practitioners as well as for upper-level undergraduates and graduate students in clinical rehabilitation counseling and psychology and in other rehabilitation health care disciplines, such as mental health counseling, social work, nursing, occupational therapy, physical therapy, speech and language therapy, and recreation. The chapters are written from a clinical rehabilitation perspective, using rehabilitation examples when appropriate. Authors include a case example in each chapter to highlight the application of theories and techniques in working with rehabilitation-specific problems of people with chronic illnesses and disabilities. In this second edition, the authors focus on scientific evidence supporting the effectiveness of the theory and technique used in their chapters.

It is not our philosophy that people with chronic illnesses and disabilities necessarily require different theories or interventions than nondisabled people. In fact, the opposite is true. People with chronic illnesses and disabilities or the agencies serving them may, however, present special needs or have special goals that require certain emphases and modifications in the application of particular theories and techniques. Although general textbooks on the theories and techniques of counseling and psychotherapy provide excellent discussions of those approaches, they need, in our opinion, to be supplemented with material that is specific to applications in rehabilitation settings. It is this need, especially, that this book attempts to fulfill.

We are pleased to be part of this particular project for several reasons. First, it gave us an opportunity to work with rehabilitation and mental health professionals from around the United States and Australia, who are clearly among the most esteemed leaders and academic scholars in our field. We are proud that many of these authors were once graduate students at the University of Wisconsin–Madison, and others have been professional associates of ours for many years. Some have worked with us in the past on scholarly projects, and we have known others through our work with professional associations. Still others we knew initially only by reputation, but we are now extremely pleased to have had the opportunity to work with them on this volume.

Another reason for our pleasure in undertaking this project is our love of counseling. To us, counseling is the core of the rehabilitation and recovery process, and it is, in all its variant aspects, the reason why most students and professionals are attracted to the field. The provision of vocational, psychosocial, and mental health counseling services to persons with chronic illnesses and disabilities is the unique contribution that rehabilitation professionals, generally, make to any multidisciplinary (or even interdisciplinary) effort to improve the lives of people with disabilities. We sincerely hope that the offerings in this book will not only excite and inform the reader about the counseling function and process, but also will ultimately benefit the literally thousands of clients with whom the readers will eventually have contact.

**An Instructor's Manual and PowerPoint slides are also available to supplement the text. To obtain an electronic copy of these materials, faculty should contact Springer Publishing Company at textbook@springerpub.com.**

*Fong Chan, PhD, CRC*
*Norman L. Berven, PhD*
*Kenneth R. Thomas, DEd*

## An Introduction to Counseling for Rehabilitation and Mental Health Professionals

*Norman L. Berven, Kenneth R. Thomas, and Fong Chan*

As stated in the Preface, the purpose of this volume is to provide state-of-the-art treatment that pertains to the dominant theories and techniques of counseling and psychotherapy from a rehabilitation perspective. This initial chapter presents several introductory topics, including definitions and terminology, the importance of counseling in professional practice in rehabilitation, a historical context for understanding theories of counseling and psychotherapy, and the efficacy of counseling and psychotherapy. In addition, a brief overview of the remainder of the book is provided.

### DEFINITIONS AND TERMINOLOGY

#### Counseling and Psychotherapy

*Counseling* and *psychotherapy* are commonly used terms, but they often mean different things to different people. Generally, *counseling* and *psychotherapy* are defined as encompassing a counseling relationship in which a professional interacts with one or more individuals seeking assistance in dealing with difficulties and in making changes in their lives and, in the context of rehabilitation settings, the individuals seeking assistance have disabilities or other special needs. The process may occur not only in a traditional office setting but also in a wide variety of community settings that provide opportunities for interaction between professionals and individuals who are seeking assistance.

According to the *Scope of Practice for Rehabilitation Counseling*, developed by the Commission on Rehabilitation Counselor Certification (CRCC, n.d., p. 2), counseling as a treatment intervention is defined as follows:

> The application of cognitive, affective, behavioral, and systemic counseling strategies which include developmental, wellness, pathologic, and multicultural principles of human behavior. Such interventions are specifically implemented in the context of a professional counseling relationship and may include, but are not limited to, appraisal; individual, group, marriage, and family counseling and psychotherapy; the diagnostic description and treatment of persons with mental emotional, and behavioral disorders or disabilities; guidance and consulting to facilitate normal growth and development, including educational and career development; the utilization of functional assessments and career counseling for persons requesting assistance in adjusting to a disability or handicapping condition; referrals; consulting; and research.

Counseling and psychotherapy share much in common with other human interactions that individuals may find helpful when they are struggling with problems, life decisions, or desired changes in their lives, whether the interactions occur with professionals, family members, or friends. A variety of rehabilitation health professionals, other than those with the specific titles of "counselor" or "psychotherapist," attempt to understand the behavior and needs of others and to collaborate with them in devising strategies to accomplish change, including rehabilitation medicine specialists and other physicians, occupational therapists, physical therapists, speech and language therapists, audiologists, rehabilitation teachers, orientation and mobility specialists, and recreation therapists. The effectiveness of services provided by rehabilitation health professionals depends on the professionals' success in accomplishing a variety of professional tasks, such as the following: establishing a therapeutic working relationship with individuals served; communicating with individuals in facilitative, helpful ways; obtaining information from individuals in a comprehensive and thorough manner; helping clients to tell their stories and explain their problems and needs; understanding and conceptualizing behavior and problems in ways that will facilitate treatment and service planning; and facilitating follow-through on commitments and compliance with treatment and service plans that individuals have decided to pursue. All of the aforementioned professional tasks may be conceptualized as components of counseling and related interactions, and professionals from a variety of rehabilitation health professions can thus benefit from an understanding of counseling theories and techniques.

Distinctions between the terms *counseling* and *psychotherapy* are ambiguous and have often been controversial. Some authors, such as Gelso and Fretz (1992), suggest that psychotherapy, in contrast to counseling, has greater depth and intensity, with typically longer duration, addressing personality reorganization and reconstruction, as opposed to the more reality-based problems addressed in counseling. Some would also suggest that psychotherapy is used to provide treatment or services to individuals with severe pathology, whereas counseling is applied to more "normal" problems of living, decision making, and personal growth, such as the often-quoted views of Tyler (1958). In addition, Sharf (2012) points out that terminology sometimes varies according to the setting in which practice occurs, with the term *psychotherapy* being more popular in medical settings and *counseling* in educational and human service settings. However, many authors (e.g., Patterson, 1986) have long advocated that the definitions of psychotherapy and counseling overlap substantially and that the distinctions between the two are at best differences of degree, and at worst, arbitrary and meaningless. The views of Patterson and other authors will be followed here; the terms *counseling*, *psychotherapy*, and *therapy* are used interchangeably throughout the book.

## Individuals Seeking Assistance From Rehabilitation and Mental Health Professionals

Different terms are also commonly used to refer to individuals engaged in treatment or service with rehabilitation health professionals, including *patient*, *client*, *consumer*, and *customer*. *Patient* has been traditionally used by physicians, nurses, and other medical professionals, and by practitioners in inpatient hospital treatment and in mental health. In addition, practitioners who identify themselves as psychotherapists are more likely to use *patient* than those identifying themselves as counselors. *Client* has been commonly used in rehabilitation counseling and in community-based rehabilitation programs, with *consumer* emerging more recently and *customer* even more recently. There are different connotations associated with the various terms. For example, *patient* may imply a medical model to some professionals in conceptualizing needs, with a concomitant tendency on the part of the people receiving services to defer to service providers in making treatment and service decisions. In contrast, the other alternative terms may be viewed as implying greater sharing of decision making or even complete control of decisions on the part of the individual served. Advances in the disability rights movement, emphasizing consumerism and empowerment (e.g., Campbell, 1991; Holmes, 1993), have heightened sensitivity to terminology and its effects on people with disabilities, and the newer terms of *consumer* and *customer* have thus emerged. Terminology has become highly controversial. For example, Thomas (1993) has argued passionately that the term *client* is preferable, whereas Nosek (1993) has argued with similar passion that the term *consumer* should be used. Partly for historical reasons, including attempts to preserve some of the terminology used by theorists in their original work, the terms *client* and *consumer*, and sometimes *patient*, are used interchangeably, and it is hoped that no readers will be offended by any of the terminology used.

## IMPORTANCE OF COUNSELING AS A PROFESSIONAL FUNCTION

Rehabilitation counseling is one profession in which considerable research has been devoted to empirically defining roles, functions, and knowledge and skill domains for professional practice, and counseling has repeatedly emerged as an essential function (e.g., Leahy, Shapson, & Wright, 1987; Leahy, Szymanski, &

Linkowski, 1993; Muthard & Salomone, 1969; Rubin et al., 1984). In the seminal role and function study in rehabilitation counseling, Muthard and Salomone (1969) reported that state vocational rehabilitation counselors divide their time roughly into thirds: one third to counseling and guidance; one third to clerical work, planning, recording, and placement; and one third to professional growth, public relations, reporting, resource development, travel, and supervisory and administrative duties. In a recent study, Leahy, Chan, Sung, and Kim (2013) surveyed certified rehabilitation counselors to examine the perceived importance of knowledge areas underlying credentialing in rehabilitation counseling, identifying four essential domains: (a) job placement, consultation, and assessment; (b) case management and community resources; (c) individual, group, and family counseling and evidence-based practice; and (d) medical, functional, and psychosocial aspects of disability. The latter two represent knowledge domains (counseling and psychosocial interventions) in counseling and are related specifically to the content of this book.

The knowledge domains identified by Leahy et al. (2013) reflect the current practice of rehabilitation counseling and clinical rehabilitation counseling in private for-profit, private not-for-profit, and public rehabilitation settings. Regardless of practice settings, however, it is well documented that vocational adjustment is greatly affected by psychosocial issues and needs (O'Brien, Heppner, Flores, & Bikos, 1997). Not surprisingly, Rubin et al. (1984) found that affective counseling was one of the most important functions of rehabilitation counselors and that counselors spend considerable time focusing on the psychological counseling process aimed at changing the client's feelings and thoughts regarding self and others.

Because of the generic professional counselor licensure movement in the United States, many rehabilitation counseling programs are changing from requiring 48 credit hours for master's degrees to 60 credit hours. In a move that will certainly accelerate this trend, the Council on Rehabilitation Education (CORE) and the Council for Accreditation of Counseling and Related Educational Programs (CACREP) has developed a new set of standards, requiring 60 credits of graduate study, for the accreditation of graduate programs in clinical rehabilitation counseling. Nearly all states have passed legislation to regulate licensed professional counselors that includes rehabilitation counselors, and rehabilitation counselors are expected to have a solid grounding in theories and techniques for changing human behavior in a rehabilitation and mental health counseling context. Similarly, many other rehabilitation health professionals, including rehabilitation nurses, occupational health nurses, social workers, and occupational, physical, speech and language, and recreation therapists, have become increasingly aware of the effects of psychosocial factors on rehabilitation outcomes and the importance of one-to-one and group interactions in professional practice. As a result, professional education programs in various rehabilitation health professions have begun to incorporate interviewing techniques, counseling interventions, and psychosocial adjustment content into their training curricula.

## HISTORICAL CONTEXT FOR THEORIES OF COUNSELING AND PSYCHOTHERAPY

Psychological, sociocultural, and systemic theories typically guide the process of counseling and psychotherapy, facilitating the understanding of behavior and the formulation of intervention strategies that hold promise for accomplishing the desired changes. In fact, it is difficult to imagine a practitioner being able to function with any degree of effectiveness without the guidance of at least some basic theoretical direction. As stated by Prochaska and Norcross (1999, p. 5):

> Without a guiding theory or system of psychotherapy, clinicians would be vulnerable, directionless creatures, bombarded with literally hundreds of impressions and pieces of information in a single session . . . theory describes the clinical phenomena, delimits the amount of relevant information, organizes that information, and integrates it all into a coherent body of knowledge that prioritizes our conceptualization and directs our treatment.

### Early Historical Roots

The historical development of counseling and psychotherapy has been elaborated in a recent book by Norcross, Vandenbos, and Freedheim (2011). Arguably, the first psychotherapeutic treatment of a potential rehabilitation client took place outside of Vienna between 1880 and 1882. The "counselor" was a Viennese physician named Joseph Breuer, and the patient was Bertha Peppenheim. Bertha, who is better known as Anna O, presented an array of symptoms, including paraphasia, a convergent squint, severe disturbances of vision, paralyses of her upper and lower extremities, eating and drinking disturbances, and a severe nervous cough (Breuer & Freud, 1893–1895/1966; Freud, 1910/1955). The treatment itself, which consisted primarily of hypnosis and catharsis, provided only temporary relief of Bertha's "conversion hysteria," and she experienced several relapses and hospitalizations after the premature termination of the treatment (Jones, 1953; Summers, 1999). However, the long-term ramifications of the treatment would eventually prove to exceed the wildest dreams of either Bertha or the physician. Breuer, who was a close friend, mentor, and early benefactor of Freud, was even credited by Freud, at least initially (e.g., Freud, 1910/1955), for the creation of psychoanalysis. During the treatment, Bertha herself originated such famous terms as "the talking cure" and "chimney sweeping," thus demonstrating remarkable insight into the dynamics of these early psychotherapeutic interventions and providing her own very substantial contribution to counseling and psychotherapy. Although the treatment itself was essentially a disaster, with Bertha having a hysterical pregnancy with Breuer as the alleged father, and Breuer abandoning the treatment in fear of losing his professional reputation (Jones, 1953), the basis was laid for Freud's later, lifelong development of his theories and therapies of psychoanalysis.

One of Freud's dreams was that the benefits of psychoanalysis could eventually be spread to the general populace by using a cadre of trained, nonmedical therapists. It was, in fact, Freud's strong belief that psychoanalytically trained "lay persons" rather than physicians would make the best therapists (Freud, 1926/1959). Although this dream was never realized, especially in the United States, where a very restrictive medical community virtually prevented non-physicians from receiving psychoanalytic training under the auspices of the American Psychoanalytic Association, Bertha's "talking cure" provided the basis for a variety of counseling and psychotherapeutic interventions, both psychoanalytic and otherwise.

From a rehabilitation standpoint, Bertha would have been, at least eventually, a remarkable success story. Despite her subsequent hospitalizations, she went on to have a distinguished career as a social worker, feminist, and writer, and is, in fact, one of the most important individuals in the history of European social welfare. Although modern-day rehabilitation professionals use methods that are vastly different in scope and form from those used by Breuer, the goal of helping distressed individuals live more productive and happy lives is essentially the same.

### More Recent Evolution of Theoretical Approaches

From the early roots of psychoanalysis, a variety of theoretical approaches to counseling and psychotherapy have developed, as indicated in a recent review by Lambert (2013). Garfield and Bergin (1994, p. 3), in an earlier review of the evolution of theoretical approaches, indicated that Freud's psychoanalytic theory, along with derivatives due to some of his followers, such as Alfred Adler, Carl Jung, Karen Horney, and Harry Stack Sullivan, was "from the end of the nineteenth century to about the 1960s, the dominant influence." The client-centered or person-centered theoretical approach, developed by Carl Rogers (1942), represented one of the major early departures from psychoanalytic theory, emphasizing the potential of people to self-actualize and the therapeutic qualities of empathy, unconditional positive regard, and genuineness that could nourish and release this positive growth potential toward constructive personality and behavior change. The emergence of behavior therapy, although beginning many years before, did not gain popularity until the 1950s, with the publication of Wolpe's (1958) book on reciprocal inhibition as an approach to psychotherapy. In the 1960s, the community mental health movement brought a new focus on the mental health needs of low-income people, along with community-based treatment and crisis intervention. Long-term psychotherapy, particularly psychoanalytic approaches, was generally used primarily by middle- and upper-income people, and briefer forms of counseling and psychotherapy became more popular, with the rise of many different theoretical orientations.

A proliferation of approaches to counseling and psychotherapy has emerged over the years. Garfield (1982) identified 125 different approaches to psychotherapy in existence in the 1960s, and in the 1980s, Herink (1980) identified more than 250 and Kazdin (1986) estimated more than 400, with most having received little or no systematic empirical evaluation. Adding to the variety of theoretical approaches in use is the popularity of eclecticism among practitioners, drawing from and integrating concepts and techniques from multiple theoretical approaches, rather than adhering to a single approach. Jensen, Bergin, and Greaves (1990) surveyed practitioners in psychiatry, clinical psychology, social work, and marriage and family therapy and found that 68% of respondents identified themselves as eclectics. Thus, a wide variety of theoretical approaches to counseling and psychotherapy are in use by professional practitioners in rehabilitation and health settings, with many drawing from and attempting to integrate multiple approaches in their work.

Prochaska and Norcross (1999), compiling data from three different surveys (Norcross, Karg, & Prochaska, 1997; Norcross, Strausser, & Missar, 1988; Watkins, Lopez, Campbell, & Himmell, 1986), identified predominant theoretical orientations of practitioners in counseling and psychotherapy in the United States, including clinical psychologists, counseling psychologists, psychiatrists, social workers, and counselors. As found in other studies, eclectic orientations were the most frequently indicated among all of the respondent groups, varying from 27% of the clinical psychologists to 53% of the psychiatrists. Psychoanalytic/psychodynamic orientations were indicated by a large number of psychiatrists (35%) and social workers (33%) and also by a number of clinical psychologists (18%), counseling psychologists (12%), and counselors (11%). Cognitive behavioral orientations tended to be most predominant among psychologists and counselors, with 27% of clinical psychologists indicating either cognitive or behavioral orientations, in addition to 19% of counseling psychologists and 16% of counselors. Humanistic orientations tended to be most predominant among counseling psychologists and counselors, with 21% of counselors indicating either Rogerian/person-centered or existential/humanistic orientations, in addition to 14% of counseling psychologists.

Because large numbers of practitioners in counseling and psychotherapy indicate that their orientations are eclectic, it should also be informative to ask eclectic practitioners about the theoretical orientations that they draw on in forming their eclectic orientations. Jensen et al. (1990) asked this question of the 283 eclectic practitioners in their study and found a mean of 4.4 theories identified as influential in their practice, including dynamic (72%), cognitive (54%), behavioral (49%), and humanistic (42%), among those theories most frequently identified. On the basis of the available evidence, it would appear that a diverse array of theoretical orientations influences the practice of counseling and psychotherapy. In addition, it would appear that individuals who follow an eclectic orientation may often be influenced by diverse theoretical orientations themselves, suggesting the importance of understanding a variety of different theories of counseling and psychotherapy.

## EFFICACY OF COUNSELING AND PSYCHOTHERAPY

Over the past several decades, psychotherapy researchers have devoted concerted efforts to examining the efficacy of counseling and psychotherapy. Wampold (2001) examined thousands of studies regarding the efficacy of psychotherapy using meta-analysis and concluded that at least 70% of psychotherapeutic effects are due to common factors, whereas only 8% are due to specific ingredients. The remaining 22%, which is unexplained, is due in part to client differences. Common factors are ingredients that all forms of counseling and psychotherapy share in common, existing across all forms and types as they are typically practiced. For Wampold (2001), the common factors include goal setting, empathic listening, and such considerations as the following:

- Allegiance (i.e., the degree to which the practitioner is committed to the belief that the therapy is beneficial to the client)
- The therapeutic alliance, defined pantheoretically by Wampold to include
  - The client's affective relationship with the therapist
  - The client's motivation and ability to accomplish work collaboratively with the therapist
  - The therapist's empathic response to and involvement with the client
  - Client and therapist agreement about the goals and tasks of therapy

Conversely, specific ingredients, as distinguished from the common factors, include actions or techniques that are both essential and unique to a particular theory. Wampold (2001) has clearly demonstrated an important empirical link between common factors in the counseling relationship and outcomes. However, counselors must still formulate hypotheses about client problems and facilitate interactions with clients based on certain theoretical orientations. It can be argued that not every counselor will be comfortable with only one form or approach to counseling and psychotherapy. Conversely, the same is probably true for clients seeking assistance from rehabilitation counseling professionals. In order to maximize the effects of the common factors, tailoring counseling interventions to the individual differences and needs of rehabilitation clients might be critical. In a multimodal way, the method of treatment would depend, at the very least, on the needs, context, expectations, personality, and problems of the individual seeking help, and methods are carefully tailored and custom made (Lazarus, 1981). The effectiveness of the multimodal method will depend on (a) the implementation of the correct techniques in the proper manner and (b) the practitioner's ability to be an "authentic chameleon," who can change according to the needs of the client for a counselor or therapist who is directive, supportive, reflective, cold, warm, tepid, formal, or informal.

## OVERVIEW OF SECTIONS AND CHAPTERS

In providing coverage of counseling theories and techniques for rehabilitation health professionals, this book is organized into sections, with each section comprising multiple chapters. After the present introductory section, the following sections are included: Counseling Theories, Basic Techniques, Special Considerations, and Professional Issues.

The Counseling Theories section provides reviews of 10 different theoretical approaches to counseling and psychotherapy, with an emphasis on their

applications in rehabilitation settings. To the extent possible, each chapter is organized according to the following structure: History, Major Concepts, Theory of
Personality, Description of the Counseling Process, Rehabilitation Applications,
Case Study, Research Findings/Scientific Evidence, and Prominent Strengths
and Limitations. Thus, in addition to discussing the major components of each
theoretical approach, practical applications in rehabilitation health practice are
emphasized, including case examples to demonstrate applications. In addition,
in contrast to the first edition, a much greater emphasis has been placed on evidence-based practice in this second edition. As previously discussed, there are
literally hundreds of theoretical approaches to counseling and psychotherapy
that have been developed, so the selection of theories to include was not an easy
task. In general, an attempt was made to select the most prominent theoretical
approaches, while also attempting to represent a broad spectrum of theories that
have potential applicability in rehabilitation and mental health settings.

The Counseling Theories section is divided into three subsections, representing major categories of theoretical approaches. The first subsection is Humanistic
Approaches, including three chapters that cover person-centered, solution-
focused brief therapy and gestalt approaches. In addition to the term *humanistic*,
these approaches could also have been categorized as experiential, existential,
and relationship oriented. In addition, Seligman and Reichenberg (2014) categorized person-centered and gestalt theories as "treatment systems emphasizing
emotions and sensations," and Patterson and Watkins (1996) categorized person-
centered and gestalt approaches as "perceptual-phenomenological." Solution-
focused brief therapy is included in this Humanistic Approaches section, although
others may argue that it is not a particularly good fit in this section.

As indicated previously in this chapter, humanistic approaches would
appear to be most widely used by counselors and counseling psychologists,
among the various disciplines that practice counseling and psychotherapy.
Because of their application in initiating counseling relationships and facilitating
client exploration, including the exploration of emotions, some textbooks (e.g.,
James & Gilliland, 2003) place humanistic theories as the first theories covered.
In addition, humanistic theories, particularly person centered, emphasize the
relationship between counselor and client, and this emphasis has been influential in the evolution of many other theoretical approaches. Finally, gestalt theory
provides the basis for somatopsychology, which is one of the primary theoretical
approaches to understanding the impact of and adaptation to disability.

The second subsection under the Counseling Theories is Cognitive and
Behavioral Approaches, composed of four chapters covering behavioral and cognitive behavioral approaches, rational emotive behavior therapy, and trait–factor
theory. These four approaches are all systematic and action oriented, and authors
of textbooks on theories of counseling and psychotherapy have used terms such
as *action* (Corey, 2001) and *action-oriented* (James & Gilliland, 2003) therapies to
refer to this category of approaches. As indicated in the surveys of practitioners
discussed previously, cognitive and behavioral approaches are highly influential in the work of many clinical psychologists, counseling psychologists, and

counselors. Cognitive and behavioral approaches do not ignore emotions, but they tend to view emotions as a product of the ways that an "individual perceives, interprets, and assigns meaning" to events (Warwar & Greenberg, 2000, p. 585), and interventions designed to influence emotions are primarily directed at thoughts and behaviors. Trait–factor theory is related to the other cognitive and behavioral approaches in providing a systematic and rational approach to making career and life decisions, and although the trait–factor theory has not always been included in textbooks on theories of counseling and psychotherapy, it is included here because of the emphasis in many rehabilitation settings on facilitating client decisions and the frequent use of trait–factor principles by practitioners.

The third subsection under Counseling Theories is Psychodynamic Approaches, with two chapters covering psychoanalytic therapy and Adlerian therapy. Psychodynamic approaches follow from Sigmund Freud's psychoanalysis and, as in the surveys previously cited, are popular among contemporary practitioners in counseling and psychotherapy, particularly among psychiatrists and social workers, but also those from other disciplines. In addition, as discussed by Corey (2001, pp. 7–9), the psychoanalytic model has been a major influence on all of the other formal systems of psychotherapy. Some are basically extensions of psychoanalysis, others are modifications of analytic concepts and procedures, and still others are positions that emerged as a reaction against psychoanalysis. Many of the other theories of counseling and psychotherapy have borrowed and integrated principles and techniques from psychoanalytic approaches. Adlerian therapy was included because, as indicated by James and Gilliland (2003, p. 2), "of all of the psychoanalytic therapies, it is undoubtedly the most widely used and practiced approach." In addition, relative to other psychodynamic theories, Adlerian constructs and techniques have been frequently applied to understanding people with disabilities and to professional practice in rehabilitation settings, and it has been described as being highly consistent with the contemporary emphasis on client and consumer empowerment in rehabilitation (Bishop, 1999).

Part III, the Basic Techniques section, begins with a chapter on basic counseling skills, which are primary to many theoretical approaches to counseling, and a chapter on motivational interviewing techniques follows. Motivational interviewing has become very popular in rehabilitation and mental health settings to move individuals ahead in accomplishing their goals, and it uses a number of techniques that are covered in the basic counseling skills chapter. The next two chapters focus on group and family counseling, respectively, which are two types of counseling interactions that have a number of unique features relative to individual counseling. Finally, the section concludes with a chapter on career counseling, which represents an important specific component of counseling in rehabilitation settings.

Part IV, the Special Considerations section, describes counseling and service considerations that are related to specific types of disabilities. As was true in selecting counseling theories, there were many potential choices as to the specific types of disability and client groups to include. The chapters in the section address three broad disability groups: substance abuse, physical disabilities, and psychiatric disabilities. A fourth chapter in the section addresses multicultural considerations in counseling and psychotherapy, a particularly important and timely topic.

Part V, the Professional Issues section, focuses on two general topics that are directly related to the practice of counseling in rehabilitation settings. The first chapter focuses on clinical supervision, a critical function in monitoring and improving the quality of service and treatment provided to clients; in addition, supervision is a critical function in facilitating the professional development of practitioners as well as the learning and development of students preparing for professional practice careers. The second chapter in the section focuses on risk management in professional practice, including ethical issues.

In conclusion, this book provides an overview of prominent theoretical approaches to counseling and psychotherapy, along with some of the ways in which they can be applied in rehabilitation settings to assist people with disabilities. In addition, special considerations related to specific types of disabilities are presented, along with a discussion of selected professional issues related to professional practice. It is hoped that the content will be helpful to professional practitioners and to students in rehabilitation health professions in better understanding counseling and psychotherapy practice and the potential applications of theories and techniques in rehabilitation settings.

## REFERENCES

Bishop, M. (1999). Decision making in client-directed rehabilitation counseling: An Adlerian approach. *Journal of Applied Rehabilitation Counseling, 30*(2), 32–37.

Breuer, J., & Freud, S. (1966). Studies in hysteria. In J. Strachey (Ed. & Trans.), *The standard edition of the complete psychological works of Sigmund Freud* (Vol. 2). London, UK: Hogarth Press. (Original work published 1893–1895)

Campbell, J. F. (1991). The consumer movement and implications for vocational rehabilitation services. *Journal of Vocational Rehabilitation, 1*, 67–75.

Commission on Rehabilitation Counselor Certification (CRCC). (n.d.). *Scope of practice for rehabilitation counseling.* Rolling Meadows, IL: Author.

Corey, G. (2001). *Theory and practice of counseling and psychotherapy* (6th ed.). Belmont, CA: Brooks/Cole.

Freud, S. (1955). Five lectures on psycho-analysis. In J. Strachey (Ed. & Trans.), *The standard edition of the complete psychological works of Sigmund Freud* (Vol. 11). London, UK: Hogarth Press. (Original work published 1910)

Freud, S. (1959). The question of lay analysis: Conversations with an impartial person. In J. Strachey (Ed. & Trans.), *The standard edition of the complete psychological works of Sigmund Freud* (Vol. 20, pp. 183–258). London, UK: Hogarth Press. (Original work published 1926)

Garfield, S. L. (1982). Eclecticism and integration in psychotherapy. *Behavior Therapy, 13*, 610–623.

Garfield, S. L., & Bergin, A. E. (1994). Introduction and historical overview. In A. E. Bergin & S. L. Garfield (Eds.), *Handbook of psychotherapy and behavior change* (4th ed., pp. 3–18). New York, NY: Wiley.

Gelso, C. J., & Fretz, B. R. (1992). *Counseling psychology.* Ft. Worth, TX: Harcourt Brace.

Herink, R. (Ed.). (1980). *The psychotherapy handbook: The A to Z guide to more than 250 different therapies in use today.* New York, NY: Meridian/New American Library.

Holmes, G. E. (1993). The historical roots of the empowerment dilemma in vocational rehabilitation. *Journal of Disability Policy Studies, 4*(1), 1–19.

James, R. K., & Gilliland, B. E. (2003). *Theories and strategies in counseling and psychotherapy* (5th ed.). Boston, MA: Allyn & Bacon.

Jensen, J. P., Bergin, A. E., & Greaves, D. W. (1990). The meaning of eclecticism: New survey and analysis of components. *Professional Psychology: Research and Practice, 21*, 124–130.

Jones, E. (1953). *The life and work of Sigmund Freud* (Vol. 1). New York, NY: Basic Books.

Kazdin, A. E. (1986). Comparative outcome studies of psychotherapy: Methodological issues and strategies. *Journal of Consulting and Clinical Psychology, 54*, 95–105.

Lambert, M. J. (2013). Introduction and historical overview. In M. J. Lambert (Ed.), *Bergin and Garfield's handbook of psychotherapy and behavior change* (6th ed., pp. 3–20). Hoboken, NJ: Wiley.

Lazarus, A. (1981). *The practice of multimodal therapy*. New York, NY: McGraw-Hill.

Leahy, M. J., Chan, F., Sung, C., & Kim, M. (2013). Empirically derived test specifications for the certified rehabilitation counselor examination. *Rehabilitation Counseling Bulletin, 56*, 199–214.

Leahy, M. J., Shapson, P. R., & Wright, G. N. (1987). Rehabilitation counselor competencies by role and setting. *Rehabilitation Counseling Bulletin, 31*, 94–106.

Leahy, M. J., Szymanski, E. M., & Linkowski, D. (1993). Knowledge importance in rehabilitation counseling. *Rehabilitation Counseling Bulletin, 37*, 130–145.

Muthard, J. E., & Salomone, P. R. (1969). The roles and functions of the rehabilitation counselor. *Rehabilitation Counseling Bulletin, 13*, 81–168.

Norcross, J. C., Karg, R. S., & Prochaska, J. O. (1997). Clinical psychologists and managed care: Some data from the Division 12 membership. *Clinical Psychologist, 50*, 4–8.

Norcross, J. C., Strausser, D. J., & Missar, C. D. (1988). The process and outcomes of psychotherapists' personal treatment experiences. *Psychotherapy, 25*, 36–43.

Norcross, J. C., Vandenbos, G. R., & Freedheim, D. K. (2011). *History of psychotherapy: Continuity and change* (2nd ed.). Washington, DC: American Psychological Association.

Nosek, M. A. (1993). A response to Kenneth R. Thomas' commentary: Some observations on the use of the word "consumer." *Journal of Rehabilitation, 59*(2), 9–10.

O'Brien, K. M., Heppner, M. J., Flores, L. Y., & Bikos, L. H. (1997). The career counselling self-efficacy scale: Instrument development and training applications. *Journal of Counseling Psychology, 44*, 112.

Patterson, C. H. (1986). *Theories of counseling and psychotherapy* (4th ed.). New York, NY: Harper & Row.

Patterson, C. H., & Watkins, C. E., Jr. (1996). *Theories of psychotherapy* (5th ed.). Boston, MA: Allyn & Bacon.

Prochaska, J. O., & Norcross, J. C. (1999). *Systems of psychotherapy: A transtheoretical approach* (4th ed.). Pacific Grove, CA: Brooks/Cole.

Rogers, C. R. (1942). *Counseling and psychotherapy*. Boston, MA: Houghton Mifflin.

Rubin, S. E., Matkin, R. E., Ashley, J., Beardsley, M. M., May, V. R., & Onstott, K. (1984). Roles and functions of certified rehabilitation counselors. *Rehabilitation Counseling Bulletin, 27*, 199–224.

Seligman, L. W., & Reichenberg, L. W. (2014). *Theories of counseling and psychotherapy: Systems, strategies, and skills* (4th ed.). Boston, MA: Pearson.

Sharf, R. S. (2012). *Theories of psychotherapy & counseling: Concepts and cases* (5th ed.). Belmont, CA: Brooks/Cole.

Summers, F. L. (1999). *Transcending the self: An object relations model of psychoanalytic therapy*. Hillsdale, NJ: Analytic Press.

Thomas, K. R. (1993). Commentary: Some observations on the use of the word "consumer." *Journal of Rehabilitation, 59*(2), 6–8.

Tyler, L. E. (1958). Theoretical principles underlying the counseling process. *Journal of Counseling Psychology, 5*, 3–10.

Wampold, B. E. (2001). *The great psychotherapy debate: Models, methods, and findings.* Mahwah, NJ: Erlbaum.

Warwar, S., & Greenberg, L. S. (2000). Advances in theories of change and counseling. In S. D. Brown & R. W. Lent (Eds.), *Handbook of counseling psychology* (3rd ed.). New York, NY: Wiley.

Watkins, C. E., Lopez, F. G., Campbell, V. L., & Hummell, C. D. (1986). Contemporary counseling psychology: Results of a national survey. *Journal of Counseling Psychology, 33*, 301–309.

Wolpe, J. (1958). *Psychotherapy by reciprocal inhibition.* Stanford, CA: Stanford University Press.

CHAPTER

2

# Person-Centered Counseling

*John See and Brian Kamnetz*

> *It is as though he listened and such listening as his enfolds*
> *us in a silence in which at last we begin to hear what we are*
> *meant to be.*
> —*Lao-tse, 500 BCE*

## LEARNING OBJECTIVES

The goal of the chapter is to facilitate understanding of the development and current practice of the person-centered approach to counseling. Special emphasis is placed on the six "necessary and sufficient" conditions of successful person-centered counseling and description of the three facilitative conditions in terms of the "common factors" of successful counseling. Following are the learning objectives for the chapter:

1. Readers will be able to describe Rogers's facilitative conditions and what is meant by the phrase "necessary and sufficient."
2. Readers will be able to explain how the basic tenets of the person-centered approach can be applied in rehabilitation settings. Specifically, readers will be able to explain how rehabilitation professionals can incorporate client-centered techniques or themes into their work with clients, along with limitations of the approach.
3. Readers will be able to describe Rogers's theory of personality, how it interfaces with his theory of therapy, and how it can facilitate conceptualization of client concerns and problems.
4. Readers will be able to briefly explain what is meant by "evidence-based practice" and what the positive and negative effects have been for psychotherapy and counseling.

## ORIGIN OF THE PERSON-CENTERED APPROACH

Carl Rogers (1902–1987) is considered by many to be the most important psychotherapist in American history (Kirschenbaum & Henderson, 1989; "The Most Influential Therapists," 2007; Smith, 1982). Further, Rogers's work will continue to influence research and practice in counseling and psychotherapy for many years to come (Kirschenbaum & Jourdan, 2005). Best known as the originator of person-centered psychotherapy and counseling, Rogers also pioneered therapeutic encounter groups and extended his theories of psychotherapy to the entire range of helping professions, including teaching, parenting, social work, and even international conflict resolution. He authored 16 books and more than 200 articles, with millions of copies printed in over 60 languages.

Today, Rogers and his person-centered principles remain very much in the mainstream. Since his death in 1987, more books, chapters, and journal articles have been written on person-centered topics than had been written during his entire career. Approximately 200 professional organizations around the world are dedicated to continuing his work, along with more than 50 person-centered/experiential journals worldwide. This international movement is more broadly based now than it was during Rogers's lifetime (Kirschenbaum & Jourdan, 2005).

*Psychotherapy Networker* ("The Most Influential Therapists," 2007) published a poll of more than 2,500 counselors, social workers, and psychologists that found Rogers again to be the most influential psychotherapist in America, by a landslide. Aaron Beck, founder of cognitive behavioral therapy (CBT), was voted the second most influential. This same survey found that 95% of the respondents had an eclectic approach to therapy, with the majority (69%) using CBT in some combination with other therapies. An interesting anomaly was that only 31% admitted to using Rogerian techniques, although the majority had voted for him as the person who had influenced them the most during the previous 25 years.

Rogers started his remarkable career in 1928 as a clinical psychologist working with children in Rochester, New York. He then worked at Ohio State University (1939–1945), the University of Chicago (1945–1957), and his alma mater, the University of Wisconsin (1957–1963). The last leg of his journey was spent in La Jolla, California, at the Center for Studies of the Person (1964–1987).

During his wide-ranging clinical experience, Rogers developed many ideas that were new and often counter to the prevalent views in psychiatry and counseling. Other psychotherapists worked with *patients*, a label that to Rogers evoked a sick person who relinquished control to a professional who was far better able to understand the problem and prescribe a cure. Rogers (1942, p. 253) observed somewhat sarcastically, "Even in our phonographic recordings we find these counselors deciding with assurance such diverse issues as how to study history, how to get along with one's parents, how to solve the issue of racial discrimination, and what is the proper philosophy of life." Rogers derisively referred to such directive practice as counselor-centered counseling (Kirschenbaum, 2009). Alternatively, *client-centered counseling* allowed the client to retain personal dignity and to work as an equal in the counseling process.

Rogers's first major theoretical contribution came in the early 1940s when, as a young psychologist, he audaciously advocated the belief that humans were basically good and could be trusted to direct their own lives (Rogers, 1942). This perspective was anathema to the then-prevalent Freudian view of therapy as the process of helping people manage their lives by controlling their darker impulses. In addition to this more optimistic view of human nature, he also formulated a revolutionary treatment approach based more on the personal characteristics of the therapist and the resulting relationship with the client, than on any techniques or formal training. He challenged the psychotherapy community by formally articulating the belief that the therapist's "facilitative conditions" of empathy, positive regard, and genuineness were the necessary and sufficient conditions for therapy (Rogers, 1957). Nothing more was needed; nothing less would do. *This revolutionary idea meant that the medium as well as the essence of therapy was simply the relationship between the therapist and the client.* These new humanistic formulations, so elegant and so powerful, would become the heart of the person-centered approach and the "quiet revolution" that Rogers was leading.

By the early 1970s, Rogers had moved beyond his seminal work on individual psychotherapy and had turned to other person-centered applications in education, marriage therapy, and encounter groups. In the final decades of his life, he took person-centered principles to the ultimate level of facilitating world peace. He and his colleagues conducted person-centered conflict resolution groups with warring factions, such as the Catholics and Protestants in Northern Ireland, Blacks and Whites in the Union of South Africa, and the antagonists in conflicts in El Salvador, Guatemala, and other Latin countries (Kirschenbaum & Henderson, 1989). His thoughts on international diplomacy might well be required reading for all leaders seeking rapprochement in a troubled world. He was nominated for the Nobel Peace Prize shortly before his death.

## MAJOR CONCEPTS

The basis of Rogers's grand conception was the notion of self-actualization. Put simply, humans have the inherent (almost magical) capacity to grow in a positive direction and to realize their full potential, if they are (lucky enough to be) nourished by the unconditional positive regard and understanding of significant others. This pivotal idea, like the theme of a great symphony, would recur again and again in different variations of person-centered practice throughout Rogers's life.

Of all of the major counseling theories, person-centered theory most epitomizes democratic and libertarian ideals. It is the ultimate statement about tolerance, acceptance, and willingness to allow others to live as they see fit. It most explicitly informs people that if they want to help others to blossom, then they must accept or prize them unconditionally while simultaneously staying out of their way and allowing them to move toward self-actualization. Rogers (1980) was eventually to suggest a universal formative tendency that extended the idea of self-actualization to the entire universe. Over the past half-century, this seemingly simple idea has grown into a far-reaching philosophical system with implications for virtually all areas of human interaction. This formative tendency could be seen in rock crystals, as well as living organisms, as they all seemed to grow in the direction of complexity, interrelatedness, and order. There are obvious philosophical and spiritual implications in the theory (Kirschenbaum, 2009). Some have found ecclesiastical or deterministic overtones, whereas others have found almost the opposite, a total freedom from authority.

## Theory of Personality

Rogers's theory of personality derives from his clinical practice, in which he saw people move naturally in the direction of wholeness and health. He also saw the negative emotions (e.g., anxiety, anger, jealousy, self-destruction), but these were viewed as secondary reactions to frustrations, whereas the overarching tendency was to heal or grow in a positive direction. The working principles discussed in the following text are an adaptation of an earlier discussion by See (1986, pp. 138–139, adapted with permission).

### Actualizing Tendency

According to Rogers, humans have an instinctive need to grow and develop in a positive direction. As the acorn follows its biological blueprint and develops into a healthy, mature tree, so humans tend to follow their inherent blueprints and move in the direction of complexity, autonomy, and, ultimately, a fulfilled and harmonious life. However, before this natural tendency can operate, it must be liberated by a loving and nonjudgmental environment that encourages and invites the child to follow his or her natural inclinations. If the environment is strongly nurturing, then the organism may approach its full potential.

### Self-Concept

According to Rogers, the central personality construct is the picture that individuals have of themselves. It is the perceptual gestalt and sum total of all of the thoughts, feelings, values, and relationships within the experiential field. It is material consciously acknowledged about the self. It is more or less what individuals would say about themselves if they were to write a candid and exhaustive autobiography—in other words, who individuals think they are. The self-concept determines to a large extent how individuals behave.

### Organismic Valuing Process

Infants evaluate experiences and behavior according to the feelings elicited. Behavior produces good feelings if it furthers the actualizing tendency of the organism. Infants do not need to be told what is right or wrong; they automatically sense it in an intuitive way. Both good and bad experiences become part of the self-concept and are accurately symbolized in awareness. Because adults lose much of this natural and wholesome reactivity to the world, the task of therapy is to help them relearn how to listen to these organismic messages from within. To the extent that adults can recapture the childlike ability to trust feelings, they become more autonomous, more alive, and more congruent.

## Need for Positive Regard

During the early stages of development, a powerful secondary need emerges that can work for or against the organismic valuing process. This is the need for love or positive regard from significant others.

Unconditional positive regard (alternative terms are acceptance, warmth, caring, nonpossessive love, and prizing) has no strings attached, and is not based on behavior; if the child performs better or worse, the parent may be more or less proud, but will not love the child any more or less. When significant others provide unconditional positive regard, infants are encouraged to develop according to the actualizing tendency and will learn of their potential by directly experiencing the world. Because humans are instinctively good and act in ways that enhance the organism, this self-directed search for identity can be trusted to result in a well-developed and congruent personality.

Certainly, there will be many occasions when parental guidance or discipline is essential. For example, children cannot be given the option of deciding whether they will attend school, consume alcohol, or play with loaded guns. There are safety, health, and legal constraints that simply are not negotiable, and responsible parents must set standards. But there are also vast domains of childhood existence in which it is safe and wholesome for them to choose for themselves what is best.

Things go badly for developing individuals when the acceptance or love provided them by significant others is dependent on how they behave. Conditional love cripples development because it requires that individuals listen to others rather than to themselves. When individuals conform in order to obtain love, they are living according to values introjected by others, or what Rogers calls the "conditions of worth." This emotional blackmail results in individuals who deny their own actualizing tendency and relinquish the right to discover their own uniqueness. In the extreme, they may become conforming, authoritarian types with rigid self-concepts.

## Inner Conflict and Anxiety

Inner conflict results when individuals are torn between doing what comes naturally and what others expect. When individuals accept the values of others in order to gain positive regard, those values are internalized and become part of the personality. If the individual then behaves or thinks in ways that are inconsistent with those introjected values, the self-concept is violated, and the person loses self-esteem and suffers anxiety. The mother who spanked the boy 30 years ago for masturbatory activity has long been gone from this world, yet the adult-child becomes anxious when he thinks of sex.

Individuals defend against anxiety and threats to self-esteem by developing self-concepts that will be less open to new, and therefore possibly disturbing, experiences. They begin to distort reality through the use of defense mechanisms, such as denial, projection, and reaction formations. By putting tight reins on emotions, they can live out their lives in a stable but unfulfilled state. In order for therapy to be effective, there must be a weakening of these defenses to the point where the individual can sense the incongruity between the self-concept and the experiencing self. It is this identity crisis and the ensuing anxiety that may motivate the person to seek help and engage in the counseling process.

## CLASSICAL PERSON-CENTERED THERAPY

In classical person-centered psychotherapy (PCT), Rogers proposed that treatment is no more or less than the therapeutic relationship between the counselor and the client. If that relationship is characterized by six necessary and sufficient conditions (Table 2.1), then constructive personality change will take place (Rogers, 1957).

This seemingly simple formula would become one of the most controversial ideas in the entire realm of psychotherapy. The phrase "necessary and sufficient" was the ribbon around the package; it had strong heuristic value because it implied a declaration of war on the established therapies of the day. Later in this chapter, some modifications are discussed that have evolved over the years to Rogers's original theory of therapy.

To begin to appreciate the importance of the six conditions of therapy, beginning counselors need to become steeped in the material; they need to study and observe person-centered practice and then experience it directly in supervised laboratory or practicum settings. The following quotation from Rogers (1980, pp. 114–117) in his book *A Way of Being* gives an excellent sense of how he saw the facilitative conditions contributing to the process of therapy:

> What do I mean by a person-centered approach? It expresses the primary theme of my whole professional life, as that theme has become clarified through experience, interaction with others, and research. I smile as I think of the various labels I have given to this theme during the course of my career—non-directive counseling, client-centered therapy, student-centered teaching, group-centered leadership. Because the fields of application have grown in number and variety, the label "person-centered approach" seems the most descriptive.
>
> The central hypothesis of this approach can be briefly stated....Individuals have within themselves vast resources for self-understanding and for altering their self-concepts, basic attitudes, and self-directed behavior; these resources can be tapped if a definable climate of facilitative psychological attitudes can be provided.
>
> There are three conditions that must be present in order for a climate to be growth-promoting. These conditions apply whether we are speaking of the relationship between therapist and client, parent and child, leader and group, teacher and student, or administrator and staff. The conditions apply, in fact, in any situation in which the development of the person is a goal. I have described these conditions in previous writings; I present here a brief summary from the point of view of psychotherapy, but the description applies to all of the foregoing relationships.
>
> The first element could be called *genuineness* [italics added], realness, or congruence. The more the therapist is himself or herself in the relationship, putting up no professional front or personal facade, the greater is the likelihood that the client will change and grow in a constructive manner. This means that the therapist is openly being the feelings and attitudes that are flowing within at the moment. The term "transparent" catches the flavor of this condition: the therapist makes himself or herself transparent to the client; the client can see right through what the therapist

**TABLE 2.1 Necessary and Sufficient Conditions for Psychotherapy**

| ROGERS'S SIX "NECESSARY AND SUFFICIENT" CONDITIONS | ROLE OF THERAPIST | ROLE OF CLIENT |
|---|---|---|
| 1. Two persons are in psychological contact | To have sufficient training to understand the role of the facilitative conditions, including the person-centered philosophy behind them | To be cognitively and emotionally capable of making psychological contact |
| 2. The client is in a state of incongruence, being vulnerable or anxious | No role except to recognize what propels the client into the therapeutic relationship | To recognize the psychological state and to seek relief |
| 3. The therapist is congruent or integrated in the relationship | To enter the relationship as the genuine self (within professional boundaries), not hiding behind professional or personal facades | To be in the relationship |
| 4. The therapist experiences unconditional positive regard for the client | To extend nonpossessive love, acceptance, or caring to the client, valuing the client as a person regardless of behaviors that may be unattractive | To be in the relationship |
| 5. The therapist experiences an empathic understanding of the client's internal frame of reference and endeavors to communicate this experience back to the client | To accept the centrality of the client in the relationship, to experience the client's subjective inner world as if being the client (without losing sight of the "as if" quality), and through attentive and spoken behaviors, demonstrate this understanding to the client | To be in the relationship |
| 6. The communication to the client of the therapist's empathic understanding and unconditional positive regard is to a minimal degree achieved | To have sufficient training to communicate these things and to monitor the relationship for indications that the communication is successful | To have the capacity and be active enough in the relationship to perceive the communications of the therapist |

*Note:* Items in the first column are Carl Rogers's six facilitative conditions, which he believed were necessary and sufficient to produce positive psychological change. To aid readers in understanding the facilitative conditions in the counseling relationship, the authors have added corresponding roles of the counselor and of the client.

is in the relationship; the client experiences no holding back on the part of the therapist. As for the therapist, what he or she is experiencing is available to awareness, can be lived in the relationship, and can be communicated, if appropriate. Thus, there is a close matching, or congruence, between what is being experienced at the gut level, what is present in awareness, and what is expressed to the client.

The second attitude of importance in creating a climate for change is acceptance, or caring, or prizing—what I have called *unconditional positive regard* [italics added]. When the therapist is experiencing a positive, acceptant attitude toward whatever the client is at that moment, therapeutic movement or change is more likely to occur. The therapist is willing for the client to be whatever immediate feeling is going on—confusion, resentment, fear, anger, courage, love, or pride. Such caring on the part of the therapist is nonpossessive. The therapist prizes the client in a total rather than a conditional way.

The third facilitative aspect of the relationship is *empathic understanding* [italics added]. This means that the therapist senses accurately the feelings and personal meanings that the client is experiencing and communicates this understanding to the client. When functioning best, the therapist is so much inside the private world of the other that he or she can clarify not only the meanings of which the client is aware but even those just below the level of awareness.

This kind of sensitive, active listening is exceedingly rare in our lives. We think we listen, but very rarely do we listen with real understanding, true empathy. Yet listening, of this very special kind, is one of the most potent forces for change that I know.

How does this climate which I have just described bring about change? Briefly, as persons are accepted and prized, they tend to develop a more caring attitude toward themselves. As persons are empathically heard, it becomes possible for them to listen more accurately to the flow of inner experiencings. But as a person understands and prizes self, the self becomes more congruent with the experiencings. The person thus becomes more real, more genuine. These tendencies, the reciprocal of the therapist's attitudes, enable the person to be a more effective growth-enhancer for himself or herself. There is a greater freedom to be the true, whole person.

## CASE STUDY

The following excerpt from an interview carried out by Carl Rogers in 1983 illustrates some of the basic skills used in person-centered counseling (Raskin & Rogers, 1995, p. 144, reproduced with permission):

Therapist (T-1):   OK, I think I'm ready. And you . . . ready?

Client (C-1):   Yes.

T-2:   I don't know what you might want to talk about, but I'm very ready to hear. We have half an hour, and I hope that in that half an hour we can get to know each other as deeply as possible, but we don't need to strive for anything. I guess that's my feeling. Do you want to tell me whatever is on your mind?

*(continued)*

*(continued)*

C-2: I'm having a lot of problems dealing with my daughter. She's 20 years old; she's in college; I'm having a lot of trouble letting her go. . . . And I have a lot of guilt feelings about her; I have a real need to hang on to her.

T-3: A need to hang on so you can kind of make up for the things you feel guilty about—is that part of it?

C-3: There's a lot of that. . . . Also, she's been a real friend to me, and filled my life. . . . And it's very hard . . . a lot of empty places now that she's not with me.

T-4: The old vacuum, sort of, when she's not there.

C-4: Yes. Yes. I also would like to be the kind of mother that could be strong and say, you know, "Go and have a good life," and this is really hard for me to do that.

T-5: It's very hard to give up something that's been so precious in your life, but also something that I guess has caused you pain when you mentioned guilt.

C-5: Yeah, and I'm aware that I have some anger toward her that I don't always get what I want. I have needs that are not met. And, uh, I don't feel I have a right to those needs. You know. . . . She's a daughter; she's not my mother—though sometimes I feel as if I'd like her to be mother to me. It's very difficult for me to ask for that and have a right to it.

T-6: So it may be unreasonable, but still, when she doesn't meet your needs, it makes you mad.

C-6: Yeah, I get very angry, very angry with her.

PAUSE

T-7: You're also feeling a little tension at this point, I guess.

C-7: Yeah. Yeah. A lot of conflict . . .

T-8: Umm-hmm . . .

C-8: A lot of pain.

T-9: A lot of pain. Can you say anything more what that's about?

C-9: (sigh) I reach out for her, and she moves away from me. And she steps back and pulls back. . . . And then I feel like

*(continued)*

*(continued)*

> a really bad person. Like some kind of monster, that she
> doesn't want me to touch her and hold her like I did when
> she was a little girl. . . .

T-10: It sounds like a very double feeling there. Part of it is,
"Damn it, I want you close." The other part of it is, "Oh my
God, what a monster I am to not let you go."

C-10: Umm-hmm. Yeah. I should be stronger. I should be a grown
woman and allow this to happen.

Raskin made the following observation on this case study (Raskin &
Rogers, 1995, p. 148):

> The interview just quoted reveals many examples of the way in which
> change and growth are fostered in the person-centered approach. Rogers's
> straightforward statements in opening the interview (T-1 and T-2) allow the
> client to begin with a statement of the problem of concern to her and to initiate
> dialogue at a level comfortable for her. Just as he does not reassure, Rogers does
> not ask questions. In response to C-2, he does not ask the myriad questions
> that could construct a logical background and case history for dealing with the
> presenting problem. Rogers does not see himself as responsible for arriving
> at a solution to the problem as presented, or determining whether this is the
> problem that will be focused on in therapy, or changing the client's attitudes.
> The therapist sees the client as having these responsibilities and respects her
> capacity to fulfill them.

Often the use of reflections, as illustrated by Rogers in this case study,
is misconstrued by beginning counselors. They see reflections as a passive
technique that simply parrots back, almost facetiously, what the client has
said: "I hear you saying you are feeling depressed, and you are going to
jump out the window." While somewhat humorous, nothing could be
further from the truth. A careful examination of Rogers's reflections reveals
them to be highly perceptive, selective, and provocative. They have a
laserlike quality that focuses on the deeper emotional meanings that need
to be explored. Watching Rogers in the widely available "Gloria" tapes
(Rogers, Perls, Ellis, & Shostrom, 1965) will quickly illustrate this point.
He is constantly repeating the essence of the client's statements, but in a
facilitative way that encourages her to go ever deeper with self-exploration.
Inadequate reflections that are mechanical and do not go beyond the surface
will be seen as tedious and stultifying by many clients. On the other hand,
sensitive reflections can offer the profound expression of empathy usually
associated with client gain.

## HISTORICAL BENCHMARKS OF PERSON-CENTERED THERAPY
### (a.k.a. the Saga of the Dodo Bird)

During the past half-century, many forces have altered the face of psychotherapy and have had a direct impact on the person-centered brand. The following developments are generally sequential and include considerable overlap.

1. **Early on, the dodo bird exclaimed, "Everybody has won and all must have prizes."**
   This famous phrase from Lewis Carroll's *Alice's Adventures in Wonderland* was first directed at psychotherapy by Saul Rosenzweig (1936), who could not see any differences in client outcome between the existing schools of therapy. Over the past 50 years, this verdict of therapeutic parity has been confirmed repeatedly in hundreds of studies, but given widespread consideration only after meta-analytic reviews began emerging in the 1980s (Smith, Glass, & Miller, 1980). The good news was that all bona fide therapies seemed to work equally well; the confusing news was that there did not seem to be any difference between them. This remains one of the most perplexing mysteries in the field of psychotherapy—how can therapies that look so different have similar client outcomes?

   This phenomenon, sometimes called the equivalence paradox, had a friendly ramification for the person-centered school, which had been slipping in popularity in the United States since the 1970s. Now at least all schools of psychotherapy were equal, and none had to worry about being abandoned due to obsolescence. The person-centered adherents were now secure in the knowledge that they were just as good as the next guy.

2. **Theorists puzzling over the equivalence paradox formulated a construct called the "common factors," which are believed to be the nonspecific therapeutic ingredients shared by all successful brands of psychotherapy.**
   These common factors account for a larger proportion of client gain than any of the specific techniques used by the various schools of therapy, so they are considered extremely important in the healing process. They are thought to include such things as emotional support, the placebo effect, hope, talking about problems, and being in a therapeutic relationship. Although still somewhat a mystery, they are estimated to account for up to 70% of the outcome variance in psychotherapy (Wampold, 2001).

3. **Examination of the common factors suggested that some of the most potent ingredients were precisely the facilitative conditions that Carl Rogers had espoused 50 years earlier: empathy, positive regard, and genuineness.**
   These facilitative conditions seemed to overlap and complement the working alliance to create the therapeutic relationship, which is at the very heart of all credible therapy systems. There is more than a little irony in Rogers's (1957, p. 102) comments about the connection between the facilitative conditions and the other psychotherapies: "The techniques

of the various therapies are relatively unimportant except to the extent that they serve as channels for fulfilling one of the conditions." How remarkably prophetic his words were, and how tersely they framed the equivalence paradox and the common factors we still struggle with today.

C. H. Patterson (1986, p. 562) made a similar point in his *Theories of Counseling and Psychotherapy*:

> Considering the obstacles to research on the relationship between therapist variables and therapy outcomes and the factors that militate against achieving significant relationships, the magnitude of the evidence for the effectiveness of empathic understanding, respect or warmth, and therapeutic genuineness is nothing short of astounding. The evidence for the necessity, if not the sufficiency, of these therapist qualities is incontrovertible. There is little or no evidence for the effectiveness of any other variables or techniques or for the effectiveness of other methods or approaches to psychotherapy in the absence of these conditions.

It is important to note that Patterson is not making the claim that the conditions are sufficient, only that they are necessary. His final phrase, "in the absence of these conditions," suggests that, if the facilitative conditions were removed from the other therapies, then the techniques that remained would likely be a weak residue of questionable value. In other words, the therapeutic relationship is the platform or stage on which more specialized techniques must operate. Other techniques, such as behavioral and cognitive behavioral, cannot exist in isolation from the therapeutic relationship, and they are probably much less important.

4. **Beginning in the mid-1990s, the evidence-based practice movement, which most academics eagerly supported, had unfortunately produced some dire consequences for psychotherapy.**
   In particular, various "expert" panels had consistently shown a preference for the cognitive behavioral approaches over the humanistic–experiential approaches. A widely shared belief advocated that there were strong biases working against a fair representation of the insight therapies on the approved lists used for reimbursement by government agencies, funding organizations, hospitals, and insurance companies (Elliott, 2002; Elliott, Greenberg, Watson, Timulak, & Freire, 2013; Kirschenbaum & Jourdan, 2005; Norcross & Wampold, 2011). Lambert (2013) described the situation as follows:

> The controversies generated from the initial report came mainly from practitioners who saw the report as rigid, if not dogmatic, and as having an agenda that was biased in favor of a small number of therapies that were promoted by Task Force members (e.g., criteria were set up that would give an advantage to highly structured short-term behavioral and cognitive-behavioral treatments advocated by many Task Force members). But strong criticism came from psychotherapy researchers as well (Garfield, 1996; Nathan, 1998; Strupp, 1997). (Lambert, 2013, p. 6)

This modern phenomenon is seen as an existential threat to many of the established insight therapies, including PCT.

Parenthetically, it should be noted that the criticism of the American Psychological Association (APA) Division 12 Task Force and the funding entities that have engaged in the ill-advised use of the "lists" should not be construed as criticism of the thousands of dedicated and highly principled therapists who successfully use cognitive behavioral techniques on a regular basis. Nor should the criticism be seen as directed at the cognitive behavioral techniques themselves, which have been shown beyond a doubt to be highly effective with a wide range of mental health problems.

*The dodo bird is getting nervous. Maybe all therapies aren't*
*equal after all.*

5. **The humanistic–experiential schools, including Rogerians, have responded with alarm to the aforementioned threats to their professional existence.**

This challenge has generated, or at least contributed to, a large upsurge of empirical research that favorably compares humanistic–experiential psychotherapies (HEPs) with the other theoretical approaches. This research is discussed at length later in the chapter.

The growing appreciation for the common factors, as well as the working alliance, signals a renaissance of sorts among the insight-oriented schools, where singular importance is attached to the therapeutic relationship. This renaissance, however, does not equate to a rebirth of the old classical therapies so much as to a renewed commitment to those select elements, which are evidence based and which fit with the historical trend toward eclecticism and integration.

6. **It seems we are all Rogerians now.**

Despite the declining use of classical PCT, there is growing national and international popularity for a wide range of modern derivatives and related therapies that subscribe to Rogerian ideas and principles. Even Aaron Beck, founder of CBT, stated, "Therapists who are good at the technical end of cognitive therapy fall flat on their faces when it comes to the more complex case." Beck continued, "Empathy, sensitivity, considerateness—together with the ability to put them together with technical aspects—is the combination needed" (Bloch, 2004, p. 866).

It is now widely understood that the facilitative conditions, in some fashion, should be included in virtually all eclectic or integrated therapy systems, as well as in nontherapy settings where positive human relationships are desired, such as education, child rearing, health care, business, and diplomacy.

The ongoing appeal of the person-centered message may be partially explained by the previously mentioned poll ("The Most Influential Therapists," 2007), which showed Rogers to still be the most influential psychotherapist in the United States, even though few practitioners actually subscribed to his classic brand of therapy. This strange disconnect may have more to do with philosophical values than with science. Most likely, Rogers's legacy is alive and vibrant because of his profound wisdom, which still touches us at the deepest personal level while simultaneously providing us with greater hopefulness and understanding of the human condition.

The following passage from the Preface to *Client-Centered Therapy* (Rogers, 1951, pp. x–xi) reminds us of how charismatic and personally relevant Rogers's words could be:

> This book is about the suffering and the hope, the anxiety and the satisfaction, with which each therapist's counseling room is filled. It is about the uniqueness of the relationship each therapist forms with each client, and equally about the common elements which we discover in all these relationships. This book is about the highly personal experiences of each one of us. It is about a client in my office who sits there by the corner of the desk, struggling to be himself, yet deathly afraid of being himself--striving to see his experience as it is, wanting to *be* that experience, and yet deeply fearful of the prospect. This book is about me, as I sit there with that client, facing him, participating in that struggle as deeply and sensitively as I am able. It is about me as I try to perceive his experience, and the meaning and the feeling and the taste and the flavor that it has for him. It is about me as I bemoan my very human fallibility in understanding that client, and the occasional failures to see life as it appears to him, failures which fall like heavy objects across the intricate, delicate web of growth which is taking place. It is about me as I rejoice at the privilege of being a midwife to a new personality—as I stand by with awe at the emergence of a self, a person, as I see a birth process in which I have had an important and facilitating part.

## RESEARCH SUPPORTING PERSON-CENTERED COUNSELING

### New Outcome Research

The meta-analysis of humanistic–experiential psychotherapies (Elliott et al., 2013) in the sixth edition of the *Handbook of Psychotherapy and Behavior Change* is decidedly good news for PCT as well as the other humanistic–experiential therapies. This extensive review offers compelling evidence that places HEPs nearly on a par (see Boxes 2.1, 2.2, and 2.3) with the CBTs that have won such widespread approval from the various endorsement panels (APA Division 12 Task Force on Empirically Supported Treatments in the United States; National Institute for Clinical Excellence in the United Kingdom).

In a sense, this review is both a revelation and a resurrection coming at a time when so much adverse publicity has surrounded the mistaken belief that manualized CBTs are far superior to HEPs for treating mental health disorders. The strong research support for the CBTs in the treatment of many emotional disorders is not being questioned. However, as this review illustrates, there

**BOX 2.1**

## Four Lines of Evidence Supporting HEPs

After analyzing roughly 200 counseling outcome studies, Elliott et al. (2013, p. 523) reported four lines of evidence supporting the use of humanistic–experiential psychotherapies (HEPs) as effective alternatives to other approaches and offered these conclusions:

1. "Overall, HEPs are associated with *large pre–post client change*. These client changes are maintained over early and late follow-up." (ES = .96)
2. "In *controlled studies*, clients in HEPs generally show large gains relative to clients who receive no therapy, regardless of whether studies are randomized or not. This allows the causal inference that HEP, in general, causes client change; or rather, speaking from the clients' perspective, we can say that clients use HEP to cause themselves to change." (ES = .81)
3. "In *comparative outcome studies*, HEPs in general are statistically and clinically equivalent in effectiveness to other therapies, regardless of whether studies are randomized or not." (ES = −.02)
4. "Overall, CBT appears to have a trivial advantage over HEPs. However, this effect seems to be due to non-bona fide treatments usually labeled by researchers as supportive (or sometimes nondirective), which are generally less effective than CBT. These therapies are typically delivered when there is a negative researcher allegiance and in non-bona fide versions... when researcher allegiance is controlled for statistically, *HEPs appear to be equivalent to CBT in their effectiveness.*"

*Note*: See Box 2.2 for explanation of effect size (ES) statistics.

are numerous disorders for which the treatment of choice could just as legitimately be one of the humanistic–experiential psychotherapies, including PCT (see Box 2.3).

Elliott et al. (2013, p. 525) strongly recommend that the lists of empirically supported treatments in the United States and the United Kingdom need to be updated to reflect the type of scientific evidence presented in this report: "HEPs should be offered to clients in national health service contexts and other mental health settings, and paid for by health insurance, especially for the well-evidenced client populations highlighted." The report concludes with this final suggestion, "Like CBT [cognitive behavioral therapy], HEPs [humanistic–experiential psychotherapies] are evidence-based for a wide range of client presenting problems. In fact, we argue that the education of psychotherapists is incomplete and unscientific without a greater emphasis on these approaches, to the ultimate detriment of clients" (Elliott et al., 2013, p. 526).

**BOX 2.2**

## Brief Review of ES Statistics

This table gives a brief overview of how statistical results are commonly reported in meta-analytical reviews such as those used in this chapter. The effect size (ES) is the metric that allows comparisons to be made and conclusions drawn from the aggregation of multiple studies. When differences between treatments are measured, they are reported as $d$ and the cutoff is .20 for small effects, .50 for medium effects, and .80 for large effects.

When the study is looking at relationships or associations between variables, then the pertinent measure is $r$, the correlation coefficient, and the cutoff scores are .10 for small effects, .30 for medium effects, and .50 for large effects. The results in this section, New Outcome Research, report effect sizes using the $d$ index. The results in the next section, New Process Research, look at how therapeutic relationship variables correlate with client success, and the ES uses the $r$ index.

| Interpretation of ES Statistics | | | | |
|---|---|---|---|---|
| $d$ | $r$ | Cohen's Benchmark | Type of Effect | Success Rate of Treated Patients (%) |
| 1.0 | | | Beneficial | 72 |
| .80 | .50 | Large | Beneficial | 69 |
| .50 | .30 | Medium | Beneficial | 62 |
| .20 | .10 | Small | Beneficial | 55 |
| .00 | .00 | No effect | | 50 |
| -.20 | -.10 | | Detrimental | 45 |

*Source*: Adapted from Norcross (2011, p. 12).

Two recent naturalistic U.K. studies that were not included in the aforementioned meta-analysis warrant special attention. They fall under the rubric "practice-oriented research," described by Castonguay, Barkham, Lutz, and McAleavey (2013) as a new research paradigm, which lacks the scientific rigor of the standard efficacy trials, but has the advantage of representing real-world clinical practice. Both of these studies were long term with large samples, and both measured client outcome using the Clinical Outcomes in Routine Evaluation Outcome Measure (CORE-OM), which is a standardized assessment instrument. The first study (Gibbard & Hanley, 2008, p. 215) was a 5-year evaluation of 697 clients who received person-centered counseling in a primary care setting. The pre–post therapy effect size was 1.2, which exceeds Cohen's benchmark of .8 for large effects. The authors state, "The results indicate that person-centered counseling is effective for clients with common mental health problems, such as anxiety and depression. Effectiveness is not limited to individuals with mild to moderate symptoms of recent onset, but extends to people with moderate to severe symptoms of longer duration."

**BOX 2.3**

## HEPs and the Treatment of Emotional Disorders

This extensive analysis of counseling outcome studies indicated, among other things, that the following six emotional disorders respond to treatment with humanistic–experiential psychotherapies (HEPs) at the listed levels of effectiveness (Elliott et al., 2013, p. 523):

1. For *depression*, HEPs have been extensively researched to the point where the claim of <u>efficacious and specific</u> can be supported in general.
2. For *relationship and interpersonal problems*, EFT meets the criteria as an <u>efficacious and specific</u> treatment.
3. For *coping psychologically with chronic medical conditions* (cancer, MS, HIV, chronic pain, etc.), it appears that HEPs meet the criteria as <u>efficacious</u> treatments.
4. For *habitual self-damaging activities*, the analysis shows that HEPs meet the criteria as <u>efficacious</u> treatments for substance misuse.
5. For *anxiety problems overall*, the evidence is mixed but sufficient to warrant a general verdict of <u>possibly efficacious</u>. However, for the treatment of panic and generalized anxiety, the analysis shows that HEPs may be less efficacious than CBT.
6. For *psychotic conditions such as schizophrenia*, the authors state, "We continue to recommend a cautious verdict of <u>possibly efficacious</u>, in spite of a recent UK guideline contra-indicating humanistic counseling for clients with this condition."

The second study (Stiles, Barkham, Twigg, Mellor-Clark, & Cooper, 2008) was considerably more ambitious, involving 5,613 patients who were treated in 32 National Health Service settings with variations of PCT, CBT, or psychodynamic therapy (PDT). All three treatment groups showed a marked improvement, with an overall pre–post therapy effect size of 1.39. Stiles et al. indicated that the results were consistent with the dodo verdict: Everybody has won, and all must have prizes.

*The dodo bird is smiling. He loves getting back to parity.*

### New Process Research (Evidence-Based Therapy Relationships)

This section highlights recent findings (Norcross, 2011) on the relationship variables considered most important to the therapeutic process, specifically the facilitative conditions and the working alliance, two main variables that were deliberately omitted by the APA Division 12 Task Force (Task Force on Promotion and Dissemination of Psychological Procedures, 1995) in its controversial review of empirically supported treatments. The APA Division 12 Task

Force (1995) had not even looked at therapeutic relationships; all they had studied were therapy treatments or techniques that met fairly narrow criteria (i.e., manualized, controlled efficacy trials, with discrete populations). What this meant, in effect, was that the long-term, insight therapies, such as client-centered and psychodynamic approaches, which focus on personality change rather than symptom removal, would not even be eligible to enter the race for third-party reimbursement.

Criticisms from renowned psychotherapy researchers (e.g., Wampold, Norcross, Lambert) give a sense of how negative the reactions were to the treatment lists and the exclusion of the therapeutic relationship from the study. For example, Wampold (2001, p. 225), in his seminal work, *The Great Psychotherapy Debate*, said of the task force's work, "The bias is distinctly toward behavioral and cognitive-behavioral treatments, reducing the likelihood of acceptance of humanistic, experiential, or psychodynamic therapies." Further, Norcross and Lambert (2011, p. 7) observed of the task force's report, "While scientifically laudable in their intent, these efforts have largely ignored the therapy relationship and the person of the therapist. . . . Not only is the language offensive on clinical grounds to some practitioners, but the research evidence is weak for validating treatment methods in isolation from the therapy relationship and the individual patient."

It was partly in response to such criticism that the APA sponsored the Task Force on Evidence-Based Therapy Relationships, with John Norcross as chairperson. The extensive review and recommendations of this new task force appear in *Psychotherapy Relationships That Work: Evidence-Based Responsiveness, Second Edition* (Norcross, 2011). The remainder of this section highlights findings that seem especially relevant to the future of PCT and the other humanistic–experiential therapies.

The task force identified 12 elements in the therapeutic relationship that seemed most likely to cause or be related to positive client outcome. These elements included Rogers's facilitative conditions, whereas the rest were versions of, or closely related to, the working alliance (see Box 2.4).

In his concluding remarks, Norcross (2011) opined that practically all of the relationship variables they studied would have been considered "demonstrably effective" if they had been judged by the less rigorous standards used in the APA's Division 12 Task Force (1995) study on treatment effects (p. 426). The Norcross Task Force offered numerous conclusions, but the following three seem especially relevant to the person-centered perspective (p. 423):

1. "The therapy relationship makes substantial and consistent contributions to psychotherapy outcome independent of the specific type of treatment.
2. The therapy relationship accounts for why clients improve (or fail to improve) at least as much as the particular treatment method.
3. Efforts to promulgate best practices or evidence-based practices (EBPs) without including the relationship are seriously incomplete and potentially misleading."

**BOX 2.4**

### Statistical Effects of Facilitative Conditions

The American Psychological Association's Task Force on Evidence-Based Therapy Relationships, with John Norcross (2011) as chairperson, identified 12 elements in the therapeutic relationship that seemed most likely to cause or be related to positive client outcome.

Rogers's facilitative conditions were all included among the 12 elements and found to have small to medium effect sizes: empathy, $r = .30$, produces a medium effect size, which accounts for 9% of the outcome variance in therapy and was judged to be "demonstrably effective"; positive regard, $r = .27$, produces a medium effect size and a moderate association with positive therapy outcomes and was judged to be "probably effective"; and congruence, $r = .24$, produces a small to medium effect size and accounts for approximately 6% of the variance in treatment outcome and was judged to be "promising but insufficient research to judge." These all were roughly equivalent to the alliance effect size of $r = .275$, which accounted for about 8% of variance in therapy outcome and was judged to be "demonstrably effective."

Norcross (2011, p. 11) put these effect sizes in perspective with the following statement about successful therapy: "We do not expect large, overpowering effects of any one of its facets. Instead, we expect to find a number of helpful facets. And that is exactly what we find in the following chapters—beneficial, medium-sized effects of several elements of the complex therapy relationship."

Norcross (2011, p. 11) elaborated on the empathy effect size of $r = .30$ as follows: "This is a medium effect size. That translates into happier and healthier clients: patients with empathic therapists tend to progress more in treatment and experience a higher probability of eventual improvement."

The implications of these three conclusions, if taken seriously by rehabilitation professions, will go a long way toward bringing counseling practices into compliance with the best available science. The task force also made many recommendations for practice, training, and research, which seem quite timely and meaningful for the humanistic–experiential schools and for the helping professions in general (see Box 2.5). It is gratifying to see that the APA Task Force offers these important conclusions and recommendations to all mental health professionals.

Although this exhaustive study certainly certifies the importance of the *therapeutic relationship* and places it on an equal footing with the *therapeutic treatments*, on a lesser note, there is still disagreement about the nature of the elements within the therapeutic relationship itself. One particular sticking point for the person-centered school is the qualitative difference they see between the

**BOX 2.5**

## APA Task Force Recommendations for Practice and Training

Among many recommendations of the APA's Task Force on Evidence-Based Therapy Relationships (Norcross & Wampold, 2011, pp. 424–425) were the following, which highlight the facilitative conditions and seem especially supportive of the person-centered therapies:

- Practitioners are encouraged to make the creation and cultivation of a therapy relationship, characterized by the elements found to be *demonstrably* and *probably* effective [emphasis added], a primary aim in the treatment of patients.
- Training and continuing-education programs are encouraged to provide competency-based training in the *demonstrably* and *probably* effective [emphasis added] elements of the therapy relationship.
- Mental health organizations as a whole are encouraged to educate their members about the improved outcomes associated with using evidence-based therapy relationships, as they frequently now do about evidence-based treatments.

*Note:* The phrase "elements found to be *demonstrably* and *probably* effective" includes empathy and positive regard.

facilitative conditions and the broader working alliance. In their view, empathy, positive regard, and genuineness represent uniquely human qualities of the counselor that are not easily turned "on" and "off," whereas the working alliance seems to be a practical formula for how the client and therapist might collaborate in therapy; it refers to things like personal bonding and establishing the goals and tasks of therapy. In this comparison, Rogerians question whether the facilitative conditions will be fully valued as prerequisites for therapy, or might they be relegated to a lesser status and obscured by the more mundane activities of the alliance?

Another cautionary view was expressed by Schmid and Mearns (2006, p. 178), who provide the following distinction:

> The nature of the therapeutic relationship that we are describing is qualitatively different from the so-called working alliance. . . . Often it is thought that this is all that Carl Rogers was saying—that the relationship, to some degree, is important in all therapies. In fact, what we normally accept as the working alliance generally represents a very superficial level of relationship . . . we are looking for a deeper sense of meaning than simply a working alliance.

One common observation is that the facilitative conditions are core ingredients within the broader working alliance. Wampold (2001, p. 211) stated, "Empathy and the formation of the working alliance, for example, are intricately and inextricably connected." If this were chemistry, we might be asking which is the more important, the atom or the molecule?

Finally, the concluding paragraph in the Norcross report (Norcross & Wampold, 2011) reminds us of our professional obligation to use all scientific evidence in our quest to understand and cultivate the therapeutic relationship:

> As Carl Rogers (1980, p. 429) compellingly demonstrated, there is no inherent tension between a relational approach and a scientific one. Science can and should inform us about what works in psychotherapy—be it a treatment method, an assessment measure, a patient behavior, an adaptation method, or yes, a therapy relationship.

## RELATED THERAPIES

Although PCT is the main topic of this chapter, it might be helpful to mention several closely related therapies, most of which were strongly influenced by the work of Carl Rogers. All are considered person centered and place a premium on the subjective inner experiencing of the individual, and all consider an empathetic and positive client–therapist relationship to be central to therapy. All fall under the rubric humanistic–experiential psychotherapy. PCT (Rogers, 1961) is the most prominent, followed by gestalt therapy (Perls, Hefferline, & Goodman, 1951), emotion-focused therapy (also known as process–experiential; Greenberg, Rice, & Elliott, 1993), existential (Yalom, 1980), and focusing-oriented experiential therapy (Gendlin, 1996).

Additionally, there are developments within other major schools that approximate Rogerian principles, such as motivational interviewing (Lundahl, Kunz, Brownell, Tollefson, & Burke, 2010), which is often considered behavioral, but which has obvious client-centered components. And from the cognitive behavioral school, the following approaches have emerged: mindfulness-based cognitive therapy (Segal, Williams, & Teasdale, 2001), acceptance and commitment therapy (Hayes, Strosahl, & Wilson, 1999), and compassion-focused therapy (Gilbert, 2009). And of course, virtually all microcounseling and peer counseling training programs use client-centered principles to one degree or another.

## COMMUNITY APPLICATIONS OF PERSON-CENTERED PRINCIPLES

The following paragraphs give illustrations of well-known community-based programs that incorporate client-centered principles as key elements: public schools, motivational interviewing (MI), state vocational rehabilitation agencies, and parent effectiveness training (PET).

### Public Schools

Impressive research on student-centered teaching has been accumulating for many years. In one of their studies, Aspy and Roebuck (1974) rated 550 elementary- and secondary-level teachers on the facilitative conditions (empathy, positive regard, and genuineness) and then correlated the ratings with a large number of student performance criteria. The findings seemed quite encouraging. The students of highly rated teachers showed greater gains in academic work as well as a number of nonacademic outcomes, such as greater creative problem-solving skills, more positive self-concept, fewer discipline problems, and lower absence rates, along with possibly increased IQ scores.

Now, a recent meta-analysis on teacher–student relationships (Cornelius-White, 2007) has supported the age-old certitude that kids have regarding the link between liking the teacher and doing well in the classroom. This study analyzed results from 119 studies going back over half a century and involving over 300,000 students. The teacher variables that had above-average associations with positive student outcomes were empathy, warmth, positive relationships, non-directivity, and encouraging thinking and learning. The student behaviors that were positively correlated with the teacher variables were "participation, critical thinking, satisfaction, math achievement, drop-out prevention, self-esteem, verbal achievement, positive motivation, social connection, IQ, grades, reduction in disruptive behavior, attendance, and perceived achievement" (p. 134). Although there were wide variations, the mean correlations were above average, compared with other educational innovations. Cornelius-White (2007, p. 134) concluded, "Researchers, policy makers, teachers, administrators, students, parents, and others involved in schooling can advocate for increasing the awareness and practice of positive learner-centered relationships." Because of the breadth and scope of this study and the heterogeneous nature of teaching, it seems reasonable that these findings can be generalized, within limits, to other professions that share characteristics with teaching, such as rehabilitation counseling.

### Motivational Interviewing

MI is a popular tool in the treatment of individuals with various disabilities, especially chemical dependency and other addictions. It is an integrated treatment approach that has been around for over 30 years. It includes behavioral, cognitive behavioral, and client-centered elements. MI therapists employ client-centered counseling skills, especially accurate empathy, in encouraging clients to explore their experiences and ambivalence (Miller & Moyers, 2007).

MI is usually a short-term treatment that attempts to mobilize the client's inner resolve to make positive changes and commit to a long-term treatment program; however, as a stand-alone treatment, MI has been found to be as effective as CBT or 12-step programs. Meta-analyses show the effect size of MI to range from low ($d = .26$) to moderate ($d = .41$), with the high variability among studies possibly due to differences in participant characteristics (Emmelkamp, 2013).

### State–Federal Vocational Rehabilitation

In a nationwide study of practicing rehabilitation counselors, Bozarth and Rubin (1978) investigated the relationship of the facilitative conditions exhibited by counselors to rehabilitation gain exhibited by their clients. This 5-year study of 160 rehabilitation counselors and 1,000 clients concluded, among other things, that "the counselors were at least as high on levels of empathy, respect, and genuineness dimensions as many other professional groups, including experienced psychotherapists in private practice" (p. 178). With reference to client gain, "the higher levels of the interpersonal skills, even though falling on the operational scale definition of minimally facilitative, tended to be related to higher vocational gain at closure, higher monthly earnings at follow-up, positive psychological change 10 months or more following intake, and greater job satisfaction at follow-up" (p. 178).

### Parent Effectiveness Training

Founded in 1962, PET is one of the oldest skill-based training programs for parents. Its founder, Dr. Thomas Gordon, was recognized worldwide for his humane and democratic form of child-rearing that placed priority on communication, conflict resolution, and relationship building. His primary text sold over 5 million copies, and over a million people participated in his training courses. A meta-analysis of the effects of PET showed an overall effect of .33 standard deviation units, which was significantly higher than alternative treatments. PET had a positive effect on parents' knowledge and behavior and on children's self-esteem (Cedar & Levant, 1990). According to the Gordon Training International website, Gordon studied with Carl Rogers and applied his concepts to nontherapeutic situations for parents, teachers, and others (Stinnett, 2012).

## PERSON-CENTERED PRINCIPLES IN REHABILITATION COUNSELING

Rogers intended his person-centered approach to reach well beyond the boundaries of formal psychotherapy. It applies to any helping profession or situation in which the intention is to promote the welfare or growth of another human being (Rogers, 1980). It applies as much to the relationships between rehabilitation counselors and their clients as it does to relationships between parents and children or teachers and students. Whatever the situation, if the goal is self-actualization, then the means to that end is the therapeutic relationship, as defined by the facilitative conditions.

Rogerian counseling comes in many shapes and colors. At one extreme is the classical form of psychotherapy, which is long-term, nondirective, and adheres closely to the "necessary and sufficient" facilitative conditions set forth by Rogers (1957). This would be the most sophisticated level of application, requiring an advanced degree with extensive formal training in psychotherapy. At the other extreme would be the type of client-centered orientation seen in peer counseling programs in high schools, colleges, and community settings where volunteers can be trained in a matter of weeks to provide elementary interviewing skills that place a focus on listening, using open-ended questions, and reflecting feelings. The use of person-centered techniques in rehabilitation counseling lies somewhere between these extremes.

Over the years, numerous authorities in rehabilitation have recognized the critical role of the facilitative conditions in rehabilitation settings (e.g., Rubin & Roessler, 2008; See, 1986; Thomas, Thoreson, Parker, & Butler, 1998). According to Rubin and Roessler (2008, p. 283):

A quality relationship (i.e., one characterized by empathy, respect, genuineness, concreteness, and cultural sensitivity) facilitates client progress by providing a situation that the client will want to maintain, by enabling the client to verbalize real concerns, and by making the counselor a potent reinforcer in the client's life. Although a necessary element, a good relationship is not sufficient for ensuring positive rehabilitation outcomes. As Kanfer and Goldstein (1991) pointed out, a client should expect a counselor to be both "technically proficient" and empathic, respectful, and genuine. Rehabilitation counselor skills must be sufficiently comprehensive so that it is unnecessary for clients to make a choice between the two.

## PHASES IN PERSON-CENTERED VOCATIONAL REHABILITATION

Client movement through a person-centered vocational rehabilitation process can be conceptualized as phased activity that roughly parallels the case management process itself. This is not a strict formula but rather a flexible guideline to help counselors stay mindful of the critical importance of the facilitative conditions and how they might be used (Box 2.6). The more the focus is on the client's inner subjective world (feelings), the more the need for a deliberate application of the facilitative conditions. When the focus moves to concrete skill development

**BOX 2.6**

### Phases in Person-Centered Vocational Rehabilitation Settings

These phases are not set in concrete. They are approximations to a reality that is continually changing. They will have utility only to the extent they help counselors incorporate the facilitative conditions into the individualized work with their clients.

**Phase 1**
The first phase is characterized by the initial sessions and the diagnostic workup, along with the exploration of feelings and the engendering of hope. Rapport is established, and the client comes to trust and value the counselor. Here, the facilitative conditions are extremely important as the client struggles to find the words to symbolize the inner conflict and begins to develop an awareness of an emerging self with permission to engage in the rehabilitation process. A friendly and sincere demeanor accompanied by nonthreatening reflections of feeling can be very encouraging for most clients at this early stage.

**Phase 2**
Having made the existential determination that change is possible and desirable, the client will be ready to work with the counselor in considering options, goals, and strategies. This phase typically involves critical thinking and logical deduction as the client and counselor work together to analyze and integrate information they collected during the diagnostic and vocational evaluation phase.

*(continued)*

**BOX 2.6 (*continued*)**

Depending on the rehabilitation setting, this phase generally culminates with a formal statement specifying the vocational goal and the intermediate steps that will be necessary to reach the goal. In a state vocational rehabilitation agency, this agreement is viewed as a formal contract and signed by the client and counselor. It can be seen that this phase is somewhat analogous to the working alliance in psychotherapy that calls for collaboration between the therapist and patient in the determination of the goals and tasks of therapy.

The Council on Rehabilitation Education (CORE; 2010, p. 28) requires that master's-level rehabilitation counseling students be able to "utilize career/occupational materials to assist the individual with a disability in vocational planning." Clearly, CORE sees the vocational aspect of the rehabilitation counseling process as being centered on the client, with the counselor in an assistive role.

This phase is not as dependent on the facilitative conditions as the first phase, but, to the extent the client becomes anxious, confused, angry, or begins to lose motivation, there will still be many opportunities for the counselor to use genuineness, unconditional positive regard, and empathic understanding.

**Phase 3**
The third phase can be characterized as the action or implementation stage, in which the rehabilitation plan is implemented, and the client actually begins a new job or training program. The counseling approaches that could have the most utility at this stage are action or behaviorally oriented approaches that can be used to focus on real-world problems and day-to-day challenges, such as the many fears and anxieties associated with social interactions, dealing with authority figures, travel in the community, financial obligations, and the frequent pressures associated with life-changing events.

For many clients, this stage is uncharted territory, and the looming prospect of success or failure can be quite unnerving. Genuineness, unconditional positive regard, and empathic understanding are often blended with other counseling orientations, but are used primarily to help the client deal with negative feelings that arise during the implementation of the rehabilitation plan. Anxiety and self-doubt can jeopardize the rehabilitation program. The best preventative medicine during this final phase may simply be the support and reassurance offered by a concerned and empathetic rehabilitation counselor.

or knowledge acquisition, the facilitative conditions necessarily give way to the more pedagogical orientations associated with formal education and training.

Always, there will be the obligation for the counselor to move adroitly between the tasks that require a focus on the delivery of "real-world" services and the task of responding sensitively to the emotional needs of clients. Rehabilitation counselors will seldom be expected to engage in long-term, client-centered therapy, but they will have the continual opportunity and obligation to promote a safe, positive learning environment where the client is encouraged to acquire new vocational or daily-living skills while simultaneously acquiring more self-esteem and confidence.

As with competent high school teachers, competent rehabilitation counselors will be able to sense when the client is in need of special attention from a friendly, respectful, and understanding counselor. The facilitative conditions are not simply elements that can be manipulated for therapy purposes; they are requisite personality dimensions of all fully functioning helpers, and as such, they have a very special mission in the rehabilitation and recovery process.

It is well to remember that the facilitative conditions are not a toolbox of techniques, but rather a constellation of personality traits and attitudes that will enhance most human interactions. The intensity and focus may be conceptualized along a sliding scale that can and should vary with the circumstance. For example, when the client is trying to deal with some deep interpersonal conflict, the counselor should respond with a level of the facilitative conditions similar to those recommended by Rogers for psychotherapy. On the other hand, when there is not a compelling psychological issue involved, the counselor can reasonably lighten up and return to a more normal interaction style where the facilitative conditions are de-emphasized or allowed to hover in the background until further notice. The rehabilitation practitioner's function is to offer professional services as needed along a continuum from insight to action, remembering along the way to offer clients as much autonomy as they can handle, while still providing the emotional support they need.

## SPECIAL CONSIDERATIONS FOR PERSON-CENTERED COUNSELING IN REHABILITATION SETTINGS

### Use of Confrontation

Confrontation has found an increasing role in PCT. Many people mistakenly believe that person-centered principles are limited to techniques of attending and reflecting, seeing the therapist as supportive without being challenging (Corey, 2001), thus precluding confrontation. This view is in error. Confrontation is actually an area of development in the person-centered approach, especially in Europe; according to Lietaer (1984, p. 54), Rogers did not object to therapists influencing clients, including through confrontation, as long as the therapist does not control or manipulate the client, exert pressure, or otherwise exert power within the counseling relationship.

Discussion of confrontation requires caution because of wide-ranging definitions in the academic literature. At one extreme (opposite of person centered) is harsh confrontation, which can include threatening a client with consequences (such as a spouse leaving) if the client does not change behaviors (Polcin, 2003). Near the other (person centered) end of the spectrum is the "empathic confrontation" of Ivey, Ivey, and Zalaquett (2014, p. 236), defined as "an influencing skill that invites clients to examine their stories for discrepancies between verbal and nonverbal communication, between expressed attitudes and behaviors, or conflict with others." The later position fairly well illustrates the person-centered stance on confrontation.

### Confusion Regarding the Person-Centered Label

The term "person centered" has become ubiquitous across a wide range of disciplines and, although there is agreement on the general meaning, there is also considerable latitude in how the term is applied. It is often considered synonymous with "client centered" and "nondirective," although these two terms are more closely associated with psychotherapy proper, whereas "person centered" encompasses a broader range of activities, including education, parenting, social work, conflict resolution, health care, and medicine. Rogers coined this broader term in the 1970s when he was leading large workshops on community building and world peace (Cain & Seeman, 2001).

In medical rehabilitation, there is a confusing variety of closely related meanings similar to Rogers's conceptualization (Leplege et al., 2007). One meaning states that it is necessary to recognize the impact that a condition being dealt with may have on a person and to see the difficulties through the person's eyes. Another meaning states that it is important for professionals to recognize the strengths and capabilities of the person. Another views the affected person as the primary expert on himself or herself, rather than simply the object of treatment. According to Leplege et al., these nuanced differences need not confuse service providers if they can avoid bogging down over the definitional differences and simply implement the key operational components. It seems reasonable to extend that same advice to practitioners in rehabilitation and related fields: To the best of one's ability, within the given context, practice genuineness, unconditional positive regard, and empathic understanding.

### Contradictions of Person-Centered Theory in Rehabilitation Settings

The classical Rogerian model has many qualities that will facilitate and enhance the rehabilitation process, but there are also several limitations or contradictions that need to be recognized. These limitations are inherent in the context in which the model is used. If the context is individual psychotherapy, then the classical model will be appropriate for clients who are motivated to explore emotional problems or personal adjustment issues. However, when the context is a real-world service delivery system, such as state–federal vocational rehabilitation agencies or community-based agencies (e.g., schools, prisons, hospitals, group homes), then the clients and the goals are likely to be rather different, and the underlying assumptions will need to be modified. At risk of oversimplification, classical Rogerian therapists believe that resolving the intrapsychic problems of clients will empower them to navigate real-world challenges on their own. And although this may be true of some clients at some levels, the majority of rehabilitation clients do not need formal psychotherapy; what they often need is clear direction and assistance with a wide range of services germane to disabilities and the world of work.

Two Rogerian concepts that are especially problematic for state vocational rehabilitation agency counselors are the ideas of "nondirectiveness," and the "necessity and sufficiency" of the facilitative conditions. Both of these concepts are central to Rogers's theory of psychotherapy, but they are not central, or even helpful, to many of the coordinating activities in which rehabilitation counselors engage. To illustrate, if these Rogerian abstractions are taken literally and imposed on the rehabilitation process, they would preclude the use of formal diagnostic evaluations and the establishment of goals. They would preclude the offering of vocational and career advice, and they would preclude a focus on skill development and behavioral change. Clearly, it would be illogical, if not impossible, for state vocational rehabilitation agency counselors to function under such restrictions.

### Lack of Real-Life Experience

One of Rogers's basic assumptions is that "individuals have within themselves vast resources for self-understanding and for altering their self-concepts, basic attitudes, and self-directed behavior" (Rogers, 1980, p. 114). This statement implies that clients have sufficient familiarity with the outer world to weigh options and make choices based on reality testing. In vocational rehabilitation, clients have often not experienced the world of work and so do not have a basis for forming accurate self-concepts as workers. Whereas persons without disabilities spend a major part of their lives testing and adjusting the self against real experiences in the environment (Super, 1990), persons with early-onset or congenital disabilities may have been deprived of these natural developmental experiences and consequently can be vocationally immature as adults. Likewise, clients who acquire a disability later in life can also face serious challenges. In extreme cases (e.g., severe traumatic brain injury), the disability may largely invalidate the prior experiences on which vocational decisions were made. For many such clients, vocational rehabilitation becomes a crash course in careers. They are expected to learn in months or years what others have spent a lifetime absorbing, and they will likely need vocational exploration and training more than psychotherapy because their vocational uncertainty is largely due to a lack of knowledge rather than deep inner conflict.

### Level-of-Needs Hierarchy

Many rehabilitation clients are more in need of security than self-actualization. They are operating closer to the bottom of Maslow's needs hierarchy than the top, and until they achieve physical and psychological security, they will not have the energy or interest required for self-exploration. Some years ago, an irreverent wag observed that it's hard to think about self-actualization when you're "up to your ass in alligators." About the only time that the facilitative conditions could actually harm clients is when counselors are so ideologically driven that they cannot see the alligators and insist on using insight-oriented therapy while ignoring more fundamental needs, such as paying the rent or putting food on the table. Security trumps autonomy most of the time for most people.

## Cross-Cultural Conflict

Although cross-cultural interactions have been a fertile ground for the application of person-centered principles, there have been concerns that person-centered values may conflict with the values of other cultures. For example, the person-centered emphasis on individualism, with the implied de-emphasis on family, friends, and authorities, can run counter to the community-centered tenets of some cultures. Also seen as problematic is the person-centered emphasis on feelings and subjective experiences. This emphasis assumes an ability by the client to verbalize feelings and a willingness to share them in the moment with the therapist. Persons from some cultures may be reluctant or unable to participate adequately in these introspective techniques (Freeman, 1993; Usher, 1989).

## CONCLUSIONS

The 21st century has seen the dawning of a new chapter in psychotherapy and counseling. With the passing of the icons (Rogers, Perls, Ellis, and, of course, Freud), it is no longer necessary to feel like an apostate when thinking of combining the better elements from various theories, and that is essentially what has been happening for the past several decades. Indeed, pure Rogerians and Freudians are quickly becoming extinct.

Concurrently, there has been a substantial improvement in the tools and sophistication of the researchers who can now retrieve and analyze huge amounts of data as they explore the new terrain of evidence-based therapy. The good news is that this scientific orientation can provide a deeper understanding of the nature of psychotherapy and counseling. The bad news is that powerful funding sources (government agencies and insurance companies) seeking economic advantage or profits have often used the science to promote short-term, manualized therapies of the behavioral and cognitive behavioral variety. This has produced a strong backlash from the insight-oriented schools that point out the many ways the research model is flawed or has been misused; in particular, they criticize the omission of the large body of evidence showing how critically important the therapeutic relationship is.

The upshot has been a considerable increase in research supporting the humanistic–experiential brands of therapy, including person centered. As the pendulum swings, and the evidence-based practice movement continues to self-correct, one is reminded of Rogers's famous quote about scientific inquiry, "The facts are always friendly" (Rogers, 1961, p. 25).

Carl Rogers's contributions to the helping professions and society have been enormous. Rogers, Sigmund Freud, and B. F. Skinner are probably the three most influential behavioral scientists of the 20th century. Each staked out a radically new way of viewing human nature.

Freud, the pessimist, warned of the undercurrents, viewing people as possessed by demons and forces that needed to be tamed. The role of psychotherapy and civilization was to create a veneer of sociability that would allow people to live in harmony with themselves and their neighbors. This theory was the origin and inspiration of the psychoanalytic movement and much of psychiatry. It was essentially a medical model to diagnose and treat mental illness.

B. F. Skinner, the disinterested scientist, had an entirely different view. He believed that human nature was neither good nor bad; it was simply a product of the environment. The organism, human or otherwise, learned according to the predictable principles of operant and respondent conditioning. The challenge to society is to engineer the environment so that individuals develop in directions that are socially desirable. Different forms of reinforcement and extinction are the basic tools of the behavior therapies.

Carl Rogers, the optimist, saw the angels instead of the demons. He believed that people were innately good, with the capacity to self-actualize. This capacity, however, could only be unlocked by nurturing relationships with significant others. This perspective is the core of most humanistic and existential therapies. Some feel that Rogers's facilitative conditions (empathy, positive regard, and genuineness) come close to an operational definition of love. The person-centered approach is especially relevant for the rehabilitation professions because of its life-affirming values and its emphasis on growth and maximizing human potential.

Each of these remarkable thinkers contributed substantially to an understanding of human nature. Their ideas have transcended psychotherapy and psychology and find expression in virtually all levels of modern discourse. The well-informed helping professional will see these theories, and their many derivatives, as powerful tools for understanding and working with clients.

The past several decades have seen an obvious decline in the use of classical person-centered psychotherapy, along with other long-term insight-oriented therapies. Paradoxically, however, there has been a growing conviction regarding the importance of the facilitative conditions as "common factors" that exert a positive influence in virtually all settings where humans interact. The importance of the facilitative conditions in the helping professions is now so well established that it would seem to constitute an ethical violation to ignore or disregard them. On the other hand, taken alone, they would rarely be sufficient to promote the type of client gain that is associated with vocational rehabilitation programs. The sufficiency argument weakens the further the rehabilitation process moves along the continuum from insight to action. Because rehabilitation is so firmly rooted in the real world, clients must be offered concrete and practical services along with the therapeutic relationship.

## DISCUSSION EXERCISES

1. What are the takeaway messages from the recent literature review on outcome research by Elliott et al., 2013?
2. What are the takeaway messages from the recent literature review on process research by Norcross (2011)?
3. How did Carl Rogers's personal experiences lead to the development of the person-centered approach?
4. You are a counseling client. Review the six "necessary and sufficient" conditions, and for each one, describe how you feel. How does each contribute to therapeutic outcome?
5. What are the basic "person-centered" tenets?
6. Think of your own personal career goal. What role will understanding of the three facilitative conditions play in the way you choose to interact with your clients?

## REFERENCES

Aspy, D. N., & Roebuck, F. N. (1974). From humane ideas to humane technology and back again many times. *Education, 95*, 163–171.

Bloch, S. (2004). A pioneer in psychotherapy research: Aaron Beck. *Australian and New Zealand Journal of Psychiatry, 38*, 855–867.

Bozarth, J. D., & Rubin, S. E. (1978). Empirical observations of rehabilitation counselor performance and outcome: Some implications. In B. Bolton & M. E. Jaques (Eds.), *Rehabilitation counseling: Theory and practice* (pp. 176–180). Baltimore, MD: University Park Press.

Cain, D., & Seeman, J. (Eds.). (2001). *Humanistic psychotherapies: Handbook of research and practice*. Washington, DC: American Psychological Association.

Castonguay, L. G., Barkham, M., Lutz, W., & McAleavey, A. (2013). Practice oriented research: Approaches and applications. In M. J. Lambert (Ed.), *Bergin & Garfield's handbook of psychotherapy and behavior change* (6th ed., pp. 85–133). Hoboken, NJ: Wiley.

Cedar, B., & Levant, R. F. (1990). A meta-analysis of the effects of parent effectiveness training. *American Journal of Family Therapy, 18*, 373–384.

Corey, G. (2001). *Theory and practice of counseling and psychotherapy* (6th ed.). Belmont, CA: Brooks/Cole.

Cornelius-White, J. (2007). Learner-centered teacher-student relationships are effective: A meta-analysis. *Review of Educational Research, 77*, 113–143.

Council on Rehabilitation Education (CORE). (2010). *Accreditation manual for rehabilitation counselor education programs*. Rolling Meadows, IL: Author.

Elliott, R. (2002). Render unto Caesar: Quantitative and qualitative knowing in research on humanistic therapies. *Person-Centered and Experiential Psychotherapies, 1*, 102–117.

Elliott, R., Greenberg, L. S., Watson, J., Timulak, L., & Freire, E. (2013). Research on humanistic-experiential psychotherapies. In M. J. Lambert (Ed.), *Bergin and Garfield's handbook of psychotherapy and behavior change* (6th ed., pp. 495–538). Hoboken, NJ: Wiley.

Emmelkamp, P. M. G. (2013). Behavior therapy with adults. In M. J. Lambert (Ed.), *Bergin and Garfield's handbook of psychotherapy and behavior change* (6th ed., pp. 393–446). Hoboken, NJ: Wiley.

Freeman, S. C. (1993). Client-centered therapy with diverse populations: The universal within the specific. *Journal of Multicultural Counseling and Development, 21*, 248–254.

Garfield, S. L. (1996). Some problems associated with "validated" forms of psychotherapy. *Clinical Psychology: Science and Practice, 3,* 218–229.

Gendlin, E. T. (1996). *Focusing-oriented psychotherapy.* New York, NY: Guilford.

Gibbard, I., & Hanley, T. (2008). A five-year evaluation of the effectiveness of person-centred counselling in routine clinical practice in primary care. *Counselling and Psychotherapy Research, 8,* 215–222.

Gilbert, P. (2009). *The compassionate mind.* London, UK: Constable & Robinson.

Greenberg, L. S., Rice, L. N., & Elliott, R. (1993). *Facilitating emotional change.* New York, NY: Guilford.

Hayes, S. C., Strosahl, K. D., & Wilson, K. G. (1999). *Acceptance and commitment therapy: An experiential approach to behavior change.* New York, NY: Guilford.

Ivey, A. E., Ivey, M. B., & Zalaquett, C. P. (2014). *Intentional interviewing and counseling: Facilitating client development in a multicultural society* (8th ed.). Belmont, CA: Brooks/Cole.

Kirschenbaum, H. (2009). *The life and work of Carl Rogers.* Alexandria, VA: American Counseling Association.

Kirschenbaum, H., & Henderson, V. L. (1989). *The Carl Rogers reader.* Boston, MA: Houghton Mifflin.

Kirschenbaum, H., & Jourdan, A. (2005). The current status of Carl Rogers and the person-centered approach. *Psychotherapy: Theory, Research, Practice, Training, 42,* 37–51.

Lambert, M. J. (2013). Introduction and historical overview. In M. J. Lambert (Ed.), *Bergin and Garfield's handbook of psychotherapy and behavior change* (6th ed., pp. 3–20). Hoboken, NJ: Wiley.

Leplege, A., Gzil, F., Cammelli, M., Lefeve, C., Pachoud, B., & Ville, I. (2007). Person-centeredness: Conceptual and historical perspectives. *Disability and Rehabilitation, 29,* 1555–1565.

Lietaer, G. (1984). Unconditional positive regard: A controversial basic attitude in client-centered therapy. In R. F. Levant & J. M. Sclien (Eds.), *Client-centered therapy and the person-centered approach: New directions in theory, research, and practice* (pp. 41–58). New York, NY: Praeger.

Lundahl, B. W., Kunz, C., Brownell, C., Tollefson, D., & Burke, B. L. (2010). A meta-analysis of motivational interviewing: Twenty-five years of empirical studies. *Research on Social Work Practice, 20,* 137–160.

Miller, W. R., & Moyers, T. B. (2007). Eight stages in learning motivational interviewing. *Journal of Teaching in the Addictions, 5,* 3–17.

Nathan, P. E. (1998). Practice guidelines: Not yet ideal. *American Psychologist, 53,* 290–299.

Norcross, J. (Ed.). (2011). *Psychotherapy relationships that work: Evidence-based responsiveness* (2nd ed.). New York, NY: Oxford University Press.

Norcross, J. C., & Lambert, M. J. (2011). Evidence-based therapy relationships. In J. Norcross (Ed.), *Psychotherapy relationships that work: Evidence-based responsiveness* (2nd ed., pp. 3–21). New York, NY: Oxford University Press.

Norcross, J. C., & Wampold, B. E. (2011). Evidence-based therapy relationships: Research conclusions and clinical practices. In J. Norcross (Ed.), *Psychotherapy relationships that work: Evidence-based responsiveness* (2nd ed., pp. 423–430). New York, NY: Oxford University Press.

Patterson, C. H. (1986). *Theories of counseling and psychotherapy* (4th ed.). New York, NY: Harper & Row.

Perls, F. S., Hefferline, R. F., & Goodman, P. (1951). *Gestalt therapy.* New York, NY: Delta.

Polcin, D. L. (2003). Rethinking confrontation in alcohol and drug treatment: Consideration of the clinical context. *Substance Use and Misuse, 38,* 165–184.

Raskin, N. J., & Rogers, C. R. (1995). Person-centered therapy. In R. J. Corsini & D. Wedding (Eds.), *Current psychotherapies* (5th ed., pp. 144–149). Itasca, IL: Peacock.

Rogers, C. R. (1942). *Counseling and psychotherapy*. Boston, MA: Houghton Mifflin.

Rogers, C. R. (1951). *Client-centered therapy: Its current practice, implications, and theory*. Boston, MA: Houghton Mifflin.

Rogers, C. R. (1957). The necessary and sufficient conditions of therapeutic personality change. *Journal of Consulting Psychology, 21*, 93–103.

Rogers, C. R. (1961). *On becoming a person*. Boston, MA: Houghton Mifflin.

Rogers, C. R. (1980). *A way of being*. Boston, MA: Houghton Mifflin.

Rogers, C. R., Perls, F. S., Ellis, A., & Shostrom, E. L. (1965). *Three approaches to psychotherapy*. Corona Del Mar, CA: Psychological & Educational Films.

Rosenzweig, S. (1936). Some implicit common factors in diverse methods of psychotherapy. *American Journal of Orthopsychiatry, 6*, 412–415.

Rubin, S. E., & Roessler, R. T. (2008). *Foundations of the vocational rehabilitation process* (6th ed.). Austin, TX: Pro-Ed.

Schmid, P. F., & Mearns, D. (2006). Being-with and being-counter: Person-centered psychotherapy as an in-depth co-creative process of personalization. *Person-Centered and Experiential Psychotherapies, 5*, 174–190.

See, J. D. (1986). A person-centered perspective. In T. F. Riggar, D. R. Maki, & A. W. Wolf (Eds.), *Applied rehabilitation counseling* (pp. 135–147). New York, NY: Springer Publishing Company.

Segal, Z. V., Williams, J. M. G., & Teasdale, J. D. (2001). *Mindfulness-based cognitive therapy for depression: A new approach to preventing relapse*. New York, NY: Guilford.

Smith, D. (1982). Trends in counseling and psychotherapy. *American Psychologist, 37*, 802–809.

Smith, M. L., Glass, G. V., & Miller, T. I. (1980). *The benefits of psychotherapy*. Baltimore, MD: Johns Hopkins University Press.

Stiles, W. B., Barkham, M., Twigg, E., Mellor-Clark, J., & Cooper, M. (2008). Effectiveness of cognitive-behavioural, person-centred, and psychodynamic therapies in UK primary-care routine practice: Replication in a larger sample. *Psychological Medicine, 38*, 677–688.

Stinnett, W. (2012). *Acceptance, empathy, and genuineness: Not a weakness*. Retrieved April 2, 2013, from http://www.gordontraining.com/leadership-training/acceptance-empathy-and-genuineness-not-a-weakness/

Strupp, H. H. (1997). On the limitation of therapy manuals. *Clinical Psychological Science and Practice, 4*, 76–82.

Super, D. E. (1990). A life-span, life-space approach to career development. In D. Brown, L. Brooks, & Associates (Eds.), *Career choice and development: Applying contemporary theories to practice* (2nd ed., pp. 197–261). San Francisco, CA: Jossey-Bass.

Task Force on Promotion and Dissemination of Psychological Procedures. (1995). Training in and dissemination of empirically-validated psychological procedures: Report and recommendations. *Clinical Psychologist, 48*, 3–23.

The most influential therapists of the past quarter-century. (2007). *Psychotherapy Networker, 31*(2). Retrieved from http://www.questia.com/library/p61464/psychotherapy-networker/i2474331/vol-31-no-2-march-april

Thomas, K. R., Thoreson, R., Parker, R., & Butler, A. (1998). Theoretical foundations of the counseling function. In R. M. Parker & E. M. Szymanski (Eds.), *Rehabilitation counseling: Basics and beyond* (3rd ed., pp. 225–268). Austin, TX: Pro-Ed.

Usher, C. H. (1989). Recognizing cultural bias in counseling theory and practice: The case of Rogers. *Journal of Multicultural Counseling and Development, 17*, 62–71.

Wampold, B. E. (2001). *The great psychotherapy debate: Models, methods, and findings*. Mahwah, NJ: Erlbaum.

Yalom, I. (1980). *Existential psychotherapy*. New York, NY: Basic Books.

# Solution-Focused Brief Therapy

*Ebonee T. Johnson, Garrett Huck, Jessica Brooks, Erin Moser,*
*John Blake, and Fong Chan*

## LEARNING OBJECTIVES

The purpose of this chapter is to provide students with an understanding of the major tenets of solution-focused brief therapy (SFBT) and its usefulness within rehabilitation settings. This chapter reviews the origins of SFBT, describes the nature of SFBT as a counseling framework, and provides descriptions of specific therapy techniques. Additionally, this chapter will discuss research supporting the use of SFBT and its applications in rehabilitation settings. Learning objectives are to assist the reader in doing the following:

1. Understand SFBT's social constructivist underpinnings as well as its theoretical foundations, origins, and development.
2. Describe a solution-focused therapist's perspective on the human capacity for change and goal achievement.
3. Define the nature of therapy from a solution-focused perspective and understand the nature of the therapist–client relationship and the process of therapy.
4. Identify commonly used SFBT techniques, how they are thought to be effective, their application, and how the approach might be useful in different rehabilitation settings.
5. Discuss the current state and future directions of SFBT research.

## HISTORICAL DEVELOPMENT

SFBT was originally conceptualized in the 1980s as an approach to family counseling by de Shazer, Berg, and colleagues at the Brief Family Therapy Center in Milwaukee, Wisconsin (de Shazer, 1985). Its international and cross-disciplinary popularity thrives as it provides an alternative to the more time-intensive traditional problem-focused therapy approaches. SFBT appears to be an economical, strengths-based approach to counseling (Lewis & Osborn, 2004), with research evidence available to support its efficacy (e.g., Bannick, 2007; Kim, 2008; Stams, Dekovic, Buist, & de Vries, 2006).

Over the past two decades, SFBT has become a popular therapy/counseling approach used by practitioners from many specialty areas (de Shazer & Berg, 1997; Henden, 2011; Metcalf, 1998) to treat a variety of mental health issues, including alcohol and substance abuse (Berg & Miller, 1992; de Jong & Berg, 1997), posttraumatic stress disorder (PTSD; Berg & Dolan, 2001), personality disorders (Bakker & Bannink, 2008), and depression (de Jong & Berg, 1997). It has also been used for everyday life issues, such as work-related stressors, family conflicts, domestic violence, bereavement, and self-esteem problems (de Jong & Berg, 1997). SFBT is useful in treating children and adolescents (Berg & Steiner, 2003), adults (Berg & Miller, 1992), and couples and families (de Shazer, 1985). Likewise, SFBT is appropriate within eclectic and integrated approaches to counseling as it works well in combination with such other approaches as motivational interviewing (Lewis & Osborn, 2004).

## SOCIAL CONSTRUCTIVIST ORIGINS OF SFBT

SFBT was developed from a social constructivist framework that values clients' perspectives within their sociocultural context (Corey, 2013). Theoretical assumptions about human nature include how people attain knowledge about themselves and the world around them and their capacity for change. "What is known or understood derives from communities of understanding rather than an individual operating as an isolated psychological entity" (Cottone, 2007, p. 193). These assumptions are consistent with social constructivism theory (SCT), which posits that people cannot achieve knowledge that is truly objective or independent of the self and environment. This position also aligns with the four SCT assumptions conceptualized by Burr (2003): (a) Knowledge that is taken for granted should be critically evaluated; (b) language and communication are bound by time, place, and culture; (c) knowledge is constructed by interactions with the social environment; and (d) social constructions or negotiated realities impact the social world as opposed to being detached from it.

Individuals, therefore, construct their own realities and can never hope to identify a true, universal reality (Neimeyer, 1993). Accordingly, individuals achieve knowledge, understanding, and meaning through interactions with both their physical and social environment. The future is both created and negotiable, and an individual is not locked into a particular set of behaviors determined by history, social stratum, or psychological diagnosis (de Shazer et al., 2007).

SFBT theory further assumes that individuals are healthy and capable and have the ability to develop creative solutions that enhance their lives (Biggs & Flett, 2005). Generally, people learn how to overcome hardships in life at least at one point in time. Yet, life's difficulties can become chronic, depending on the way in which the individual and others around them react, including therapists. Such experiences contribute to how individuals develop knowledge and the ways in which they perceive themselves and the world around them. As an individual's reality is only one of many possible realities, individuals possess the power to facilitate behavioral change if afforded a supportive environment that allows them to reconstruct perspectives on life. Individuals are both resilient and able to achieve their goals and reach potential; it simply needs to be brought into their consciousness and activated (Burwell & Chen, 2006).

SFBT, therefore, presumes that individuals possess within themselves the essential ingredients to develop a new self, modify worldviews, and implement behavior changes. If therapy assists an individual in recognizing his or her competencies and builds on potentials, strengths, and resources, the individual can reconstruct life perspective and cope with (or resolve) current or similar problems in the future. When this is accomplished, the individual can regulate negative emotions, identify and make appropriate behavioral changes, and, ultimately, lead a more satisfying life.

## SFBT AS A COUNSELING FRAMEWORK

The SFBT counseling process involves a practitioner working conjointly with a client to critically evaluate his or her subjective perceptions of reality in order to construct a new or modified version of reality as a catalyst for change (Bannink, 2007; Corey, 2013). As SFBT is a time-limited counseling modality, the primary focus is on identifying positive solutions to difficult behavioral problems, rather than on causes, deficiencies, or limitations (Burwell & Chen, 2006). In order to problem solve, clients engage in adaptive practices that assist them with reconstructing various life perspectives in a few counseling or therapy sessions. SFBT stresses that incremental behavior change is the most effective and efficient way to help people improve their lives (Seligman & Reichenberg, 2010).

Early in the first session, the therapeutic conversation shifts from discussing the nature of the presenting problem (i.e., shifting away from being problem focused) to questioning and discussing how the client has been successful in coping with the problem (i.e., becoming solution focused), using SFBT techniques to modify or create a new perception of reality (Bannink, 2007). Throughout therapy, the practitioner (a co-constructionist) refrains from an in-depth conceptualization of the problem and redirects the client's attention to solutions (Berg, 1995). Using the client's expertise, the source for a solution lies within the individual, and the therapy process is guided toward identifying what currently works, doing more of what works, and discarding what does not work (Bannink, 2007). This complete process occurs over a short period of time and is, therefore, considered a cost-effective counseling approach (Corcoran & Pillai, 2009). The therapy concludes when the client has achieved a working perspective and has implemented effective personal solutions.

The SFBT framework incorporates a variety of concepts and approaches to treatment, including the unique client–therapist relationship; identification and creation of solutions based on client experiences; the planful use of questioning techniques, compliments, and feedback; and experimentation and homework to achieve solutions to behavioral or life problems. Examples are included through-out the following sections to illustrate how SFBT works as a time-limited coun-seling approach.

### The Client–Therapist Relationship

SFBT therapists adhere to an optimistic and hopeful orientation toward clients as individuals capable of tapping into their own internal coping resources, once provided the necessary support to do so (Biggs & Flett, 2005; Burwell & Chen, 2006; Cotton, 2010). Accordingly, therapists aim to maintain an expectation that positive change is inevitable (Trepper et al., 2012). The counselor/therapist views the client as expert regarding his or her own circumstances and, consequently, supports client autonomy for treatment decision making. A solution-focused therapist fosters a collaborative therapeutic alliance instead of a hierarchical therapist–client relationship.

According to the SFBT theory, significant therapeutic gains are achieved by emphasizing what can be done to enhance the present and the future and that there is only marginal value in dwelling on the referral problem or past issues (de Shazer et al., 2007). The therapist does not form notions about the nature or possible causes of behavioral problems, but rather assumes a nonpathological view of clients (Bannink, 2007). SFBT therapists also collaborate with their clients to identify relative strengths and the ability to solve problems, establish treat-ment goals, and identify and implement reasonable solutions from individual perspectives and experiences (Kim, 2008). Further, therapists and clients work as a team to pursue solutions that fit with the direction clients want to go rather than where they may have been (Burwell & Chen, 2006).

### Focus on What Is Working and Craft Solutions From Client Experience

The SFBT therapist assists a client to identify strategies useful for problem solv-ing in the past, while discarding strategies that do not work. Typically, this is achieved by the therapist planfully asking present- and future-oriented questions that focus the client on what is already working in his or her life (Trepper et al., 2012). A behavioral paradox is described by de Shazer and colleagues (2007) in which people continue trying the things that they have used in the past, even when evidence contradicts their effectiveness. Therefore, if what an individual is currently doing is not working, it is the role of the therapist to assist the indi-vidual in deciding what does work or what might work. Solution-focused thera-pists suggest that what worked in the past will likely work again in the future and, therefore, it is more beneficial to assist clients in developing awareness of instances when they have successfully solved a problem, even if the problem eventually came back (Trepper et al., 2012). For example, a client may identify instances in which he or she had coped with the problem, even to a minimal degree. Then, if the therapist proceeds to assist the client in identifying the types of resources he or she used to cope, the client can then build on that successful solution.

Another essential part in the search for what is working for the client occurs when the therapist assists the client in identifying *exceptions*. An exception is described by de Shazer (1988) as whatever was happening when the problem was not occurring or when the problem occurred to a lesser degree. Trepper and colleagues (2012) suggest that even when a client cannot think of a solution that can be repeated, most will be able to provide recent examples of times when the problem was not present. Although exceptions may seem similar to the idea of past strategies that have worked, they are marked by one key difference: Exceptions are the "something" that happened instead of the problem with or without the individual's intention or understanding (Trepper et al., 2012).

What sets SFBT apart from more traditional problem-focused therapies is that it dismisses the conventional belief that the presenting problem, or elaboration of the problem, is useful in therapy (Biggs & Flett, 2005; Bliss & Bray, 2009). It was suggested by de Shazer (1991) that identifying problems is not critical to setting and achieving therapeutic goals, as the effective solution may not necessarily be related to the problem. Rather, in SFBT, the therapist and client concentrate on identifying and creating positive solutions to behavioral problems. Once a client identifies a possible solution, the therapist's role is to encourage the client to continue to do what seems to already be working (de Shazer et al., 2007). As the individual becomes aware of appropriate resources of dealing with the problem in the past, the therapist's role is to assist the client in generating additional solutions that apply to the present problem or any future problems.

Therapy assists clients in focusing on what helps them make changes, not the factors that have made their lives difficult. Clients learn to frame goals in which a solution is present, rather than focusing on the absence of the problem. Further, individuals are encouraged to establish small, manageable goals in order to achieve an effective or longer term solution (de Shazer et al., 2007). Achieving relatively small tasks will typically appear less overwhelming, and thus more achievable, building a foundation of successes that can foster the confidence needed to pursue larger and seemingly more difficult goals to achieve.

## SFBT CORE COUNSELING TECHNIQUES

SFBT originated from an empirical base and a social constructivist theory. Over the course of several years, de Shazer and colleagues (2007) spent hundreds of hours observing and identifying types of techniques in therapy that appeared to work. Based on their analyses of therapist's and client's responses and progress, several core counseling/therapy techniques emerged, including questioning to facilitate solutions, planned compliments and feedback, and use of clinical experiments and homework assignments.

## Questioning Techniques That Facilitate Personal Solutions

The planful use of questioning is both the primary method of communication and key intervention tool in SFBT, which contrasts with other counseling approaches that use directives or interpretations as primary tools in intervention (Trepper et al., 2012). SFBT therapists/counselors infrequently interpret and very rarely challenge or confront a client. Coping, exception, miracle, scaling, and relationship questions are used to assist clients to develop their vision of a preferred future drawing from their past successes, strengths, and the resources with which to achieve their vision of reality. Questions are almost always focused on the present or the future (de Shazer et al., 2007) and are phrased in solution-focused language (Bliss & Bray, 2009). The client is encouraged to respond with solution-oriented language to develop his or her goals for change.

At the beginning of the first session, the therapist asks how things have changed since the client decided to seek counseling. A solution-focused conversation is elicited by asking questions about changes since the client made the appointment to see a therapist. Later, questions may focus on what has improved since the last session or how the client managed to find solutions as the problem reappeared. These questions provide information about previously used coping strategies and when exceptions to the problem occurred (Bannink, 2006).

### Coping Questions

Coping questions are described by Trepper et al. (2012) as questions that focus on getting the client to report on the status of the problem and how the client managed to cope, despite the ongoing presence of those problems. An example of a coping question is, "How have you managed to keep your problems from getting worse?" This type of question elicits information to identify coping strategies that have worked and strategies that can be used in the future. In addition, client answers highlight whether the problem has stabilized or has been alleviated. Verbalizing such information can alleviate frustration for clients who may not realize that they are making progress.

### Exception Questions

Exception questions help clients identify times when problems are not present and reasons why the problems did not interfere with their day-to-day activities (Seligman & Reichenberg, 2010). Client answers provide feedback not only about instances identified when the problem did not occur or occurred with less severity but also about strengths and coping resources embedded within identified exceptions. In turn, clients may find that they can use these as resources in the future (de Jong & Berg, 2002). Biggs and Flett (2005) suggest that as clients gain awareness of instances when the problem is not present, they should be encouraged to predict when they will likely overcome the problem, and later be asked to account for the accuracy of their prediction. Biggs and Flett also suggest that the act of predicting exceptions increases the frequency of such predictions and that, as more regular exceptions are noted, the problem appears more distant. Examples of exception questions include, "In what situation do you feel better already?" (Bannink, 2006, p. 156) and "What was different about that moment?" (Bannink, 2006, p. 157).

### Miracle Questions

Miracle questions are used to help a client to articulate a desired or better future in which problems would no longer exist (Bannink, 2006). Miracle questions are commonly raised at some point during the first counseling session. The therapist proposes a "miracle scenario," followed by a question, to help the client identify changes that need to occur in order for a problem to end. Bavelas, McGee, Philips, and Routledge (2000) suggest that the miracle question also provokes the client to notice different events in the world when the problem disappears. The following example from Berg and Dolan (2001, p. 7) suggests how the process works:

> I am going to ask you a rather strange question [pause]. The strange question is this: [pause] After we talk, you will go back to your work (home, school), and you will do whatever you need to do the rest of today, such as taking care of the children, cooking dinner, watching TV, giving the children a bath, and so on. It will become time to go to bed. Everybody in your household is quiet, and you are sleeping in peace. In the middle of the night, a miracle happens and the problem that prompted you to talk to me today is solved! But because this happens while you are sleeping, you have no way of knowing that there was an overnight miracle that solved the problem [pause]. So, when you wake up tomorrow morning, what might be the small change that will make you say to yourself, "Wow, something must have happened—the problem is gone!"

A client may provide a number of responses to this question. Being given time to ponder often results in multiple examples of how life might change if the problem were no longer present (Trepper et al., 2012). By examining specific responses, the client can imagine a perception of what life would be like without the problem, and that would serve as a benchmark for subsequent tasks and goals (Berg & Dolan, 2001). For example, if the client stated that he or she would be in better physical health if the problem disappeared, an appropriate solution-based goal that could follow would be engaging in more health-promoting behaviors. Alternatively, if a client rejects the idea of a miracle, then the therapist rephrases the questioning to achieve the same desired outcome along these lines: "Imagine that the problem that brought you here disappeared tomorrow. What would tomorrow look like? How would it be different from today?"

### Scaling Questions

Scaling questions assist a client in measuring progress, identifying exceptions, exploring next steps, and assessing the level of self-determination (Burwell & Chen, 2006). A scaling question asks a client to rate how things are going on any given day using a 10-point scale. For example, a therapist asks the client, "On a scale of 1 to 10, with 1 meaning that the problem is the worst it's ever been, and 10 meaning that the problem is solved, where do you feel that you are today?"

If the client reports making positive progress, his or her rating can facilitate a discussion about exceptions and how those exceptions occurred. In addition, the discussion may then lead to the client identifying steps or strategies with which to move further up the scale.

### Relationship Questions

Relationship questions elicit feedback about how perceptions of significant others are meaningful and whether these viewpoints influence if and how the client can succeed in solving the problem (de Jong & Berg, 2002). Relationship questions presuppose that significant others will notice something different about the client once a problem is gone. Examples of relationship questions include, "What will your husband notice that is different about you once you solve this problem?" and "What will your coworkers think of you when this problem is no longer present?" These questions can yield added information about what the client expects to be different once the problem disappears. The answers and discussion that follow will also provide insights, which the client can use to choose tasks to address goals, while also providing the therapist with insights about the client's interpersonal relationships. For example, a relationship question may clarify why the client's problem is more problematic in only certain relationships.

## Compliments and Feedback

A common practice in SFBT is to take a short break near the end of each counseling session (Trepper et al., 2012). The break can provide the client with an opportunity to reflect on what occurred during the session and generate feedback or conclusions. It also allows therapists the opportunity to consult with colleagues, if necessary, and prepare constructive feedback and compliments. After the break, the counselor can share compliments and feedback to encourage the client (Biggs & Flett, 2005). Compliments validate the tasks that the client does well, highlight what is working, and promote continuation of effective problem-solving behaviors and strategies. This feedback technique both acknowledges the reality of a client's struggles and sends a message that the therapist is attentive, cares, and fully expects that successful solutions will come about during the course of therapy.

According to de Shazer (1988), compliments and feedback "normalize" a client experience, restructure the meaning of the problem, and provide insight as to client competencies for solution building. The effects of such normalizing occur when compliments underscore that many perceived problems are common and understandable (Burwell & Chen, 2006). Compliments also help reframe problems and demonstrate progress to the client, in spite of any ongoing struggles. Finally, compliments help a client to recognize specific competencies through affirmations and bridging statements. Affirmations validate and provide positive feedback regarding a client's use of coping resources. Bridging statements provide transitions to the next step in treatment by linking identified strengths to a recognized problem-solving strategy. From an analysis of exit interviews with clients, Campbell, Elder, Gallagher, Simon, and Taylor (1999) reported that providing such planful compliments was the greatest benefit of SFBT as the feedback helped clients better understand their situations and share in a sense of hope and optimism.

### Clinical Experiments and Homework Assignments

SFBT therapists continuously encourage clients to do more of what is working outside therapy. Trepper et al. (2012, p. 5) suggest that therapists "gently nudge clients to do more of what has previously worked or to try changes they have brought up that they would like to try." At the end of each session, the therapist typically summarizes possible experiments and homework based on the client's unique situation and suggestions of activities or solution-based strategies that the client may want to try. For instance, if a client reports that physical stress and quality of sleep are improving since starting a workout routine, the therapist should encourage the client to maintain use of exercise as a known effective strategy. For client-identified experiments, Trepper and colleagues (2012, p. 12) suggest, "What emanates from the client is better than if it were to come from the therapist." These suggestions were made for the following reasons. First, what the client suggests, whether directly or indirectly, is familiar. Second, clients typically assign to themselves more of what has already worked or something they really want to try. In both cases, the homework is tied to their goals and their solutions. Finally, when a client determines the homework assignments, this eliminates any tendency that a client might have to resist outside intervention, no matter how well intended the suggestion or source.

### CASE STUDY

The following case example illustrates the use of scaling questions with a vocational rehabilitation client at the Department of Veterans Affairs, who sought help to cope with his anger management problems. The client is a U.S. Army combat veteran with a diagnosis of PTSD. He is pursuing an associate's degree and has difficulty in the classroom due to irritability and anger outbursts associated with his diagnosis.

**Therapist:** On the phone, you mentioned an issue that is concerning you.

**Client:** Yeah, I've been pretty stressed about keeping my temper under control at the college. A lot of the other students are just spoiled kids and they don't understand much about the real world or the importance of respect. A lot of what I hear during class discussions ends up making me furious, and well … I have a tough time hiding it, which has caused me some real problems.

*(continued)*

*(continued)*

**Therapist:** OK. Let's get a sense of how this is affecting you and where you want to go with it. Can you rate the situation on a scale from 1 to 10, where 1 is as bad as it gets and 10 is perfect? For example, at a 1, every time a student made a statement during class that you didn't totally agree with or approve of, you would completely lose your cool, shout at the student and refuse to participate in class. On the other hand, at a 10, even after a student has made a string of very objectionable comments, you would be able to continue to participate meaningfully in class without displaying any outward signs of anger.

**Client:** Well, if you know my history since I've been back from Afghanistan, you know that there isn't much chance of me hitting a 10 [uneasy laughter].

**Therapist:** You can think of the extremes of the scale as hypothetical. I just want to understand your sense of the issue and what you think needs to happen for the situation to be workable.

**Client:** Right, right. Well, I'd have to say that the situation has been at about a 3. I mean, I know I'm in college, and I expect that I'm going to run into some half-baked ideas, but when people start spouting off about things they know absolutely nothing about, I can't handle it. I see red, and in the moment I couldn't care less about the consequences. I don't storm out of class every time, but I have walked out of a couple of the last five or six classes I've attended. And I know that there have been several times that I've really scared some students, including students I like and respect.

**Therapist:** OK, so we'll say the situation is currently at a 3. And you should accept some credit for the effort it's taken to keep it at a 3. You're right, the environment at the college doesn't mesh perfectly with your values, and the fact that you've persisted and that you've decided to change your behavior shows how committed you are to completing your degree. Thinking about our scale, where do you think the situation needs to be in order for you to consider it acceptable?

**Client:** Well, I'm not going to pretend I don't have opinions, and if my actual behavior isn't out of line I doubt I'll land in hot water for sharing my perspective. I have as much right to participate as any other student. I just want to be able to make honest contributions to class without flying off the handle and scaring the hell out of everybody. If things held to a 6 or a 7, I think I'd be in safe territory.

*(continued)*

(*continued*)

> **Therapist**: All right, for now let's shoot for moving from a 3 to a 6. Thinking about our scale, where 1 is completely uncontrolled anger responses and 10 represents complete control, how will you know when you've moved from a 3 to a 6?
>
> This brief case example highlights three central components of scaling questions. First, scaling questions serve to facilitate initial and ongoing assessments. The client and the rehabilitation counselor have established an agreed-upon baseline and a framework for measuring progress. Second, scaling questions require that the focus of counseling is defined in the client's terms rather than the rehabilitation counselor's terms. Note that the client renders the assessment of current behavioral functioning and the identification of target behavior. Third, scaling questions facilitate the identification of solutions and chart client successes. The stage is set at the close of the case study for dialogue geared toward identifying exceptions to the problem and explicitly recognizing future successes (Trepper et al., 2012).

## RESEARCH IN SUPPORT OF SFBT EFFECTIVENESS

Stams, Dekovic, Buist, and de Vries (2006) conducted a meta-analysis of published and unpublished data from 21 outcome studies that involved 1,421 participants from studies with weak and strong research designs. Their analysis found that SFBT had a small to moderate effect size and better outcomes than no-treatment conditions, but the effect size was not greater than problem-focused therapy conditions. Nonetheless, the authors indicated that SFBT had a positive effect and satisfied client need for autonomy in less time than problem-focused therapy groups.

Corcoran and Pillai (2009) conducted a meta-analysis of 10 studies that used quasiexperimental or true experimental designs. For 4 of the 10 studies, the SFBT treatment demonstrated moderate to high effect sizes on therapy outcomes ($d = 0.59$–$3.00$). Participants in these four studies improved significantly on measures of depression, self-esteem, orthopedic rehabilitation, and marital and family relationships. Also, the largest effect sizes were found in true experimental studies.

Kim (2008) examined 22 experimental and quasiexperimental studies and psychosocial outcome measures for externalizing behavior, internalizing behavior, and family and relationship problems. Externalizing behavior problems refer to hyperactivity or conduct issues, whereas internalizing problems refer to low self-esteem, depression, or anxiety. He found small but positive treatment effects favoring SFBT groups over control groups on the outcome measures ($d = 0.13$–$0.26$). However, only the magnitude of the effect for internalizing behavior problems was statistically significant at the $p < .05$ level. Kim and Franklin (2009) expanded on Kim's (2008) meta-analysis, adding seven additional studies of SFBT for children and adolescents in school settings. This systematic review concluded that SFBT might be an effective intervention to decrease maladaptive emotions and improve coping with conduct and behavioral problems among at-risk students.

Woods, Bond, Humphrey, Symes, and Green (2011) also reported support for the use of solution-focused methods with children. This review found that 34 of 38 best evidence studies yielded positive psychosocial outcomes for SFBT interventions with children. SFBT children showed reduced internalizing problems (e.g., anxiety, depression, self-esteem, and self-efficacy) and externalizing behavioral problems (e.g., aggression, truancy, and cooperation). Eight of the studies also reported that some outcomes were better for SFBT participants than for either the standard intervention or a control condition.

More recently, Macdonald (2012) evaluated international studies for SFBT in the literature databases and identified a total of 120 empirical studies. These empirically based international datasets included more than 5,000 cases and 60% overall success rates within approximately three to five treatment sessions. Twenty-three randomized controlled trials were found among these studies. In 12 out of 23 studies, SFBT was found more effective when compared to a control condition. Similarly, Gingerich and Peterson (2013) reviewed 43 studies to determine the effectiveness of SFBT and found that 32 (74%) of the studies reported significant psychosocial benefits from SFBT.

### Evidence Supporting SFBT in Rehabilitation Settings

There are very few randomized controlled trials validating the efficacy of SFBT as an evidence-based practice for rehabilitation clients. Only two studies were found that examined the effects of SFBT on employment and psychosocial outcomes for persons with disabilities who were on long-term sick leave. Nystuen and Hagen (2006) attempted to determine the effects of SFBT among employees on long-term leave for psychological problems or musculoskeletal pain and found that a solution-focused intervention was no more effective than traditional psychotherapy on standard outcome measures. However, SFBT participants returned to work and showed improved health-related quality of life following treatment. Thorslund (2007) examined the effects of SFBT among employees on long-term leave for musculoskeletal problems, some of whom were experiencing depression as a secondary condition. The study found that persons in the SFBT group returned to work at a significantly higher rate than the usual care group. The SFBT group also worked more days and improved their psychological health by the end of treatment. Each study demonstrated that persons with chronic illness and disability benefit from a solution-focused intervention that includes return to work and increased quality of life as evidenced by reduced psychological symptoms associated with their chronic pain.

A comprehensive literature review by Schott and Conyers (2003) also supports the use of solution-focused interventions in psychiatric rehabilitation for persons with severe and persistent mental illness and its potential for rehabilitation counseling. They emphasize that the constructivist foundations for SFBT and psychiatric rehabilitation overlap in the following assumptions, practices, and principles: Self-determination (i.e., client is expert) is both the goal of and is central to the respective therapeutic process, focus in treatment is on individual strengths to achieve solutions rather than holding to a problems framework or diagnosis for planning treatment, commitment throughout therapy is to individual self-actualization, and cultural sensitivity is maintained through a collaborative therapeutic working alliance between coequals across the process.

## POTENTIAL APPLICATION OF SFBT IN REHABILITATION

Rehabilitation professionals working in state vocational rehabilitation agencies and community-based rehabilitation organizations typically have large caseloads. By using SFBT, practitioners can provide quality services in which time management is essential. There is also external pressure for rehabilitation professionals to provide cost-effective, empirically supported treatments due to the changing fiscal environment with state and federal budget cuts and the implementation of systems of managed care (Biggs & Flett, 2005). As a framework for assisting persons with disabilities, SFBT has been found effective in addressing such internalized problems as depression (Ormel & Von Korff, 2000), anxiety (Brenes et al., 2005), and substance abuse (Cardoso, Wolf, & West, 2009), in addition to aiding women with disabilities who are more prone to physical abuse and domestic violence (Chang et al., 2003). Finally, SFBT reflects the strengths-based, positive psychology framework of providing services to persons with disabilities first introduced by Wright (1983) and advocated by Seligman and colleagues in contemporary psychology (Seligman, Steen, Park, & Peterson, 2005).

Considering these factors, SFBT provides a resolution to the concerns of key stakeholders in rehabilitation settings (Biggs & Flett, 2005; Olney, Gagne, White, Bennett, & Evans, 2009; Smith, 2005). For practitioners, SFBT is an empirically supported treatment that is useful in facilitating behavioral changes for a variety of clinical situations and clientele. SFBT addresses ethical obligations to provide the best possible services (beneficence) in the midst of scarce resources (justice), such as time, money, and staffing (Chan, Tarvydas, Blalock, Strauser, & Atkins, 2009). For persons with disabilities who seek services to address their vocational and psychosocial needs, this is a person-centered, goal-oriented, and strengths-based approach, with the potential to maximize rehabilitation outcomes while simultaneously promoting client autonomy.

Nevertheless, the effectiveness of SFBT in various rehabilitation settings has not been firmly established, and methodologically rigorous studies are needed. Especially needed are randomized controlled trials with specific disability groups in order to determine the usefulness of the SFBT approach for persons with disabilities. The potential of SFBT for vocational rehabilitation derives largely from theory and practice of SFBT to augment treatment for psychological problems and everyday life stressors for persons with and without disabilities. Although further research on its efficacy is needed, support for the application of SFBT in rehabilitation counseling includes the following.

## Theory

- SFBT was originally designed and extensively studied for addressing such everyday life issues as work-related stressors, family conflicts, domestic violence, bereavement, and self-esteem problems (de Jong & Berg, 1997).
- SFBT is a goal-oriented, strengths-based, solution-focused approach that continues to gain acceptance among educators and practitioners in rehabilitation counseling and psychotherapy.
- SFBT reflects the strengths-based, positive psychology framework of providing services to persons with disabilities that was first introduced by Wright (1983) and advocated by others in contemporary psychology (e.g., Seligman, Steen, Park, & Peterson, 2005).
- SFBT is a person-centered, goal-oriented, and strengths-based approach with the potential to maximize rehabilitation outcomes while simultaneously promoting client autonomy.
- SFBT is a goal-oriented, strengths-based, solution-focused approach to psychological and life issues that are commonly addressed in rehabilitation counseling for individuals with various disabilities.
- SFBT shares assumptions and theoretical constructs consistent with those ascribed to in vocational rehabilitation theory and practice and is client-centric, addressing key needs and concerns of all stakeholders involved in improving the status of a client.
- SFBT aligns with core assumptions and principles adhered to in rehabilitation counseling.
- SFBT's main focus is to support client autonomy, using client expertise in the context of a cooperative and collaborative working alliance (Stams, Dekovic, Buist, & de Vries, 2006).
- SFBT addresses ethical obligations to provide the best possible services (beneficence) in the midst of scarce resources (justice), such as time, money, and staffing (Chan et al., 2009).

## Research

- Although research does not illustrate larger effect sizes when compared to traditional counseling approaches, outcomes are better than nontreatment conditions and comparable to traditional therapies.
- SFBT has been used to treat children and adolescents (Berg & Steiner, 2003), adults (Berg & Miller, 1992), and couples and families (de Shazer, 1985).
- SFBT has been explored/applied to the treatment of a wide variety of mental health issues, including alcohol and substance abuse (de Jong & Berg, 1997; Berg & Miller, 1992), PTSD (Berg & Dolan, 2001), personality disorders (Bakker & Bannink, 2008), and depression (de Jong & Berg, 1997); and the research suggests that outcomes are comparable to problem-oriented approaches.

- SFBT has been found effective in addressing such internalized problems as depression (Ormel & Von Korff, 2000), anxiety (Brenes et al., 2005), and substance abuse (Cardoso, Wolf, & West, 2009), in addition to aiding women with disabilities who are more prone to physical abuse and domestic violence (Chang et al., 2003), all of which are problems in populations often seen on rehabilitation counseling caseloads.

### Practice

- SFBT offers an empirically supported treatment that appears to facilitate behavioral changes with a variety of clinical groups.
- SFBT clinical studies suggest a well-defined process with the potential to advance counseling and therapies that address psychological problems and everyday life stressors for persons with and without disabilities.
- SFBT evidence suggests that comparable effects on psychosocial problems can be achieved in a time-limited frame.
- SFBT appears to combine well with other eclectic and integrated approaches, such as motivational interviewing (Lewis & Osborn, 2004).
- SFBT may provide an empirical alternate where caseload size and budget limitations drive the choice toward services that are both of high quality and time efficient.
- SFBT may be a useful approach for rehabilitation counselors dealing with large caseloads in state vocational rehabilitation agencies and community-based rehabilitation organizations (Biggs & Flett, 2005).
- SFBT, as a time-limited approach, may reduce pressures on rehabilitation professionals to provide cost-effective, empirically supported treatments that result from a changing fiscal environment with state and federal budget cuts and implementation of systems of managed care (Biggs & Flett, 2005).
- Rehabilitation clinicians, educators, and researchers advocate for SFBT in service for persons with disabilities as it addresses key needs and concerns of all stakeholders involved.
- SFBT offers the possibility of a resolution to the concerns of key stakeholders in the rehabilitation field (Biggs & Flett, 2005).

### CONCLUSIONS

The review of theory, research, and potential for application in rehabilitation practice in this chapter suggests the following recommendations:

### Efficacy Research

Although there has not been an overabundance of well-designed studies on the effectiveness of SFBT for people with chronic illness and disability, current evidence suggests the following about SFBT: (a) It is more useful than control conditions or no treatment (Newsome, 2004); (b) it is at least equivalent to other psychosocial interventions (Gingerich & Eisengart, 2000); (c) it shows that significantly fewer sessions can result in comparable outcomes (Littrell, Malia, & Vanderwood, 1995; Trepper, Dolan, McCollum, & Nelson, 2006); and (d) it may be particularly effective for addressing internalizing problems, such as depression (e.g., Gingerich & Peterson, 2013; Kim, 2008). Furthermore, some psychotherapy models that share techniques related to the SFBT approach (e.g., motivational interviewing) demonstrate positive results and may lend additional support for SFBT (Lewis & Osborn, 2004).

Therefore, there is a need for clinical trial research comparing SFBT to both short-term and long-term treatment programs (Knekt et al., 2008), with an applied focus on persons with disabilities. This research should overcome methodological limitations of past research designs in order to better understand the clinical efficacy of SFBT (Corcoran & Pillai, 2009). Specifically, future research studies should aim to randomize participants to both treatment and comparison conditions and collect follow-up data in order to examine the longitudinal effects of treatment (Corcoran & Pillai, 2009). As SFBT is applied with various disability populations, researchers and clinicians will be able to aggregate studies using meta-analytic procedures to elucidate the utility of SFBT in rehabilitation practice.

### SFBT Training for Rehabilitation Professionals

In addition to a need for clinical research to identify the strengths and limitations of SFBT, there is also a need for individualized training to further educate rehabilitation health professionals in SFBT methods and practices. SFBT began to be developed in 1980, when de Shazer and Berg (1997) started seeing clients in their living room with a video camera. What started out as an attempt to identify what made a difference, without any focus on providing evidence to support the benefits of SFBT, has now evolved into much more. Clinically, there is no rigid protocol or handbook for solution-focused therapists (and their clients), but there are certain aspects of SFBT that are easily recognizable and serve as indicators that SFBT is occurring (de Shazer & Berg, 1997).

In order for rehabilitation and mental health professionals to use SFBT, they must be familiar with the characteristic features of SFBT, which include (a) the therapist asking the "miracle question" at some point during the first interview; (b) at least once during the first and subsequent interviews, the client will be asked to rate something on a scale of "0 to 10" or "1 to 10"; (c) the therapist will take a break at some point during the interview; and (d) after the break, the therapist will compliment the client, which will sometimes (frequently) be followed by a homework assignment or suggestion (frequently called an "experiment"; de Shazer & Berg, 1997). Once a therapist becomes familiar with these techniques, whether or not he or she is practicing SFBT can easily be identified. Another key aspect that therapists must focus on when preparing to use SFBT is the importance of developing the same fluency when asking about hopes and achievements as when asking about problems and causes (Iveson, 2002). These key features and characteristics are important for therapists to identify and become familiar with before providing SFBT to clients. Development of techniques and recognition of the focus of SFBT can assist therapists with providing appropriate services to individuals in need and can be a great benefit to those served.

## ACKNOWLEDGMENTS

The contents of this chapter were developed with support from the Rehabilitation Research & Training Center on Evidence-Based Practice in Vocational Rehabilitation at the University of Wisconsin–Madison and the University of Wisconsin–Stout, and with funding provided by the National Institute on Disability and Rehabilitation Research, U.S. Department of Education (Grant H133B100034). The ideas, opinions, and conclusions expressed, however, are those of the authors and do not represent recommendations, endorsements, or policies of the U.S. Department of Education.

## DISCUSSION EXERCISES

1. Define what a "solution-focused" approach in therapy is, and how such an approach might differ from traditional counseling modalities.
2. SFBT suggests that in order for people to improve their lives effectively, attempts at behavior change should be incremental. How might a solution-focused therapist assist a client with creating a goal that has incremental steps? Provide an example.
3. Describe a solution-focused perspective on the importance of an individual's past, and identify why a primary focus is given to the present and the future.
4. Solution-focused therapists use a number of different types of questioning in order to assist clients with identifying goals in therapy, as well as potential plans of action for achieving their goals. Identify three types of questions commonly used in SFBT, and describe what the intention of these specific question types are in therapy.
5. Describe how a solution-focused approach may be particularly useful in vocational rehabilitation settings.

## REFERENCES

Bakker, J. M., & Bannink, F. P. (2008). Oplossingsgerichte therapie in de psychiatrische praktijk [Solution focused brief therapy in psychiatric practice]. *Tijdschrift voor Psychiatrie, 50*(1), 55–59.

Bannink, F. P. (2006). *1001 solution-focused questions*. New York, NY: Norton.

Bannink, F. P. (2007). Solution-focused brief therapy. *Journal of Contemporary Psychotherapy, 37*, 87–94.

Bavelas, J. B., McGee, D., Philips, B., & Routledge, R. (2000). Microanalysis of communication on psychotherapy. *Human Systems: The Journal of Systemic Consultation & Management, 11*, 47–66.

Berg, I. K. (1995). Solution-focused brief therapy with substance abusers. In A. M. Washton (Ed.), *Psychotherapy and substance abuse: A practitioner's handbook* (pp. 223–242). New York, NY: Guilford.

Berg, I. K., & Dolan, Y. (2001). *Tales of solutions: A collection of hope-inspiring stories.* New York, NY: Norton.

Berg, I. K., & Miller, S. D. (1992). *Working with the problem drinker: A solution focused approach.* New York, NY: Norton.

Berg, I. K., & Steiner, T. (2003). *Children's solution work.* New York, NY: Norton.

Biggs, H. C., & Flett, R. A. (2005). Rehabilitation professionals and solution-focused brief therapy. In H. Biggs (Ed.), *Proceedings of the inaugural Australian Counseling and Supervision Conference: Integrating research, practice, and training.* Carseldine, Australia: Queensland University of Technology. Retrieved from http://eprints.qut.edu.au/3796/1/3796_1.pdf

Bliss, E. V., & Bray, D. (2009). The smallest solution focused particles: Towards a minimalist definition of when therapy is solution focused. *Journal of Systemic Therapies, 28,* 62–74.

Brenes, G. A., Guralnik, J. M., Williamson, J. D., Fried, L. P., Simpson, C., Simonsick, E. M., & Penninx, B. W. (2005). The influence of anxiety on the progression of disability. *Journal of the American Geriatrics Society, 53,* 34–39.

Burr, V. (2003). *Social constructionism.* New York, NY: Routledge Chapman & Hall.

Burwell, R., & Chen, C. (2006). Applying the principles and techniques of solution-focused therapy to career counselling. *Counselling Psychology Quarterly, 19,* 189–203.

Campbell, J., Elder, J., Gallagher, D., Simon, J., & Taylor, A. (1999). Crafting the "tap on the shoulder": A compliment template for solution-focused therapy. *American Journal of Family Therapy, 27,* 35–47.

Cardoso, E., Wolf, A. W., & West, S. L. (2009). Substance abuse: Models, assessment, and interventions. In F. Chan, E. Cardoso, & J. A. Chronister (Eds.), *Understanding psychosocial adjustment to chronic illness and disability: A handbook for evidence-based practitioners in rehabilitation* (pp. 399–434). New York, NY: Springer Publishing Company.

Chan, F., Tarvydas, V., Blalock, K., Strauser, D., & Atkins, B. J. (2009). Unifying and elevating rehabilitation counseling through model-driven, diversity-sensitive evidence-based practice. *Rehabilitation Counseling Bulletin, 52,* 114–119.

Chang, J. C., Martin, S. L., Moracco, K. E., Dulli, L., Scandlin, D., Loucks-Sorrel, M. B., & Bou-Saada, I. (2003). Helping women with disabilities and domestic violence: Strategies, limitations, and challenges of domestic violence programs and services. *Journal of Women's Health, 12,* 699–708.

Corcoran, J., & Pillai, V. (2009). A review of the research on solution-focused therapy. *British Journal of Social Work, 39,* 234–242.

Corey, G. (2013). *Theory and practice of counseling and psychotherapy.* Belmont, CA: Brooks/Cole.

Cotton, J. (2010). Question utilization in solution-focused brief therapy: A recursive frame analysis of Insoo Kim Berg's solution talk. *Qualitative Report, 15,* 18–36.

Cottone, R. R. (2007). Paradigms of counseling and psychotherapy, revisited: Is social constructivism a paradigm? *Journal of Mental Health Counseling, 29,* 189–203.

de Jong, P., & Berg, I. K. (1997). *Interviewing for solutions.* Pacific Grove, CA: Brooks/Cole.

de Jong, P., & Berg, I. K. (2002). *Interviewing for solutions* (2nd ed.). Pacific Grove, CA: Brooks/Cole.

de Shazer, S. (1985). *Keys to solution in brief therapy.* New York, NY: Norton.

de Shazer, S. (1988). *Clues: Investigating solutions in brief therapy.* New York, NY: Norton.

de Shazer, S. (1991). *Putting difference to work.* New York, NY: Norton.

de Shazer, S., & Berg, I. K. (1997). "What works?" Remarks on research aspects of solution-focused brief therapy. *Journal of Family Therapy, 19,* 121–124.

de Shazer, S., Dolan, Y., Korman, H., Trepper, T., McCollum, E., & Berg, I. K. (2007). *More than miracles: The state of the art of solution-focused brief therapy*. London, UK: Routledge.

Gingerich, W. J., & Eisengart, S. (2000). Solution focused brief therapy: A review of the outcome research. *Family Process, 39*, 477–498.

Gingerich, W. J., & Peterson, L. T. (2013). Effectiveness of solution-focused brief therapy: A systematic qualitative review of controlled outcome studies. *Research on Social Work Practice, 23*(3), 266–283. Retrieved from http://rsw.sagepub.com/content/early/2013 /01/22/1049731512470859

Henden, J. (2011). Appendix A: The evidence base for solution focused therapy. In J. Henden (Ed.), *Beating combat stress: 101 techniques for recovery* (pp. 115–124). Hoboken, NJ: Wiley.

Iveson, C. (2002). Solution-focused brief therapy. *Advances in Psychiatric Treatment, 8*, 149–156.

Kim, J. S. (2008). Examining the effectiveness of solution-focused brief therapy: A meta-analysis. *Research on Social Work Practice, 18*, 107–116.

Kim, J. S., & Franklin, C. (2009). Solution-focused brief therapy in schools: A review of the outcome literature. *Children and Youth Services Review, 31*, 464–470.

Knekt, P., Lindforss, O., Harkanen, T., Valikoski, M., Virtala, E., Laaksonen, M. A., . . . Renlund, C. (2008). Randomized trial on the effectiveness of long-and short-term psychodynamic psychotherapy and solution-focused therapy on psychiatric symptoms during a three-year follow-up. *Psychological Medicine, 38*, 689–704.

Lewis, T. F., & Osborn, C. J. (2004). Solution-focused counseling and motivational interviewing: A consideration of confluence. *Journal of Counseling and Development, 82*, 38–48.

Littrell, J. M., Malia, J. A., & Wood, M. (1995). Single-session brief counseling in a high school. *Journal of Counseling & Development, 73*, 451–458.

Macdonald, A. J. (2012). *Solution-focused brief therapy evaluation list*. Retrieved from http://www.solutionsdoc.co.uk/sft.html

Metcalf, L. (1998). *Solution focused group therapy*. New York, NY: Free Press.

Neimeyer, R. (1993). An appraisal of constructivist psychotherapies. *Journal of Consulting and Clinical Psychology, 61*, 221–234.

Newsome, W. S. (2004). Solution-focused brief therapy group work with at-risk junior high school students: Enhancing the bottom line. *Research on Social Work Practice, 14*, 336–343.

Nystuen, P., & Hagen, K. B. (2006). Solution-focused intervention for sick listed employees with psychological problems or muscle skeletal pain: A randomized control trial. *BioMed Central Public Health, 6*, 69–77. Retrieved from http://www.biomedcentral. com/1471-2458/6/69

Olney, M. F., Gagne, L., White, M., Bennett, M., & Evans, C. (2009). Effective counseling methods for rehabilitation counselors: Motivational interviewing and solution-focused therapy. *Rehabilitation Education, 23*, 233–244.

Ormel, J., & Von Korff, M. V. (2000). Synchrony of change in depression and disability: What next? *Archives of General Psychiatry, 57*, 381–382.

Schott, S. A., & Conyers, L. M. (2003). A solution-focused approach to psychiatric rehabilitation. *Psychiatric Rehabilitation Journal, 27*, 43–50.

Seligman, L., & Reichenberg, L. (2010). *Theories of counseling and psychotherapy: Systems, strategies, and skills* (3rd ed.). Upper Saddle River, NJ: Pearson.

Seligman, M. E. P., Steen, T. A., Park, N., & Peterson, C. (2005). Positive psychology progress: Empirical validation of interventions. *American Psychologist, 60*, 410–421.

Smith, I. C. (2005). Solution-focused brief therapy with people with learning disabilities: A case study. *British Journal of Learning Disabilities, 33*, 102–105.

Stams, G. J., Dekovic, M., Buist, K., & de Vries, L. (2006). Effectiviteit van oplossingsgerichte korte therapie: Een meta-analyse [Efficacy of solution focused brief therapy: A meta-analysis]. *Gedragstherapie, 39*, 81–95.

Thorslund, K. W. (2007). Solution-focused group therapy for patients on long-term, sick leave: A comparative outcome study. *Journal of Family Psychotherapy, 18,* 11–24.

Trepper, T. S., Dolan, Y., McCollum, E. E., & Nelson, T. (2006). Steve de Shazer and the future of solution-focused therapy. *Journal of Marital and Family Therapy, 32,* 133–139.

Trepper, T. S., McCollum, E. E., de Jong, P., Korman, H., Gingerich, W. J., & Franklin, C. (2012). Solution-focused brief therapy manual. In C. Franklin, T. Trepper, W. Gingerich, & E. McCollum (Eds.), *Solution-focused brief therapy: A handbook of evidence-based practice* (pp. 20–36). New York, NY: Oxford University Press.

Woods, K., Bond, C., Humphrey, N., Symes, W., & Green, L. (2011). *Systematic review of solution focused brief therapy (SFBT) with children and families* (Education Research Report 179). London, UK: Department for Education, University of Manchester. (eScholarID: 149106)

Wright, B. (1983). *Physical disability: A psychosocial approach.* New York, NY: HarperCollins.

# Gestalt Therapy

*Charles Edmund Degeneffe and Ruth Torkelson Lynch*

## LEARNING OBJECTIVES

The goal of this chapter is to provide readers with an appreciation of gestalt therapy as an effective counseling approach in rehabilitation. The chapter reviews the history, theory of personality, specific techniques, and applications in working with persons with disabilities in rehabilitation settings. The chapter also reviews how the philosophy of gestalt therapy is in many ways consistent with traditional values in rehabilitation counseling. As learning objectives, the reader is assisted in achieving the following:

1. Gain awareness of the unique philosophy and assumptions of gestalt theory and therapy and the ways in which gestalt therapy views the nature of human maladjustment.
2. Develop skills in applying gestalt therapy techniques to facilitate greater client self-awareness and self-direction.
3. Appreciate the applicability of gestalt therapy in providing counseling support to persons with disabilities.
4. Understand the research evidence supporting the use of gestalt therapy
5. Acknowledge the overall strengths and limitations of gestalt therapy.

## FOUNDATIONS OF GESTALT THERAPY

Frederich (Fritz) Perls is widely credited with the development of gestalt therapy (e.g., Cottone, 1992; Feder & Ronall, 1980; Polster & Polster, 1973; Shepard, 1975; Wulf, 1998). Fritz Perls initially practiced as a neuropsychiatrist and was also influenced by the theater (as an actor in the Golden Twenties in Berlin), which resulted in his emphasis on nonverbal communication. Early in his career while training and practicing as a psychoanalyst, he was influenced by the work of Max

Wertheimer, Wolfgang Kohler, and Kurt Koffka, all of whom believed that the psychological framework of humans was constructed from wholes, rather than collections of small and discrete units (Kogan, 1983; Passons, 1975). He was also influenced through his work with Kurt Goldstein, whose theory of holism and conceptualizations on figure–ground formulations established major underpinnings in gestalt theory and therapy (Gilliland, James, & Bowman, 1994).

Gestalt therapy focuses on present experience and the cultivation of the awareness of "how" clients arrive at their predicaments, in contrast to psychoanalysis, which is rooted in the unconscious, the past, and asks "why?" (Angermann, 1998). Gestalt therapists adhere to the belief that humans have limited self-awareness in not being able to view their lives holistically but live rather through the lens of their pasts, their fantasies, and their perceived flaws and abilities (Seligman & Reichenberg, 2010).

In addition to his early teachers, Fritz Perls was influenced by his work with his wife Laura, whom he considered to be a cofounder of gestalt therapy, as well as Paul Goodman, who coauthored a major gestalt therapy textbook with Perls. Though they agreed on many aspects of gestalt therapy, the two did appear to have differences in some of their therapeutic approaches. Although Laura Perls promoted increased levels of permissiveness in the therapist–client relationship, Fritz Perls emphasized control. Though she worked closely with her husband on many aspects of the development of gestalt theory as an approach to psychotherapy, Laura Perls's contributions have largely been obscured (Kogan, 1983).

Fritz Perls lived in the United States from 1947 until his death in 1970 (Allen, 1986; Kogan, 1983). During that time, gestalt therapy gained acceptance and recognition as a new psychotherapy, in part due to a human potential movement in the United States following World War II. During that time period, people began to seek a private understanding of meaning and values for their lives, and psychologists Abraham Maslow and Carl Rogers were important contributors. The themes of the human potential movement were consistent with the philosophical notions of understanding the nature of human personality as described by Fritz Perls in promoting gestalt therapy. The growth of gestalt therapy was also facilitated by the overall presence of psychotherapy as well as psychology as an academic discipline in the United States after World War II (Kogan, 1983).

In 1951, Fritz and Laura Perls founded the first gestalt therapy institute in New York City, followed by institutes established in such locations as Esalen, California, and Cleveland, Ohio. Initially, gestalt therapy was used for group counseling, although its use in individual therapy is now more common, and it is the most widely used form of humanistic psychotherapy practiced in Europe (Strumpfel & Goldman, 2002). In addition to professionals who identify themselves as gestalt therapists, many who practice psychotherapy from other theoretical orientations incorporate elements of gestalt therapy into their work. Moreover, persons from various other professional disciplines use elements of the gestalt approach (e.g., Kelly & Howie, 2011).

## MAJOR CONCEPTS OF GESTALT THERAPY

### Theoretical Underpinnings

Gestalt therapy is based on a set of assumptions regarding what it means to be human. It is distinguished from other forms of therapy by the ways in which human personality is conceptualized. Gestalt theory postulates that humans are products of the dynamic interrelation of their mind, soul, sensations, thoughts, emotions, and perceptions, and not through discrete parts of the person (Livneh & Sherwood, 1991). Gestalt theorists do not subscribe to dichotomous concepts, such as "mind" and "body," "real" and "emotional," and "unconscious" and "conscious." The focus on wholes explains the appellation "gestalt," which is a German word meaning the organization of a meaningful whole (Coven, 1978).

A central concept of this view of human nature is that the whole is greater than the sum of the parts. The organism functions as a whole. For example, difficulty in marriage will influence job performance, and failure in school is likely to affect interpersonal relationships (Patterson & Welfel, 2000). The concept of the whole also applies to interactions within the person, including the relationship between the physiological and psychological aspects of a person. As an example, emotion may be expressed through physical means, requiring a counselor to carefully observe both nonverbal and verbal behavior in order to fully understand a person. In fact, Perl's approach to learning about oneself does not focus much on words or thoughts, but rather on the feeling and awareness that are communicated through the body's nonverbal messages (Axelson, 1999).

Gestalt therapists stress that people have the ability to define their own reality and make their own choices (Coven, 1978), which is the basic force that shapes human life:

> Every individual, every plant, every animal has only one inborn goal—to actualize itself as it is. A rose is a rose is a rose. A rose is not intent to actualize itself as a kangaroo. An elephant is not intent to actualize itself as a bird. In nature—except for the human being—constitution, and healthiness, potential growth, is all one unified something. (Perls, 1969, p. 31)

Gestalt therapy is based on a collection of beliefs on what it means to be a human being. Passons summarized the beliefs as the following:

1. Man is a whole who is (rather than has) a body, emotions, thoughts, sensations, and perceptions, all of which function interrelatedly.
2. Man is part of his environment and cannot be understood outside of it.
3. Man is proactive rather than reactive. He determines his own responses to external and proprioceptive stimuli.
4. Man is capable of being aware of his sensations, thoughts, emotions, and perceptions.
5. Man, through self-awareness, is capable of choice and is thus responsible for covert and overt behavior.

6. Man possesses the wherewithal and resources to live effectively and to restore himself through his own assets.
7. Man can experience himself only in the present. The past and the future can be experienced only in the now through remembering and anticipating.
8. Man is neither intrinsically good nor bad. (Passons, 1975, p. 14)

### Gestalt Therapy Theory of Personality

When an individual makes choices in life that meet personal needs, homeostasis has been achieved. The natural inclination to move toward homeostasis is termed organismic self-regulation. Humans are seen as constantly striving for balance in their lives, and this balance is threatened by events outside oneself as well as by internal conflict (Patterson & Welfel, 2000). Further, the natural inclination is for humans to move toward growth (Murdock, 2013). Human needs are understood by the person through a figure–ground conceptualization. Figures are perceived by the person as an immediate need, while also providing the strategies required to meet the need. Ground represents the physical and psychological environments having relation to a need and its fulfillment (Thomas, Thoreson, Parker, & Butler, 1998). When the figure is successfully achieved, it retreats to the background, permitting another figure to emerge in the foreground (Grossman, 1990).

People often find difficulty in reaching homeostasis because they do not know how to locate and engage with the figures in their environments that will assist them in meeting their needs. To fulfill needs, persons make contact with their environments (Murdock, 2013); contact is achieved through the use of all of the senses, which include looking, listening, touching, talking, smelling, tasting, and moving (Polster & Polster, 1973). In addition, contact requires the support that comes from internal characteristics and collective experiences. According to Laura Perls (1976, p. 225):

> Support is everything that facilitates the ongoing assimilation and integration for a person, a friendship, or a society: primary physiology (like breathing and digestion), upright posture and coordination, sensitivity and mobility, language, habits and customs, social manners and relationships, and everything else that we have learned and experienced during our lifetime.

Individuals may experience difficulties in successfully making contact due to limitations of internal psychological growth. These areas of limitation include introjection, projection, retroflection, deflection, and confluence (Gilliland et al., 1994; Murdock, 2013; Polster & Polster, 1973).

Introjection refers to the failure to assimilate facts, ethics, ideas, and norms from the surrounding environment. Rather than assimilating, individuals "swallow" these concepts whole and are not able to integrate them into their personalities, resulting in feelings of phoniness, superficiality, and separation from others. Introjectors often fail to clarify preferences and expectations, such as blindly following societal rules without consideration of one's personal value system. Projection refers to placing responsibility for occurrences in life onto others. Common words in a projector's lexicon include *they, them, she, he,* and *you.* Projectors often feel powerless to effect change in their lives. Retroflection involves directing behavior toward the self that one would like to direct toward others. These behavioral impulses can be either antagonistic or loving. Retroflectors restrict interaction with their environments. Deflectors interact with their environments on a chance basis. They either do not spend energy or they place misguided focus on trying to make contact and, as a result, do not get from the environment what is required to have needs satisfied. With confluence, individuals lack a boundary between the self and the environment, and also with others. Confluence is often characterized by fear about recognizing or valuing differences and distinctions from others.

Other problems areas that people experience in their attempts to meet life needs include unfinished business and fragmentation (Passons, 1975). Unfinished business refers to unfulfilled needs, unexpressed feelings, or other uncompleted important events in a person's life. The focus of the unfinished business often dominates the person's attention and awareness. Moreover, it encumbers the ability to attend to other life needs. Tobin (1983, pp. 373–374) provided an example of unfinished business in the following vignette of a worker's feeling toward his supervisor:

> A simple example would be the employee who feels angry toward his boss but, because he is frightened of being fired, decides not to express his feelings. Until he expresses his anger in some way, he is left with the physical tension that results from the impasse between the physical excitation of the anger and the inhibiting force that suppresses the emotion. He may try to deal with this unfinished situation in indirect ways, e.g., by having fantasies about telling his boss off or about the death of the boss in an accident, or by taking it out on his wife and children when he goes home that night. No matter what he does, he is tense and anxious and has a nagging feeling of not having done something he should have done.

Fragmentation refers to denying or disowning essential needs of life (e.g., companionship) or to continuous dimensions of the self, such as thoughts, traits, values, and actions becoming polarized (Gilliland et al., 1994). For example, an individual may identify with being only masculine or only feminine, failing to recognize dimensions of both characteristics within the self. Passons (1975, p. 19) exemplified the limiting effects of dichotomization when he stated, "A person cannot feel the fullness of his strength unless he permits himself to experience enough of his weakness to be able to appreciate the contrast between the two."

Believing that instinct plays a part in motivating behavior, Fritz Perls emphasized a "hunger" instinct that motivates persons to take in elements of the environment. Although gestalt theorists would view this instinct as driving the organism, behavior would not be seen as either "bad" or "good," but rather as "effective" or "ineffective" (Patterson & Welfel, 2000).

## GESTALT COUNSELING PROCESS

The purpose of counseling in the gestalt system is to encourage personal growth. Simply put, gestalt is an integrative approach to counseling, rooted in an existential orientation (Whitmore, 1991). Compared to counseling approaches that stress the importance of reflective listening, gestalt therapy instead focuses on a client's nonverbal behavior (Seligman & Reichenberg, 2010), based on the assumption that nonverbal behavior provides a more reliable indicator of what the client truly feels and believes. Because client feelings are emphasized, and the client is seen as responsible for his or her own coping behavior, gestalt counseling falls toward the affective and client-centered end of the continuum of counseling theories (Patterson & Welfel, 2000). Gestalt therapy is best used with individuals who seek self-growth and understanding. A basic premise of gestalt therapy is that "individuals who are in touch with themselves, who are aware of the present, and who have a good clear sense of self and environment, when confronted by decision making are able to make decisions that are congruent with their needs and self-concepts" (Cottone, 1992, p. 142).

In the gestalt approach, clients come for help because they are feeling that their lives are incomplete and their needs are unmet (Allen, 1986). People often develop a sense of hopelessness over the direction of their lives and do not have awareness as to how they can help themselves (Passons, 1975). The central focus of intervention involves work toward assimilating feelings; cognitions; beliefs; perceptions; and past, present, and future events to help in developing self-awareness and meeting desired life needs. In this process of assimilating experience, addressing unfinished business, learning how to meet needs, and working toward becoming whole, the client works toward closure, otherwise known as "completing the unfinished gestalt" (Gilliland et al., 1994).

A key assumption in gestalt therapy is that clients need to learn to accept responsibility for their behaviors and choices in life (Livneh & Sherwood, 1991). In his reference to Perls, Passons (1975) stressed that responsibility does not mean that clients try to meet others' expectations. Rather, taking responsibility refers to clients' understanding of their own unique and individual abilities in achieving what they want out of life. As Perls (1969, p. 38) stated:

> So what we are trying to do in therapy is step-by-step to re-own the disowned parts of the personality until the person becomes strong enough to facilitate his own growth, to learn to understand where are the holes, what are the symptoms of the holes. And the symptoms of the holes are always indicated by one word: avoidance.

Indicative of the emphasis on taking responsibility in gestalt therapy, Allen (1986) noted that clients are continually asked to use personalizing pronouns, such as *I*, *me*, and *my*, rather than *it* or *you*, when describing their feelings and experiences. Allen suggested that nonpersonalizing pronouns allow clients to distance themselves from their situations. Allen also stressed that by asking clients to make statements from their questions, they can reown and take responsibility for their belief systems.

In addition to the emphasis on client responsibility, gestalt therapy has a here-and-now orientation. There is a focus on the present behavior of the client and the meaning of the client's posture, breathing, mannerisms, gestures, voice, and facial expressions, referred to as contact functions (Polster & Polster, 1973). For example, clients who bow their heads or clench their fists are challenged by the therapist to recognize the feeling associated with the observed behavior (Thomas et al., 1998). Consistency between verbal statements and nonverbal behaviors is sought (e.g., "You say you were hurt and embarrassed but you are laughing"). Confrontation might also be used in response to discrepant components of verbal statements that the client makes and also to omissions—what the client is not saying—in order to move closer and closer to an authentic awareness and acceptance of experiences (Patterson & Welfel, 2000). The focus on what the client communicates nonverbally derives from a belief in gestalt therapy that clients too often focus on their intellectual awareness without an adequate appreciation of what their body senses may be differently communicating (Seligman & Reichenberg, 2010).

Attention to a client's senses is characteristic of the holistic orientation in gestalt therapy that involves the client cognitively, emotionally, sensorially, and physically (Coven, 1978). Indicative of the focus, gestalt therapists believe that the present is the most important area of attention since the past is gone and the future has not yet arrived. In gestalt therapy, the counselor attempts to have clients restate past and future events in present terms (Allen, 1986).

In gestalt therapy, the nature of the relationship between the client and counselor is a dynamic, two-way encounter, referred to as the "I–thou" relationship (Yontef, 1983). Simkin (1976) suggested that in the I–thou relationship, the counselor works on a horizontal level with the client. In describing the horizontal nature of the I–thou relationship, Simkin (1976, p. 79) stated, "For me, I see many therapists not sharing themselves nor encouraging the patient to invade the therapist's privacy. In the vertical relationship the 'I' remains private and hidden and deliberately or inadvertently fosters dependency and transference."

Gestalt counseling is not interpretive (i.e., the counselor does not interpret behavior), but the counselor needs sufficient diagnostic skills to recognize defensive attempts to hide rather than be authentic (i.e., to reflect his or her internal state accurately; Patterson & Welfel, 2000). Gestalt therapists use an assessment method called patterning rather than traditional diagnosis, which is a process of listening to the client and observing verbal and nonverbal gestures, requiring a creative combination of therapeutic skills and theory with the therapist's awareness of his or her own past experiences and responses (Angermann, 1998). Such observation allows a picture or pattern to emerge about the client and the environment (e.g., family, relationships, peer groups).

Cottone (1992) reflected that there is no final determination or interpretation in gestalt therapy but, rather, the counselor enters into dialogue to facilitate growth of both the counselor's and the client's personality through interpersonal interactions. Although the counselor is active in the process of therapy, interpretation of events, experiences, and even dreams is the client's responsibility. Change is allowed to unfold as clients become who they really are, rather than expending energy on being someone they are not (Angermann, 1998).

## GESTALT STRATEGIES

Fritz Perls thought that the term *technique* sounded manipulative and controlling, but in reality he used several methods to engage and to influence clients (Cottone, 1992). Angermann (1998, p. 39) relates that "Gestaltists are not 'stuffy' people; they refer to their therapeutic techniques as rules and games." As part of achieving the goals of counseling in gestalt therapy, the counselor attempts to engage the client in a multitude of experiential techniques where, in the safety of the therapeutic relationship (Gilliland et al., 1994), the client is able to work through with the therapist the nature of what in the client's life is keeping him or her from fulfilling life's needs. Moreover, experiments can help illustrate previously unrecognized skills and capabilities that clients already have that may be needed in achieving future goals (Polster & Polster, 1973). Gestalt techniques focus on enhancing active awareness. Commonly used experiential techniques include dream work, "focusing questions," role-playing via the empty chair technique, the exaggeration game, the "I take responsibility" game, and enactment.

Gestalt therapists view dreams as an existential message from one part of the self to another part (Appelbaum, 1983). Dreams can also be helpful in learning about the present relationship with the counselor, as well as the relationships with other group members during group therapy (Polster & Polster, 1973). In dream work, clients are asked to describe their dreams as if the dream was presently occurring. Following this report, clients may then be requested to play out the various parts of the dream. This could occur by asking the client to engage in a conversation with parts of the self that were represented in the dream (Gilliland et al., 1994). "Focusing questions" are designed to get the client to attend to certain experiences in the present, such as "How are you feeling now?" or "What are you thinking now?"(Cottone, 1992).

As implied by its name, the empty chair technique involves having the client speak to an empty chair. It is used to help clients reclaim what they have rejected (e.g., a physically abusive childhood) and to teach them to use things perceived as painful and difficult (e.g., memories) to enhance their awareness and well-being (Zinker, 1977). The empty chair technique is a role-playing strategy applied to situations that require an integration of opposing parts of one's personality or a resolution of unfinished business. For example, it could be used to help a client communicate unexpressed feelings of anger toward a parent who died during the client's childhood. In such a scenario, the client would verbally express these feelings to the deceased parent, whom the client would imagine to be sitting in the empty chair. The client may then be asked to sit in the empty chair and assume the role of the parent, who will then communicate back to the child. The counselor functions as a "director" instructing the client to play various roles (Haney & Leibsohn, 1999).

In the exaggeration game, the client is asked to exaggerate a view that has been expressed and viewed by the counselor as defensive. The intention is for the client to see the inaccuracy, as the affect and content become exaggerated, so that the client may take back part of the original defensive statement (Patterson & Welfel, 2000).

The "I take responsibility" game works similarly to the exaggeration game, because the client is asked to repeat a questionable statement and follow it with the words "I take responsibility for what I have said." The client must alter the original statement if, in retrospect, he has doubts about it. He would not otherwise feel able to take responsibility for the statement (Patterson & Welfel, 2000).

With enactment, clients are asked to act out in a dramatic manner an aspect of themselves (Polster & Polster, 1973). Enactment often addresses issues related to personal characteristics or to unfinished business, both from the distant and recent past. Through this exercise, clients often gain new insights into abilities, behaviors, and personal characteristics that had not been available to their conscious awareness. Polster and Polster (1973, p. 276) presented an example of enactment as used during a group session:

> One example concerns Maeta, a young woman who described herself as "being all tied up in knots." So, I asked her to tie herself up in knots and play out her own personal metaphor. This she did, twisting her arms, legs and body around in convoluted fashion, literally tying herself up. I asked her how she felt all tied up this way, and Maeta replied that she felt immobilized, tightly constricted and tense. What did she feel like doing? She felt like getting untied, and I directed her to do this gradually, untwisting one limb at a time and experiencing each of these loosenings separately. As she did this, she was surprised to realize that she was fearful of untying herself! No matter how painful and paralyzing being tied up in knots was, it was at least an identity of sorts, and if she got completely untied, she didn't know who or what she might become!

## GESTALT APPLICATIONS IN REHABILITATION

The gestalt approach to psychotherapy and counseling provides a theoretical model that would appear to have utility in the provision of rehabilitation counseling and related interventions for people with disabilities. The central tenets include (a) a holistic view of self, (b) an understanding of the person and the environment (i.e., figure and ground), (c) a temporal emphasis on the here and now, (d) a horizontal relationship between client and counselor, and (e) an acknowledgment that awareness in the here and now leads to change (Cottone, 1992). These tenets would appear to be clearly consistent with traditional values in rehabilitation counseling and related professions.

It has been argued in the rehabilitation literature that gestalt theory and therapy may have benefit in working with persons with disabilities (Allen, 1986; Coven, 1978; Grossman, 1990; Livneh & Sherwood, 1991; Thomas et al., 1998), even though it has received relatively little attention compared to a number of counseling approaches. Gestalt theory has a focus on self-awareness, self-completion, self-integration, self-responsibility (Allen, 1986), as well as holism (Livneh & Sherwood, 1991), and that focus is particularly relevant when working with persons with disabilities. Because one of the tasks of clients in counseling is to envision, conceptualize, and realize a new identity (e.g., after the onset of a chronic illness or occurrence of an injury), the sustained work to "finish a gestalt" can be effective in rehabilitation. A goal of gestalt therapy is "to aid the client to complete gestalts from the past, have richer experiences of self and others in the present, and to open a future full of new meanings that are always in formation" (Berger, 1999, p. 33). Further, gestalt therapists believe in the importance of clients finding their own way (Seligman & Reichenberg, 2010), a practice consistent with the ideal of the right of self-determination among persons with disabilities. These attributes of gestalt therapy have the potential to enhance rehabilitation practice.

Livneh and Antonak (1997) noted that consumers of rehabilitation services, those with chronic illness and disability, face a potential array of psychological, emotional, and social stresses. Sources of these stresses include prognosis, performance of daily activities, impact on family and friends, and fulfilling of life roles. Although a central aim of gestalt therapy is to help clients move away from an overreliance on the environment for support toward self-support, the theory does not ignore the fact that, at times, clients have a need for healthy or nonmanipulative support from their environment (Bull, 1997). On a clinical level, gestalt therapy may help rehabilitation clients adapt to the consequences of their impairments (e.g., Imes, Clance, Gailis, & Atkeson, 2002).

Gestalt therapy offers a number of experiential techniques for use in a rehabilitation counseling relationship. Many of these techniques may be helpful to rehabilitation clients in addressing anger (both internal and external), denial, depression, and other aspects of adapting and living with disability. Gestalt therapy interventions can help clients become more aware of their feelings about living with disability, as well as ways in which they can achieve greater happiness and fulfillment in the future. Of particular utility in counseling persons with disabilities is the focus on self-responsibility and personalizing pronouns, in addition to the gestalt experiential games of unfinished business, exaggeration, and dialogue (Livneh & Sherwood, 1991). As an example, Grossman (1990) noted that through the empty chair technique, a client could engage in a dialogue with that part of the body (e.g., a lost limb, a prosthesis, or a phantom limb) that may have contributed to creating an internal conflict between the able and disabled aspects of the client's personality.

Gestalt therapy interventions can be effective in helping persons with disabilities come to terms and bring closure to their feelings regarding what a disability has taken from their lives (Coven, 1978). Instead of only directing clients toward what their residual capabilities are, there is recognition of what has been lost. Counselors can prompt the client to discuss losses with phrases such as "what I now can't do is..." and "I'm frustrated by..." (Coven, 1978, p. 145). Further, in discussing the theory's applicability to women, Murdock (2013) noted that gestalt therapy promotes an ideal of growth and worth that is not dependent on others' views. This philosophy likewise has implications for how persons with disabilities choose to perceive their inherent value.

In addition to its usefulness for addressing adjustment to disability issues, gestalt therapy is also commonly used in other rehabilitation contexts, such as the treatment of alcoholism (Clemmens, 1997), group counseling (Fedar & Ronall, 1980; Harman, 1996), and family counseling (Polster & Polster, 1973). Moreover, it has been used with other disability groups, including persons with intellectual disabilities, emotional disturbances, generalized anxiety disorder, discomfort, psychosomatic disorders, and anomie; children and adolescents (Thomas et al., 1998); and persons with HIV/AIDS (Siemens, 2000), eating disorders (Angerman, 1998), and posttraumatic stress disorder (PTSD; Cohen, 2003; Perera-Diltz, Laux, & Toman, 2012). Cohen argued that gestalt therapy should in fact be viewed as the treatment approach of choice, given its focus on the present, body movements, and nonverbal behavior, all necessary components that Cohen believes are necessary for the successful treatment of PTSD. Cohen laments, however, that little research exists to demonstrate its treatment efficacy for this population.

Siemens (2000) noted the usefulness of the gestalt approach for counseling persons with HIV/AIDS. Because a tremendous amount of shame toward the outside world remains in the lives of HIV-infected persons, Siemens noted that individuals may hide through retroflection to avoid exposure in the social community. However, there has also been a shift in perspective about HIV/AIDS from a terminal illness to a chronic illness, with resulting changes in expectations for self-support, leading to confusion for persons who are HIV infected, many of whom had withdrawn from daily life events (including working and caring for a home). Gestalt therapy can address the retroflection process (i.e., aggression turned toward the self) and encourage the individual to realize a more accurate sense of self in the present.

There are several goals of counseling for individuals with eating disorders that Angermann (1998, p. 38) asserts can be effectively addressed, using gestalt therapy

> (a) to bring awareness to internal physical and emotional states (somatic perception); (b) to understand how the client avoids contact and how boundary disturbances serve adaptive functions; (c) to integrate the self and self-image into a unified whole (address fragmentation); and (d) to examine unfinished business as it affects the present situation and blocks awareness and integration.

As an example of this application, clients may be assisted in distinguishing between reality in their environment and the confabulations in their head. For individuals with eating disorders, these dichotomies are present in the ways in which they see themselves and believe that others see them (e.g., physically), what they think of themselves (e.g., worthless, ugly), and what they assume others think of them (Angermann, 1998). The counselor might use the exaggeration technique to bring awareness to the amount of time that a person already gives to various obsessions in her inner world rather than facing the outer world. Another useful strategy might be the empty chair technique for the child self and the adult self when a client with eating disorders has assumed the role of caretaker in the family at an early age (e.g., alcoholic parents) and is trapped by a focus on the needs and expectations of others.

Coven (1978) suggested that the philosophies, theories, techniques, and rules associated with gestalt therapy could be used in carrying out rehabilitation for individual clients and could be extended beyond a clinical level to a wider service system level. Yontef (1997) has suggested that gestalt therapy has valuable applications in clinical supervision. On a clinical level, gestalt perspectives could facilitate functions, such as helping clients in task completion and rehabilitation closure, responding to feelings of vocational and personal inadequacy, and facilitating the process of achieving personal–vocational wholeness. For purposes of clinical supervision, a counselor can effectively help counselors in training to recognize, understand, contain, and appropriately express emotions with awareness and present-centeredness. On a broader service system level, gestalt principles could enhance client choice of services, increase the accessibility of rehabilitation professionals to their clients, and reduce the time required to go through the rehabilitation process. These types of system-level, gestalt-based ideas appear to be consistent with many recent changes in the ways in which rehabilitation services are delivered to persons with disabilities, which focus on self-determination, consumer empowerment, and normalization (e.g., Degeneffe & Terciano, 2012). Especially relevant are the gestalt ideas of humans defining their own realities and the attention that should be given to the holistic needs of the individual.

It is hypothesized that rehabilitation professionals who are familiar and identify with the philosophies and beliefs in the gestalt approach may be more likely to support contemporary changes in the disability service system. These changes are consistent with the "I–thou" relationship between the counselor and client, in which clients are the ones who determine what is wanted in life and, in turn, have a significant say and personal responsibility for the ways in which they choose and use rehabilitation services.

Gestalt therapy requires clients to be able to engage in a collaborative and often intense relationship with the counselor that addresses feelings of detachment, lack of joy in life, and a sense that life is not being fully lived. As such, it may not be a suitable approach for all clients receiving rehabilitation services. Gestalt therapy has limited applicability for clients out of touch with reality, those in crisis, and those seeking assistance with a narrowly defined issue or need (e.g., being in an unsatisfying job; Seligman & Reichenberg, 2010).

However, based on her review of the literature and her clinical experience in Denmark, Arnfred (2012) argued that gestalt therapy can be effectively used with persons with schizophrenia to help promote contact with other clients in group therapy and to assist them in developing greater self-awareness. She noted, however, that there is no agreement on the extent to which counselors should change behavior, enter the psychotic world of the client, use acting-out experiments, and employ enactment exercises. Also, Baalen (2010) provided a comprehensive case study review of his use of gestalt therapy with a woman with bipolar disorder who had experienced symptoms, including psychosis, hyperactivity, and sleep-lessness. Baalen described his long-term treatment relationship with the client using gestalt therapy by addressing polarities in her life; the phenomenological meaning of her life; and her relationships with her lover, colleagues, and the space where she did her artwork. He described his work with the client as relational, and reported that she remained in therapy for 3 years without taking medication and experienced no further bipolar disorder episodes.

---

### CASE STUDY

John is a 38-year-old man who 6 months previously experienced a spinal cord injury as the result of an automobile accident. He is paralyzed below the waist and lives alone in an apartment. At the insistence of his parents, John has agreed to participate in counseling. They have expressed to John their concerns that he is not adjusting well to his disability. John appears angry most of the time and has shut himself off from family and friends. When asked by others how he is feeling, John's usual response is to say things are fine and then to change the subject. The following excerpts are taken from a counseling session. In the session, John addresses his feelings about counseling and his current relationship with his parents.

Co:  What are your reasons for coming to counseling?

Cl:  My parents thought I needed it. They are concerned I haven't done well since my accident.

Co:  I see. How do you feel about being here today?

Cl:  It's all right I guess. It sounds like a good idea.

Co:  John, I want you to say that last sentence again. This time I want you to use "I" instead of "it" when telling me your feelings on being here.

Cl:  Why? What difference will that make?

Co:  Because you are making a statement about yourself. The way you phrased your statement doesn't sound like you are talking about your personal feelings toward counseling.

Cl:  OK, here I go again. I think counseling is a good idea.

Co:  Do you hear the difference in the two statements?

Cl:  Yeah, I don't feel like I meant it the second time I told you.

Co:  So, how do you feel about your parents asking you to come to counseling?

*(continued)*

*(continued)*

Cl: I understand why. They are just looking out for me. I guess it makes sense. (The counselor notices that John makes a fist with his right hand when he conveys his answer.)

Co: Do you see what you did with your right hand when you told me that?

Cl: It's in a fist.

Co: What do you think that means?

Cl: I'm not sure. I didn't even realize I did that.

Co: John, I want you to put both of your hands in a fist for 10 seconds. When you do this, I want you to concentrate on how you feel.

Co: (After 10 seconds) How do you feel now?

Cl: I feel frustrated and upset.

This exchange illustrates the counselor's efforts to have John become self-aware of his feelings about counseling. By having John restate his original statement in terms of "I" and not "it," and having him focus on his nonverbal behavior, the counselor has facilitated the process of John owning and recognizing his true feelings. Later in the session, the counselor engages John in a discussion on his current relationship with his parents.

Co: How are things with your parents?

Cl: We get along OK. Sometimes though, they interfere too much in my life.

Co: How do they interfere?

Cl: They call every day. They come to my place and make sure I have enough food and that my personal care attendant is doing his job correctly.

Co: Have you told them how you feel about how much they are involved in your life?

Cl: No.

Co: Why not?

Cl: They are trying to help me. I couldn't say how I feel to their faces.

Co: John, I want you to try an experiment. I want you to talk to that empty chair next to us and pretend that you are actually talking to your parents about your feelings.

*(continued)*

*(continued)*

Cl:   OK, but this seems a bit strange. I've never done anything like this before.

Co:   That's OK. Just give it a shot.

Cl:   Mom and Dad, I appreciate what you try to do for me. But I want to live my own life. I'm 38 years old and I can do things for myself.

Co:   Are you angry with them?

Cl:   Yeah, but I understand why they interfere.

Co:   I don't want you to focus on their feelings. I want you to focus on how you feel and I want you to express your anger.

Cl:   Mom and Dad, you embarrass me when you come over and check my cabinets for food. You make me angry when you interrogate my attendant on how he does things. (John's face becomes flushed and he begins to raise his voice.) Live your own life and let me live mine! I can't worry about making sure you're satisfied on what goes on with my life! Let me worry about that.

With the empty chair technique, John gets the experience of actually saying out loud what he has been feeling about his relationship with his parents. He begins to allow himself to consciously feel what he has tried to suppress and, for the first time, he has an experience related to what he might actually say in the future to his parents. Later in the session, the counselor asked John to pretend that he was his own parent who is speaking to him about why they are so involved in his life. The use of the empty chair may be part of a foundation on which John will develop a better relationship with his parents, especially on issues related to autonomy, choice, and independence. He can learn to recognize his feelings prior to an actual interaction, to acknowledge those feelings, and to rehearse an approach that will convey his feelings without necessarily being hurtful (which would end up to be counterproductive).

## RESEARCH FINDINGS IN GESTALT THERAPY

Early research on the processes and outcomes of gestalt therapy is limited (Allen, 1986; Fagan & Shepherd, 1970; Simkin, 1976) and has not been as extensive as research with other counseling theories (Murdock, 2013), due both to methodological factors (Fagan & Shepherd, 1970; Thomas et al., 1998) and philosophical considerations (Allen, 1986; Livneh & Sherwood, 1991). As previously mentioned, gestalt therapy is a form of existential psychotherapy and, as such, the measurement of therapeutic outcomes poses several difficulties (May & Yalom, 1995), as goals often focus on deep layers of client self-perception and a search for life meaning. This type of focus is often difficult, and sometimes impossible, to quantify. As Fagan and Shepherd (1970, p. 241) stressed:

> Most often, hard data are difficult to obtain: the important variables resist quantification; the complexity and multiplicity of variables in therapist, patient, and the interactional processes are almost impossible to unravel; and the crudeness and restrictiveness of the measuring devices available cannot adequately reflect the subtlety of the process.

Beyond these methodological considerations, gestalt therapists have traditionally been philosophically resistant to measuring formally the outcomes of their interventions. In his reference to Simkin, Allen (1986) noted that gestalt therapists largely do not see the benefits of research methodology or formal psychodiagnostic evaluation. Moreover, gestalt therapists often subscribe to the belief that the most efficacious tool for evaluating client outcomes is clinical judgment. They commonly believe that therapeutic outcome can be evaluated by subjective indicators, such as client change in outlook, adequate self-expression, the ability to extend awareness to the verbal level, and the assumption of responsibility (Livneh & Sherwood, 1991, p. 531).

There have been recent efforts in psychology to expand the extent to which components of gestalt therapy are evaluated and are based on established methods. Thomas and colleagues (1998) noted that there have been recent efforts to integrate a variety of theoretical and empirical outcomes from mainstream psychology into the ways in which gestalt therapy is conducted. Indicative of the growing emphasis on quantitative evaluation, Greenberg, Elliott, and Lietaer (1994) conducted a review of previous research on gestalt therapy concerning psychotherapy outcome, therapeutic process, and specific therapeutic task interventions. Regarding outcome, Greenberg and colleagues (1994) cited research indicating that gestalt therapy was equally effective in the treatment of depression as compared to nondirective therapy plus bibliotherapy. Moreover, gestalt therapy was found to be equally effective as compared to behavioral therapy on client outcomes, using measures of target complaints, personal orientation, and adjustment. They also noted that psychotherapy process research has identified common counseling strategies used in gestalt therapy, including in-session advisement, reflections, interpretations, disclosure, questions, and information. Research on psychotherapy process variables has also indicated that gestalt therapists most often focused on issues related to the here and now, experiences, and feelings, and a majority of the time they have used action verbs in responses to clients.

Finally, Greenberg et al. (1994) reviewed research on two gestalt therapy interventions, the two-chair and empty chair dialogue techniques. Based on several studies comparing two-chair dialogue with nongestalt interventions, the two-chair dialogue was found to be a superior strategy in working with clients experiencing splits or conflicts between two aspects of self. Two-chair dialogue was effective in helping clients achieve enhanced depth of experiencing, focusing ability, and decision-making skills. Regarding the empty chair dialogue, research has indicated that it can be an effective method for addressing unfinished business.

In a more recent review of the extant research on gestalt therapy, Strumpfel and Goldman (2002) reviewed 60 studies on gestalt therapy that addressed microprocesses (i.e., moment-by-moment processes in gestalt therapy counselor–client interactions) and long-term macroprocesses (i.e., outcome data on gestalt therapy's use with different populations). Strumpfel and Goldman suggested that microprocess studies have provided clinicians with models that inform the proper use of gestalt therapy techniques and how best to effect client change in therapy. With regard to outcome data, 75% of the reviewed studies only used gestalt therapy approaches, whereas the remaining 25% combined gestalt techniques with other techniques in process-experiential therapy. In providing their conclusion to their review of outcome data, Strumpfel and Goldman (2002, p. 212) stated:

> Outcome studies have shown the effects of Gestalt therapy to be equal to or greater than other therapies for a variety of disorders. Whereas the methodological weaknesses of earlier studies sometimes obscured the strength of effects, newer studies have shown Gestalt therapy to be most promising, especially with affective and personality disturbances, and most recently, with psychosomatic disturbances and chemical addictions. Furthermore, the effects of therapy are stable in the follow-up studies 1 to 3 years after the cessation of treatment.

Over the previous 10 years, in a continued departure from its early foundations, gestalt therapy practitioners and scholars increasingly stress the importance of research to demonstrate gestalt therapy's utility as an evidence-based counseling approach. In articulating the reasons for this direction in gestalt therapy, Philip Brownell, a well-recognized scholar and clinician on modern gestalt therapy, noted:

> Over the last decade, Gestalt therapists have become increasingly interested in research. In the face of growing concern in the wider field of psychotherapy for evidence to support practice, Gestalt therapists began to realize that the burden for producing evidence supporting Gestalt therapy would fall upon themselves rather than the usual mix of experimental psychologists and researchers in established academic institutions. The dominant paradigm of cognitive behavioral therapy preoccupied most such research, and there still remains relatively little awareness of contemporary Gestalt therapy. With the looking linkage between research evidence and public policy, and the growing movement toward treatment guidelines, Gestalt therapy was in danger of becoming quite marginalized. We live in an age in which policy is marching on; it is influenced by psychology-as-science. Already the situation in Germany, in which Gestalt therapy had indeed become disenfranchised, had become a sobering reality. (Fisher, 2012, p. 5)

Despite these calls for action, there appears to be continued resistance among some gestalt therapy practitioners to demonstrate the effectiveness of their work. As Cohen (2003, p. 49) concluded, for example, on the lack of research on gestalt therapy interventions for PTSD: "Of course, these grim findings do not indicate that gestalt therapists fail to treat patients suffering from PTSD. They do indicate that gestalt therapists do not bother to report their work and they refrain from sharing it with their colleagues."

Indicative of his call for an enhanced focus on developing evidence-based knowledge on gestalt therapy, Brownell (2008) edited the *Handbook for Theory, Research, and Practice in Gestalt Therapy,* stressing the need for research on gestalt therapy. The book reviews both quantitative- and qualitative-based studies demonstrating gestalt therapy's utility and includes chapters on establishing "research communities" among those interested in conducting studies about gestalt therapy. Also, in April 2013, an international conference devoted to gestalt therapy research was cohosted by the Association for the Advancement of Gestalt Therapy and the Gestalt International Study Center (Fisher, 2012).

## STRENGTHS AND LIMITATIONS OF THE GESTALT APPROACH

Gestalt therapy has made a number of contributions to counseling and psychotherapy in general (Gilliland et al., 1994). Gestalt therapy has identified the importance of attending not only to the client's verbal statements and cognitive processing but also to the client's existential understanding of what is happening in therapy and in the client's life. In contrast to different types of therapies that stress technique rather than process, it has brought a creative approach to therapy, as gestalt therapists approach each encounter with clients as a unique existential experience. They attempt to respond to the client in ways that are uniquely focused on the needs and personality of each individual client. In addition to its applicability to disability issues, gestalt therapy works well for many different types of counseling needs, including gender issues, crisis, and poverty, as well as with interaction groups. Finally, gestalt therapy has emphasized the idea that significant therapeutic meaning can come from a client's nonverbal behavior and language.

Gestalt therapy works best for people whose enjoyment of life seems to be minimal and who appear to be internally restrictive and overly socialized, restrained, and constricted, those often referred to as neurotic, phobic, perfectionist, ineffective, and depressed (Shepherd, 1970). Gestalt therapy also works best for clients who are cerebral, referred to by Simkin (1976, p. 35) as being "up in the head." Clients who experience gestalt therapy should be willing to change and take responsibility for their emotional, cognitive, and physical behavior (Passons, 1975). Gestalt therapy does not work as well for clients who are less organized, more severely disturbed, or psychotic (Shepherd, 1970) and, because of these limitations, it may be ruled out as a counseling approach of choice for some rehabilitation clients.

Another limitation of gestalt therapy is the extensive training required of its practitioners, including participating in gestalt therapy as a counselee as a part of training, which may limit its use by rehabilitation counselors (Thomas et al., 1998). Clients may have a wide range of reactions to the dynamic and experiential nature of gestalt therapy, leading to the need for extensive training on the part of practitioners, and counselors thus need to have a solid understating of what exactly will work for each individual client (Passons, 1975).

Despite its limitations, practitioners in rehabilitation can use many of the techniques, philosophies, and focus of gestalt therapy in working with and understanding their clients. The theory offers a client-focused, process-oriented, existential approach for understanding people with disabilities participating in rehabilitation, facilitating their growth and awareness. Its philosophy and theory are generally consistent with values that have long been held in rehabilitation and can provide important elements and techniques for use in counseling.

## DISCUSSION EXERCISES

1. What are the areas of life in whch people commonly take a polarized perspective on an issue or topic?
2. In your own life, are there areas of "unfinished business" that you think about?
3. Compared to other counseling approaches commonly used with persons with disabilities, such as motivational interviewing and cognitive behavioral therapy, what are the advantages and disadvantages of using a gestalt approach?
4. Why do you think gestalt therapy has not received as much research attention as other counseling approaches? How does its lack of empirical research support (compared to other counseling approaches) make you feel about using a gestalt approach in your work?

## REFERENCES

Allen, H. A. (1986). A gestalt perspective. In T. F. Riggar, D. R. Maki, & A. W. Wolf (Eds.), *Applied rehabilitation counseling* (pp. 148–157). New York, NY: Springer Publishing Company.

Angermann, K. (1998). Gestalt therapy for eating disorders: An illustration. *Gestalt Journal, 21,* 19–47.

Appelbaum, S. A. (1983). A psychoanalyst looks at gestalt therapy. In C. Hatcher & J. Aronson (Eds.), *The handbook of gestalt therapy* (3rd ed., pp. 753–778). New York, NY: Jason Aronson.

Arnfred, S. M. H. (2012). Gestalt therapy for patients with schizophrenia: A brief review. *Gestalt Review, 16,* 53–68.

Axelson, J. A. (1999). *Counseling and development in a multicultural society.* Pacific Grove, CA: Brooks/Cole.

Baalen, D. V. (2010). Gestalt therapy and bipolar disorder. *Gestalt Review, 14,* 71–88.

Berger, G. (1999). Why we call it gestalt therapy. *Gestalt Journal, 22,* 21–35.

Brownell, P. (2008). *The handbook for theory, research, and practice in gestalt therapy.* Newcastle, UK: Cambridge Scholars.

Bull, A. (1997). Models of counselling in organizations. In M. Carroll & M. Walton (Eds.), *Handbook of counseling in organizations* (pp. 29–41). Thousand Oaks, CA: Sage.

Clemmens, M. C. (1997). *Getting beyond sobriety: Clinical approaches to long-term recovery.* San Francisco, CA: Jossey-Bass.

Cohen, A. (2003). Gestalt therapy and post-traumatic stress disorder: The irony and the challenge. *Gestalt Review, 7,* 42–55.

Cottone, R. (1992). *Theories and paradigms of counseling and psychotherapy.* Boston, MA: Allyn & Bacon.

Coven, A. B. (1978). The Gestalt approach to rehabilitation of the whole person. *Journal of Applied Rehabilitation Counseling, 9*(4), 143–147.

Degeneffe, C. E., & Terciano, J. (2012). Rosa's law and the language of disability: Implications for rehabilitation counseling. *Rehabilitation Research, Policy, and Education, 25,* 163–172.

Fagan, J., & Shepherd, I. L. (Eds.). (1970). *Gestalt therapy now: Theory, techniques, and applications.* Palo Alto, CA: Science & Behavior Books.

Fedar, B., & Ronall, R. (1980). *Beyond the hot seat: Gestalt approaches to group.* New York, NY: Brunner/Mazel.

Fisher, S. L. (2012). Editorial: The gestalt research tradition: Figure and ground. *Gestalt Review, 16,* 3–6.

Gilliland, B. E., James, R. K., & Bowman, J. T. (1994). *Theories and strategies in counseling and psychotherapy* (3rd ed.). Needham Heights, MA: Allyn & Bacon.

Greenberg, L. S., Elliott, R., & Lietaer, G. (1994). Research on experiential psychotherapies. In A. E. Bergin & S. L. Garfield (Eds.), *Handbook of psychotherapy and behavior change* (4th ed., pp. 509–539). New York, NY: Wiley.

Grossman, E. F. (1990). The gestalt approach to people with amputations. *Journal of Applied Rehabilitation Counseling, 21*(1), 16–21.

Haney, H., & Leibsohn, J. (1999). *Basic counseling responses: A multimedia learning system for the helping professions.* Pacific Grove, CA: Brooks/Cole.

Harman, R. L. (1996). *Gestalt therapy techniques: Working with groups, couples, and sexually dysfunctional men.* Northvale, NJ: Jason Aronson.

Imes, S. A., Clance, P. R., Gailis, A. T., & Atkeson, E. (2002). Mind's response to the body's betrayal: Gestalt/existential therapy for clients with chronic or life-threatening illnesses. *Journal of Clinical Psychology, 58,* 1361–1373.

Kelly, T., & Howie, L. (2011). Exploring the influence of gestalt therapy training on psychiatric nursing practice: Stories from the field. *International Journal of Mental Health Nursing, 20,* 296–304.

Kogan, J. (1983). The genesis of gestalt therapy. In C. Hatcher & J. Aronson (Eds.), *The handbook of gestalt therapy* (3rd ed., pp. 235–258). New York, NY: Jason Aronson.

Livneh, H., & Antonak, R. F. (1997). *Psychological adaptation to chronic illness and disability.* Gaithersburg, MD: Aspen.

Livneh, H., & Sherwood, A. (1991). Application of personality theories and counseling strategies to clients with physical disabilities. *Journal of Counseling and Development, 69,* 525–538.

May, R., & Yalom, I. (1995). Existential psychotherapy. In R. J. Corsini & D. Wedding (Eds.), *Current psychotherapies* (5th ed., pp. 262–292). Itasca, IL: Peacock.

Murdock, N. L. (2013). *Theories of counseling and psychotherapy.* Boston, MA: Pearson.

Passons, W. R. (1975). *Gestalt approaches in counseling.* New York, NY: Holt, Rinehart & Winston.

Patterson, L. E., & Welfel, E. R. (2000). *The counseling process* (5th ed.). Belmont, CA: Wadsworth/Thomson Learning.

Perera-Diltz, D. M., Laux, J. M., & Toman, S. M. (2012). A cross-cultural exploration of posttraumatic stress disorder: Assessment, diagnosis, recommended (gestalt) treatment. *Gestalt Review, 16,* 69–87.

Perls, F. S. (1969). *Gestalt therapy verbatim.* Lafayette, CA: Real People Press.

Perls, L. (1976). Comments on the new directions. In E. W. L. Smith (Ed.), *The growing edge of gestalt therapy* (pp. 221–226). New York, NY: Brunner/Mazel.

Polster, E., & Polster, M. (1973). *Gestalt therapy integrated* (3rd ed.). New York, NY: Brunner/Mazel.

Seligman, L., & Reichenberg, L. W. (2010). *Theories of counseling and psychotherapy: Systems, strategies, and skills* (3rd ed.). Boston, MA: Pearson.

Shepard, M. (1975). *Fritz*. New York, NY: Saturday Review Press.

Shepherd, I. L. (1970). Limitations and cautions in the gestalt approach. In J. Fagan & I. L. Shepherd (Eds.), *Gestalt therapy now: Theory, techniques, applications* (pp. 234–238). Palo Alto, CA: Science & Behavior Books.

Siemens, H. (2000). The gestalt approach: Balancing hope and despair in persons with HIV/AIDS. *Gestalt Journal, 23*, 73–79.

Simkin, J. S. (1976). *Gestalt therapy mini-lectures*. Millbrae, CA: Celestial Arts.

Strumpfel, U., & Goldman, R. (2002). Contacting gestalt therapy. In D. J. Cain & J. Seeman (Eds.), *Humanistic psychotherapies: Handbook of research and practice* (pp. 189–220). Washington, DC: American Psychological Association.

Thomas, K. R., Thoreson, R., Parker, R., & Butler, A. (1998). Theoretical foundations of the counseling function. In R. M. Parker & E. M. Szymanski (Eds.), *Rehabilitation counseling: Basics and beyond* (3rd ed., pp. 225–268). Austin, TX: Pro-Ed.

Tobin, S. A. (1983). Saying goodbye in gestalt therapy. In C. Hatcher & J. Aronson (Eds.), *The handbook of gestalt therapy* (3rd ed., pp. 371–385). New York, NY: Jason Aronson.

Whitmore, D. (1991). *Psychosynthesis counselling in action*. Newbury Park, CA: Sage.

Wulf, R. (1998). The historical roots of gestalt therapy. *Gestalt Journal, 21*, 81–92.

Yontef, G. (1997). Supervision from a gestalt therapy perspective. In A. E. Bergin & S. L. Garfield (Eds.), *Handbook of psychotherapy and behavior change* (4th ed., pp. 147–163). New York, NY: Wiley.

Yontef, G. M. (1983). The theory of gestalt therapy. In C. Hatcher & J. Aronson (Eds.), *The handbook of gestalt therapy* (3rd ed., pp. 213–222). New York, NY: Jason Aronson.

Zinker, J. (1977). *Creative process in gestalt therapy*. New York, NY: Brunner/Mazel.

# CHAPTER 5

# Cognitive Behavioral Therapy

*Elizabeth A. Boland, Timothy N. Tansey, and Jessica Brooks*

## LEARNING OBJECTIVES

The main goal of this chapter is to introduce cognitive behavioral therapy (CBT) approaches and provide a summary of the research that has been conducted using CBT applications for people with diverse disabilities and presenting conditions. Learning objectives are to facilitate knowledge and understanding of the following:

1. General cognitive and behavioral strategies, techniques, and interventions
2. Personality theory associated with CBT
3. The ways in which CBT methods can be applied to individuals with diverse disabilities
4. The scientific evidence supporting CBT as an evidence-based practice

## OVERVIEW OF CBT

From its origin in the early 1960s (Ellis, 1962), CBT approaches revolutionized the prevailing schools of thought in counseling and psychology (Hayes, 2004). The first versions of CBT sought to achieve behavior change as a direct outcome of thought modification (Kazdin, 1978). In other words, CBT interventions treat inner events as if they were behaviors (Pilgrim, 2011). This was a dramatic shift in thinking from the predominant counseling approaches of the time, namely, psychodynamism (Freud, 1923/1961) and behaviorism (Wolpe, 1958). Informed by groundbreaking research in cognitive psychology, these early cognitive behavioral therapists (e.g., Beck, 1967) began to draw interest to their practice through their astute observations of particular cognitive errors among various client groups. Thereafter, a new domain of psychotherapy research was formed that began to identify the distinctive types of cognitive distortions and methods to correct them (Hayes).

Today, CBT approaches often focus on detecting, testing, and changing dysfunctional beliefs, assumptions, and thoughts as the main method of treatment, with the ultimate goal of behavior change (Dobson & Dozois, 2010). CBT is conceptualized as a collaborative investigation undertaken by the counselor and the client. This collaborative relationship facilitates the exploration of thinking patterns and beliefs that an individual holds that may lead to maladaptive behaviors, erroneous beliefs about oneself and others, and debilitating relationships with the world (Beck & Weishaar, 2014; James & Gilliland, 2003). CBT, like all therapeutic systems, seeks to improve an individual's emotional health, while building a new repertoire of adaptive behaviors. It focuses on the empirical investigation of a person's thinking patterns and cognitive assumptions, which theoretically drives maladaptive, erroneous thoughts and behaviors (Beck & Weishaar).

## THEORETICAL FOUNDATIONS

CBT is grounded in theoretical concepts from cognitive psychology, which assert that psychological disorders can be traced to both inappropriate learning and maladaptive thinking. The broad mental ability of cognition (from the Latin, *cognito*, to know or to learn) is itself subsumed by information-processing functions that lead to conclusions about one's situation, which, in turn, control affect and behavior. At a basic level, CBT views the adaptive processing of information as being crucial to an organism's survival (Beck & Weishaar, 2014). The theory gives credence to the importance of learning and environmental influences on personality development, while emphasizing information processing and cognitive mediation in the development and treatment of psychological disorders (James & Gilliland, 2003). Based on these emphases, CBT asserts that change is brought about by influencing an individual's cognitive system, which, in turn, modifies the way the person perceives, interprets, and assigns meaning to life experiences (Table 5.1). As described by Beck and Weishaar, attitudes or central beliefs, called cognitive vulnerabilities, predispose individuals going through life experiences to interpret their situations in a biased way.

A person's cognitive system interacts with the other information-processing systems (i.e., affective, motivational, and physiological systems) to respond

**TABLE 5.1  Principles of Cognitive Behavioral Therapy**

| Access hypothesis | The content and process of our thinking is knowable. |
|---|---|
| Mediation hypothesis | Our thoughts mediate our emotional responses. |
| Change hypothesis | Due to our ability to mediate our emotional responses and because our cognitions are knowable, we can intentionally modify our responses to events in our environments. |

to data from both physical and social surroundings (Beck & Weishaar, 2014). If the response stems from a maladaptive conclusion, the counselor will assist the person in testing the hypothesis that led to that conclusion. In current cognitive theory, all systems work together as modes that consist of networks of cognitive, behavioral, affective, and motivational schemas, which are components of personality and serve to interpret life experiences. Some modes are primal and are tied to survival; however, they can be maladaptive when they are triggered by misinterpretations or react excessively. The development of psychological disorders and, conversely, the development of positive emotional responses and coping behaviors, are assumed to rely on one's evaluations of environmental stimuli interacting with personal innate dispositions, along with cognitive vulnerabilities. In CBT, the counselor works with the client to override these primal modes by replacing them with purposeful thinking, intentional goals, problem solving, and long-term planning.

Cognitive distortions, or systematic errors in reasoning, are present during psychological concerns and disturbances. According to Beck (1967), there are six different and distinct categories of cognitive distortions, including (a) arbitrary inference, (b) selective abstraction, (c) overgeneralization, (d) magnification and minimization, (e) personalization, and (f) dichotomous thinking (see Table 5.2). Arbitrary inference involves deriving a conclusion without any evidence or in direct opposition to evidence. Selective abstraction occurs when an individual magnifies and interprets a life experience based on one detail taken out of context. Overgeneralization involves creating an overall rule from one or a few isolated experiences and applying it to all situations. Magnification and minimization occur when a person interprets a situation as either extremely more significant or less significant than it actually is. Personalization occurs when a person ascribes an external life experience to himself or herself without data upholding a causal relationship. In dichotomous thinking, an individual classifies a situation in one of two extremes.

CBT overlaps somewhat with several other psychotherapy systems, sharing techniques and/or philosophical preferences with rational emotive behavior therapy (REBT; Ellis, 1962), behavior therapy (Wolpe, 1958), and social learning theory (Bandura, 1977). CBT derives some of its viewpoints from Kelly's (1955) personal constructs and also acknowledges Sullivan's (1953) interpersonal therapy as informing its philosophical base. Constructivists also share some techniques and points of view with CBT (Ramsay, 1998; Winter & Watson, 1999). Although CBT uses a wide range of counseling techniques, many of which were developed from the aforementioned theoretical orientations, it is not merely an "eclectic" approach. As Beck (1993) asserted, "Cognitive therapy is best viewed as the application of the cognitive model of a particular disorder with the use of a variety of techniques designed to modify the dysfunctional beliefs and faulty information processing characteristic of each disorder" (p. 194). Therefore, the techniques chosen by a cognitive behavioral counselor are used for specific purposes, based on the counselor's cognitive conceptualization of the client and his or her treatment plan (Freeman, Pretzer, Fleming, & Simon, 1990).

**TABLE 5.2 Cognitive Distortions**

| Arbitrary inference | Occurs when an individual reaches a conclusion without evidence supporting the conclusion or despite being provided evidence that contradicts the conclusion. Example: An individual believes that a coworker does not like him/her despite the coworker sending a get-well card after the individual missed work due to illness. |
|---|---|
| Selective abstraction | Occurs when a person magnifies the importance of a specific detail or point, often removed from the original context, at the expense of other available information. Example: An individual attends a party and afterward believes he or she was not really welcome after focusing on one awkward look directed his or her way and disregards all the positive glances and conversations of the evening. |
| Overgeneralization | Occurs when a person uses information from a limited number of observations to create a broad conceptualization or belief and then applies this conceptualization to unrelated situations or interactions. Example: An individual believes that since a job interview did not go well, all future interviews will not go well. |
| Magnification | Occurs when a person believes an event or outcome as being extremely more significant than it actually is. Example: An individual believes that missing a single class due to illness will cause the teacher to completely lose respect for him or her, and that in turn he or she will fail the final exam, not graduate from college, have limited job prospects, and will never be able to support self or family. |
| Minimization | Occurs when a person believes an event or outcome as being extremely less significant than it actually is. Example: An individual believes that failing the final exam, worth most of the grade in a class, will not have a negative impact on the final grade because he or she earned some extra credit during the course. |
| Personalization | Occurs when a person believes that the actions of others are intended as a direct, personal message to the person regardless of the actual intent behind those actions. Example: An individual believes that when a server at a restaurant spilled soup on his or her lap, it was on purpose because the server does not like him or her. |
| Dichotomous thinking | Occurs when an individual classifies outcomes or incidents into one of two extreme conclusions. Example: An individual believes that people are either completely honest or unable to be truthful without recognizing the large gray area that may exist. |

## THERAPEUTIC STRATEGIES AND TECHNIQUES

As mentioned previously, CBT uses a broad variety of both cognitive and behavioral strategies, leaving a clinician with hundreds of interventions to choose from for use with any given client (James & Gilliland, 2003; O'Kearney, 1998). Consequently, counselors should aim to be selective in their use of the slew of available CBT techniques, and they should use evidence-based practice when carefully examining the utility and efficacy of a technique for a particular client (Chan, Rosenthal, & Pruett, 2008). As often as possible, counselors should only use specific strategies and techniques that have already been effectively tested and applied to their particular client groups. Despite these individual differences in treatment needs, all CBT approaches are based on the following set of general principles that can be applied to most clients (Beck, Liese, & Najavits, 2005):

- Therapy is based on a unique cognitive conceptualization of each patient.
- A strong therapeutic alliance is essential.
- Therapy is goal oriented.
- The initial focus of therapy is on the present.
- Therapy is time sensitive.
- Therapy sessions are structured, with active participation.
- Clients are taught to identify and respond to dysfunctional thoughts.
- Therapy emphasizes psychoeducation and relapse prevention. (p. 482)

These treatment principles can provide a solid foundation that therapists can couple with specific CBT strategies and techniques.

*Cognitive conceptualization* refers to a thorough examination of the presenting problem and associated thoughts, as well as emotional, behavioral, and physiological reactions (Beck et al., 2005). All applications of this general approach focus on distinct cognitive problems that are conceptualized as the causes of psychological distress (Dobson & Dozois, 2010). Therapists start by helping clients to find patterns expressed in their automatic, fleeting, and persistent thoughts in order to identify underlying dysfunctional core beliefs about themselves, the world, and other people (e.g., "I am stupid"; Seligman & Reichenberg, 2010). Therapists can then help clients to recognize maladaptive behavior patterns that they use to cope with negative thinking (e.g., avoiding social situations, abusing drugs). As pointed out by Beck et al., from the onset of therapy, cognitive behavioral therapists should also work to develop a positive, respectful, collaborative, and *strong therapeutic alliance*. This will help to ensure that clients are trusting and open with therapists—providing elicited feedback to the therapist and other contributions.

At the first session and throughout treatment, cognitive behavioral therapists should also ask clients to formulate specific and realistic objectives by using open-ended questions, such as "What would you like to work on by the end of therapy?" (Beck et al., 2005). In addition, therapists should encourage the development of short-term goals and assess the client's degree of motivation toward change. Cognitive behavioral therapists assume that individuals have control over their own thoughts and actions, permitting clients to be active agents in their own lives (Dobson & Dozois, 2010). This *goal-directed therapy* should initially only *focus on present* issues in the client's life in order to help stay focused on the problem at hand. The therapist can use Socratic dialogue to help the client to discover current maladaptive thoughts and related problems. The Socratic dialogue consists of asking informative questions, listening, summarizing, and then asking synthesizing questions that apply the information obtained to the person's original belief (Freeman et al., 1990).

The treatment duration for CBT is *time sensitive,* as it aims to effect change rapidly, yet its time frame can vary depending on client needs (Beck et al., 2005; Dobson & Dozois, 2010). As a result, CBT sessions are carefully *structured, with active participation* highlighted, in order to optimize efficiency and effectiveness (Seligman & Reichenberg, 2010). Therapists regularly evoke feedback from clients to monitor their understanding of treatment methods, as well as inherent interest in session content. With the receipt of honest feedback, therapists can modify strategies and techniques based on the client's individual abilities and preferences. In addition, therapeutic homework assignments are regularly used and considered an integral component of CBT, but the homework is customized to the client to enhance the relevance and likelihood of completion. Through CBT, clients often find a reduction in acute symptoms and mood stability, as well as the acquisition of adaptive behavioral and cognitive coping strategies (e.g., assertiveness skills, relaxation, mindfulness, reframing; Beck et al., 2005; James & Gilliland, 2003). After symptom reduction, therapists and clients may begin to experiment with decreasing sessions. According to Seligman and Reichenberg, treatment termination can usually occur after 4 to 14 sessions when dealing with straightforward problems.

Another commonality across CBT approaches is the central goal of helping clients learn to *identify and respond to dysfunctional thoughts.* The therapist reinforces the theoretical assumptions of CBT at each session to help teach clients to self-monitor, evaluate, and modify maladaptive thinking patterns (Beck et al., 2005). Clients learn to investigate whether a given thought is valid or inaccurate and, depending on their findings, they may either problem solve ways to respond to the thought or accept the resultant implications of the internal event. Therapists typically use questioning and standardized tools (e.g., thought records), as opposed to persuading or listening strategies, to help clients use this scientific method. The specific cognitive techniques emphasized rely on an individual's misinterpretations of stimuli and provide mechanisms for testing them, investigating their rational basis, and revising them if they fail an empirical or logical test or identify alternative thinking patterns (Craighead, Craighead, Kazdin, & Mahoney, 1994; Shafran & Somers, 1998).

Collectively, all of these treatment principles underscore the value assigned to *psychoeducation and relapse prevention* in CBT. Helping clients to learn the therapeutic model and gain new skills is the driving force in CBT sessions, and therapists often tailor and modify sessions according to client needs (Swett & Kaplan, 2004). Moreover, effective therapists will frequently create alternative systems to accommodate learning difficulties, cognitive disabilities, or other problems (Beck et al., 2005). For instance, therapists may audiotape sessions or provide written brief summaries to clients. By learning about the therapeutic process, clients can deal with recurring or new problems on their own through employing CBT concepts and methods, which can help to prevent a relapse in symptoms (Dobson & Dozois, 2010). *Relapse prevention* is also underscored at final sessions by reviewing completed goals, new skills, and potential barriers to ongoing success.

A wide variety of procedures and techniques fall under the umbrella of CBT and, predictably, several subsystems of CBT have been developed, each with varying degrees of cohesiveness to cognitive and behavioral theories (e.g., Beck, 1983; Ellis, 1979; Goldfried, 1980; Hayes & Strosahl, 2004; Meichenbaum, 1995;

Nezu, 1987). However, most practitioners of CBT use a combination of cognitive and behavioral strategies (Spiegler & Guevremont, 1993; Tarrier et al., 1999). The cognitive techniques emphasize discovering and testing the person's beliefs, investigating their source and foundation, modifying them if they do not stand up to an empirical or rational test, and learning to use problem-solving, mindfulness, or acceptance-based strategies (Beck & Weishaar, 2014), while behavioral methods focus on diminishing maladaptive behaviors and increasing adaptive behaviors (see Chapter 7 in this volume for additional information on behavioral strategies).

## CBT IN THE CONTEXT OF REHABILITATION COUNSELING

In actual practice, most individuals who participate in rehabilitation counseling will experience multiple, mutually exacerbating problems (physical and/or emotional), which are mediated by self-appraisal, beliefs about personal worth, social support, and problem-solving proclivities, and CBT may be applied to such problems and needs. Psychosocial factors in adjustment to disability have always been a major focus of philosophy and practice in rehabilitation counseling.

CBT approaches psychosocial adjustment as a collaborative task between a counselor and client that focuses on identifying and changing negative cognitions associated with disability (Beck & Weishaar, 2014). Incurring a disability can place individuals at a higher risk for depression due to globalized negative self-statements (e.g., "I'm worthless because I can't work"), which affect self-regard, mood, and behavior. CBT interventions can be directed toward minimizing negative biases, increasing positive risk taking, developing life skills, and facilitating realism in client self-appraisals.

Increasingly, the rehabilitation research literature has applied CBT approaches to people with disabilities, especially individuals with schizophrenia and other psychotic disorders (e.g., Farhall & Thomas, 2013), multiple sclerosis (e.g., Hind et al., 2014), chronic pain (e.g., Morley, Eccleston, & Williams, 1999), and intellectual disabilities (e.g., Nicoll, Beail, & Saxon, 2013). For people with multiple sclerosis and chronic pain, CBT interventions have led to marked improvements in mood as well as a reduction in pain symptoms. Although people with psychotic disorders have also indicated positive changes in mood after CBT, studies also show that they may experience significant decreases in the positive and negative symptoms of schizophrenia (e.g., Wykes, Steel, Everitt, & Tarrier, 2008). Lindsay (1999) cites strong evidence that people with intellectual disabilities are particularly prone to serious emotional and behavioral disorders, including depression, anxiety, and anger, and refers to 50 clinical cases evidencing positive effects of CBT treatment on long-lasting behavior change in clients with intellectual disabilities.

Over the past several decades, the application of CBT to individuals with schizophrenia, in particular, has become an evidence-based practice in rehabilitation settings with a range of cognitive and behavioral techniques and strategies, usually delivered together with pharmacological interventions (Farhall &

Thomas, 2013). However, it is important to note that treatment adaptations need to be made to cognitive methods when working with people with severe and persistent mental illness (Morrison & Barratt, 2010). For instance, therapists should initially suspend beliefs about the validity of delusional content in order to help facilitate the working dialogue. Eventually, therapists can help clients to further interpret explanations for specific events and experiences that triggered delusions—teaching them to consider and even test out alternative hypotheses. More recent developments in CBT for individuals with psychotic disorders include targeting other major processes that contribute to psychosis, such as probabilistic reasoning or biases to make external and personal attributions for negative events (e.g., Moritz, Veckenstedt, Randjbar, Vitzthum, & Woodward, 2011; Ross, Freeman, Dunn, & Garety, 2011). Additionally, another new research domain includes the application of contemporary CBT methods to people with psychotic disorders, such as mindfulness and acceptance-based strategies (Morris, Johns, & Oliver, 2013).

Notwithstanding the emerging evidence, researchers cite the potential difficulties in applying CBT to people with varying cognitive limitations. For example, individuals with central nervous system processing disorders, as found in some types of brain injuries, intellectual disabilities, learning disabilities, cerebral vascular accidents, alcoholism, and several subtypes of psychosis, among other disorders, may not have the capacity to accurately self-assess, provide valid self-reports, or process abstract concepts (Kroese, 1998). If these capabilities are significantly compromised, a client may not be a good candidate for CBT intervention.

A recent study by Oathamshaw and Haddock (2006) provided empirical evidence to confirm these opinions. The investigators evaluated the cognitive skills necessary to participate in CBT among people with intellectual disabilities and psychotic disorders. The findings suggested that all participants found any task that involved cognition to be more challenging. Yet, individuals were able to complete certain tasks that required self-monitoring, such as finding links among behaviors, events, and feelings. The authors concluded that individuals with cognitive limitations seem to benefit from some CBT methods, but may struggle with tasks solely focused on cognition (e.g., cognitive mediation, recognizing thoughts).

Although there is a well-developed conceptual framework for CBT applications, the research base to support its use in rehabilitation settings is still limited. In general, more research is needed regarding the utility of this theory when applied to persons with disabilities.

## CBT AS AN EVIDENCE-BASED PRACTICE

Identifying the evidence in support of CBT theory and corresponding techniques allows for careful examination of the utility and efficacy of the theory. Evidence-based practice relies on a hierarchy of evidence in determining those practices for which there is empirical support (Pruett, Swett, Chan, Rosenthal, & Lee, 2008). Evaluations of CBT have included comparisons of outcomes to no treatment, other talk therapies, and pharmacological agents in randomized and nonrandomized treatment designs and through meta-analyses of the results of these studies.

## CBT and Anxiety Disorders

CBT is considered an evidence-based, first-line treatment for people with a variety of anxiety disorders, such as social phobias, obsessive-compulsive disorders, and posttraumatic stress disorders (PTSDs; Hofmann & Smits, 2008). A recent review of meta-analyses (Hofmann, Asnaani, Vonk, Sawyer, & Fang, 2012) indicated that CBT is much more likely to reduce symptoms of generalized anxiety than no-treatment or pill placebo groups and is as equally efficacious as pharmacological treatments, relaxation methods, and supportive therapies. Furthermore, there is emerging evidence for Internet-based or Internet-guided self-help CBT in the immediate treatment of anxiety (Coull & Morris, 2011; Öst, 2008).

For the treatment of the disorder of social phobia, CBT has been shown to be effective in reducing anxiety in comparison to waitlist and other types of control groups (Gil, Carrillo, & Sánchez Meca, 2000; Gould, Buckminster, Pollack, Otto, & Yap, 1997; Oberlander, Schneier, & Liebowitz, 1994), with superior performance over pharmacological interventions in the long term (Fedoroff & Taylor, 2001). In addition, multiple meta-analyses have identified CBT as useful in the treatment of obsessive-compulsive and severe anxiety disorders (e.g., Bruce, Spiegel, & Hegel, 1999; Butler, Chapman, Forman, & Beck, 2006; Hofmann & Smits, 2008; Hofmann & Spiegel, 1999). Randomized controlled trials demonstrate a large effect size for CBT in the treatment of obsessive-compulsive disorder and show similar effectiveness to anxiety medications (Eddy, Dutra, Bradley, & Westen, 2004; Ruhmland & Margraf, 2001). CBT has also been recognized as an option in the treatment of PTSD (Meadows & Foa, 1999). In addition, CBT has been found equal in effectiveness to an emerging evidence-based therapy for PTSD, namely, eye movement desensitization and reprocessing (EMDR; Bisson & Andrew, 2007; Seidler & Wagner, 2006); however, a systematic review of 23 randomized controlled trials found that CBT had lower remission rates when compared to EMDR or supportive therapies (Mendes, Mello, Ventura, de Medeiros Passarela, & de Jesus Mari, 2008).

## CBT in the Treatment of Other Psychiatric Disorders

Depression and related mood disorders are common psychiatric disorders that are often found among people with disabilities, as either primary or secondary diagnoses. Depression has especially high rates in people with neuropathological conditions, such as stroke (Lezak, Howieson, Bigler, & Tranel, 2012), brain injury (Dixon, Layton, & Shaw, 2005), and multiple sclerosis (Rao, 1990). Mood disorders are also more common among individuals with spinal cord injuries (Elliott & Frank, 1996), chronic pain (Alexy, Webb, Crismore, & Mark, 1996), and psychotic disorders (Bustillo, Lauriello, & Keith, 1999). Devins and Binik (1996) also found dysphoria to be common in a mixed population of individuals with disabilities or chronic illnesses. Therefore, evidence-based CBT strategies geared toward depression treatment would likely be useful to chronic illness and disability populations.

Overall, based on a number of meta-analyses, CBT has been identified as equally effective in the treatment of depression for the general population, when compared to controls, but not necessarily more effective than other psychotherapies in the treatment of mood disorders, including depression (Baardseth et al., 2013; Hofmann et al., 2012; Wampold, Minami, Baskin, & Tierney, 2002). CBT has also shown some efficacy in reducing the risk of recurrence of mood symptoms (Blackburn, Eunson, & Bishop, 1986; Miranda, Gross, Persons, & Hahn, 1998; Segal, Gemar, & Williams, 1999).

Some researchers have claimed that CBT is more effective in treating mood disturbance than either pharmacotherapy or other psychotherapeutic systems (e.g., Bowers, 1990; Dobson, 1989). However, well-controlled research has not fully supported these assertions (Hollon & Beck, 2013). In the treatment of bipolar disorder, CBT has been evaluated both as an intervention to reduce symptoms experienced and as an adjunct treatment to pharmacological therapy. CBT has been found to reduce clinical symptoms and improve adherence to pharmacological therapy, although it appears to be less effective in reducing relapse in persons with bipolar disorders (Szentagotai & David, 2010). Recently, a meta-analysis of well-controlled studies indicated that CBT had a small but significant effect on symptoms of mania (Gregory, 2010). Due to the paucity of evidence regarding the practical significance of CBT for manic symptoms in persons with bipolar disorders, there is a need for further research.

A large number of randomized controlled trials of CBT with individuals with schizophrenia have been published, and many studies note positive therapeutic benefits observed, even 5 years after treatment termination (Turkington et al., 2008). More specifically, the use of CBT has also been found to reduce the experience of both positive and negative symptoms of schizophrenia (Lawrence, Bradshaw, & Mairs, 2006; van der Gaag, Valmaggia, & Smitt, 2014), although treatment of about 16 to 20 sessions was found typically necessary to achieve positive outcomes (Sarin, Wallin, & Widerlöv, 2011). In addition, several studies have found that individuals with schizophrenia have shown improved community functioning and work performance when CBT is used as an adjunct to pharmacotherapy (Bustillo et al., 1999; Chadwick & Lowe, 1990; Lysaker, Bond, Davis, Bryson, & Bell, 2009). A meta-analysis of 34 controlled-trial studies found that individuals experienced a reduction in psychotic symptoms as well as improvement in mood symptoms and social functioning (Wykes et al., 2008). Another recent meta-analysis demonstrated that CBT led to a 26% reduction in readmission rates in comparison to routine treatment interventions (National Collaborating Centre for Mental Health, 2009). Therefore, CBT for individuals with psychotic disorders appears to be more effective than standard interventions alone, but there is not enough evidence to document greater effectiveness when compared to other psychological treatments (Lynch, Laws, & McKenna, 2010).

### CBT and Intellectual Disabilities

Although CBT research is still lacking for people with intellectual disabilities, the largest area of interest has involved anger problems for this client group. People with intellectual disabilities have very high prevalence rates of anger control problems, and this is rapidly becoming a popular area of study. A recent meta-analysis evaluated nine studies, and indicated large effect sizes for the treatment of anger issues (Nicoll et al., 2013). Although these study findings are optimistic, there were methodological limitations in the studies reviewed, including small sample sizes and lack of comparison group controls. Another recent study used the rigorous research design of a randomized controlled trial, applying group CBT to individuals with mild to moderate intellectual disabilities (Oathamshaw & Haddock, 2006). The results demonstrated significantly improved anger control after a 12-week program. The results of this study, along with other research results, suggest that individuals with intellectual disabilities may have the skills to participate in modified CBT programs that do not involve techniques with a strong emphasis on cognition. Additional research is needed to explore the potential utility of modified CBT programs for people with intellectual disabilities.

## CASE STUDY

Linda is a 45-year-old divorced female with a high school education, who has not worked in the past 7 years. She has prior work experience as a medical transcriptionist. Linda was diagnosed 5 years previously with systemic lupus erythematosus (SLE or lupus), in addition to rheumatoid arthritis. She was referred for counseling services by her rehabilitation counselor, due to difficulties in adjustment to her disabilities. Linda reports that her disabilities were a contributing factor to her divorce from her husband of 20 years. Following her divorce, she applied and was approved for Social Security Disability Insurance benefits.

At her initial interview with her therapist, Linda expressed feeling "worthless," "of no value," and "totally damaged." Her overall presentation suggested that she was experiencing anxiety, depressed mood and affect, and persistent death wishes, but with no suicidal ideation or intent. Linda reported having a very small, close social support network consisting of a few friends who lived in the same state, but not in close proximity. Her parents were deceased, and she had little contact with her only sibling, an older brother living several states away. Linda had regular contact with one of her two adult children and had a "bitter" relationship with her ex-husband, choosing to talk through her daughter rather than directly with him. During the initial sessions, her therapist suggested that Linda would benefit from treatment focus on addressing cognitive interpretations. Clinical testing revealed no difficulties with Linda's verbal abstraction, short-term memory, information processing speed, or intellect.

Initial CBT interventions centered on identifying Linda's distorted cognitions and relating them to her subsequent negative feelings and maladaptive behaviors. Linda stated that she was "taught to be a good girl and not

*(continued)*

*(continued)*

make waves" by her punitive, depressed mother. Linda was able to see how these messages were at least partially responsible for her feelings of anxiety ("I will be punished for not working") and depression ("I'm no good because I don't contribute; in fact, I take money from the government, which makes me even worse"). These messages, which formed the basis for much of her self-talk, also influenced her lack of assertiveness toward a male friend with whom she was interested in developing a romantic relationship ("Good girls don't ask men for dates" and "Who could care about me?").

Linda was asked to consciously monitor her thoughts and note examples of negative self-talk and globalized self-demeaning statements. When she recognized such an internal event, Linda was instructed to replace the thought with a neutral or positive self-statement, thereby encouraging her to lessen the pernicious impact of constant self-destructive ideation.

As therapy progressed, Linda was able to acknowledge feelings of anger and resentment that she had repressed or incorrectly attributed to her own inadequacies. A variety of imagery techniques were used, in which she imagined confronting people, events, and even her own physical problems. She was able to decenter herself from being "the source of all wrong," and reattribute several negative life events into a more rational, reality-based focus.

Imagery was also used to increase Linda's assertiveness. She imagined herself being able to "reach out and grab some life" despite her serious physical limitations. Emotional risk taking was also overtly rehearsed by asking her male acquaintance for a date.

Linda was able to use the skills that she learned in therapy in the context of her everyday life. She began to think of herself as "a worthwhile human" who was not "consigned to life's junk pile" as a result of her disabilities. She was able to act more freely and directly in her own best interest, when she successfully challenged her dysfunctional cognitions and replaced them with self-affirming, reality-based thoughts. She felt better able to defend against her ex-husband's derisive comments and set stronger boundaries with her son.

Linda continues to experience negative physical effects from her disabilities, but they no longer fully dictate her mood or her self-perception. Although she is often ill or fatigued, she can now separate these experiences from her self-evaluations and, as a result, is far less angry, anxious, and depressed. She is also enjoying her relationship with her significant other, and he was thrilled when she asked him for that date.

## CONCLUSIONS

CBT clearly has a place in rehabilitation counseling practice, and a growing body of research and a variety of anecdotal accounts confirm its efficacy in helping people adjust to disability. However, the possible shortcomings of CBT must be acknowledged, relative to its use in people with disabilities. Because CBT was originally used for treating individuals with depression and anxiety, but without cognitive limitations, its methods may not be useful for clients with particular disabilities served in rehabilitation settings. Rehabilitation counselors should use the available research evidence to inform how they select, organize, and implement CBT strategies and methods when working with clients with disabilities, especially when cognitive limitations are present. Additional research findings on CBT are needed to obtain a clearer picture of when, where, with whom, and under which circumstances CBT techniques might be used most effectively in rehabilitation settings.

## ACKNOWLEDGMENTS

The contents of this chapter were developed with support from the Rehabilitation Research & Training Center on Evidence-Based Practice in Vocational Rehabilitation (RRTC-EBP VR) at the University of Wisconsin–Madison and the University of Wisconsin–Stout and with funding provided by the National Institute on Disability and Rehabilitation Research, U.S. Department of Education (Grant H133B100034). The ideas, opinions, and conclusions expressed, however, are those of the authors and do not represent recommendations, endorsements, or policies of the U.S. Department of Education.

## DISCUSSION EXERCISES

1. Identifying and reshaping cognitive distortions is one area of focus in CBT. What, if any, benefits are associated with cognitive distortions? If there are potential benefits, how should a counselor identify which distortions to address and when should they be addressed in the counseling relationship?
2. CBT overlaps with other theories, such as REBT, behavior therapy, and social learning theory. What common elements exist between CBT and these other theoretical approaches? How is CBT different?
3. In thinking about the therapeutic process in CBT, would you recommend using this theoretical approach with all clients, regardless of the nature of their disabilities? Would CBT be more or less effective with clients with different types of disabilities? If so, which disabilities and why?
4. You have been asked to work with a client with a physical disability, who was recently fired from her job. The client, on intake, reveals that one of her coworkers would say hurtful things to her at work. She believes that all her coworkers and her supervisor are racist, based on this interaction with the coworker, despite reporting that the others were always nice to her and did not make similar statements. The client now believes she will be unable to work because all employers and coworkers will discriminate and say harmful things to her. What cognitive distortion might this client be experiencing? Discuss how you would identify and ultimately address these distortions using CBT.

# REFERENCES

Alexy, W., Webb, P., Crismore, L., & Mark, D. (1996). Utilizing psychological assessment in rehabilitating patients with occupational musculoskeletal injuries. *Journal of Back and Musculoskeletal Rehabilitation, 7*, 41–51.

Baardseth, T. P., Goldberg, S. B., Pace, B. T., Wislocki, A. P., Frost, N. D., Siddiqui, J. R., . . . Wampold, B. E. (2013). Cognitive-behavioral therapy versus other therapies: Redux. *Clinical Psychology Review, 33*, 395–405.

Bandura, A. (1977). *Social learning theory.* Englewood Cliffs, NJ: Prentice Hall.

Beck, A. (1983). Cognitive therapy of depression: New perspectives. In P. Clayton (Ed.), *Treatment of depression: Old controversies and new perspectives* (pp. 191–233). New York, NY: Raven Press.

Beck, A. T. (1967). *Depression: Clinical, experimental, and theoretical aspects.* New York, NY: Hoeber. Republished as *Depression: Causes and treatment.* Philadelphia, PA: University of Pennsylvania Press [1972].

Beck, A. T. (1993). Cognitive therapy: Past, present, and future. *Journal of Consulting and Clinical Psychology, 61*, 194–198.

Beck, A. T., Liese, B. S., & Najavits, L. M. (2005). Cognitive therapy. In R. J. Frances, S. I. Miller, & A. H. Mack (Eds.), *Clinical textbook of addictive disorders* (3rd ed., pp. 473–501). New York, NY: Guilford.

Beck, A. T., & Weishaar, M. E. (2014). Cognitive therapy. In D. Wedding & R. J. Corsini (Eds.), *Current psychotherapies* (10th ed., pp. 231–264). Belmont, CA: Brooks/Cole.

Bisson, J., & Andrew, M. (2007). Psychological treatment of post-traumatic stress disorder (PTSD). *Cochrane Database of Systematic Reviews*, (3), CD003388.

Blackburn, I. M., Eunson, K. M., & Bishop, S. (1986). A two-year naturalistic follow-up of depressed patients treated with cognitive therapy, pharmacotherapy and a combination of both. *Journal of Affective Disorders, 10*, 67–75.

Bowers, W. (1990). Treatment of depressed in-patients: Cognitive therapy plus medication, relaxation plus medication, and medication alone. *British Journal of Psychiatry, 156*, 73–78.

Bruce, T., Spiegel, D., & Hegel, M. (1999). Cognitive-behavioral therapy helps prevent relapse and recurrence of panic disorder following alprazolam discontinuation: A long-term follow-up of the Peoria and Dartmouth studies. *Journal of Consulting and Clinical Psychology, 67*, 151–156.

Bustillo, J. R., Lauriello, J., & Keith, S. J. (1999). Schizophrenia: Improving outcome. *Harvard Review of Psychiatry, 6*, 229–240.

Butler, A. C., Chapman, J. E., Forman, E. M., & Beck, A. T. (2006). The empirical status of cognitive-behavioral therapy: A review of meta-analyses. *Clinical Psychology Review, 26*, 17–31.

Chadwick, P. D., & Lowe, C. F. (1990). Measurement and modification of delusional beliefs. *Journal of Consulting and Clinical Psychology, 58*, 225–232.

Chan, F., Rosenthal, D. A., & Pruett, S. R. (2008). Evidence-based practice in the provision of rehabilitation services. *Journal of Rehabilitation, 74*(2), 3–5.

Coull, G., & Morris, P. G. (2011). The clinical effectiveness of CBT-based guided self-help interventions for anxiety and depressive disorders: A systematic review. *Psychological Medicine, 41*, 2239–2252.

Craighead, L. W., Craighead, W. E., Kazdin, A. E., & Mahoney, M. J. (1994). *Cognitive and behavioral interventions: An empirical approach to mental health problems.* Needham Heights, MA: Allyn & Bacon.

Devins, G. M., & Binik, Y. M. (1996). Facilitating coping with chronic physical illness. In M. Zeidner & N. S. Endler (Eds.), *Handbook of coping: Theory, research, and applications* (pp. 640–696). New York, NY: Wiley.

Dixon, T. M., Layton, B. S., & Shaw, R. M. (2005). Traumatic brain injury. In H. H. Zaretsky, E. F. Richter III, & M. G. Eisenberg (Eds.), *Medical aspects of disability: A handbook for the rehabilitation professional* (3rd ed., pp. 119–150). New York, NY: Springer Publishing Company.

Dobson, K. S. (1989). A meta-analysis of the efficacy of cognitive therapy for depression. *Journal of Consulting and Clinical Psychology, 57,* 414–419.

Dobson, K. S., & Dozois, D. J. A. (2010). Historical and philosophical bases of the cognitive-behavioral therapies. In K. S. Dobson (Ed.), *Handbook of cognitive-behavioral therapies* (pp. 3–38). New York, NY: Guilford Press.

Eddy, K. T., Dutra, L., Bradley, R., & Westen, D. (2004). A multidimensional meta-analysis of psychotherapy and pharmacotherapy for obsessive-compulsive disorder. *Clinical Psychology Review, 24,* 1011–1030.

Elliott, T. R., & Frank, R. G. (1996). Depression following spinal cord injury. *Archives of Physical Medicine and Rehabilitation, 77,* 816–823.

Ellis, A. (1962). *Reason and emotion in psychotherapy.* New York, NY: Stuart.

Ellis, A. (1979). The practice of rational-emotive therapy. In A. Ellis & J. M. Whitely (Eds.), *Theoretical and empirical foundations of rational-emotive therapy* (pp. 61–100). Monterey, CA: Brooks/Cole.

Farhall, J., & Thomas, N. (2013). Cognitive and behavioural therapies for psychosis. *Australian and New Zealand Journal of Psychiatry, 47,* 508–511.

Fedoroff, I. C., & Taylor, S. (2001). Psychological and pharmacological treatments of social phobia: A meta-analysis. *Journal of Clinical Psychopharmacology, 21,* 311–324.

Freeman, A., Pretzer, J., Fleming, B., & Simon, K. (1990). *Clinical applications of cognitive therapy.* New York, NY: Plenum.

Freud, S. (1961). The ego and the id and other works. In J. Strachey (Ed. & Trans.), *The standard edition of the complete psychological works of Sigmund Freud* (Vol. 19, pp. 1–66). London, UK: Hogarth. (Original work published 1923)

Gil, P. J. M., Carrillo, F. X. M., & Sánchez Meca, J. (2000). Effectiveness of cognitive-behavioural treatment in social phobia: A meta-analytic review. *Psicothema-Oviedo, 12,* 346–352.

Goldfried, M. R. (1980). Toward the delineation of therapeutic change principles. *American Psychologist, 35,* 991–999.

Gould, R. A., Buckminster, S., Pollack, M. H., Otto, M. W., & Yap, L. (1997). Cognitive-behavioral and pharmacological treatment for social phobia: A meta-analysis. *Clinical Psychology: Science and Practice, 4,* 291–306.

Gregory, V. L. (2010). Cognitive-behavioral therapy for mania: A meta-analysis of randomized controlled trials. *Social Work in Mental Health, 8,* 483–494.

Hayes, S. C. (2004). Acceptance and commitment therapy, relational frame theory, and the third wave of behavioral and cognitive therapies. *Behavior Therapy, 35,* 639–665.

Hayes, S. C., & Strosahl, K. D. (Eds.). (2004). *A practical guide to acceptance and commitment therapy.* New York, NY: Springer Publishing Company.

Hind, D., Cotter, J., Thake, A., Bradburn, M., Cooper, C., Isaac, C., & House, A. (2014). Cognitive behavioural therapy for the treatment of depression in people with multiple sclerosis: A systematic review and meta-analysis. *BMC Psychiatry, 14,* 5–36.

Hofmann, S. G., Asnaani, A., Vonk, I. J., Sawyer, A. T., & Fang, A. (2012). The efficacy of cognitive behavioral therapy: A review of meta-analyses. *Cognitive Therapy and Research, 36,* 427–440.

Hofmann, S. G., & Smits, J. A. (2008). Cognitive-behavioral therapy for adult anxiety disorders: A meta-analysis of randomized placebo-controlled trials. *Journal of Clinical Psychiatry, 69,* 621–632.

Hofmann, S. G., & Spiegel, D. A. (1999). Panic control treatment and its applications. *Journal of Psychotherapy Practice and Research, 8,* 3–11.

Hollon, S. D., & Beck, A. T. (2013). Cognitive and cognitive-behavioral therapies. In M. J. Lambert (Ed.), *Bergin and Garfield's handbook of psychotherapy and behavior change* (6th ed., pp. 393–442). Hoboken, NJ: Wiley.

James, R. K., & Gilliland, B. E. (2003). *Theories and strategies in counseling and psychotherapy* (5th ed.). Boston, MA: Allyn & Bacon.

Kazdin, A. E. (1978). *History of behavior modification: Experimental foundations of contemporary research.* Baltimore, MD: University Park Press.

Kelly, G. (1955). *The psychology of personal constructs.* New York, NY: Norton.

Kroese, B. S. (1998). Cognitive-behavioral therapy for people with learning disabilities. *Behavioural and Cognitive Psychotherapy, 26,* 315–322.

Lawrence, R. R., Bradshaw, T. T., & Mairs, H. H. (2006). Group cognitive behavioural therapy for schizophrenia: A systematic review of the literature. *Journal of Psychiatric and Mental Health Nursing, 13,* 673–681.

Lezak, M. D., Howieson, D. B., Bigler, E. D., & Tranel, D. (2012). *Neuropsychological assessment* (5th ed.). New York, NY: Oxford University Press.

Lindsay, W. R. (1999). Cognitive therapy. *Psychologist, 12,* 238–241.

Lynch, D., Laws, K. R., & McKenna, P. J. (2010). Cognitive behavioural therapy for major psychiatric disorder: Does it really work? A meta-analytical review of well-controlled trials. *Psychological Medicine, 40,* 9–24.

Lysaker, P. H., Davis, L. W., Bryson, G. J., & Bell, M. D. (2009). Effects of cognitive behavioral therapy on work outcomes in vocational rehabilitation for participants with schizophrenia spectrum disorders. *Schizophrenia Research, 107,* 186–191.

Meadows, E. A., & Foa, E. B. (1999). Cognitive-behavioral treatment of traumatized adults. In P. A. Saigh & J. D. Bremner (Eds.), *Posttraumatic stress disorder: A comprehensive text* (pp. 376–390). Needham Heights, MA: Allyn & Bacon.

Meichenbaum, D. H. (1995). Cognitive-behavioral therapy in historical perspective. In B. M. Bongar & L. E. Beutler (Eds.), *Comprehensive textbook of psychotherapy: Theory and practice* (pp. 140–158). New York, NY: Oxford University Press.

Mendes, D. D., Mello, M. F., Ventura, P., de Medeiros Passarela, C., & de Jesus Mari, J. (2008). A systematic review on the effectiveness of cognitive behavioral therapy for posttraumatic stress disorder. *International Journal of Psychiatry in Medicine, 38,* 241–259.

Miranda, J., Gross, J. J., Persons, J. B., & Hahn, J. (1998). Mood matters: Negative mood induction activates dysfunctional attitudes in women vulnerable to depression. *Cognitive Therapy and Research, 22,* 363–376.

Moritz, S., Veckenstedt, R., Randjbar, S., Vitzthum, F., & Woodward, T. S. (2011). Antipsychotic treatment beyond antipsychotics: Metacognitive intervention for schizophrenia patients improves delusional symptoms. *Psychological Medicine, 41,* 1823–1832.

Morley, S., Eccleston, C., & Williams, A. (1999). Systematic review and meta-analysis of randomized controlled trials of cognitive behaviour therapy and behaviour therapy for chronic pain in adults, excluding headache. *Pain, 80,* 1–13.

Morris, E. M. J., Johns, L. C., & Oliver, J. E. (2013). *Acceptance and commitment therapy and mindfulness for psychosis.* New York, NY: Wiley–Blackwell.

Morrison, A. P., & Barratt, S. (2010). What are the components of CBT for psychosis? A Delphi study. *Schizophrenia Bulletin, 36,* 136–142.

National Collaborating Centre for Mental Health. (2009). *Schizophrenia: The NICE guideline on core interventions in the treatment and management of schizophrenia in adults in primary and secondary care (National clinical practice guideline, updated edition).* London, UK: Royal College of Psychiatrists & British Psychological Society.

Nezu, A. M. (1987). A problem-solving formulation of depression: A literature review and proposal of a pluralistic model. *Clinical Psychology Review, 7,* 121–144.

Nicoll, M., Beail, N., & Saxon, D. (2013). Cognitive behavioural treatment for anger in adults with intellectual disabilities: A systematic review and meta-analysis. *Journal of Applied Research in Intellectual Disabilities, 26*, 47–62.

Oathamshaw, S. C., & Haddock, G. (2006). Do people with intellectual disabilities and psychosis have the cognitive skills required to undertake cognitive behavioural therapy? *Journal of Applied Research in Intellectual Disabilities, 19*, 35–46.

Oberlander, E. L., Schneier, F. R., & Liebowitz, M. R. (1994). Physical disability and social phobia. *Journal of Clinical Psychopharmacology, 14*, 136–143.

O'Kearney, R. (1998). Responsibility appraisals and obsessive-compulsive disorder: A critique of Salkovskis's cognitive theory. *Australian Journal of Psychology, 50*, 43–47.

Öst, L. G. (2008). Efficacy of the third wave of behavioral therapies: A systematic review and meta-analysis. *Behaviour Research and Therapy, 46*, 296–321.

Pilgrim, D. (2011). The hegemony of cognitive-behaviour therapy in modern mental health care. *Health Sociology Review, 20*, 120–132.

Pruett, S. R., Swett, E. A., Chan, F., Rosenthal, D. A., & Lee, G. K. (2008). Empirical evidence supporting the effectiveness of vocational rehabilitation. *Journal of Rehabilitation, 74*, 56–63.

Ramsay, J. R. (1998). Postmodern cognitive therapy: Cognitions, narratives, and personal meaning-making. *Journal of Cognitive Psychotherapy, 12*, 39–55.

Rao, S. M. (1990). Multiple sclerosis. In J. L. Cummings (Ed.), *Subcortical dementia* (pp. 164–180). New York, NY: Oxford University Press.

Ross, K., Freeman, D., Dunn, G., & Garety, P. (2011). A randomized experimental investigation of reasoning training for people with delusions. *Schizophrenia Bulletin, 37*, 324–333.

Ruhmland, M., & Margraf, J. (2001). Effektivität psychologischer Therapien von generalisierter Angststörung und sozialer Phobie: Meta-Analysen auf Störungsebene [Effectiveness of psychological therapies for generalized anxiety disorder and social phobia: Meta-analyzes on fault plane]. *Verhaltenstherapie, 11*, 27–40.

Sarin, F., Wallin, L., & Widerlöv, B. (2011). Cognitive behavior therapy for schizophrenia: A meta-analytical review of randomized controlled trials. *Nordic Journal of Psychiatry, 65*, 162–174.

Segal, Z. V., Gemar, M., & Williams, S. (1999). Differential cognitive response to a mood challenge following successful cognitive therapy or pharmacotherapy for unipolar depression. *Journal of Abnormal Psychology, 108*, 3–10.

Seidler, G. H., & Wagner, F. E. (2006). Comparing the efficacy of EMDR and trauma-focused cognitive-behavioral therapy in the treatment of PTSD: A meta-analytic study. *Psychological Medicine, 36*, 1515–1522.

Seligman, L., & Reichenberg, L. W. (2010). *Theories of counseling and psychotherapy*. Upper Saddle River, NJ: Pearson.

Shafran, R., & Somers, J. (1998). Treating adolescent obsessive-compulsive disorder: Applications of the cognitive theory. *Behaviour Research and Therapy, 36*, 93–97.

Spiegler, M. D., & Guevremont, D. C. (1993). *Contemporary behavior therapy* (2nd ed.). Pacific Grove, CA: Brooks/Cole.

Sullivan, H. S. (1953). *The interpersonal theory of psychiatry*. New York, NY: Norton.

Swett, E. A., & Kaplan, S. P. (2004). Cognitive-behavioral therapy. In F. Chan, N. L. Berven, & K. R. Thomas (Eds.), *Counseling theories and techniques for rehabilitation health professionals* (pp. 159–176). New York, NY: Springer Publishing Company.

Szentagotai, A., & David, D. (2010). The efficacy of cognitive-behavioral therapy in bipolar disorder: A quantitative meta-analysis. *Journal of Clinical Psychiatry, 71*, 66–72.

Tarrier, N., Pilgrim, H., Sommerfield, C., Faragher, B., Reynolds, M., Graham, E., . . . Barrowclough, C. (1999). A randomized trial of cognitive therapy and imaginal exposure in the treatment of chronic posttraumatic stress disorder. *Journal of Consulting and Clinical Psychology, 67*, 13–18.

Turkington, D., Sensky, T., Scott, J., Barnes, T. R., Nur, U., Siddle, R., . . . Kingdon, D. (2008). A randomized controlled trial of cognitive-behavior therapy for persistent symptoms in schizophrenia: A five-year follow-up. *Schizophrenia Research, 98,* 1–7.

van der Gaag, M., Valmaggia, L. R., & Smit, F. (2014). The effects of individually tailored formulation-based cognitive-behavioural therapy in auditory hallucinations and delusions: A meta-analysis. *Schizophrenia Research, 156,* 30–37.

Wampold, B. E., Minami, T., Baskin, T. W., & Tierney, S. C. (2002). A meta-(re)analysis of the effects of cognitive therapy versus 'other therapies' for depression. *Journal of Affective Disorders, 68,* 159–165.

Winter, D. A., & Watson, S. (1999). Personal construct psychotherapy and the cognitive therapies: Different in theory but can they be differentiated in practice? *Journal of Constructivist Psychology, 12,* 1–22.

Wolpe, J. (1958). *Psychotherapy by reciprocal inhibition.* Stanford, CA: Stanford University Press.

Wykes, T., Steel, C., Everitt, B., & Tarrier, N. (2008). Cognitive behavior therapy for schizophrenia: Effect sizes, clinical models, and methodological rigor. *Schizophrenia Bulletin, 34,* 523–537.

# Rational Emotive Behavior Therapy

*Malachy Bishop and Allison R. Fleming*

## LEARNING OBJECTIVES

The goal of this chapter is to introduce the history and major concepts of rational emotive behavior therapy (REBT); to describe the counseling process, counseling relationship, and counseling techniques associated with this therapy; to describe REBT's application in rehabilitation counseling; and to review the current REBT evidence base and research.

As learning objectives, readers will be able to identify, describe, and apply major theoretical and philosophical concepts and to accomplish the following:

1. Understand the concept of rationality as defined in REBT, and describe and define rational and irrational beliefs and the biological and social influences on the development of irrational beliefs.
2. Describe the interrelationship among cognition, behavior, and emotion in REBT theory and the ABC framework.
3. Define psychological health and disturbance.
4. Describe the nature of the REBT counseling relationship and commonly used techniques and methods.
5. Discuss the state and direction of REBT research.

## OVERVIEW OF REBT

REBT is an active–directive form of counseling and psychotherapy in which practitioners employ cognitive, behavioral, and emotive (or affective) techniques in order to help people achieve and maintain constructive change. This change occurs through an educational counseling process aimed at helping clients to understand the following: (a) that they largely create their own psychological disturbances and problems; (b) that they do this by maintaining irrational beliefs;

and (c) that they can learn to address and overcome their problems by learning to detect, question, challenge, and reject their irrational beliefs as illogical and unconstructive and developing rational beliefs that are "true, sensible, and constructive" (Dryden, 2005, pp. 322–323).

The fundamental tenet of REBT is that events, incidents, or adversities themselves do not lead to emotional disturbance; rather, it is the irrational beliefs, dogmatic musts, and imperative demands that people hold about these events that lead people to become disturbed and to engage in the self-defeating emotions and dysfunctional behaviors that hinder goal attainment. Alternately, if people can take primary responsibility for their emotional problems and work in a determined fashion to combat the irrational thinking that underpins them, the result will be a minimizing of self-defeating upsets and an enhanced chance for happiness and satisfaction (Yankura & Dryden, 1994).

In the decades since REBT was developed, it has become an important and influential theory and method of cognitive behavioral counseling and psychotherapy (Weinrach, 2006). Many aspects of REBT make it appropriate and effective for use in the rehabilitation setting in work with clients with chronic illnesses or disabilities.

## HISTORY

Albert Ellis was the founder and chief proponent of REBT until his death in 2007. Ellis was born in Pittsburgh in 1913 and at age 4 moved with his family to New York, where he remained for the rest of his life. Ellis was the oldest of three children. He described his father as a minimally successful businessman who was frequently away from home and showed little affection for his children (Ellis, Abrams, & Abrams, 2012). Ellis described his mother as emotionally distant, self-absorbed, and as having a bipolar affect. As a child, Ellis developed a strong sense of responsibility for his younger siblings and of self-sufficiency. Ellis was often sick during childhood and was hospitalized several times, primarily due to kidney disease (Sharf, 2012). Ellis attributed much of the development of REBT to his challenges and experiences early in life and his approaches to resolving problems. For example, at the age of 19 in an attempt to overcome his shyness with girls, he made himself ask out 100 girls in 1 month. Although unsuccessful in getting a date, the experience helped him overcome his shyness, and this direct approach to resolving his fears clearly is reflected in the techniques he would later advocate with his clients.

After obtaining his undergraduate degree in business administration in 1934 and briefly pursuing careers in business and fiction writing, he began writing nonfiction, including lay counseling documents in the area of human sexuality (Ellis et al., 2012). He completed his master's degree in clinical psychology in 1943 and engaged in part-time private practice while pursuing his PhD, which he completed at Teachers College, Columbia University, in 1947. After completing his degree, he sought training in psychoanalysis, completed his personal analysis, and began practicing under the supervision of a training analyst at the Karen Horney Institute.

Ellis practiced classical analysis and psychoanalytically oriented therapy for several years. During this time he became increasingly disillusioned with what he considered to be the passivity, inefficiency, and ineffectiveness of psychoanalysis (Ellis, 2005). He noted that despite developing insight into, or understanding of, events from their early childhood, clients rarely lost their symptoms. Further, they continued to retain the tendency to create new ones. Ellis proposed that this was not only because of the irrational beliefs that they had developed in their youth but also because they were currently continuing to construct dysfunctional demands of themselves and others and were continually reindoctrinating themselves with these irrational demands.

By 1953, Ellis had almost completely rejected the psychoanalytic approach (Yankura & Dryden, 1994). For 2 years, he "intensively studied hundreds of other methods" and as a result of this research and his clinical experiences, developed rational therapy in 1955 (Ellis, 1996, p. 5). Ellis subsequently renamed his theory rational emotive therapy (RET) in 1961 and rational emotive behavior therapy (REBT) in 1993. In describing the rationale for these changes in the name of the therapy, Ellis pointed out that they reflected a clarification and inclusion of elements that had always been present in the theory, rather than a philosophical or practical shift in the theory or practice of REBT (Ellis, 1995a).

Ellis first presented rational therapy publicly in a paper delivered at the American Psychological Association annual conference in 1956. Due to the current widespread acceptance and popular use of cognitive or cognitive behavioral theories and techniques, some of the concepts and ideas associated with REBT may today seem familiar, even to those new to the theory. At the time Ellis introduced REBT, however, the ideas were innovative and unfamiliar in a psychotherapy landscape dominated by psychoanalysis and, as it was known at that time, client-centered therapy (DiGiuseppe, 2011).

Ellis cited a wide variety of influences in the development of REBT (Ellis, 1995b, 1996, 2005). These included a number of philosophical influences, including existential philosophy and Asian philosophers, such as Confucius, Lao-Tsu, and Buddha. Stoic philosophy was a primary influence, and he was particularly inspired by the stoic philosophers Epictetus, Seneca, and Marcus Aurelius, who stated that happiness or misery result not from events but from the perceptions and thinking about those events. Other influences included behavior theory and therapy, Karen Horney's "tyranny of the shoulds" (Horney, 1965), and the theory and therapy of Alfred Adler (Ellis, 1973). Ellis credited Adler with the realization that people's behavior stems from their ideas and called Adler "the modern psychotherapist who was the main precursor of REBT" (Ellis, 1995b, p. 167).

Ellis maintained an extraordinary work ethic in his clinical work, training REBT therapists and writing throughout his life, until his death at age 93. Ellis published 75 books and almost 800 articles and numerous book chapters (Sharf, 2012). In 1959, he organized the Institute for Rational Living, a site for training, therapy, and research, which was renamed the Albert Ellis Institute in 1996. Ellis served as president emeritus of the institute until his death in 2007.

# MAJOR THEORETICAL CONCEPTS

## View of Human Nature

From the REBT perspective, people are seen as fluid and complex biopsychosocial beings, with a strong tendency to establish and pursue goals. People are seen as being happiest when they establish important life goals and purposes and are actively striving to achieve them (Dryden, 2012, p. 191). The fundamental and universal human goals include the need "to survive, to be relatively free from pain, and to be reasonably satisfied or content" (Ellis, 1991, p. 142). More specific subgoals may include the following: (a) to be happy when alone; (b) to be happy with others, in both intimate relationships and wider social relationships; and (c) to be happy with educational, vocational, economic, and recreational activities.

Because humans are primarily concerned with their own survival and happiness, from an REBT perspective, people are described as essentially hedonistic (Dryden, David, & Ellis, 2010). Yet REBT holds that people should embrace a long-range rather than short-term hedonism. Although it is important to achieve some of their short-term goals, people are encouraged to maintain a focus on long-range goals and purposes and also to recognize the social nature of the world in which they are pursuing their goals and purposes (Dryden et al., 2010, p. 229). Focusing too much on immediate wants and seeking instant gratification can lead to situations that inhibit or threaten one's ability to work to obtain long-term goals. Further, REBT emphasizes that people should realize that they live in a social world, in which achieving their goals often involves cooperation with or assistance from others, such that social interest and a cooperative attitude toward the goals of others promotes the pursuit and achievement of one's own goals (Dryden, 2012; Dryden et al., 2010).

## Rationality

The concept of rationality holds a preeminent position in REBT theory and practice. From an REBT perspective, what is rational is broadly defined as that which helps a person to achieve his or her goals or purposes and that leads to healthy results. Alternately, irrational is whatever prevents a person from achieving his or her goals and leads to unhealthy results for the person and his or her relationships (Dryden, 2012, 2013). Because people have unique goals and purposes, the precise meaning of rationality depends on the individual and the situation and therefore cannot be defined in an absolute sense (Dryden et al., 2010).

"In REBT theory, rational beliefs are deemed to be at the core of psychological health and a primary goal of REBT is to help clients to change their irrational beliefs into rational beliefs" (Dryden, 2013, p. 39). Rational beliefs are characterized as being logical, flexible, consistent with reality, and consistent with one's long-term goals. A rational belief or expectation is expressed in terms of what we want or would like to happen, or as a preference, while at the same time recognizing that we may not have, and do not have to get, what we want. People who hold rational beliefs and expectations experience positive feelings of satisfaction when they get what they want, and experience healthy negative feelings, such as disappointment, sadness, healthy anger, or regret when they do not (Dryden, 2012). These healthy negative feelings may serve to motivate continued efforts toward the eventual attainment of one's goals or desires.

For example, a job seeker who approaches a job interview maintaining a set of rational beliefs may say to herself: "Although it would, for a variety of reasons, be nice to obtain this position, many other people may also be interviewing for the position, including some people who may be more skilled or experienced (or better interviewers) than I. Since I cannot control the employer's decision, all I can do is to do my best." If she then learns that she did not obtain the position, it would be natural for her to experience such feelings as disappointment, a healthy anger, and sadness. These emotions are healthy in that they do not prevent further goal pursuit, and may motivate her to take productive action, like trying to find out how she can do even better the next time so that eventually she can reach her goal of obtaining a job.

Irrational beliefs are rigid, illogical, inconsistent with one's long-term goals, and unhealthy. Irrational beliefs are expressed as demands (e.g., "Things *have to* work out the way I think they should"), as musts (e.g., "I *must* have what I want"), or as all-or-nothing absolutes (e.g., "I am *always* treated unfairly" or "I will *never* succeed"). A job seeker maintaining irrational beliefs about an upcoming interview might express such beliefs as "I must get this job. I really cannot bear to continue to live without a job for another week. I deserve this job and the employer should give it to me because no one else can do it better than me." If this person does not get the position, he or she will likely experience unhealthy negative emotions, such as depression, unhealthy anger or rage, guilt, or shame. Because these unhealthy negative emotions are likely to be associated with behaviors that negatively affect the health of the person's relationships, such as withdrawal, isolation, procrastination, inactivity, escapism, or substance abuse, they hinder rather than promote the person's long-term goal pursuit and achievement.

The distinction between rational and irrational beliefs is a unique and central focus of REBT and one that Ellis and others have written about extensively (e.g., Dryden, 2013; Weinrach, 2006). In his early REBT writings, Ellis (1962, pp. 60–88) proposed a set of specific irrational beliefs that he saw as being the most frequent causes of emotional upset. These are presented in Table 6.1. In more recent works, Ellis and colleagues have suggested that irrational beliefs and attitudes can be characterized in terms of three main "musts" or demands (Dryden, 1990, 2012; Ellis, 1994, 1996):

1. Demands about the self: "I absolutely must, at practically all times, be successful and demonstrate competency in my endeavors and win the approval of virtually all the significant people in my life." Such beliefs are often associated with feelings of anxiety, depression, shame, and guilt, and such behaviors as avoidance, withdrawal, and substance abuse or addiction.

**TABLE 6.1  Specific Irrational Beliefs Frequently Associated With Emotional Upset**

1. The idea that it is a dire necessity for an adult human being to be loved or approved by virtually every significant person in his community
2. The idea that one should be thoroughly competent, adequate, and achieving in all possible respects if one is to consider oneself worthwhile
3. The idea that certain people are bad, wicked, or villainous and that they should be severely blamed and punished for their villainy
4. The idea that it is awful and catastrophic when things are not the way one would very much like them to be
5. The idea that human unhappiness is externally caused and that people have little or no ability to control their sorrows and disturbance
6. The idea that if something is or may be dangerous or fearsome, one should be terribly concerned about it and should keep dwelling on the possibility of its occurring
7. The idea that it is easier to avoid than to face certain life difficulties and self-responsibilities
8. The idea that one should be dependent on others and should need someone stronger than oneself on whom to rely
9. The idea that one's past history is an all-important determiner of one's present behavior and that because something once affected one's life, it should indefinitely have a similar effect
10. The idea that one should become quite upset over other people's problems and disturbances
11. The idea that there is invariably a right, precise, and perfect solution to human problems and that it is catastrophic if this solution is not found

2. Demands about others: "Other people must practically always treat me considerately, kindly, fairly, and lovingly. If they don't, then it is awful and they are no good and deserve no joy in their lives." These beliefs often underpin feelings of anger, rage, passive aggressiveness, and resentment, and aggressive or violent behaviors.

3. Demands about the world/living conditions: "I need and must have the things I want. Conditions under which I live must be comfortable, pleasurable, and rewarding. If they are not, I can't stand it, it is terrible." Feelings that are associated with such beliefs include rage, self-pity, and low frustration tolerance. Behaviors that may coincide include withdrawal, procrastination, and addiction.

### The Interrelationship Among Cognition, Behavior, and Emotion

Ellis always maintained that the basic human processes of thinking, emoting (feeling or affect), and behaving are not separate, but interrelated, generally simultaneous, and overlapping (Dryden, 2012). Ellis (1996, p. 14) provided the following example to highlight the interrelated nature of the components:

> When you think negatively ("I'm an inadequate person when I fail to win John's [or Joan's] approval!"), you tend to *feel* badly (e.g., anxious) and act dysfunctionally (e.g., beg for approval or avoid John [or Joan]). When you *feel* anxious, you tend to *think* negative thoughts and to *act* compulsively or avoidantly. When you act compulsively, you tend to *think* and *feel* negatively.

As a consequence of the overlapping nature of these elements, the most effective method of therapy is one that engages the client at all three levels.

## Psychological Disturbance and Psychological Health

The REBT view of psychological health rests on the fundamental tenet of REBT that emotional upsets and disturbances largely arise from irrational beliefs that people hold about events that occur in their lives. In order for a person to become psychologically or emotionally disturbed, he or she must first make an evaluation, and based on his or her beliefs about the event, relationship, or situation under consideration, conclude that it is terrible, awful, and unbearable, as opposed to simply inconvenient, unpleasant, or disagreeable (Weinrach, 2006). REBT theory suggests that people who maintain a personal philosophy of demanding and "musturbation" (i.e., insisting that things *must* go as they want, and that others and the world in general *must* meet their needs and desires) tend to come to exaggerated and extreme conclusions about their experiences (Dryden et al., 2010). These extreme conclusions include awfulizing, low frustration tolerance, and self-depreciation.

Awfulizing refers to exaggerating how bad a thing is or believing that something that is unpleasant, inconvenient, or disagreeable is terrible, awful, or the worst thing that could happen. Low frustration tolerance refers to the exaggerated conclusion that one cannot bear the frustration of not having a demand met when and how one believes it should be met. Self-depreciation refers to making generalized or global self-evaluations based on beliefs about oneself, others, or the world in general. For example, a student who does poorly on an important test and concludes, based on his or her irrational self-related demands, "I am a total failure" is making a global, self-depreciating evaluation about his or her whole self, rather than that aspect of the self that is relevant to the situation.

REBT identifies two major categories of psychological disturbances: ego disturbance and discomfort disturbance. Ego disturbance is associated with self-depreciation or giving oneself a global negative rating, when rigid demands of the self, others, and the world are not met. Discomfort disturbance refers to the inability to tolerate threats to comfort and comfortable conditions (Dryden et al., 2010). Some common examples of discomfort disturbance are low frustration tolerance or overreaction to unpleasant life circumstances.

Whereas irrational beliefs and dogmatic demands about one's self, others, and the world lead to psychological disturbance and emotional upset, the central feature of psychologically healthy people is the ability to develop and maintain flexible, rational beliefs. People who develop healthy personalities maintain logical and flexible thinking, foster self-enhancing beliefs, have a sense of mastery and control over their destiny, and are aware that they are capable of changing their thoughts (Dryden, 2011; Ellis, 1989). Ellis (1994) described flexible beliefs that are at the core of psychological health as including nonawfulizing beliefs, acceptance beliefs, and discomfort tolerance beliefs.

Non-awfulizing beliefs involve making a nonextreme evaluation when nondogmatic desires or preferences are not met (e.g., "It is unfortunate that I did not get what I want, but it is not awful" or "It is bad, but not the worst thing that could happen, and I can keep trying"). Acceptance beliefs reflect an unconditional self-acceptance. Specifically, this means refusing to give oneself

**TABLE 6.2 Ellis's Criteria for Positive Mental Health**

1. Enlightened self-interest
2. Social interest
3. Self-direction
4. Acceptance of ambiguity and uncertainty
5. Scientific thinking
6. Commitment to and being vitally absorbed in important projects
7. Flexibility
8. Calculated risk-taking
9. Acceptance of reality

a global negative rating and realizing that people are so complex, multidimensional, and fluid that such a rating is unrealistic and illogical. Accompanying this belief is acknowledging that people make mistakes, but that this does not mean that they are bad or worthless. The healthy response to discomfort disturbance is to accept (a) that sometimes we do not get what we want and that we cannot control every outcome and (b) that discomfort, frustration, and undesirable circumstances are a part of life and that they can be tolerated. Acceptance is distinguished, however, from resignation. When possible, it is healthy to work to change or modify the undesirable event or circumstances, but when they cannot be changed, the healthy and rational response is to accept this reality and continue to pursue and find meaning in other goals (Dryden, 2011). A comprehensive list of the criteria for positive mental health, proposed by Ellis (1979), is presented in Table 6.2.

### Biological and Social Influences on Development

A fundamental REBT principle is that people are born with the potential for rational (healthy, logical, and constructive), as well as irrational (harmful, rigid, and defeatist), thoughts, feelings, and behaviors. Consistent with the humanistic theories of Abraham Maslow and Carl Rogers, Ellis posited that people have innate tendencies for self-preservation, happiness, communion with others, and self-actualization. However, Ellis also asserted that people have inborn and primarily biological tendencies toward self-defeat, self-sabotage, self-destruction, perfectionism, thought avoidance, procrastination, and growth avoidance (Ellis, 1979, 2003).

Ellis offered a number of arguments supporting his hypothesis that there is a biologically based tendency toward irrationality (Ellis, 1976, 1979). Selected examples are presented in Table 6.3. Despite the strong emphasis on the inherent biological influence toward irrationality, it is important to note that REBT is not a deterministic theory; rather, it is humanistic, seeing people as capable, growth oriented, and having inherent worth (Dryden, 1990). People are seen as having the unique ability to think about their own thinking. Because of this, they are also capable of learning and understanding that for the most part they are choosing

**TABLE 6.3  Evidence Supporting a Biological Basis for Irrationality**

1.  Virtually all people demonstrate self-defeating tendencies and irrationalities, regardless of family background, culture, or ethnicity. Irrationality has been consistently observed in social and cultural groups throughout history.
2.  Many of the irrational beliefs run counter to the teachings of parents, teachers, and other social influences.
3.  Even bright and competent individuals who give up a set of irrational beliefs tend to adopt a new set, and individuals who tend to think rationally will sometimes revert to irrational beliefs.
4.  Insight into one's own irrational thoughts and behaviors only partially helps to change them.
5.  People often revert to irrational behavior and thoughts even after they have worked hard to overcome them.

*Note:* Supporting evidence selected from Ellis (1976, 1979).

their upsetting and disturbing beliefs and behaviors and are capable of changing these behaviors. Habits only stay habits when they are left alone, and self-defeating and irrational ideas remain so only when they are accepted without question (Young, 1974).

REBT also recognizes that tendencies toward irrationality and emotional disturbance can be influenced by familial and other social influences (Ellis, 1993, 2003; Yankura & Dryden, 1994). A person's sense of self is to a great extent influenced by the complex social interactions that he or she experiences, and parents, families, friends, and other social groups influence the development of beliefs and expectations. Importantly, however, Ellis noted that although social influences may have contributed to the development of a person's irrational beliefs, it is the individual himself or herself who is choosing to maintain them and, as a result, reindoctrinate himself or herself with them in the present (Walen, DiGiuseppe, & Dryden, 1992, p. 358). "Even when they accept such dysfunctional beliefs from others, they tend to reconstruct them and actively carry them on; and they are not merely affected years later by the fact that they accepted these beliefs but by their continuing to promulgate them and to act on them" (Ellis, 2003, p. 221).

### The ABC Framework

In the course of pursuing their goals, people often experience adversities or circumstances that are not in accord with their demands. The ABC model presents an REBT framework for understanding the mechanics of how people respond in such circumstances (Ellis, 1977). In the ABC model, the *A* stands for the activating event or adversity that acts to block goal attainment. The *A* can be the situation in which the person experienced his or her disturbed feelings, or it can be the specific part of the situation to which the person responds with disturbance (Dryden, 2012). The *B* represents the beliefs, both rational and irrational, that the individual holds regarding the activating event. The *C* connotes the emotional and behavioral consequences that result from holding particular beliefs about *A* (Ellis, 1991, 1996; Yankura & Dryden, 1994).

Whereas people often believe that *A* is the direct cause of their emotional and behavioral response or consequence *C*, Ellis made clear through this model that it is not the adversity or activating event, but the individual's beliefs *B* about *A* that largely determine one's emotional and behavioral reactions. If the person's beliefs and expectations about the adversity or thwarted goal pursuit are rational (i.e., flexible, logical, and expressed as preferences, hopes, and wishes), then, as noted earlier in this chapter, they will experience appropriate and healthy negative emotions. For example, if the adverse event were the loss of a job, a person might respond with a self-statement such as "I wish I had not lost my job, but I did. It is unfortunate, but I can certainly continue with my life and eventually find happiness in another position." Alternately, if the person's beliefs and expectations are irrational (characterized by rigidity and absolutist musts, shoulds, and oughts), then the self-statements may sound more like this: "I should never have lost my job. It is awful that I lost my job, and my being let go proves that I am a worthless person" (Dryden, 1990; Ellis, 1996).

For many clients, simply understanding the theory behind the ABC framework can be a therapeutic insight. The awareness (a) that one's emotional and behavioral response to adversity is not determined by external factors and (b) that people choose to disturb and upset themselves by holding and actively maintaining irrational beliefs about the events in their lives can be a critical therapeutic insight in that it leads to the empowering idea that the client can change the consequences by changing his or her beliefs.

Since its original presentation, Ellis and colleagues have continued to evaluate and extend the ABC framework both as a conceptual model and as a counseling tool. Although the ABC framework appears fairly straightforward and simple (and indeed, like all good models, it is a simple and effective means of representing the relationship among *A*, *B*, and *C* for clients and counselors), the integrative and dynamic nature of human cognition, behavior, and affect make the reality of human experience somewhat more complicated. For example, REBT recognizes that, in addition to disturbing themselves about events and circumstances, people often disturb themselves about disturbing themselves. In this case, being disturbed becomes an activating event. This dynamic of being disturbed about being disturbed (or thinking about thinking about thinking) is referred to as metadisturbance (Dryden, 2012).

Considering the situation of the aforementioned woman who lost her job can provide an example of metadisturbance. If, largely due to her irrational beliefs about the importance of her job, the woman were to become depressed, she might then begin to disturb herself about being depressed due to her irrational beliefs about depression (e.g., "Depression is weakness, and feeling depressed proves that I am a weak person"). In addition to disturbing herself about her emotional response, she might also begin to disturb herself about her behavioral or cognitive response to her emotional response (Dryden, 2012), which are possibilities that suggest the potential complexity and expanding nature of metadisturbance.

Ellis also added a *D* and an *E* to the ABC model. The *D* represents the active disputing of irrational beliefs, and the *E* represents an effective new philosophy, emotion, and behavior. In REBT counseling, the counselor will often explain the ABC framework to the client and then teach the client the process of effectively disputing irrational beliefs. This involves four components: detecting, defining, discriminating, and debating (Ellis, 1977). First, the client learns to detect or identify his or her rigid and extreme beliefs. The client learns to accurately define the beliefs by focusing on the language that the client uses when referring to the beliefs. The client learns to discriminate rational from irrational beliefs through an understanding of the nature and characteristics of irrational beliefs (e.g., rigid, extreme, illogical demands). Then, the client learns the process of effectively debating irrational beliefs by challenging the underlying logic. The process of debating irrational beliefs is further described later in the chapter. Finally, at *E*, the client is encouraged to develop a more effective, rational, and functional philosophy to replace the irrational beliefs.

## DESCRIPTION OF THE COUNSELING PROCESS

The process of REBT counseling is essentially one of educating clients in the skill of identifying and effectively disputing irrational beliefs. Change occurs through an educational counseling process in which clients come to learn that they can overcome their problems by learning to detect, challenge, and reject their irrational beliefs as illogical and unconstructive and develop rational beliefs that are more likely to help them achieve their goals (Dryden, 2005). The overriding goal of REBT is to help clients acquire a more realistic, rational, and tolerant philosophy of life (Ellis, 1995b).

Beyond symptom relief or a short-term response to a client's presenting problem, the goal of REBT counselors is to teach REBT counseling, so that clients learn to dispute and change their irrational beliefs on their own and, as a result, develop a more effective and rational personal philosophy. This long-term view is related to Ellis's perspective that irrational beliefs are "like very stubborn weeds" that are hard to get rid of (Dryden, 2011). Changing one's beliefs requires a forceful, energetic approach and continued vigilance and persistence.

REBT is an active–directive and problem-focused therapy, and counselors will often use time-saving and efficient tools, such as questionnaires, self-help forms, and homework, for example, the reading of or listening to psychoeducational materials. There are also certain procedures and techniques, viewed as inefficient and indirect, which are not likely to be seen in an REBT counseling session, including the use of standard diagnostic tests (Yankura & Dryden, 1994). In addition, an REBT counselor is not likely to spend a great deal of time, if any at all, discussing the client's problem history. Such "obsessing" is seen as inefficient and having little to do with the client's present disturbances (Ellis, 1979, p. 95). Clients are encouraged to narrate their activating experiences in a relatively brief and nonobsessive manner.

REBT counselors should be aware that clients often enter counseling with beliefs and values that will act to prevent therapeutic change, and these beliefs must, therefore, be addressed immediately in the counseling process. These beliefs place the cause and responsibility on external and often uncontrollable factors. Examples include blaming one's current attitudes and conditions on poor parenting, critical friends, or a stress-filled work environment, or expecting that the counselor, or the simple experience of being in counseling, will somehow magically produce results for the client. REBT therapists help clients to understand that wherever the beliefs may have started, they are currently choosing to disturb and upset themselves by maintaining these irrational beliefs in the present. Further, the client must come to understand that the process of changing one's beliefs requires hard and sustained effort. Ellis posited that before counseling can be effective, the counselor must convey three main insights of REBT to the client (Yankura & Dryden, 1994, p. 48):

1. You largely choose to disturb yourself about the unpleasant events in your life, even though you may be influenced to do so by external factors.
2. Regardless of how or when you acquired your present self-disturbing and self-defeating beliefs, you are choosing to maintain them in the present, and that is why you are disturbed now. Your past history and your present life conditions affect you, but they do not disturb you.
3. There is no magical way for you to change your personality and your tendencies to upset yourself. This change will require work and practice.

## COUNSELING TECHNIQUES

As a multimodal therapy, REBT allows for considerable flexibility on the part of the practitioner in terms of techniques and procedures (George & Christiani, 1995). Practitioners employ cognitive, emotive, and behavioral techniques, as appropriate, to the client and the situation. In the following text, we describe several techniques that may be used by an REBT counselor.

### Cognitive Techniques

The most common cognitive technique, particularly early on, is the active disputation of the client's irrational beliefs, attitudes, and self-talk. Four specific disputing strategies have been identified as being particularly effective and helpful (Beal, Kopec, & DiGiuseppe, 1996):

1. Logical disputes: The aim of this strategy is to weaken the client's affinity for an irrational belief by pointing out the faulty logic. Common leads in this type of disputing would be: "Does it follow logically from what you have said that...?" or "Does that seem consistent to you?"
2. Empirical disputes: In this strategy, the counselor invites the client to provide evidence for the irrational belief and tries to show that the client's belief is inconsistent with empirical reality. For example, the counselor may say, "Where is the evidence for your belief that... (e.g., you are worthless)?"

3. Functional disputes: The aim of this strategy is to show the client that it is not pragmatic to continue to hold the irrational belief and that he or she is paying emotional and behavioral consequences for continuing to do so. Common leads here are "Does your holding this belief get you what you want in life?" or "Can you tell me what feelings you are experiencing as a result of that belief?"

4. Rational alternative disputes: In disputing and attempting to restructure or modify maladaptive beliefs, it is necessary to keep in mind that one is not likely to change a belief, despite overwhelming evidence to the contrary, unless an alternative belief of equal or superior value is offered. The counselor should encourage the client to identify an effective alternative replacement belief that is more logical, more empirically sound, and provides fewer emotional and behavioral consequences. If the client cannot, the counselor will suggest alternatives. Examples are "It would be very disappointing if I didn't get X, but it would not be terrible, awful, or the end of the world" or "If they don't like me, that is perhaps unfortunate, but it does not mean that I am a bad or worthless person."

Other cognitive techniques include:

- Rational self-statements. This technique involves having clients repeatedly remind themselves of rational beliefs in the form of short coping self-statements. Dryden (2012) suggested that clients who do not have the cognitive or intellectual skills to perform cognitive disputing may be encouraged to carry cards with their rational self-statements written on them and repeat them at various times during the day between sessions.

- Referenting. In this technique, the client is encouraged to identify both the positive and negative referents of a particular concept and so develop a more holistic perspective. For example, if the client is focusing on the positive aspects of a particular self-defeating behavior, this exercise helps him or her to acknowledge the negative results and increases the motivation to change.

- Using REBT with others. Using REBT with and teaching friends and others about REBT allow clients to reinforce and practice thinking through rational disputes and reinforces their learning between sessions (Dryden, 2012).

- Semantic precision. This method is used to help the client to become aware of language use that serves to perpetuate irrational beliefs. As an example, a client might be asked to restate the phrase "I can't do that" as "I have not done that yet." Similarly, clients are taught to reframe their perspective in order to redefine a situation in a more positive light (e.g., rather than seeing oneself as a victim, one can choose to see oneself as a survivor).

## Behavioral Techniques

- Homework. The assignment of homework is a particularly important aspect of REBT and may include completion of self-help forms, which the counselor provides, teaching the basics of REBT to others, or psychoeducational methods, such as reading or listening to REBT books and audio.
- Skills training. REBT counselors may use techniques to teach and help clients acquire and use social skills, assertiveness skills, interviewing skills, and relaxation techniques.
- Shame-attacking exercises. In order to demonstrate the irrational nature of the fear of embarrassment or shame, which prevents certain actions or behaviors, clients are given assignments directly related to their particular fears. For example, a client may be assigned the task of approaching strangers and initiating conversations, asking a silly question at a lecture, or singing out loud. In completing these assignments, clients learn that they can train themselves to not be controlled by fear about the responses or potential responses of others.
- In vivo exposure. Clients are frequently encouraged to fully expose themselves to feared events or situations, in order to learn that they can face and deal constructively with adversity; though, in practice, the client and counselor may negotiate progressive compromises depending on how ready the client is to fully enter such situations (Dryden, 2012).

## Emotive Techniques

REBT counselors will not spend much time, if any, exploring with clients the emotions experienced in relation to the presenting problem. However, because of the interactive nature of cognition, behavior, and emotion, selective emotive exercises and techniques are employed to help clients become aware of and change dysfunctional and goal-hindering emotional responses. Some of these techniques are

- Rational emotive imagery. Using imagery, clients mentally practice thinking, feeling, and acting the way they would like to behave in real life. Clients can also imagine the worst thing that could happen related to a given situation, imagine the experience of inappropriate emotions, and then mentally see themselves changing the emotions and experiencing more productive or appropriate ones.
- Role-playing. In-session role-playing may be used to show clients the interpersonal and emotional effects of their irrational beliefs. Clients can also use this method to rehearse new and more effective behaviors and to experience the resulting positive emotions.
- Humor. Humor is used to show clients that part of the problem may be that they are taking things too seriously. Dramatic exaggerations, irony, and feigned incredulity are examples of humor often used by REBT practitioners.

## COUNSELOR–CLIENT RELATIONSHIP

The counselor–client relationship has been well defined in the REBT model. The counselor's role is primarily that of an educator. Ellis (1973, 1980, 1994) characterized the REBT counselor as active–directive with most clients, risk-taking, intelligent and knowledgeable, vigorous in detecting and disputing irrational ideas, and persistent and empathic. Flexibility is encouraged, and although Ellis was well known for having a "particularly forceful version" of the active–directive approach, other REBT experts recommend a more passive, gentle approach, depending on what will be most effective and appropriate for a particular client (Dryden, 2012, p. 198). REBT counselors strive to achieve unconditional acceptance of clients as fallible humans, regardless of self-defeating behavior or their maintenance of irrational beliefs (Dryden et al., 2010). The counselor's acceptance of the client may be communicated verbally, and the counselor's own self-acceptance is modeled by his or her behavior in the counseling sessions (e.g., in not seeking the client's approval). Although the importance of a therapeutic alliance and acceptance are emphasized, warmth is not, as it may lead to a reinforcement of the client's dependency and need for love and approval from others. REBT counselors interact with their clients in an open, informal style, incorporate humor, and are willing to self-disclose when sharing personal experiences and learning seems appropriate and is likely to be productive for the client.

## REHABILITATION APPLICATIONS

Many aspects of REBT are congruent with the philosophy and principles of rehabilitation counseling. These include the counselor's full and unconditional acceptance of the client; valuing the client for himself or herself; listening to the client's worldview without judging; reinforcing reality without judging the client; helping the client give up absolutist expectations about the world (Balter, 1997); and helping the client to accept changes, learn new skills, and engage in new interests. According to Balter (1997, p. 191):

> An REBT approach has strengths in the field of adjustment to and living with physical disabilities and chronic health conditions that other therapeutic approaches lack. It helps the client to reconceptualize the minor and major hassles associated with living with a disability and not to overvalue the messages given them by family, friends and "well-meaning others." REBT also values the person as having worth apart from the role s/he plays in life. This is a difficult concept for many to grasp, however it is important in helping patients accept themselves with their disabilities.

Indeed, Ellis suggested that he developed REBT as a result of living with a number of disabilities himself from the age of 5 years. "But rather than plague myself about my physical restrictions, I devoted myself to the philosophy of remaining happy in spite of my disabilities, and out of this philosophy I ultimately originated REBT in January 1955" (Ellis, 1997, p. 21).

Because it is a focused, active–directive, and intrinsically brief form of therapy (Ellis, 1996, p. 6), REBT is well suited to rehabilitation agencies and programs, such as the state–federal vocational rehabilitation system, where counseling is short term and goal oriented. In the REBT framework, people with disabilities are viewed "no differently from people who experience any other life misfortune (e.g., loss of job, loss of home, loss of loved one)" (Livneh & Sherwood, 1991, p. 532). When the focus of the counseling is the disability itself, the disability is perceived as an activating event, and counseling focuses on self-acceptance, identifying and challenging irrational beliefs and attitudes that surround the disability and helping clients to break down problems perceived as insurmountable into smaller and more manageable units (Livneh & Sherwood, 1991).

A number of REBT writers have asserted that REBT is appropriate and helpful with clients from diverse cultures, educational backgrounds, intelligence levels, and forms of disability (Balter, 1997; Ellis, 1973, 1994, 1997; Gandy, 1995; Olevitch, 1995).

Because of the focus on cognition, and the insight involved in understanding and actively modifying one's beliefs and attitudes, however, some researchers have suggested that REBT may be inappropriate and unlikely to benefit persons who are not in touch with reality, have significant brain injuries, are manic, or have moderate to severe intellectual disability (Ellis & Harper, 1979; Ostby, 1986). However, it would seem inappropriate to make generalizations based on such broad classifications, and REBT theory and techniques may be effective for persons with a wide range of intellectual, communication, and cognitive disabilities. Additional research attention to methods of effectively translating the core REBT concepts and creative modifications or adaptations of REBT techniques is warranted.

A potential limitation with using REBT in rehabilitation settings has been noted with respect to the adaptation to chronic illness and disability process. Mpofu, Thomas, and Chan (1996) noted that a hallmark REBT assumption is that people tend to develop and maintain irrational beliefs; they suggested that it is important for REBT counselors to realize that situational factors related to severe disability could result in a "genuinely awful experience" (Mpofu et al., 1996, p. 104). Care is required to ensure that clients' experiences are not casually or inappropriately described as "irrational," which may jeopardize the client–counselor relationship and interfere with identifying effective strategies to address these issues.

When applying REBT early in the adaptation process, REBT counselors may seek to dispute a client's reactions, such as denial, which are often a natural part of the adjustment process and temporarily necessary to support psychological well-being. For this reason, Calabro (1990) pointed out that there are times, particularly early in the adjustment process, when more supportive techniques are indicated. Active–directive and confrontational REBT methods can be extremely well suited to later stages in the adjustment process (Calabro, 1990; Livneh & Sherwood, 1991; Zabrowski, 1997).

Alvarez (1997) provided an example of a combination of REBT and supportive therapies applied to individuals recovering from stroke. The author suggested that once individuals have moved through the early stages of adjustment and coping and are experiencing feelings of anxiety, depression, or "feeling different," REBT methods are potentially useful in helping them identify and dispute irrational beliefs that are causing them emotional distress or interfering with their rehabilitation goals. For example:

- I cannot do anything, so therefore I am worthless.
- I must be a bad person, because I am being punished.
- What has happened to me is horrible, I will not be happy until I am better.
- Disability is unfair and should not have happened to me.
  (Alvarez, 1997, p. 241)

## CASE STUDY

Samantha G. was a 37-year-old woman who was experiencing adjustment difficulties due to an occupational injury. Samantha worked as a critical care nurse in a local hospital until she experienced a severe back injury while attempting to lift a patient. Samantha recovered from back surgery, but she was informed that she would not be able to return to work as a critical care nurse or in any other type of nursing duties that required strenuous physical demands.

Samantha agreed to begin seeing a rehabilitation counselor on an outpatient basis. The counselor quickly learned that Samantha was depressed and lacking in self-worth. Working from an REBT framework, the counselor attempted to focus on the client's primary goals. In this case, regaining vocational satisfaction and self-worth were major concerns. The therapeutic approach employed by the counselor consisted of a series of weekly counseling sessions and homework assignments.

In the counseling sessions, the counselor challenged any self-defeating verbalizations and illogical beliefs. The counselor introduced Samantha to the ABC model and helped Samantha to identify her irrational beliefs and their behavioral and emotional consequences. According to Ellis (1995b), REBT practitioners challenge clients to try to defend their ideas, show them that they contain illogical premises, analyze these ideas and actively dispute them, and show how these ideas can be replaced with more rational philosophies. In addition, the client is taught how to minimize future problems by employing logical thinking when subsequent irrational ideas and illogical deductions arise that may lead to self-defeating feelings and behaviors. In Samantha's case, discussion focused on thoughts about her occupational future.

Cl: I am so disgusted with myself. My life will be so awful if I can't return to my job.

Co: Why is it so awful that you can't return to critical nursing?

*(continued)*

*(continued)*

> Cl: Critical nursing allowed me to make a real difference. Sometimes I helped save lives.
>
> Co: Do you mean to tell me that critical nursing is the only way that you can make a difference?

The intent is to challenge or dispute the client's rigid and absolutist thinking about her life situation. The counselor pursues questioning that helps Samantha to identify her awfulizing beliefs and illicits alternative, more rational beliefs, such as "It is bad that I can no longer do this job that gave me such meaning, but it is not awful, and it is not unbearable. I can find other ways to help people in a meaningful way." Irrational beliefs are not generally given up easily. The counselor often has to be persistent. In this case, the counselor posed other questions such as the following:

> Co: Are there other ways of serving as a nurse or health care practitioner that might provide you the opportunity to make a difference in people's lives?
>
> Co: Have you ever dealt with other significant life changes?
>
> Co: How have you handled those changes?

Here, the attempt of the counselor was to demonstrate that the client is capable of successful life change. Previous successes are used to demonstrate client capabilities. For example, the client noted that her role as a mother changed as her children grew older and more independent. Samantha's acceptance of her changing parental role was emphasized in order to show that she is capable of dealing with life change.

In the ongoing counseling sessions, homework assignments were used to fortify the client's logical thinking. In this case, the client was asked to read recommended REBT books, practice REBT reasoning when dealing with her family, and talk with nurses who worked in other types of nursing settings.

Over a period of weeks, it was obvious that Samantha was becoming more flexible and rational in her thinking, emotions, and behaviors. The weekly REBT sessions and homework assignments proved to be helpful to a client who was once convinced that her life would be unfulfilling if she could not return to critical care nursing. Through persistence and hard work, the client's thinking became less illogical and self-sabotaging. Samantha returned to work in health care and was successfully adjusting to this new phase in her career and life.

## RESEARCH FINDINGS

David, Szentagitai, Kallay, and Macavei (2005) suggested that empirical outcome research on REBT can be characterized as having developed over three periods: before 1970, 1970 to 1990, and 1990 to the present. Prior to 1970, there was little empirical REBT outcome research. Between 1970 and 1990, a series of outcome studies were published in addition to several research reviews. A number of methodological problems were highlighted with respect to much of this research, and among the cognitive behavioral approaches, REBT was perhaps the least adequately empirically evaluated, with the majority of the research based on nonclinical populations and case studies (Hollon & Beck, 1994; Livneh & Wright, 1995). There has been an effort since 1990 to rectify and strengthen the base of empirical support (Bernard, 1995; Hollon & Beck, 1994), and Hollon and Beck pointed out that a lack of adequate evaluation should not be confused with a lack of efficacy, and that REBT has generally performed well in studies in which it was adequately operationalized. Additionally, the results of many high-quality studies show support for the basic theory of REBT (David et al., 2005).

As presented by David et al. (2005), research in REBT can be classified into two areas: (a) basic studies, focused on related irrational beliefs to feelings, indicators of psychological distress, behavior, and cognitions and (b) applied research, focused on outcomes associated with REBT and the efficacy of REBT, when compared with other interventions. David et al. noted that the criticisms over the quality of research have largely been aimed at applied research.

In terms of its scientific reputation, REBT has been hampered in key areas, including (a) ambiguities in the theory (e.g., nature of irrational beliefs), (b) deficiencies in the experimental design of many REBT studies, (c) the absence of studies involving large clinical groups, and (d) deficiencies in formulating the REBT hypotheses in terms of researchable questions (Bernard, 1995). In spite of these limitations, there have been a number of large-scale reviews of outcome studies supportive of the efficacy and clinical effectiveness of REBT.

McGovern and Silverman (1984) reviewed 47 studies from 1977 to 1982 and found that 31 of the 47 reported significant findings in favor of the efficacy of REBT. Another review of 89 outcome studies by Silverman, McCarthy, and McGovern (1992) yielded similarly positive results. Lyons and Woods (1991) conducted a meta-analysis of 70 REBT outcome studies. A total of 236 comparisons of REBT to baseline, control groups, cognitive behavior modification (CBM), behavior therapy, and other psychotherapies were examined. The results indicated that participants receiving REBT demonstrated significant improvement over baseline measures and control groups, whereas the comparisons among REBT, CBM, and behavior therapy produced nonsignificant differences.

A significant challenge in providing empirical support for the efficacy of REBT has been differentiating this approach from other cognitive behavioral techniques, most notably cognitive theory (CT). As part of the effort to compare REBT to CT, David, Szentagitai, Lupu, and Cosman (2008) used a manualized approach to compare REBT to CT and pharmacological interventions (Prozac) in individuals with depression in Romania. Results indicated that participants assigned to all three treatment conditions experienced a reduction in symptoms at the end of treatment, with no significant differences among groups. However, at 6-month follow-up, there were no differences between individuals who received REBT and CT with respect to symptoms, but significant differences were observed between individuals who received pharmacological intervention and REBT. These investigators also sought to compare the cost-effectiveness of these three approaches and found that, given the similar results (all reduced symptoms), REBT and CT were more cost-effective, as measured by "depression-free days" and "quality-adjusted life years" (Sava, Yates, Lupu, Szentagotai, & David, 2009).

These findings are sensitive to differences in health care costs, such as cost of medication and cost of therapy and so must be considered within those variables. The researchers failed to identify any differences in mechanisms of change among the three treatment approaches, concluding that all three appeared to impact the automatic thoughts, core beliefs, and irrational thoughts of the participants. The only area where REBT seemed to have a differential impact was with participants who were assessed for irrational beliefs indirectly (i.e., through a simulated story) rather than directly. Researchers concluded that although CT, pharmacotherapy, and REBT all seemed to result in a change in core beliefs, automatic thoughts, and irrational beliefs, CT was more likely to impact those beliefs that could be vocalized during therapy, but would not be as effective against those irrational beliefs that were more difficult to vocalize. The finding of reduction of all three mechanisms of change (core beliefs, automatic thoughts, and irrational beliefs) is consistent with Ellis's theory of the relationship between irrational beliefs and automatic thoughts (David et al., 2008).

Another approach to evaluating the effectiveness of REBT has been to link irrational beliefs to low unconditional self-acceptance, low self-esteem, and issues with emotional adjustment (Davies, 2006, 2007; Munoz-Eguileta, 2007). Using REBT to target irrational thoughts, clients can be helped to have higher levels of self-esteem, unconditional self-acceptance, and emotional adjustment. In addition, researchers have sought to differentiate among irrational beliefs, facilitating understanding as to which of the irrational beliefs in particular are most detrimental (Davies, 2007). Davies (2006, 2007) found a significant negative correlation between irrational beliefs and self-esteem as well as a causal link between beliefs and unconditional self-acceptance. Davies (2007) used priming techniques to determine whether rational, irrational, or neutral statements would impact the measured unconditional self-acceptance of participants. Results indicated that there was a significant interaction between the type of priming (rational/irrational) and measured self-acceptance at pre- and post-test phases. In other words, thinking about rational beliefs increased self-acceptance, whereas thinking about irrational beliefs reduced self-acceptance. This appeared to be a major finding in support of REBT tenets.

Although REBT still does not have the evidence-based research basis of cognitive and cognitive behavioral approaches, there is some empirical support for the theoretical basis as well as the efficacy of the approach (David et al., 2005). REBT has been applied to address issues related to disability, including adaptation and coping (Alvarez, 1997; Zaborowski, 1997). Additional research is needed to evaluate the efficacy of REBT approaches in counseling for disability-relevant issues.

## STRENGTHS AND LIMITATIONS OF REBT

Potential limitations to REBT are found in the areas of counseling for adjustment to disability and research. Another commonly noted limitation is that the REBT approach may oversimplify and neglect important aspects of the human experience when attempting to fit experiences into the ABC model (Livneh & Wright, 1995). Because of the emphasis on persuasion, suggestion, and repetition, there is potential for rehabilitation counselors, who use REBT in their practice, to impart their own values and expectations to their clients (George & Christiani, 1995). Weinrach (1996) suggested that issues relating to diversity-sensitive counseling are not adequately addressed in REBT. The REBT emphasis on independence and insight, and its active–directive and educational approach, requires that counselors be particularly aware of the values and expectations of clients from cultural backgrounds that value interdependence and family or community reliance or of those who expect and prefer a more passive interaction style. REBT has, however, been effectively applied internationally and with clients from a wide range of cultural and ethnic backgrounds and with a wide range of rehabilitation and other clinical issues (Dryden, 2012).

REBT has made a number of important contributions to the field of counseling and psychotherapy, the most distinctive of which is the explication of the concept of rationality and identification of the human tendency toward irrational beliefs (Gilliland, James, & Bowman, 1994). Ellis's challenge to the psychological status quo, in a period in which psychoanalysis was the primary approach of mental health professionals, revolutionized and helped to begin the development of cognitive behavioral therapy, challenged and changed the nature of client–counselor relationships, and increased the emerging power and responsibility of the client in the therapeutic relationship. Particular to REBT, the eclectic combination of cognitive, behavioral, and emotive techniques; the de-emphasis of the importance of the past in the light of present problems; the educational, preventive, and accepting nature of treatment; and the development of the role of the active–directive counselor have all been important contributions to the mental health professions.

## DISCUSSION EXERCISES

1. In your own words, describe the overall goals of REBT.
2. The difference between rational and irrational thinking is central to REBT. Provide an example of a rational and irrational belief that a person might hold relevant to these common life circumstances: (a) grades in school, (b) relationship with a friend, and (c) applying for a job.

3. From the REBT perspective, how are events, beliefs, and results interrelated?

4. Describe the role of the counselor according to REBT and contrast it with another theory that you have learned about previously.

5. In the chapter, we discussed the relationship between REBT and other cognitive approaches. Identify and describe characteristics of REBT that distinguish it from other cognitive therapies.

6. REBT has many potential applications; however, it is not appropriate for every client or situation. Describe a situation in which REBT may not be beneficial.

## REFERENCES

Alvarez, M. F. (1997). Using REBT and supportive psychotherapy with post-stroke patients. *Journal of Rational-Emotive & Cognitive-Behavior Therapy, 15*, 231–245.

Balter, R. (1997). Using REBT with clients with disabilities. In J. Yankura & W. Dryden (Eds.), *Special applications of REBT: A therapist's casebook* (pp. 69–100). New York, NY: Springer Publishing Company.

Beal, D., Kopec, A. M., & DiGiuseppe, R. (1996). Disputing clients' irrational beliefs. *Journal of Rational-Emotive & Cognitive-Behavior Therapy, 14*, 215–229.

Bernard, M. E. (1995). It's prime time for rational emotive behavior therapy: Current theory and practice, research recommendations, and predictions. *Journal of Rational-Emotive & Cognitive-Behavior Therapy, 13*, 9–27.

Calabro, L. E. (1990). Adjustment to disability: A cognitive-behavioral model for analysis and clinical management. *Journal of Rational-Emotive & Cognitive-Behavior Therapy, 8*, 79–102.

David, D., Szentagotai, A., Kallay, E., & Macavei, B. (2005). A synopsis of rational emotive behaviour therapy (REBT): Fundamental and applied research. *Journal of Rational-Emotive and Cognitive-Behavior Therapy, 3*, 175–221.

David, D., Szentagotai, A., Lupu, V., & Cosman, D. (2008). Rational emotive therapy, cognitive therapy and medication in the treatment of major depressive disorder: A randomized clinical trial. *Journal of Clinical Psychology, 6*, 728–746.

Davies, M. F. (2006). Irrational beliefs and unconditional self-acceptance. I. Correlational evidence linking two key features of REBT. *Journal of Rational-Emotive and Cognitive-Behavior Therapy, 24*, 113–124.

Davies, M. F. (2007). Irrational beliefs and unconditional self-acceptance. II. Experimental evidence for a causal link between two key features of REBT. *Journal of Rational-Emotive and Cognitive-Behavior Therapy, 26*, 89–101.

DiGiuseppe, R. (2011). Reflection on my 32 years with Albert Ellis. *Journal of Rational-Emotive & Cognitive-Behavior Therapy, 29*, 220–227.

Dryden, W. (1990). *Rational-emotive counselling in action.* London, UK: Sage.

Dryden, W. (2005). Rational emotive behavior therapy. In A. Freeman, S. H. Felgoise, C. M. Nezu, A. M. Nezu, & M. A. Reinecke (Eds.), *Encyclopedia of cognitive behavior therapy* (pp. 321–324). New York, NY: Springer.

Dryden, W. (2011). Albert Ellis and rational emotive behavior therapy: A personal reflection. *Journal of Rational-Emotive & Cognitive-Behavior Therapy, 29*, 211–219.

Dryden, W. (2012). Rational emotive behavior therapy (REBT). In W. Dryden (Ed.), *Cognitive behaviour therapies* (pp. 189–215). London, UK: Sage.

Dryden, W. (2013). On rational beliefs in rational emotive behavior therapy: A theoretical perspective. *Journal of Rational-Emotive and Cognitive-Behavior Therapy, 31*, 39–48.

Dryden, W., David, D., & Ellis, A. (2010). Rational emotive behavior therapy. In K. S. Dobson (Ed.), *Handbook of cognitive-behavior therapy* (3rd ed.). New York, NY: Guilford.

Ellis, A. (1962). *Reason and emotion in psychotherapy*. Secaucus, NJ: Lyle Stuart.

Ellis, A. (1973). *Humanistic psychotherapy: The rational-emotive approach*. New York, NY: Julien.

Ellis, A. (1976). The biological basis of human irrationality. *Journal of Individual Psychology, 32,* 143–168.

Ellis, A. (1977). The basic clinical theory of rational-emotive therapy. In A. Ellis & R. Grieger (Eds.), *Handbook of rational-emotive therapy* (pp. 3–34). New York, NY: Springer Publishing Company.

Ellis, A. (1979). The practice of rational-emotive therapy. In A. Ellis & J. M. Whitely (Eds.), *Theoretical and empirical foundations of rational-emotive therapy* (pp. 61–100). Monterey, CA: Brooks/Cole.

Ellis, A. (1980). Rational-emotive therapy and cognitive behavior therapy: Similarities and differences. *Cognitive Therapy and Research, 4,* 325–340.

Ellis, A. (1989). Rational-emotive therapy. In R. J. Corsini & D. Wedding (Eds.), *Current psychotherapies* (4th ed., pp. 197–238). Itasca, IL: Peacock.

Ellis, A. (1991). The revised ABC's of rational-emotive therapy (RET). *Journal of Rational-Emotive & Cognitive-Behavior Therapy, 9,* 139–172.

Ellis, A. (1993). Fundamentals of rational-emotive therapy for the 1990s. In W. Dryden & L. K. Hill (Eds.), *Innovations in rational-emotive therapy* (pp. 1–32). Newbury Park, CA: Sage.

Ellis, A. (1994). *Reason and emotion in psychotherapy* (Rev. ed.). Secaucus, NJ: Birch Lane.

Ellis, A. (1995a). Changing rational-emotive therapy (RET) to rational emotive behavior therapy (REBT). *Journal of Rational-Emotive & Cognitive-Behavior Therapy, 13,* 85–89.

Ellis, A. (1995b). Rational-emotive behavior therapy. In R. J. Corsini & D. Wedding (Eds.), *Current psychotherapies* (5th ed., pp. 162–196). Itasca, IL: F. E. Peacock.

Ellis, A. (1996). *Better, deeper, and more enduring brief therapy: The rational emotive behavior therapy approach*. New York, NY: Brunner/Mazel.

Ellis, A. (1997). Using rational emotive behavior therapy techniques to cope with disability. *Professional Psychology: Research and Practice, 28,* 17–22.

Ellis, A. (2003). Early theories and practices of rational emotive behavior theory and how they have been augmented and revised during the last three decades. *Journal of Rational-Emotive & Cognitive-Behavior Therapy, 21,* 219–243.

Ellis, A. (2005). Rational emotive behavior therapy. In R. J. Corsini & D. Wedding (Eds.), *Current psychotherapies* (7th ed., pp. 166–201). Belmont, CA: Brooks/Cole.

Ellis, A., Abrams, M., & Abrams, L. (2012). *A brief biography of Dr. Albert Ellis 1913–2007*. Retrieved from http://www.rebt.ws/albertellisbiography.html

Ellis, A., & Harper, R. (1979). *A new guide to rational living*. Hollywood, CA: Wilshire.

Gandy, G. L. (1995). *Mental health rehabilitation: Disputing irrational beliefs*. Springfield, IL: Charles C Thomas.

George, R. L., & Christiani, T. S. (1995). *Counseling: Theory and practice* (4th ed.). Needham Heights, MA: Allyn & Bacon.

Gilliland, B. E., James, R. K., & Bowman, J. T. (1994). *Theories and strategies in counseling and psychotherapy*. Englewood Cliffs, NJ: Prentice Hall.

Hollon, S. D., & Beck, A. T. (1994). Cognitive and cognitive-behavioral therapies. In A. E. Bergin & S. L. Garfield (Eds.), *Handbook of psychotherapy and behavior change* (pp. 428–466). New York, NY: Wiley.

Horney, K. (1965). *Collected works*. New York, NY: Norton.

Livneh, H., & Sherwood, S. (1991). Application of personality theories and counseling strategies to clients with physical disabilities. *Journal of Counseling and Development, 69,* 525–538.

Livneh, H., & Wright, P. E. (1995). Rational-emotive therapy. In D. Capuzzi & D. R. Gross (Eds.), *Counseling and psychotherapy: Theories and interventions* (pp. 325–352). Englewood Cliffs, NJ: Prentice Hall.

Lyons, L. C., & Woods, P. J. (1991). The efficacy of rational emotive therapy: A quantitative review of the outcome research. *Clinical Psychology Review, 11,* 357–369.

McGovern, T. E., & Silverman, M. S. (1984). A review of outcome studies of rational-emotive therapy from 1977 to 1982. *Journal of Rational-Emotive Therapy, 2,* 7–18.

Mpofu, E., Thomas, K. R., & Chan, F. (1996). Cognitive-behavioural therapies: Research and applications in counselling people with physical disabilities. *Australian Journal of Rehabilitation Counselling, 2,* 99–114.

Munoz-Eguileta, A. (2007). Irrational beliefs as predictors of emotional adjustment after divorce. *Journal of Rational-Emotive & Cognitive-Behavior Therapy, 1,* 1–15.

Olevitch, B. A. (1995). *Using cognitive approaches with the seriously mentally ill: Dialogue across the border.* Westport, CT: Praeger.

Ostby, S. (1986). A rational-emotive perspective. In T. F. Riggar, D. R. Maki, & A. W. Wolf (Eds.), *Applied rehabilitation counseling* (pp. 135–147). New York, NY: Springer Publishing Company.

Sava, F., Yates, B., Lupu, V., Szentagotai, A., & David, D. (2009). Cost-effectiveness and cost-utility of cognitive therapy, rational emotive behavioral therapy and fluoxetine in treating depression: A randomized clinical trial. *Journal of Clinical Psychology, 1,* 36–52.

Sharf, R. S. (2012). *Theories of psychotherapy and counseling: Concepts and cases* (5th ed.). Pacific Grove, CA: Brooks/Cole.

Silverman, M. S., McCarthy, M., & McGovern, T. E. (1992). A review of outcome studies of rational-emotive therapy from 1982–1989. *Journal of Rational-Emotive and Cognitive Behavior Therapy, 10,* 111–175.

Walen, S. R., DiGiuseppe, R., & Dryden, W. (1992). *A practitioner's guide to rational-emotive therapy* (2nd ed.). New York, NY: Oxford University Press.

Weinrach, S. G. (1996). Reducing REBT's "wince factor": An insider's perspective. *Journal of Rational-Emotive & Cognitive-Behavior Therapy, 14,* 63–78.

Weinrach, S. G. (2006). Nine experts describe the essence of rational-emotive therapy while standing on one foot. *Journal of Rational-Emotive & Cognitive-Behavior Therapy, 24,* 217–232.

Yankura, J., & Dryden, W. (1994). *Albert Ellis.* Thousand Oaks, CA: Sage.

Young, H. S. (1974). *A rational counseling primer.* New York, NY: Institute for Rational-Emotive Therapy.

Zaborowski, B. (1997). Adjustment to vision loss and blindness: A process of reframing and retraining. *Journal of Rational-Emotive & Cognitive-Behavior Therapy, 15,* 215–221.

# Behavior Therapy

*Jennifer L. Stoll and Jessica Brooks*

## LEARNING OBJECTIVES

The goal of this chapter is to introduce behavior therapy; to describe the major concepts, counseling approaches, and techniques of behavior therapy; to explain the related theory of personality; to describe application in rehabilitation counseling; and to review the current behavior therapy evidence base and research. Readers will be able to identify, describe, and apply major theoretical and philosophical concepts of behavior therapy and to achieve the following:

1. Understand the concept of maladaptive behaviors as described in behavior therapy and the impact of contextual and environmental influences on the development of maladaptive behaviors.
2. Describe the two main approaches of behavior therapy: classical conditioning and operant conditioning.
3. Identify commonly used behavior therapy techniques and methods, and describe the nature of the behavior therapy relationship.
4. Apply the scientific approach to evaluate the effectiveness of behavioral techniques through clearly defined, objective, and measurable goals.
5. Use behavior therapy approaches for people with disabilities.
6. Discuss the state and direction of behavior therapy research.

## BEHAVIORAL THERAPY IN REHABILITATION

Behavior therapy encompasses three distinct approaches to accomplishing the same ultimate goals of diminishing inappropriate behaviors and enhancing appropriate behaviors. The three primary approaches include classical conditioning, operant conditioning, and cognitive behavioral approaches (Craighead, Craighead, Kazdin, & Mahoney, 1994; Thieme & Turk, 2012). Both classical and operant conditioning are reviewed in this chapter. Cognitive behavioral approaches are discussed in Chapter 5 in this volume.

The purpose of the present chapter is to provide a general overview of behavior therapy when implemented within a rehabilitation context. Major concepts common to all behavior therapy approaches are covered and, for the sake of clarity, classical conditioning and operant conditioning are discussed separately in terms of history of the approach, central tenets, and treatment techniques based on the approach. This chapter also includes relevant information on the theory of personality, counseling process, rehabilitation applications, a case study, and research findings.

## APPROACHES TO BEHAVIOR THERAPY

Behavior therapy is a collection of approaches and techniques that is used to decrease maladaptive behaviors and increase adaptive ones. Although behavioral techniques may differ in the manner through which they achieve behavior change, they share three common characteristics. First, behavioral approaches emphasize the importance of current behavior rather than focusing on past behavior (Antony & Roemer, 2011; Corey, 1991; Wilson, 1995). Thus, behavior theorists treat the behavior itself rather than the underlying hypothesized causes of behavior, representing a marked contrast to more traditional models of psychotherapy (e.g., psychoanalysis), which focus on the past or historical events that contribute to the development and manifestation of maladaptive behavior. Second, behavior therapies employ the scientific approach to evaluate the effectiveness of behavioral techniques through clearly defined, objective, and measurable goals (Corey, 1991). The third common characteristic that all behavior therapies share is their use of multiple assessments conducted throughout the treatment process (Corrigan & Liberman, 1994).

In addition to the aforementioned three central communalities, Rotgers (1996) identified seven basic assumptions of behavior therapy: (a) Human behavior is largely learned rather than determined by genetics; (b) the same learning processes that create maladaptive behaviors can be used to change or eliminate them; (c) behavior is predominantly determined by contextual and environmental mediators; (d) covert behaviors, such as thoughts and feelings, are subject to change through the implementation of learning processes; (e) actual performance of new behaviors in the contexts in which they are to be performed is a critical aspect of behavior change; (f) each client is unique and requires an individualized assessment of inappropriate behavior; and (g) the cornerstone of successful treatment is a thorough behavioral assessment.

### Classical Conditioning

Classical conditioning originated with the Russian physiologist Ivan Pavlov (Kazdin, 1994). Pavlov (1927) had been investigating digestive processes in dogs when he learned that the animals would salivate not only to the taste, sight, or smell of meat powder but also when no meat powder was present, with the dogs beginning to salivate upon entering the room where experiments were being conducted. His experiments usually involved the pairing of a neutral stimulus that did not produce salivation with the presentation of meat powder, which naturally induced salivation. After multiple pairings, Pavlov found that the neutral stimulus came to produce salivation on its own.

### Central Tenets

To describe the *conditioning process*, Pavlov (1927) introduced a set of terms. He called the stimulus that naturally elicits the desired response the unconditioned stimulus (UCS) and the naturally occurring response was called the unconditioned response (UR; Craighead et al., 1994). The neutral stimulus was referred to as the conditioned stimulus (CS), because it is that stimulus that becomes "conditioned" to produce the target response (Thieme & Turk, 2012). Finally, the conditioned response (CR) is the response that is elicited subsequent to the presentation of the CS (Craighead et al., 1994). It should be noted that the CR and the UR are the same response, with the only difference being the way in which the response is achieved.

Once the relationship between the CS and CR is established, the association will disappear if the CS is repeatedly presented without the UCS. This process is referred to as *classical extinction* (Antony & Roemer, 2011; Schloss & Smith, 1994). Maintenance of a classical CR often requires "booster" sessions in which both the UCS and CS are again paired (Mueser, 1993). If classical extinction does occur, relearning the association between the CS and UCS often occurs more rapidly than was necessary to learn the task initially (Schloss & Smith, 1994). Extinction generally does not occur all at once. Rather, if the CS and UCS are paired following extinction, spontaneous recovery may occur, defined as exhibiting a CR in response to the CS after the target behavior was regarded as extinguished.

The long-term effectiveness of classical conditioning is also influenced by a variety of modifiable factors. First, the CS–UCS sequence is important because, in order for classical conditioning to occur, the CS must precede the UCS. The second important factor that influences the effectiveness of classical conditioning is the delay between presentation of the CS and UCS (Kiernan, 1975). The number of trials also influences the effectiveness of classical conditioning. Generally, the intensity and persistence of the CR is related to the number of conditioning trials, with a greater number of trials associated with greater intensity. Finally, specific characteristics of the UCS and CS may facilitate or hinder the effectiveness of the conditioning process. Generally, a CR is easier to establish when the UCS is strong and produces a rapid response (Kiernan, 1975). Subsequent to the conditioning process, the strength of the CR is determined through assessing its strength or frequency of response, the length of time between the presentation of the CS and occurrence of the CR, and the persistence of the CR (i.e., the length of time that the CR is elicited by the CS in the absence of the UCS).

After a CR has been established, an individual may demonstrate either *stimulus generalization* or *stimulus discrimination* in response to the CS (Antony &

Roemer, 2011). If stimulus generalization is demonstrated, the conditioned behavior will be performed in the presence of the CS as well as other similar stimuli (Schloss & Smith, 1994). For example, suppose a client who recently underwent a hip replacement participates in physical therapy. The therapist informs the client to remain seated until he is able to adjust the therapy equipment to the appropriate tension; however, contrary to the therapist's request, the client attempts to stand, loses her balance, and falls, with the physical therapist unable to reach her in time to prevent the fall. Subsequently, the client develops symptoms of anxiety (e.g., difficulty breathing, rapid heart rate, and perspiration) whenever she has a physical therapy session. If the client's symptoms of anxiety occur only when she works with the therapist who was near her when she fell, the client would be demonstrating stimulus discrimination. On the other hand, if the woman experiences anxiety whenever she has a physical therapy session, regardless of the therapist providing treatment, stimulus generalization would be occurring.

## Treatment Techniques

Because classical conditioning does not entail learning a new response, but rather develops an association between an existing response and a new stimulus (Craighead et al., 1994), treatment techniques based on this approach are directed toward helping clients to "unlearn" connections between specific stimuli and inappropriate behaviors, or conversely, to learn a connection between specific stimuli and appropriate behaviors (Papajohn, 1982).

One of the treatment techniques based on classical conditioning is *systematic desensitization*, which requires the client and therapist to construct a hierarchy of anxiety-producing scenes surrounding one particular fear (Thieme & Turk, 2012). Therapy requires clients to remain relaxed as they imagine each scene in the hierarchy until they reach the most anxiety-provoking scene and are able to remain relaxed (Emmelkamp, 1994). *Flooding* is another example of a therapeutic technique derived from classical conditioning (Emmelkamp, 1994) that involves exposing clients to a feared stimulus while making escape or avoidance impossible. Implosive therapy is similar to flooding except that clients imagine being placed in the fear-eliciting situation without opportunity for escape (Papajohn, 1982). Finally, *aversive therapy* is also based on principles of classical conditioning and attempts to eliminate inappropriate behavior by pairing it with a stimulus that naturally produces an unpleasant response. For example, in treating intravenous drug use, a client may be injected with a substance that induces nausea subsequent to the intravenous drug use. Consequently, the client may come to associate intravenous drug use with nausea and thereby cease to continue the behavior.

## Operant Conditioning

The two primary founders of operant conditioning are E. L. Thorndike and B. F. Skinner (Wilson, 1995). Through his studies with animals, Thorndike developed several laws of learning, the most important being the law of effect, stating that behaviors that lead to satisfaction will be reinforced, whereas behaviors that do not lead to satisfaction will not be reinforced. Like Thorndike, Skinner also believed that complex behaviors resulted from the ways that the organism interacted with or "operated" on the environment due to behavioral consequences (Corey, 1991).

## Central Tenets

The key components of operant conditioning are *reinforcement* and *punishment*. Reinforcement occurs when certain stimuli increase the frequency of a given behavior, whereas punishment happens when aversive consequences lead to decreases in the maladaptive behavior (Thieme & Turk, 2012). Reinforcement can involve either positive or negative cues. Positive reinforcement concerns the administration of a positive reward for good behavior (Craighead et al., 1994). In contrast, negative reinforcement occurs when the frequency of a behavior increases through the elimination of an aversive stimulus (Papajohn, 1982). Punishers may also be positive or negative. Positive punishment occurs when an undesired behavior decreases following administration of a particular stimulus (e.g., placing a client in physical restraints subsequent to assaulting another client; Craighead et al., 1994). In contrast, negative punishment occurs when a positive stimulus is removed following an undesired behavior (e.g., when a client involved in a residential substance abuse program loses his privilege to go out on pass due to becoming verbally aggressive toward the staff; Kiernan, 1975).

Reinforcers can be delivered through a variety of *reinforcement schedules*; however, behaviors are usually acquired more efficiently when reinforcement is delivered on a continuous schedule (i.e., the client is reinforced after each occurrence of the desired behavior; Thieme & Turk, 2012; Walker, Greenwood, & Terry, 1994). A fixed-interval schedule, for example, provides reinforcement to the client after a consistent time interval, regardless of how many times the desired behavior occurred within that time interval (e.g., a client in supported employment receives a paycheck every 2 weeks). Similarly, a fixed-ratio schedule is provided when a client is reinforced after he or she makes a specified number of the desired responses (e.g., a client is allowed to take a 5-minute break after boxing 10 packages of batteries).

Once a behavior has been acquired, however, it is best maintained through a schedule of partial or intermittent reinforcement (i.e., behavior is not reinforced after every occurrence; Gilliland, James, & Bowman, 1994). A variable-interval schedule of reinforcement involves providing reinforcement after an unpredictable period of time (e.g., incarcerated juveniles are informed that they will have six random room checks during the year, but are not informed of the dates when the checks will occur). Finally, a variable-ratio schedule of reinforcement entails the provision of reinforcement after a client demonstrates a variable number of desired responses. This type of reinforcement schedule produces the highest rates of responding, because the relationship between the response and administration of the reinforcer is unpredictable (e.g., clients participating in a residential substance abuse treatment program may earn reinforcers after submitting urine samples that are negative for drugs, but the number of negative test results varies from two to six before a client may earn a reinforcer).

Similar to classical conditioning, operant conditioning can also undergo *extinction*. In operant conditioning, this process occurs when reinforcement is withheld from a previously reinforced behavior to decrease or eliminate the undesired behavior (Wilson, 1995). Operant extinction generally does not occur immediately. Rather, abrupt removal of reinforcement will often produce a temporary increase in the frequency of the maladaptive behavior before the frequency decreases or is eliminated (Corrigan & Liberman, 1994). This temporary increase is referred to as an extinction burst. In order for operant conditioning to facilitate enduring behavioral change, the reinforcement must be meaningful enough for a client (Mueser, 1993).

There are two types of reinforcers (primary and secondary). Primary reinforcers are inherently reinforcing (Craighead et al., 1994; Gilliland et al., 1994), whereas secondary reinforcers derive their reinforcing properties through learning and experience (e.g., tokens earned in a token economy that can be exchanged for desired rewards; Craighead et al., 1994). An array of factors may affect the potency of positive reinforcement (Walker et al., 1994): (a) whether there is a contingent relationship between manifestation of the target behavior and provision of the reinforcer, (b) the immediacy of the reinforcer subsequent to demonstration of the desired behavior, (c) the magnitude or strength of the reinforcer, (d) the schedule of reinforcement, (e) the inclusion of verbal and/or physical prompting to enhance the likelihood of behavioral demonstration, and (f) the likelihood of generalizability or ease of transfer of training of the target behavior.

Another important treatment consideration is that sometimes a behavior only occurs under certain specific conditions in the environment. The environmental factors that must be present for the behavior to occur are referred to as *positive discriminative stimuli* (Kiernan, 1975). In contrast, the desired behavior will not occur in the presence of negative discriminative stimuli. Whenever the manifestation of a behavior occurs under discriminative stimuli, the behavior is said to occur under stimulus control (Kazdin, 1994). Stimulus discrimination is demonstrated when an individual with a head injury is taught how to cook successfully on a stove within a rehabilitation facility, but is unable to even turn on the stove once the individual returns home. This is in contrast to stimulus control in which a behavior occurs only under specific environmental conditions (Schloss & Smith, 1994). Sometimes similar stimuli are capable of eliciting the same behavioral response, and this phenomenon is referred to as *stimulus generalization* (Craighead et al., 1994). An example of stimulus generalization occurs when an individual with an intellectual disability mistakenly identifies all four-legged animals as "dog."

### Treatment Techniques

There are multiple treatment techniques based on operant approaches that increase the frequency of behavior through the use of punishment and/or positive reinforcement (Antony & Roemer, 2011). Treatment techniques derived from operant principles used to decrease behavior through punishment include verbal reprimands, overcorrection (i.e., overcorrecting negative behavior while also practicing positive behavior), response cost (i.e., loss of a reinforcer following undesired behavior), and time-out from reinforcement (Craighead et al., 1994; Walker et al., 1994). Other treatment techniques that emphasize positive reinforcement include shaping, differential reinforcement (Walker et al., 1994), behavioral contracts, token economies (Allyon & Azrin, 1968), and social skills training (SST; Emmelkamp, 1994).

*Shaping* involves reinforcing closer and closer approximations of the desired target behavior until the target behavior is demonstrated (Antony & Roemer, 2011). This technique is most helpful in situations in which the target behavior never or rarely occurs in the natural environment (Craighead et al., 1994).

*Differential reinforcement* occurs when all behaviors except the target behavior are positively reinforced. Because this technique also involves withholding reinforcement following a response, differential reinforcement is essentially a combination of both positive reinforcement and extinction. For example, suppose a client with a brain injury consistently chooses to eat all foods with her fingers during mealtimes. In this situation, the client is provided with positive reinforcement (e.g., verbal praise) for using the proper utensils during mealtimes, but is ignored or asked to sit at a table alone when she eats with her fingers. Depending on the goal of behavior change, differential reinforcement may be implemented in a variety of ways. The aforementioned example demonstrates differential reinforcement of incompatible behavior (DRI) because, if the client is using eating utensils (i.e., the reinforced behavior), eating with her fingers is incompatible with the desired behavior. Other variations of this technique include differential reinforcement of low rates of responding (DRL), differential reinforcement of alternative behaviors (DRA), and differential reinforcement of other behaviors (DRO; for a more detailed discussion of these techniques, refer to Craighead et al., 1994; Kazdin, 1994; Walker et al., 1994).

Behavior can also be modified through *behavioral contracts*, which are essentially agreements made between the behavior therapist and the client (Kazdin, 1994). The contract is a contingency statement that identifies behaviors that are to be changed and the reinforcers and punishers that will be instrumental in the behavior change. Although effectiveness of the behavioral contract is enhanced by client participation during contract development, effective contracts contain five additional elements: (a) identification of reinforcers, (b) identification of target behaviors, (c) a process for making alterations to the contract if attempts at behavioral change are unsuccessful, (d) identification of extra reinforcers for consistent compliance with the terms outlined in the contract, and (e) provision of frequent feedback regarding the client's progress toward behavior change.

Behavior can also be modified through a *token economy* (Ayllon & Azrin, 1968). Token economies are generally implemented in a structured environment in which desirable behaviors are reinforced with tokens, which can then be exchanged for other desired reinforcers (Corrigan & Liberman, 1994). All effective token economies have the following characteristics: (a) clearly identified and defined target behaviors, (b) reinforcers provided following presentation of the desired behavior, (c) implementation of a system of constant monitoring and evaluation of the effectiveness of the token economy, and (d) a plan implemented to assist the individual in maintaining appropriate behavior in the absence of a token economy on reintegration into the community (Gilliland et al., 1994). Consequences for inappropriate behavior may vary from one token system to another and may involve loss of tokens for undesirable behavior (i.e., response cost) or prevention of earning additional tokens for a specified amount of time.

Finally, behavior can also be modified through *SST* (Emmelkamp, 1994; Marzillier, Lambert, & Kellett, 1976), which is often implemented to enhance communication, assertiveness, problem solving, and other desired social skills (Corrigan & Liberman, 1994; Mueser, 1993). Unlike other behavioral techniques discussed previously, SST is unique in that it derives its effectiveness from a combination of operant conditioning, classical conditioning, and social learning theory. For this reason, a variety of techniques may be implemented during SST, including modeling, coaching, behavior rehearsal, feedback, reinforcement, and homework.

## THEORY OF PERSONALITY

Maladaptive behaviors are learned and can also be unlearned through either classical conditioning or operant conditioning (Antony & Roemer, 2011). From a behavioral perspective, when maladaptive behavior was originally learned, a specific function was fulfilled, and the behavior is maintained through either positive reinforcement (e.g., continuing to use heroin to experience the "high" without regard for negative physical and social consequences) or negative reinforcement (e.g., drinking in the morning to prevent withdrawal symptoms).

The presence of aversive stimuli plays a major role in both the initial development of maladaptive behavior as well as maintenance of the behavior. Through avoidance of or escape from an aversive situation, the behavior is strengthened. Nevertheless, if there is a significant quantity of aversive stimuli present during the conditioning history, persistent avoidance of these stimuli will lead to either withdrawal into a fantasy world free from aversive stimuli (e.g., a client who develops dissociative personality disorder in response to contact with an environment composed of extreme abuse and aversive situations) or emotional problems such as fear, guilt, anger, depression, and anxiety (Gilliland et al., 1994). For example, suppose a male child is inconsistently subjected to severe physical punishment from his father for trivial reasons (e.g., failing to make his bed in the morning); however, when the punishment is inflicted, the boy is unable to escape the situation because his father locks him in a closet following the beating. After the boy's father lets him out of the closet, the child is left feeling confused about why the punishment occurred, angry that he had no control over the situation and the resulting punishment, and fearful that the punishment may occur again. If the punishment does continue to occur, the boy may begin to develop maladaptive behaviors including anger, depression, guilt, and anxiety. Conversely, the boy may retreat into a fantasy world in which punishment and aversive consequences are either not present or avoided.

## COUNSELING PROCESS

The focus of the behavior therapy process is corrective learning, which encompasses the acquisition of new coping skills, enhancement of communication, and the overcoming of maladaptive emotional conflicts (Antony & Roemer, 2011; Wilson, 1995). When implementing behavior therapy, all learning occurs within a structured environment. Nevertheless, to the greatest extent possible, behavior therapists emphasize that clients should take an active role in effecting change during their activities in the real world between therapy sessions.

Kuehnel and Liberman (1986) describe behavior therapy as a six-stage process. First, a behavioral assessment is conducted, which helps to identify maladaptive behaviors. Second, a client's assets and strengths are noted to help identify strategies and approaches that may serve as templates for effective treatment interventions. The third step in the therapeutic process is relating the identified or target behaviors to the context in which they occur. Possible behavioral antecedents and consequences are specified. The fourth step entails developing a process to measure the problematic behavior(s). This is accomplished by assessing the frequency of a target behavior during a baseline period (i.e., prior to the initiation of treatment). The baseline becomes the reference point for determining treatment effectiveness. The fifth step in the process requires the identification of reinforcers. These may include activities, people, or things that will provide motivation for treatment as well as the maintenance of the desired behavior after treatment has ended. The final step in the counseling process is the development of treatment goals, which are developed jointly between the counselor and client. Generally, the client determines the behaviors that will be changed, whereas the therapist determines how the changes will best be made (Wilson, 1995).

The process of developing treatment goals has been delineated by Cormier and Cormier (1985) and involves the following steps. First, the behavior therapist explains the purpose of goals to the client. The client then identifies desired outcomes as a result of counseling. The client and therapist then jointly discuss whether the desired outcomes are outcomes that the client is committed to achieving and whether the treatment goals are realistic. This is followed by a discussion between both parties of the advantages and disadvantages of the treatment goals. Finally, the therapist and client collaboratively define the treatment goals through identifying the behaviors involved, the methods of change, and the degrees of change desired.

The length of behavior treatment duration is intended to be short term, yet guidelines for establishing the length of treatment are quite general and consist of three processes (Wilson, 1995). First, an assessment of maladaptive behavior is conducted and target behaviors are identified. Second, treatment interventions are implemented as soon as possible. Finally, progress in treatment is continually assessed against clearly defined, objective, measurable therapeutic goals. Because all clients have different therapeutic goals and life circumstances, the length of treatment, the number of sessions required, and the time spent in treatment will vary from one client to another. Thus, treatment length is determined by the rate at which clients demonstrate progress toward treatment goals (Wilson, 1995).

## THERAPEUTIC RELATIONSHIP

As indicated in the previous section, all aspects of behavior therapy are conducted jointly between the therapist and the client. It is thought that through actively participating during development of the treatment plan, the client will be more invested in behavioral change and more likely to work toward goal attainment (Corey, 1991). While developing treatment goals and implementing the treatment plan, the behavior therapist focuses on current behavior rather than underlying causes for the behavior. Any investigation of the client's past is considered important only as it relates to the present.

Behavior therapists are active and direct in their interactions with clients and typically function as consultants and problem solvers (Wilson, 1995). Historically, behavior therapists have been viewed as behavioral experts; however, more contemporary views of the behavior therapist's role emphasize the collaborative relationship between client and counselor. Furthermore, behavior therapists were often previously stereotyped as indifferent, mechanical, and manipulative technicians, but today they are often described as understanding, friendly, caring, and personal (Gilliland et al., 1994).

Although behavior therapy uses a systematic and structured approach to treatment, the therapeutic relationship is important and contributes to the process of behavioral change (Wilson, 1995). The client is more invested in treatment if the therapeutic relationship is characterized by the client's belief in the therapist's competence and regards him or her as honest and trustworthy. Nevertheless, Corey (1991) contends that the core conditions (i.e., congruence, acceptance, and empathy) are necessary but not sufficient for behavioral change to occur.

## REHABILITATION APPLICATIONS

Behavioral techniques were implemented to treat maladaptive behaviors well before the procedures were identified as a cohesive theory of counseling. Within the past few decades, these techniques have been implemented to treat multiple maladaptive behaviors of people with a wide variety of disabilities, including substance abuse (Rotgers, 1996), traumatic brain injury (TBI; Giles, Ridley, Dill, & Frye, 1997; Horton & Barrett, 1988), developmental disabilities (Griffiths, Feldman, & Tough, 1997; Madle & Neisworth, 1990), mental illness (Corrigan, McCracken, Edwards, Kommana, & Simpatico, 1997), schizophrenia (Mueser, 1993), depression (Gloaguen, Cottraux, Cucherat, & Blackburn, 1998), and chronic pain (McCracken, 1997; Slater, Doctor, Pruitt, & Atkinson, 1997). For the sake of brevity, the following portion of this chapter addresses the common application of behavior therapy to individuals with developmental disabilities as well as TBI.

## Developmental Disabilities

Within the past 30 years, behavior therapy has had a strong influence in the treatment of maladaptive behaviors of persons with developmental disabilities and intellectual disabilities. Behavioral techniques have been used to treat a variety of behaviors successfully, including toileting (Azrin & Foxx, 1971; Madle & Neisworth, 1990), pica (Paisey & Whitney, 1989), impulsivity and self-control (Schweitzer & Sulzer-Azaroff, 1988), and other challenging behaviors.

Toileting was one of the first targeted behaviors that received significant research attention from a behavioral perspective; however, Azrin and Foxx (1971) were the first to report the implementation of multiple procedures simultaneously to accomplish toilet training. Some of the techniques employed included modeling, shaping, positive reinforcement, and punishment (e.g., verbal reprimands, time-out). Over the past 25 years, additional research has been conducted on toilet training and has indicated that although other toilet-training programs exist besides those proposed by Azrin and Foxx (1971), specific behavioral techniques, including reinforcement, chaining, shaping, prompting, and punishment, are required for successful results (Madle & Neisworth, 1990).

Pica is defined as the ingestion of inedible substances (Piazza et al., 1998). This behavior occurs with as many as 25% of persons with intellectual disabilities (Danford & Huber, 1982), and, unfortunately, this behavior is often resistant to treatment (Piazza et al., 1998). Nevertheless, pica has been treated successfully through the use of various reinforcers and punishers (Paisey & Whitney, 1989) as well as other behavioral techniques. Fisher and colleagues (1994) employed behavioral assessment results to identify reinforcers and punishers from empirically derived consequences and were effective in reducing the pica behavior of three children to near-zero levels. In another study, Piazza et al. (1998) conducted functional analyses on three participants with pica. Results revealed that the pica of one participant was maintained by automatic reinforcement (e.g., oral stimulation), whereas the pica of the other two participants was maintained by a combination of both social and automatic reinforcement. The researchers then provided the participants with stimuli that either matched or did not match the function of their pica behavior. When the participants were given stimulation that did not match the sensory components of pica, the behavior was maintained. In contrast, when the individuals were given matched stimuli, pica was reduced.

Behavioral techniques have also been implemented to teach self-control and reduce impulsivity among persons with intellectual disabilities. Self-control has been defined as "behavior that results in access to a larger reinforcer after a longer delay, rather than impulsive behavior that results in a small reinforcer after a shorter or no delay" (Schweitzer & Sulzer-Azaroff, 1988). Dixon et al. (1998) conducted a study to examine the effects of concurrent fixed-duration and progressive-duration reinforcement schedules as a means of teaching self-control and increasing targeted behaviors of three individuals with developmental disabilities. Results demonstrated that by establishing a reinforcement history in which participants are gradually exposed to increasingly longer delays prior to access to a larger reinforcer and are required to demonstrate a target behavior during the delay, greater self-control and reduced impulsivity may both occur with greater frequency. These results are consistent with those of Schweitzer and Sulzer-Azaroff (1988), who argued that gradually increasing the delay to the access of a desired reinforcer might increase self-control.

A variety of applications of behavior therapy to persons with intellectual disabilities have been discussed; however, behavioral techniques have also been applied successfully to many other challenging behaviors commonly exhibited. These treatment interventions have focused on the following: (a) activities of daily living (i.e., feeding and dressing; Madle & Neisworth, 1990); (b) speech, language, and communication (Hagopian, Fisher, Sullivan, Acquisto, & LeBlanc, 1998; Lancioni, VanHouten, & Ten Hoopen, 1997); (c) community preparation (Bourbeau, Sauers, & Close, 1986; Williams & Cuvo, 1986); (d) aggressive and disruptive behavior (Lennox, Miltenberger, Sprengler, & Erfanian, 1988); (e) sleep disturbances (Didden, Curfs, Sikkema, & de Moor, 1998); and (f) reduction of cigarette smoking (Peine, Darvish, Blakelock, Osborne, & Jenson, 1998).

### Traumatic Brain Injury

Maladaptive behavior commonly occurs after the onset of TBI (Horton & Barrett, 1998). Fortunately, the behavioral approach to treatment is particularly appropriate for TBI rehabilitation (Eames & Wood, 1985; Giles et al., 1997). A variety of behavioral approaches has been employed to increase behavioral deficits or reduce behavioral excesses among persons with TBI and include positive reinforcement, time-out, and overcorrection.

Positive reinforcement involves provision of a desired reinforcer subsequent to exhibition of a desired target behavior and has been regarded as the cornerstone of behavior management techniques (Lewis & Bitter, 1991). To enhance the effectiveness of positive reinforcement among persons with TBI, Lewis and Bitter (1991) identified six guidelines: (a) Reinforcers should be provided immediately after the client demonstrates the desired response; (b) the client should be made aware of which specific behaviors will be reinforced and which will not; (c) when identifying reinforcers and behaviors to clients, speech should be slow to enhance the ability of the individual with TBI to process the information; (d) instructions should be broken down and presented in small steps; (e) a variety of reinforcers should be offered to prevent the client from satiating on one particular reinforcer; and (f) throughout the treatment process, reinforcers should be provided on a continuous schedule due to the length of time that is often required for persons with TBI to learn the association between the behavior and subsequent reinforcement. Once the association is learned, intermittent reinforcement will more effectively maintain the desired behavior.

Time-out from reinforcement involves removing the individual from all sources of reinforcement subsequent to the demonstration of maladaptive behavior. Marr (1982) proposed guidelines to enhance the effectiveness of time-out when implemented with a person with TBI. First, the individual should receive a time-out immediately after the inappropriate behavior occurs. Next, the individual must be informed of the specific behavior that resulted in the time-out. Third, the duration of time the individual remains in time-out should be brief, limited to 5 to 10 minutes. Because many individuals with TBI experience memory difficulties, if the time spent in time-out becomes too long, the individual may have minimal or no recollection of the reasons that he or she has been placed in time-out. Furthermore, impaired memory, in turn, may potentially result in escalation of the individual's behavior due to frustration over the reasons that he or she has been removed from positive reinforcement.

Overcorrection positive practice requires the individual to repeatedly perform an appropriate response or behavior that is incompatible with behavior that is targeted for reduction or elimination (Madle & Neisworth, 1990). This procedure is particularly applicable to individuals with TBI who possess impairments in memory and planning ability because it provides them with opportunities to rehearse a desired behavior over multiple trials, while simultaneously reducing the frequency of performing the maladaptive behavior.

## CASE STUDY

The following case study attempts to demonstrate the application of behavioral techniques discussed in this chapter, including positive and negative reinforcement, punishment, shaping, time-out, token economies, self-control and impulsivity, and the collaborative client–therapist relationship.

Annie is an 18-year-old Caucasian female who was born with intellectual disability, with an IQ score of 55 to 60. She lived at home with her parents and two sisters until the age of 9. At that age, due to significant behavioral problems, Annie went to live in an eight-bed group home 2 miles from her home. Although Annie could be charming and very social, her inappropriate and aggressive behaviors were the primary reason that she left home.

Annie's family frequently allowed her to have her own way and did not realize that they were actually reinforcing her behavior by continuing to do so. Annie had learned through previous instances that if she became verbally or physically aggressive, she would get what she wanted. In addition, Annie's family also learned that if they conceded to Annie's demands, Annie's verbal and physical aggression would either stop or be prevented altogether (i.e., negative reinforcement). Nevertheless, Annie continued to make demands, and her family continued to give in.

As Annie grew older, her demands continued. Her family was getting frustrated with her increasingly aggressive behavior and realized that, over the years, Annie's behavior had become uncontrollable. They sought an alternative residence for her and ultimately decided that Annie would

*(continued)*

(*continued*)

best be served in a group home. Annie stayed overnight at the group home for a "trial" visit so that she would have the opportunity to meet the staff and other residents, and the staff would have the opportunity to observe her behaviors. The group home staff felt that Annie's behaviors could be addressed and treated successfully, and Annie moved in a few days later.

On her first day living at the group home, Annie was told that the home had one rule: Respect others. Knowing Annie's behavioral history, the staff provided Annie with numerous examples of respectful behavior (e.g., not causing emotional or physical harm to another, completing assigned chores, not taking others' possessions without permission). Annie was told that for each day she demonstrated respectful behavior for the entire day, she would be able to choose a reward for herself at the end of the day (e.g., a phone call home or an ice cream sundae). Annie was given a wall calendar, and for each day that she earned a reward, she was to draw a star to remind herself that she showed appropriate behavior all day. As a means of encouraging consistent behavior over a longer period of time, Annie was told that every time she earned five stars consecutively, she could choose a larger reward (e.g., going out to eat or shopping). Finally, Annie was told that if she demonstrated disrespectful behavior toward any other resident or staff, she would be told to go to the "quiet room" for 10 minutes to think about what she had done (i.e., time-out).

Annie's first few months at the group home consisted of behavioral ups and downs. Her calendar revealed that she would go for a few days with appropriate behavior, followed by a few days of disrespectful and aggressive behavior toward others. Yet, over time, the group home staff noticed a trend in Annie's behavior. It appeared that Annie was able to demonstrate respectful behavior for a greater length of time if she chose to make a phone call to her family as her daily reward. The group home staff approached the family with this observation and asked them if they would be willing to have Annie return home for a weekend visit if she was able to demonstrate two consecutive weeks of respectful behavior; however, the family had to agree to implement the same behavioral strategies at home that were implemented at the group home (e.g., positive reinforcement and time-out). Annie's family agreed that this would be an appropriate goal for which Annie should strive, in hopes that it would increase her self-control and decrease her impulsive tendencies.

The idea was discussed with Annie, who became very excited when she heard that she could go home for the entire weekend. Annie had indeed demonstrated an improvement in her maladaptive behaviors since coming to live in the group home, and the staff decided to implement the idea for a weekend home visit. Initially, it took Annie almost 2 months to achieve 2

(*continued*)

(*continued*)

consecutive weeks of respectful behavior; however, as Annie's time living at the group home continued to increase, the frequency of her inappropriate behaviors continued to decrease. Eventually, she was able to earn weekend visits home almost always twice per month.

## RESEARCH FINDINGS

Behavior therapy has long been established as a major form of psychotherapy, and behavioral techniques have addressed a broad range of psychological and rehabilitation issues (Wilson, 1995). In a classic meta-analysis, Smith, Glass, and Miller (1980) reviewed approximately 100 controlled studies on behavior therapy and cognitive behavioral therapy (CBT) interventions for individuals with mental health disorders. Their findings suggested that behavior therapy, as well as CBT, outperformed placebo treatments, with mean effect sizes ranging from .73 to 1.13. Another meta-analysis on behavior therapy evaluated 69 studies published from 1977 to 1986 (Bowers & Chum, 1988). Bowers and Clum reported that the effects of behavior therapy were twice the effects of nonspecific treatments. Other early meta-analytic studies and systematic literature reviews provided support for the effectiveness of behavior therapy for specific mental health disorders, such as agoraphobia (e.g., Trull, Nietzel, & Main, 1988) and obsessive-compulsive disorder (OCD; e.g., Stanley & Turner, 1996; van Balkom et al., 1994). In the case of treatment outcome research for OCD, Stanley and Turner reported that about 63% of individuals with OCD in behavior therapy tend to obtain positive benefits.

Over time, behavioral therapy methods have been successfully applied to other health problems, including depression (e.g., Dobson, 1989; Ekers, Richards, & Gilbody, 2007; Gloaguen et al., 1998), pain (Morley, Eccleston, & Williams, 1999), insomnia (e.g., Morin, Culbert, & Schwartz, 1994; Murtagh & Greenwood, 1995), and substance abuse (e.g., Dutra et al., 2008; Griffith, Rowan-Szal, Roark, & Simpson, 2000; Prendergast, Podus, Finney, Greenwell, & Roll, 2006). Despite the fact that behavior therapy has been consistently shown to be equally effective to CBT in treating health problems like depression, it is not routinely recommended as the standard treatment in rehabilitation or health care settings. Emerging research has even suggested that behavioral strategies alone may facilitate enduring therapeutic changes for people with depression that are comparable to comprehensive CBT methods (Gortner, Gollan, Dobson, & Jacobson, 1998; Jacobson et al., 1996).

These results were extended in a recent randomized design study on therapies for adults with major depression (Dimidjian et al., 2006). The findings demonstrated that behavioral activation strategies were comparable to antidepressant medication among more severely depressed patients, and both behavioral activation and medications produced significantly more benefits than cognitive therapy. Hence, there appears to be value in helping clients with straightforward behavioral strategies, such as goal setting, self-monitoring, activity scheduling, and problem solving. Taken together, these research findings have helped to reignite clinical interest in behavioral therapy approaches (Ekers, Richards, & Gilbody, 2007).

Successful implementation of behavioral techniques has now been noted in a variety of settings, including medicine, education, and rehabilitation. With regard to rehabilitation settings, applications are discussed in the following section when used with individuals with developmental disabilities and TBIs; however, behavior therapy has also been effectively implemented with individuals with many other types of disabilities, including mental illness (Corrigan et al., 1997), schizophrenia (Mueser, 1993) and chronic pain (McCracken, 1997; Slater et al., 1997).

### Developmental Disabilities

To date, behavior therapies have been recognized among clinicians for their utility in treating maladaptive behaviors in adults and children with developmental disabilities, with more recent documentation of their effectiveness through meta-analyses of research results. For instance, Harvey, Boer, Meyer, and Evans (2009) conducted a meta-analysis using data from various behavioral intervention studies on children. The authors reported significant findings and indicated mean effect sizes ranging from .24 to .57. In particular, skills replacement, consequence manipulation combined with systems change, and traditional antecedent interventions yielded the most positive results. However, when examining the clinical effectiveness of the individual types of behavior therapies, there seems to be a paucity of available evidence. Although various clinical trials and single-subject studies have evaluated the usefulness of specific types of behavior interventions, the majority of the research has methodological limitations (Virués-Ortega, 2010).

Recently, Virués-Ortega (2010) used more rigorous research methods to analyze the long-term effects of applied behavioral analysis (ABA) interventions in young children with autism. The findings demonstrated that comprehensive ABA interventions facilitated medium to large effects on intellectual functioning, language development, acquisition of daily living skills, and social functioning. More specifically, individuals with autism showed better language-related outcomes, in addition to receptive and expressive language, with average effect sizes approaching 1.50. A recent systematic review (Spreckley & Boyd, 2009) examined the effectiveness of six randomized comparison trials testing a variant of ABA, called applied behavior intervention, for preschool children with autism spectrum disorders. The results indicated insufficient evidence to support the effectiveness of applied behavioral interventions.

A growing body of research has also provided evidence for another popular type of behavior therapy, early intensive behavioral intervention (EIBI; Eikeseth, 2009). One recent meta-analysis (Reichow, 2012) reviewed data from five earlier meta-analyses on EIBI for young children with autism spectrum disorders. For both IQ scores and adaptive behavior measures, the combined meta-analytic findings showed that there were mean effect sizes ranging from $g = .38$ to 1.19 and $g = .30$ to 1.09, respectively. In addition, four out of the five meta-analyses concluded that EIBI was an effective intervention model for children with autism spectrum disorders. However, various systematic reviews have concluded that although EIBI generally has demonstrated significant positive outcomes for young children with autism, there are large individual differences in treatment response, and most children require ongoing specialized services (Eikeseth, 2009; Howlin, Magiati, & Charman, 2009; Matson & Smith, 2008; Rogers & Vismara, 2008).

## Traumatic Brain Injury

Although rehabilitation research papers published in over 20 peer-reviewed journals have applied behavioral interventions to people with acquired brain injury, the frequency of these publications has remained low over the past few decades (Heinike & Carr, 2014). Gurdin, Huber, and Cochran (2005) evaluated the effectiveness of behavioral interventions in 20 studies and reported evidence to support the use of behavioral interventions in either reducing problem behavior or increasing adaptive skills in children and adolescents with brain injuries across multiple treatment settings. In addition, Ylvisaker et al. (2007) reviewed the effects of 65 behavioral intervention trials (traditional contingency management, positive behavior interventions and supports, or a combination of the two) for children and adults with behavior disorders following TBI. The authors indicated that at least one target behavior was enhanced in each study, and most reductive procedures led to significant social outcomes. Ylvisaker et al. concluded that contingency management procedures or positive behavior supports should be considered evidence-based treatment options.

Finally, Cattelani, Zettin, and Zoccolotti (2010) expanded on the review by Ylvisaker et al. (2007) by also examining the effects of behavior treatment options different from ABA (i.e., behavior analytic, cognitive behavioral, and comprehensive holistic rehabilitation approaches). The authors determined that comprehensive holistic rehabilitation interventions should be implemented as a standard treatment, whereas ABA and CBT should only be considered evidence-based treatment options for adults with psychosocial and behavioral problems after the onset of an acquired brain injury.

More recently, Heinike and Carr (2014) reviewed the brain injury research and concluded that reinforcement and antecedent treatment techniques in behavior therapy were deemed well established as skill acquisition interventions, and self-management was deemed probably efficacious. Furthermore, differential reinforcement, antecedent interventions, and punishment were determined to be well established as behavior reduction interventions for persons with brain injury, and both self-management and extinction were deemed probably efficacious for decreasing challenging behaviors. Even though the effect sizes were found to be very large for this population, none of the behavior interventions for individuals with brain injury were considered evidence-based methods.

Within the extant rehabilitation literature, there has been limited research available on the application of behavior therapy to other behavioral problems. Nonetheless, a recent meta-analysis (McGuire et al., 2014) reviewed data from eight randomized controlled trials for comprehensive behavioral interventions and habit reversal training for individuals with Tourette syndrome and chronic tic disorders. The results showed that the behavioral therapies led to medium to large effect sizes relative to comparison conditions, which are similar to treatment effects derived by meta-analyses on antipsychotic medication trials. Moderator analyses demonstrated that larger treatment effects were observed among older participants, those with more therapeutic contact, and less co-occurring attention deficit hyperactivity disorder (ADHD). Moreover, a current systematic literature review (Nye et al., 2013) evaluated the usefulness of eight experimental and quasi-experimental behavioral intervention studies in treating children with stuttering disorders. The results indicated significant positive effects of approximately 1 standard deviation unit when compared to nontreatment control groups, but there were not significant differences for studies comparing two active behavior treatments.

In summary, research findings on the effectiveness of behavior therapy suggest that the effects are at least comparable to other psychosocial interventions (e.g., Ekers, Richards, & Gilbody, 2007) and that it is effective for health behaviors, especially for problems with depression (e.g., Ekers et al., 2007), pain (Morley et al., 1999), insomnia (e.g., Smith et al., 2002), and substance abuse (e.g., Dutra et al., 2008). In addition, preliminary empirical studies demonstrate that behavior therapies may be useful for both adults and children with developmental disabilities (e.g., Eikeseth, 2009) as well as TBI (Heinicke & Carr, 2014). There is also early, yet promising research that shows that behavior activation strategies may be more beneficial than cognitive therapies for adults with severe depression (Dimidjian et al., 2006). Future empirical studies should aim to investigate the processes for long-lasting behavior change, as it remains possible that behavioral strategies work through underlying cognitive mechanisms to yield their enduring effects (Bandura, 1977).

## DISCUSSION EXERCISES

1. Describe the behavioral explanation for individual differences in human nature.
2. From the behavioral perspective, how are antecedents, behaviors, and reinforcers interrelated?
3. What are some operant conditioning strategies for effectively reducing maladaptive behaviors in people with disabilities?
4. What can be done to promote generalization when implementing systematic desensitization? What can help to prevent a relapse in anxiety symptoms?

5. In the beginning of this chapter, we mentioned the relationship between traditional behavior therapy approaches and CBT methods. Identify and describe the characteristics of traditional behavior therapy (e.g., classical conditional approaches) that distinguish it from CBT.
6. Behavior therapy is considered generally applicable, so is it necessary to consider cultural diversity? Explain your rationale.

## REFERENCES

Antony, M. M., & Roemer, L. (2011). *Behavior therapy*. Washington, DC: American Psychological Association.

Ayllon, T., & Azrin, N. H. (1968). *The token economy*. New York, NY: Appleton-Century-Crofts.

Azrin, N. H., & Foxx, R. (1971). A rapid method of toilet training the institutionalized retarded. *Journal of Applied Behavior Analysis, 4*, 89–99.

Bandura, A. (1977). Self-efficacy: Toward a unifying theory of behavioral change. *Psychological Review, 84*, 191–215.

Bourbeau, P. E., Sowers, J. A., & Close, D. W. (1986). An experimental analysis of generalization of banking skills from classroom to bank settings in the community. *Education and Training of the Mentally Retarded, 21*, 98–107.

Bowers, T. G., & Clum, G. A. (1988). Relative contribution of specific and non-specific treatment effects: Meta-analysis of placebo-controlled behavior therapy research. *Psychological Bulletin, 103*, 315–323.

Cattelani, R., Zettin, M., & Zoccolotti, P. (2010). Rehabilitation treatments for adults with behavioral and psychosocial disorders following acquired brain injury: A systematic review. *Neuropsychology Review, 20*, 52–85.

Corey, G. (1991). *Theory and practice of counseling and psychotherapy* (4th ed.). Pacific Grove, CA: Brooks/Cole.

Cormier, W. H., & Cormier, L. S. (1985). *Interviewing strategies for helpers: Fundamental skills and cognitive behavioral interventions* (2nd ed.). Pacific Grove, CA: Brooks/Cole.

Corrigan, P. W., & Liberman, R. P. (1994). Overview of behavior therapy in psychiatric hospitals. In P. W. Corrigan & R. P. Liberman (Eds.), *Behavior therapy in psychiatric hospitals* (pp. 1–38). New York, NY: Springer Publishing Company.

Corrigan, P. W., McCracken, S. G., Edwards, M., Kommana, S., & Simpatico, T. (1997). Staff training to improve implementation and impact of behavioral rehabilitation programs. *Psychiatric Services, 48*(10), 1336–1338.

Craighead, L. W., Craighead, W. E., Kazdin, A. E., & Mahoney, M. J. (1994). *Cognitive and behavioral interventions: An empirical approach to mental health problems*. Needham Heights, MA: Allyn & Bacon.

Danford, D. E., & Huber, A. M. (1982). Pica among mentally retarded adults. *American Journal on Mental Deficiency, 87*, 141–146.

Didden, R., Curfs, L. M. G., Sikkema, S. P. E., & de Moor, J. (1998). Functional assessment and treatment of sleeping problems with developmentally disabled children: Six case studies. *Journal of Behavior Therapy and Experimental Psychiatry, 29*, 85–97.

Dimidjian, S., Hollon, S. D., Dobson, K. S., Schmaling, K. B., Kohlenberg, R. J., Addis, M. E., . . . Jacobson, N. S. (2006). Randomized trial of behavioral activation, cognitive therapy, and antidepressant medication in the acute treatment of adults with major depression. *Journal of Consulting and Clinical Psychology, 74*, 658–670.

Dixon, M. R., Hayes, L. J., Binder, L. M., Manthey, S., Sigman, C., & Zdanowski, D. M. (1998). Using a self-control training procedure to increase appropriate behavior. *Journal of Applied Behavior Analysis, 31*, 203–210.

Dobson, K. S. (1989). A meta-analysis of the efficacy of cognitive therapy for depression. *Journal of Consulting and Clinical Psychology, 57,* 414–419.

Dutra, L., Stathopoulou, G., Basden, S., Leyro, T., Powers, M., & Otto, M. (2008). A meta-analytic review of psychosocial interventions for substance use disorders. *American Journal of Psychiatry, 165,* 179–187.

Eames, P., & Wood, R. (1985). Rehabilitation after severe brain injury: A follow-up study of a behavior modification approach. *Journal of Neurology, Neurosurgery, and Psychiatry, 48,* 613–619.

Eikeseth, S. (2009). Outcome of comprehensive psycho-educational interventions for young children with autism. *Research in Developmental Disabilities, 30,* 158–178.

Ekers, D., Richards, D., & Gilbody, S. (2008). A meta-analysis of randomized trials of behavioral treatment of depression. *Psychological Medicine, 38,* 611–623.

Emmelkamp, P. M. (1994). Behavior therapy with adults. In A. E. Bergin & S. L. Garfield (Eds.), *Handbook of psychotherapy and behavior change* (4th ed., pp. 379–427). New York, NY: Wiley.

Fisher, W. W., Piazza, C. C., Bowman, L. G., Kurtz, P. F., Sherer, M. R., & Lachman, S. R. (1994). A preliminary evaluation of empirically derived consequences for the treatment of pica. *Journal of Applied Behavior Analysis, 26,* 23–36.

Giles, G. M., Ridley, J. E., Dill, A., & Frye, S. (1997). A consecutive series of adults with brain injury treated with a washing and dressing retraining program. *American Journal of Occupational Therapy, 51,* 256–266.

Gilliland, B. E., James, R. K., & Bowman, J. T. (1994). *Theories and strategies in counseling and psychotherapy* (3rd ed.). Boston, MA: Allyn & Bacon.

Gloaguen, V., Cottraux, J., Curcherat, M., & Blackburn, I. (1998). A meta-analysis of the effect of cognitive therapy in depressed patients. *Journal of Affective Disorders, 49,* 59–72.

Gortner, E. T., Gollan, J. K., Dobson, K. S., & Jacobson, N. S. (1998). Cognitive-behavioral treatment for depression: Relapse prevention. *Journal of Consulting and Clinical Psychology, 66,* 377–384.

Griffith, J. D., Rowan-Szal, G. A., Roark, R. R., & Simpson, D. D. (2000). Contingency management in outpatient methadone treatment: A meta-analysis. *Drug and Alcohol Dependence, 58,* 55–66.

Griffiths, D., Feldman, M. A., & Tough, S. (1997). Programming generalization of social skills in adults with developmental disabilities: Effects on generalization and social validity. *Behavior Therapy, 28,* 253–269.

Gurdin, L. S., Huber, S. A., & Cochran, C. R. (2005). A critical analysis of data-based studies examining behavioral interventions with children and adolescents with brain injuries. *Behavioral Interventions, 20,* 3–16.

Hagopian, L. P., Fisher, W. W., Sullivan, M. T., Acquisto, J., & LeBlanc, L. A. (1998). Effectiveness of functional communication training with and without extinction and punishment: A summary of 21 inpatient cases. *Journal of Applied Behavior Analysis, 31,* 211–235.

Harvey, S. T., Boer, D., Meyer, L. H., & Evans, I. M. (2009). Updating a meta-analysis of intervention research with challenging behavior: Treatment validity and standards of practice. *Journal of Intellectual and Developmental Disability, 34,* 67–80.

Heinicke, M. R., & Carr, J. E. (2014). Applied behavior analysis in acquired brain injury rehabilitation: A meta-analysis of single-case design interventions research. *Behavioral Interventions, 29,* 77–105.

Horton, A. M., & Barrett, D. (1988). Neuropsychological assessment and behavior therapy: New directions in head trauma rehabilitation. *Journal of Head Trauma Rehabilitation, 3,* 57–64.

Howlin, P., Magiati, I., & Charman, T. (2009). Systematic review of early intensive behavioral interventions for children with autism. *American Journal on Intellectual and Developmental Disabilities, 114,* 23–41.

Jacobson, N. S., Dobson, K. S., Truax, P. A., Addis, M. E., Koerner, K., . . . Prince, S. E. (1996). A component analysis of cognitive-behavioral treatment for depression. *Journal of Consulting and Clinical Psychology, 64,* 295–304.

Kazdin, A. E. (1994). *Behavior modification in applied settings* (5th ed.). Pacific Grove, CA: Brooks/Cole.

Kiernan, C. (1975). Behaviour modification. In D. Bannister (Ed.), *Issues and approaches in the psychological therapies* (pp. 241–260). New York, NY: Wiley.

Kuehnel, J. M., & Liberman, R. P. (1986). Behavior modification. In I. L. Kutash & A. Wolf (Eds.), *Psychotherapist's casebook* (pp. 240–262). San Francisco, CA: Jossey-Bass.

Lancioni, G. E., Van Houten, K., & Ten Hoopen, G. (1997). Reducing excessive vocal loudness in persons with mental retardation through the use of a portable auditory feedback device. *Journal of Behavior Therapy and Experimental Psychiatry, 28,* 123–128.

Lennox, D. B., Miltenberger, R. G., Sprengler, P., & Erfanian, N. (1988). Decelerative treatment practices with persons who have mental retardation: A review of five years of the literature. *American Journal on Mental Retardation, 92,* 492–501.

Lewis, F. D., & Bitter, C. J. (1991). Applied behavior analysis and work adjustment training. In B. T. McMahon (Ed.), *Work worth doing: Advances in brain injury* (pp. 137–165). Boca Raton, FL: CRC Press–St. Lucie Press.

Madle, R. A., & Neisworth, J. T. (1990). Mental retardation. In A. S. Bellack & M. Hersen (Eds.), *International handbook of behavior modification and therapy* (2nd ed., pp. 731–762). New York, NY: Plenum.

Marr, J. N. (1982). Behavioral analysis of work problems. In B. Bolton (Ed.), *Vocational adjustment of disabled persons* (pp. 127–147). Baltimore, MD: University Park Press.

Marzillier, J. S., Lambert, C., & Kellett, J. (1976). A controlled evaluation of systematic desensitization and social skills training for socially inadequate psychiatric patients. *Behavior Research and Therapy, 14,* 225–228.

Matson, J. L., & Smith, K. R. (2008). Current status of intensive behavioral interventions for young children with autism and PDD-NOS. *Research in Autism Spectrum Disorders, 2,* 60–74.

McCracken, L. M. (1997). "Attention" to pain in persons with chronic pain: A behavioral approach. *Behavior Therapy, 28,* 271–284.

McGuire, J. F., Piacentini, J., Brennan, E. A., Lewin, A. B., Murphy, T. K., Small, B. J., & Storch, E. A. (2014). A meta-analysis of behavior therapy for Tourette syndrome. *Journal of Psychiatric Research, 50,* 106–112.

Morin, C. M., Culbert, J. P., & Schwartz, S. M. (1994). Nonpharmacological interventions for insomnia. *American Journal of Psychiatry, 151,* 1172–1180.

Morley, S., Eccleston, C., & Williams, A. (1999). Systematic review and meta-analysis of randomized controlled trials of cognitive behavior therapy and behavior therapy for chronic pain in adults, excluding headache. *Pain, 80,* 1–13.

Mueser, K. T. (1993). Schizophrenia. In A. S. Bellack & M. Hersen (Eds.), *Handbook of behavior therapy in the psychiatric setting* (pp. 269–292). New York, NY: Plenum.

Murtagh, D. R., & Greenwood, K. M. (1995). Identifying effective psychological treatments for insomnia: A meta-analysis. *Journal of Consulting and Clinical Psychology, 63,* 79–89.

Nye, C., Vanryckeghem, M., Schwartz, J. B., Herder, C., Turner, H. M., & Howard, C. (2013). Behavioral stuttering interventions for children and adolescents: A systematic review and meta-analysis. *Journal of Speech, Language, and Hearing Research, 56,* 921–932.

Paisey, T. J. H., & Whitney, R. B. (1989). A long-term case study of analysis, response suppression, and treatment maintenance involving life-threatening pica. *Behavioral Residential Treatment, 4,* 191–211.

Papajohn, J. C. (1982). *Intensive behavior therapy: The behavioral treatment of complex emotional disorders.* New York, NY: Pergamon.

Pavlov, I. P. (1927). *Conditioned reflexes: An investigation of the physiological activity of the cerebral cortex* (G. V. Anrep, Trans. & Ed.). London, UK: Oxford University Press.

Peine, H. A., Darvish, R., Blakelock, H., Osborne, J. G., & Jenson, W. R. (1998). Non-aversive reduction of cigarette smoking in two adult men in a residential setting. *Journal of Behavior Therapy and Experimental Psychiatry, 29,* 55–65.

Piazza, C. C., Fisher, W. W., Hanley, G. P., LeBlanc, L. A., Worsdell, A. S., Lindauer, S. E., & Keeney, K. M. (1998). Treatment of pica through multiple analyses of its reinforcing functions. *Journal of Applied Behavior Analysis, 31,* 165–189.

Prendergast, M., Podus, D., Finney, J., Greenwell, L., & Roll, J. (2006). Contingency management for treatment of substance use disorders: A meta-analysis. *Addiction, 101,* 1546–1560.

Reichow, B. (2012). Overview of meta-analyses on early intensive behavioral intervention for young children with autism spectrum disorders. *Journal of Autism and Developmental Disorders, 42,* 512–520.

Rogers, S. J., & Vismara, L. A. (2008). Evidence-based comprehensive treatments for early autism. *Journal of Clinical Child & Adolescent Psychology, 37,* 8–38.

Rotgers, F. (1996). Behavioral therapy of substance abuse treatment: Bringing science to bear on practice. In F. Rotgers, D. S. Keller, & J. Morgenstern (Eds.), *Treating substance abuse: Theory and technique* (pp. 174–201). New York, NY: Guilford.

Schloss, P. J., & Smith, M. A. (1994). *Applied behavior analysis in the classroom.* Boston, MA: Allyn & Bacon.

Schweitzer, J. B., & Sulzer-Azaroff, B. (1988). Self-control: Teaching tolerance for delay in impulsive children. *Journal of the Experimental Analysis of Behavior, 50,* 173–186.

Slater, M. A., Doctor, J. N., Pruitt, S. D., & Atkinson, J. H. (1997). The clinical significance of behavioral treatment for chronic low back pain: An evaluation of effectiveness. *Pain, 71,* 257–263.

Smith, M. L., Glass, G. V., & Miller, T. I. (1980). *The benefits of psychotherapy.* Baltimore, MA: Johns Hopkins University Press.

Smith, M. T., Perlis, M. L., Park, A., Smith, M. S., Pennington, J., Giles, D. E., & Buysse, D. J. (2002). Comparative meta-analysis of pharmacotherapy and behavior therapy for persistent insomnia. *American Journal of Psychiatry, 159,* 5–11.

Spreckley, M., & Boyd, R. (2009). Efficacy of applied behavioral intervention in preschool children with autism for improving cognitive, language, and adaptive behavior: A systematic review and meta-analysis. *Journal of Pediatrics, 154,* 338–344.

Stanley, M. A., & Turner, S. M. (1996). Current status of pharmacological and behavioral treatment of obsessive-compulsive disorder. *Behavior Therapy, 26,* 163–186.

Thieme, K., & Turk, D. C. (2012). Cognitive-behavioral and operant-behavioral therapy for people with fibromyalgia. *Reumatismo, 64,* 275–285.

Trull, T. J., Nietzel, M. T., & Main, A. (1988). The use of meta-analysis to assess the clinical significance of behavior therapy for agoraphobia. *Behavior Therapy, 19,* 527–538.

van Balkom, A. J., van Oppen, P., Vermeulen, A. W., van Dyck, R., Nauta, M. C., & Vorst, H. (1994). A meta-analysis on the treatment of obsessive-compulsive disorder: A comparison of antidepressants, behavior, and cognitive therapy. *Clinical Psychology Review, 14,* 359–381.

Virués-Ortega, J. (2010). Applied behavior analytic intervention for autism in early childhood: Meta-analysis, meta-regression and dose-response meta-analysis of multiple outcomes. *Clinical Psychology Review, 30,* 387–399.

Walker, D., Greenwood, C. R., & Terry, B. (1994). Management of classroom disruptive behavior and academic performance problems. In L. W. Craighead, W. E. Craighead, A. E. Kazdin, & M. J. Mahoney (Eds.), *Cognitive and behavioral interventions: An empirical approach to mental health problems* (pp. 215–234). Boston, MA: Allyn & Bacon.

Williams, G. E., & Cuvo, A. J. (1986). Training apartment upkeep skills to rehabilitation clients: A comparison of task analytic strategies. *Journal of Applied Behavior Analysis, 19,* 39–51.

Wilson, G. T. (1995). Behavior therapy. In R. J. Corsini & D. Wedding (Eds.), *Current psychotherapies* (5th ed., pp. 197–228). Itasca, IL: Peacock.

Ylvisaker, M., Turkstra, L., Coehlo, C., Yorkston, K., Kennedy, M., Sohlberg, M. M., & Avery, J. (2007). Behavioral interventions for children and adults with behavior disorders after TBI: A systematic review of the evidence. *Brain Injury, 21,* 769–805.

# Trait–Factor Theory and Counseling Process

*John F. Kosciulek, Brian N. Phillips, and Michelle C. Lizotte*

## LEARNING OBJECTIVES

The goals of this chapter are to provide a historical overview of the trait–factor theory, including a definition of major constructs; to describe the trait–factor counseling process and theoretical assumptions; to review empirical evidence supporting trait–factor approaches and areas in need of further study; and to provide specific applications of the trait–factor approach in rehabilitation counseling. After reading the chapter, readers should be able to:

1. Discuss major historical milestones in the development of the trait–factor approach.
2. List the three broad factors believed to be involved in the wise choice of a vocation.
3. Explain the evolution of trait–factor to person–environment theory.
4. Weigh the evidence for using a trait–factor approach in rehabilitation counseling.

## HISTORY OF THE TRAIT–FACTOR APPROACH

The trait–factor counseling approach rests on the assumptions that people have different traits, that occupations require a particular combination of worker characteristics, and that effective vocational counseling matches a person's traits with job requirements (Parsons, 1909). Because trait–factor counseling has proven effective in assisting people with disabilities in securing employment (Dawis & Lofquist, 1984; Hershenson & Szymanski, 1992), it has been widely used in rehabilitation counseling (Kosciulek, 1993; Lynch & Maki, 1981; Schmitt & Growick, 1985; Thomas, Thoreson, Butler, & Parker, 1992).

The origins of the trait–factor approach can be traced to Parsons's (1909) proposition that vocational choice involves the individual, the work environment, and an understanding of the relationship between the two. Parsons developed the first major theory of vocational counseling, based on the assumptions that people have different traits, that occupations require a particular combination of worker characteristics, and that effective vocational guidance matches a person's traits with job requirements. The objective of vocational guidance, according to Parsons, is to match a person's traits with a particular combination of worker characteristics. He advocated that individuals should gain a full understanding of their personal attributes, including both strengths and weaknesses, along with a thorough understanding of the conditions of success in given occupations. Parsons developed his approach in response to the dramatic social, political, and economic upheavals that were occurring in the United States in the early 20th century. Trait–factor counseling offered a pragmatic approach to the resultant problems of occupational choice and adjustment, particularly among young adults (Swanson, 1996). Parsons's ideas provided the impetus for research and continued development of the trait–factor approach (Kosciulek, 1993).

Through the efforts of researchers affiliated with the Minnesota Employment Stability Research Institute at the University of Minnesota, Parsons's ideas were expanded after his death. Drawing from differential psychology, the Minnesota group developed tests and other psychometric instruments that provided career counselors and clients with tools to conduct the personal analysis necessary for effective vocational decision making. Early applications of the instruments developed by the Minnesota group included assessment of the vocational abilities of unemployed people during the Great Depression and classifying and assigning military personnel during World War II. Many of the vocational tests and occupational information systems used in career counseling today (e.g., Minnesota Importance Questionnaire) are direct descendants of the Minnesota research (Chartrand, 1991). One of the members of the Minnesota group, E. G. Williamson, emerged as the major spokesperson for the Minnesota point of view, a term often used synonymously with trait–factor counseling.

The trait–factor approach was the sole method of career counseling until the emergence of client-centered therapy in the 1950s (see Chapter 2 in this volume). Associated with the introduction of Carl Rogers's (1942) publication, *Counseling and Psychotherapy*, the emergence of client-centered therapy corresponded not only with a decline in trait–factor counseling, specifically, but also with an overall decline in career counseling in general (Crites, 1981). According to Chartrand (1991), the maturation and ensuing sophistication of developmental and social learning approaches also had the effect of displacing trait–factor counseling as the unique approach to career counseling.

### Evolution of the Trait–Factor Counseling Approach

When client-centered therapy became the preferred mode of counseling, a concomitant value was placed on the role of the client–counselor relationship as the means for therapeutic change. The role of the counselor was accordingly de-emphasized, and so, in turn, was the role of the counselor as the expert in the counseling relationship. Trait–factor counseling was perceived and criticized as being overly directive (Swanson, 1996). In addition, the trait–factor approach was criticized as oversimplifying the complexities of counseling people with a wide range of career problems and causing counselors to underserve the needs of clients (Krumboltz, 1994). Further, Crites (1981) stated that trait–factor counseling ignored the psychological realities of decision making that lead to indecision and unrealism in career choice. His often-referenced characterization of trait–factor counseling was "three interviews and a cloud of dust."

According to Rounds and Tracey (1990), however, after an approximate 20-year hiatus, reports of the death of trait–factor counseling were greatly exaggerated. In revisiting the original works of Williamson (1965, 1972), it was noted that influential reviewers had misinterpreted the writings and had made assumptions without corresponding documentation. Brown (1990) argued that counselors who applied a simplistic formulation of Williamson's model did not fully understand the approach. Brown further observed that in the ensuing years, no other career counseling approach or theory had satisfactorily replaced "trait-oriented" thinking. Rounds and Tracey (1990) also reported that Holland's (1973, 1985) research and conceptualizations have expanded and clarified the original Parsonian assumptions of matching people and occupations, leading to current trait–factor practices that are more flexible, efficient, and effective. Rounds and Tracy stated that the present vocational assessment practice is linked historically to trait–factor conceptions of vocational counseling, and further, that current assessment processes continue to be influenced by the original Parsonian assumptions.

Zytowski and Borgen (1983) described how trait–factor counseling has evolved from Parsons's developmental model to a congruence model. The congruence model focuses on matching and choice processes, in which the person's work personality matches the demands and characteristics of the job (Zanskas & Strohmer, 2010). As discussed by Zytowski and Borgen, primary assumptions of the model include the following: (a) Well-adapted individuals within an occupation share certain psychological characteristics, (b) measurable and practical differences exist among people and occupations, (c) outcome is a function of individual–environment fit, and (d) person and job characteristics demonstrate sufficient time and situation consistency to justify prediction of outcome over the long term.

## MAJOR TRAIT–FACTOR COUNSELING CONCEPTS

Parsons (1909) believed that choosing a vocation was more important than securing work, and he postulated that there were three broad factors involved in the wise choice of a vocation. The first factor was knowledge of self, aptitudes, interests, ambitions, resources, and limitations. The second was knowledge of the requirements and conditions of success, advantages and disadvantages of specific jobs, compensation, opportunities, and prospects in different lines of work. The third factor was accurate reasoning on the relation of these two groups of facts.

Traits offered a definition of human behavior in terms of categories such as aptitudes and interests that could be integrated into constellations of individual characteristics called factors. Traits, and assessment instruments that measure the traits, make up one major set of ingredients in trait–factor theory. The second major set of ingredients is composed of job factors or requirements, which are often gleaned from job analyses. Individual traits are then compared to job factors to determine potential matches. In the trait–factor counseling approach, traits and factors are first defined and operationalized. A problem-solving matching method is then applied that leads to predictable outcomes across varied individuals and work environments (Gilliland, James, & Bowman, 1994; McKay, Bright, & Pryor, 2005).

### Underlying Assumptions of the Trait–Factor Approach

As discussed by Kosciulek (1993), the trait–factor counseling approach rests on the assumption that people have different traits and that occupations require a particular combination of worker characteristics. In the trait–factor approach, effective vocational guidance matches the person's traits with job requirements. In the development of his model, however, Parsons (1909) was mostly concerned with the process of career choice, rather than job placement, and it was not until later formulations of the trait–factor theory (e.g., Williamson, 1972) that environmental factors were stressed.

Key assumptions of the trait–factor counseling approach include the following: (a) Each person is keyed to a few correct occupations, (b) clients need vocational guidance to avoid wasting time and risking the selection of an inappropriate occupation, (c) correct occupations influence other personal decisions over time, (d) occupational decisions remain constant, (e) trait–factor counseling provides information about many relevant aspects of life, (f) life is generally predictable, and (g) the trait–factor approach provides a basis for action as well as providing a number of useful comparisons of individual traits to job tasks. Another key assumption is that clients will generally have personal problems solved or already under control (Schmitt & Growick, 1985). However, it is also accepted that vocational adjustment has much to do with life adjustment in general and, for many individuals, career factors spill over into other aspects of their lives (Gilliland et al., 1994).

Other researchers (e.g., Crites, 1981; Klein & Weiner, 1977) have reviewed the general assumptions of trait–factor counseling. In addition, Brown (1990) and Kosciulek (1993) have summarized current thinking on the underlying assumptions and propositions of trait–factor theory as follows:

1. Each individual has a unique set of traits that can be measured reliably and validly.
2. Occupations require that workers possess certain very specific traits for success, although a worker with a rather wide range of characteristics can still be successful in a given job.

3. The choice of an occupation is a rather straightforward process, and matching is possible.
4. The closer the match between personal characteristics and job requirements, the greater the likelihood of success (as indicated by productivity and satisfaction).

### Trait–Factor Counseling Process

Williamson (1965, 1972) articulated an empirically oriented counseling process guided by Parsons's concept of matching people and work environments. Williamson emphasized the importance of reliably and accurately assessing career problems and individual characteristics. He viewed counseling as facilitating self-understanding, realistic planning, and decision-making skills (Chartrand, 1991).

Williamson (1972) described a six-step counseling process that included analysis, synthesis, diagnosis, prognosis, counseling, and follow-up. The first three steps involve the gathering of demographic and clinical information, synthesizing that information to determine client strengths and limitations, and then drawing inferences based on those strengths and developmental needs. A diagnosis is based on both the nature and cause of the career development or vocational decision-making problem (Brown, 1990).

The counselor next formulates a prognosis by estimating the probability of client adjustment under different conditions or choice options. The prognosis is then followed by a rational, problem-solving approach to counseling that includes follow-up after the client makes a career decision. In the trait–factor counseling process, the counselor assumes a tutorial or advisory role with the client. Typical trait–factor counseling activities include assisting the client in obtaining data about self or jobs, presenting and discussing alternative options and actions, and attempting to help the client reach the best choice or decision (Rounds & Tracey, 1990).

## APPLICATIONS OF THE TRAIT–FACTOR APPROACH TO REHABILITATION COUNSELING

Several authors have shown the utility of the trait–factor approach for rehabilitation counseling practice. Hershenson and Szymanski (1992, p. 282) pointed out that the foundation of trait–factor theory could be found in most current rehabilitation practices in both the public and private sectors. They went on to state that job-matching systems, analysis of transferable skills, and ecological assessment processes used in supported employment are "obvious manifestations of trait–factor theory in current rehabilitation practice." Further, Lynch and Maki (1981) presented a structure for vocational rehabilitation services based on a trait–factor approach, viewing the rehabilitation counselor as a problem solver, with the goal of assisting clients in achieving optimal functional independence.

In the trait–factor approach, vocational difficulties are viewed as resulting from a lack of information and the inability to make effective decisions. Hence, consistent with the rehabilitation philosophies of empowerment and consumer choice (Kosciulek, 1999), the trait–factor approach to rehabilitation counseling attempts to improve client problem-solving and decision-making skills, promoting self-determination. A client's vocational and personality traits are considered to be measurable and stable but not rigid. Lynch and Maki (1981) considered the assessment of client interests, aptitudes, and skills to be the core of trait–factor rehabilitation counseling.

Schmitt and Growick (1985) also examined the trait–factor approach from a rehabilitation perspective. These authors viewed trait–factor counseling as most useful when little or no prospect for independent client change appears possible. They suggested that rehabilitation counselors might successfully apply trait–factor methods in persons with mental, physical, or emotional impairments who find job selection difficult and confusing. They viewed the rehabilitation counselor as a mediator in facilitating the placement and adjustment process.

Thomas et al. (1992) reported that trait–factor counseling closely parallels the practice of most rehabilitation counselors, particularly in state vocational rehabilitation agencies. The goals of trait–factor counseling are characterized as being generally congruent with the broader goals of rehabilitation. Thomas et al. reported that trait–factor counseling techniques are usually well within the repertoire of skills of many rehabilitation counselors and are deemed appropriate in most rehabilitation settings. The existing literature thus strongly suggests that the trait–factor counseling approach is useful for rehabilitation counseling in meeting the needs of persons with disabilities.

Support for the use of trait–factor counseling in rehabilitation has been provided through research conducted to test the validity of the Minnesota Theory of Work Adjustment (MTWA; Dawis & Lofquist, 1984). Because the MTWA was developed specifically to address the needs of persons with disabilities, it has provided rehabilitation counselors with a systematic and reliable model for applying trait–factor counseling methods. Consistent with the general trait–factor approach, the MTWA focuses on matching an individual with a work environment. Lofquist and Dawis (1969, p. 46), originators of the theory, defined work adjustment as the "continuous and dynamic process by which the individual seeks to achieve and maintain correspondence with the work environment." In the MTWA, the work adjustment process involves matching the person's abilities and work-related needs, respectively, with the ability requirements and reinforcer system of the work environment. The match between the person's abilities and the ability requirements of the work environment determines satisfactoriness (i.e., the extent to which the person is able to perform the job). The match between the person's needs and the reinforcer systems of the work environment determine the person's satisfaction with the job. Tenure, the length of time the person stays on the job, is a function of both satisfaction and satisfactoriness (Hershenson & Szymanski, 1992).

While providing a theoretical framework for vocational rehabilitation programs serving persons with disabilities, the MTWA also offers a way to conceptualize disability, to identify vocational assessment information needed, to suggest counseling procedures, and to evaluate the effectiveness of rehabilitation counseling (Dawis & Lofquist, 1984). However, because it is based on a trait–factor approach, the MTWA is susceptible to the same criticisms as general trait–factor theory.

## SCIENTIFIC EVIDENCE SUPPORTING THE TRAIT–FACTOR APPROACH

Evidence-based rehabilitation counseling practice is the integration of the best available research with clinical expertise in the context of client characteristics and preferences (Kosciulek, 2010). In evidence-based rehabilitation counseling practice, the practitioner assesses current and past research, clinical guidelines, and other information resources, with the goal of providing the most effective rehabilitation counseling services. As the most researched career development theory, trait–factor theory offers an extensive research base for consideration (Furnham, 2001). Measured outcomes that are expected to correlate with congruence include job satisfaction, performance, commitment, well-being, intentions for tenure and actual tenure, with job satisfaction being the most commonly studied outcome.

Although trait–factor or person–environment theory considers fit holistically, most empirical studies have used Holland's six personality profiles for operationalizing and testing fit outcomes. This limited operationalization of fit has not shown as strong an effect between congruence and job satisfaction as might have been expected, with congruence accounting for no more than 5% of the variance in job satisfaction across several meta-analyses (Assouline & Meir, 1987; Tranberg, Slane, & Ekeberg, 1993; Tsabari, Tziner, & Meir, 2005). However, evidence still supports the broader theoretical tenets of person–environment fit (Cable & DeRue, 2002; Furnham, 2001; Rehfuss, Gambrell, & Meyer, 2011; Verquer, Beehr, & Wagner, 2003), particularly when fit is operationalized and measured using more than one dimension (e.g., abilities, needs, and values).

As previously mentioned, much of the vocational rehabilitation process assumes fit to be of great importance. The relatively little research regarding fit has been mixed at best. Beveridge and Fabian (2007) conducted a study with 171 vocational rehabilitation clients in Maryland and found a connection between congruent vocational goals and wages, but not between congruent vocational goals and vocational satisfaction. Bond, Campbell, and Becker (2012) found no relationship between congruence and the criterion variables of job start, job satisfaction, and job tenure in the first job after receiving vocational rehabilitation services. Despite unfavorable results, it does not seem reasonable to assume that fit does not matter; rather, it appears necessary to better understand fit and its relationship to successful employment outcomes.

It seems clear that the measurement of person–environment fit is much more complicated as a construct than is typically conveyed in research. Future research on person–environment fit should consider what personal traits and environmental factors are most salient in which contexts, with great attention being paid to how salient environmental factors are measured. It is easy to recognize how two positions in the same occupation, but in different organizations, may differ in ways that influence perceived fit, and these differences are not recognized in occupational coding systems, such as the *Dictionary of Occupational Titles*. Arnold (2004) made several suggestions for improving research efforts to link congruence with successful vocational outcomes using Holland's theory; these suggestions include expanding the theory to include more constructs, improving measurement of the environment, and improving the precision of congruence measures.

Further, there is a dearth of research on the implementation of person–environment theory in counseling settings. No research articles could be found in the vocational rehabilitation literature that measured job outcomes, using the method of implementing person–environment theory as the predictor. This combination of current knowledge suggests the need for greater caution in implementing what is sometimes erroneously viewed as a simple matching of person and environment, until critical congruencies are identified, and methods for implementation in vocational rehabilitation settings can be validated.

## LIMITATIONS OF THE TRAIT–FACTOR APPROACH FOR REHABILITATION COUNSELING

Numerous authors have addressed the limitations of trait–factor counseling. Hershenson and Szymanski (1992) stated that trait–factor approaches do nothing to compensate for the limited early experiences of persons with congenital disabilities or to suggest supportive interventions that can permit persons with disabilities to enter, function, and sustain themselves in the work environment. Hershenson and Szymanski further reported that the focus of the theory on current individual traits ignores the potential of people with significant disabilities to perform most jobs with appropriate assistive devices and job modifications.

Gilliland et al. (1994) refuted the trait–factor counseling assumption that clients can "see the light" if the facts and consequences of behavior are presented. Weinrach (1979) interpreted Williamson's (1972) supposition that people are rational beings as an overly cognitive view that fails to consider affective processes. He also characterized trait–factor counselors as overly directive and authoritarian. The rehabilitation counselor who is controlling and avoids the emotional impact of work may fail to assist individuals with disabilities with successful adjustment to the work environment (Kosciulek, 1993).

Crites (1981) criticized trait–factor approaches on the grounds that they are atheoretical, analytic, and atomistic in their orientation. The rehabilitation counselor who falls into what Crites described as test and tell counseling that unfolds as three interviews and a cloud of dust is most likely not providing individualized or comprehensive services (Kosciulek, 1993). Hershenson and Szymanski (1992) questioned how trait–factor counseling approaches could describe the human personality in all its dimensions when client motivation is not considered in the counseling process. Finally, Kosciulek concluded that trait–factor counseling may be prone to ignoring interactions of a familial, social, economic, or political nature, which are variables that are critical to successful employment and independent living for persons with disabilities. In sum, a lack of comprehensiveness in trait–factor counseling is a consistent point of attack by critics.

As described in the following section, recent advances in trait–factor counseling theory, however, provide rehabilitation counselors with a model for overcoming the limitations of trait–factor counseling approaches. The person × environment (P × E) fit approach (Chartrand, 1991; Kosciulek, 1993; Rounds & Tracey, 1990), which is an updated perspective on trait–factor counseling, extends beyond the assessment of individual abilities and work factors and captures the dynamic nature of person–environment interactions. Hence, many of the previous criticisms of trait–factor counseling are no longer fully warranted.

### Contemporary Trait–Factor Counseling: The P × E Fit Approach

During the 1990s, a general conceptual shift from a trait-oriented to a P × E perspective occurred in the rehabilitation, counseling, and psychology literature. The focus of trait–factor theory has moved from a static matching view to a more dynamic interpretation of persons selecting and shaping environments (Hershenson, 1996; Pervin, 1987; Tansey, Mizelle, Ferrin, Tschopp, & Frain, 2004). From a P × E perspective, the guiding questions in rehabilitation counseling have become the following: (a) What kinds of personal and environmental factors are salient in predicting vocational choice and adjustment? (b) How is the process of person and environment interaction best characterized (Kosciulek, 1993)?

Chartrand (1991) described three basic assumptions that have been transmitted from original trait–factor vocational counseling to the P × E fit approach. First, people are viewed as capable of making rational decisions. Affective processes are not ignored; rather, a cognitive orientation guides the search for intervention tactics. Rehabilitation counseling is embodied as a cognitive approach that emphasizes learning processes (Kosciulek, 1993).

Second, people and work environments differ in reliable, meaningful, and consistent ways. This assumption does not mean that a person with a disability prefers and best performs a specific job. Rather, it implies that important work behaviors, skill patterns, and working conditions can be identified to organize both people and work environments. The third assumption states that the better the congruence between personal characteristics and job requirements, the greater the likelihood of success. This means that knowledge of person and environmental patterns can be used to inform people about the probability of satisfaction and adjustment to different work settings (Kosciulek, 1993). The P × E fit approach moves beyond the assumption of congruence to include the notion of dynamic reciprocity (Rounds & Tracey, 1990); that is, P × E is a reciprocal process, with individuals shaping the environment and the environment influencing individuals.

The counseling style in P × E counseling is generally a supportive, teaching approach with the types of treatment and intervention recommended as a function of the level of the client's information-processing abilities. A teaching approach is well suited for clients who are motivated and willing, but may lack the skills, understanding, ability, or confidence to effect change (Chartrand, 1991).

In the P × E fit approach, clients are considered as capable of rational decision making. It is also assumed that reliable and meaningful individual differences can be assessed and that psychometric instruments may be used to predict relevant personal and occupational criteria (Chartrand, 1991). Given time pressures, it is usually conducted within a brief counseling framework. In further consideration of time–money economy, P × E principles are well suited for group counseling (Lunneborg, 1983). A specific example of a rehabilitation-related P × E group counseling approach is the job club (Azrin & Besalel, 1980), which is used in providing job development and placement services.

As the job club illustrates, trait–factor counseling in rehabilitation has generally been thought of in relation to career counseling and job placement. However, Rounds and Tracey (1990) proposed that the P × E approach has a broader range of applications than just vocational problems. More specifically, a P × E problem-solving framework that integrates components of decision making and information processing could be applied to a diverse array of clients with varying needs and goals. Support for this concept can be drawn from Blustein and Spengler (1995). These researchers found that a P × E career counseling approach resulted in significant and positive noncareer outcomes, including improved self-concept (self-esteem and interpersonal competence), more positive personal attitudes, an increased internal locus of control, and decreased levels of anxiety. This extended application of the P × E approach lends support to the expanded MTWA conceptual framework proposed by Lofquist and Dawis (1991) that includes the interrelationship among personal, interpersonal, and environmental factors.

The current P × E interaction model expands the original formulations of trait–factor counseling. It differs from earlier trait–factor theory in that the P × E approach considers the joint contribution of two variables, person and environment, in the prediction of behavior. Trait–factor formulations, on the other hand, were generally focused on the contributions of person-centered traits (Chartrand, Strong, & Weitzman, 1995). The P × E model generates information that is pragmatically useful in understanding the world of work and how people fit into it. Therefore, the contemporary P × E fit counseling approach serves as a useful model for the provision of vocational counseling in a variety of settings, including rehabilitation counseling for persons with disabilities.

## CONCLUSIONS

Persons with disabilities often seek rehabilitation services to enhance the match between themselves and their work, home, or community environments. The trait–factor counseling approach has proven effective for assisting people with disabilities in securing and maintaining employment (Dawis & Lofquist, 1984; Hershenson & Szymanski, 1992), and it has been widely used in rehabilitation counseling (Lynch & Maki, 1981; Schmitt & Growick, 1985; Thomas et al., 1992). However, numerous criticisms and limitations of trait–factor counseling have been cited in the career counseling and rehabilitation literature (e.g., Gilliland et al., 1994; Kosciulek, 1993). In this chapter, an updated perspective on trait–factor counseling, the P × E fit approach, was considered as a potentially useful model for counseling persons with disabilities in rehabilitation settings. This approach compensates for previous criticisms of trait–factor counseling by considering the reciprocal and dynamic relationship between the individual and the environment. Through ecological P × E rehabilitation counseling, persons with disabilities can be empowered to maximize the quality of their interpersonal and vocational life activities.

## DISCUSSION EXERCISES

1. What are some of the unique strengths and weaknesses of applying a trait–factor approach to the career development and job planning of people with disabilities?
2. The labor market today looks very different than it did when the trait–factor approach was originally created. Do you think the changes in the labor market increased or decreased the applicability of a trait–factor approach in selecting a job?
3. Reflect for a moment on your career choice. Discuss as a group some of the factors that influenced career choices, and identify the three steps of trait–factor theory as they arise. What things influenced your career choice not tied to the trait–factor theory?
4. Discuss whether a great trait–factor match in career planning ensures a high level of job satisfaction. Provide a rationale for your opinion.
5. Discuss ways for handling a situation in which the client's perceived occupational match appears to be problematic to the counselor as a result of gaps in ability, values, pay, or other factors.

## REFERENCES

Arnold, J. (2004). The congruence problem in John Holland's theory of vocational decisions. *Journal of Occupational and Organizational Psychology, 77*, 95–113.

Assouline, M., & Meir, E. I. (1987). Meta-analysis of the relationship between congruence and well-being measures. *Journal of Vocational Behavior, 31*, 319–332.

Azrin, N. H., & Besalel, V. A. (1980). *Job club counselor's manual: A behavioral approach to vocational counseling.* Austin, TX: Pro-Ed.

Beveridge, S., & Fabian, E. (2007). Vocational rehabilitation outcomes: Relationship between individualized plan for employment goals and employment outcomes. *Rehabilitation Counseling Bulletin, 50*, 238–246.

Blustein, D. L., & Spengler, P. M. (1995). Personal adjustment: Career counseling and psychotherapy. In W. B. Walsh & S. H. Osipow (Eds.), *Handbook of vocational psychology: Theory, research, and practice* (2nd ed., pp. 295–329). Hillsdale, NJ: Erlbaum.

Bond, G. R., Campbell, K., & Becker, D. R. (2012). A test of the occupational matching hypothesis for rehabilitation clients with severe mental illness. *Journal of Occupational Rehabilitation, 23*, 261–269.

Brown, D. (1990). Trait and factor theory. In D. Brown, L. Brooks, & Associates (Eds.), *Career choice and development* (pp. 13–36). San Francisco, CA: Jossey-Bass.

Cable, D. M., & DeRue, D. S. (2002). The convergent and discriminant validity of subjective fit perceptions. *Journal of Applied Psychology, 87*, 875–884.

Chartrand, J. M. (1991). The evolution of trait-and-factor career counseling: A person x environment fit approach. *Journal of Counseling and Development, 69*, 518–524.

Chartrand, J. M., Strong, S. R., & Weitzman, L. M. (1995). The interactional perspective in vocational psychology: Paradigms, theories, and research practices. In W. B. Walsh & S. H. Osipow (Eds.), *Handbook of vocational psychology: Theory, research, and practice* (2nd ed., pp. 35–65). Hillsdale, NJ: Erlbaum.

Crites, J. O. (1981). *Career counseling: Models, methods, and materials.* New York, NY: McGraw-Hill.

Dawis, R. V., & Lofquist, L. H. (1984). *A psychological theory of work adjustment.* Minneapolis, MN: University of Minnesota Press.

Furnham, A. (2001). Vocational preference and P-O fit: Reflections on Holland's theory of vocational choice. *Applied Psychology: An International Review, 50*, 5–29.

Gilliland, B. E., James, R. K., & Bowman, J. T. (1994). *Theories and strategies in counseling and psychology* (3rd ed.). Boston, MA: Allyn & Bacon.

Hershenson, D. B. (1996). Work adjustment: A neglected area in career counseling. *Journal of Counseling & Development, 74*, 442–446.

Hershenson, D. B., & Szymanski, E. M. (1992). Career development of people with disabilities. In R. M. Parker & E. M. Szymanski (Eds.), *Rehabilitation counseling: Basics and beyond* (2nd ed., pp. 273–303). Austin, TX: Pro-Ed.

Holland, J. L. (1973). *Making vocational choices: A theory of careers.* Englewood Cliffs, NJ: Prentice Hall.

Holland, J. L. (1985). *Making vocational choices: A theory of vocational personalities and work environments* (2nd ed.). Englewood Cliffs, NJ: Prentice Hall.

Klein, K. L., & Weiner, Y. (1977). Interest congruency as a moderator of the relationship between job tenure and job satisfaction and mental health. *Journal of Vocational Behavior, 10*, 91–98.

Kosciulek, J. F. (1993). Advances in trait-and-factor theory: A person x environment fit approach to rehabilitation counseling. *Journal of Applied Rehabilitation Counseling, 24*(2), 11–14.

Kosciulek, J. F. (1999). Consumer direction in disability policy formulation and rehabilitation service delivery. *Journal of Rehabilitation, 65*(2), 4–9.

Kosciulek, J. F. (2010). Evidence-based rehabilitation counseling practice: A pedagogical imperative. *Rehabilitation Education, 24*, 205–212.

Krumboltz, J. D. (1994). Improving career development theory from a social learning perspective. In M. L. Savickas & R. W. Lent (Eds.), *Convergence in career development theories: Implications for science and practice* (pp. 9–31). Palo Alto, CA: CPP Books.

Lofquist, L. H., & Dawis, R. V. (1969). *Adjustment to work: A psychological view of man's problems in a work-oriented society.* New York, NY: Appleton-Century-Crofts.

Lofquist, L. H., & Dawis, R. V. (1991). *Essentials of person–environment correspondence counseling.* Minneapolis, MN: University of Minneapolis Press.

Lunneborg, P. W. (1983). Career counseling techniques. In W. B. Walsh & S. H. Osipow (Eds.), *Handbook of vocational psychology: Applications* (Vol. 2). Hillsdale, NJ: Erlbaum.

Lynch, R. K., & Maki, D. R. (1981). Searching for structure: A trait-factor approach to vocational rehabilitation. *Vocational Guidance Quarterly, 30*, 61–68.

McKay, H., Bright, J. E. H., & Pryor, R. G. L. (2005). Finding order and direction from chaos: A comparison of chaos career counseling and trait matching. *Journal of Employment Counseling, 42*, 98–112.

Parsons, F. (1909). *Choosing a vocation.* Boston, MA: Houghton Mifflin.

Pervin, L. A. (1987). Person–environment congruence in light of the person–situation controversy. *Journal of Vocational Behavior, 31*, 222–230.

Rehfuss, M. C., Gambrell, C. E., & Meyer, D. (2011). Counselors' perceived person–environment fit and career satisfaction. *Career Development Quarterly, 60,* 145–151.

Rogers, C. R. (1942). *Counseling and psychotherapy: Newer concepts in practice.* Boston, MA: Houghton Mifflin.

Rounds, J. B., & Tracey, T. J. (1990). From trait-and-factor to person–environment fit counseling: Theory and process. In W. B. Walsh & S. H. Osipow (Eds.), *Career counseling: Contemporary topics in vocational psychology* (pp. 1–44). Hillsdale, NJ: Erlbaum.

Schmitt, P., & Growick, B. (1985). Trait-factor approach to counseling: Revisited and reapplied. *Journal of Applied Rehabilitation Counseling, 16,* 100–106.

Swanson, J. (1996). The theory is the practice: Trait-and-factor/person environment fit counseling. In M. L. Savickas & W. B. Walsh (Eds.), *Handbook of career counseling theory and practice* (pp. 93–108). Palo Alto, CA: Davies-Black.

Tansey, T. N., Mizelle, N., Ferrin, J. N., Tschopp, M. K., & Frain, M. (2004). Work related stress and the demand-control support framework: Implications for the p x e model. *Journal of Rehabilitation, 70,* 34–41.

Thomas, K. R., Thoreson, R., Butler, A., & Parker, R. M. (1992). Theoretical foundations of rehabilitation counseling. In R. M. Parker & E. M. Szymanski (Eds.), *Rehabilitation counseling: Basics and beyond* (2nd ed., pp. 207–247). Austin, TX: Pro-Ed.

Tranberg, M., Slane, S., & Ekeberg, S. E. (1993). The relation between interest congruence and satisfaction: A meta-analysis. *Journal of Vocational Behavior, 42,* 253–264.

Tsabari, O., Tziner, A., & Meir, E. I. (2005). Updated meta-analysis on the relationship between congruence and satisfaction. *Journal of Career Assessment, 13,* 216–232.

Verquer, M. L., Beehr, T. A., & Wagner, S. H. (2003). A meta-analysis of relations between person–organization fit and work attitudes. *Journal of Vocational Behavior, 63,* 473–489.

Weinrach, S. G. (1979). Trait-and-factor counseling: Yesterday and today. In S. G. Weinrach (Ed.), *Career counseling: Theoretical and practical perspectives* (pp. 59–69). New York, NY: McGraw-Hill.

Williamson, E. G. (1965). *Vocational counseling.* New York, NY: McGraw-Hill.

Williamson, E. G. (1972). Trait-factor theory and individual differences. In B. Stefflre & W. H. Grant (Eds.), *Theories of counseling* (pp. 136–176). New York, NY: McGraw-Hill.

Zanskas, S., & Strohmer, D. C. (2010). Rehabilitation counselor work environment: Examining congruence with prototypic work personality. *Rehabilitation Counseling Bulletin, 53,* 143–152.

Zytowski, D. G., & Borgen, F. H. (1983). Assessment. In W. B. Walsh & S. H. Osipow (Eds.), *Handbook of vocational psychology* (Vol. 2). Hillsdale, NJ: Erlbaum.

# CHAPTER 9

# Psychodynamic Therapy

*Hanoch Livneh and Jerome Siller*

## LEARNING OBJECTIVES

The goals of this chapter are to acquaint the reader with the historical antecedents and conceptual underpinnings of psychodynamic psychotherapy (PDPT), with particular emphasis on its psychoanalytic background; psychodynamic applications to rehabilitation and chronic illness and disability (CID) studies; and research findings that help to appreciate the effectiveness of PDPT, as well as the usefulness of psychodynamic applications, to various rehabilitation and CID-related needs. Readers will achieve the following learning objectives:

1. Become familiarized with the historical antecedents of PDPT.
2. Understand the key concepts of PDPT, including its views on personality structure and the therapeutic process.
3. Get acquainted with the role of defense mechanisms as they apply to adaptation to, and coping with, CID.
4. Understand the impact of CID on body image.
5. Understand the ensued psychosocial reactions to loss and the onset of CID.
6. Understand the psychodynamics that underlie attitudes toward people with CID.
7. Gain awareness of existing empirical support for psychodynamic theory and its concepts, with particular emphasis on their role within the rehabilitation context.
8. Gain awareness of the effectiveness of PDPT.

## HISTORY

Within counseling and psychotherapy, psychodynamically based interventions are distinguished by a focus on the importance of early experience and the role of unconscious mental functioning. In common with other approaches to counseling and psychotherapy, considerable attention is paid to familial, social, vocational, and other aspects of life. It is the manner in which these nonpsychodynamic "realities" are viewed analytically that claims distinctiveness. Character change is usually the goal of psychodynamically oriented treatments, striving to facilitate self-understanding. Alleviation of symptoms, in effect, is viewed as a by-product of characterological change. Psychoanalytic theories of personality development and structures serve as the basis for interventions to facilitate self-awareness, through which the consequences of developmental distortions, conflicts, and arrested development can be changed.

Within psychoanalysis and its various offshoots there is much variation in theory and treatment procedures. Classical psychoanalytic treatment is not typically feasible within rehabilitation settings, but a variety of psychodynamic concepts and procedures clearly have a place. Specific rehabilitation procedures can be informed by these concepts, including those that are not specifically psychodynamic (e.g., interventions involving mourning experiences). Sharp distinctions among various psychoanalytic "schools" or between psychoanalysis and psychotherapy in this context are not necessary. However, to convey the developing nature of psychoanalytic thought and treatment and its present status, a historical view of psychoanalysis follows. By focusing on the vicissitudes of mainstream psychoanalysis, the fundamental thrusts of psychodynamic thinking and applications to rehabilitation may be represented.

Pine (1988) depicted how clinical psychoanalysis has led to the development of four conceptually separate perspectives on the functioning of the human mind: psychologies of drive, ego, object relations, and self. The four perspectives overlap and add to the understanding of both theory and clinical treatment. In addition, expression of the four perspectives can be found in both psychodynamic and nonpsychodynamic approaches to counseling and psychotherapy.

In Freud's drive theory, mental life emerges from strong urges and wishes, shaped by early bodily and family experiences, which serve to power conscious and unconscious fantasies and behaviors. Many fantasies are experienced as dangerous and engender anxiety, guilt, shame, inhibition, symptom formation, and pathological character traits. Early bodily and family experiences are influential in determining personality and, as pointed out by Siller (1976), early bodily experiences can be particularly important in the development of persons with physical disabilities or deformities. Fundamental concepts of the drive theory include a presupposition of universal laws that govern all mental life, both normal and abnormal; psychic determinism; the human organism as an energy system; a personality structure with the constructs of id, ego, and superego; and a complex of other interrelated concepts, including an active unconscious with primary and secondary process modes of thought, repression, resistance, and transference.

Among widely used terms originating in the drive theory are the *id*, *psychosexuality*, *libido*, *fixation*, *repression*, *defense mechanisms*, *narcissism*, *the pleasure principle*, and *metapsychology*.

The catchphrase "where id was there ego shall be" (Freud, 1933/1964, p. 80) characterizes the therapeutic goal of treatment based on the drive theory, with interpretation of the force of unconscious processes and the analysis of resistance and transference as the forces for change. Developments beyond pure instinct theory facilitated an oncoming ego psychology, and structural theory was also introduced (Freud, 1923/1961), along with a signal theory of anxiety (Freud, 1926/1959). Freud postulated, in place of conscious and unconscious systems in mental life, new structures of the id, ego, and superego, explicating their roles in intrapsychic conflict. According to Freud, anxiety is the fundamental phenomenon and focal problem of neurosis. He expanded the concept of anxiety from earlier conceptions where it was seen to result from the discharge of repressed somatic tensions (libido). Freud saw anxiety as a signal of danger to the ego and differentiated among three types: reality, neurotic, and moral anxiety. Defenses were then conceptualized as ego functions, and psychoanalytic treatment expanded from its initial somatic base. In addition to the translation of id forces into consciousness as a treatment goal, analysis of ego functions also came to be emphasized (Freud, 1926/1959).

Ego psychology emerged during the 1930s as the preeminence of the id began to be shared with that of the ego. Functions of the ego were emphasized in terms of capacities for adaptation, reality testing, and defense. Hartmann (1939/1964) introduced a significant emphasis on adaptation to the average expectable environment, attempting to systematize and resolve contradictions in psychoanalytic theory. His conceptions included disagreements with major propositions of Freudian thinking in the development and functioning of the ego, the importance of ego structure in the totality of personality, and the relationship of the person to reality. In addition to the Freudian conception of the id existing at birth and the ego developing out of the id, Hartmann suggested that life begins with an undifferentiated phase during which both the ego and id form out of the totality of the individual's psychological inheritance. Ego development was viewed as an interactive function of biology and environment where heredity and maturation interact with the environmental forces of learning.

Ego psychology expanded psychoanalytic theory to encompass normal as well as abnormal phenomena. Psychoanalytic theory became more receptive to the idea of environmental forces serving as key influences in psychological development. Consciousness and cognitions came to have importance, and therapeutic interventions were then geared to all levels of personality, with the present and recent past then viewed as relevant, along with conscious awareness. Interpretations, although still symbolically based, tend to be less so, with current situations, needs, and explanations given more attention. Object relations theory continued the movement of psychoanalytic thought from drive and instinct theory and has had a profound influence in extending psychoanalytic theory and intervention. The psychology of object relations differs appreciably from the transactional or interpersonal theories of Harry Stack Sullivan, Karen Horney, and Erich Fromm. The latter positions stress the social and interactive nature of human relations and tend to downplay intrapsychic events. Object relations theory focuses on internalization of psychic events and intrapsychic processes. It is the representation and symbolization within the person of the other, rather than the actual transaction between them that serves as the focus.

As characterized by Sandler and Rosenblatt (1962), through conscious and unconscious memories derived from early childhood, an internal drama occurs in which individuals enact one or more of the roles. New experiences are not experienced entirely as new, but are rather processed through internal images that are to varying degrees based on childhood experience. Consistent with the psychoanalytic orientation, these internal dramas are dominated by experience with the primary objects of childhood. What the child experiences, however, is not a "true" representation of the relationship, as object relation consists of memories structured by feelings and wishes active at the time of the experience. As with ego psychology, object relations psychology readily fits within the psychoanalytic model and provides insights into such classical conceptions as transference and countertransference, early psychic development, and ongoing subjective states. The fourth and most recent psychology identified by Pine (1988, p. 574) is self-experience and is the source of much contemporary attention: "What I shall work with as the domain of psychology of self-experience is subjective experience specifically around feelings of self-definition in relation to the object." This domain involves seeing the individual in terms of the ongoing subjective state, particularly around issues of boundaries, continuity, and esteem, reactions to imbalances in that subjective state (Sandler, 1960). Attention is also paid to such central features of the subjective state as degree of differentiation of the self from other, separateness of boundaries, and loss or absence of boundaries.

Self-psychology, as developed by Heinz Kohut, has moved away from customary psychoanalytic thought. Kohut (1971, 1977) approached self-psychology in terms of narcissistic development. He conceptualized the emerging self as composed of the grandiose and idealizing lines of development. Phase-appropriate minor "failures" in empathy of "good-enough" parents, can lead to healthy development. Disturbances in the self arise from severe, phase-inappropriate, and/or chronic frustration of the child's needs for mirroring of grandiosity and for models worthy of idealizing.

The present writers hold with Pine (1988) that all four of the psychologies used as the organizing basis for this review are legitimately psychoanalytic, along with some others that are not mentioned because of space restrictions, and psychoanalysis conceptualizes a complex and multifaceted view of functioning that only psychoanalysis provides. The aforementioned considerations are not intended as "jurisdictional" quibbling but rather to alert those not operating within the psychodynamic/psychoanalytic perspective to the vitality, flexibility, and growth within this framework for application to the multinatured demands of rehabilitation.

## MAJOR CONCEPTS

Psychodynamic theoretical systems, while varying in many ways from classical psychoanalysis and its later derivatives, draw considerably from the psychoanalytic theoretical base. Fundamental techniques and concepts of treatment from psychoanalysis are expanded, transformed, or dropped, depending on the thrust of a particular psychodynamic orientation. In moving to psychodynamic, as contrasted with psychoanalytic counseling and psychotherapy, certain constraints and procedures appropriate to the psychoanalytic process may be relieved and a wider assortment of interventions considered.

A core concept form early psychoanalysis that persists in psychodynamic theory is hedonism, striving for pleasure and avoiding pain. In Freud's instinct theory, Eros, the life drive, is based on general biological energy (libido), which is guided by the pleasure principle and is expressed through self-love, love of others, and the uninhibited pursuit of pleasure. This drive is located in the unconscious and is represented by the id. The core of personality evolves out of a need to reach a compromise between the "pleasure principle" and the "reality principle," the latter embodying parental and societal demands, restrictions, and obligations in the act of seeking gratification. A second major drive proposed by Freud, Thanatos, the death drive, has never received general acceptance and is not discussed here.

Other basic concepts include the idea of a dynamic unconscious, the basic importance of early developmental history and experience, and the preeminent nature of repression. It has already been noted in this chapter that contemporary thinking has not been receptive to the energy theory of drives and other aspects of libido theory, including the well-known development of psychosexual stages. Thus, the libido theory and psychosexual stages are not fundamental concepts in psychodynamic theory, but the concepts of psychosexuality and character neurosis are important.

Primary perspectives in psychoanalysis include the following: (a) a physiological perspective emphasizing biological development; (b) a psychological perspective concerning inner psychological states of consciousness and unconsciousness; and (c) a sociocultural perspective, including the importance of early, family-based experiences in shaping the life (psychological reality) of the individual and the influence of sociocultural beliefs, values, demands, and expectations on families and child-rearing practices (Fine, 1973; Ford & Urban, 1998; Maddi, 1989). Modern psychodynamic models borrow from earlier psychoanalytic concepts, but typically focus on a restricted range of personal and interpersonal domains, such as separation/autonomy versus merger/independence tendencies, interpersonal transactions, and in disability, work by Siller on attitude structure and Shontz on adjustment to disability.

## THEORY OF PERSONALITY

As characterized by Dewald (1978), basic elements of personality emerge from the inevitable conflicts experienced by the infant and young child in their interactions with important people in their environment and are elaborated in various intrapsychic functions and mental processes. Constitutional determinants are highly influential, and the process leads to the establishment of the "core" of personality and psychic function. The core psychic functions and patterns of organization are reasonably well established in most individuals with the passage through the Oedipal phase, and in ordinary psychic development, these core psychological functions undergo repression with the onset of latency. As Dewald pointed out, following Rappaport (1960, p. 536), "'psychic structures' merely describes and defines specific individual psychological functions that, once established, tend to be stereotyped, automatic, unconscious, and tend to have a slow spontaneous rate of change. In other words, the core structures tend to be established early, and to remain relatively unchanged as the basic foundations of subsequent personality development."

Dewald (1978) emphatically rejected the idea that personality development ceases around the time of resolution of the Oedipus phase or that there is a direct causal relationship between psychic functioning in the adult and the core psychic structures established during childhood (the genetic fallacy). A major contribution to organizing the theoretical structure of psychoanalysis, by identifying the minimum number of assumptions on which the system of psychoanalysis is based, was offered by Rappaport and Gill (1959), supplemented by others such as Arlow and Brenner (1964) and Fine (1973). The clinical implications of this conceptualization, as Greenson (1967, pp. 21–22) indicated, are "that in order to comprehend a psychic event thoroughly, it is necessary to analyze it from six different points of view—the topographic, dynamic, economic, genetic, structural, and adaptive."

- **Topographic:** Human consciousness includes a complex hierarchical layering from unconscious (perceived as the most significant determinant of behavior) to preconsciousness, to consciousness. Whereas unconscious activities are governed by primary thought processes, the remaining two are mostly influenced by secondary thought processes.
- **Genetic:** Human behavior follows a temporal process whereby present personality can be explained by earlier life experiences. Present behaviors, including personality traits and neurotic symptoms, are therefore determined by psychosexual phases of development from early childhood and cumulative experience. Biological–constitutional as well as experiential factors are stressed.
- **Dynamic:** Human behavior is determined by the interplay of dynamic impulses or drives. These desire are typically composed of libidinal (sexual) and aggressive drives. Hypotheses concerning instinctual drives, defenses, ego interests, and conflicts are based on this point of view, and examples of dynamics are ambivalence, overdetermination, and symptom formation.
- **Economic:** Human behavior requires energy. As such, it draws, disposes of, and is regulated by psychological energy. This energy feeds psychic structures and process. The processes of binding and neutralizing energy are referred to as cathexes (to objects, such as people).

- **Structural:** Human behavior relies on the interaction among three main personality structures—the id, ego, and superego. These structures are persisting functional units. The id is the storehouse of all drives and instincts. The ego is composed of a group of functions that coordinate and organize behavior, including the ego anxiety-minimizing defense mechanisms. The superego is the product of moral and social values. The primary function of the ego is seen as mediating conflicting demands from the id, superego, and external reality.
- **Adaptive:** Human behavior has to conform to the demands of the external reality, in particular, social reality.

It should be noted that contemporary psychoanalytic theorists have addressed the aforementioned basic metapsychological assumptions in various ways. For example, although all agree on unconscious motivators and the role of early developmental processes, there are varying positions on the value of psychosocial as contrasted with psychosexual stages and the psychological structures of id, ego, and superego, among other concepts.

Some additional points of view have been proposed, including the following:

- **Psychosocial:** Human behavior is strongly influenced by social forces, especially the early familial context.
- **Gestalt:** Human behavior is multiply determined and multifaceted. Despite its conceptual differentiation into perceptual, motor, cognitive, and affective aspects and the spatial and temporal contexts within which it occurs, it is ultimately integrated and indivisible.
- **Organismic:** Human behavior is not performed in isolation, but rather is a reflection or component of the total personality. Thus, it must be explained within the structural and functional framework of the total personality. Clinically, behavior performed in isolation from the context or the rest of the personality generally reflects pathology.

The enormous complexity and richness of the points of view or propositions (also referred to as metapsychological assumptions) should be juxtaposed with less ambitious conceptualizations. Although full elaboration of the different assumptions involved rarely can be made, it does target an approach that attempts to appreciate real persons in real-life contexts. This complexity is particularly apparent in the area of diagnosis. Diagnostic evaluation from the psychodynamic point of view provides understanding of the psychological state of the person. Psychodynamic approaches deal with such psychological dimensions as growth, experience, family, society, self, relationships, intrapsychic phenomena, symbolization, subjectivity, spirituality, needs, character, defenses, and behavior, among countless others. They also deal with constitution, temperament, and heredity and their roles in interaction with the foregoing dimensions. The whole person is always involved, and diagnosis focuses on such dimensions as ego strength, character style, and insight, with formal objective labels rapidly becoming irrelevant once the course of psychotherapy has been determined.

Major dissatisfaction with the prevalent, and even mandated, diagnostic systems of the American Psychiatric Association's *Diagnostic and Statistical Manual of Mental Disorders* (*DSM*) and the *International Classification of Diseases* (*ICD*) come from psychodynamic and other positions. Many of the criticisms stem from the efforts of the *DSM* and *ICD* to develop an atheoretical, purely descriptive nosology for psychiatric disorders. A comprehensive and systematic alternative, reflecting the complexity and subjectivity of human functioning and dysfunctioning, has been offered by a collaboration Task Force of the Alliance of Psychoanalytic Organizations. The conclusions of this collaboration were published in 2006 in the *Psychodynamic Diagnostic Manual* (*PDM*). "The...PDM is a diagnostic framework that attempts to characterize an individual's full range of functioning—the depth as well as the surface of emotional, cognitive, and social patterns. It emphasizes individual variation as well as commonalities....The PDM is based on current neuroscience, treatment outcome research, and other empirical investigations" (PDM Task Force, 2006, p. 1).

## THE PROCESS OF PSYCHODYNAMIC COUNSELING

Psychodynamic counseling is not a lesser form of psychological intervention than psychoanalysis or any of its variants. It is intended for different purposes and often for different populations. In classical psychoanalysis, there are rather stringent requirements for "suitability." For example, in an encyclopedic presentation of the psychoanalytic theory of neurosis of that time, Fenichel (1945) presented indications and contraindications for psychoanalytical treatment. Specific contraindications for psychoanalytic treatment were elaborated on by Fenichel and include age, insufficient intelligence, unfavorable life situations, triviality of a neurosis, urgency of a neurotic symptom, severe disturbance of speech, lack of a reasonable and cooperative ego, certain secondary gains, and schizoid personalities. As psychoanalytic theory has developed, inroads have been made in a number of areas affecting some of these contraindications. For example, older persons in many instances have been found to be suitable for psychoanalytic interventions. Modifications in psychoanalytic technique have opened analytic and analytically based approaches to those with borderline, schizoid, and even psychotic diagnoses. Considerable progress has been made in understanding pre-Oedipal psychic states, and hard-and-fast distinctions between transference and narcissistic neuroses continue to erode as a result.

Fundamental concepts of psychoanalytic therapy involve free association, abreaction, transference, resistance, and interpretation (of symptoms, dreams, fantasies, defenses, and character style). Greenson (1967, Chapter 1) offered a review of the components of classical psychoanalytic technique, which serves as the basis for what follows.

**Free association** has priority and is the major method of producing material in psychoanalysis, but free association is used only selectively in psychoanalytically oriented psychotherapies.

**Transference** is defined by Greenson (1967, p. 33) as "the experiencing of feelings, drives, attitudes, fantasies, and defenses toward a person in the present which are inappropriate to that person and are a repetition, a displacement of reactions originating in regard to significant persons of early childhood." Transference repetitions bring into the analysis some material that otherwise is inaccessible. Freud also used the term *transference neurosis* to describe that constellation of transference reactions in which the analyst and the analysis have become the center of the patient's emotional life, and the patient's neurotic conflicts are relived in the analytic situation (Freud, 1914/1958). For ordinary rehabilitation purposes, establishment of a transference neurosis is neither necessary nor appropriate.

**Resistance** refers to all the forces within the patient that oppose the procedures and processes of psychoanalytic work. Resistance, regardless of its source, operates through the ego, both consciously and unconsciously. Resistance is seen through repetitions of all of the defense operations that the patient has used in his or her past life. A major task of psychoanalytic therapy is to thoroughly and systematically analyze resistance to uncover how the patient resists, what is being resisted, and why the resistance occurs. Ultimately, resistances are efforts to ward off a traumatic state.

In psychoanalysis, a wide variety of therapeutic procedures are used, all having the direct aim of furthering self-insight. Others do not add insight, but strengthen those ego functions that are required for gaining insight. Greenson (1967) used abreaction as an example of a nonanalytic procedure that may permit a sufficient discharge of instinctual tension to reduce feelings of endangerment and render the ego secure enough to work analytically. The most important analytic procedure is interpretation, with all others subordinated to it both theoretically and practically. Exceptions, however, to the unique position of interpretation have arisen, particularly with those stressing direct experience and less cognitive approaches.

The crux of actually "analyzing" a psychic phenomenon usually involves four distinct procedures (Greeenson, 1967). These include *confrontation, clarification, interpretation,* and *working through*.

- **Confrontation** is the first step in analyzing a psychic phenomenon. The phenomenon in question has to be made explicit to the patient's awareness. Greenson provides, as an example, failure to show up for a session, which was interpreted by the analyst as related to a general tendency to avoid unpleasantness. In the previous session, "controversial" material had been discussed that made her feel that the analyst was angry at her [supposed] misbehavior. The specific fear, embedded in a general avoidance of possible unpleasantness, was then confronted in the next session. "You missed your last session not because you 'forgot' but you were frightened that I was going to be angry with you!"
- **Clarification** refers to those activities that aim at placing the psychic phenomenon being analyzed in sharp focus. Significant details have to be identified and separated from extraneous matter. The particular variety

or pattern of the phenomenon in question has to be singled out and isolated. Greenson used his patient's characteristic avoidance of her anger by projecting it on to others as shown by invoking instances in which she feared retaliation from her own "boldness" [hostility]. The clarification demonstrated how she projected her anger onto others, and her subsequent fear of rejection.

- **Interpretation** is the "procedure which distinguishes psychoanalysis from all other psychotherapies because in psychoanalysis interpretation is the ultimate and decisive instrument….To interpret means to make an unconscious phenomenon conscious….To make conscious the unconscious meaning, source, history, mode, or cause of a given psychic event" (Greenson, 1967, p. 39). In the instance of the cited patient, the interpretation offered was that she was transferring [repeating] toward the analyst complex feelings of ambivalence toward her father, based on both correct and distorted images of him. Specifically, she had the unconscious belief that opposition toward him would lead to rejection and even abandonment. Her family history and personal recollections suggested that, although her father was somewhat authoritarian with the children, she greatly distorted the extent of his wrath. Typically, an indication of a correct and timely interpretation is the response of the person, such as the flow of associations.

- **Working through** is the final step of the analyzing process. "Working through refers to a complex set of procedures and processes which occur after an insight has been given. The analytic work, which makes it possible for an insight to lead to change, is the work of working through. It refers in the main to the repetitive, progressive, and elaborate explanations of the resistances which prevent an insight from leading to change" (Greenson, 1967, p. 42). Change actually occurs through the working through. For the aforementioned patient, one aspect of working through involved demonstrating the many situations wherein hostile feelings on her part were projected onto others, particularly parental figures. The expectation of retaliatory punishment and rejection could then be seen as her own childlike fear of abandonment for noncompliance and willfulness. Insight regarding her use of projection as a resistance against contacting her own hostile feelings was followed up as its many guises were revealed. Self-affirmation began to be distinguished from hostility and selfishness as fears of abandonment abated.

**Termination** of psychotherapy is arrived at by mutual and satisfactory agreement that the major goals of treatment have been attained by patient and analyst and that the transference has been resolved.

A final concept, the **working alliance**, completes this survey of major analytic concepts and processes. "The working alliance is the relatively nonneurotic, rational relationship between the patient and analyst which make it possible for the patient to work purposefully in the analytic situation….The working alliance along with the neurotic suffering provide the incentive for doing the analytic work; the bulk of the raw material is provided by the patient's neurotic transference reactions" (Greenson, 1967, pp. 46–47).

It is the focus on unconscious determinants and the role of transference that distinguishes PDPT (Patton & Meara, 1992). As with other counseling approaches, immediate imperatives regarding coping; dealing with affective responses; negotiating familial, functional, social, and vocational consequences; and combating stigmatization dominate encounters. Contents influenced by a psychodynamic orientation regarding loss, grief, self-image, shame, anger, and depression, although not exclusive to psychodynamic exploration, are given a particular slant because practical and socially directed interventions are not necessarily helpful. The role and need for mourning of loss of function and/or body part and its status as an object loss can be lost in procedures directed toward functional restoration.

Typical rehabilitation situations do not justify the elaborate therapeutic activity of psychoanalysis. Specific contributions to understanding the relationships of psychodynamic orientations and concepts to counseling can be found in Bordin (1980), Gelso and Carter (1985), and Robbins (1989). Thomas and Siller (1999, pp. 193–194) have noted that

> Long-term characterological analysis in the overwhelming majority of rehabilitation situations is not feasible for practical reasons. Short-term, focused psychoanalytic exploration at best inevitably will be the most available....Apart from practical questions of short-term versus long-term, there is the theoretical issue of relative usefulness of intensive character as contrasted with a more focused exploration. First, relatively few persons in the general population meet the criteria or have the desire for intensive character analysis. For most persons newly disabled, the imperatives almost always are elsewhere such as for functional restoration and the medical situation. With this understanding persons newly disabled in most instances will be unsuitable for intensive characterological interventions. . . .Sufficient help can be obtained for both those newly disabled and those with longer lasting conditions through the use of more focused interventions. Intensive character analysis is the choice when the presence of disability is secondary in importance to the general needs and character of the person.

## REHABILITATION APPLICATIONS

Psychodynamic applications to rehabilitation and disability studies may be conveniently classified under four broad domains: (a) the use of defense mechanisms by people with CIDs during the process of psychosocial adaptation; (b) the effect of CID on the person's body image and self-perception; (c) the study of reactions to loss, trauma, and CID (e.g., mourning, grief, depression, denial, anger); and (d) the meaning and structure of attitudes toward people with CID.

### Study of Defense Mechanisms Within the Context of Coping With Physical Disability

A major contribution of psychoanalysis and ego psychology to the understanding of how the onset of chronic illnesses, life-threatening conditions, and physical and sensory disabilities affects the individual is the study of the ego defense mechanisms. Defense mechanisms are broadly viewed as unconscious processes that are mobilized when the ego is unable to ward off anxiety and other disturbing emotions or cope with unacceptable impulses (Freud, 1936/1946). To succeed in alleviating these debilitating internal states, the ego may resort to a number of psychological defense maneuvers, including:

1. **Repression:** Expelling conscious awareness of those intrapsychic conflicts and painful experiences (e.g., the person with a visible, congenital disability repressing feelings of shame triggered by early-life reactions of significant others).

2. **Projection:** Casting out or externalizing unconscious forbidden and unacceptable wishes, needs, and impulses and attributing them to others (e.g., the person with a recently acquired disability who attributes lack of progress during rehabilitation to medical staff incompetence rather than to own lack of effort; the individual who blames environmental conditions for the onset of lung cancer rather than to long-term smoking).

3. **Rationalization:** Using after-the-fact, false justifications for engaging in unacceptable or embarrassing behaviors, so that negative emotions or consequences can be prevented (e.g., the person with hearing loss who attempts to attribute lack of participation in a conversation to boredom or fatigue).

4. **Denial:** Among the plethora of definitions of denial, a leading contender among the psychoanalytically derived ones is an amalgam of affective and cognitive processes that seek to defuse, distort, or repudiate an encounter with both internal or external painful (anxiety-provoking, threat-inducing) stimuli (e.g., the person with spinal cord injury who, after many years of being a wheelchair user, still insists that he will be soon walking again). More often, however, rather than blatant reality-defying denial, it is the minimization of CID implications or the apprehension associated with the anticipated attitudes of others that is being denied.

5. **Sublimation:** Adopting beneficial and socially sanctioned behaviors to express forbidden and socially unacceptable wishes and impulses (e.g., a person with sudden-onset orthopedic disability whose anger toward, and wishes to retaliate against, an indifferent society are channeled into artistic endeavors or to benevolent behaviors toward other people, including those with CID).

6. **Reaction formation:** Substituting and expressing responses and feelings that are opposites of those that are forbidden (e.g., parents who demonstrate extreme manifestations of loving behaviors or overprotectiveness, rather than feelings of aversion and rejection, toward their child who was born with a severe physical deformity).

7. **Regression:** The reverting to childlike behaviors first exhibited by the individual during an earlier developmental stage (e.g., a recently disabled individual whose temper tantrums are activated when wishes are not immediately gratified).

8. **Compensation:** Seeking to excel in functionally related (direct or primary compensation) or mostly unrelated (indirect or secondary compensation) activities or behaviors to make up for disability-triggered loss (e.g., the person who lost sight at an early age and became a successful musician).

Brief discussions of these and other defense mechanisms in the context of rehabilitation and disability studies can be found in Caplan and Shechter (1987), Castelnuovo-Tedesco (1981), Cubbage and Thomas (1989), Grzesiak and Hicok (1994), Kruger (1981–1982), Livneh (1986, 2009), and Neiderland (1965).

Finally, related concepts, although not traditionally regarded as defense mechanisms, are primary and secondary gain. Primary gain refers to those symptoms and behaviors directly linked to alleviation of the stress-inducing affect. Secondary gain, on the other hand, addresses some form of social exploitation (e.g., familial, occupational), permitting the individual not to engage in previously performed roles and activities (e.g., the person with low back pain who refuses to discontinue receiving Social Security benefits or resume household chores despite condition improvement). Tertiary gains have also been observed, and they refer to benefits gained by individuals other than, but associated with, the one with CID, including financial and psychological benefits.

## Disability Impact on Body Image and Self-Perception

Body image is viewed as the unconscious representation of one's own body (Schilder, 1950) and, more recently, as a fabric of "psychological experiences, feelings and attitudes that relate to the form, function, appearance and desirability of one's own body which is influenced by individual and environmental factors" (Taleporos & McCabe, 2002, p. 971). Following the early contributions of Head (1920), who proposed that people create a set of reference models (schemata) of their own body structure, Schilder expanded those notions to conceptualize body image as residing at the core of self-image, self-concept, and personal identity. This mental picture reflects a three-dimensional image of symbolic and emotional significance that includes personal, interpersonal, environmental, and temporal dimensions (Cash & Pruzinsky, 2002; McDaniel, 1976; Shontz, 1975).

Chronic illnesses and disabilities are thought to alter, even to distort, the body image and, therefore, also the self-concept, because the imposed physical changes must be confronted by the person (Falvo, 2005). Furthermore, problems that stem from the new disability-associated reality (e.g., pain, disfigurement, sensory and mobility limitations, cognitive distortions) all threaten the stability of the body image and necessitate changes in its structure, perception, and dynamic operations (Bramble, 1995). Successful psychosocial adaptation to a disabling condition includes the integration of the imposed physical changes into a reconstructed body image and, consequently, personal identity. Unsuccessful adaptation, in contrast, is marked by physical experiences and psychiatric symptoms that often include psychogenic pain; chronic fatigue and energy depletion; feelings of anxiety, embarrassment, shame, self-pity, depression, anger, social withdrawal, and attempts at denying loss or impaired functioning of the involved body part(s).

In the context of psychoanalytic theorizing, the onset of adventitious CID is tantamount to a profound narcissistic injury, because narcissism and the development of body image progress in parallel routes during the course of normal human development (Grzesiak & Hicok, 1994). Moreover, as the body (or part of the body) is the initial object being cathected by the developing ego (Siller, 1988; Szasz, 1957), the body image is invested with archaic and symbolic meanings. Injury to the body, therefore, particularly at early developmental stages, often results in identity confusion, impoverished self-esteem, and emotional distress (Greenacre, 1958; Thomas & Siller, 1999).

In a similar vein, Neiderland (1965) and Castelnuovo-Tedesco (1981) contended that an early body defect leads to a narcissistic injury (at times referred to a narcissistic ego impairment) and, therefore, to an unresolved conflict, because of its concreteness, permanency, and association with archaic forms of anxiety (e.g., body disintegration anxiety, separation anxiety, castration anxiety). This unresolved narcissistic injury results in a disrupted body image and, consequently, may lead to an unrealistic self-concept that, although often distorted, may also give rise to heightened artistic and cognitive creativity. When the narcissistic injury expresses itself in a compensatory fashion, it may lead to increased aggressiveness, excessive vulnerability, impaired object relations, self-aggrandizement, and possibly delusional beliefs (Catelnuovo-Tedesco, 1978, 1981; Grzesiak & Hicok, 1994; Krystal & Petty, 1961; Neiderland, 1965).

Of utmost importance is the developmental stage during which the disability was acquired. Narcissistic injuries during the separation–individuation, Oedipal, and adolescent stages are thought to render the individual most vulnerable to body image distortion, self-representation instability, and self-concept traumatization (Castelnuovo-Tedesco, 1981; Earle, 1979). Loss or removal of body parts is fraught with potential psychological disturbances, and their gain or addition (e.g., organ transplantation) could be equally disturbing. The transplant situation triggers heightened life–death anxieties, because the transplant organ is often obtained from a deceased person or from a donor whose life may now be in greater jeopardy (e.g., kidney donors). The transplant could result in thoughts of having robbed the donor of vital organs and the accompanying feelings of guilt, self-blame, and fear of punishment (Castelnuovo-Tedesco, 1978). Further discussion of the role of body image in the context of disability studies may be found in Block and Ventur (1963) and Lussier (1980).

## Psychosocial Reactions to Loss and Disability

Numerous theoretical and clinical accounts of the nature, structure, and temporal sequencing of psychosocial reactions to the onset of CID have been provided in the literature. Central to all of the accounts is the assumption that a discernable order of reactions exists to account for the ways that the individual responds, copes with, or reacts to the newly acquired condition. Among psychoanalytically influenced writings are those of Bellak (1952), Blank (1961), Cubbage and Thomas (1989), Degan (1975), Engel (1962), Gunther (1971), Kruger (1981–1982), Krystal and Petty (1961), Langer (1994), Neff and Weiss (1961), Nemiah (1964), Pollock (1961), Siller (1976), Thomas (1994), and Thomas and Siller (1999).

Most of the aforementioned writers view the process of psychosocial adaptation to the onset of CID as (a) reflecting a symbolic transition from possessing a "normal" or "whole" body ("former self") to that which is not complete or whole ("present self"); (b) having to accept a loss of previously attained physical, psychological, and social selves; (c) creating a need for a period of mourning (grieving) for the lost body part or function that, on its successful resolution, leads to a reconstructed self-image as a person with CID; (d) being determined by the symbolic meaning (both in its narcissistic and self-esteem connotations, as well as its functional impairment) of the CID and body parts involved to the individual and society; (e) influenced to a large extent by unconscious wishes, needs, and fears that include, among others, castration and separation anxieties, fear of loss of love objects, and dependency needs; and (f) following a complex series of psychic activities in which cathexes are first withdrawn from the injured ego, as well as from the outside world, and then after a period of denial (serving as a defensive role in minimizing the CID and its consequences) and energies are gradually reinvested in a new body and self images, alternative needs, wishes and gratifications, and the reestablishment of contact with a newly perceived reality.

The following reactions of adaptation to the CID experience (often viewed as mostly internally determined psychosocial phases) are typically addressed in the psychoanalytically derived literature: (a) shock, disbelief, and chaotic disruption; (b) anxiety (injury, loss, and disability, such as blindness and amputation, are said to reawaken archaic castration anxiety); (c) grief, mourning, and depression to real object loss (and the necessitated changes in narcissistic investments, emotional cathexes, and self-image); (d) denial of illness or disability (denial of affect associated with the nature, functional implications, prognosis, extent, or seriousness of the condition); (e) anger and aggression (turned inwardly and resulting in feelings of guilt and shame or turned outwardly to trigger feelings of other-blame and need for revenge); and (f) adjustment, reintegration, and restitution (a successful resolution of the lost object decathexis, "work of mourning," and reformation of the self-image).

## Attitudes Toward People With CID

The origins, formation, and structure of attitudes toward people with CID have been addressed extensively from a psychodynamic perspective. Earlier psychoanalytic views posited that negative societal attitudes toward people with CID may be traced to (a) the belief that CID is a (divine) punishment for sinful acts committed by the individual; (b) the projection of one's unacceptable impulses and wishes on those with CID (those who were justly punished) as they are least likely to retaliate; (c) the perception that if CID, as a punishment, was inflicted unjustly, then the person with CID is motivated to commit an evil act to counteract the injustice and is, therefore, dangerous and should be avoided; (d) unresolved conflicts over scopophilia and exhibitionism, during early psychosexual stages of development that trigger fascination/attraction versus repulsion/avoidance conflict when being exposed to a person with visible CID (e.g., aesthetically or cosmetically disfigured person); (e) "guilt by association" that may render a nondisabled person, who interacts with people with CID, as maladjusted or of inferior social status, thus resulting in social ostracism; (f) guilt of being nondisabled when the other person has lost an important body part or function and is permanently affected by it (akin to the "survivor's guilt" phenomenon); (g) CID as a reminder of death, because loss and CID symbolize death and destruction, thereby rekindling existential anxiety and archaic fears of annihilation and further serving as reminders of mortality; (h) CID as a threat to one's perceived intact body image that reawakens earlier castration anxiety, along with fears of losing physical integrity and personal safety; (i) anxiety triggered by aesthetic, visceral aversion that further fuels concerns about the observer fragile appearance; and (j) a "requirement for mourning" of the loss of intact body that serves to safeguard the nondisabled person's entrenched values and beliefs about the importance and sacredness of the human body (Barker, Wright, Meyerson, & Gonick, 1953; Blank, 1957; Chan, Livneh, Pruett, Wang, & Zhang, 2009; Degan, 1975; Greenberg, Pyszczynski, & Solomon, 1997; Hirschberger, Florian, & Mikulincer, 2005; Livneh, 1982; Livneh et al., 2014; Siller, 1976, 1984; Siller, Chipman, Ferguson, & Vann, 1967; Thomas, 1995; Wright, 1983).

Siller and associates (Siller, 1970, 1984; Siller et al., 1967), in a multifaceted and extended series of studies, investigated the structure of attitudes toward persons with various disabilities. They concluded that attitudes toward persons with disabilities are multidimensional in nature and typically reflect such components as interaction strain, rejection of intimacy, generalized rejection, authoritarian virtuousness, inferred emotional consequences, distressed identification, and imputed functional limitations, each of which may have different developmental and personological roots. He has, further, suggested that for those with CID who have gained awareness of the responses toward them can empower productive actions to positively control social interactions as well as to bolster their own self-regard. In this regard, important work from a nonanalytic perspective on coping versus succumbing responses by Wright (1983) and others demonstrate that the self-presentation of those with CID becomes an important determinant in creating a climate for a meaningful social interaction.

## CASE STUDY

Mr. J. B. was referred by his attorney for psychological counseling, in part, to support a legal action for damages received while at work and, in part, to provide psychological support for emotional distress in connection with his disability. The first session occurred approximately 1 year after an accident at work in which Mr. J. B. was hit and pinned against a wall by a cart that lurched forward due to a mechanical failure of a restraining part. Injuries included a crushed left leg that required an above-knee amputation and "minor" head injuries requiring stitches in the temporal area. Neuropsychological testing revealed difficulty in attending and concentrating; slow motor speed, but within normal limits; no perceptual or auditory dysfunction; no evidence of aphasia, but significant impairment in linguistic skill, with an IQ in the average range and memory within normal limits. The cognitive difficulties, particularly in attention and concentration, appeared to be symptoms of postconcussion syndrome, possibly accounting for the self-reported memory difficulties. About 3 months later, he was fitted for prosthesis and began physical therapy and walking instructions that were continued at the time first seen in counseling.

Mr. J. B. was 49 years old at the time of the accident and had been working as the manager of the machine shop when injured. He was born and raised in Greece prior to moving to the United States about 10 years before the injury. His wife and two children still lived in Greece, and long periods of separation from his family had become a way of life.

He appeared to be a pragmatic, sincere, and serious family- and work-oriented person, who was accustomed to working methodically, independently, and responsibly. The aftermath of his injuries was devastating, and he was trying to reconstitute himself functionally through applying himself to the prosthetic program. His emotional state was more problematic, as he had no clear reference as to how to cope with strong feelings of stigmatization, shame, and diminished self-regard. He was seen for psychological counseling once per week for almost 6 months.

The first five sessions were focused mostly on information, limited mostly to the accident and present rehabilitation efforts, daily life, and background status. As focus shifted from the "external" situation to feelings about insecurities and fear of the future, a modified form of psychoanalytic psychotherapy was used. Report of dreams was encouraged, but interpretations were conservatively advanced and limited to issues germane to rehabilitation. A major stimulus for the shift to psychodynamic intervention was emotional distress created by realization that prosthetic restoration had reached a plateau and was being terminated, far short of achieving his expectations.

*(continued)*

*(continued)*

The first three sessions concentrated on the themes of prosthetic restoration and his insecurity about his function in mobility, language, and memory. At the fourth session, he began to speak of his sensitivity and awkwardness in being seen by people who knew him from before the accident, separation from his family, and feelings of "being less than a man." Transference occurred to the therapist as a rational authority, viewing the therapist impersonally as a possible vehicle of benefit with expert status regarding disability. He experienced despair about his ultimate ability to use his prosthesis comfortably and effectively, although he was actively walking and exercising. Major resistances then appeared to be based in denial of the functional consequences of his amputation and concealment of the affect of shame. He was also concerned about his short-term memory.

The nature of counseling changed by the sixth session, as he was distraught about the failure of the prosthesis to return him to his original functional status. The therapist confronted him, indicating that he was underestimating the value of his prosthesis, as it was enabling him to move and travel quite well. Referring to a phrase he had already used, "I feel less of a man," an interpretation was offered that, "You are feeling inadequate as a person, both physically and sexually, and in most respects your fantasy of being made whole by the prosthesis has been exploded." A main purpose of treatment in restoring his self-regard and appreciation of himself in a realistic context was suggested. His emotional distress enabled expansion of counseling from the prosthetic and functional focus to questions of self-regard, manhood, social worth, and more. His reticence about opening up emotionally to a stranger lessened, and a new phase began.

The extended and only partially successful efforts at prosthetic restoration complicated body and self-image adaptation. Socket adjustments were frequently being made. Phantom sensations were present, but did not seem to be a general concern. At the sixth session, when asked if anything was bothering him, he replied, "One of the worst times for me comes when retiring for the night. Taking off the prosthesis gives me the reality that I'm missing my leg." Talking about sleep and having to see his stump opened two lines of inquiry: the nature of his dreams and the process of mourning his lost part and status.

He generally did not have disturbing dreams, although there was a recurrent dream about a feeling of falling in space. He was not attuned to probing his dreams and was unable to pursue an associative path. Asked whether he had such dreams before the injury and whether he felt that they were now connected with the injury, he indicated that he did not remember having them before, but that they might be connected to his balance and walking with prosthesis. While agreeing that it was a likely connection,

*(continued)*

(*continued*)

subsequent intervention was designed to go beyond the physical to more general insecurities. In effect, the therapeutic direction was to confront and to clarify the resistance through which he was trying to contain the unpleasantness of his self-feelings as a diminished man by focusing on the functional/physical realm. Counseling returned to issues previously touched on at a more intellectualized level, such as stigmatization and fear of the future, with an extended perspective based on transference and resistance.

The next session continued with urging him to further address feelings about seeing his stump. There appeared to be mixed feelings about his level of impairment, and the discussion was directed to the connection between his despair and his embarrassment at being seen by those who knew him from before. He observed that he was less uncomfortable at home with his brother's family (where he lived), and for the first time, the session was almost entirely directed toward emotional matters.

Prior adaptations to the expectations of his family and self now needed revision to restore value in his own eyes. Returning to an early theme of the need to mourn, the concept of mourning of his loss of limb was discussed, along with impaired mobility and self-regard. As he was getting more comfortable with and less defensive about such considerations, the naturalness of mourning, placed in the context of all significant losses, became more acceptable and not a sign of weakness and unmanliness. During this period, there was an exacerbation of disturbing dreams involving potential danger (e.g., being on a ship in a hurricane, recurring thoughts of the accident). Work on interpreting dreams, along with discussions about his past and present relationships and feelings, helped to expand his sense of self, and the disturbed dreams became less threatening. Near the end of counseling, he was much more active and insightful as to how determining he was in creating his emotional state.

After some 20 sessions, Mr. J. B. left for a visit to family in Greece. Soon afterward, a settlement was reached in his legal action, and he returned to Greece permanently. A telephone follow-up indicated that sensitivities, anxieties, and mood swings continued, but that he had a generally better feeling about his condition. Encountering former friends or coworkers had become easier. There were few disturbing dreams, and when they occurred, he thought of them along the lines that we had addressed. He also commented about more appreciative feelings toward his prosthesis.

The counseling experience was successful to the extent that a lessening of most of the complaints was achieved, and the ability to appreciate the value of his prosthesis was enhanced by attention to the magical thinking surrounding it. Facilitating mourning by interpreting denial of affect and questions of "manhood" helped to make the prosthesis a support rather

(*continued*)

*(continued)*

than a failure of fantasies about restoration. Technically, the major vehicle of change resided in a shift in transference. Rather than seeing the counselor as an objective and impersonal "disability expert," a more positive transference developed, seeing the counselor as a source of help with feelings and as someone who would not devalue him when he revealed his self-doubts and fears. Analytic tools of dream analysis, interpretation, confrontation, clarification, insight, and working through, and analysis of resistance were used, but primarily in an adulterated and selective way.

## RESEARCH FINDINGS

Due to the scope and focus of this chapter, it is not reasonable to provide a comprehensive coverage of the extensive research findings generated by psychodynamic theory and therapy. Three broad research trends are evident in the extant literature: (a) the study of psychoanalytically derived concepts, such as defense mechanisms, the nature and function of dreams, and unconscious motivation; (b) the effectiveness of psychodynamic therapy; and (c) CID and rehabilitation-applied research (e.g., the symbolic meaning of loss and CID onset, the structure of attitudes toward people with CID, body image and CID).

### Research on Freudian Theory

Freud was quite skeptical of the value of empirical research on psychoanalytic concepts and procedures. For him, each session was an experiment in itself, and psychoanalysis needed no further support. For many years, research on psychoanalytic theory and practice did little to dispel this notion. More recent work is more reflective of the true character of the phenomena studied, and optimism is increasing regarding the possibility of subjecting psychoanalytic concepts to more adequate verification (e.g., Bornstein & Masling, 1998; Fisher & Greenberg, 1978, 1985; Westen, 1998). Significant problems, however, must be recognized. As a psychological specialty that stresses unconscious phenomena, it deals with derivatives of the unconscious not directly reflected in behavioral acts. In addition, the complexity and abstractness of many psychoanalytic concepts renders them difficult to measure. The tautological nature of some of the constructs also may preclude direct refutation of their existence and operation. Yet, an enormous body of empirical research has been accumulated on psychoanalytic theory and practice.

The results are equivocal, but as Kline (1981) concludes after a major critical review of earlier empirical research on psychoanalytic theory: (a) Much of the theory's metapsychology contrasts with traditional scientific jargon and cannot, therefore, be readily subjected to any kind of empirical test or be readily refuted (e.g., id, death instinct, pleasure principle) and (b) much of psychoanalytic theory consists of empirical propositions, which can be tested, and many of the compo-nents of psychoanalytic theory have been supported (e.g., repression, projection, the Oedipus complex). Kline (1981, pp. 446–447) concluded, "The status of psy-choanalytic theory must now be clear. It must be retained not as a whole but only after rigorous objective research has revealed what parts are correct or false or in need of modification." The reader may find additional review sources on empiri-cal studies in Bornstein and Masling (1998), Fisher and Greenberg (1978, 1985), Ford and Urban (1998), and Maddi (1989).

Despite the equivocal empirical support, psychodynamic theory and research have greatly enriched psychological testing by introducing projec-tive techniques into the mainstream of assessment. Projective tools include the Rorschach inkblot technique, Thematic Apperception Test (TAT), Draw-A-Person Test, House–Tree–Person Test, the various word association procedures, the Blacky (Pictures) Test, Rosenzweig Picture–Frustration Study, and the more recent measures of defense mechanisms, including the Defense Mechanisms Inventory (DMI; Gleser & Ihilevich, 1969) and the Repression–Sensitization (R-S) scale (Byrne, 1961). Westen (1998), therefore, in his commentary on Freud's scientific contributions, concluded that a large body of empirical literature has been aggregated to support Freud's theoretical propositions on unconscious pro-cesses, the early life origins of certain personality dispositions and aberrations, the dynamics of psychosocial developmental processes, and the cognitive repre-sentations of the self and others.

### Effectiveness of Psychoanalytically Derived Psychodynamic Therapy

It has been argued that adequate empirical studies to assess the effectiveness of psychoanalytically oriented therapy are scarce because of its complexity and the virtually impossible task of trying to control the many variables involved (Arlow, 2000). Moreover, Fisher and Greenberg (1985, p. 41) speculated that comparisons of therapeutic efficacy between psychoanalytic therapy and other therapeutic approaches are doomed to failure because "the evidence indicates that there is no one conception of what psychoanalytic therapy is," and many analysts do not view change, especially behavioral change, as a primary ther-apeutic goal. In addition, psychoanalytic-based therapy is typically suited for a narrower range of psychiatric conditions (e.g., patients who seek long-term investments and in-depth personality changes), requires a longer period of time and more frequent sessions to establish its full impact, and does not lend itself readily to strict lab (experimental) conditions, all essential requirements for comparative empirical research (Doidge, 1997; Fonagy, 1982; Leichsenring, 2005; Messer, 2004; Milton, 2002).

Earlier efforts by Fenichel (1930) and Knight (1941), as well as occasional studies by the American Psychoanalytic Association (Arlow, 2000; Fisher & Greenberg, 1985), have suggested that successful therapeutic outcomes typi-cally have ranged from a low of 25% (for patients diagnosed with psychoses) to a high of 65% to 75% (for patients diagnosed with neuroses). In his reviews,

Prochaska (1984) concluded that (a) the efficacy of psychoanalytic therapy had not been adequately assessed and (b) when compared to other forms of therapy, psychoanalytic treatment had not been shown to be superior to other, less time-consuming, forms of psychotherapy.

With the emergence of comparative, meta-analytic studies in the 1980s and 1990s (Lipsey & Wilson, 1993; Prioleau, Murdock, & Brody, 1983; Shapiro & Shapiro, 1982; Smith, Glass, & Miller, 1980), psychoanalytic and other psychodynamic therapies have been judged to be equal to slightly less effective than cognitive behavioral therapies (effectiveness studies are typically conducted under clinical practice conditions, in contrast to efficacy studies, which use the "gold standard" of randomized control trials [RCTs], although this distinction is often blurred in most of the literature).

Dynamic therapies have clearly demonstrated their effectiveness when compared to no-treatment control groups. For example, Bachrach, Galatzer-Levy, Skolnikoff, and Waldron (1991) concluded that studies on long-term efficacy of psychoanalytic therapy were mostly methodologically flawed. Yet, from these studies, and from numerous anecdotal clinical reports, it appears that it is beneficial for the majority of self-selected clients. In support of their claims, Bachrach and his colleagues have cited extensive evidence from several long-term, well-known clinical research projects, including those conducted by the Menninger Foundation Psychotherapy Research Project, the Columbia Psychoanalytic Center Research Project, the Boston Psychoanalytic Institute Prediction Studies, and the New York Psychoanalytic Institute Studies, among others.

As methodological improvements occur, and more appropriate evaluation and research studies are reported, increasing evidence is anticipated to be forthcoming to substantiate the value of psychoanalytic psychotherapies. *Psychoanalytic Inquiry* (Lazar, 1997) published a supplement to their journal, with 12 articles supporting psychoanalytic therapies in various terms, including cost-effectiveness, clinical effectiveness, and public health. For example, Doidge (1997) reviewed the empirical evidence for psychoanalytic therapies and psychoanalysis and indicated that they are the most widely practiced of the more than 100 different types of psychotherapy. The results of studies consistently confirm the effectiveness of psychoanalytic therapy when used with appropriate patient populations, with improvement rates ranging from 60% to 90%. For other detailed earlier reviews of the efficacy of psychoanalytic therapies, the reader is referred to Fisher and Greenberg (1985), Meltzoff and Kornreich (1970), Prochaska and Norcross (1994), and Roth and Fonagy (1996).

With the exponential growth of empirical outcome research on therapeutic interventions, yielded by RCTs and evidence-based practice (EBP) approaches during the past 15 to 20 years, the number of related meta-analytic studies has also expanded immensely. Among the plethora of reported meta-analytic studies on the efficacy of psychotherapy, a good portion was devoted to examining the success of PDPTs, in general, and psychoanalytic-oriented therapies (PAOTs), more specifically. These meta-analytic studies spanned a wide range of treated psychiatric disorders, including personality disorders (i.e., borderline and antisocial personality disorders [PDs], Cluster C PDs, depression, anxiety, posttraumatic stress disorder [PTSD], and eating disorders [i.e., bulimia and anorexia nervosa]).

Findings from a series of publications by Leichsenring and his colleagues (Leichsenring, 2001, 2005, 2009; Leichsenring & Leibing, 2003; Leichsenring & Rabung, 2008; Leichsenring, Rabung, & Leibing, 2004) indicate the following:

1. PDPT, when applied to PD, yielded overall mean effect sizes ranging from 1.08, for self-reported measures, to 1.79, for observer-rated measures. These effect sizes translated to an average of 59% recovery rate from PD when measured 15 months after termination of treatment.

2. Short-term PDPT yielded significant effect sizes of 1.39 and 1.59 at treatment conclusion and follow-up, respectively. Furthermore, these effect sizes were significant for a number of outcome measures, including general psychiatric symptoms and social functioning. These effect sizes suggest success rates of over 90% for short-term PDPT. In all comparisons, the short-term treatments were superior to no-treatment control and treatment-as-usual (TAU) groups.

3. For patients with complex psychiatric disorders (i.e., PDs, chronic psychiatric disorders, multiple psychiatric disorders), PAOT yielded effect sizes that significantly surpassed those achieved by TAU, low-dose treatment comparison, or untreated groups. These treatments were also significantly more effective than short-term types of PDPT.

4. Long-term PDPT yielded significantly (a) higher overall effectiveness, (b) reduced target problems, and (c) improved personality functioning as compared to short-term forms of PDPT (effect sizes averaging 1.8, indicating that, on the average, these patients (mostly diagnosed with PDs, depressive or anxiety disorders) were better than 96% of the patients treated by the various comparisons groups. Furthermore, many of these effect sizes increased significantly from treatment completion to follow-up.

Based on these findings, Leichsenring (2009, p. 19) concluded that PDPT "was either more effective than placebo therapy, supportive therapy, or TAU or as effective as CBT." Additionally, long-term PDPT, with complex psychiatric disorders, consistently yielded large effect sizes and proved superior to no treatment or shorter types of therapy.

In a comprehensive review of the literature on PDPT, Fonagy, Roth, and Higgitt (2005) examined the available empirically based evidence for both short-term PDPT (defined as weekly treatments extending up to about 20 sessions) and long-term PDPT. Based on their review, the authors concluded that (a) short-term PDPTs have been shown to be more effective when compared to waiting-list patient groups or to general outpatient treatment in reducing levels of depression and anxiety; (b) long-term PDPT was successful in achieving up to 80% success rate (as evaluated by patients, their therapists, and independent experts) at a 6.5-year follow-up study of treated German patients; and (c) PAOT fared well when compared to dialectical behavior therapy (DBT), in reducing depression (including suicidality), increasing social functioning, and increasing Global Assessment of Functioning (GAF) scores, among patients with borderline PD.

Another systematic review of the literature on the effectiveness of PDPT by de Maat, de Jonghe, Schoevers, and Dekker (2009), focused on long-term (defined as consisting of at least 50 weekly sessions) PAOT. According to these authors, the majority of the reviewed PDPT studies ($N = 10$) dealt with patients presenting with moderate/mixed pathologies. These studies yielded large mean effect sizes (.78 at closure and .94 at follow-up). More specifically, mean effect sizes were 1.03 for symptom reduction (e.g., depression, anxiety) and .54 for personality change. In a somewhat similar fashion, PAOT studies ($N = 4$) that focused on moderate/mixed pathology also yielded large mean effect sizes of .87 at closure and 1.18 at follow-up, further indicating a mean effect size of 1.38 for symptom reduction and .76 for personality change. Success rates derived from these effect sizes, according to the authors, suggest a weighted mean of 70% according to therapists and 73% according to patients, and 71% overall success rate at closure and 54% at follow-up.

Finally, in a recent review and commentary on the efficacy of PDPT, Shedler (2010) concluded that "empirical evidence supports the efficacy of psychodynamic therapy" (p. 98) and that the yielded effect sizes by this therapy are "as large as those reported for other treatments that have been actively promoted as 'empirically supported' and 'evidence-based'" (p. 107). Furthermore, Shedler maintains that the efficacy of PDPT has been demonstrated for a wide range of psychiatric disorders and patients, as well as providing therapeutic gains that have lasted over time. He concludes his argument by stating that PDPT "promotes inner capacities and resources that allow a richer and more fulfilling life" (Shedler, 2010, p. 106).

Efficacy of psychotherapy is a complex and thorny issue. Psychodynamic-based therapies do not foster an immediate, direct, and readily discernable cause-and-effect link, and their effects are more diffuse and character related. Goals and outcomes that focus on behavioral change, as customarily pursued in traditional RCT studies, only depict one isolated aspect of the complex nature of human experience.

### Applied Research in Disability and Rehabilitation

Body Image and Adaptation to CID

In a series of studies, Druss and associates (Druss, 1986; Druss, O'Connor, Prudden, & Stern, 1968; Druss, O'Connor, & Stern, 1969, 1972) explored changes in body image and psychosocial adaptation of patients who underwent colostomy and ileostomy, following chronic ulcerative colitis and bowel cancer. The authors noted that, immediately after surgery, patients experienced shock and depressive reactions. Loss of a highly valued organ, the sense of mutilation, and heightened body awareness appeared evident. Furthermore, support was found for the notion of parallelism between surgery and feelings of castration and between the stoma and phallus. Research on disturbances of body image was also reported following spinal cord injury and brain injuries (Arnhoff & Mehl, 1963; Fink & Shontz, 1960; Mitchell, 1970; Nelson & Gruver, 1978; Shontz, 1956; Wachs & Zaks, 1960) and following limb amputation (Bhojak & Nathawat,1988; Centers & Centers, 1963; Gallagher, Horgan, Franchignoni, Giordano, & MacLachlan, 2007; Rybarczyk, Nicholas, & Nyenhuis, 1997; Rybarczyk, Nyenhuis, Nicholas, Cash, & Kaiser, 1995).

## Castration Anxiety, Death Anxiety, Object Representations, and Attitudes Toward People With CID

The relationships between attitudes toward people with CID and several psychoanalytic-derived personality constructs have been investigated. A number of empirical studies focused on the relationship between castration anxiety and intrapsychic perceptions (expressed as endorsed attitudes) among people with physical disabilities. The authors (Baracca, 1991; Fine, 1973; Follansbee, 1981; Gladstone, 1977; all cited in Thomas & Siller, 1999) investigated the effects of castration anxiety and level of object representation on attitudes toward persons with CID, using the Siller et al. (1967) Disability Factor Scales–General (DFS–G) measure. The findings suggested, albeit tentatively, the following: (a) Heightened castration anxiety is positively associated with more negative attitudes toward those with CID; (b) among preschool children, those who scored higher on castration anxiety (using the Blacky test) also manifested more negative attitudes toward others with CID; (c) increased narcissistic vulnerability was found to be associated with more negative attitudes; and (d) those with more rigid defense mechanisms (using the DMI) were more rejecting of persons with physical disabilities (object relations theory views defense as a central function of the ego in its efforts to ward off anxiety and stress, both triggered by threat to one's own body integrity).

Finally, negative attitudes toward those with physical disabilities are posited by psychoanalytic theory to be linked to fears of insults to one's own body integrity (e.g., castration anxiety) and also to loss of one's life (i.e., death anxiety). Indeed, it was conjectured that archaic fears of physical deterioration and death are triggered when faced with situations that constitute symbolic reminders of death, such as the presence of a person with a visible disability. Empirical support for these notions was reported by Enders (1979), Fish (1981), and Livneh (1985). Furthermore, findings obtained from research spawned by terror management theory (TMT) have suggested that death-related cognitions and emotions resulted in withdrawal from, and fear of, people with disabilities, as well as greater attributions of blame (negative attitudes) toward those who were severely injured in accidents (Hirschberger, 2006; Hirschberger et al., 2005). These findings thus lend further support to the notion that cognitive or actual exposure to people with CID increases awareness of one's own mortality as well as triggers defensive negative attitudes toward this group.

Loss, Mourning, and Disability

Psychoanalytic theory regards the mourning process as a gradual decathexis of the mental representation of, and the affective investments in, the lost object (Frankiel, 1994). Disability-related conceptualizations equate the mourning process, engendered by the death of significant others (interpersonal loss) with that triggered by loss of body parts or functions (personal loss). Research by Parkes (1972a, 1972b, 1975), comparing the psychosocial reactions of widows and people with amputation, indicated that similar phases of grief and realization (e.g., shock, denial, depression, anger, acceptance) as well as defensive processes were experienced by both groups.

## PROMINENT STRENGTHS AND LIMITATIONS

### General Strengths

- Psychoanalytically derived psychodynamic insights have been applied to therapy, dream interpretation, humor, child-rearing practices, educational and learning experiences, vocational development and occupational choice, history, religion and mythology, art, music, literature, political and social organizations, anthropology, psychological testing (projective techniques), and daily human experiences (slips of the tongue, gestures, symptomatic acts).
- Psychoanalytic theory provides the clinician with an extremely rich perspective on human emotions, cognitions, and behaviors. It affords therapists the opportunity to explore human functioning at its deepest and most complex levels.

### Rehabilitation-Related Strengths

- Psychoanalytic-derived psychodynamic concepts are well entrenched in rehabilitation practice (e.g., defense mechanisms, coping strategies, secondary gain, body image).
- Adopting a psychodynamic perspective enables rehabilitation practitioners to focus on subjective and unique meanings of loss, grief, and CID for both the individual and his or her family members.
- The psychodynamic approach affords the rehabilitation practitioner a dynamic and developmental perspective on the process of adaptation to CID across the life span (Cubbage & Thomas, 1989; Thomas, 1994; Thurer, 1986).

### General Limitations

- Problems of tautology, refutability, and controlled research make global assessment of the theory and its elements exceedingly difficult. There is no consensual global theory and, although various elements have received support, others have not, and many simply have not been adequately defined or tested (e.g., carthexis, id, libido).

- Clinical observations from case studies are often anecdotal in nature, uncontrolled for bias, and may not be representative of the general clinical population.
- Some classical psychoanalytic concepts, such as castration anxiety, penis envy, libido, and development of the woman's superego, have been strongly criticized as being gender biased.
- Psychodynamic therapy focuses primarily on intrapsychic issues and conflicts and frequently neglects broader social contexts (e.g., family dysfunction, social problems). This limitation, while operating in certain instances particularly in the past, seems archaic in the face of reality of modern psychoanalysis. The role of the family and society was fundamental to psychoanalysis from the beginning, and nonlibidinal object relations, self theory, and adult relationships abound as prime factors in current theoretical developments and clinical work.
- Assessment measures of clients' affective status and behavior have been judged to possess low validity and reliability (e.g., projective techniques); are highly subjective; and often lack standardization in administration, scoring, and interpretation (Ford & Urban, 1998; Liebert & Spiegler, 1990; Maddi, 1989; Prochaska & Norcross, 1994).

### Rehabilitation-Related Limitations

- Earlier, a rationale for short-term focused psychoanalytic exploration in the rehabilitation context was offered. However, time constraints, lack of trained personnel, inability to meet the prerequisites of verbal capacity, diminished personal insight, and limitations induced by certain cognitive impairments (e.g., clients with intellectual disabilities, clients who sustained brain injury, clients with severe mental illness) are realities in rehabilitation.
- Psychoanalytically derived therapy emphasizes long-term, abstract, reflective, insight-building processes, and gradual personality reconstruction, whereas rehabilitation focuses on short-term, "here and now," concrete and pragmatic goals, emphasizing daily functional activities and vocational and independent living pursuits.
- The goal of psychoanalytically driven therapy in rehabilitation is likely to focus on symptom alleviation and anxiety reduction rather than personality reconstruction, analyzing defenses, gaining self-insight, and projecting hopes and wishes into the future. As stated by Siller (1969, p. 294), "The aim of [rehabilitation] is to assist the person toward reformulating a self that approves of continuing to be despite important discontinuities with its past identity. Specifically this means the promotion of a new self-image predicated on worth, rather than on deficiency and self-contempt." Clinically, awareness of psychodynamics may help in understanding why some people with CID can, and others cannot, reconstitute positive feelings toward the self or to adopt a coping, rather than succumbing, life orientation. Rehabilitation requires a larger canvas within a team environment,

merging medical attention, functional performance, skill acquisition, education, and adaptation to CID. Psychoanalytic sensitivity to unconscious issues, such as mourning and object loss, can be invaluable for an individual with a recently acquired CID. Psychodynamic interventions, therefore, have a prominent role to play within the larger rehabilitation context.

## DISCUSSION EXERCISES

1. Discuss what types of clients will be most, and least, suitable for PDPT.
2. Discuss which criteria PDPT would use to assess successful therapeutic outcomes.
3. Discuss the various psychosocial reactions to sudden-onset CID and how they manifest themselves in specific conditions (e.g., spinal cord injury, traumatic brain injury, amputation, heart failure).
4. Discuss the origins and structure of attitudes toward people with CID and how their negative impact could be minimized.

## REFERENCES

Arlow, J. A. (2000). Psychoanalysis. In R. J. Corsini & D. Wedding (Eds.), *Current psychotherapies* (6th ed., pp. 16–53). Itasca, IL: Peacock.

Arlow, J. A., & Brenner, C. (1964). *Psychoanalytic concepts and structural theory.* New York, NY: International Universities Press.

Arnhoff, F. N., & Mehl, M. C. (1963). Body image deterioration in paraplegia. *Journal of Nervous and Mental Disease, 134,* 88–92.

Bachrach, H., Galatzer-Levy, R., Skolnikoff, A., & Waldron, S. (1991). On the efficacy of psychoanalysis. *Journal of the American Psychoanalytic Association, 39,* 871–916.

Barker, R. G., Wright, B. A., Meyerson, L., & Gonick, M. R. (1953). *Adjustment to physical handicaps and illness: A survey of the social psychology of physique and disability* (Rev. ed.). New York, NY: Social Science Research Council.

Bellak, L. (1952). Introduction. In L. Bellak (Ed.), *Psychology of physical illness* (pp. 1–14). New York, NY: Grune & Stratton.

Bhojak, M. M., & Nathawat, S. S. (1988). Body image, hopelessness, and personality dimensions in lower limb amputees. *Indian Journal of Psychiatry, 30,* 161–165.

Blank, H. R. (1957). Psychoanalysis and blindness. *Psychoanalytic Quarterly, 26,* 1–24.

Blank, H. R. (1961). The challenge of rehabilitation. *Israel Medical Journal, 20,* 127–142.

Block, W. E., & Ventur, P. A. (1963). A study of the psychoanalytic concept of castration anxiety in symbolically castrated amputees. *Psychiatric Quarterly, 37,* 518–526.

Bordin, E. S. (1980). A psychodynamic view of counseling psychology. *Counseling Psychologist, 9,* 62–70.

Bornstein, R. F., & Masling, J. M. (Eds.). (1998). *Empirical perspectives on the psychoanalytic unconscious.* Washington, DC: American Psychological Association.

Bramble, K. (1995). Body image. In I. M. Lubkin (Ed.), *Chronic illness: Impact and interventions* (3rd ed., pp. 285–299). Boston, MA: Jones & Bartlett.

Byrne, D. (1961). The repression-sensitization scale: Rational, reliability, and validity. *Journal of Personality, 29,* 334–349.

Caplan, B., & Shechter, J. (1987). Denial and depression in disabling illness. In B. Caplan (Ed.), *Rehabilitation psychology desk reference* (pp. 133–170). Rockville, MD: Aspen.

Cash, T. F., & Pruzinsky, T. (Eds.). (2002). *Body image: A handbook of theory, research, and clinical practice*. New York, NY: Guilford.

Castelnuovo-Tedesco, P. (1978). Ego vicissitudes in response to replacement or loss of body parts: Certain analogies to events during psychoanalytic treatment. *Psychoanalytic Quarterly, 47*, 381–397.

Castelnuovo-Tedesco, P. (1981). Psychological consequences of physical defects: A psychoanalytic perspective. *International Review of Psychoanalysis, 8*, 145–154.

Centers, L., & Centers, R. (1963). A comparison of the body images and amputee and non-amputee children as revealed in figure drawings. *Journal of Projective Techniques, 27*, 158–165.

Chan, F., Livneh, H., Pruett, S., Wang, C. C., & Zheng, L. X. (2009). Societal attitudes toward disability: Concepts, measurements, and interventions. In F. Chan, E. D. Cardoso, & J. A. Chronister (Eds.), *Understanding psychosocial adjustment to chronic illness and disability: A handbook for evidence-based practitioners in rehabilitation* (pp. 333–367). New York, NY: Springer Publishing Company.

Cubbage, M. E., & Thomas, K. R. (1989). Freud and disability. *Rehabilitation Psychology, 34*, 161–173.

Degan, M. J. (1975). The symbolic passage from the living to the dead for the visibly injured. *International Journal of Symbology, 6*, 1–14.

de Maat, S., de Jonghe, F., Schoevers, R., & Dekker, J. (2009). The effectiveness of long-term psychoanalytic therapy: A systematic review of empirical studies. *Harvard Review of Psychiatry, 17*, 1–23.

Dewald, P. A. (1978). The process of change in psychoanalytic psychotherapy. *Archives of General Psychiatry, 35*, 535–542.

Doidge, N. (1997). Empirical evidence for the efficacy of psychoanalytic psychotherapies and psychoanalysis: A review. In S. G. Lazar (Ed.), Extended dynamic therapy: Making the case in an age of managed care. *In Psychoanalytic Inquiry* (Suppl., pp. 102–150). Hillsdale, NJ: Analytic Press.

Druss, R. G. (1986). Psychotherapy of patients with serious undercurrents of medical illness (cancer). *Journal of the American Academy of Psychoanalysis, 14*, 459–472.

Druss, R. G., O'Connor, J. F., Prudden, J. F., & Stern, L. O. (1968). Psychological response to colectomy. *Archives of General Psychiatry, 18*, 53–59.

Druss, R. G., O'Connor, J. F., & Stern, L. O. (1969). Psychologic response to colectomy. II. Adjustment to a permanent colostomy. *Archives of General Psychiatry, 20*, 419–427.

Druss, R. G., O'Connor, J. F., & Stern, L. O. (1972). Changes in body image following ileostomy. *Psychoanalytic Quarterly, 41*, 195–206.

Earle, E. (1979). The psychological effects of mutilating surgery in children and adolescents. *Psychoanalytic Study of the Child, 34*, 527–546.

Enders, J. E. (1979). Fear of death and attitudinal dispositions toward physical disability. *Dissertation Abstracts International, 39*, 7161A (University Microfilms No. 79-11825).

Engel, G. L. (1962). *Psychological development in health and disease*. Philadelphia, PA: Saunders.

Falvo, D. R. (2005). *Medical and psychosocial aspects of chronic illness and disability* (3rd ed.). Boston, MA: Jones & Bartlett.

Fenichel, O. (1930). *Ten years of the Berlin Psychoanalytic Institute (1920–1930)*. Berlin, Germany: Berlin Psychoanalytic Institute.

Fenichel, O. (1945). *The psychoanalytic theory of neurosis*. New York, NY: Norton.

Fine, R. (1973). Psychoanalysis. In R. Corsini (Eds.), *Current psychotherapies* (pp. 1–33). Itasca, IL: Peacock.

Fink, S. L., & Shontz, F. C. (1960). Body-image disturbances in chronically ill individuals. *Journal of Nervous and Mental Diseases, 131*, 234–240.

Fish, D. E. (1981). Counselor effectiveness: Relationship to death anxiety and attitudes toward disabled persons. *Dissertation Abstracts International, 42,* 1488A (University Microfilms No. 81-21927).

Fisher, S., & Greenberg, A. P. (1985). *The scientific credibility of Freud's theories and therapy.* New York, NY: Columbia University Press.

Fisher, S., & Greenberg, R. P. (Eds.). (1978). *The scientific evaluation of Freud's theories and therapy: A book of readings.* New York, NY: Basic Books.

Fonagy, P. (1982). The integration of psychoanalysis and experimental science: A review. *International Journal of Psychoanalysis, 9,* 125–145.

Fonagy, P., Roth, A., & Higgitt, A. (2005). Psychodynamic psychotherapies: Evidence-based practice and clinical wisdom. *Bulletin of the Menninger Clinic, 69,* 1–58.

Ford, D. H., & Urban, H. B. (1998). *Contemporary models of psychotherapy: A comparative analysis* (2nd ed.). New York, NY: Wiley.

Frankiel, R. V. (Ed.). (1994). *Essential papers on object loss.* New York, NY: New York University Press.

Freud, A. (1946). *The ego and the mechanisms of defense.* New York, NY: International Universities Press. (Original work published 1936)

Freud, S. (1958). Remembering, repeating, and working through. In J. Strachey (Ed. & Trans.), *The standard edition of the complete psychological works of Sigmund Freud* (Vol. 12, pp. 145–156). London, UK: Hogarth Press. (Original work published 1914)

Freud, S. (1959). Inhibitions, symptoms, and anxiety. In J. Strachey (Ed. & Trans.), *The standard edition of the complete psychological works of Sigmund Freud* (Vol. 20, pp. 75–173). London, UK: Hogarth Press. (Original work published 1926)

Freud, S. (1961). The ego and the id. In J. Strachey (Ed. & Trans.), *The standard edition of the complete psychological works of Sigmund Freud* (Vol. 19, pp. 3–66). London, UK: Hogarth Press. (Original work published 1923)

Freud, S. (1964). New introductory lectures on psychoanalysis. In J. Strachey (Ed. & Trans.), *The standard edition of the complete psychological works of Sigmund Freud* (Vol. 22, pp. 3–182). London, UK: Hogarth Press. (Original work published 1933)

Gallagher, P., Horgan, O., Franchignoni, F., Giordano, A., & MacLachlan, M. (2007). Body image in people with lower limb amputation: A Rasch analysis of the Amputee Body-Image Scale (ABIS). *American Journal of Physical Medicine and Rehabilitation, 86,* 205–215.

Gelso, C. J., & Carter, J. A. (1985). The relationship in counseling and psychotherapy: Components, consequences, and theoretical antecedents. *Counseling Psychologist, 13,* 155–243.

Gleser, G. C., & Ihilevich, D. (1969). An objective instrument for measuring defense mechanisms. *Journal of Consulting and Clinical Psychology, 33,* 51–60.

Greenacre, P. (1958). Early physical determinants in the development of the sense of identity. *Journal of the American Psychoanalytic Association, 6,* 612–627.

Greenberg, J., Pyszczynski, T., & Solomon, S. (1997). Terror management theory of self-esteem and cultural worldviews: Empirical assessments and conceptual refinements. In P. M. Zanna (Ed.), *Advances in experimental social psychology* (Vol. 29, pp. 61–141). San Diego, CA: Academic Press.

Greenson, R. R. (1967). *The technique and practice of psychoanalysis.* New York, NY: International Universities Press.

Grzesiak, R. C., & Hicok, D. A. (1994). A brief history of psychotherapy and physical disability. *American Journal of Psychotherapy, 48,* 240–250.

Gunther, M. S. (1971). Psychiatric consultation in a rehabilitation hospital: A regression hypothesis. *Comprehensive Psychiatry, 12,* 572–585.

Hartmann, H. (1964/1939). *Essays on ego psychology: Selected problems in psychoanalytic theory.* New York, NY: International Universities Press.

Head, H. (1920). *Studies in neurology* (Vol. II). London, UK: Oxford University Press.

Hirschberger, G. (2006). Terror management and attributions of blame to innocent victims: Reconciling compassionate and defensive responses. *Journal of Personality and Social Psychology, 91*, 832–844.

Hirschberger, G., Florian, V., & Mikulincer, M. (2005). Fear and compassion: A terror management analysis of emotional reactions to physical disability. *Rehabilitation Psychology, 50*, 246–257.

Kline, P. (1981). *Fact and fantasy in Freudian theory* (2nd ed.). London, UK: Methuen.

Knight, R. P. (1941). Evaluation of the results of psychoanalytic therapy. *American Journal of Psychiatry, 98*, 434–446.

Kohut, H. (1971). *The analysis of the self.* New York, NY: International Universities Press.

Kohut, H. (1977). *The restoration of the self.* New York, NY: International Universities Press.

Kruger, D. W. (1981–1982). Emotional rehabilitation of the physical rehabilitation patient. *International Journal of Psychiatry in Medicine, 11*, 183–191.

Krystal, H., & Petty, T. A. (1961). The psychological process of normal convalescence. *Psychosomatics, 2*, 366–372.

Langer, K. G. (1994). Depression and denial in psychotherapy of persons with disabilities. *American Journal of Psychotherapy, 48*, 181–194.

Lazar, S. G. (Ed.). (1997). Extended dynamic therapy: Making the case in an age of managed care. In *Psychoanalytic Inquiry* (Suppl.). Hillsdale, NJ: Analytic Press.

Leichsenring, F. (2001). Comparative effects of short-term psychodynamic psychotherapy and cognitive-behavioral therapy in depression: A meta-analytic approach. *Clinical Psychology Review, 21*, 401–419.

Leichsenring, F. (2005). Are psychodynamic and psychoanalytic therapies effective? A review of empirical data. *International Journal of Psychoanalysis, 86*, 841–868.

Leichsenring, F. (2009). Psychodynamic psychotherapy: A review of efficacy and effectiveness studies. In R. A. Levy & J. S. Ablon (Eds.), *Handbook of evidence-based psychodynamic psychotherapy* (pp. 3–27). New York, NY: Humana Press.

Leichsenring, F., & Leibing, E. (2003). The effectiveness of psychodynamic therapy and cognitive behavior therapy in the treatments of personality disorders: A meta-analysis. *American Journal of Psychiatry, 160*, 1223–1232.

Leichsenring, F., & Rabung, S. (2008). Effectiveness of long-term psychodynamic psychotherapy: A meta-analysis. *Journal of the American Medical Association, 300*, 1551–1565.

Leichsenring, F., Rabung, S., & Leibing, E. (2004). The efficacy of short-term psychodynamic psychotherapy in specific psychiatric disorders: A meta-analysis. *Archives of General Psychiatry, 61*, 1208–1216.

Liebert, R. M., & Spiegler, M. D. (1990). *Personality: Strategies and issues* (6th ed.). Pacific Grove, CA: Brooks/Cole.

Lipsey, M. W., & Wilson, D. B. (1993). The efficacy of psychological, educational, and behavioral treatment: Confirmation from meta-analysis. *American Psychologist, 48*, 1181–1209.

Livneh, H. (1982). On the origins of negative attitudes toward people with disabilities. *Rehabilitation Literature, 43*, 338–347.

Livneh, H. (1985). Death attitudes and their relationships to perceptions of physically disabled persons. *Journal of Rehabilitation, 51*, 38–41, 80.

Livneh, H. (1986). A unified approach to existing models of adaptation to disability: I. A model of adaptation. *Journal of Applied Rehabilitation Counseling, 17*(1), 5–16, 56.

Livneh, H. (2009). Denial of chronic illness and disability: Part I. Theoretical, functional and dynamic perspectives. *Rehabilitation Counseling Bulletin, 52*, 225–236.

Livneh, H., Chan, F., & Kaya, C. (2014). Stigma related to physical and sensory disabilities. In P. W. Corrigan (Ed.), *The stigma of disease and disability: Understanding causes and overcoming injustices* (pp. 93–120). Washington, DC: American Psychological Association.

Lussier, A. (1980). The physical handicap and the body ego. *International Journal of Psychoanalysis, 61*, 179–185.

Maddi, S. R. (1989). *Personality theories: A comprehensive analysis* (5th ed.). Chicago, IL: Dorsey.

McDaniel, J. (1976). *Physical disability and human behavior* (2nd ed.). New York, NY: Pergamon.

Meltzoff, J., & Kornreich, M. (1970). *Research in psychotherapy*. Chicago, IL: Aldine.

Messer, S. B. (2004). Evidence-based practice: Beyond empirically supported treatments. *Professional Psychology: Research and Practice, 35*, 580–588.

Milton, M. (2002). Evidence-based practice: Issues for psychotherapy. *Psychoanalytic Psychotherapy, 16*, 160–172.

Mitchell, K. R. (1970). The body image barrier variable and level of adjustment to stress induced by severe physical disability. *Journal of Clinical Psychology, 26*, 49–52.

Neff, W. S., & Weiss, S. A. (1961). Psychological aspects of disability. In B. B. Wolman (Ed.), *Handbook of clinical psychology* (pp. 785–825). New York, NY: McGraw-Hill.

Neiderland, W. G. (1965). Narcissistic ego impairment in patients with early physical malformation. *Psychoanalytic Study of the Child, 20*, 518–534.

Nelson, M., & Gruver, G. G. (1978). Self-esteem and body-image concept in paraplegics. *Rehabilitation Counseling Bulletin, 21*, 108–113.

Nemiah, J. C. (1964). Common emotional reactions of patients to injury. *Archives of Physical Medicine and Rehabilitation, 45*, 621–623.

Parkes, C. M. (1972a). *Bereavement: Studies of grief in adult life*. New York, NY: International Universities Press.

Parkes, C. M. (1972b). Components of the reaction to loss of limb, spouse or home. *Journal of Psychosomatic Research, 16*, 343–349.

Parkes, C. M. (1975). Psychosocial transitions: Comparison between reactions to loss of limb and loss of spouse. *British Journal of Psychiatry, 127*, 204–210.

Patton, M. J., & Meara, N. M. (1992). *Psychoanalytic counseling*. New York, NY: Wiley.

Pine, F. (1988). The four psychologies of psychoanalysis and their place in clinical work. *Journal of the American Psychoanalytic Association, 36*, 571–596.

Pollock, G. H. (1961). Mourning and adaptation. *International Journal of Psychoanalysis, 42*, 341–361.

Prioleau, L., Murdock, M., & Brody, N. (1983). An analysis of psychotherapy versus placebo studies. *Behavioral and Brain Sciences, 6*, 275–310.

Prochaska, J. O. (1984). *Systems of psychotherapy: A transtheoretical analysis* (2nd ed.). Chicago, IL: Dorsey.

Prochaska, J. O., & Norcross, J. C. (1994). *Systems of psychotherapy: A transtheoretical analysis* (3rd ed.). Pacific Grove, CA: Brooks/Cole.

Psychodynamic Diagnostic Manual (PDM) Task Force. (2006). *Psychodynamic diagnostic manual*. Silver Spring, MD: Alliance of Psychoanalytic Organizations.

Rappaport, D. (1960). The structure of psychoanalytic theory. In *Psychological Issues* 6 (Vol. 2). New York, NY: International Universities Press.

Rappaport, D., & Gill, M. M. (1959). The points of view and assumptions of metapsychology. *International Journal of Psychoanalysis, 40*, 153–162.

Robbins, S. B. (1989). Role of contemporary psychoanalysis in counseling psychology. *Journal of Counseling Psychology, 36*, 267–278.

Roth, A., & Fonagy, P. (1996). *What works for whom? A critical review of psychotherapy research*. New York, NY: Guilford.

Rybarczyk, B. D., Nicholas, J. J., & Nyenhuis, D. L. (1997). Coping with a leg amputation: Integrating research and clinical practice. *Rehabilitation Psychology, 42*, 242–256.

Rybarczyk, B. D., Nyenhuis, D. L., Nicholas, J. J., Cash, S. M., & Kaiser, J. (1995). Body image, perceived social stigma, and the prediction of psychosocial adjustment to leg amputation. *Rehabilitation Psychology, 40*, 95–110.

Sandler, J. (1960). The background of safety. *International Journal of Psychoanalysis, 41*, 352–356.

Sandler, J., & Rosenblatt, B. (1962). The concept of the representational world. *Psychoanalytic Study of the Child, 17*, 128–145.

Schilder, P. (1950). *The image and appearance of the human body*. New York, NY: International Universities Press.

Shapiro, D. A., & Shapiro, D. (1982). Meta-analysis of comparative therapy outcome studies: A replication and refinement. *Psychological Bulletin, 92*, 581–604.

Shedler, J. (2010). The efficacy of psychodynamic psychotherapy. *American Psychologist, 65*, 98–109.

Shontz, F. C. (1956). Body-concept disturbances of patients with hemiplegia. *Journal of Clinical Psychology, 12*, 293–295.

Shontz, F. C. (1975). *The psychological aspects of physical illness and disability*. New York, NY: Macmillan.

Siller, J. (1969). Psychological situation of the disabled with spinal cord injuries. *Rehabilitation Literature, 30*, 290–296.

Siller, J. (1970). The generality of attitudes toward the disabled. In *Proceedings of the 78th Annual Convention of the American Psychological Association* (Vol. 5, pp. 697–698). Washington, DC: American Psychological Association.

Siller, J. (1976). Psychosocial aspects of disability. In J. Meislin (Ed.), *Rehabilitation medicine and psychiatry* (pp. 455–484). Springfield, IL: Charles C Thomas.

Siller, J. (1984). The role of personality in attitudes toward those with physical disabilities. In C. J. Golden (Ed.), *Current topics in rehabilitation psychology* (pp. 201–227). Orlando, FL: Grune & Stratton.

Siller, J. (1988). Intrapsychic aspects of attitudes toward persons with disabilities. In H. E. Yuker (Ed.), *Attitudes toward those with physical disabilities* (pp. 58–67). New York, NY: Springer Publishing Company.

Siller, J., Chipman, A., Ferguson, L. T., & Vann, D. H. (1967). *Attitudes of the nondisabled toward the physically disabled*. New York, NY: New York University School of Education.

Smith, M. L., Glass, G. V., & Miller, T. I. (1980). *The benefits of psychotherapy*. Baltimore, MD: Johns Hopkins University Press.

Szasz, T. S. (1957). *Pain and pleasure*. New York, NY: Basic Books.

Taleporos, G., & McCabe, M. P. (2002). Body image and physical disability: Personal perspectives. *Social Science & Medicine, 54*, 971–980.

Thomas, K. R. (1994). Drive theory, self-psychology, and the treatment of persons with disability. *Psychoanalysis and Psychotherapy, 11*, 45–53.

Thomas, K. R. (1995). Attitudes toward disability: A phylogenetic and psychoanalytic perspective. In J. Siller & K. R. Thomas (Eds.), *Essays and research on disability* (pp. 121–128). Athens, GA: Elliott & Fitzpatrick.

Thomas, K. R., & Siller, J. (1999). Object loss, mourning, and adjustment to disability. *Psychoanalytic Psychology, 16*, 179–197.

Thurer, S. (1986). A psychodynamic perspective. In T. F. Riggar, D. R. Maki, & A. W. Wolf (Eds.), *Applied rehabilitation counseling* (pp. 102–111). New York, NY: Springer Publishing Company.

Wachs, H., & Zaks, M. S. (1960). Studies of body image in men with spinal cord injury. *Journal of Nervous and Mental Diseases, 131*, 121–125.

Westen, D. (1998). The scientific legacy of Sigmund Freud: Toward a psychodynamically informed psychological science. *Psychological Bulletin, 124*, 333–371.

Wright, B. A. (1983). *Physical disability: A psychosocial approach* (2nd ed.). New York, NY: Harper & Row.

# Adlerian Therapy

*Mary O'Connor Drout, Rochelle V. Habeck, and Warren R. Rule*

## LEARNING OBJECTIVES

This chapter informs readers of major concepts in Adlerian theory, with an emphasis on the contemporary relevance of Adlerian approaches for rehabilitation counselors and related professionals. The importance of a holistic understanding of individuals, as well as the significance of one's social context, is highlighted. As learning objectives, readers will achieve the following:

1. Develop an understanding of key concepts, including holistic understanding of individuals, the significance of social context in Adlerian approaches, and the importance of goal-directed behavior and "lifestyle."
2. Understand the counseling process in Adlerian approaches and the role of the counselor in providing encouragement while facilitating change.
3. Consider the level of evidence-based support for Adlerian approaches.
4. Appreciate the relevance of Adlerian theory in rehabilitation counseling, including the significance of the environment, the need to address problems in the environment, and implications for social justice.

## HISTORY

Alfred Adler was a physician, psychologist, and educator. His ideas have had a wide-ranging influence on multiple psychological therapeutic approaches, including gestalt, humanistic, reality, person-centered, and rational emotive behavior therapies (Corey, 2005). Adler's approach, known as "individual psychology," stresses the "indivisible" nature of each individual. Adler also believed in the importance of understanding individuals within social units, such as families; he maintained that people cannot be understood apart from their social context (Mosak & Maniacci, 1999). Adler's pioneering emphasis on the social, phenomenological, holistic, and goal-directed nature of people has maintained its application and popularity over time. Adler's focus on unity, that the whole person is something beyond the sum of the parts, and the importance of social context for fully understanding individuals, combine to make this approach particularly relevant for use with people with disabilities in rehabilitation settings (Rule, 1984a).

Alfred Adler (1870–1937), founder of individual psychology, was trained as a physician in Austria. Adler joined Freud's Psychoanalytic Society for a 10-year period, but his evolving beliefs in holism; the goal directedness of behavior; and the importance of social, family, and cultural influences led him to part ways with Freud. He believed in the creativity of the individual, influenced, but not firmly shaped, by heredity and the environment; his approach has been described as "soft determinism" as opposed to "hard determinism" (Ansbacher & Ansbacher, 1956). In light of the prevailing views at the time, Adler's departure from Freud was significant, and represented a great contrast to Freudian focus on unconscious and biological drives and psychosexual development.

Adler and others formed the Society of Individual Psychology in 1912 (Carlson & Englar-Carlson, 2012). The name of the society may be misleading, as it does not reflect Adler's pioneering emphasis on social context and the social embeddedness of personality. The choice of the term *individual* was based on the Latin *individuum* and was intended to reflect the indivisible and holistic nature of personality (Mosak & Maniacci, 1999).

When Adler immigrated to the United States in 1935, he was already widely known for his work in school reform and family education, and he was in demand as a speaker. His advocacy for social justice and his teachings were clearly influenced by his earlier experience of serving the "working class" as a physician and his personal history as a Jewish person in this period. In 1952, Rudolf Dreikurs founded the first Adler Institute in Chicago, currently known as Adler University, to further Adler's work. The Adler School, along with other institutes, societies, and the *Journal of Individual Psychology*, continues to provide instruction and information on the application of Adlerian approaches and psychotherapy to a wide variety of clients, issues, and societal challenges. Adler enjoyed success in his time, and the popularity of his theory continues today.

## MAJOR CONCEPTS AND THEORY OF PERSONALITY

### Holistic Nature of People

Adler believed in the holistic and indivisible nature of people, in contrast to Freud's conceptualization of the tripartite structure of id, ego, and superego. This Adlerian concept promoted the understanding of people as whole "individuals" versus a "collection of parts," which fits compatibly with the holistic perspective of rehabilitation. Adler believed that the person's wholeness or holistic nature is irreducible so that, considering parts of the personality separately inherently undermines understanding the individual. The way in which individuals organize themselves as whole people influences their perceptions of themselves and others and has a large bearing on their goals and behavioral interactions with others. One cannot "dissect" parts of the personality without losing some understanding of the main pattern or theme that runs through a person's life, which is necessary for understanding the behavior of the person. In rehabilitation, the focus on "person first" language supports this holistic approach for understanding and considering the whole person, rather than reducing the person and addressing needs as if they can be known from disabling characteristics as reflected in labeling language, such as "para" or "quad" (e.g., Wright, 1983). To illustrate this concept, Adler used the analogy of music, which cannot be fully appreciated by studying each note alone; rather, one needs to have the context of the other notes in order to experience the melody.

### Social Interest and Social Context

Adler is sometimes described as the first community psychologist, because he emphasized the importance of social interest (*gemeinschaftsgefühl*), an internal feeling of connectedness to others and their well-being, to the well-being of the individual. To Adler, social interest includes one's sense of belonging and ultimately striving and participating with others to improve one's community and the world, as the hallmark of the fully developed person. As Mosak and Maniacci (1999, p. 113) stated, "We have an obligation to people and life in general, and if our sense of community is strong, we take them into account in our actions and leave to posterity a better world." The importance of one's social interest was so significant in Adler's view that he equated social interest with mental health.

Ansbacher and Ansbacher (1956) noted that Adler's approach could be properly referred to as "context" psychology. Adler believed that people are social beings and that behavior can only be fully understood in a social context. He regarded personal problems basically as social or interpersonal problems. Key to the social nature of personality is the desire and need to belong. Each individual strives to find a place of significance in the eyes of others. The goal of obtaining a "place of somebodyness" is handled differently, depending on the early experiences and social context that have shaped the perceptions and goals of the person. According to this view, a life challenge (such as a disability) would be handled uniquely by different people, because both the perceived "place of somebodyness" and the social context or interpersonal world varies from person to person (Rule, 2004).

Because people are socially embedded in their needs and identity, the goals that a person pursues and the behaviors, attitudes, and convictions a person displays are seen as directly related to the innate desire to enhance oneself within a social context. Thus, in attempting to understand another person, a fundamental question would be, "How is this person seeking to be known by others?" The answer holds important implications for rehabilitation.

## Family Constellation and Birth Order

Adler is also sometimes considered to be one of the first family therapists. He recognized the importance of the family in the development and formation of personality and, unlike Freud, he worked, spoke, and wrote about his work with children and families (Mosak & Maniacci, 1999). The family constellation that surrounds the child includes the family atmosphere and emotional tone of the home, presence of siblings, their age differences and birth order, parental influences and expectations, parenting styles and family values, neighbors, and peers. Adler maintained that children form conclusions early in life that appear to be drawn from experiences related to this first social group. These conclusions (or beliefs) are drawn from a host of childhood impressions and experiences and become the goals that underlie the person's patterns in life. Adler believed these early conclusions are formed before approximately age 6 or 7 and go a long way toward determining the dimly conscious goals that comprise the individual's life pattern. After this age, the individual has begun to broaden the range of influences received from his or her first social group, the family, to those of the next social group, the school.

Because the family is the first social group that children encounter, one's attempt to stake out psychological "territory" in reaching self-significance or belonging in this first social group has implications for how individuals assume roles in later nonfamily groups (Carlson, Watts, & Maniacci, 2006). Thus, Adlerians give considerable emphasis to family constellation for understanding patterns of behavior. Accordingly, in psychotherapy, assessment carefully considers aspects of the family constellation, such as sibling age differences, order of birth, genders, favoritism, uniqueness, alliance groups, developmental patterns of siblings, and feeling of clients about their positions. Adlerians consider the importance of birth order, but view the *psychological* position of birth order, the role children adopt in relation to others as being more important than simply their actual ordinal birth order (Carlson et al., 2006; Corey, 2005).

Adlerians typically recognize five psychological birth order positions: *only child*—this child may not learn to share or cooperate with other children, has to use parents as role models, and may be perfectionists who set high goals; *oldest child*—for a time is the only child who is used to being number one and, therefore, develops the tendency to be independent, to be dependable, to be hardworking, and to do what is "right"; *second child*—the second child competes for attention with the oldest from the time of birth and often seeks to achieve successes in opposite areas of success from the oldest; *middle child*—this child may feel "squeezed" by siblings; many assume the role of peacemaker and diplomat; *youngest child*—the youngest is the "baby" of the family and tends to go his or her own way, often in areas not already pursued by siblings; he or she may crave stimulation and excitement (Carlson & Englar-Carlson, 2012; Corey, 2005).

## Goal Directedness

Adler believed that all behavior, including emotions, is goal directed, espousing a purposive or teleological explanation of behavior (Corey, 2005). Stated another way, *all things that people do have a purpose and are a function of their ideas, both conscious and dimly conscious, about consequences to be obtained in the future* (Rule, 2004). However, even though people may be aware of thinking, feeling, or acting in a certain way, most of the time they are unaware of the goals that are operating at a less conscious level and at work in all aspects of their daily lives. Behaviors that seemingly cannot be explained become more understood as the goal or purpose comes to light.

Adler believed that a person's pattern of long-range goals is organized around the subjectively determined concept of the self-ideal. These goals are informed by "private logic," one's deeply established beliefs that were based on perceptions and understandings of early childhood experiences (Carlson & Englar-Carlson, 2012) discussed in the previous section, which constitute the only "slice of life" from which a child can generalize. Considerable emphasis is placed, in attempting to understand a person and discern the underlying goals, on the psychological "territory" that the individual chose to stake out as his or her own in an attempt to feel that "others take notice of me when I am like this." Individuals learn at an early age through trial and error what goals will be most apt to help them move toward a place of significance, and they begin to experiment with behaviors that are most useful in implementing the goals. Not surprisingly, individuals also learn behaviors, including emotions, in keeping with the dimly conscious goals of the lifestyle that safeguard their vulnerabilities and sense of self-esteem. Generally speaking, this pattern of goals allows individuals to evaluate, to understand, to predict, and to control experience (Mosak, 2005).

The person, in his or her private logic, continually moves through life with this self-ideal as a general reference point and strives, at a dimly conscious level, to become like the imagined self, which he or she believes is necessary for attaining significance in the eyes of others and a real feeling of security. This striving provides the main thrust that motivates people to move, on a daily basis and throughout their lives, from a position of felt inferiority or noncoping to a position of overcoming or coping. Adler believed that this results in a pattern of complementary goals that are organized around a "fictional final goal" of the ideal self and what must be obtained to secure one's place in life. In addition, this pattern flows in this unified direction or "line of movement" as people move toward their goals in a variety of ways (Mosak & Maniacci, 1999).

Our goal-directed behaviors, emotions, and cognitions surrounding this self-ideal are thus based on subjective interpretation of experience. Depending on the circumstances in our early life experiences, our goals may be fueled by "faulty logic." The significance of this was noted by Adler (as cited in Mosak & Maniacci, 1999, p. 53), who commented, "The greatest tragedy about human nature might be that we make such great decisions about ourselves and our world when we are so small and know so little."

### The Five Life Tasks

Adler identified three life tasks as essential for full development of the individual: coping with problems of social relationships (community), coping with problems of work, and coping with the problems of love. Subsequently, Adlerians recognize two additional life tasks: coping with the self and understanding existence (Mosak & Maniacci, 1999). Adlerians believe that everyone takes a position, with varying degrees of success or failure, on these five areas of living. If one of the tasks is evaded, difficulties may ultimately unfold in the other tasks as well, or the pattern that works well in one or two of the tasks may not serve as well in the others. Unsuccessful attempts to navigate a major life task can result in psychopathology; challenges in meeting life tasks often bring one to seek therapy and should also be considered when encountered in the rehabilitation process in order to better facilitate successful outcomes.

### The Organizing Structure of the Lifestyle

The organizing structure for Adler's major concepts and theory of personality is the concept of "style of life," usually shortened to "lifestyle," a term that he originated. The term *lifestyle*, when used in this context, means something considerably more than contemporary uses of the word convey, which make it difficult to appreciate the fullness of this overarching concept in Adler's thinking and approach that this term represents. A broad definition is "that unity in each individual, in his thinking, feeling, acting, in his so-called conscious and unconscious, in every expression of his personality" (Ansbacher & Ansbacher, 1956, p. 175).

Adlerians believe that personality is expressed in present and future choices and is reflected in one's line of movement. The lifestyle is seen as the individual's holistic pattern of beliefs and goals that the person uses for interacting with others and for measuring self-worth. The characteristic ways that people strive and move toward goals are based on their lifestyle, which can be described as a "roadmap of life" or "strategy for living" (Corey, 2005), which then represents the characteristic ways that people strive and move toward goals.

Because the lifestyle shapes our present and future, yet so much of it is formed by age 6 or 7, Adlerians recognize that early childhood experiences are very significant and, thus, ascribe great importance to early recollections and to parenting. The lifestyle develops in children as an attempt to "make sense out of and control the data from the environment and their own bodies; they receive information, both internally and externally, that needs to be processed" (Mosak & Maniacci, 1999, p. 33). Children respond to cues from both their internal and external environments while they attempt to move forward with inherent motivation for growth. As they strive, they become aware of their "incompleteness," which leads to inferiority feelings that typically motivate effort and growth. Children strive for significance to move from this subjectively felt inferiority position toward self-conceived/fictional goals of superiority and security. The lifestyle is built on this private logic, not typically recognized by the person; yet it guides interpretations of the experiences that one encounters. With difficult or painful early life experiences, one develops faulty logic based on mistaken conclusions.

The lifestyle is pervasively at work in everyone's daily life. As highlighted previously, the lifestyle expresses itself broadly and often only dimly in the conscious (e.g., in selection of friends, in work, in love relationships, in definition of success and failure, in spirituality, in self-regard, in automobiles purchased, and in views taken toward the limitations of a disability). The overriding mental pattern is regarded by Adlerians as the unity that reflects the *key cognitive* dimensions on which a person takes a sensitive position (Rule, 2004). This mental pattern is useful to the individual, because it works in terms of the person's subjective perspective. Just as blinders on a horse serve to focus, and to limit, perspective and to get the horse through heavy traffic, so do selective perceptions and goals get people through life. This overriding mental pattern, in turn, influences the individual's feelings and behaviors in reaction to life's challenges. Thus, this unique pattern of thinking, the lifestyle, with its built-in limiters, leads people to their successes and failures and to their greatest strengths and weaknesses.

Because of the consistency of the cognitive nature of the lifestyle, it is often helpful to the individual to have an awareness of this unique lifestyle pattern when facing decisions or facing problems. This awareness is especially worthwhile, due to the fact that the lifestyle, the time-tested pattern of basic attitudes and expectations, becomes most obvious when the person is experiencing stress. The lifestyle concept, as well as the appearance-under-stress phenomenon, has useful implications for rehabilitation practitioners.

Therapy and other therapeutic or significant life events allow for change in one's lifestyle convictions (Carlson & Englar-Carlson, 2012). Adlerians see development as "an ongoing process in which the person is continually creating (or recreating) him or herself. He or she is always in the process of becoming" (Mosak & Maniacci, 1999, p. 20).

## DESCRIPTION OF THE COUNSELING PROCESS

Adlerian therapists believe that all people can grow and change and that this is desirable. So, they optimistically support this potential in clients and view the process of change to be one of encouraging the client's growth and development (Carlson & Englar-Carlson, 2012). When clients encounter difficulties, counselors seek to help identify what needs to be changed and then to help clients understand how they have a part in creating the difficulty and can take responsibility for change. In essence, the goal of Adlerian counseling is to identify goals and assumptions in the cognitive map that interfere with successful living in any of the main life tasks and to help modify these toward a sense of belonging and useful social interest. The Adlerian counseling process involves four broad components: relationship development, assessment that focuses on the client's lifestyle or cognitive map, facilitating self-understanding, and supporting change through reorientation.

### Relationship

The change process rests on the foundation of a positive relationship. The Adlerian approach requires the establishment of a highly collaborative, egalitarian, and cooperative relationship, characterized by mutual respect and trust (Corey, 2005). The counselor must not accept the position of expert, but steadfastly maintain an active, optimistic, and supportive partnership with the client throughout the process of learning and change. The relationship provides the basis for the development of the subsequent phases, as well as providing a secure context for helping the client explore himself or herself in relationship to the disability and providing for the exchange of information needed for the rehabilitation process (e.g., medical, vocational, procedural).

### Lifestyle Assessment

The assessment phase focuses on the person in his or her social and cultural context, valuing the subjective understanding and unique world of this individual (Carlson & Englar-Carlson, 2012). One can think of this process as having two parts. In the subjective interview, clients are very actively helped to tell their stories, with follow-up questions to understand client functioning in the five tasks of life and to help reveal their approaches toward life's tasks, their unique strengths in coping, their blind spots, and what may account for their concerns (Corey, 2005). The subjective interview is often concluded with "The Question," asking the client how his or her life would be different if the problem did not exist (Carlson et al., 2006). Sometimes the answer to this question indicates the purpose for which individuals are experiencing significant difficulties, or from what life task they wish to retreat, or from what demands or threats they are defending themselves.

The second part of the assessment process, the objective interview, includes gathering information about current concerns and how they began, social history, and coping efforts with life tasks, in addition to a lifestyle assessment (Corey, 2005). There are a number of useful interview forms available for conducting lifestyle assessments; examples include the Lifestyle Personality Inventory (Wheeler, Kern, & Curlette, 1991) and manuals developed by Shulman and Mosak (1988) and Powers and Griffith (1995). Central components of the lifestyle interview are the person's early childhood history, family constellation, and early memories, as this is where one acquires most of one's view of the way life works; in addition, gender roles, expectations, one's position in relation to the forces governing early life, and the ways that one adopts for striving to reach the goals perceived as necessary for living are also addressed. The interview questions about the family constellation are straightforward—asking about birth order and sibling relations, sibling rankings on possible areas of competition (e.g., intelligence, pleasing, having own way, athletics, appearance, temper), sibling interrelationships, parental relations, family values, and cultural context—and help reveal the client's perception of the conditions and family climate during their early years and how this contributed to the way one views oneself and others (Corey, 2005).

#### Eliciting Specific Early Recollections

In completing the lifestyle assessment, importance is given to the client's early specific recollections as a way to understand the person's beliefs about the self and others, coping patterns and strengths, and assumptions that interfere. Adlerians rely on the selectivity of memory as providing information that is useful to the individual's lifestyle. Adlerians believe that recollections are remembered that coincide with one's present outlook on self, others, or life. Thus, the person's early recollections reflect the same patterns that are operating currently in the person's cognitive map; they are reminders that the individual carries around regarding personal limits and the meaning of circumstances (Ansbacher & Ansbacher, 1956). Most individuals can remember events, both real and even imagined, before approximately age 6 or 7 when children typically enter the larger social arena with school entry. Each early recollection, when considered in the context of the accompanying feelings about the remembered incident, reflects a current expectation. Adlerians focus on the manifest content of the early memory, not on hidden, symbolic meanings. Moreover, each recollection supplements and rounds out the outlook reflected by the other early recollections; themes in the remembered early environment reflect the dimly conscious notions and goals the client is presently using.

### Other Sources of Lifestyle Information

Supplemental sources are discussed by Lombardi (1973), including the importance of other case history data (knowing about clients), expressive behavior (observing clients), grouping (interacting with clients), and symptomatic behavior (clients' telltale signs). Much can also be learned from what the client avoids in life, what the client criticizes in others, and as Goethe contended, nothing is more revealing than what makes one laugh (Rule, 2004).

## Facilitating Self-Understanding

Adlerians believe that lifestyle behaviors serve important purposes, and they also believe that the goals of the lifestyle must be identified and understood by the counselor and client to serve as the foundation for any change that needs to occur. Thus, the counselor's focus in interpreting the assessment findings is to promote insight, in a sense a confrontation, in which the client examines the beliefs and goals the behavior may be serving (Carlson & Englar-Carlson, 2012). Adlerians believe that the lifestyle operates in service of the person's primary goal in relating to others and the world based on the conclusions drawn from experiences with the person's early world. The emphasis for the practitioner is on relating patterns of lifestyle movement, grounded in childhood conclusions, to understand the person's main way of relating to others and achieving a feeling of significance (Corey, 2005). These same patterns reveal the person's preferred mode for coping with life and preserving the self when dealing with stress and challenge. The practitioner is interested in using the assessment information to help the client become more aware of these conclusions and patterns and to be able to see how the goals one's lifestyle serves may also be contributing, however consciously, to difficulties that the client is experiencing currently.

Assessment information is summarized and shared in a collaborative manner with the client, in the context of the trusting and egalitarian relationship, with interpretations and suggestions offered in tentative terms for the client's input and discussion. Using the lifestyle material to see what conclusions about self, others, and life that the person has drawn, the practitioner helps identify the goals the person seems to have used in striving to be a coping, significant person (Carlson et al., 2006). In addition to broad, overriding goals, the counselor helps the client identify specific convictions that may relate to current concerns, such as issues related to disability.

The focus is placed on the current behavior and situation of the client, using awareness developed from the assessment, to clarify the client's underlying goals and beliefs and to better understand what may be contributing to present problems and what one can do to change this. Helping the person to identify and gain insight about mistaken beliefs being held as part of one's cognitive map and that are contributing to present problems is an essential part of this phase before change can be addressed. Various terms for describing common behavioral patterns, the goals served, and their potential pitfalls have been offered (e.g., Mosak, 1971).

### Reorientation (Supporting Change)

Reorientation emphasizes education and change and builds on the practitioner's and the client's awareness of the client's lifestyle or cognitive map and its relationship to current concerns. Expressed another way, now that they both have insight into the client's daily implementation of the lifestyle, a springboard for agreed-upon change has been created. Self-defeating features of the lifestyle can be identified, and goals and homework strategies for overcoming them can be established. Beyond this, a broader educational perspective can be used to explore the interrelatedness among thinking, feeling, and doing, especially how thoughts are usually at the root of emotions that energize behavior; to encourage a belief in a significance of self that is not a function of comparisons with others or self-rankings; and to foster increased empathy or social interest toward others (Carlson et al., 2006). The aim is to assist the client in developing a perspective toward life that is more fully functioning, identifying and addressing fears, thoughts, and patterns that interfere with adaptive functioning in life's main tasks. In this phase, the client is supported in moving from insight to action, using the encouraging relationship to help sustain motivation, and making choices that are more consistent with the goals truly desired (Carlson & Englar-Carlson, 2012).

Encouragement is a central Adlerian concept at this stage and should be a major component of all strategies. Despite the conveyance of encouragement, however, the clinician places responsibility with the client for his or her own approach to a given situation. The counselor serves as a coach or teacher to help clients acquire the skills and behaviors to create more functional patterns in their lifestyles. The focus is kept on the (future-oriented) goals of a behavior or feeling, because this focus reduces the likelihood that the client will feel burdened by, or use to one's "advantage," the "whys" or "causes" of behavior. The "whys" or "causes" reflect past, unchangeable reasons, whereas "goals" indicate future-oriented, changeable targets. Because the process creates increased awareness of the goals one's old behaviors attempted to serve, the client becomes less likely to pursue them now that one recognizes how these work to one's ultimate disadvantage. Adler is said to have expressed this point in an unforgettable metaphor: Once the therapist has spat into the client's soup, the client can continue to eat the soup, but it won't taste as good (Carlson et al., 2006).

Bitter and Nicoll (2000) articulated the application of Adlerian brief therapy and how it can be used in a short period to provide focus and effective change. Mosak and Maniacci (1998) offered a large number of situation-specific procedures in counseling and psychotherapy that are tailored to Adlerian applications (for a detailed description, interested readers are encouraged to the review their book, *Tactics in Counseling and Psychotherapy*). Compatible strategies and techniques from other approaches (e.g., rational emotive behavioral, gestalt, behavioral, cognitive behavioral, and family therapy) may be incorporated at this stage as well. The facilitative use of humor to help clients develop lifestyle awareness and recognize lifestyle goals in their thoughts and behaviors is valued in this approach. Awareness can also be accomplished through the use of fables, parables, metaphors, cartoons, recordings, photographs, and so on. The use of humor and Adlerian tactics and strategies are handled in a spirit of true encouragement (not necessarily praise), conveying worth, acceptance, and uniqueness of the client.

## ENCOURAGEMENT AS A SPECIAL FOCUS

Adler saw encouragement as the foundation of psychotherapy (Main & Boughner, 2011), including the development of social interest of the client. The counselor's role is to develop and enhance by helping the client to create alternatives that replace discrepant behaviors with goal-enhancing actions. This requires encouragement, a process that focuses on the person's resources, strengths and assets, recognizes client efforts and positive movement, and adopts an optimistic position. Carlson and Englar-Carlson (2012, p. 99) point out that encouragement is especially useful with people from groups who are marginalized in our culture and have experienced constant discouragement, noting, "The use of encouragement and acceptance can be an extremely validating and supportive process with sociopolitical ramifications for both the client and the therapist." The German term Adler used for encouragement, Ermutigung, means "to encourage through action"; in this context, action by the therapist to instill courage in the client to engage the community (Main & Boughner, 2011). Adler held that "courage is found only on the side of life that advances community" (Ansbacher & Ansbacher, 1978, p. 399).

This German word Alder chose emphasizes the active role and responsibility on the part of the therapist to motivate the client to join with others and engage in community, which is highly compatible with and results from the goals of rehabilitation. Encouragement was much more than theory to Adler; in this approach, encouragement is a method that is positive and requires action (Main

& Boughner, 2011). Accomplishing this requires the development of a counseling relationship with sufficient intimacy and trust to inspire actionable hope and possibility, leading Adlerians to define encouragement as "the affective aspect of therapy" (Main & Boughner, 2011, p. 270), which Adler himself embodied in his work and proponents find so difficult to convey. Adlerian therapists use an eclectic variety of techniques, but all within a framework of encouragement.

Reaching rehabilitation goals and overcoming obstacles, internal and external, requires courage and is the less visible, yet essential, work of the counselor and client. Adler recognized that the process of developing courage is not linear and thus requires considerable patience and commitment on the part of the counselor. Main and Boughner (2011) summarize from Adlerian scholars that maintaining encouragement relies on structuring the relationship as cooperative and equalitarian and attributing success to the client to foster autonomy, hope, and resilience; staying coolheaded and not engaging with the client in battle when behaviors are discrepant with goals; and positioning oneself carefully in relation to the client's discouragement or opposition. Adler developed indirect and direct techniques (e.g., paradoxical, compliance based, action oriented) to help the therapist sustain encouragement in the face of client responses to obstacles and change. The positive actions and change that must be undertaken by the client rest on the client's need for belonging and for useful contribution, which the counselor and client awaken together. They emphasize that cocreating this emotional basis for change requires the therapist's deep belief in a client's abilities to contribute to the community, and that when clients believe in this possibility, they will be able to risk change. Sustaining the case for change (e.g., reaching rehabilitation goals) will depend on the extent to which clients have access to actionable hope and believe they are entitled to equity.

"Encouraged people are willing to take risks and do things that lead toward growth" (Carlson & Englar-Carlson, 2012, p. 98); Carlson and Englar-Carlson describe discouragement as the feeling of not belonging or being useful, which can come from within the person's own cognitions or from adverse life circumstances and conditions outside the person, from the familial to societal level. This perspective is clearly relevant to considering the effect of social barriers—be they architectural or policy based or attitudinal in nature—on the person and what is required to overcome them. By joining with and encouraging clients and normalizing their difficulties, a pathway can be created for reaching even the most discouraged people. Encouragement and prescriptive actions are linked to the lifestyle assessment, which has given the client (and counselor) a new, meta-perspective about oneself and one's life. As Main and Boughner (2011, p. 274) summarize from Adler and his followers, clients "do not thirst so much for information as they thirst for motivation, resolve, or the courage to change."

In rehabilitation, clients may be balancing learning how to reach goals and believing they can. Adler believed that people will put learning into practice and take action once they are sufficiently inspired to believe and hope they can change the course of their lives. Adler's articulation of the role of encouragement has great value for rehabilitation counseling.

## REHABILITATION APPLICATIONS

In addition to encouragement, many aspects of the Adlerian approach are consistent with current perspectives in positive rehabilitation approaches. Of particular importance are the goal and future orientation of Adlerian perspectives, the empowering and egalitarian relationship between counselor and client, the value of holistic understanding of the person, and the importance of developing social interest.

Clearly, the goal focus and future orientation of the Adlerian approach align well with the purpose and nature of rehabilitation. The Adlerian approach is also positive, hopeful, and action based (Main & Boughner, 2011), as is the rehabilitation process. Described as an optimistic approach, Adlerians believe that people can learn and change, and, as in rehabilitation, Adlerians stress the importance of skill training and an educational model of treatment (Carlson & Englar-Carlson, 2012), with learning as a foundational aspect of the process (Shifron, 2010). Although the social context of early childhood may have shaped a great deal of the lifestyle, Adler held a strong belief in the creative power of the individual as giving agency to determine one's future.

The egalitarian relationship in Adlerian counseling is of central importance to the premise of its effectiveness. Consistent with contemporary rehabilitation, the client must be an empowered participant, an active, copartner with the counselor in the Adlerian process. Within a framework of encouragement, the counselor focuses on the client's assets and strengths, helping the client engage and strengthen these in problem-solving interventions to reach identified goals. This approach is highly consistent with optimal rehabilitation counseling values and methods.

The holistic understanding of the individual that is fundamental to an Adlerian approach is compatible with a comprehensive view of rehabilitation. Tools such as lifestyle analysis provide a uniquely comprehensive lens that incorporates the personal meanings of the individual within his or her social context, which can help discern what significance the impairment or disability may have for this person in this circumstance. Understanding the client's lifestyle can help the counselor and client understand discrepancies in the client's behavior on plans or assigned tasks toward professed goals. Analysis may identify lifestyle goals and mistaken beliefs that serve as barriers to adjustment to disability or success in rehabilitation, for example, those involving competition, dependency, fears of loss of liberty, inferiority, or views of authority. Instead of viewing these stalemates in progress as lack of client motivation or as client resistance, the Adlerian perspective would consider the behavior in light of the lifestyle, create and replace it with alternative, growth-enhancing behaviors (Watts, 2000), and assist the client in different ways to develop social interest. Through this process of reorientation, one involves and assists the client in overcoming barriers to success.

This individual-focused perspective for understanding the significance of disability also reduces the focus on a comparative frame of reference that has been associated with "succumbing" to disability (Wright, 1983). This person-centered approach can help the client and counselor focus on the particular strengths and assets and goals of the individual. In these ways, the Adlerian approach is consistent with a more complete consideration of disability and can facilitative perspective for personal adjustment, consistent with Wright's coping versus succumbing model. The role of the counselor would be to consider how the lifestyle impacts the significance of the disability and the goals for rehabilitation and to help the client use this information for accomplishing his or her real aims. Rather than viewing problems in adjustment or in rehabilitation progress from a pathology perspective, Adlerians see adjustment as a process and would likely view this impasse as evidence of discouragement. Adler explained that when we are in favorable situations, our style of life cannot be seen clearly. But in new situations when confronted with difficulty, the style of life becomes visible quickly (Rule, 2004). In the rehabilitation context, one may see defenses in service of the lifestyle as a client experiences difficulty with a goal. Seen from this light, the counselor can help clients see how to advance efforts and encourage them to achieve their goals in more effective ways.

Adler's assumption that finding social meaning in our lives is the basis for mental health is very consistent with values that underlie the philosophy and policy support for vocational rehabilitation. Both hold that increasing participation in community and in work has inherent worth to the individual and will mutually promote the well-being of the client as well as the interests of the supporting community. With these guiding assumptions, Adler encouraged his patients to connect with others and find joy in service (Main & Boughner, 2011). The focus of rehabilitation on goals of productive engagement and social participation are clearly consistent with the assumptions underlying Adlerian theory regarding the need of the individual for belonging and meaningful contribution. Rehabilitation counselors encourage the involvement of their clients in peer support, advocacy efforts, and activities of centers for independent living as ways to find supportive relationships and opportunities to serve others confronting similar challenges. Rehabilitation counselors also assist the individual in removing or overcoming barriers outside the person in his or her environment. Mosak (2005, p. 63) notes, "The Adlerian is not interested in curing sick individuals or a sick society, but in reeducating individuals and in reshaping society." The goals of both rehabilitation and of Adlerian approaches simultaneously serve the personal adjustment needs of the individual as well as the goals of the community.

## CASE STUDY

Sally J. was a 43-year-old female, who married for the second time 2 years prior to her automobile accident in which her left leg was crushed. Despite a successful medical recovery, including prosthesis, she was referred for counseling. Sally complained of feeling depressed and worthless. Her two children from her first marriage were living away from home. Her husband was the only source of income for the household.

*(continued)*

*(continued)*

As the result of exploratory discussion, it seemed that the client blamed her accident for most of her unhappiness, feared that her relatively new husband would leave her because of her disfigurement, and found herself withdrawing socially as she continued to become increasingly depressed. The counselor gathered lifestyle information, using an Abbreviated Lifestyle Form, designed by Rule (1984b), and introduced this process in roughly the following manner:

> Sally, sometimes it is helpful to be in touch with some pretty broad attitudes and goals that are at work in major areas of a person's life. We are talking here about important beliefs that an individual has learned about herself, other people, and life that she probably is not completely aware of but influence her nonetheless. One way that I have found very useful in trying to help someone identify these beliefs is by taking a look at impressions from early childhood a person continues to believe and that may be contributing to a person's difficulties. You and I could discuss a few of your early impressions and then explore how these may be operating right now, in your everyday life. Want to give it a try?

The client described herself in childhood as being the oldest of three, with a brother 3 years younger and a sister 5 years younger. She did not get along with her brother and saw him as bossy, deceitful, and her mother's favorite. She got along better with her sister, whom she viewed as cute, charming, and her father's favorite. She described herself as shy, with her feelings easily hurt, yet having a good sense of humor. She regarded her father as somewhat distant, intimidating, and having a drinking problem; he expected her to be perfect. Sally described her mother as attractive, easygoing, even submissive, and easy to please; she gave Sally no indication that she should have been different than she was. The family atmosphere was portrayed as tense and unpredictable. Sally's three early recollections were:

1. Age 3. I remember when my brother was born. That afternoon, Mom was holding him, looking at him and kissing his head. I was mostly watching from the kitchen.
   Feeling? Sad, jealous.
   Most vivid part? The look on her face.
2. Age 3 ½. I remember one time lying on the grass in my backyard. It was a clear, sunny day and the breeze was blowing gently. I was looking at the different shapes of the clouds and how they were slowly moving.
   Feeling? Content, curious.
   Most vivid part? The soft look of the clouds.

*(continued)*

*(continued)*

3. Age 5. I was in kindergarten. The teacher, Miss Moore, went around the room looking at the crayon drawings we were doing at our desks. She lifted mine up, looked at it and said, "Nice work."
   Feeling? Proud, special.
   Most vivid part? Miss Moore looking at it.

As noted previously, the counselor relies on the selectivity of long-term memory as being an indicator of present expectations of self, others, and life. The lifestyle information seems to suggest that Sally is very sensitive to losing a place of importance, and that she regards herself as quiet and fragile, while wishing to be perfect. Her sensitivity to being unappreciated and to not measuring up is coupled with a desire to maintain a low profile. Gender-guiding lines in her social context indicated that men can be powerful and challenging; women are expected to be accepting. Several areas were noted in the client's lifestyle patterns for potentially useful focus: her achievement orientation, her strong preference for engaging life visually, and her capacity for humor.

Sally agreed with the counselor's interpretation of these issues that touched a tender nerve. Based especially on her lifestyle sensitivities, the therapist made a special effort to emphasize to her, throughout the therapy process, the importance of speaking out if she felt that what she said was being taken lightly. (Rule [1984c] has addressed the key issue of therapist self-awareness and blind spots as an interactive factor with client vulnerability.) Considerable discussion was initially devoted to how these sensitivities were at work in her daily life, particularly how some of these notions converged to result in the irrational expectation that her husband would leave her and that others could not accept her because of her lost leg. These lifestyle beliefs included her sensitivity to losing a place of importance, seeking to measure up or be perfect, tending to expect males to challenge or to distance, and emphasizing—and thereby expect others to emphasize—the visual aspects of life (e.g., her leg).

Becoming aware of and disputing these cognitive expectations were part of the initial strategy for change or reorientation. The push-button technique (Mosak & Maniacci, 1998) was used to teach Sally that thoughts largely control emotions. Ellis's (1994) A-B-C-D-E techniques, which are quite compatible with Adler's approach, were used to encourage her and to help her dispute her tendency to rate herself based on others', especially her husband's, total approval. The goal of increasing her unconditional self-acceptance was further strengthened by Ellis's shame-attacking exercises and rational emotive imagery, which built on her visual propensity; she was to imagine herself being self-accepting, regardless of her worst fear of others' disapproval of her or her amputated leg. Later on, systematic exercises

*(continued)*

*(continued)*

were used daily, which capitalized on her ability to generate humor; these homework procedures were developed by Rule for increasing internal locus of control using self-modeled humor by a visual method (Rule, 1979) and by an auditory self-imaging procedure (Rule, 1977).

After Sally achieved considerable progress with the cognitive strategies, the therapist used role-playing with Sally to increase her assertiveness skills with others, particularly in communicating her concerns with her husband. Although he was reluctant to participate in joint counseling, he responded mostly favorably to her new-found approach to communication.

To further build on the client's strengths and to increase her choices for attaining a place of lifestyle significance in keeping with the strengths of her self-ideal, the therapist explored her keen visual orientation. Assessment revealed an aptitude for and a strong pattern of interest in artistic pursuits. Following several courses in drawing and in painting at a community college, Sally achieved great satisfaction from teaching artistic expression to seniors at a nearby center as a volunteer.

In summary, the application of the lifestyle counseling process involves the realms of feeling, thinking, and behaving. A useful metaphor is that the interaction of relationship factors (feeling oriented) is the key that opens the door to the dark room; the lifestyle self-understanding (thinking oriented) creates light in the room; and the reorientation methods (action oriented) rearrange the room and the furniture to meet the wishes of the individual.

## RESEARCH FINDINGS

There are a number of challenges with Adlerian theory and its application for evaluating this approach with the currently accepted evidence hierarchy. Adler was more of a pragmatist than a theoretician. As a result, Adlerian theory is often criticized for having concepts that are general and simplistic and, therefore, hard to define and operationalize. Adler has also been criticized for not providing sufficiently specific procedures for key aspects of the approach, such as lifestyle interpretation and reorientation. When used in applied settings, like schools, Adlerian theory is often embedded in other interventions, so its specific impact is difficult to assess. With these constraints and predilections of Adlerians, review of Adlerian literature illustrates that there is limited use of what has been described as higher level evidence, such as randomized controlled trials. Review of Adlerian literature demonstrates a preference for use of single case studies (Mosak, 2005). As a result, though many have referred to extensive research investigations based on Adlerian approaches (e.g., Stewart, 2012), there is limited support for the constructs of Adlerian theory that meet high levels of evidence in the accepted evidence hierarchy. Nevertheless, there is other important evidence to consider.

The Adlerian construct of lifestyle has been investigated extensively. Kern, Gormley, and Curlette (2008) summarized the results of 41 studies using the Basic Adlerian Scales for Interpersonal Success–Adult Form (BASIS–A) inventory, which assesses lifestyle themes with five primary scales, including belonging/social interest, going along, taking charge, wanting recognition, and being cautious. Kern et al. maintain the BASIS–A is a viable research and clinical tool. They found research applications ranging from aspects of personality to pathology, adjustment, career, leadership, and organizational behavior in the literature. Kern et al. also advocate for increasing the base of empirical support for Adlerian theory.

Adler's early recognition of the importance of the social contexts of the family and education in one's development has led to a long and rich application of his ideas in parenting education, academic programming, and student preparation. The approach that Adler and Dreikers developed decades ago still forms the basis of many current parent education programs that are considered best practice, namely, that children learn best with logical versus arbitrary consequences, that encouragement is powerful, and that assisting children to develop internalized discipline, to feel self-worth, and to find a place in and value community will yield positive outcomes. Empirical examination in these areas provides support for Adlerian theory, yet also demonstrates the challenge of parceling out the specific impact of Adlerian theory when it has been infused with other interventions. For example, Brigman, Villares, and Webb (2011) cite meta-analytic support for the use of individual psychology approaches to improve student achievement and behaviors and to help students develop and grow. They reviewed programs for school-based counselors grounded in individual psychology principles that emphasize students' strengths, social interest, belonging, and encouragement. These principles are clearly reflective of, yet not unique to, individual psychology and include other principles as well. Villares, Brigman, and Peluso (2008) offer evidence for a Ready to Learn (RTL) program, in which early elementary school students in a randomized comparison group study received an RTL intervention informed by individual psychology and scored significantly higher on listening comprehension and behavior related to academic and social skills. The holistic RTL approach intervention included students, teachers, school counselors, and parents. RTL combined the Adlerian principles of addressing the need to belong, encouragement, and social skills, along with intervention for cognitive skills, so it is difficult to ascribe the RTL-measured outcomes, such as gains in student achievement, solely to the Adlerian elements. Gfroerer, Kern, and Curlette (2004) compared the impact of democratic and authoritative parenting styles as addressed in the individual psychology's parenting education model. They found support for this model in Baumrind's (1996) longitudinal research findings, associating positive outcomes with an authoritative parenting style, along with the protective effects of the sense of community (democratic style) against adolescent risk-taking behaviors. These findings support Adlerian assertions about the importance of a sense of belonging and social interest.

Adler's consideration of birth order has also received extensive attention in the literature. In reviewing the empirical literature, Stewart (2012) notes that the vast majority of the hundreds of birth order studies have relied on *actual* rather than *psychological* birth order. This distinction is a critical one for Adler's followers, who emphasize that it is one's functional rather than actual birth order position that shapes social context and development. However, instruments assessing psychological birth order may have limited applicability due to changes in family structure since Adler's time. Stewart notes that the most commonly used assessment of psychological birth order, the White–Campbell Psychological Birth Order Inventory (PBOI; Campbell, White, & Stewart, 1991), can be further refined by considering changes in family structure, such as the impact of large increases in single-parent households.

Examining research about Adlerian constructs, such as social interest and the need to belong, illustrates the challenge of terminology in generating research support for Adlerian theory. For example, noting that Adlerians do not agree on what constitutes "social interest," a key element of Adlerian theory, Bass, Curlette, Kern, and McWilliams (2002) investigated social interest using five self-report instruments of social interest found in Adlerian literature. They found low correlations among the measures of social interest. Similarly, Gere and MacDonald (2010) reviewed the literature to examine support for the Adlerian concept of the need to belong. Although they found evidence for strong positive effects of feelings of belonging on cognition, emotion, and behavior, as well as negative effects with its absence, they also noted many inconsistencies warranting further investigation.

## PROMINENT STRENGTHS AND LIMITATIONS

In evaluating strengths of the Adlerian approach, Corey (2005, pp. 118–119) concluded:

> Adler was far ahead of his time, and most of the contemporary therapies have incorporated at least some of his ideas. Individual Psychology assumes that people are motivated by social factors; are responsible for their own thoughts, feelings, and actions; are the creators of their own lives, as opposed to helpless victims; and are impelled by purposes and goals, looking more toward the future than the past.

Strengths of the Adlerian approach, which resonate in rehabilitation, include its strengths-based, creative, and positive perspective; the importance of a holistic understanding of individuals; a focus on health and wellness as opposed to pathology; and the key significance of one's social context or community. A person's earliest social system is the family, and Adler was a pioneer in recognizing the importance of family systems; later Adlerians have provided extensive focus on how to support the family, increase parenting effectiveness, and provide community supports for families.

The Adlerian emphasis on social context led to the consideration of multiculturalism long before others, recognizing that "social embeddedness" naturally leads to consideration of the unique aspects of a client's culture. The practice of Adlerian therapy lends itself to assisting diverse groups, and Adlerian practitioners have addressed issues of ethnicity, gender, racism, sexual orientation, disability, and social equality (Carlson et al., 2006).

The issue as to where to intervene for issues related to disability helps illustrate how multiculturalism can be seen as both a strength and weakness in the Adlerian approach. The person–environment interaction and the corresponding importance of social context have an important history in reframing rehabilitation and approaches to understanding disability espoused by Wright (1983) and expressed in Hahn's (1985) minority group model of disability. In its conceptualization of disability, the World Health's Organization's (2001) *International Classification of Functioning, Disability and Health (ICF)* meshes well with the Adlerian consideration of social context; for example, as disability and functioning occur in context, environmental factors are important (Peterson, 2005).

Although the Adlerian approach is lauded for being multicultural (e.g., Ansbacher & Ansbacher, 1978; Carlson et al., 2006), caution regarding a "western" focus in Adlerian approaches has been raised (e.g., Carlson & Englar-Carlson, 2012; Corey, 2005). Adlerian approaches can be construed as relying on the "self" as the focus of change. However, in recognizing the importance of the environment, the *ICF* model illustrates the potential for consideration of environmental factors, including social policy and the built environment, to allow for greater participation and inclusion for persons with disability. Calls for Adlerians to attend to social justice issues (e.g., Todman & Mansager, 2009) recognize the importance of change efforts at the environmental level.

A frequently noted criticism of the Adlerian approach is its emphasis on general concepts that are hard to define and quantify, and some of Adler's concepts have been evaluated as simplistic and commonsense. The breadth of scope in the Adlerian approach (e.g., the individual, the family, parenting, the social context, the importance of community) likely perpetuates difficulties in defining and then assessing (especially in an evidence-based approach) the efficacy of exclusively Adlerian precepts. Indeed, the degree to which Adlerian concepts have been found in other theories (e.g., cognitive behavioral therapy [CBT], gestalt, existential approaches, and family theories) demonstrates both the significance of Adler's contributions and the challenge in isolating what is exclusively Adlerian. Nonetheless, the key aspects of Adlerian approaches suggest that this theory is compatible with the rehabilitation perspective and has much to offer practitioners in helping people with disabilities to live connected, self-directed lives (see Carlson & Englar-Carlson, 2012).

## ACKNOWLEDGMENTS

The authors wish to acknowledge the extensive contributions of Dr. Warren Rule in enriching the field of rehabilitation counseling. He is posthumously listed as third author to recognize his work in the first edition of this text and also to honor his many contributions in integrating Adlerian theory with rehabilitation and promoting social interest through his writing, teaching, and practice.

## DISCUSSION EXERCISES

1. Discuss the importance of early experiences and the family constellation in Adlerian theory.
2. Explain the implications of Adler's belief that all behavior is goal directed in the counseling process.
3. Articulate the organizing structure of the lifestyle.
4. Describe the stages of the counseling process in Adlerian approaches and articulate the role of the counselor.
5. Consider the Adlerian value for the importance of social context in understanding an individual; contrast this with the role of social context in another theoretical approach.

## REFERENCES

Ansbacher, H. L., & Ansbacher, R. W. (Eds.). (1956). *The individual psychology of Alfred Adler.* New York, NY: Basic Books.

Ansbacher, H. L., & Ansbacher, R. W. (Eds.). (1978). *Cooperation between the sexes: Writings on women, love and marriage, sexuality and its disorders.* Garden City, NY: Anchor Books.

Bass, M. L., Curlette, W. L., Kern, R. M., & McWilliams, A. E., Jr. (2002). Social interest: A meta-analysis of a multidimensional construct. *Journal of Individual Psychology, 58,* 4–33.

Baumrind, D. (1996). The discipline controversy revisited. *Family Relations, 45,* 405–414.

Bitter, J., & Nicoll, W. G. (2000). Adlerian brief therapy with individuals: Process and practice. *Journal of Individual Psychology, 56,* 31–44.

Brigman, G., Villares, E., & Webb, L. (2011). The efficacy of individual psychology approaches for improving student achievement and behavior. *Journal of Individual Psychology, 67,* 408–419.

Campbell, L. F., White, J., & Stewart, A. E. (1991). Relationship between psychological and actual birth order. *Individual Psychology: The Journal of Adlerian Theory, Research, and Practice, 47,* 130–140.

Carlson, J., Watts, R., & Maniacci, M. (2006). *Adlerian therapy: Theory and practice.* Washington, DC: American Psychological Association.

Carlson, J. D., & Englar-Carlson, M. (2012). Adlerian therapy. In J. Frew & M. D. Spiegler (Eds.), *Contemporary psychotherapies for a diverse world* (1st ed., pp. 87–129). New York, NY: Routledge/Taylor & Francis.

Corey, G. (2005). *Theory and practice of counseling and psychotherapy* (7th ed.). Belmont, CA: Cengage Brooks/Cole.

Ellis, A. (1994). *Reason and emotion in psychotherapy revised.* New York, NY: Carol Publishing.

Gere, J., & MacDonald, G. (2010). An update of the empirical case for the need to belong. *Journal of Individual Psychology, 66,* 93–115.

Gfroerer, K. P., Kern, R. M., & Curlette, W. L. (2004). Research support for individual psychology's parenting model. *Journal of Individual Psychology, 60,* 379–388.

Hahn, H. (1985). Toward a politics of disability: Definitions, disciplines, and policies. *Social Science Journal, 22,* 87–105.

Kern, R. M., Gormley, L., & Curlette, W. L. (2008). BASIS-A Inventory empirical studies: Research findings from 2000 to 2006. *Journal of Individual Psychology, 64,* 280–309.

Lombardi, D. N. (1973). Eight avenues of lifestyle consistency. *Individual Psychologist, 10,* 5–9.

Main, F. O., & Boughner, S. R. (2011). Encouragement and actionable hope: The source of Adler's clinical agency. *Journal of Individual Psychology, 67,* 269–291.

Mosak, H. H. (1971). Lifestyle. In A. Nikelly (Ed.), *Techniques for behavior change* (pp. 77–81). Springfield, IL: Charles C Thomas.

Mosak, H. H. (2005). Adlerian psychotherapy. In R. J. Corsini & D. Wedding (Eds.), *Current psychotherapies* (7th ed., pp. 52–95). Belmont, CA: Brooks/Cole.

Mosak, H. H., & Maniacci, M. (1998). *Tactics in counseling and psychotherapy.* Itasca, IL: Peacock.

Mosak, H. H., & Maniacci, M. (1999). *A primer of Adlerian psychology: The analytic–behavioral–cognitive psychology of Alfred Adler.* New York, NY: Brunner-Routledge.

Peterson, D. (2005). International classification of functioning, disability and health: An introduction for rehabilitation psychologists. *Rehabilitation Psychology, 50,* 105–112.

Powers, R. L., & Griffith, J. (1995). *The individual psychology client workbook.* Chicago, IL: American Institute of Adlerian Studies.

Rule, W. (1977). Increasing self-modeled humor. *Rational Living, 12,* 7–9.

Rule, W. (1979). Increased internal-control using humor with lifestyle awareness. *Individual Psychologist, 16,* 16–26.

Rule, W. (1984a). *Lifestyle counseling for adjustment to disability.* Rockville, MD: Aspen.

Rule, W. (1984b). Abbreviated lifestyle form. In W. Rule (Ed.), *Lifestyle counseling for adjustment to disability* (pp. 343–346). Rockville, MD: Aspen.

Rule, W. (1984c). Lifestyle self-awareness and the practitioner. In W. Rule (Ed.), *Lifestyle counseling for adjustment to disability* (pp. 319–330). Rockville, MD: Aspen.

Rule, W. R. (2004). Adlerian therapy. In F. Chan, N. L. Berven, & K. R. Thomas (Eds.), *Counseling theories and techniques for rehabilitation health professionals* (pp. 53–75). New York, NY: Springer Publishing Company.

Shifron, R. (2010). Adler's need to belong as the key for mental health. *Journal of Individual Psychology, 66,* 10–29.

Shulman, B., & Mosak, H. (1988). *Manual for lifestyle assessment.* Muncie, IN: Accelerated Development.

Stewart, A. E. (2012). Issues in birth order research methodology: Perspectives from individual psychology. *Journal of Individual Psychology, 68,* 75–106.

Todman, L. C., & Mansager, E. (2009). Social justice: Addressing social exclusion by means of social interest and social responsibility. *Journal of Individual Psychology, 65,* 311–318.

Villares, E., Brigman, G., & Peluso, P. R. (2008). Ready to learn: An evidence-based individual psychology linked curriculum for prekindergarten through first grade. *Journal of Individual Psychology, 64,* 403–415.

Watts, R. E. (2000). Adlerian counseling: A viable approach for contemporary practice. *TCA Journal, 28,* 11–23.

Wheeler, M. S., Kern, R. M., & Curlette, W. L. (1991). Life-style can be measured. *Individual Psychology: Journal of Adlerian Theory, Research & Practice, 47,* 229–240.

World Health Organization. (2001). *International classification of functioning, disability and health (ICF).* Geneva, Switzerland: Author.

Wright, B. A. (1983). *Physical disability: A psychosocial approach* (2nd ed.). New York, NY: Harper & Row.

## CHAPTER
## 11

# Basic Counseling Skills

*Norman L. Berven and Jill L. Bezyak*

### LEARNING OBJECTIVES

Basic counseling skills, which are the focus of this chapter, are essentially relationship-building and empathic listening skills, drawing out client stories and concerns in depth, along with the surrounding context. Thus, basic counseling skills serve as the foundation for working collaboratively with clients in understanding and conceptualizing their concerns and problems in ways that can be addressed, along with developing counseling, service, and intervention plans to address the concerns in collaboration with the client. The skills are basic to virtually all theoretical orientations in counseling, which help counselors conceptualize problems and develop plans for interventions and other services. The goals of this chapter are to facilitate understanding and development of the skills to apply in counseling, regardless of a counselor's theoretical orientation. Following are the learning objectives to be addressed:

1. Develop knowledge of the importance of the counseling relationship and build skills that can facilitate therapeutic relationships and the ability to encourage clients to share and elaborate on their stories and concerns.
2. Develop knowledge and skill in applying basic attending behaviors in counseling.
3. Develop knowledge of the different ways that questions can be formulated and build skill in using both direct and indirect open questions and follow-up questions in counseling.
4. Develop knowledge of and skill in using the active listening responses of encouragers and restatements, paraphrases, reflections of feeling, and summarizations.
5. Develop skill in integrating the basic listening skills to structure a counseling session.

## FACILITATIVE RELATIONSHIP AND COMMUNICATION SKILLS

### Basic Therapeutic Conditions

Virtually all theoretical approaches to counseling and psychotherapy emphasize the importance of strong therapeutic or working relationships with clients.
The client-centered approach, now commonly known as the person-centered
approach, has been particularly prominent in recognizing the importance of the
relationship. Rogers (1942, 1951; Chapter 2 in this volume) hypothesized that the
basic therapeutic conditions of empathy, genuineness, and unconditional positive regard are the necessary **and** sufficient conditions for constructive change
through counseling and psychotherapy (Rogers, 1957). However, although virtually all theoretical approaches to counseling and psychotherapy recognize the
importance of these conditions in accomplishing constructive change, they are
now typically viewed as necessary **but not** sufficient, thus suggesting that interventions are also necessary that go beyond the basic conditions. The working
alliance is a related concept, emphasizing the critical importance of the emotional
bond between client and counselor, in addition to agreement between counselor
and client on therapeutic goals and tasks to be undertaken in the counseling
relationship (Bordin, 1994). There is substantial empirical evidence to support
the importance of the therapeutic relationship, with extensive meta-analyses
conducted to document the contributions of the relationship to success in counseling across many different types of interventions and treatments (Norcross &
Wampold, 2011).

Rogers (1957, p. 99) refers to empathy as a unique type of understanding
in the counseling relationship, entering the client frame of reference to understand the perceptions of client experiences from their own frames of reference, to
"sense the client's private world as if it were your own, but without ever losing
the 'as if' quality." Rogers (1957, p. 98) refers to unconditional positive regard as
nonjudgmental and nonevaluative, as "experiencing a warm acceptance of a client's experience as being part of that client ... neither approval nor disapproval
of the client ... simply acceptance." Rogers (1957, p. 97) refers to genuineness on
the part of counselors as being "within the confines of this relationship, a congruent, genuine, integrated person ... not presenting a façade" and not denying his
or her own feelings to him or herself.

Rogers (1957) goes on to point out that the therapeutic conditions of empathy, unconditional positive regard, and genuineness must not only be experienced by counselors but also must be communicated effectively so that clients are
able to perceive the empathy and acceptance that counselors feel toward them.

### Microcounseling or Microskills

A number of attempts have been undertaken to operationalize the communication of the therapeutic conditions in the form of basic counseling skills. As discussed by Hill and Knox (2013), three of the most visible and researched programs
to train counselors in these skills are human relations training (HRT; Carkhuff,

1969), interpersonal process recall (IPR; Kagan, 1984), and microcounseling or microskills (Ivey, 1971). As pointed out by Ridley, Kelly, and Mollen (2011, p. 801), "For more than four decades, the microskills approach has been the dominant paradigm of training in counseling psychology and other mental health specialties, especially for entry level trainees." As noted in the *Intentional Interviewing and Counseling* text by Ivey, Ivey, and Zalaquett (2014), now in its eighth edition, the microcounseling or microskills approach has been used in more than 1,000 university and related training programs in counseling. In rehabilitation counseling training programs specifically, Dalgin, Bruch, and Barber (2010) noted that 83% of the programs required microskills training prior to practicum, and another 3% reported microskills training as a part of practicum training. A number of textbooks are available to facilitate preparation in basic counseling skills by Ivey and colleagues (e.g., Evans, Hearn, Uhlemann, & Ivey, 2011; Ivey et al., 2014) and by other authors (e.g., Cormier, Nurius, & Osborn, 2013; Egan, 2014; Hill, 2014), all of which cover the basic skills addressed in the present chapter along with other counseling skills.

The specific skills that are covered here, namely, attending, questioning, minimal encouragers, paraphrases, reflections of feeling, and summarizations, are particularly important in the initial stages of counseling. In the initial stages, the focus of counseling is on building the base of a strong working relationship, in addition to understanding client concerns and stories. In addition, specific types of interviews emphasize these skills, including intake interviews and other types of assessment and clinical interviews (Berven, 2008, 2010). However, the skills can also be useful at subsequent points in counseling, when the focus is on listening; for example, a client may want to report on experiences with a homework assignment, and the counselor attempts to facilitate the telling of the story.

It is important to point out that microskills go well beyond the basic skills to be covered here, including, for example, self-disclosure, interpretation, reframing, and empathic confrontation (e.g., see Ivey et al., 2014). In addition, Ridley, Mollen, and Kelly (2011) have suggested that the range of microskills be expanded to a variety of other counseling competencies, including not only counseling behaviors but also cognitive and affective skills. According to the counseling model proposed by Hill (2014), the microskills covered in this chapter are particularly important in the initial exploration stage of counseling, with the goals of attending, observing, listening, and exploring both thoughts and feelings, prior to the stages of insight and action. In the initial stages of counseling, there is typically an emphasis on listening and attempting to understand as fully as possible the client's concerns and stories.

Ivey et al. (2014) indicate that microcounseling training has been supported through more than 450 empirical studies to document effectiveness. Both verbal and nonverbal components of communication are emphasized, as the nonverbal component is a major part of communication; in other words, it is not only the words spoken that are important, but also the ways and manner in which those words are spoken. Listening effectively and making an attempt to understand what a client is communicating is at the core of the counseling process, and, because many people are probably better "talkers" than "listeners," the development and refinement of active listening skills is important. It is certainly important to listen in order to hear and understand client stories. In addition, because many individuals are not particularly good listeners, being listened to can be a refreshing change and a powerful tool in relationship building, showing the client that the counselor cares enough to give undivided attention to hearing and understanding the client's message.

## ATTENDING

Attending skills may be defined as the verbal and nonverbal counseling skills that communicate the therapeutic conditions, show clients that counselors are focusing their attention on them and what they have to say, facilitate strong therapeutic relationships, and encourage and reward continued client communication (Hill, 2014; Ivey et al., 2014). As already noted, all interpersonal communication includes both verbal and nonverbal channels. The nonverbal channel is composed of at least two components, kinesic and paralinguistic. Kinesic components include both eye contact and body language, the latter comprising more specific components. Paralinguistic components of communication include the voice qualities of volume, pitch, pace, and fluency. As also previously noted, much of communication occurs through nonverbal channels, particularly the communication of emotion (e.g., a smile, a red face, a raised voice with increased volume). Further, when the verbal and nonverbal components of a message conflict (e.g., a person saying the words, "I am NOT angry," with a red face, a loud voice, and a shaking finger), the nonverbal message is the more likely to be believed.

### Specific Attending Skills

**Eye contact** is one of the most important attending skills, showing clients that counselors are paying attention and that they are interested in what clients have to say. Failure to maintain eye contact may be interpreted by clients as disinterest, discomfort with the client or the topic being discussed, or distraction or preoccupation with other matters as opposed to what the client is communicating. Facilitative eye contact involves simply looking at the person in a natural way, without "glaring" or "staring." Some breaks in eye contact are perfectly natural, while still maintaining a focus on the client. Counselors are more likely to maintain eye contact with clients as they are talking, maybe glancing away occasionally as they are collecting their thoughts and responding. One important function of eye contact is the regulation of turn-taking in communication, with the speaker sometimes breaking eye contact, occasionally glancing away while talking, and then looking at the other person when it is his or her turn to talk. Because of the importance of eye contact in communication, it is more common for two people to interrupt one another while talking on the telephone, as opposed to face-to-face conversations, because the absence of eye contact makes it more difficult to effectively regulate turn-taking.

**Body language and facial expression** represent another component of attending behavior. Facilitative body language typically includes facing a client directly and leaning slightly toward the client, with a comfortable posture and arms unfolded, not slouching and not ramrod straight. Natural physical gestures are consistent with facilitative body language, consistent with the content and flow of the conversation, not sitting totally still and stiff. Smiles and head nods, again not overdone, and facial expressions conveying attention and concern are also components of facilitative body language.

**Paralinguistics or vocal qualities** are also components of attending behavior, including volume, pitch, and pace or speed of talking. Facilitative communication is characterized by volume that is moderate, not too loud and not too soft; pace or speed of speaking that is moderate, not too quick and not too slow; and pitch that is appropriately modulated according to the words and ideas being communicated, as opposed to flat and monotone.

One of the most important components of paralinguistics is latency in responding, which refers to the delay from the time that a client finishes speaking until the counselor begins a response. Latency can vary from a very long delay to a very short or even nonexistent delay, jumping in before the client has actually finished speaking and interrupting the client. Interruptions and short delays in communication may often be perceived as aggressiveness, whereas very long delays may be perceived as passivity. In addition, if counselors frequently interrupt clients or demonstrate very short response latencies, they may be perceived as more concerned with what they themselves have to say than what the client has to say, and clients may then see the counselor as not truly listening and paying attention. Longer latencies in responding may be particularly important with clients who tend to speak slowly, with long pauses, perhaps pondering before speaking, as a counselor may miss additional important things that the client has to say when jumping in too quickly. Attempts to lengthen latencies in responding may be difficult for counselors who tend to typically communicate in a fast-paced manner, but doing so may be very helpful in improving listening and attending skills, getting more important information from clients in interviews, and building rapport.

Silence can be anxiety provoking in conversation, both for counselors and clients, and counselors may rush in to fill the silence and respond too quickly. Sometimes, particularly when clients look like they are thinking or contemplating what they might say, it is often important to wait until the counselor perceives that the client has finished talking. In addition, when counselors are thinking about what they are going to say next, which can often occur, especially with beginning counselors, this can be a major distraction from listening to all that a client is communicating. It is typically beneficial to try to focus total attention on what a client is communicating and then taking a moment to reflect on what has been communicated in order to think about what to say in response, accepting that a few moments of silence will be okay.

**Verbal tracking** is one of the most important of the active listening skills and is also one of the most difficult to master. Verbal tracking occurs when counselor responses follow from client leads, continuing on the same or a related topic that follows directly from what the client is communicating, as opposed to introducing new topics. Verbal tracking leads to more organized interviews as opposed to interviews that seem to "bounce around" from topic to topic. One of the benefits of verbal tracking is that clients will likely perceive counselors as listening to what they have to say, as verbal tracking can only be accomplished if the counselor hears what the client is communicating. In addition, verbal tracking can serve to facilitate understanding of client stories by exploring what the client is communicating in greater depth, not leaving topics until they are more fully explored. Thus, verbal tracking can produce many important benefits in counseling and are basic to some of the other microskills yet to be discussed in this chapter.

### General Considerations on Attending

If counselors do not actually experience a sense of warmth, caring, and interest toward a client, it is difficult to convince the client otherwise. However, clients may not always perceive these qualities on the part of the counselor, even when the counselor experiences them, and basic attending skills may serve to communicate those qualities to clients. Basic attending skills can demonstrate that counselors care enough to pay attention to clients and what they are communicating, also helping to build a strong working relationship or rapport (Ivey et al., 2014). Attending skills help to "grease the wheels" and help clients to open up and tell their stories in greater depth. From a behavioral perspective, attending skills can be viewed as reinforcing client communication, with counselor attention serving as the reinforcer.

Many counselors may engage in note taking during counseling, either jotting down handwritten notes or entering information by computer during a counseling session. Such note taking can detract counselor attention from clients and what they are communicating. Thus, to the extent possible, it may be beneficial to minimize note taking during counseling or interviewing sessions, perhaps allowing a few minutes after a session to then make notes while information is still fresh in the mind of the counselor. If counselors have forms to complete or other information to obtain from clients in an initial interview or at other points in counseling, it may be helpful to first allow clients to talk and express what they have to say, and later in the session say something like, "Before we get back to talking, there are some forms that we have to complete, so maybe we can take care of that at this point."

As previously discussed, verbal tracking is probably the most difficult of the attending skills to master, because tracking requires listening and perceiving what clients are communicating. Often counselors may be thinking about what they are going to say next while the client is talking, detracting from listening to the client. Alternatively, counselors will typically benefit by devoting their full attention to what clients are communicating, waiting until they have finished, and then thinking about what the client has communicated and formulating a response to follow that topic or to switch to a new topic. As is true in any conversation, counselors may be at a loss as to what to say at any point in a counseling session. As noted previously, counselors can get back on track by taking a moment of silence to think about what the client has communicated and what part of that communication may be helpful to follow up.

Basic attending skills can influence perceptions of counselors on the part of clients in positive ways, and these skills can help clients open up and tell their stories and elaborate on their concerns. In addition, these skills can be readily learned, although verbal tracking may be more challenging to master, and Ivey and colleagues (e.g., Ivey et al., 2014) have developed procedures to teach these skills with documentation to support their effectiveness.

## QUESTIONS

Questions are essential in interviewing and counseling, as they are in all human interaction. However, counselors vary in the extent to which they rely on questions, as opposed to other types of responses, and also in the ways in which questions are formulated, both of which can influence client responses, in addition to client perceptions of the counselor and relationship or rapport building (Ivey et al., 2014).

### Open-Ended and Closed-Ended Questions

Closed-ended and open-ended questions represent two general ways of formulating questions. Closed-ended questions can be answered with one or a small number of words (e.g., "Do you like school?"), whereas open-ended questions request more elaborate responses (e.g., "What things do you most like about school?"). It is important to note that some questions, which are technically yes–no questions, actually function like, and can be considered to be, open-ended (e.g., "Can you tell me about school?" is technically a yes–no question, but the response requested is clearly not a yes–no response).

Open-ended questions may be further divided into direct and indirect open-ended questions. Direct open questions would be clearly seen as questions ending with a question mark (e.g., "What is school like for you?"). In contrast, indirect open questions do not end with a question mark, although they function like questions (e.g., "Tell me about school" or "I'm interested in knowing more about what school is like for you"). Open questions, whether direct or indirect, can be open to different degrees (e.g., "What is school like for you?" vs. "What do you enjoy about school?" vs. "What is the single thing that you enjoy most about school?"). Sometimes a client may not be able to handle the degree to which a question is open. For example, a counselor may say, "Please tell me about yourself" to which the client may reply, "Well, what do you want to know?" indicating that he or she is having difficulty answering, so the counselor may follow up with a less open alternative, "Well, I'm interested in knowing about your family."

Closed-ended questions tend to provide very specific direction to a client and are thus highly efficient in getting specific information sought (Cormier et al., 2013); for example, it is much more efficient to learn a client's age by asking "How old are you?" as opposed to "Please tell me about yourself" and hoping that age will be a part of the response. Because of the efficiency provided by closed-ended questions, a great deal of specific information can be obtained in a short amount of time. In addition, for some clients, closed-ended questions from counselors are less threatening because the counselor assumes more responsibility for the interaction, with the client simply giving short answers to direct, specific questions. Finally, closed-ended questions give the counselor greater control over the interaction and the responses that are likely to come from the client; because of the control given to the questioner, attorneys conducting a cross-examination will frequently use closed-ended questions (e.g., "Is it not true that you disliked Mr. Jones, the victim of this crime?").

Open-ended questions also have advantages. Although closed-ended questions may sometimes produce a longer client response than a simple "yes" or "no," open-ended questions generally tend to produce much longer and more elaborate responses than closed-ended questions. Thus, open-ended questions will typically elicit more extensive and detailed information, which can then be followed up by the counselor, and clients will tend to do more of the talking and counselors less (Ivey et al., 2014). Open-ended questions also put more of the control for the interaction in the hands of clients, giving them more freedom to tell their stories. Because of the more elaborate responses that open-ended questions produce, attorneys conducting a direct examination of their own witnesses will often use more open-ended questions (e.g., "Please tell the court about your relationship with Mr. Jones").

### Uses and Types of Open-Ended Questions

#### Opening New Topics of Discussion

Open questions are typically used to open an interview (Ivey et al., 2014), whether an initial interview (e.g., "What brings you in to see me today?" or "Please tell me about yourself" or "I'm interested in knowing what's on your mind, so where would you like to start?") or a subsequent interview (e.g., "What has been happening with you since we last talked?" or "At the end of our last interview, you were all set to follow up on that job lead that you were excited about, and I'm interested in knowing all about it"). Open-ended questions are also typically used to open a new topic of discussion in an interview after transitioning from the previous topic (e.g., "Tell me about the role that your sister might be playing in these difficulties that you've been having" or "How about the relationship with your other boss?").

#### Obtaining Information

Who, what, where, or why questions elicit specific facts or information (e.g., "In the office where you work, who seems to take the major responsibility for getting those types of things done?" "What responsibilities in your office would you most like to have?"). "Why" questions can sometimes come across as challenging and may thus provoke defensiveness, and this can be due to the experiences that we have had with "why" questions dating back to our childhood (e.g., "Johnny, why is your room always such a mess?" or "Johnny, why can't you be nice to your little sister?" or "Johnny, why do you persist in tormenting me?"). "Why" questions (e.g., "You're unhappy with your work situation, so why don't you do something about it?") can easily be rephrased as "what" questions (e.g., "You're unhappy with your work situation, so what do you see as your options to deal with it?"), so the use of "why" questions can be minimized relatively easily, avoiding their possible disadvantages (Cormier et al., 2013).

### Following Up on Client Communications to Explore Topics in Greater Depth

Questions can be used for verbal tracking to stay with a topic and explore it in further depth. Some very simple open-ended follow-up questions can be used to accomplish this purpose (e.g., "Could you tell me more about that?" or "Please tell me more" or "Can you go a little further with that?").

In contrast to these more general follow-up questions seeking elaboration, other follow-up questions can attempt to obtain greater detail in understanding client stories and communications (e.g., "Can you tell me more specifically what you mean?" or "When you say that she is sometimes combative, can you tell me what you mean by 'combative'?"). A particularly helpful type of follow-up question asks for specific examples (e.g., "Can you give me an example of a typical day at work for you?" or "Can you give me a specific example of a time when he said something that specifically bothered you in that way?"). Asking for specific examples can be extremely helpful in more fully understanding a client's story and communications (Ivey et al., 2014).

Consistent with the attending skill of verbal tracking, follow-up questions can be used to stick with topics and explore them more fully. Leaving topics and moving on to new topics more quickly may provide a more superficial picture of client stories, and counselors may often not explore topics in sufficient depth. Following is an example, beginning with no follow-up and, instead, moving on to a new related topic:

Co: Have you been looking for work?

Cl: Yes, every single day I have been looking and working hard at it, but I haven't been able to find anything.

Co: That's got to be really frustrating. How is the money holding out after being unemployed for so long?

Following is an alternative, following up on the client's last response:

Cl: Yes, every single day I have been looking and working hard at it, but I haven't been able to find anything.

Co: I'm interested in knowing more about your job hunt. … Can you tell me more about it?

Cl: Well, like I said, it's every single day … a real grind?

Co: Well, let's take yesterday as an example. Perhaps you can tell me specifically what you did yesterday in your job hunt.

Cl: OK, yesterday. … It was pretty much like all of the days … I got my cup of coffee and sat down with the newspaper first thing in the morning and looked at the job ads and, just like all or the other days, there was absolutely nothing worthwhile, so I went on with my day.

The counselor follow-up in this alternative interchange brought out a more specific picture of the client's job hunt, much different from the picture from the first interchange, showing the value of following up and not leaving topics too quickly.

## Building Skills in Formulation and Use of Questions

### Closed Versus Open-Ended Questions

An interview that is composed almost entirely of questions may sound much like an interrogation rather than a counseling or interview session (Ivey et al., 2014). This is particularly true if the questions are predominantly closed-ended, tending to elicit "yes–no" or other very short client responses to the counselor questions; a preponderance of closed-ended questions will also typically reduce the proportion of talk time on the part of the client versus the counselor, making it more difficult to get a thorough and in-depth understanding of client stories. Closed-ended questions tend to be commonly used in day-to-day communication because of their efficiency in getting some information and then moving on. Thus, people generally tend to be more skilled in asking closed rather than open-ended questions and tend to automatically phrase questions in a closed-ended format, so work is needed to build skill in using open-ended questions as a part of the repertoire of questioning skills.

It is relatively easy to rephrase a closed question into an open-ended format (e.g., "Do you want to go to the technical school?" can be rephrased as "What are your thoughts about going to technical school?"). So, skill in formulating questions in an open-ended format can be developed through practice in regular day-to-day conversations, taking a moment to think about the question that you are about to ask, determining whether it is closed or open-ended and, if closed-ended, rephrase it in an open-ended format. One possible goal of such practice is to work toward the point of being able to carry on a conversation, say for 20 minutes, without asking a single closed-ended question. Working toward this goal is not meant to imply that closed-ended questions are "bad," but rather to become as skilled in formulating questions in an open-ended format as in asking closed-ended questions; as this skill is established in the repertoire of questioning skills, open-ended questions can be readily formulated whenever they are judged to best serve a purpose at any point in an interaction. In addition, using more indirect open questions, as opposed to direct open questions, can also make a difference in the tone of an interview or counseling session, making it sound less like an interrogation, and the use of indirect open questions can be practiced in a similar manner, consciously reformulating direct open questions into an indirect format.

## Using Follow-Up Questions

Again, because there is often an emphasis on efficiency in day-to-day communication, little follow-up may often occur. In interviewing and counseling, depth of understanding may often be more important than efficiency, and more extensive follow-up will be critical in accomplishing greater depth of understanding (Ivey et al., 2014). As with open-ended questions, it is possible to practice listening to what a person has to say in a conversation and using follow-up questions to get more specific information (e.g., "Can you tell me more about that?" or "When you say that he can be difficult to deal with, can you tell me more specifically what you mean?" or "Can you give me an example when he seemed difficult to deal with?").

## ACTIVE LISTENING RESPONSES

Active listening responses provide alternatives to questions, facilitating follow-up and verbal tracking. Nearly all active listening responses focus on some aspect of what the client has communicated and indicate what you have heard in the client's message. Active listening responses may focus on the content of a client response or on the affective component of what the client has communicated. Because they require that the counselor listen in order to respond to the client's message, active listening responses show the client that the counselor is paying attention and listening (Ivey et al., 2014). In addition, they provide alternatives to questions, reducing the reliance on questions as a general type of counseling response.

## Encouragers

Head nods and "uh-huhs" represent minimal nonverbal and verbal encouragers (Ivey et al., 2014). Unlike other active listening responses, they do not feed back to clients what the counselor has heard them say. However, they reinforce client communication and increase the likelihood of continued talk about whatever immediately preceded them. Other verbal encouragers involve the simple verbatim restatement of a key word or phrase in a client communication. For example,

> Cl: The things he says make me really, really angry!

> Co: The things he says?

Alternatively, the counselor might focus on another part of this brief message.

> Co: Really angry?

If stated by the counselor in a definitive tone of voice, rather than a questioning tone of voice as indicated in the aforementioned alternative responses, the client is likely to say in response something like, "Yes, the things he says," or to the second alternative, "You bet I get angry!" However, if stated in a questioning tone of voice with a rise in pitch at the end of the response, the client is likely to expand on "the things that he says" in response to the first alternative or to expand on feelings of anger in response to the second alternative, even though the counselor response has been only minimal.

In other words, the restatement type of encouragers that are used with a questioning tone of voice can serve to invite the client to expand on the part of the previous response that is restated by the counselor. Thus, a restatement of a word or phrase can substitute for a question (e.g., "What kinds of things does he say?"), eliciting a similar response on the part of the client as a question might do. A restatement of a key word or phrase in the content part of a message will facilitate expansion of that content, whereas a restatement of a key word or phrase in the affective or feeling part of a message will facilitate further talk and expansion regarding the affect communicated. In fact, it is possible to conduct an interview that is quite productive in facilitating client communication and the telling of a story, relying primarily on encouragers. The use of restatements depends on listening to a client response, identifying a key word or phrase that may be worth following up and expanding on, and then restating that key word or phrase, typically using a questioning tone of voice.

### Paraphrases

Paraphrases summarize or reflect the content in a client response, as opposed to the affective or feeling component of the message, using the counselor's own words to summarize or rephrase what the counselor has heard the client say (Ivey et al., 2014). Unlike an encourager, which repeats verbatim a word or phrase that the client has stated, a paraphrase does not "parrot" what the client has stated, but rather states the essence of what the client has communicated using new words that often will clarify the client's message and the thoughts underlying that message. The purpose of a paraphrase is to both show the client that the counselor is listening and to encourage the client to expand on the content of what has already been communicated. In addition, in highlighting the most important parts of the client's communication, without some of the peripheral parts of the message, a paraphrase can help clients clarify their thoughts.

A paraphrase of a client response is composed of several components (Ivey et al., 2014). First, the counselor must be paying attention and listening to what the client is communicating, including key words used by the client. The counselor must then think about and process what has been heard in order to formulate a paraphrase. A paraphrase always includes a summary that captures the essence of what the client has communicated, using the counselor's own words, which is the defining characteristic of a paraphrase. However, a paraphrase often also includes one or more of the client's own key words. In addition, the paraphrase may, although not always, include a stem (e.g., "So you seem to be saying …" or "So it looks to you like …" or "It sounds like you're thinking that …"). Finally, a paraphrase may have a check for accuracy (e.g., "Am I hearing you correctly?" or "Have I got that right?").

A paraphrase may attempt to be all-inclusive in summarizing the essence of an entire client response, even a lengthy response. Alternatively, a paraphrase of a client response, particularly a lengthy one, may focus only on a part of the response, encouraging the client to expand on that part that the counselor might see as useful to explore (Cormier et al., 2013). For example:

Cl:  I don't know what to think. Sometimes the possibility of taking this new job sounds really good to me, but on the other hand, the job that I have is OK, I'm doing a good job, and I know that I can stay there as long as I want, and I know that I will never have to move away, and I know that my wife really likes living here.

Co:  So there are some things about the new job that really sound good to you.

This paraphrase would encourage the client to talk more about and explore some of the specific things about the new job that are attractive to him. Alternatively,

Co:  So staying put in your current job has some advantages, too.

This paraphrase would encourage the client to talk more about and explore things about the current job that are appealing. Yet another possibility:

Co:  So your wife has some thoughts about this decision, too.

Another option might be to summarize the alternative sides of the decision to be made.

Co:  So on the one hand the new job has some big advantages, but there are some good things about your current job, too, and your wife also has some thoughts about this, too.

Paraphrases may stick closely to what has been explicitly communicated by a client or may go beyond what the client has stated explicitly to infer what the client seems to be saying implicitly. For example,

Co:  So there is some risk in moving into this new job, where your current job offers you a great deal of security.

If a paraphrase is accurate in capturing an implicit message being communicated by a client, it can stimulate a greater depth of exploration. However, even if the paraphrase accurately captures an implicit message, but is too far ahead of a client's awareness, the client may deny the accuracy of the paraphrase in the next response or may even respond defensively.

Paraphrases can produce a number of benefits in counseling. As just noted, a client response can be accurately paraphrased only if the counselor is listening carefully to what the client is communicating, so the paraphrase is a clear indication that the counselor is paying attention and listening. Further, the perception of a client that the counselor is listening and attempting to understand can contribute substantially to the development of a good working relationship or rapport. In addition, a paraphrase can serve as an alternative to questions in helping clients to explore and talk about their concerns, the context surrounding their concerns, their thoughts and, more generally, expanding on and telling their stories in greater depth. Finally, because paraphrases highlight the essence of what has been communicated, they may help clients clarify their thoughts.

### Reflections of Feeling

In contrast to paraphrases, reflections of feeling focus on the affective component of client responses, encouraging the exploration of feelings as opposed to the content (Ivey et al., 2104). Because the communication of feelings often occurs through nonverbal channels, the verbal components of a client response may or may not explicitly state the feeling being communicated, and a client may not be fully aware of the feelings being expressed (Cormier et al., 2013). The exploration of feelings is often a major component of counseling, as feelings may play important roles in concerns brought to counselors. For example, clients may often talk about needing to "sort out" their feelings in attempting to resolve a conflict or make a decision, and reflections of feeling may play an important role in understanding those concerns and the surrounding context. In addition, dysfunctional feelings, such as fear and anxiety, can pose major barriers to pursuing and achieving goals and may even be primary concerns brought to counselors.

Reflections of feeling also have several components (Ivey et al., 2014). As with paraphrases, reflections of feeling require that the counselor listen to what the client is communicating and to process and think about what has been heard, considering both the verbal and nonverbal components of a client response, as nonverbal channels are particularly important in the communication of affect. A reflection of feeling always includes a feeling label, which is the defining characteristic of this type of response (e.g., "You are angry" or "You are feeling very discouraged"). In addition, because the focus of the exploration of feelings in counseling may be in the present rather than the past, often termed "the here and now," reflections of feeling often use the present verb tense (e.g., "You feel angry about what he said" as opposed to "You felt angry when he said that"). A reflection of feeling may also provide a context for the feeling reflected (e.g., "You are feeling _____ about _____" or "You are feeling _____ because _____"). In addition, as with a paraphrase, a stem may be included, and a check for accuracy may also be included. Finally, because conflicting feelings are often important in counseling in sorting out those conflicting feelings, reflections may highlight those conflicting feelings (e.g., "So, on the one hand you are feeling _____ but at the same time you are also feeling _____.").

Reflections of feeling encourage clients to continue talking and exploring the feelings communicated in greater depth. As with paraphrases, reflections of feeling may have different degrees of inference in the extent to which they go beyond the feelings explicitly communicated in the words spoken by clients, but perhaps communicated through nonverbal channels. Going beyond what has been communicated explicitly may facilitate greater depth of exploration and, as indicated for paraphrases, clients may not accept the reflections or may even react defensively, particularly if they are not aware of the feelings they are communicating implicitly, or if the reflection is not particularly accurate. Also, as true for paraphrases, reflections of feeling can serve as alternatives to questions in encouraging exploration of feelings. Finally, clients may not be accustomed to being listened to, particularly when they are communicating feelings, and reflections can thus communicate caring and attempts to understand, facilitating the development of working relationships with clients.

## Summarizations

Summarizations are also listening responses, similar to paraphrases and reflections of feeling, and they may focus on content or feelings communicated by clients or both (Ivey et al., 2014). The difference from paraphrases and reflections of feeling is that, rather than focusing on an immediately previous client response, they focus on a more extended series of client responses. Summarizations can have several important uses in counseling. They can be used at the end of an interview, summarizing what has occurred in the interview and highlighting the things that counselors may particularly want clients to remember and reflect on prior to the next interview. Similarly, summarizations may be used at the beginning of an interview, summarizing what occurred in the previous session or sessions and then using this summary to move into the current interview. Summarizations may also be used to summarize an extended interaction of a topic just discussed in an interview before transitioning into another topic. Such a use of summarizations can also occur when a client seems to be rambling, to wrap up the topic and transition into a new one. Summarizations are, of course, active listening responses and clearly demonstrate to a client that a counselor has listened and heard what has been communicated and also show that the counselor is attempting to understand what the client is communicating.

## A General Interview Strategy

Active listening responses can be organized into a general strategy for organizing and conducting interviews, particularly in the early stages of counseling, which tend to focus on developing an understanding of client concerns and surrounding context and facilitating the telling of client stories. An interview can begin with an open question or open invitation to talk, perhaps preceded by a summarization of what the counselor recalls from previous information received about the client (e.g., a referral source) or communicated by the client. The counselor then uses follow-up questions, encouragers, paraphrases, and reflections of feeling to explore in greater depth what the client is communicating. When it is time to move on to the next topic, the counselor summarizes what has been communicated and then transitions into the next topic with an open question.

As is true of conversations in general, counselors may sometimes be at a loss as to what to say next, particularly less experienced counselors who may also be uncomfortable with silence. In those instances, one strategy is for counselors to give themselves a moment to think about what a client has communicated previously and identify a specific aspect on which to follow up. This strategy not only allows the client to elaborate on an important topic, but it also provides further clarification for the counselor, which will prompt the counselor to use one of the responses previously discussed to continue the interview. Another strategy for the counselor is to remain silent and use the amount of time necessary to collect his or her thoughts and continue the interview. It is important to remember that a brief period of silence will not halt the flow of the interview, and it will likely improve the counselor's next steps.

## EVIDENCE SUPPORTING BASIC COUNSELING SKILLS

A number of reviews and meta-analyses have been provided regarding basic counseling or helping skills training, including the research on the microcounseling or microskills approach (Alberts & Edelstein, 1990; Baker & Daniels, 1989; Baker, Daniels & Greely, 1990; Daniels & Ivey, 2007; Ford, 1979; Hill & Knox, 2013; Ridley, Kelly, & Mollen, 2011; Russell, Crimming, & Lent, 1984). As noted previously, Ivey et al. (2014) indicate that more than 450 empirical studies have been conducted to support the microcounseling or microskills approach. As has generally been true of other reviews of research on microcounseling, Ridley et al. (2011, p. 816) criticize the hundreds of studies conducted for methodological limitations and for the limited focus of the research in documenting the effects of training over short time intervals and using primarily novice counselors as research participants; however, they go on to state, "Even with their flaws, the hundreds of studies examining the microskills approach to counselor training are truly impressive." Ridley et al., along with the other reviewers of this body of research, have pointed out that effects have typically been documented in terms of the production of the target skills in training with students, often beginning students, and research has rarely looked at the effects of training on the effectiveness of counselors with clients in real-life counseling sessions.

There is ample evidence regarding the importance of the therapeutic relationship in the efficacy of counseling and psychotherapy. Based on evidence from more than two dozen reviews of research, Norcross and Wampold (2011) concluded that the therapeutic relationship plays a major role in therapeutic effectiveness, independent of the types of treatments used, and they state that behaviors that promote positive therapeutic relationships should be emphasized in manuals and guidelines for specific therapeutic treatments. The behaviors and skills that are the focus of the present chapter, which are a major component of microskills and other helping skills training, are intended to be behaviors that promote positive therapeutic relationships. In addition, Daniels and Ivey (2007) reviewed research, documenting that clients of helpers trained in microskills express greater satisfaction with their counselors and counseling and perceive

greater rapport with their counselors, consistent with a positive therapeutic relationship; that the clients tend to talk more in counseling sessions, whereas their
counselors talk less; that the clients tend to make more self-focused statements
and statements focusing on affect; and that the clients tend to engage in more
self-disclosure. Thus, there is some documentation of the therapeutic effects of
the basic counseling skills that are covered in the present chapter, although more
research would be helpful to document the effects in actual counseling sessions,
including effects on counseling outcomes.

## CONCLUSIONS

As reviewed in this chapter, basic counseling skills serve as the foundation for an
effective, therapeutic relationship with clients. They serve as a tool for communicating empathy, unconditional positive regard, and genuineness, as described by
Rogers (1951, 1957). The facilitative conditions advocated by Rogers are recognized
as necessary to the counseling relationship, and basic counseling skills, as described
in this chapter, are also important to the development of a counseling relationship.
    Initially, attending skills help to communicate the therapeutic conditions
and to focus attention on clients, which encourages continuing communication.
Questions elicit information from clients, and different types of open-ended
questions can have a particularly important place in counseling in opening new
topics of discussion and in following up for elaboration and specificity of information communicated. Active listening responses provide alternatives to questions and also allow clients to expand on topics and share additional information.
Encouragers, paraphrases, reflections of feelings, and summarizations all provide opportunities to learn more from clients regarding the content of their stories and the feelings attached to these stories. The basic counseling skills covered
in this chapter can be helpful to counselors, regardless of theoretical orientation,
in building relationships, listening to client concerns and stories, and developing the understanding needed to develop treatment and service plans. It is also
important to note that the microskills of open-ended questions, reflective listening (paraphrases and reflections of feeling), and summarizations are central
microskills in motivational interviewing (Miller & Rollnick, 2002, 2013), which
has empirical support as an evidence-based practice, with considerable applicability in rehabilitation settings (see Chapter 12 in this volume).

## DISCUSSION EXERCISES

1. Review the three facilitative conditions described by Carl Rogers and
   describe an encounter in which you experienced unconditional positive
   regard. How was it communicated to you, and how did it feel to receive
   unconditional positive regard?
2. Consider times when you experienced uncomfortable silence. What is
   the source for that discomfort? How might that knowledge influence the
   use of silence in counseling?

3. Compare two experiences when you felt an individual was truly listening to you and one when that was not the case. What was different in those two experiences? How did each one make you feel?

4. Think about the last time you talked with a group of people. During those conversations: Who did you find yourself looking at and talking to most frequently? Why do you think that was the case?

5. Think of interviewers that you have seen on television talk shows that you have found particularly effective in eliciting information. What do you think makes them particularly effective?

## REFERENCES

Alberts, G., & Edelstein, B. (1990). Therapist training: A critical review of skill training studies. *Clinical Psychology Review, 5,* 497–511.

Baker, S. B., & Daniels, T. G. (1989). Integrating research on the microcounseling program: A meta-analysis. *Journal of Counseling Psychology, 36,* 213–222.

Baker, S. B., Daniels, T. G., & Greeley, A. T. (1990). Systematic training of graduate level counselors: Narrative and meta-analytic reviews of three major programs. *Counseling Psychologist, 18,* 355–421.

Berven, N. L. (2008). Assessment interviewing. In B. F. Bolton & R. M. Parker (Eds.), *Handbook of measurement and evaluation in rehabilitation* (4th ed., pp. 241–261). Austin, TX: Pro-Ed.

Berven, N. L. (2010). Clinical interviews. In E. Mpofu & T. Oakland (Eds.), *Assessment in rehabilitation and health* (pp. 158–171). Upper Saddle River, NJ: Merrill.

Carkhuff, R. R. (1969). *Human and helping relations* (Vols. 1 & 2). New York, NY: Holt, Rinehart, & Winston.

Cormier, S., Nurius, P. S., & Osborn, C. J. (2013). *Interviewing and change strategies for helpers* (7th ed.). Belmont, CA: Brooks/Cole.

Dalgin, R. S., Bruch, L. A., & Barber, G. (2010). Rehabilitation counseling practicum: A national survey of design and implementation. *Rehabilitation Education, 24,* 75–84.

Daniels, T., & Ivey, A. (2007). *Microcounseling: Making skills training work in a multicultural world.* Springfield, IL: Charles C Thomas.

Egan, G. (2014). *The skilled helper: A problem-management and opportunity-development approach to helping* (10th ed.). Pacific Grove, CA: Brooks/Cole.

Evans, D. R., Hearn, M. T., Uhlemann, M. R., & Ivey, A. E. (2011). *Essential interviewing: A programmed approach to effective communication* (8th ed.). Pacific Grove, CA: Brooks/Cole.

Ford, J. (1979). Research on training counselors and clinicians. *Review of Education Research, 49,* 87–130.

Hill, C. E. (2014). *Helping skills. Facilitating exploration, insight, and action* (4th ed.). Washington, DC: American Psychological Association.

Hill, C. E., & Knox, S. (2013). Training and supervision in psychotherapy. In M. J. Lambert (Ed.), *Bergin and Garfield's handbook of psychotherapy and behavior change* (pp. 775–811). Hoboken, NJ: Wiley.

Ivey, A. E. (1971). *Microcounseling: Innovations in interviewing training.* Springfield, IL: Charles C Thomas.

Ivey, A. E., Ivey, M. B., & Zalaquett, C. P. (2014). *Intentional interviewing and counseling* (8th ed.). Belmont, CA: Brooks/Cole.

Kagan, N. (1984). Interpersonal process recall. Basic methods and recent research. In D. Larson (Ed.), *Teaching psychological skills: Models for giving psychology away* (pp. 229–244). Monterey, CA: Brooks/Cole.

Miller, W. R., & Rollnick, S. (2002). *Motivational interviewing: Preparing people for change* (2nd ed.). New York, NY: Guilford.

Miller, W. R., & Rollnick, S. (2013). *Motivational interviewing: Helping people change* (3rd ed.). New York, NY: Guilford Press.

Norcross, J. C., & Wampold, B. E. (2011). Evidence-based therapy relationships: Research conclusions and clinical practices. In J. C. Norcross (Ed.), *Psychotherapy relationships that work: Evidence-based responsiveness* (2nd ed., pp. 423–430). New York, NY: Oxford.

Ridley, C. R., Kelly, S. M., & Mollen, D. (2011). Microskills training: Evolution, reexamination, and call for reform. *Counseling Psychologist, 39,* 800–824.

Ridley, C. R., Mollen, D., & Kelly, S. D. (2011). Beyond microskills: Toward a model of counseling competence. *Counseling Psychologist, 39,* 825–864.

Rogers, C. R. (1942). *Counseling and psychotherapy.* Boston, MA: Houghton Mifflin.

Rogers, C. R. (1951). *Client-centered therapy.* Boston, MA: Houghton Mifflin.

Rogers, C. R. (1957). The necessary and sufficient conditions of therapeutic personality change. *Journal of Consulting Psychology, 21,* 95–103.

Russell, R. K., Crimmings, A. M., & Lent, R. W. (1984). Counselor training and supervision: Theory and research. In S. D. Brown & R. W. Lent (Eds.), *Handbook of counseling psychology* (pp. 625–750). New York, NY: Wiley.

CHAPTER

12

# Motivational Interviewing

*Trevor J. Manthey, Jessica Brooks, Fong Chan, Linda E. Hedenblad, and Nicole Ditchman*

## LEARNING OBJECTIVES

The goal of this chapter is to provide readers with an appreciation of motivational interviewing (MI) as an effective counseling approach in rehabilitation settings. The chapter provides an overview of MI, its conceptual framework, counseling techniques, scientific evidence supporting the effectiveness of MI, and rehabilitation applications. As learning objectives, readers should:

1. Increase their familiarity with the history and major concepts of MI.
2. Understand the use of the core microskills, principles, processes, and language strategies associated with MI.
3. Have a greater understanding about the existing empirical support for MI.
4. Be knowledgeable about practical applications of MI in rehabilitation counseling.

## MOTIVATION AND COUNSELING

Historically, client motivation has been considered one of the essential ingredients needed to provide effective counseling (Chan, Shaw, McMahon, Koch, & Strauser, 1997; Cook, 2004; Thomas, Thoreson, Parker, & Butler, 1998; Thoreson, Smits, Butler, & Wright, 1968), and client motivation has been shown to play a key role in the success of rehabilitation counseling and services in particular (Larson, 2008; Manthey, Jackson, & Evans-Brown, 2011; Wagner & McMahon, 2004; Wright, Smits, Butler, & Thoreson, 1968). Thoreson and colleagues (1968) suggested that vocational rehabilitation (VR) clients may lack motivation due to feelings of hopelessness and passivity, unrealistic service goals, fear of losing

Social Security and other benefits and aid, and unstable job markets. Although external factors can indeed influence client behavior, internalized and intrinsic motivation have been found to have a stronger effect on treatment engagement and compliance (Edmunds, Ntoumanis, & Duda, 2006; Ng et al., 2012). Therefore, it is important for rehabilitation counselors and other health professionals to assess client feelings and values related to behavior change, in addition to external forces that impact motivation (Cook, 2004).

Oftentimes, counselors may perceive clients as having little or no internalized motivation for tasks and goals in rehabilitation counseling and services. In addition, rehabilitation service systems are frequently set up to assess the severity of a client's disability and the significance of barriers to rehabilitation in order to determine eligibility for services. For example, the state–federal VR program eligibility determination process can add considerable wait time to the actual receipt of services. This assessment, along with a complex counseling process that requires counselors to provide a lot of information, may lead counselors to take on an "expert" advice-giving role, and may in turn position clients in a less empowered role, ultimately impacting their engagement and motivation. Therefore, it is important to consider the client's perspective in order to enhance motivation (Cook, 2004).

Clients often have competing interests, values, and conflicts related to rehabilitation plans, and it is important for counselors to learn how to effectively help individuals to explore and resolve this ambivalence. Recently, the MI counseling approach has received considerable attention in rehabilitation because of its focus on helping clients deal with ambivalence. MI is useful for changing counselors' attitudes toward helping clients and provides a framework for counselors to use specific techniques to increase client motivation in order to achieve goals and successful rehabilitation outcomes (Manthey et al., 2011; Wagner & McMahon, 2004).

## HISTORY

MI is described as a client-centered, directive, yet nonconfrontational counseling approach to enhancing motivation for change by exploring and resolving ambivalence (Miller & Rollnick, 2002, 2013). MI was initially designed to treat alcohol-related problems (Miller, 1983) and was an alternative to the confrontational and coercive approaches prevalent in substance abuse treatment at the time (Miller & Rollnick, 2002). MI has since been applied to a wide range of health behavior issues (Miller & Rose, 2009). Following its origin in the 1980s, there have been more than 800 publications on MI (complete bibliography available at www.motivationalinterview.org). Several recent meta-analyses of MI outcome studies have supported its use for eliciting behavioral change in clients with problems related to substance abuse as well as mental health, health promotion, and treatment adherence (e.g., Burke, Arkowitz, & Menchola, 2003; Hettema, Steele, & Miller, 2005; Lundahl, Tollefson, Gambles, Brownell, & Burke, 2010; Rubak, Sandbæk, Lauritzen, & Christensen, 2005; Vasilaki, Hosier, & Cox, 2006). These empirical studies also suggest that MI approaches are not necessarily more effective than other psychosocial interventions, but that MI yields comparable results in shorter treatment periods (e.g., Burke et al., 2003) and is appropriate for a broad range of client groups and issues (Lundahl et al., 2010). MI is a brief intervention that is essential to the generally fast-paced counseling practice in rehabilitation settings (Manthey et al., 2011; Wagner & McMahon, 2004).

William Miller and Steven Rollnick have written three books articulating the progression of MI as an intervention over time. The first book describes MI as a way to help people resolve their ambivalence with regard to substance use specifically (Miller & Rollnick, 1991). Their second book describes MI as an approach to helping people resolve ambivalence and move toward change in a broad variety of settings (Miller & Rollnick, 2002). The third describes new skills and processes developed within MI based on contemporary research and theory (Miller & Rollnick, 2013).

MI is often compared to the transtheoretical (stages of change) model (Prochaska, DiClemente, & Norcross, 1992) due to its emphasis on addressing motivation early in the precontemplation and contemplation stages of the behavior change process (Hettema et al., 2005). However, several misconceptions about MI have become common, which Miller and Rollnick (2009) have attempted to address. For instance, although MI has been commonly paired with the Prochaska et al. stages of change model, some have misconstrued the two to be equivalent (Miller & Rollnick, 2009). Counselors do not need to learn the stages of change model in order to obtain or use MI skills (Madson, Loignon, & Lance, 2009; Miller & Moyers, 2006), and doing so may be confusing for some learners (Miller & Rollnick, 2009).

Other misconceptions are that MI is easy to learn, a way to manipulate or trick people, an advanced pros and cons list or decisional balance, equivalent to cognitive behavioral therapy (CBT) that requires assessment feedback, a reiteration of client-centered therapy, and a panacea (Miller & Rollnick, 2009). MI is not any of these things. Instead, counselors use MI as a way to help individuals resolve their internal ambivalence about change by facilitating a strategic conversation in which people articulate and hear their own desires, abilities, reasons, and needs for change. Hearing their own reasons for change increases individuals' motivation and commitment for change and ultimately leads individuals to decide to make positive behavior changes on their own (Miller & Rose, 2009). The counselor avoids confrontation or coercion while helping individuals take ownership of their own change process (Miller & Rollnick, 2013).

## MAJOR CONCEPTS

MI has evolved out of humanistic theoretical approaches (e.g., Rogers, 1979) that have also served as a foundation for rehabilitation counseling (Wagner & McMahon, 2004). Miller and Rollnick (2002) describe MI as a strategic use of general counseling techniques to foster behavioral change. The general counseling skills are used for specific effects based on client language. It is the strategy, use, timing, and ratio of these general counseling skills that can sometimes become difficult to learn (Madson et al., 2009) and is how MI differentiates itself from other counseling techniques (Miller & Rollnick, 2013).

**TABLE 12.1 Overview of MI Terms**

| SPIRIT OF MI (PACE) | MI MICROSKILLS (OARS) | GENERAL MI PRINCIPLES | MI PROCESSES | TYPES OF LANGUAGE |
|---|---|---|---|---|
| Partnership | Open-ended questions | Expressing empathy | Engaging | Discord talk |
| Acceptance | Affirmations | Developing discrepancy | Focusing | Sustain talk |
| Compassion | Reflections | Rolling with resistance | Evoking | Change talk |
| Evocation | Summary statements | Supporting self-efficacy | Planning | Commitment talk |

*Note:* The columns in this table are used to group concepts only. Rows are not meant to indicate equivalence. MI, motivational interviewing.

## "Spirit" of MI

The fundamental essence or "spirit" of MI is achieved by developing a positive client–counselor relationship to reduce resistance and to promote client understanding, choices, and autonomy (Manthey et al., 2011). The spirit of MI is articulated through the acronym PACE: partnership, acceptance, compassion, and evocation (Miller & Rollnick, 2013). The counselor fosters an equal partnership, helps the client feel accepted through empathic listening and avoidance of confrontation, focuses on what is best for the client rather than what is easiest or convenient for the counselor, and evokes the client's own thoughts about change (see Table 12.1 for an overview of MI terminology).

## Definitions of MI

In the latest edition of Miller and Rollnick's (2013) MI book, MI has been articulated using three distinct definitions: (a) a basic definition, (b) a practical or pragmatic definition, and (c) a technical or "how to" definition. Each definition is meant for different audiences and emphasizes different elements and are defined as follows:

1. MI is a collaborative conversation style for strengthening a person's own motivation and commitment to change.
2. MI is a person-centered counseling style for addressing the common problem of ambivalence about change.
3. MI is a collaborative, goal-oriented style of communication with particular attention to the language of change. It is designed to strengthen personal motivation for and commitment to a specific goal by eliciting and exploring the person's own reasons for change within an atmosphere of acceptance and compassion.

## MI Microskills

There are four general counseling skills termed the "microskills" that are used strategically within MI. These microskills are *o*pen-ended questions, *a*ffirmations, *r*eflections, and *s*ummary statements (OARS; Miller & Rollnick, 2002). An in-depth description of each of these skills is outside the scope of this chapter (see Chapter 11 in this volume for additional information on basic counseling microskills of open-ended questions, reflections, and summarizations). However, a brief description of OARS is appropriate to illustrate how these general microskills are used differently and strategically within MI.

### Open-Ended Questions

Open-ended questions are probes not easily answered with a "yes/no" or brief answer. Asking open questions invites clients to think more deeply about an issue and take time to elaborate on reasons for making desired changes. This approach encourages clients to do most of the talking while the counselor listens attentively and supports elaboration. Answers to these questions provide reasons for why change is necessary or desirable from the clients' perspectives (Levensky, Forcehimes, O'Donohue, & Beitz, 2007). Examples of open questions are

- "What brought you here today?"
- "What do you like about working?"
- "Why are you considering returning to work?"

### Affirmations

Affirmations are statements that recognize client strengths and involve reframing behaviors or concerns as evidence of positive client qualities. Affirmations can be a compliment, an acknowledgment, or statement of appreciation. Affirmations support client self-efficacy, foster rapport, reinforce client efforts, and encourage open exploration. Affirmation is the key to facilitating the MI principle of supporting self-efficacy. The following are examples of affirmation:

- "It is great that you want to be more self-sufficient, that is an admirable goal."
- "I know how hard it is for you to manage your disability and yet you stay resilient."
- "Despite all of the difficulties you have faced, you stay persistent. You are clearly not someone who gives up."

### Reflections

Reflections are statements a counselor makes that mirror back to the client elements of what the client has just expressed or stated previously. This is often termed reflective listening. Reflective listening is considered foundational to implementing MI successfully (Miller & Rollnick, 2002). More than simply repeating what a client has said, reflective listening involves accurately reflecting what the client has said, while also incorporating what the client is experiencing, but has yet to verbalize.

Reflections are versatile and can be used in many ways to accomplish different effects (Miller & Rollnick, 2013). For instance, reflections can be used to steer a conversation, emphasize one side of a client's ambivalence, develop discrepancy, help articulate unspoken content, increase or decrease emotional content, express compassion/empathy, identify strengths, increase confidence or importance, help the client talk more about change, or simply to let the client know the counselor is listening. Each of the reflective listening strategies identified is used when needed and illustrates how the nuances of MI provide strategy and purpose to generalist counseling techniques. The following are examples of reflection:

- "Part of you is worried that you might lose your benefits and another part of you wonders whether there might be greater earning potential in the future."
- "You are upset that your mom says you need to be here and you feel pretty fed up."
- "You want to work with someone who is actively trying to understand what it is like to have a disability."

### Summary Statements

Summary statements are a type of reflection that allow the counselor to review what has been discussed in all or part of the counseling session. Summary statements pull together several elements that the client has shared. Summaries can be used to link or collect these elements together and can also be used to transition to new topics. Summary techniques are useful for synthesizing and reinforcing content discussed in the counseling session. After listening to client needs, desires, abilities, and reasons for change, the counselor distills and integrates what he or she is hearing and offers these reflections back to the client in a few sentences as a summary. Summaries can be effectively used to communicate interest and care, highlight ambivalence about change, and promote the identification of discrepancies. Summary statements sometimes end with an invitation to allow the client opportunity to provide feedback. The following are examples of summary statements:

- "Let me see if I've got this right, one thing you told me about yourself is that your family is your highest priority, also you want to find a job where you can provide and model positive work for your children, and you want to find something that will help you achieve the dream of owning a home."
- "Earlier you mentioned fear about losing your benefits, later you mentioned fear about getting older, and just now you mentioned worry about discrimination."
- "Part of you is worried that if you get a job you might lose your benefits, at the same time there are several things you are hoping to achieve, such as greater life satisfaction, feeling better about yourself, being able to move out from your mom's place, and perhaps increase your earning potential."

The MI skills are used with a different strategic purpose during each of the four processes of MI (Miller, 2012; Miller & Rollnick, 2013): (a) engaging, (b) focusing, (c) evoking, and (d) planning, and the skills are described in more detail in the subsequent section, MI Counseling Process.

## MI Principles

Microskills are used to support the guiding MI principles: (a) expressing empathy, (b) developing discrepancy, (c) rolling with resistance, and (d) supporting self-efficacy (Rollnick & Miller, 1995).

### Expressing Empathy

The counselor is expected to express empathy for the client to build rapport and create a safe environment where the client feels understood. Counselors should share their understanding of the clients' situations, perceptions, strengths, hopes, and concerns. This principle is designed to enable clients to feel listened to in a nonjudgmental environment where the client and counselor recognize multiple options at hand (Wagner & McMahon, 2004).

### Developing Discrepancy

This principle guides counselors to gently explore discrepancies between the clients' desired futures and their current behavior. This should be done by focusing on the client's point of view, not the counselor's reasons as to why change is important. By bringing discrepancies to the client's attention, the client may be more willing to explore how current behaviors may not be leading to his or her desired future.

### Rolling With Resistance

When clients express points of view that may not appear desirable to the counselor, it is still important for the counselor to create a calm and supportive environment and to not react or fight against the client's competing motivations. This is especially important when the client is argumentative, defensive, or becomes withdrawn. If the counselor remains open and calm, the client's exploration of issues is more likely to occur (Miller, Benefield, & Tonigan, 1993).

### Supporting Self-Efficacy

Counselors are responsible for finding opportunities to build client self-efficacy in working toward their personal goals. Clients may recognize that a change is needed, but they may not be willing to put forth effort or commit to making a change unless they believe that they are able to succeed. As client self-efficacy improves, confidence in the ability to make a change also improves.

## MI Language Types

There are four types of client language to which MI counselors should pay attention in order to find clues to the most helpful process of MI counseling discussion.

These four types of language are discord talk, sustain talk, change talk, and commitment talk.

## Discord Talk

Discord talk (or resistant talk) is client language that indicates that there are issues with the helping relationship. Discord is often emotionally based and relationally oriented (e.g. "You don't care about me"; "You just want me to get any job"; "I could be working in the fast-food industry for all you care"; "You don't have a disability, so you don't get it!"). If discord persists, the counselor should move to the engagement process to repair the relationship.

## Sustain Talk and Change Talk

Sustain talk and change talk are two sides of the same coin, representing opposing sides of ambivalence. Sustain talk occurs when individuals talk about why they feel like they are not able to change (e.g., "I'm worried I'll lose my benefits"; "It's too hard"), and change talk occurs when individuals talk about why they might want to change (e.g., "I feel better about myself when I am working"; "I want to provide a better life for my kids"). There are times when a counselor may want to maintain balance between these two types of language and, in the literature, this is termed *equipoise* (Miller, 2012; Miller & Rollnick, 2013). In general, however, the goal in MI is most often to help individuals talk more about why they want to modify their behaviors or actions (change talk) rather than why they feel stuck (sustain talk). As counselors become skillful at helping people talk more about why they might change, they learn skills to help consolidate a client's change language into commitment.

## Commitment Talk

Commitment language is an indication that the individual has made a decision and is no longer ambivalent, at least for the time being. Commitment can be statements of intent or a willingness to take small steps (e.g., "I'm going to do this!"; "I'll update my résumé tonight"). Counselors firm up commitment by moving into the planning process and evoking a realistic plan that builds confidence and addresses barriers.

## MI COUNSELING PROCESS

There are four counseling processes articulated in MI: engagement, focusing, evoking, and planning (Miller & Rollnick, 2013). These four processes can be viewed as building on one another, each process being foundational and requisite to proceeding to the next (see Figure 12.1). Although on the surface the four processes of MI might seem linear, they are not, and counselors will revisit prior processes based on client language and circumstance as needed (Miller & Rollnick, 2013).

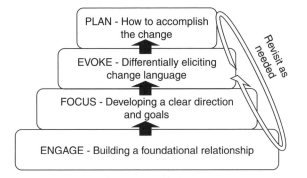

**FIGURE 12.1** The four processes of motivational interviewing.

## Engaging

During the engagement process, the counselor's goal is to build a working alliance and foundational relationship with the client. It is difficult to work with a client if there is a lack of trust, or if discord is present (Miller & Rollnick, 2013). During the engagement process, the counselor will try to express empathy for the client's situation and concerns. The counselor should also avoid confronting resistance; instead, the counselor will "roll with resistance" (Miller & Rollnick, 2002) and explore the discord or resistance to help the client articulate his or her underlying concerns empathically. Alternative perspectives from the client are invited rather than forced. The purpose of this process is not to get the client to change but to use the microskills to establish or reestablish a working relationship.

## Focusing

The focusing process helps the client and counselor come to an agreement about the direction of the counseling interaction. The focusing process is about finding that direction and, within it, more precise attainable objectives (Miller & Rollnick, 2013). In this process, the microskills are used to negotiate an agenda, empower the client to choose and own the behavior change topic, and (once a target behavior is identified) either keep the client on topic or remap the agenda.

## Evoking

Once a target behavior is identified, the counselor develops the discrepancy between the client's current behavior and the client's underlying values or long-term goals (Miller & Rollnick, 2002). One of the primary means for developing discrepancy is to elicit change talk. Eliciting change talk means using the microskills to encourage the client to talk about desires, abilities, reasons, and needs for change (Miller & Rollnick, 2013). One of the main characteristics of MI that differentiates it from other supportive therapies is that MI is designed to elicit change talk rather than simply waiting for it to occur. Consistent with the characterization of the MI spirit as "evocative," the MI counselor strategically aims to elicit change talk, which can then be explored and strengthened. Miller and Rollnick (2002) have described many methods for eliciting change talk, including asking evocative questions (e.g., "In what ways might change be a good thing?") and avoiding questions that are likely to lead to resistance (e.g., "Why haven't you changed?"). When change talk is elicited, the counselor may use reflection, affirmation, or requests for elaboration to elicit further change talk. The goal is to help clients to talk more about their personal reasons to change rather than the reasons they are stuck or do not want to change (sustain talk). Throughout this process, preference is given to the client's ideas about change. The counselor uses evocation to draw the content from the client rather than telling the client why the counselor thinks he or she should change.

## Planning

The planning process occurs when the counselor and client determine steps for change. As in evocation, preference is given to how the client envisions the change taking place rather than how the counselor thinks change should happen (Miller & Rollnick, 2013). Often counselors move to the planning process too early in the MI interaction. If this occurs, the client may push back or continue to be ambivalent, which are clues indicating that the counselor has moved ahead to planning too quickly. If this occurs, the counselor should move back to a previous process. In planning, the counselor uses the skills to help clients articulate their own plan for change.

## THEORY OF PERSONALITY

When first developed, MI did not have a theory of change or personality attached to it. Rather, MI was developed by paying attention in clinical interactions to behaviors that preceded positive movement toward change (Miller & Rollnick, 2002), using a bottom-up, inductive reasoning approach (Vansteenkiste, Williams, & Resnicow, 2012). In other words, MI was developed by paying attention to what worked well in clinical interactions and attempting to attach theories as to why certain aspects of MI seemed to be effective (e.g., Apodaca & Longabaugh, 2009; Markland, Ryan, Tobin, & Rollnick 2005; Miller & Rose, 2009). Since that time, process and outcome studies have been conducted on MI that have led to the formulation of theories regarding the mechanisms of MI (Miller & Rose, 2009). Instead of having one grand theory about personality and why people change, scholars have linked the mechanisms of MI to a number of different theories (e.g., Hohman, 2012). Some personality theories and constructs with which scholars have linked MI include conflict and ambivalence (Orford, 1985), reactance (Brehm & Brehm, 1981), person-centeredness (Rogers, 1951, 1957), cognitive dissonance (Festinger, 1957), self-determination (Ryan & Deci, 2002), self-perception (Bem, 1972), self-affirmation (Steele, 1988), self-efficacy (Bandura, 1999), value theory (Rokeach, 1973), and the strengths perspective (Saleebey, 2006). Although exploring each of these personality theories and constructs in detail is beyond the scope of this chapter, it is important to briefly summarize each in order to high-light how different aspects of MI incorporate their concepts and propositions.

## Ambivalence

Ambivalence means feeling or thinking two ways about something (Orford, 1985) and is often theoretically conceptualized as a negative predictor of attitude strength (Conner & Armitage, 2008). One of the primary assumptions in MI is that ambivalence about change is normal (Miller & Rollnick, 1991). Motivation for making changes will increase and decrease at different times throughout interactions with counselors based on where clients are in their ambivalence (Arkowitz, Westra, Miller, & Rollnick, 2008).

## Reactance

Brehm and Brehm (1981) postulated that reactance occurs when clients perceive a threat to their autonomy or freedom. Clients seek to reduce the perceived threat by defending their right to not change and by opposing suggestions by counselors in other ways. The idea in MI is that pushing against, confronting, cajoling, persuading, or coercing someone to change has the opposite of the intended effect, actually triggering reactance.

## Person-Centered Theory

MI incorporates elements of person-centered theory (Rogers, 1951; Chapter 2 in this volume), such as unconditional positive regard and belief in the absolute worth of the person (Rogers, 1957). One of the tenets of MI is that acceptance of the individual facilitates change, whereas perceived expectation of change generates discord or resistance (Miller & Rollnick, 2002). In person-centered counseling, clients are viewed as experts on their own lives and are the ones who know best about the personal and environmental context surrounding the problems they are seeking to solve (Rogers, 1957).

## Cognitive Dissonance

Cognitive dissonance occurs when individuals engage in behaviors that conflict with their internal values (Festinger, 1957). The internal conflict that results from cognitive dissonance causes individuals either to make behavioral changes or to justify the conflicting behavior in some way. In MI, the principle of developing discrepancy through empathic reflections is used to increase cognitive dissonance strategically in a way that evokes change (Dracott & Dabbs, 1998).

## Self-Determination

The self-determination theory posits that people endeavor to experience positive growth (Ryan & Deci, 2002). This theory suggests that the more the environment supports autonomy, competence, and relationships, the more likely clients will be motivated, whether internally or externally. In MI, there are skills that are explicitly used to build motivation, support autonomy, increase confidence, and build positive relationships (Markland et al., 2005).

## Self-Perception

The self-perception theory argues that people understand themselves and what they believe about themselves better when they hear themselves speak in their interactions with other people (Bem, 1972). In MI, this idea is taken very seriously, and intentional efforts are made to help people talk more about why they want to change as opposed to why they are stuck. The more people hear themselves talk about their reasons to change, the more they will believe it for themselves. The reverse can also occur if people hear themselves talk more about why they do not want to change. For that reason, MI is intentional in how the counselor helps the client talk about his or her problem, evoking the conversations that support change.

## Self-Affirmation

In the self-affirmation theory, individuals need to perceive themselves as competent in order to protect their self-worth and to avoid resistant reactions to feelings of inadequacy (Steele, 1988). Throughout MI, and in particular during the engagement process, the counselor endeavors to build a relationship with clients to help them feel valued, heard, and competent (Miller & Rollnick, 2013).

## Self-Regulation

The self-regulation theory posits that people have immediate impulses that can get in the way of long-term goals, if they are not regulated by internal controls (Kanfer, 1987). The extent to which people are driven by internal goals will determine how likely they will be to assert impulse control and, therefore, assert control over their environment (Fenton-O'Creevy, Nicholson, Soane, & Willman, 2003). MI intentionally helps enhance client goals for behavior change with the idea that the more important the individual perceives the goal to be, the more self-control he or she will exert when the desire for immediate gratification becomes stronger or persistent.

## Self-Efficacy

Social cognitive theory asserts that an individual's self-efficacy—the perceived confidence to accomplish a task—influences whether he or she will be able to accomplish behavior change (Bandura, 1999). When individuals experience low self-efficacy, they may avoid attempts at changing, whereas people who experience high self-efficacy will be more likely to attempt and succeed at difficult behavior changes (Bandura, 1999; Chou, Ditchman, Pruett, Chan, & Hunter, 2009). In MI, self-efficacy is supported through the strategic use of affirmations, building of confidence, and the development of realistic steps toward change (Miller & Rollnick, 2013).

## Value Theory

The primary thinking behind value theory is that individuals naturally strive to act more consistently with the values that are underlying principles in their lives (Rokeach, 1973).

In MI, special attention is given to core values, so that clients can identify how their behaviors either fit or do not fit with their personal beliefs (Miller & Rollnick, 2002).

## Strengths Perspective

Key to the strengths perspective is the notion that individuals do not change, and are less likely to recover, in systems or relationships that emphasize client problems and deficits (Saleebey, 2006). Instead, the strengths perspective posits that a stronger and more effective helping relationship is related to the counselor's ability to help clients recognize, talk about, and use the strengths that they already possess. MI is viewed as a strengths-based practice (Manthey, Knowles, Asher, & Wahab, 2011.) When clients talk more about the problems and barriers that get in the way of making a change in the future—instead of their hopes, desires, and abilities for making the change—it is more likely that clients will choose not to change (Amrhein, Miller, Yahne, Knupsky, & Hochstein, 2004; Amrhein, Miller, Yahne, Palmer, & Fulcher, 2003).

MI was developed inductively through paying attention to what seemed to be producing positive results in the moment within clinical interactions. Therefore, there was no single theory of personality that drove the development of MI as an intervention. Instead, there are many theories that may influence why MI seems to be effective. Hohman (2012, pp. 27–28) weaves many of these theories together and ties them to MI concepts in the following statement.

> [In] combining these theories, we see that clients have a need for connection, competence, and autonomy (self-determination theory) and when this autonomy or self-worth is threatened (reactance theory and self-affirmation theory), clients tend to react in a way to preserve these things (sustain talk and/or resistance). They listen to themselves describe why they can't or won't change or they reduce the importance of the problem (self-perception theory, dissonance theory). Clients who feel engaged, valued, and connected to their [counselor] (client centered theory) are more likely to see themselves as competent and capable (self-efficacy theory, self-perception theory) and become more open to discussing reasons and need for change (change talk). And research tells us that the more clients talk about change, the more likely they are to embark on this change.

MI steers away from focusing on elements, such as psychoanalytic concepts of repression, threats to self-image, pathogenic beliefs, or secondary gain (Arkowitz et al., 2008). It also does not focus on distorted beliefs, homework assignments, or placing the counselor as the expert in the counseling relationship (Arkowitz et al., 2008). MI is focused on the present and future values, goals, and behaviors of clients who are describing their ambivalence about change. Foundational to MI is the assumption that a person's ambivalence about change is normal (Miller & Rollnick, 2002). Arguing or trying to convince someone to change is avoided, because this typically results in the person verbally defending the status quo, thus reinforcing the maladaptive behavior. In MI, a client's ambivalence is purposely explored, with the goal of increasing the motivation for change. A major role of the counselor is to explore client goals and values and to elicit statements, thoughts, and emotions that support behavior change (Miller & Rollnick, 2002).

Instead of confronting or pushing against an individual's ambivalence in order to get the client to resolve it, counselors work *with* the client's ambivalence to help the client articulate his or her ultimate goals and values. In other words, many clients will fight against changing their behavior if the counselor does not accept them for who they are—including their perceived faults. Alternatively, if individuals feel like the counselor *does* accept them as they are; they may be more willing to contemplate changing. This is a paradox for many counselors, who may view their responsibility as actively changing client behavior. The goal of MI is for counselors to develop a skill set that helps clients feel accepted for who they are, avoiding creation of an atmosphere in which clients feel like they are not accepted, do not have worth, or feel forced to change. MI also uses targeted communication strategies to help individuals articulate their own internal reasons for change. The more individuals hear their own reasons for change, the more motivated they will be to change their behaviors (Miller & Rollnick, 2012). Thereafter, counselors can work with enhanced motivation to consolidate commitment and begin making incremental steps toward change.

## REHABILITATION APPLICATIONS

There has been a call to expand the use of evidence-based practices within rehabilitation counseling (Chan, Tarvydas, Blalock, Strauser, & Atkins, 2009), and MI has been recognized as one of these practices (Chan et al., 2011). The primary objective of MI is to assist clients in resolving ambivalence and increasing motivation for positive behavior change. MI has broad applicability across human service and counseling specialties. The current empirical evidence illustrates that MI has been successfully used in a variety of settings with diverse client groups, that intersect with employment and rehabilitation, including substance abuse (Vasilaki et al., 2006), health care (e.g., Britt, Hudson, & Blampied, 2004; Rollnick, Miller, & Butler, 2008), forensics (McMurran, 2009), and outpatient mental health programs (Cleary, Hunt, Matheson, & Walter, 2009).

MI could be effective in improving outcomes in VR programs by maneuvering work barriers and highlighting career values. Rehabilitation clients may perceive barriers when they negatively view outcomes that are consequences to finding employment, such as workplace discrimination (Cook, 2004). However, certain career-related outcomes, such as contributing to society, may hold positive value for clients. MI can provide useful techniques to help individuals when exploring and making career choices. For instance, when developing discrepancy during the MI process, rehabilitation counselors can help clients to outline the pros and cons of career decisions, comparing positive and negative outcome expectations.

Even though studies have not yet examined the effectiveness of MI in VR settings, researchers postulate that it might be a useful approach for increasing motivation related to finding and maintaining employment (Manthey, 2009; Manthey, Jackson, & Evans-Brown, 2011; Wagner & McMahon, 2004). Wagner and McMahon identified several rehabilitation contexts in which MI might be appropriate, including managing medical issues and adjusting to physical disability, adjusting to cognitive impairment, improving psychosocial functioning, and returning to work. Scholarly work specific to returning to work has argued that MI may be appropriate for career coaching (Brooks, 2005), supported education (Manthey, 2011), supported employment (Larson, 2008), employment assessments (Graham, Jutla, Higginson, & Wells, 2008), building employment-focused self-efficacy (Chou et al., 2009), as an adjunct to other rehabilitation interventions (Vong, Cheing, Chan, So, & Chan, 2011), and engaging people with disabilities in job-seeking behaviors (Mannock, Levesque, & Prochaska, 2002). MI has been suggested as an employment intervention for juvenile offenders who use drugs (Leukefeld et al., 2003), for individuals with psychiatric disabilities (Lloyd, Tse, Waghorn, & Hennessy, 2008), intellectual disabilities (Rose, Saunder, Hensel, & Kroese, 2005), sex workers (Yahne, Miller, Irvin-Vitela, & Tonigan, 2002), mandated clients, and clients from lower economic status (Muscat, 2005).

## CASE STUDY

The following is a short case study meant to illustrate how MI concepts might be used within a rehabilitation context.

Brian is a 28-year-old male who has been mandated to see a VR counselor. Brian has a learning disability, experiences depression, and has a back injury. Brian is not happy discussing his employment concerns with a VR counselor.

### Engaging

Co:  Hi, Brian, thanks for coming in today. [Affirmation]

Cl:  I'm not sure I'm glad to see you.

*(continued)*

(*continued*)

Co: You're not happy to be here. Tell me more about that. [Reflection, open question]

Cl: I just think this is going to be a big waste of time.

Co: It's hard to imagine a way our interactions together might work out. [Reflection]

Cl: Yeah, my wife and my mother are also on my case to go back to work, but they are on my case about everything lately.

Co: Your wife and mother care about you and it is coming across as them telling you what to do. And you don't like it. [Reflection]

Cl: Yeah, I suppose they care about me, but I think they care more about me "lazing about the house."

Co: So you're feeling pushed around and you're worried I might do the same thing to you. [Reflection]

Cl: Well, I have heard horror stories from other people. You know, people who've come here to get help with getting work, but then they end up being forced to work in a fast-food place.

Co: You want to work at job that you find meaningful. [Reflection]

Cl: Yeah! The last thing I want to do is be forced to work at a fast-food place, a thrift store, or loading boxes in the back of a truck. I have a hard enough time not feeling bad about myself as it is. I have some pride.

Co: I'm hearing loud and clear that the last thing you want is to feel forced to take a job that you feel is demeaning. [Reflection]

Cl: I'm glad because, that is just something I am not willing to do.

Co: Well, Brian, this really is up to you. Although there are some guidelines, where we go with this process and where you decide to work will largely be driven by you. As a counselor I certainly strive to avoid helping people get jobs that they find demoralizing. [Affirmation and giving information]

Cl: Well, thank you, I don't want to work in a place that feels like hell.

Co: And yet you still decided to come in here and talk to me despite the fear that you might end up in a demeaning job. You came partly because your family is telling you to. What are they telling you about work? What are their concerns? [Reflection and open question]

Cl: Well, they're worried I am going to just play computer games all the time and not do anything of value with my life.

(*continued*)

*(continued)*

Co:  And you're not concerned about that, you feel like they are way off base. [Reflection]

Cl:  Well, I don't know that they are way off base. I know I should be doing other things with my time too. I mean being on the computer isn't the only thing I do, but I suppose it isn't always the best thing for me either.

Co:  So there is a part of you that thinks your family isn't acknowledging all of the good things you do and at the same time there is a small part of you that thinks that going back to work might be valuable and be a good way to spend your time. [Reflection]

Cl:  I suppose so. I mean I've thought about going back to work for awhile, but I just don't know if I can do it now. I don't know if I have the stamina for it.

Co:  What happened? [Open question]

Cl:  I fell off a ladder while cleaning my gutters and ruptured three discs and broke my leg. My leg is better now but my back is still bothering me a lot.

Co:  Your back injury is getting in your way and you can't do the things you used to do. [Reflection]

Cl:  Well, yeah, I was into construction and would do all sorts of demanding things. I would put my body through the ringer and be fine the next day. But now I can't seem to even stand for 5 minutes without my body wearing down and my back starting to ache. I can't even lift 20 lbs these days.

Co:  So you're worried about your body's ability to go back to work and despite this you've been thinking about potentially finding work for a long time. [Reflection]

Cl:  Yeah, for a while now.

The goal in the engaging process is for the client to feel listened to and understood in order to build a relationship. If resistance or discord is present, it is not confronted, but instead it is explored, and new perspectives are invited through empathic reflections. The microskills of MI were used to strategically help Brian express his concerns about employment, avoiding confrontation and allowing Brian to tell his story.

### Focusing

Co:  You're feeling forced to be here, your back injury is giving you a hard time, and you have some worries about what might happen here. At the same time there is a part of you that is considering

*(continued)*

*(continued)*

> returning to work, feels like work might be valuable, and you have been thinking about work for a while now. So given all of this, what would you like to do with me here today? What do you think might be helpful for you? [Summary and open question]

Cl: Well, honestly, I'm not sure, I've never done this before.

Co: This is all new. [Reflection]

Cl: Well, I've had friends come here but this is the first time I've been here.

Co: Would it be alright if I shared with you some of the things I have talked about with other people in similar situations? [Asking permission and closed question]

Cl: Sure.

Co: Well, some people come here and they aren't sure about whether returning to work is right for them or whether VR is right for them. What we often do is have a conversation about the VR process and what it might mean for them if they were to return to work. Others find it helpful to try vocational interest and aptitude assessments to determine meaningful areas for employment that they haven't tried or thought of before. Still others discuss options for finding work outside of VR, because truly VR isn't for everyone. Working with VR really is up to you. Perhaps you've even thought about something else we could talk about that I haven't listed. What do you think? [Giving information in a menu of options and open question]

Cl: I think helping me decide whether or not I should go back to work would be a good place to start. The interest inventories sound interesting too, but perhaps I should decide first before I head down that route.

The focusing process helps the individual take ownership of the topic of conversation, come to consensus about the direction of counseling, and set an agenda for the session. Throughout the processes of MI, the goal is to help clients to be in the driver's seat by evoking their expression of thoughts and ideas. With Brian, this was accomplished by asking permission, providing a menu of options, and using the OARS skills specifically to help him narrow down the topic for today.

### Evoking

Co: So you'd like to start out talking about whether or not to return to work. That's a great idea. So what have been your thoughts about what it might be like if you returned to work?

*(continued)*

*(continued)*

Cl: Well, like I said before I'm worried about how I'll feel. I'm worried that my body won't take it well.

Co: Yes, you've mentioned that several times, you'd like to find work that wouldn't be damaging to your body.

Cl: Well, there's more to it than that. I have a learning disability too, I went into construction because I didn't think I could do office work. It's hard for me to read material and learn things and my spelling is horrible. So I thought construction was my only option, so now that I can't do that I feel like I don't have any options at all.

Co: So what you are interested in is something that you can do that will be easy on your back, but will also be a job that wouldn't force you to do a lot of writing in front of other people.

Cl: Yeah, I know there is spell check and stuff that wasn't around before, so I suppose if I didn't have to write in front of people in the moment, that would be better.

Co: What would that be like for you, if you could find a job that was easier on your back and didn't require you to write in front of people?

Cl: Well, that would be great! I'd love that, I mean, I'd still be worried about my learning disability in other ways, but for the most part I could see myself being really happy with that.

Co: What would make you feel happy about that?

Cl: Well, I would feel like I had value as a person again. Right now I just feel like a drain on everyone around me. My mom and wife didn't think they'd have to be taking care of me at 28 years old. And my mom wouldn't have to deal with me and my wife living with her again. And I didn't get married just so that I could sit around and be depressed all the time. I mean, who wants that?

Co: So not working has contributed to you being depressed.

Cl: Totally. I know this is going to sound stereotypical. But as a man I've never envisioned myself as not being a bread winner and it has really sucked feeling dependent on other people.

Co: You feel like going back to work might help you feel less depressed and maybe even happy. You might also become more independent.

Cl: I suppose so. It would be really nice to have our own apartment again. It is no fun being married and living with your mother.

Co: So finding a job that would allow you to move out and have some privacy would be really important to you.

*(continued)*

*(continued)*

Cl: Oh, god yes, it's no fun trying to be intimate while your mom is in the house.

Co: So having a good relationship with your wife is important too. You've also mentioned her several times. You feel like going to work successfully might help your relationship with her.

Cl: Well, don't get me wrong, she can sometimes be a pain, but she also stuck with me even after my accident. She even stayed with me when we had to move into my mom's house. So, yeah, it would be real nice to be able to feel like I was reciprocating more.

Co: And you think that maybe getting a job that balances physical demands on your back with some of your concerns about your learning disability might be a way you could reciprocate.

Cl: I suppose so. I never thought about it that way before, but I suppose so.

Co: So what would it be like 5 years from now if you didn't return to work? What would that be like for you?

Cl: Well, in some ways it might be relief, because I have a feeling this is going to be really hard, but in other ways it might be exactly how things are now. Well, maybe not exactly, I don't know how long my wife would stick around. She might leave me eventually if I continue on this way.

Co: You really do care for her, and you're worried that she might not be in your life if something doesn't change.

Cl: Well, it isn't just that I'd need to go back to work, I'd have to be less depressed too. I know I'm draining on everyone around me when I get into that place.

Co: You've been depressed a lot since you got into the accident and couldn't work.

Cl: Yes, all the time. I can't seem to shake it.

Co: And you're thinking that perhaps things aren't okay as they are, that going back to work and maybe even working on your depression in other ways might be helpful.

Cl: I guess you're right on that.

Co: So the last thing you want is work that makes you feel demeaned and you're also worried about what work might mean for you physically and with your learning disability. At the same time you feel that if you could find work that balanced your back and

*(continued)*

*(continued)*

learning issues you would find that rewarding and it might help with your relationships, might help you feel more independent, and might help you reciprocate more with your wife. You also don't like how not working makes you feel and you're thinking that perhaps getting a job might be part of a plan to help you address depression.

Cl: Yep, I think you nailed it there. That's what I'm thinking and really things can't stay the way they are forever.

Co: So going through VR to try and return to work really is up to you, and you have a lot that you are considering, including this idea that you aren't happy with how things are.

Cl: Well, I think I'm going to give this a try.

In the evoking process, the strategy is to help clients feel heard and empathized with as they discuss reasons why they are stuck. The counselor then transitions the conversation to help clients speak about the reasons that they might want to change. The microskills of MI are used to help clients articulate their own desires, abilities, reasons, and needs for change. In Brian's case, the counselor expressed empathy through reflective listening as Brian discussed his concerns about back pain and his learning disability. The counselor then strategically shifted the focus of the conversation through well-placed open questions and reflections to help Brian talk more about his desires and reasons for change.

### Planning

Co: That's great, Brian. I'm really looking forward to working with you! You mentioned earlier that one of the things you might be interested in doing is interest and assessment inventories, what other things might you be interested in doing while going through VR?

Cl: Well, I don't know really, I suppose I need help with my résumé. I haven't even looked at it since my accident.

Co: So, once you have an idea about what type of job you'd like to try for, you'd also be interested in adjusting or tweaking your résumé.

Cl: Yep.

Co: That's a really good idea. Having a good résumé can be very helpful when returning to the job market.

Cl: Thank you.

*(continued)*

(*continued*)

> Co:  Would it be okay if I shared with you some of the VR processes that often people experience while they are here?
>
> Cl:  Sure.
>
> Co:  Well, first, we fill out some forms and assess the barriers to employment, such as your learning disability and back injury. From there, we have a wide variety of options, including retraining, a trial work experience, and so forth.
>
> During the planning process, the goal is to evoke information from the client on how she or he might perceive accomplishing his or her goal. It is helpful to ask permission and provide information by presenting a menu of options. Here, the counselor helps Brian begin to envision the future VR interactions. The counselor uses MI microskills to help Brian feel autonomous in their interactions.

## RESEARCH FINDINGS

Since the publication of the classic text on MI by Miller and Rollnick (1991), the research base on MI has been rapidly growing. More than 250 outcome studies on MI have been published (Wagner & Conners, 2010), along with over 100 randomized controlled trials, in addition to a number of meta-analyses and systematic reviews (e.g., Burke et al., 2003; Hettema, Steele, & Miller, 2005; Westra, Arkowitz, & Dozois, 2009). MI has earned its standing as an evidence-based treatment and is currently listed on the National Registry of Evidence-Based Practices and Programs (2012).

### Effectiveness of MI

The first systematic reviews of the empirical literature on MI concluded that the evidence available at the time supported the utility of MI approaches for substance abuse problems, hypertension, bulimia, and diabetes treatment adherence (Burke, Arkowitz, & Dunn, 2002; Dunn, DeRoo, & Rivara, 2001; Noonan & Moyers, 1997). There were mixed results on the effectiveness of MI in the areas of smoking, exercise, and diet and no support found for implementing adaptations of MI with HIV risk behaviors (Burke et al., 2002). In later studies, Burke and colleagues sought to understand better how, why, and for whom MI works. Burke et al. (2003) conducted the first meta-analysis on 30 controlled clinical trials examining the effectiveness of adaptations of MI. These approaches demonstrated significant effect sizes (Cohen's $d$ ranging from .25 to .57) compared with no-treatment and/or placebo controls for problems with alcohol, drugs, and diet and exercise, but not for smoking or HIV risk behaviors. The results did not show that MI approaches were more effective than other active treatment approaches. Nonetheless, MI approaches yielded comparable results in shorter treatment periods (three to four fewer sessions than other psychosocial interventions). Despite low power for moderator analyses, the results indicated significant moderators for different MI approaches (i.e., higher doses of treatment and delivering it as a motivational prelude to other clinical services resulted in better outcomes in substance abuse studies).

After MI gained momentum in the field of addictions, clinical health professionals started to show an interest in applying these evidence-based methods to other health behavior problems (Knight, McGowan, Dickens, & Bundy, 2006). A meta-analysis and systematic review by Rubak et al. (2005) appraised the empirical evidence for MI in health problem areas of physiological and psychological disorders. The study reviewed 72 randomized controlled trials on MI, and the meta-analytic findings showed a significant effect size estimate for the outcome measures of body mass index, total blood cholesterol, systolic blood pressure, blood alcohol concentration, and standard ethanol content, whereas that for cigarettes per day and for glycated hemoglobin ($HbA_{1c}$) was not significant (combined effect sizes included 0). Additionally, abbreviated MI sessions of 15 minutes indicated an effect in 64% of the studies. Another systematic review also investigated the efficacy of MI interventions in health care settings (Knight et al., 2006). This study reviewed the outcomes from eight studies on diabetes, asthma, hypertension, hyperlipidemia, and heart disease. The majority of the studies found positive results for the effects of MI on psychological, physiological, and lifestyle change outcomes. Future research using MI with health behavior problems is needed, but the collective results imply that it may outperform the traditional advice giving in health care settings.

A recent meta-analysis by Lundahl, Kunz, Brownell, Tollefson, and Burke (2010) was based on 25 years of empirical evidence on MI to determine how it compares with other interventions. A total of 119 studies were included in the meta-analysis, with outcomes related to substance use (tobacco, alcohol, drugs, marijuana), health-related behaviors (diet, exercise, safe sex), gambling, and engagement in treatment variables. They found a smaller overall effect size of $g = .22$ (95% confidence interval or .17–.27). Although MI did not perform better than other treatments, such as CBT and 12-step interventions, MI interventions on average required significantly less time (over 100 fewer minutes) to produce equal effects and were durable at the 2-year mark and beyond. MI is also effective for increasing client engagement in treatment and intention to change. There were several delivery and client variables that significantly moderated outcomes, including assessment feedback, delivery time, manualization, delivery mode (group vs. individual), and client ethnicity. The strength of the delivery method of motivational enhancement therapy (MET; an adaption of MI techniques) was also highlighted in a recent review of published systematic reviews on the effectiveness of psychotherapy modalities for alcohol abuse problems (Martin & Rehm, 2012). The findings demonstrated that therapies with the strongest empirical evidence include MET, in addition to other brief interventions and CBT. MET coupled with physiotherapy has also been found to be effective for promoting functioning outcomes for individuals experiencing low-back pain (Vong et al., 2011).

There is also emerging evidence that MI appears to have cross-cultural transferability. Reviews of clinical trials have found the effect size of MI to be twice as large when those receiving treatment have come from predominantly minority populations in the United States compared with the majority White population (Hettema et al., 2005; Lasser et al., 2011). Other studies have demonstrated MI's application to diverse groups, including African Americans (Hettema et al., 2005; Resnicow et al., 2001, 2005) and Native Americans (Foley et al., 2005). Although this research is still relatively limited, MI's relevance to counseling with diverse cultural groups appears promising.

Using rigorous scientific methods, such as meta-analytic techniques, has helped to establish the efficacy of MI in treating a myriad of health and behavior problems (e.g., Hettema, 2006; Lundahl & Burke, 2009). However, it is largely unknown *how* MI produces its beneficial effects. A systematic review by Apodaca and Longabaugh (2009) was the first major attempt to dissect and summarize the empirical evidence for its underlying mechanisms of change. The authors reviewed evidence from 19 MI outcome studies that provided data on at least one link for a causal chain model. The conceptual model used in this study examined various clinician and client constructs. The four MI constructs of clinician behavior included spirit, consistent behaviors, inconsistent behaviors, and clinician use of specific techniques. In addition, five MI constructs of client behavior were assessed: change talk/intention, readiness to change, involvement/engagement, resistance, and discrepancy. The results indicated that effect sizes were mixed for the majority of the causal links. The most reliable data were only found for client change talk/intention and client experience of discrepancy, which were found to be related to improved outcomes and for inconsistent clinician behavior, which was associated with poorer outcomes.

### Fidelity

Fidelity has been an important element in the history of MI. Many counselors have stated that they were practicing MI when in actuality they were not (Miller & Rollnick, 2009). Likewise, some research has been conducted on interventions that have been labeled as MI, but technically were something else (Miller & Rollnick, 2013). However, when counselors or researchers overly manualize an MI intervention, its effectiveness appears to lessen (Miller & Rollnick, 2013). Research into how counselors best learn MI seems to indicate that counselors should obtain some form of ongoing fidelity measurement and coaching for MI skills to be adequately learned and retained (Madsen et al., 2009), but that being overly rigid in MI application (e.g., the development of forms or manuals in the absence of having an MI conversation) can also be detrimental (Miller & Rollnick, 2013). Therefore, it is important for rehabilitation counselors seeking to learn MI to obtain some form of fidelity measurement and coaching while at the same time avoiding interventions that are based on MI but are overly manualized.

## PROMINENT STRENGTHS AND LIMITATIONS

One of the primary strengths of MI is its versatility. MI is a strengths-based intervention that is geared toward helping individuals resolve ambivalence, enhance motivation, and increase commitment to a specific behavior change (Manthey et al., 2011). Ambivalence is a common issue experienced by almost anyone contemplating making a life change (Prochaska et al., 1992) and may be one reason why MI has been adopted for so many different applications, groups, and settings (Miller & Rollnick, 2013). In rehabilitation counseling, there are major issues of ambivalence that often need to be resolved (e.g., ambivalence about one's ability to handle competitive employment after developing a disability or ambivalence about losing disability benefits if one returns to work) as well as seemingly trivial issues (e.g., ambivalence about dressing for a job interview). Although further research still needs to be conducted to determine whether MI's effectiveness will extend to the specific scenarios within rehabilitation, in a pragmatic sense, MI may be a beneficial skill for counselors, when common issues of ambivalence and motivation emerge during the rehabilitation process.

Although the research conducted in other helping arenas is promising, one of the primary limitations of MI in rehabilitation is the lack of research specific to rehabilitation counseling and VR. Using MI to resolve ambivalence and increase motivation is not the only tool rehabilitation counselors should be using (Wagner & McMahon, 2004). Indeed, even Miller describes the highest level of skillfulness in MI as being able to determine when to use MI, when not to use it, and the ability to smoothly transition in and out of MI (Miller & Moyers, 2006). MI is not an intervention that will address every issue. For instance, MI was not developed to fix a dysfunctional service system or to create job opportunities for large groups of people with disabilities during a downturn in the economy. Addressing these large-scale issues requires different tools and skill sets. Nor is MI always used as a direct treatment for specific disabilities or symptoms (Miller & Rollnick, 2013). Instead, MI is often used as an engagement strategy to help clients resolve their ambivalence about seeking help for a disability or related symptoms, such as helping a client with a psychiatric disability work through ambivalence about taking medications (Manthey, Blajeski, & Monroe-DeVita, 2012); helping an individual with a learning disability resolve ambivalence regarding whether or not to disclose his or her disability to a campus accommodations office; helping an individual decide to seek treatment for depression; or ambivalence previously mistaken for a lack of motivation or desire to change, leading to unsuccessful closures.

It is important to note several additional strengths of MI highlighted in the research review. Research findings on the effectiveness of MI suggest that (a) it is more useful than placebo conditions or no treatment (Burke et al., 2003), (b) it is at least equal to other psychosocial interventions (Burke, Dunn, Atkins, & Phelps, 2004), (c) it yields comparable results in briefer treatment periods (Vasilaki et al., 2006), (d) it is effective for a wide range of addictive and health behaviors (Hettema & Hendricks, 2010; Lundahl et al., 2010), and (e) it may increase the efficacy of treatment programs when used at onset to increase engagement

(Miller & Rose, 2009). In addition, prospective therapy modalities that modify or integrate counseling techniques (e.g., enhancing MI with feedback or combining MI with CBT) demonstrate promising results and may offer further evidence for adaptations to MI (Hettema et al., 2005; Westra et al., 2009).

In summary, MI is a brief intervention that fits within the shortening counseling time frames allowed in modern practice in rehabilitation settings. MI is a strengths-based counseling style that helps clients resolve ambivalence by facilitating a conversation in which clients talk themselves into change. This is accomplished through purposively using open-ended questions, reflection, affirmations, and summary statements to guide clients through four MI processes: engaging, focusing, evoking, and planning. By paying attention to client language, counselors are able to identify when to use each of the four MI processes and strategically help clients articulate their own reasons for change. Although there are limitations to MI, it is a counseling style that may prove more efficient in addressing many issues relevant to rehabilitation counseling.

## ACKNOWLEDGMENTS

The contents of this chapter were developed with support from the Rehabilitation Research and Training Center on Effective Vocational Rehabilitation Service Delivery Practices at the University of Wisconsin–Madison and the University of Wisconsin–Stout and with funding provided by the National Institute on Disability and Rehabilitation Research, U.S. Department of Education (Grant H133B100034). The ideas, opinions, and conclusions expressed, however, are those of the authors and do not represent recommendations, endorsements, or policies of the U.S. Department of Education.

## DISCUSSION EXERCISES

1. How might you use the microskills of MI differently during each of the four processes (engaging, focusing, evoking, and planning)?
2. What do you think the evidence of MI, as reviewed here, suggests about its applications in rehabilitation counseling?
3. How can MI be used to help rehabilitation clients meet their goals?
4. What do you think are the drawbacks and benefits of an intervention built inductively through clinical practice?
5. How do you think you would go about building your MI skills?

## REFERENCES

Amrhein, P. C., Miller, W. R., Yahne, C. E., Palmer, M., & Fulcher, L. (2003). Client commitment language during motivational interviewing predicts drug use outcomes. *Journal of Consulting and Clinical Psychology, 71*(5), 862–878.

Amrhein, P. C., Miller, W. R., Yahne, C., Knupsky, A., & Hochstein, D. (2004). Strength of client commitment language improves with therapist training in motivational interviewing. *Alcoholism: Clinical and Experimental Research, 28*, 74A.

Apodaca, T. R., & Longabaugh, R. (2009). Mechanisms of change in motivational interviewing: A review and preliminary evaluation of the evidence. *Addiction, 104,* 705–715.

Arkowitz, H., Westra, H. A., Miller, W. R., & Rollnick, S. (2008). *Motivational interviewing in the treatment of psychological problems.* New York, NY: Guilford.

Bandura, A. (1999). *Self-efficacy: Toward a unifying theory of behavioral change.* New York, NY: Psychological Press.

Bem, D. J. (1972). Self-perception theory. In L. Berkowitz (Ed.), *Advances in experimental social psychology* (Vol. 6, pp. 1–62). New York, NY: Academic Press.

Brehm, S. S., & Brehm, J. W. (1981). *Psychological reactance: A theory of freedom and control.* New York, NY: Academic Press.

Britt, E., Hudson, S. M., & Blampied, N. M. (2004). Motivational interviewing in health settings: A review. *Patient Education and Counseling, 53,* 147–155.

Brooks, K. (2005). "You would think...": Applying motivational interviewing and career coaching concepts with liberal arts students. *Journal of Career Planning and Employment, 65,* 28–36.

Burke, B. L., Arkowitz, H., & Dunn, C. (2002). The efficacy of motivational interviewing. In W. R. Miller & S. Rollnick (Eds.), *Motivational interviewing: Preparing people for change* (2nd ed., pp. 217–250). New York, NY: Guilford.

Burke, B. L., Arkowitz, H., & Menchola, M. (2003). The efficacy of motivational interviewing: A meta-analysis of controlled clinical trials. *Journal of Consulting and Clinical Psychology, 71,* 843–860.

Burke, B. L., Dunn, C. W., Atkins, D. C., & Phelps, J. S. (2004). The emerging evidence base for motivational interviewing: A meta-analytic and qualitative inquiry. *Journal of Cognitive Psychotherapy, 18,* 309–322.

Chan, F., Shaw, L., McMahon, B. T., Koch, L., & Strauser, D. (1997). A model for enhancing consumer-counselor working relationships in rehabilitation. *Rehabilitation Counseling Bulletin, 41,* 122–137.

Chan, F., Sung, C., Muller, V., Wang, C. C., Fujikawa, M., & Anderson, C. A. (2011). Evidence-based practice and research utilization. In D. Maki & V. Tarvydas (Eds.), *The professional practice of rehabilitation counseling* (pp. 391–412). New York, NY: Springer Publishing Company.

Chan, F., Tarvydas, V., Blalock, K., Strauser, D., & Atkins, B. (2009). Unifying and elevating rehabilitation counseling through model-driven, diversity sensitive, evidence-based practice. *Rehabilitation Counseling Bulletin, 52,* 114–119.

Chou, C. C., Ditchman, N., Pruett, S., Chan, F., & Hunter, C. (2009). Application of self-efficacy related theories in psychosocial interventions. In F. Chan, E. Cardoso, & J. A. Chronister (Eds.), *Understanding psychosocial adjustment to chronic illness and disability: A handbook for evidence-based practitioners in rehabilitation* (pp. 243–276). New York, NY: Springer Publishing Company.

Cleary, M., Hunt, G. E., Matheson, S., & Walter, G. (2009). Psychosocial treatments for people with co-occurring severe mental illness and substance misuse: Systematic review. *Journal of Advanced Nursing, 65,* 238–258.

Conner, M., & Armitage, C. J. (2008). Attitudinal ambivalence. In W. D. Crano & R. Prislin (Eds.), *Attitudes and attitude change* (pp. 261–286). New York, NY: Psychology Press.

Cook, D. W. (2004). Counseling people with physical disabilities. In F. Chan, N. L. Berven, & K. R. Thomas (Eds.), *Counseling theories and techniques for rehabilitation health professionals* (pp. 328–341). New York, NY: Springer Publishing Company.

Dracott, S., & Dabbs, A. (1998). Cognitive dissonance 2: A theoretical grounding of motivational interviewing. *British Journal of Clinical Psychology, 37,* 355–364.

Dunn, C., Deroo, L., & Rivara, F. P. (2001). The use of brief interventions adapted from motivational interviewing across behavioral domains: A systematic review. *Addiction, 96,* 1725–1742.

Edmunds, J., Ntoumanis, N., & Duda, J. L. (2006). A test of self-determination theory in the exercise domain. *Journal of Applied Social Psychology, 36,* 2240–2265.

Fenton-O'Creevy, M., Nicholson, N., Soane, E., & Willman, P. (2003). Trading on illusions: Unrealistic perceptions of control and trading performance. *Journal of Occupational and Organisational Psychology, 76,* 53–68.

Festinger, L. (1957). *A theory of cognitive dissonance.* Evanston, IL: Row, Peterson.

Foley, K., Duran, B., Morris, P., Lucero, J., Jiang, Y., & Baxter, B. (2005). Using motivational interviewing to promote HIV testing at an American Indian substance abuse treatment facility. *Journal of Psychoactive Drugs, 37,* 321–329.

Graham, V., Jutla, S., Higginson, D., & Wells, A. (2008). The added value of motivational interviewing within employment assessments. *Journal of Occupational Psychology, Employment and Disability, 10,* 43–52.

Hettema, J., Steele, J., & Miller, W. R. (2005). Motivational interviewing. *Annual Review of Clinical Psychology, 1,* 91–111.

Hettema, J. E. (2006). *A meta-analysis of motivational interviewing across behavioral domains.* Albuquerque, NM: University of New Mexico. Retrieved from ProQuest.

Hettema, J. E., & Hendricks, P. S. (2010). Motivational interviewing for smoking cessation: A meta-analytic review. *Journal of Consulting and Clinical Psychology, 78,* 868–884.

Hohman, M. (2012). *Motivational interviewing in social work practice.* New York, NY: Guilford.

Kanfer, F. H. (1987). Self-regulation and behavior. In H. Heckhausen, P. M. Gollwitzer, & F. E. Weinert (Eds.), *Jenseits des Rubikon* (pp. 286–299). Heidelberg, Germany: Springer-Verlag.

Knight, K. M., McGowan, L., Dickens, C., & Bundy, C. (2006). A systematic review of motivational interviewing in physical health care settings. *British Journal of Health Psychology, 11,* 319–332.

Larson, J. E. (2008). User-friendly motivational interviewing and evidence-based supported employment tools for practitioners. *Journal of Rehabilitation, 74,* 18–30.

Lasser, K. E., Murillo, J., Lisboa, S., Casimir, A. N., Valley-Shah, L., Emmons, K. M., . . . Ayanian, J. Z. (2011). Colorectal cancer screening among ethnically diverse, low-income patients: A randomized controlled trial. *Archives of Internal Medicine, 171,* 906–912.

Leukefeld, C., McDonald, H., Staton, M., Mateyoke-Scrivner, A., Webster, M., Logan, T., & Garrity, T. (2003). An employment intervention for drug-abusing offenders. *Federal Probation, 67,* 27–31.

Levensky, E. R., Forcehimes, A., O'Donohue, W. T., & Beitz, K. (2007). Motivational interviewing: An evidence-based approach to counseling helps patients follow treatment recommendations. *American Journal of Nursing, 107,* 50–58.

Lloyd, C., Tse, S., Waghorn, G., & Hennessy, N. (2008). Motivational interviewing in vocational rehabilitation for people living with mental ill health. *International Journal of Therapy and Rehabilitation, 15,* 572–578.

Lundahl, B., & Burke, B. L. (2009). The effectiveness and applicability of motivational interviewing: A practice-friendly review of four meta-analyses. *Journal of Clinical Psychology, 65,* 1232–1245.

Lundahl, B. W., Kunz, C., Brownell, C., Tollefson, D., & Burke, B. L. (2010). A meta-analysis of motivational interviewing: Twenty-five years of empirical studies. *Research on Social Work Practice, 20*(2), 137–160.

Lundahl, B. W., Tolefson, D., Gambles, C., Brownell, C., & Burke, B. (2010). Meta-analysis of motivational interviewing: Twenty five years of research. *Research on Social Work Practice, 20*(2), 137–160.

Madson, M., Loignon, A., & Lance, C. (2009). Training in motivational interviewing: A systematic review. *Journal of Substance Abuse Treatment, 36,* 101–109.

Mannock, T., Levesque, D. A., & Prochaska, J. M. (2002). Assessing readiness of clients with disabilities to engage in job seeking behaviors. *Journal of Rehabilitation, 68,* 16–23.

Manthey, T. (2009). Training motivational interviewing in a vocational rehabilitation context. *MINT Bulletin, 15*(1), 9–13.

Manthey, T. (2011). Using motivational interviewing to increase retention in supported education. *American Journal of Psychiatric Rehabilitation, 14*, 120–136.

Manthey, T. J., Blajeski, S., & Monroe-DeVita, M. (2012). Motivational interviewing and assertive community treatment: A case for training ACT teams. *International Journal of Psychosocial Rehabilitation, 16*, 5–17.

Manthey, T. J., Knowles, B., Asher, D., & Wahab, S. (2011). Strengths-based practice and motivational interviewing. *Advances in Social Work, 12*, 126–151.

Manthey, T., Jackson, C., & Evans-Brown, P. (2011). Motivational interviewing and vocational rehabilitation: A review with recommendations for administrators and counselors. *Journal of Applied Rehabilitation Counseling, 42*(1), 3–14.

Markland, D., Ryan, R. M., Tobin, V. J., & Rollnick, S. (2005). Motivational interviewing and self-determination theory. *Journal of Social and Clinical Psychology, 24*, 811–831.

Martin, G. W., & Rehm, J. (2012). The effectiveness of psychosocial modalities in the treatment of alcohol problems in adults: A review of the evidence. *Canadian Journal of Psychiatry, 57*, 350–358.

McMurran, M. (2009). Motivational interviewing with offenders: A systematic review. *Legal and Criminological Psychology, 14*, 83–100.

Miller, W. R. (1983). Motivational interviewing with problem drinkers. *Behavioural Psychotherapy, 11*, 147–172.

Miller, W. R. (2012). Equipoise and equanimity in motivational interviewing. *Motivational Interviewing: Training, Research, Implementation, Practice, 1*(1), 31–32. doi:10.5195/mitrip.2012.10

Miller, W. R., Benefield, R. G., & Tonigan, J. S. (1993). Enhancing motivation for change in problem drinking: A controlled comparison of two therapist styles. *Journal of Counseling and Clinical Psychology, 61*, 455–461.

Miller, W. R., & Moyers, T. B. (2006). Eight stages in learning motivational interviewing. *Journal of Teaching in the Addictions, 5*(1), 3–17.

Miller, W. R., & Rollnick, S. (1991). *Motivational interviewing: Preparing people to change addictive behavior*. New York, NY: Guilford.

Miller, W. R., & Rollnick, S. (2002). *Motivational interviewing: Preparing people for change* (2nd ed.). New York, NY: Guilford.

Miller, W. R., & Rollnick, S. (2009). Ten things that motivational interviewing is not. *Behavioral and Cognitive Psychotherapy, 37*, 129–140.

Miller, W. R., & Rollnick, S. (2013). *Motivational interviewing: Helping people change* (3rd ed.). New York, NY: Guilford.

Miller, W. R., & Rose, G. S. (2009). Toward a theory of motivational interviewing. *American Psychologist, 64*, 527–537.

Muscat, A. (2005). Ready, set, go: The transtheoretical model of change and motivational interviewing for "fringe" clients. *Journal of Employment Counseling, 42*, 179–192.

National Registry of Evidence-Based Practices and Programs. (2012). *Motivational interviewing*. Substance Abuse and Mental Health Services Administration. Retrieved from http://www.nrepp.samhsa.gov/

Ng, J. Y., Ntoumanis, N., Thøgersen-Ntoumani, C., Deci, E. L., Ryan, R. M., Duda, J. L., & Williams, G. C. (2012). Self-determination theory applied to health contexts: A meta-analysis. *Perspectives on Psychological Science, 7*, 325–340.

Noonan, W. C., & Moyers, T. B. (1997). Motivational interviewing. *Journal of Substance Use, 2*, 8–16.

Orford, J. (1985). *Excessive appetites: A psychological view of addictions*. New York, NY: Wiley.

Prochaska, J. O., DiClemente, C. C., & Norcross, J. C. (1992). In search of how people change: Applications to addictive behaviors. *American Psychologist, 47*, 1102–1144.

Resnicow, K., Jackson, A., Blissett, D., Wang, T., McCarty, F., & Rahotep, S. (2005). Results of the Healthy Body Healthy Spirit trial. *Health Psychology, 24,* 339–348.

Resnicow, K., Jackson, A., Wang, T., De, A. K., McCarty, F., & Dudley, W. N. (2001). A motivational interviewing intervention to increase fruit and vegetable intake through black churches: Results of the eat for life trial. *American Journal of Public Health, 91,* 1686–1693.

Rogers, C. R. (1951). *Client-centered therapy.* Boston, MA: Houghton Mifflin.

Rogers, C. R. (1957). The necessary and sufficient conditions of psychotherapeutic personality change. *Journal of Consulting Psychology, 2,* 95–103.

Rogers, C. R. (1979). The foundations of the person-centered approach. *Education, 100,* 98–107.

Rokeach, M. (1973). *The nature of human values.* New York, NY: Free Press.

Rollnick, S., & Miller, W. R. (1995). What is motivational interviewing? *Behavioural and Cognitive Psychotherapy, 23,* 325–334.

Rollnick, S., Miller, W. R., & Butler, C. C. (2008). *Motivational interviewing in health care: Helping patients change behavior.* New York, NY: Guilford.

Rose, J., Saunder, K., Hensel, E., & Kroese, B. (2005). Factors affecting the likelihood that people with intellectual disabilities will gain employment. *Journal of Intellectual Disabilities, 9,* 9–23.

Rubak, S., Sandbaek, A., Lauritzen, T., & Christensen, B. (2005). Motivational interviewing: A systematic review and meta-analysis. *British Journal of General Practice, 55,* 305–312.

Ryan, R. M., & Deci, E. L. (2002). Overview of self-determination theory: An organismic-dialectical perspective. In E. L. Deci & R. M. Ryan (Eds.), *Handbook of self-determination research* (pp. 3–33). Rochester, NY: University of Rochester Press.

Saleebey, D. (2006). *The strengths perspective in social work practice* (4th ed.). New York, NY: Longman.

Steele, C. M. (1988). The psychology of self-affirmation: Sustaining the integrity of the self. In L. Berkowitz (Ed.), *Advances in experimental and social psychology* (Vol. 21, pp. 261–302). San Diego, CA: Academic Press.

Thomas, K. R., Thoreson, R., Parker, R., & Butler, A. (1998). Theoretical foundations of the counseling function. In R. M. Parker & E. M. Szymanski (Eds.), *Rehabilitation counseling: Basics and beyond* (pp. 225–268). Austin, TX: Pro-Ed.

Thoreson, R. W., Smits, S. J., Butler, A. J., & Wright, G. N. (1968). *Counselor problems associated with client characteristics (Wisconsin studies in vocational rehabilitation).* Madison, WI: University of Wisconsin Regional Rehabilitation Research Institute.

Vansteenkiste, M., Williams, G. C., & Resnicow, K. (2012). Toward systematic integration between self-determination theory and motivational interviewing as examples of top-down and bottom-up intervention development: Autonomy or volition as a fundamental principle. *International Journal of Behavioral Nutrition and Physical Activity, 9,* 2–11.

Vasilaki, E. I., Hosier, S. G., & Cox, W. M. (2006). The efficacy of motivational interviewing as a brief intervention for excessive drinking: A meta-analytic review. *Alcohol and Alcoholism, 41,* 328–335.

Vong, S. K., Cheing, G. L., Chan, F., So, E. M., & Chan, C. C. (2011). Motivational enhancement therapy in addition to physical therapy improves motivational factors and treatment outcomes in people with low back pain: A randomized controlled trial. *Archives of Physical Medicine and Rehabilitation, 92,* 176–183.

Wagner, C. C., & Conners, W. (2010). *Motivational interviewing: Motivational interviewing bibliography 1983–2007.* Virginia, VA: Mid-Atlantic Addiction Technology Transfer Center.

Wagner, C. C., & McMahon, B. T. (2004). Motivational interviewing and rehabilitation counseling practice. *Rehabilitation Counseling Bulletin, 47,* 152–161.

Westra, H. A., Arkowitz, H., & Dozois, D. J. (2009). Adding a motivational interviewing pretreatment to cognitive behavioral therapy for generalized anxiety disorder: A preliminary randomized controlled trial. *Journal of Anxiety Disorders, 23,* 1106–1117.

Wright, G. N., Smits, S. J., Butler, A. J., & Thoreson, R. W. (1968). *A survey of counselor perceptions.* Madison, WI: University of Wisconsin, Regional Rehabilitation Research Institute.

Yahne, C. E., Miller, W. R., Irvin-Vitela, L., & Tonigan, J. S. (2002). Magdalena pilot project: Motivational outreach to substance abusing women sex workers. *Journal of Substance Abuse Treatment, 23,* 49–53.

# Group Procedures

*Nicole Ditchman, Eun-Jeong Lee, and Ruth A. Huebner*

## LEARNING OBJECTIVES

This chapter provides an overview of group procedures in rehabilitation from an evidence-based perspective. Specifically, it will (a) discuss the application of group procedures in rehabilitation, including counseling, psychotherapy, and psychoeducation formats; (b) highlight the major theoretical approaches that guide group work; and (c) review the empirical support for group procedures. As learning objectives, readers should:

1. Have an understanding of the research related to the therapeutic benefits of group procedures.
2. Be familiar with theoretical approaches that can uniquely be applied to group intervention models.
3. Be able to identify recommended practices for group leadership styles and techniques, along with empirically supported guidelines for group formation and process considerations.
4. Have an understanding of ethical and legal issues impacting group process.

## BASIC CONCEPTS

Humans have always been social beings, seeking the comfort of others in times of loss, the safety of others in times of threat, the wisdom of others in times of change, and the joy of others in times of celebration. Thus, it is no surprise that group procedures are used frequently as a part of treatment and service provision in rehabilitation settings. Groups are sometimes used as stand-alone treatments, but they are also commonly integrated into comprehensive treatment plans that might include some combination of other services, individual treatment and counseling, and/or medication.

Groups can be used for therapeutic and educational purposes with a variety of clients for a variety of purposes. Today, the benefits of groups are increasingly being recognized in rehabilitation and mental health settings. Counseling and psychoeducation groups fit particularly well in today's managed-care health system because they can be designed to be brief, cost-effective treatments. In fact, most groups today are not unstructured personal growth groups, but, rather, short-term groups targeting specific client populations and designed to remediate or prevent particular problems (Corey & Corey, 2006). Moreover, the group process has unique therapeutic and learning advantages (Corey, 2012). An emerging body of research demonstrates that group methods are effective, that the benefits are maintained over time, and that best practices in group procedures are associated with positive outcomes (Barlow, 2008; Bednar & Kaul, 1994).

Presently, group counseling is generally thought of as a specialized mode of treatment, and there is no recognized certifying body for group counselors or specialists established under the American Psychological Association (APA) or the American Counseling Association (ACA; Cottone & Tarvydas, 2007). However, there are divisions in both professional organizations dedicated to the study and practice of group counseling—namely, APA's Division 49 (Society of Group Psychology and Group Psychotherapy) and the ACA's Association for Specialists in Group Work (ASGW). Separate from these professional organizations, the American Group Psychotherapy Association (AGPA) offers certification for group psychotherapists. All three of these associations provide best practice guidelines and resources for counselors and psychologists who are engaged in group work.

## Definition of the Group

According to ASGW (2000, pp. 329–330), group work can be defined as

> a broad professional practice involving the application of knowledge and skill in group facilitation to assist an interdependent collection of people to reach their mutual goals, which may be intrapersonal, interpersonal, or work related. The goals of the group may include the accomplishment of tasks related to work, education, personal development, personal and interpersonal problem solving, or remediation of mental and emotional disorders.

There are many types of groups, including task and work groups, psychoeducational groups, counseling groups, psychotherapy groups, self-help groups, and peer support groups (Corey & Corey, 2006). Variations among types may include degree of structure used, specificity of tasks and objectives, and characteristics of group members. Common group goals include self-exploration, personal growth, and building of inner resources. In essence, group members come together to form a social system, with norms and expectations, and they interact with one another and the leader.

In group counseling, the group context and the group process constitute the treatment intervention. The therapeutic effects originate within the group context based on the fundamental assumption that the presence of others provides opportunities for self-exploration, learning, and cohesion that is unique relative to individual counseling approaches. The general therapeutic effects are described in both the classic and the current literature on group procedures (Corey & Corey, 2006; Posthuma, 1998; Yalom & Leszcz, 2005) and are associated with group processes regardless of the theoretical approach.

### General Therapeutic Factors

Although a number of different theoretical orientations can impact how a practitioner leads a group, there is a relatively well-established body of research supporting a number of common factors associated with the effectiveness of group procedures (Corey & Corey, 2006; Posthuma, 1998; Yalom & Leszcz, 2005). Yalom and Leszcz (2005) reviewed empirical data and expert clinical observations centered on the mechanisms of change that are common to virtually all group interventions. Of these factors, there is emerging consensus that cohesion is the most central and is the best definition of the therapeutic relationship in groups (Bernard et al., 2008; Burlingame et al., 2002; Yalom & Leszcz, 2005). Cohesion is a function of a number of potential alliances in groups, including member-to-member, member-to-group, and member–leader relationships (Burlingame et al., 2002). Cohesion of groups has been positively associated with clinical outcomes in a number of published studies (Tschuschke & Dies, 1994). Table 13.1 reviews additional therapeutic factors identified by Yalom and Leszcz (2005), along with specific considerations for some clients with disabilities.

## APPLICATION OF THEORIES TO GROUP PROCEDURES

Multiple theoretical approaches, derived in large part from methods and theories applied to individual counseling (Bednar & Kaul, 1994), have also been applied to group counseling. It is less common to see strict adherence to a single theory; rather, many counselors function within an integrative, continually developing framework that aligns with their unique worldviews (Norcross & Goldfried, 2005). Four broad categories of theories are conceptualized here to illustrate the fundamental differences among theoretical approaches.

### Psychodynamic Approaches

Concepts from psychoanalysis, object relations, and interpersonal theory may be grouped together under the psychodynamic approach (see Chapters 9 and 10 in this volume). The goal of the psychodynamic group is restructuring the client's character and personality by moving unconscious conflicts into the client's awareness. Wolf and Schwartz (1963) developed group applications for basic psychodynamic techniques, such as free association, dream analysis, and transference. The goal of this intervention is to provide a climate in which clients may re-experience relationships with family members or close peers. The group

**TABLE 13.1 General Therapeutic Factors and Their Applications to Rehabilitation**

| THERAPEUTIC FACTOR | DEFINITION | APPLICATION TO REHABILITATION |
|---|---|---|
| Universality | Members recognize that other members share similar thoughts, feelings, and challenges. | The universality effect may promote acceptance of one's feelings as normal responses to a chronic illness or disability, potentially reducing catastrophizing or shame associated with the condition. |
| Instillation of hope | Members recognize that other members' success can be valuable and they develop optimism for their own progress. | In rehabilitation, the need for a sense of hope may be particularly salient for individuals who have experienced a traumatic onset of disability, such as spinal cord injury, a chronic illness, such as bipolar mood disorder, or attempts to return to work after chronic unemployment. |
| Altruism | Members of the group increase self-esteem through extending help to other members of the group. | Opportunities to alternate between giving and receiving in the group process foster role versatility. For those with chronic conditions who may have become dependent on others, this can be an important shift toward normal role functioning (Holmes & Kivlighan, 2000). |
| Imparting information | Advice or education is provided by the group leaders or members. | Imparting information is a critical element of the counseling process for many rehabilitation groups, and a didactic aspect of the rehabilitative process can be critical. Often, new information about the extent to which members share a common problem can stimulate discussion, solutions, and instillation of hope. |
| Imitative behavior | Members expand their personal knowledge and skills through vicarious learning and observing other members' progress. | Learning from others facing similar challenges can be particularly valuable for individuals with disabilities and promotes self-management of chronic conditions. |
| Interpersonal learning | Members gain personal insight through feedback provided by other members. | Wright (1983) suggested that groups generate novel solutions to problems, changes in values, or changes in fundamental expectations. This can be particularly beneficial for individuals with newly acquired disabilities to gain insight into the effects disability may have in their lives. |

| | | |
|---|---|---|
| Cohesiveness | Feelings of belonging, trust, and togetherness experienced by members of the group. | The acceptance and mutual respect shared by group members can foster self-acceptance, an important factor for clients with disabilities. At the same time, bonding with other individuals facing similar disabilities or life situations can promote a sense of community, belonging, and empowerment. |
| Development of socializing techniques | The group context can provide members with an environment that promotes adaptive and effective communication. | Members in a supportive group do not hesitate to provide constructive feedback to one another. This in turn can strengthen social skills and self-efficacy beliefs among individuals with disabilities. |
| Recapitulation of the family experience | The group provides a corrective emotional experience to reshape and reframe the member's early experiences. | Disability can have a considerable impact on the family, expected roles, and interpersonal relationships. Group processes stimulate a range of possible transference experiences and provide a safe environment to work through interpersonal conflicts and to develop new skills and healthier expectations in relationships. |
| Catharsis | Release of strong feelings about past or present experiences. | Profound emotional experiences can surface as a result of group interventions. Members who have minimized the extent of their disability may be confronted with distorted self-perceptions. Studies suggest that emotional expressiveness and self-disclosure in groups can result in lower psychological distress and improved quality of life and health status (Bower et al., 1998; Stanton et al., 2000). |
| Existential factors | Acceptance of responsibility for life decisions. | Self-efficacy is rooted in recognition that one has agency in how one's life is lived, which is an important aspect of adjustment to disability. |
| Self-understanding | Members gain insight into psychological motivation behind emotional reactions and behavior. | Accepting and understanding "self" has been known as one of the most important indicators for positive adjustment (Linkowski, 1971). This is especially relevant for a person with an acquired disability, for whom it is critical to gain a better understanding about one's self and acceptance of changes to identity and values. |

process may elicit transference and defense mechanisms. For example, one group member may remind another member of a mother, a father, a close friend, or an authority figure.

As with people in general, persons with disabilities may experience problems related to relationships, emotional distress, culture, and abuse (Patterson, McKenzie, & Jenkins, 1995). Experiences with disability may elicit stereotypical responses from others, including inaccurate perceptions of abilities, the spread of disability to all aspects of life, lowered expectations for adaptation, and distancing from others (Marshak & Seligman, 1993). Effective group leaders provide opportunities for clients to practice alternative responses, facilitating the development of social competence. The psychodynamic group process may be an unstructured approach or may be more highly structured, for example, for persons with limited cognitive abilities, for individuals who have more difficulty sharing or articulating feelings, or during the early stages of group development. Sharing memories of early life and early experience with disability, presenting photographs, making a collage of different stages of life, drawing a timeline of one's life, creating artwork, or engaging in imaging exercises may be used to activate self-awareness. The sharing and processing of these experiences among group members to enhance insight is a critical component of the psychodynamic approach.

### Experiential and Humanistic Approaches

Concepts from gestalt therapy, logotherapy, existential therapy, and person-centered therapy are grouped here under experiential and humanistic approaches (see Chapters 2, 3, and 4 in this volume). The goals of experiential approaches are to develop an understanding of self and to empower group members to change and take responsibility for their lives. The group provides a safe climate where members can explore the full range of emotions while experiencing acceptance by the group. Nonverbal behaviors are attended to as clues to masked feelings. For example, the client may say that life is fine, but downturned eyes and wringing hands may suggest otherwise. In response, the group may point out the inconsistency and help the person express more of his or her present emotional experience. The focus on the "here and now" experience is intended to increase awareness of emotions, provide catharsis, and develop congruence between actions and feelings (Yalom & Josselson, 2011).

Role-playing, emphatic group responses, reflection, modeling, and a variety of active exercises are used to elicit and experience feelings. Use of the empty chair technique may encourage a group member to mourn a disability, say goodbye to a former self, express an emotion to a specific person, or accept a disowned part of the self. For groups needing more structure, members could be asked to write down a feeling toward another group member and then express it or pair up to interview another person. Group members are encouraged to confront denial, entitlement, and anger, and then to acknowledge, own, and accept responsibility for their emotions and actions.

## Cognitive Behavioral Approaches

Concepts from behavior therapy, rational emotive therapy, cognitive behavioral therapy, reality therapy, and solution-focused therapy are grouped together here (see Chapters 5, 6, and 7 in this volume). The goal of cognitive behavioral approaches is to replace maladaptive behavior and thinking with adaptive behavior and rational cognition. The group members and leader reinforce adaptive behavior and thoughts, seek to extinguish maladaptive responses, and promote direct and vicarious learning. The cognitive behavioral focus is attractive in rehabilitation because it facilitates collaboration, focuses on presenting problems, is structured with specific goals, and can be documented for reimbursement (Bowers, 1988). Numerous examples of the application of this approach are found in the literature. Group role-plays and structured experiences may be used, for instance, to teach the social skills of asking for help, training care providers, demonstrating equipment, or interviewing for a job (Liberman, DeRisi, & Mueser, 1989). Specific cognitive distortions identified with disability, such as "I can't live with this disability" may be reframed by a group into more adaptive responses associated with improved adjustment to disability (Sweetland, 1990).

Intervention strategies used in the cognitive behavioral approach tend to be more structured, often with specific behavioral objectives (Burns & Beck, 1999). Role-playing, systematic desensitization, relaxation, meditation, assertiveness and time management training, workbooks and reading assignments, and many other techniques are used. Members may establish weekly goals, share these goals with the group, devise methods to achieve the goals, and return to share their progress and strategies that they have found to be effective. Tangible reinforcement, like tokens or stickers, may be used to visualize progress.

## Psychoeducational Approaches

Educational, support, and self-help groups that are structured around some central theme are included here under Psychoeducational Approaches. The goals of these groups are to build knowledge, develop pragmatic coping strategies, and establish social support with others having similar experiences. The group leader may be very active in planning and running a support group, leadership may rotate among members, or there may not be a formal group leader. Group membership may be stable or changing in virtually every session. Group members function as a support and knowledge base for one another and as a source of practical solutions to problems and action.

In rehabilitation, there are psychoeducational groups within inpatient, outpatient, and vocational programs. Groups can be organized to impart information about an illness or disability and to teach self-management skills; they are often organized around a particular illness or disability, such as heart conditions, arthritis, or brain injury. Job clubs may support those with chronic unemployment through a structured and intensive job search and training process (Salomone, 1996). Specific job skills for the transition from school to work may also be taught using a group format (McWhirter & McWhirter, 1996).

## GROUP PROCEDURES AND PROCESS

Group process refers to the ways in which a group develops or evolves over time from beginning to end. Group process is concerned with the dynamics that go on within the group among the members. Specific guidelines and recommendations for group formation, procedures, and process are provided by several sources, including the ASGW and the AGPA, and numerous books (e.g., Corey & Corey, 2006; Yalom & Leszcz, 2005).

### Group Formation

The theoretical approach used and the specific methods employed in a group will be dictated in part by the constraints of the environment and the needs of the individuals in the group. For example, cost-containment constraints tend to lead inpatient groups to be characterized by rapid changes in group composition and leadership and heterogeneous patient populations. Regardless of what type of group is conducted, fundamental guidelines for group formation are commonly described in the literature (e.g., Bernard et al., 2008; Corey & Corey, 2006; Thomas & Pender, 2008; Yalom & Leszcz, 2005). Important considerations regarding size, composition, location, and timing of sessions are presented in Table 13.2, along with considerations for clients with disabilities.

### Practical Considerations and Client Rights in Groups

In most settings, groups are voluntary, and participants have the right to receive help and to self-disclose at a comfortable pace. Careful screening and selection of prospective group participants are recommended. Leaders can make assessments of client readiness for a group, along with providing information and exploring concerns that potential clients may have about the group. To the extent possible, rehabilitation practitioners should select members whose needs and goals are compatible with the goals of the group, who do not impede the group process, and whose well-being is not jeopardized by the group experience. Clients generally do well in group work when they have personal goals that align with the goals of the group and are motivated and attracted to the group (Seligman, 1995).

It is recommended that each member of the group be informed of group processes, techniques, fees, and risks (Bernard et al., 2008). Starting a group can be an anxiety-provoking experience for clients, and the structure and framework of the group should be described upfront (e.g., information about location, time and day of meeting, duration of each session, frequency and number of sessions, and group size). Even policies, such as absence notifications, eating/drinking during the group, and exiting should be clarified. Group members are usually individually oriented to the group and procedures prior to the first meeting. A signed informed consent procedure that outlines the specifics of the group, confidentiality and limits to confidentiality, and the risks of group membership,

**TABLE 13.2 General Guidelines and Considerations for Group Formation**

| FORMATION CONSIDERATIONS | GENERAL GUIDELINES | ADDITIONAL REHABILITATION CONSIDERATIONS |
|---|---|---|
| Meeting place | Settings should be considered on the basis of privacy, attractiveness, and ease of face-to-face interaction. Uncluttered rooms with limited distractions are generally ideal. | Consider the transportation and accessibility needs of the clients when determining a location and space. |
| Seating arrangement | Seating should be comfortable. Sitting in a circle allows participants to see one another and provides freedom for physical movement. If two leaders are present, it is recommended they sit across from each other to avoid creating a "we vs. them" atmosphere. | Room should have accessible seating or leave space for people using wheelchairs. Individuals may need special seating accommodations and/or opportunities to adjust and move around. |
| Group size | The size of the group may depend on several factors, but generally 6–8 members are recommended for adults and 3–4 for children. | For individuals with unique disability concerns, it may be less feasible to reach these size recommendations while maintaining geographic proximity for all group members. |
| Open vs. closed group | Leaders should consider which option meets the goals of the group. Open groups allow for new members to replace those leaving, which can provide new stimulation. On the other hand, the changing composition of the group may impact cohesion, and new members may struggle because they have missed past sessions. | Group leader(s) can help new members by preparing them beforehand and helping them get integrated into the group. |
| Homogeneous vs. heterogeneous | This consideration depends on the specific goals of the group. With a specific target population, it is generally more appropriate to be able to focus exclusively on their specific needs. Similarity among members can also foster greater cohesion. On the other hand, heterogeneous groups are a more accurate reflection of the outside social structure and allow members to get feedback from diverse perspectives. | Even within disability types, there is much heterogeneity, which may make the formation of homogeneous groups more challenging. |
| Length of session time | Outpatient groups typically meet for 90 min, and inpatient groups tend to be shorter in duration. Adults functioning relatively well generally have a 2-hr group that meets weekly. | Individuals with disabilities may benefit from opportunities to take breaks during longer sessions. |
| Frequency of meetings | Groups typically meet on a weekly basis. Some groups, such as job clubs or inpatient groups, may meet daily. | Transportation availability of members is an important consideration. |
| Duration | Groups can be short term or long term. It is recommended that a termination date be set at the outset of a closed group. Longer term groups generally range from 12 weeks to a year. Colleges and universities may have weekly groups that run the course of a semester (15 weeks). | Medical procedures, hospitalizations, and changes in living arrangements may impact the ability of some individuals to maintain regular attendance in longer term groups. |

as well as a contract for group attendance and adherence to group rules, is important to consider. Specifying group guidelines in a written format is an easy way to make this information clear. For many time-limited groups, manuals are available for this purpose (e.g., Munoz & Miranda, 2000).

## Potential Risks Associated With Group Procedures

One of the most important tasks for group leaders is to create positive and cohesive group dynamics; however, there are always potential risks. Many of these risks can be minimized through careful screening and orientation of group members, contracts, ongoing group dialogue, and the leader's skills. Group leaders are expected to adhere to and practice within their profession's ethical standards, such as the Commission on Rehabilitation Counselor Certification's (CRCC's; 2010) *Code of Professional Ethics for Rehabilitation Counselors*. They need to be aware and keep up to date with state laws that might apply to their professional practice. Specific risks include

- **Threats to confidentiality:** Group counseling can lead to some complex and unique ethical concerns, particularly around privileged communication, privacy, and confidentiality issues (Cottone & Tarvydas, 2007). For example, even in the presence of a licensed or certified professional, who maintains confidentiality with his or her clients, other members in the group may not keep information private and confidential, even when asked to do so by group leaders and members. Participants must know that confidentiality cannot be guaranteed, but the group leader should also emphasize regularly the importance of confidentiality on the part of group members (CRCC, 2010).
- **Risks in self-disclosure:** Self-disclosure may directly affect cohesiveness and productivity of the group. Without disclosing personal problems, it may be difficult to solve a problem or achieve goals. However, if self-disclosure is not adequately addressed, or when issues disclosed are ignored by other members or leaders, it may result in increasing hopelessness or distress for clients.
- **Scapegoating:** Scapegoating may occur in which members are singled out in negative ways by other members. It is important for the group leader to observe problematic behaviors and use strategies to protect the individual and maintain cohesiveness and positive group dynamics.
- **Cultural issues:** Cultural differences can create misunderstandings, which may affect group dynamics. Therefore, it is critical that group leaders (a) are aware of their own biases and stereotypes, (b) recognize cultural issues inherent in the group process, and (c) respect the values and beliefs that each group member may have. Once a cultural issue arises, it may be important to have an open group dialogue to provide an opportunity for resolving the issue and fostering growth as a group.

## Leader Characteristics and Functions

Group leaders bring to every group session their personal qualities, training, values, and life experiences, along with their biases and assumptions. Leaders need to demonstrate growth-oriented lives themselves and be open to self-reflection. The classic work by Lieberman, Yalom, and Miles (1973), using factor analysis, identified four basic functions of group leaders. First, *executive function* refers to setting up the parameters of the group, establishing rules and guidelines, and keeping the group on track. *Caring* is the second function and refers to being invested in the well-being of the members of the group and effectiveness of the interventions used. Third, the leader is also responsible for *emotional stimulation,* defined as efforts to uncover and encourage expression of personal feelings and values among members. *Meaning attribution* is the final function and refers to helping members in developing their ability to understand themselves and others (Lieberman et al., 1973). Corey and Corey (2006) also describe in depth a core set of basic functions and skills that are essential for effective group leadership, including active listening, restating, and summarizing, many of the same basic counseling skills that are important in individual counseling (see Chapter 11 in this volume).

The leader must also be sensitive to the key blocks to therapeutic change that are described in the literature (e.g., Posthuma, 1998; Yalom & Leszcz, 2005). A skilled leader will recognize that any block to the group process provides an opportunity to help group members to change. In order to share group leadership among all members, the leader must relinquish control at times, trust in the capacity of others to guide their own lives, and empower others. This more submissive response of relinquishing control to the group may be difficult for professionals in rehabilitation (Huebner & Thomas, 1996). Coleading of a group may be effective if the leaders agree on procedures or model conflict resolution (Posthuma, 1998).

Self-disclosure by the group leader has been the focus of many studies (Bednar & Kaul, 1994; Kiesler, 1996; Yalom & Leszcz, 2005). The goal of effective self-disclosure is to model this behavior for group members to emulate and to convey to the group a sense of personal humanness (Posthuma, 1998). Judicious self-disclosure involves an appropriate level of detail, with the focus remaining on the client (Rachman, 1990). Although group leaders will have differing thresholds for what they are willing to share about themselves, it is important to recognize that group leaders reveal things about themselves in a number of nonverbal ways as well (e.g., body posture, voice inflection). In fact, group leaders may be more exposed in group than in individual counseling, because they interact with a range of people who elicit different facets of their identity in the presence of everyone in the group (Bernard et al., 2008).

## Peer-Led and Peer-Assisted Groups

Although groups have traditionally been led by professional practitioners, there has been movement toward recognizing the contribution of peer group facilitators, who have lived experience in common with group members. These models are commonly found in addictions/12-step programs, as well as in peer-led recovery groups for people with mental illness. Examples of approaches combining manualized self-help with peer-facilitated groups include wellness recovery action planning (WRAP; Copeland, 1997), *The Recovery Workbook* (Spaniol, Koehler, & Hutchinson, 1994), and *Pathways to Recovery* (Ridgway, McDiarmid, Davidson, Bayes, & Ratzlaff, 2002).

## Group Stages

Although different stage models of the group process are defined in the literature, there is generally consensus that the character of a group evolves in a somewhat predictable developmental process. Drawing from Tuckman's (1965) classic work on group development, Corey and Corey (2006) delineate four key stages:

- **Initial stage:** This stage can be characterized by tentativeness as members become acclimated to the group. The main objectives during this stage are orientation and exploration as members find their way, learn how to relate and behave within the group, and begin to trust members and the leader(s).
- **Transition stage:** In this stage, members begin to challenge the resistance that is a barrier to working on issues within the group, and they begin to take more risks. Members express feelings and difficulties as they work through the resistance, conflicts, and mistrust that inhibit growth.
- **Working stage:** In this stage, members actively work on issues, attempt to accomplish goals, demonstrate commitment to explore and deal with problems, and attend to the dynamics of the group. Ideally, a period of group cohesion then emerges marked by shared leadership and group responsibility, group stability, and engagement in group work.
- **Final stage:** This stage is a time of consolidating what has been accomplished and working toward applying what has been learned to making changes outside of the group. As groups disband, the group is likely to experience a period of adjournment, including grieving the loss.

Although these stages are frequently cited as occurring in groups, the stages of group process may differ for people with disabilities (Marshak & Seligman, 1993). For example, the process of grieving a loss of function may interact with the group stages to produce more anger or dependency than might otherwise be typical.

## Disability Considerations

In rehabilitation, group membership is often composed of diverse individuals with varying degrees of functional limitations and types of disabilities, which may require adaptation of group procedures (Patterson et al., 1995). There are several variables related to disability and possible accommodations that are noted in the literature that counselors need to consider when they form a group.

It will be important that future research continue investigating ways of managing disability-related factors and delineating effective strategies to promote the full inclusion of all group members.

## Group Heterogeneity

It is common for groups to be heterogeneous, because clients can come from various backgrounds (e.g., age, gender, and income) and may have varying functional abilities. In the planning stage, counselors should consider strategies for managing the heterogeneity of the group. Possible accommodations to improve the inclusion of all members may include (a) a buddy system among clients with complementary skills or collaborative subgroups, which may encourage higher functioning group members to assist lower functioning members; (b) collaborative modifications to group procedures, which promote experiences of teaching and altruism and provide the individualized attention needed among individuals with varying degrees of functioning; and (c) setting individual goals within group goals that will allow clients to monitor their own progress and still align with the overall end goals of the group.

## Cognitive Limitations

Members who have limited cognitive abilities will likely benefit from more structure from the group leader. Nonetheless, a group leader must strive to relinquish control to the group members, with the belief that all people have some, perhaps untapped, ability to manage themselves and their lives. Increasing the predictability of the group may empower members to take on leadership roles. Therefore, possible accommodations include (a) using consistent structures and agenda; (b) providing simple and brief instructions; (c) incorporating more visual cues and sensory/motor activities; and (d) providing more frequent feedback and concrete examples (Stein, 1996).

## Communication Limitations

Because the focus of groups is often verbal, limitations in verbal communication can be particularly challenging to manage. A variety of verbal and nonverbal tasks may allow all group members an opportunity to participate. Augmentative communication devices and alternative communications, such as sign language, body gestures, drawing, and writing, are also possible accommodations. Paying particular attention to nonverbal cues may help the leader recognize critical moments that signal a need to validate or explore feelings with group members who have communication barriers. All group members may benefit from learning to wait for slower communication by a member and from observing and responding to nonverbal communication among all members (Marshak & Seligman, 1993).

## Attention, Behavioral Difficulties, and Fatigue

Individuals with short attention spans, or those experiencing pain or fatigue, may find it difficult to participate in a long counseling session. Short but more frequent group sessions may be more beneficial. It may also be necessary to teach members skills to control certain behaviors and cope with levels of fatigue. Balancing active and passive activities may help participants engage in the group process. Group members who exhibit uncooperative or avoidant behavior might be invited to take over a portion of a group task, such as planning the agenda or running an activity.

### Physical and Sensory Impairments

Group members within rehabilitation settings may attend a group with an array of assistive devices (e.g., traction devices, wheelchairs, or oxygen tanks). These devices must be accommodated in a manner that allows all members of the group to see each other and interact. Marshak and Seligman (1993) caution that a forced seating arrangement to accommodate these devices may diminish group interaction and an individual's sense of control. Hearing impairments may be accommodated by looking directly at the group member with hearing loss while speaking, summarizing the elements of the group process that may have been missed, or including a scribe or interpreter in the group. Miller and Moores (1990) provide recommendations for group counseling with deaf clients who use American Sign Language (ASL), stressing the importance of the group leader having comprehensive ASL skills for most group counseling situations to minimize communication barriers. Clients with visual impairments may miss the nonverbal communication of members and be uncertain when it is their turn to speak. Assistive technologies exist to enlarge written materials or enhance hearing and should be incorporated into the group (see Livneh, Wilson, & Pullo, 2004 for a review of approaches with physical and sensory disability groups).

## REHABILITATION APPLICATIONS

In rehabilitation settings, groups are designed to address the salient needs of clients with disabilities and can be guided by a number of different theoretical orientations. For example, cognitive behavioral group interventions have been found to be effective for decreasing depressive symptoms for persons with multiple sclerosis (e.g., Forman & Lincoln, 2009), reducing aggressive behaviors among individuals with severe intellectual disabilities (Rose, 1996), and improving physical and psychological functioning among adults with chronic pain (Subramanian, 1991). For individuals with brain injuries, holistic group rehabilitation programs (e.g., Nilsson, Bartfai, & Lofgren, 2011), along with group psychotherapy focused on self-concept change (Vickery, Gontkovsky, Wallace, & Caroselli, 2006), have had positive effects.

There is also strong empirical support for the use of social skills training, which draws from cognitive behavioral and psychoeducation frameworks and often occurs in group formats. A meta-analysis by Bolton and Akridge (1995) summarized results of experimental studies of small group skills training interventions developed for use with vocational rehabilitation clients and found strong support for the use of these programs for clients with disabilities. Group interventions have also been successful in developing safety awareness and behavioral changes for women with disabilities (Hughes et al., 2010), building self-esteem and reducing depression among women with physical disabilities (Hughes, Robinson-Whelen, Taylor, Swedlund, & Nosek, 2004), helping people with HIV/AIDS return to work (Martin et al., 2012), and improving leisure independence among young adults with autism spectrum disorders (Palmen, Didden, & Korzilius, 2011).

Additionally, groups have been used in rehabilitation settings to address the needs of family members of persons with chronic illnesses or disabilities. For example, a study by Shechtman and Gilat (2005) involved 95 mothers of children with learning disabilities who engaged in twelve 90-minute group sessions based on a humanistic stage model. Findings from their study indicated that, through the supportive and therapeutic environment, parents were able to lower their stress levels and gain insight into how to continue to manage their stress levels more efficiently (Shechtman & Gilat, 2005). Within psychiatric rehabilitation, family psychoeducation has also been associated with improvements in consumer functioning and caregiver stress reduction (Dixon et al., 2001).

## CASE STUDY: JOB CLUB

The job club is a strategy that draws heavily from psychoeducational, cognitive behavioral, and social learning approaches and is frequently applied in rehabilitation settings (Salomone, 1996) and social services (Sterrett, 1998). Initially developed by Azrin, Flores, and Kaplan (1975), the job club is a highly structured group intervention. Rather than a one-size-fits-all approach, curricula are individualized to empower job seekers by providing information, training, and opportunities to practice specific aspects of the job search. Structured job club lessons and protocols are designed to assist participants in securing employment by developing readiness for work, identifying job interests, locating job leads, contacting employers, completing job applications, and developing job interview skills. The group process promotes self-efficacy and empowerment through team building, clear goals, training in skills, a buddy system, and group practice. Because obtaining a job is defined as a full-time activity, the job club may meet on a daily basis.

The research literature on the outcomes of job clubs is encouraging. This model has been applied to address the unique needs of client groups, including people with psychiatric disabilities (Corbiere, Mercier, & Lesage, 2004; Corrigan, Reedy, Thadani, & Ganet, 1995), welfare recipients (Sterrett, 1998), and international students (Bikos & Furry, 1999). The earliest reports of job club outcomes (Azrin & Philip, 1979) found that 95% of job club members with disabilities obtained jobs. Although Salomone (1996) criticized the rigor and conclusions of this study, he recognized that the high intensity of the job club is likely to improve outcomes.

## RESEARCH FINDINGS

There is mounting empirical support for the use of group procedures to promote treatment outcomes. A review by Burlingame, MacKenzie, and Strauss (2004), looking at more than 100 studies and 14 meta-analyses, found robust support for the general effectiveness of group approaches in treating mental health disorders. Further, there is fairly solid evidence that group and individual treatments are generally equal in effectiveness and that group formats have a reliable effect when used alone as well as in conjunction with other treatments (McRoberts, Burlingame, & Hoag, 1998). However, the literature does suggest that group and individual treatments achieve their results through somewhat different mechanisms (Holmes & Kivlighan, 2000). Participants in group formats tend to report higher levels of relationship, climate, and other-focused processes as being responsible for change in comparison to clients receiving individual treatment (Holmes & Kivlighan, 2000). However, further research is needed to better understand the specific mechanisms inherent in group approaches that facilitate behavior change and adjustment. There have also been concerns that most of the studies demonstrating efficacy are based on cognitive and/or behavioral approaches, whereas psychodynamic and experiential approaches have not been frequently studied (Klein, 2008).

Group cohesion continues to be an important factor that has been studied in the literature. There is convincing support for the positive relationship between group cohesion and clinical improvement (Tschuschke & Dies, 1994), and high levels of group cohesion have been directly related to symptom improvement (Budman et al., 1989), decreased premature dropout (MacKenzie, 1987), increased tenure (Yalom & Leszcz, 2005), and higher self-disclosure (Tschuschke & Dies, 1994). As research continues to connect cohesion and successful group counseling and psychotherapy outcomes, it is important to elucidate factors that promote group cohesion (see Burlingame et al., 2002, for a more expansive review of evidence-based principles related to cohesion).

The current state of research on group counseling and psychotherapy has also begun to shed some light on client and structural characteristics that may make certain individuals more amenable to the positive effects of group interventions. For example, there is consensus that pregroup preparation can be very beneficial for prospective members as well as the group as a whole (Burlingame et al., 2002; Yalom & Leszcz, 2005). However, it is less clear how much preparation is ideal and in what specific ways the group benefits from it (Piper & Ogrodniczuk, 2004). Client factors also appear to play a role in the group process. For instance, findings from recent meta-analyses suggest higher outcome effect sizes for group members with mood disorders when compared to members with posttraumatic stress disorder and members with schizophrenia in both outpatient (Burlingame, Fuhriman, & Mosier, 2003) and inpatient (Kosters, Burlingame, Nachtigall, & Strauss, 2006) groups.

## PROMINENT STRENGTHS AND LIMITATIONS

There are a number of key advantages related to the use of group approaches. First, clients may feel less alone because the group format allows them to receive support and encouragement from other group members often facing similar problems (Dies, 1993). In addition, group members can serve as role models and support figures for other members. Groups also provide a safe context for individuals to practice behaviors within a secure setting (Manor, 1994). Further, groups provide a context for the leader or counselor to directly observe how each client responds to other people and behaves in social situations in order to tailor valuable feedback in vivo. Group work is also amenable to the use and integration of multiple theoretical approaches. Finally, group counseling can be cost-effective, allowing the practitioner to devote time to more clients.

There are also limitations associated with group procedures that practitioners should recognize. First, clients may still have a need or desire for individual attention, especially if group work is used as the only treatment modality. There are also inherent concerns regarding threats to confidentiality that must be clearly presented to group members. For rehabilitation clients, disability is considerably heterogeneous and, especially for less common conditions, it may be difficult or even impossible to create a group to address a specific need. Moreover, the logistics of finding a common and accessible location and meeting time may present challenges. Finally, although there is indeed growing empirical support for the effectiveness of group approaches, more research is needed to better understand factors impacting group processes and outcomes, especially for rehabilitation client populations.

## DISCUSSION EXERCISES

1. Discuss the various types of groups that can be used in rehabilitation.
2. Discuss the major characteristics of each group counseling stage.
3. Discuss the pros and cons of having coleaders for group work.
4. Discuss the ethical concerns and client risks related to group counseling.
5. Discuss how to assess client progress in group work.

## REFERENCES

Association for Specialists in Group Work (ASGW). (2000). Professional standards for the training of group workers, 2000 revision. *Journal for Specialists in Group Work, 25*, 327–342.

Azrin, N. H., Flores, R., & Kaplan, S. J. (1975). Job-finding club: A group-assessed program for obtaining employment. *Behavior Research and Therapy, 13*, 17–27.

Azrin, N. H., & Philip, R. A. (1979). The job club method for the job handicapped: A comparative outcome study. *Rehabilitation Counseling Bulletin, 23*, 144–155.

Barlow, S. H. (2008). Group psychotherapy specialty practice. *Professional Psychology: Research and Practice, 39*, 240–244.

Bednar, R. L., & Kaul, T. (1994). Experiential group research: Can the canon fire? In A. E. Bergin & S. L. Garfield (Eds.), *Handbook of psychotherapy and behavior change* (pp. 631–663). New York, NY: Wiley.

Bernard, H., Burlingame, G., Flores, P., Greene, L., Joyce, A., Kobos, J., . . . Feirman, D. (2008). Clinical practice guidelines for group psychotherapy. *International Journal of Group Psychotherapy, 58*, 455–542.

Bikos, L. H., & Furry, T. S. (1999). The job search club for international students: An evaluation. *Career Development Quarterly, 48*, 31–44.

Bolton, B., & Akridge, R. L. (1995). A meta-analysis of skills training programs for rehabilitation clients. *Rehabilitation Counseling Bulletin, 38,* 262–273.

Bower, J. E., Kemeny, M. E., Taylor, S. E., & Fahey, J. L. (1998). Cognitive processing, discovery of meaning, CD4 decline, and AIDS-related mortality among bereaved HIV-seropositive men. *Journal of Consulting and Clinical Psychology, 66,* 979–986.

Bowers, W. A. (1988). Beck's cognitive therapy: An overview for rehabilitation counselors. *Journal of Applied Rehabilitation Counseling, 19,* 43–46.

Budman, S. H., Soldz, S., Demby, A., Feldstein, M., Springer, T., & Davis, M. S. (1989). Cohesion, alliance, and outcome in group psychotherapy. *Psychiatry, 52,* 339–350.

Burlingame, G. M., Earnshaw, D., Hoag, M., Barlow, S. H., Richardson, E. J., Donnell, I., & Villani, J. (2002). A systematic program to enhance clinician group skills in an inpatient psychiatric hospital. *International Journal of Group Psychotherapy, 52,* 555–587.

Burlingame, G. M., Fuhriman, A. F., & Mosier, J. (2003). The differential effectiveness of group psychotherapy: A meta-analytic review. *Group Dynamics: Theory, Research, and Practice, 7,* 3–12.

Burlingame, G. M., MacKenzie, D., & Strauss, B. (2004). Small group treatment: Evidence for effectiveness and mechanisms of change. In M. J. Lambert (Ed.), *Bergin and Garfield's handbook of psychotherapy and behavioral change* (pp. 647–696). New York, NY: Wiley.

Burns, D. D., & Beck, A. T. (1999). *The new mood therapy.* New York, NY: Harper.

Commission on Rehabilitation Counselor Certification (CRCC). (2010). *Code of professional ethics for rehabilitation counselors.* Schaumburg, IL: Author.

Copeland, M. E. (1997). *Wellness recovery action plan.* Brattleboro, VT: Peach Press.

Corbiere, M., Mercier, C., & Lesage, A. (2004). Perceptions of barriers to employment, coping efficacy, and career search efficacy in people with mental illness. *Journal of Career Assessment, 20,* 1–18.

Corey, G. (2012). *Theory and practice of group counseling.* Belmont, CA: Brooks/Cole.

Corey, M. S., & Corey, G. (2006). *Groups: Process and practice* (7th ed.). Belmont, CA: Thomson Brooks/Cole.

Corrigan, P. W., Reedy, P., Thadani, D., & Ganet, M. (1995). Correlates of participation and completion in a job club for clients with psychiatric disability. *Rehabilitation Counseling Bulletin, 39,* 42–53.

Cottone, R. R., & Tarvydas, V. M. (2007). *Counseling ethics and decision making* (3rd ed.). Upper Saddle River, NJ: Pearson Prentice Hall.

Dies, R. R. (1993). Research on group psychotherapy: Overview and clinical applications. In A. Alonso & H. I. Swiller (Eds.), *Group therapy in clinical practice* (pp. 473–518). Washington, DC: American Psychiatric Press.

Dixon, L., McFarlane, W. R., Lefley, H., Lucksted, A., Cohen, M., Falloon, I., . . . Sondheimer, D. (2001). Evidence-based practices for services to families of people with psychiatric disabilities. *Psychiatric Services, 52,* 903–910.

Forman, A., & Lincoln, N. (2009). Evaluation of an adjustment group for people with multiple sclerosis: A pilot randomized controlled trial. *Clinical Rehabilitation, 24,* 211–221.

Holmes, S. E., & Kivlighan, D. M. (2000). Comparison of therapeutic factors in group and individual treatment process. *Journal of Counseling Psychology, 47,* 478–484.

Huebner, R. A., & Thomas, K. R. (1996). A comparison of the interpersonal characteristics of rehabilitation counseling students and college students with and without disabilities. *Rehabilitation Counseling Bulletin, 40,* 45–61.

Hughes, R. B., Robinson-Whelen, S., Pepper, A. C., Gabriella, J., Lund, E. M., Legerski, J., & Schwartz, M. (2010). Development of a safety awareness group intervention for women with diverse disabilities: A pilot study. *Rehabilitation Psychology, 55,* 263–271.

Hughes, R. B., Robinson-Whelen, S., Taylor, H. B., Swedlund, N., & Nosek, M. A. (2004). Enhancing self-esteem in women with physical disabilities. *Rehabilitation Psychology, 49,* 295–302.

Kiesler, D. J. (1996). *Contemporary interpersonal theory and research*. New York, NY: Wiley.

Klein, R. H. (2008). Toward the establishment of evidence-based practices in group psycho-therapy. *International Journal of Group Psychotherapy, 58*, 441–454.

Kosters, M., Burlingame, G. M., Nachtigall, C., & Strauss, B. (2006). A meta-analytic review of the effectiveness of inpatient group psychotherapy. *Group Dynamics: Theory, Research, & Practice, 10*, 146–163.

Liberman, R. P., DeRisi, W. J., & Mueser, K. T. (1989). *Social skills training for psychiatric patients*. Boston, MA: Allyn & Bacon.

Lieberman, M., Yalom, I. D., & Miles, M. (1973). *Encounter groups: First facts*. New York, NY: Basic Books.

Linkowski, D. C. (1971). A scale to measure acceptance to disability. *Rehabilitation Counseling Bulletin, 14*, 236–244.

Livneh, H., Wilson, L. M., & Pullo, R. E. (2004). Group counseling for people with physical dis-abilities. *Focus on Exceptional Children, 36*, 1–18.

MacKenzie, K. R. (1987). Therapeutic factors in group psychotherapy: A contemporary view. *Group, 11*, 26–34.

Manor, O. (1994). Group psychotherapy. In P. Clarkson & M. Pokorny (Eds.), *The handbook of psychotherapy* (pp. 249–264). New York, NY: Routledge.

Marshak, L. E., & Seligman, M. (1993). *Counseling for persons with physical disabilities*. Austin, TX: Pro-Ed.

Martin, D. J., Chernoff, R. A., Buitron, M., Comulada, W. S., Liang, L., & Wong, F. L. (2012). Helping people with HIV/AIDS return to work: A randomized controlled trial. *Rehabilitation Psychology, 57*, 280–289.

McRoberts, C., Burlingame, G., & Hoag, M. (1998). Comparative efficacy of individual and group psychotherapy: A meta-analytic perspective. *Group Dynamics: Theory, Research and Practice, 2*, 101–117.

McWhirter, P. T., & McWhirter, J. J. (1996). Transition-to-work group: University students with learning disabilities. *Journal for Specialists in Group Work, 21*, 144–148.

Miller, M., & Moores, D. (1990). Principles of group counseling and their application to deaf clients. *Journal of the American Deafness and Rehabilitation Association, 23*, 82–87.

Munoz, R. F., & Miranda, J. (2000). *Group therapy manual for cognitive-behavioral treatment of depression*. Santa Monica, CA: RAND.

Nilsson, C., Bartfai, A., & Lofgren, M. (2011). Holistic group rehabilitation: A short cut to adap-tation to the new life after mild acquired brain injury. *Disability and Rehabilitation, 33*, 969–978.

Norcross, J. C., & Goldfried, M. R. (Eds.). (2005). *Handbook of psychotherapy integration* (2nd ed.). New York, NY: Oxford.

Palmen, A., Didden, R., & Korzilius, H. (2011). An outpatient group training programme for improving leisure lifestyle in high functioning young adults with ASD: A pilot study. *Developmental Neurorehabilitation, 14*, 297–309.

Patterson, J. B., McKenzie, B., & Jenkins, J. (1995). Creating accessible groups for individuals with disabilities. *Journal for Specialists in Group Work, 20*, 76–82.

Piper, W. E., & Ogrodniczuk, J. S. (2004). Brief group therapy. In J. Delucia–Waack, D. A. Gerrity, C. R. Kolodner, & M. T. Riva (Eds.), *Handbook of group counseling and psychotherapy* (pp. 641–650). Beverly Hills, CA: Sage.

Posthuma, B. W. (1998). *Small groups in counseling and therapy: Process and leadership* (3rd ed.). Boston, MA: Allyn & Bacon.

Rachman, A. W. (1990). Judicious self-disclosure in group analysis. *Group, 14*, 132–144.

Ridgway, P., McDiarmid, D., Davidson, L., Bayes, J., & Ratzlaff, S. (2002). *Pathways to recovery: A strengths recovery self-help workbook*. Lawrence, KS: University of Kansas.

Rose, J. (1996). Anger management: A group treatment program for people with mental retar-dation. *Journal of Developmental and Physical Disabilities, 8*, 133–149.

Salomone, P. R. (1996). Career counseling and job placement: Theory and practice. In E. M. Szymanski & R. M. Parker (Eds.), *Work and disability* (pp. 365–420). Austin, TX: Pro-Ed.

Seligman, M. E. P. (1995). The effectiveness of psychotherapy: The *Consumer Reports* study. *American Psychologist, 50*, 965–974.

Shechtman, Z., & Gilat, I. (2005). The effectiveness of counseling groups in reducing stress of parents of children with learning disabilities. *Group Dynamics: Theory, Research, & Practice, 9*, 275–286.

Spaniol, L., Koehler, M., & Hutchinson, D. (1994). *The recovery workbook: Practical coping and empowerment strategies for people with psychiatric disability.* Boston, MA: Center for Psychiatric Rehabilitation, Boston University.

Stanton, A. L., Danoff, S., Cameron, C. L., Bishop, M., Collins, C. A., Kirk, S. B., . . . Twillman, R. (2000). Emotionally expressive coping predicts psychological and physical adjustment to breast cancer. *Journal of Consulting and Clinical Psychology, 68*, 875–882.

Stein, S. M. (1996). Group psychotherapy and patients with cognitive impairment. *Journal of Developmental and Physical Disabilities, 8*, 263–273.

Sterrett, E. A. (1998). Use of a job club to increase self-efficacy: A case study of return to work. *Journal of Employment Counseling, 35*, 69–78.

Subramanian, K. (1991). Structured group work for the management of chronic pain: An experimental investigation. *Research on Social Work Practice, 1*, 32–45.

Sweetland, J. D. (1990). Cognitive-behavior therapy and physical disability. *Journal of Rational-Emotive Therapy and Cognitive-Behavior Therapy, 8*, 71–78.

Thomas, R. V., & Pender, D. A. (2008). Association for specialists in group work: Best practice guidelines 2007 revisions. *Journal for Specialists in Group Work, 33*, 111–117.

Tschuschke, V., & Dies, R. R. (1994). Intensive analysis of therapeutic factors and outcome in long-term inpatient group. *International Journal of Group Psychotherapy, 44*, 185–208.

Tuckman, B. W. (1965). Development sequence in small groups. *Psychological Bulletin, 63*, 384–399.

Vickery, C. D., Gontkovsky, S. T., Wallace, J. J., & Caroselli, J. S. (2006). Group psychotherapy focusing on self-concept change following acquired brain injury: A pilot investigation. *Rehabilitation Psychology, 51*, 30–35.

Wolf, A., & Schwartz, E. K. (1963). *Psychoanalysis in groups.* New York, NY: Grune & Stratton.

Wright, B. A. (1983). *Physical disability: A psychosocial approach.* New York, NY: HarperCollins.

Yalom, I., & Leszcz, M. (2005). *The theory and practice of group psychotherapy* (5th ed.). New York, NY: Basic Books.

Yalom, I. D., & Josselson, R. (2011). Existential psychotherapy. In R. Corsini & D. Wedding (Eds.), *Current psychotherapies* (9th ed., pp. 310–342). Belmont, CA: Brooks/Cole.

# CHAPTER 14

# A Family Systems and Social–Ecological Perspective for Rehabilitation Health Professionals

*Maria-Cristina Cruza-Guet, Robert A. Williams,*
*and Julie A. Chronister*

## LEARNING OBJECTIVES

Goals of this chapter are to provide rehabilitation health professionals with a set of tools (i.e., theoretical constructs) used to understand families of a person with a disability from family systems and social–ecological perspectives, to familiarize rehabilitation health professionals with specific family systems and social–ecological interventions as they relate to individuals with a disability, to increase rehabilitation counselors' sensitivity to the cultural and social context that impacts the families of a person with a disability, to introduce rehabilitation health professionals to a social–ecological approach that addresses the needs of families of an individual with a disability, and to address the limitations of family systems and social–ecological therapies as well as the implications of these approaches for training and practice in rehabilitation health. As learning objectives, readers will be able to do the following:

1. Use basic principles of family systemic theory in rehabilitations services and practices.
2. Explain the relevance of family systems therapies to rehabilitation health professions.
3. Distinguish between traditional and contemporary models of family systems theory and explain how this distinction applies to families of a person with a disability.
4. Conceptualize families of a person with a disability from a social–ecological perspective.

5. Critique traditional and contemporary family systems therapies and a social–ecological approach in addressing the needs of families of an individual with a disability.
6. Discuss current issues in training and practice of rehabilitation health as related to the application of family system theories.

## DISABILITY AND FAMILY SYSTEMS

Today, disability is conceptualized as a biopsychosocial phenomenon that reflects an interaction between the person and her or his environment, of which the family system is a critical component. According to McGoldrick and Gerson (1985), the family is the most powerful system to which a person belongs, with all members of this system being affected by the actions or experiences of any one member (Lynch & Morley, 1995). For decades, rehabilitation scholars have acknowledged the importance of understanding disability-related experiences within the family system (e.g., Accordino, 1999; Cottone, Handelsman, & Walters, 1985; Dew, Phillips, & Reiss, 1989; Gilbride, 1993; Herbert, 1989; Lynch & Morley, 1995; Power & Dell Orto, 1986, 2004; Reagles, 1982; Sutton, 1985). Family therapy scholars have also sought to understand how to address disability-related issues within a family systems framework (e.g., Chenail, Levinson, & Muchnick, 1992; Fohs, 1991; Rolland, 1999; Stavros, 1991; Woody, 1993; Zarski, Hall, & DePompei, 1987). In addition, there is some empirical evidence suggesting that family systems interventions are beneficial for the person with the disability and her or his family (e.g., Becerra & Michael-Makri, 2012; Marshall & Ferris, 2012; Pitschel-Walz, Leucht, Bauml, Kissling & Engel, 2001; Webb-Woodward & Woodward, 1982). Indeed, rehabilitation health professionals need to understand the bidirectional influence of disability and family functioning—particularly given the lack of long-term health care resources for persons with disabilities and supports for family members with caregiving responsibilities.

Despite extant scholarly contributions in this area, psychosocial and vocational rehabilitation (VR) interventions for persons with disabilities continue to focus primarily on the *individual*. This is due, in part, to academic accreditation and state licensure standards that de-emphasize family systems coursework for rehabilitation counselor training programs, coupled with structural barriers within the rehabilitation service delivery system (e.g., lack of funds in public VR for family intervention). Nonetheless, for persons living with health impairments, the degree to which the impairment becomes disabling is indeed linked to family system functioning, which in turn, influences rehabilitation outcomes. As Cottone and colleagues (1986, p. 39) stated many years ago, still salient today:

> Although it is not recommended that rehabilitation counselors attempt family therapy without specialized training, it is imperative that rehabilitation counselors are able to identify systemic problems so they do not close cases as "failure to operate" or "too severely disabled" when, in fact, the problems are manifestations of a treatable family problem. In addition, counseling techniques developed from an

intra-psychic or individual model approach may prove counter-productive or less effective than systemic interventions when the family is actively influencing the rehabilitation process.

## BASIC PRINCIPLES

A *family* is a group of two or more related individuals, whether by blood or any legal processes (e.g., marriage, adoption, and foster care) that operates as a system (Substance Abuse and Mental Health Services Administration [SAMHSA], 2004). A *system* is an organized unit or organism comprising interconnected and interdependent elements, (i.e., family members), which operate as a whole. More specifically, a system is *"more than a sum of its parts,"* and, consistent with this metaphor, a *family system* reflects the collection of individual family members and their functioning as a whole unit (Brown & Christensen, 1999). Family systems are also embedded within, and interact with, larger sociocultural systems (Bronfenbrenner, 1989a).

*Family systems theory*, which is rooted in general systems theory, social ecology model, cybernetics, and social constructionism, regards a person's psychosocial functioning as a reflection of her or his family system and, accordingly, individual behaviors are not an expression of individual difficulties, but rather, manifestations of the family functioning as a whole. Thus, within a systems framework, the family unit, not the individual, becomes the "identified client" and focus of counseling (Foley, 1984). From this perspective, individual difficulties reflect unhealthy family functioning, which is said to (a) play a specific protective role within the family (Nichols & Schwartz, 2004; Vogel & Bell, 1960); (b) reflect a family's approach to handling stress or navigating developmental transitions; and (c) be passed across generations (Bitter & Corey, 1996).

Family systems theorists propose that families have organized rules and boundaries that seek to preserve stability by maintaining a stable and relatively constant "status quo" condition, or *homeostasis* (Jackson, 1959). This capacity to remain in a state of dynamic balance reflects the influence not only of systems theory but also of cybernetics (i.e., study of the mechanisms by which a system self-regulates; Jackson, 1959). Using cybernetic concepts, theorists explain that family interaction patterns are *circular* rather than linear. As Nichols and Schwartz (2004, p. 92) put it: "Each element [family member] has an effect on the next, until the last element 'feeds back' the cumulative effect into the first part of the cycle." It is through this cyclic mechanism, known as *feedback loop* that families obtain information about themselves and the environment. Feedback loops allow families to either remain stable and maintain homeostasis or change when necessary. Similar to how a thermostat responds to a temperature that is higher or lower than the preestablished temperature (Nichols & Schwartz, 2004), when the family perceives a threat to its stability or integrity, its immediate response is to mobilize family members in a manner that restores the family to its previous homeostatic state. Feedback loops that point to a threat to the family stability are called *negative*, whereas those that signal the need for a change are denoted as *positive*.

Consider a dysfunctional interaction between a girl with autism and her parents: Each time the girl displays the capacity to engage in some independent living (i.e., negative feedback loop), such as cooking, the father punishes her as he is afraid that his daughter will get burned. In response to the strict disciplinary style of the father, the mother comforts the girl, but also prepares a meal for her, reinforcing the father's message that it is not okay to be independent. As a result of this circular interaction (i.e., from girl to father, from father to mother and daughter, and from parents to daughter), the girl remains dependent on her parents, and the family as a whole maintains an unhealthy homeostatic state by not allowing positive change to take place. If the parents decide, by a counselor's suggestion, for example, to let their child do more things on her own (i.e., positive feedback loop), the interactions among the three family members are likely to change, accommodating a new and healthier state.

Family system theorists also posit that families, in spite of their homeostatic features, experience continuous evolution and growth through an "open system" phenomenon. According to general systems theory (i.e., systems theory, but applied to living organisms only; von Bertalanffy, 1950), *open systems*, like all living organisms, have unique characteristics that distinguish them from closed systems (i.e., machines); among them (a) they have a natural tendency to thrive, or in other words, they are not only reactive to stimuli, but are proactive and creative; (b) they are capable of attaining goals through different means, an ability known as *equifinality*; and (c) they survive by virtue of exchanging resources and information with the environment (Davidson, 1983; von Bertalanffy, 1950). In the face of these exchanges, which are either inevitable or desirable, a system's homeostasis is disturbed such that it either tries to recover to its preexisting condition or accommodates to the new information or status. Healthy families are open systems that may resist initial efforts at change on the one hand, yet seek and adjust to change on the other hand (Davidson, 1983; von Bertalanffy, 1950). The mechanisms by which these changes or lack thereof occur varies, to an extent, from one theoretical model to the other, as described in subsequent paragraphs. We first review the traditional family system models and then describe those known as contemporary or 21st-century models.

## TRADITIONAL FAMILY SYSTEMS THEORIES

### Intergenerational Family Therapy

Drawing from psychoanalytic theory (attachment concepts in particular) and his research on families of a person with schizophrenia, Murray Bowen developed an approach to family therapy that is considered to be, among all systemic theories, the most theoretic in nature and the most comprehensive in explaining human behaviors (Nichols & Schwartz, 2007). Bowen (1966) conceived an individual's behaviors as dependent on and reactive to his or her relations with an *intergenerational network* of family members. In fact, from his perspective, a family could only be understood in the context of at least a three-generation analysis (Bitter & Corey, 1996). According to his theory, these relations are regulated by two polarized inner forces, which counterbalance each other: *togetherness*, which refers to the necessity to live in companionship and closeness, and *individuality* or the need for independence (Nichols & Schwartz, 2007). Thus, an individual's behaviors fall on a continuum from emotional fusion (i.e., a symbiotic-like state) to differentiation. Where an individual falls on this continuum depends on how well she or he has established secure familial attachments and has learned to manage her or his emotions, particularly anxiety.

Bowen uses the term *differentiation of the self* to refer to the process by which individuals learn to manage their emotionality (i.e., attachment-related anxiety), both interpersonally and intrapsychically and are able to think through and handle anxiety-provoking situations (triggered by either internal or external stimuli) appropriately, that is, with wisdom, flexibility, spontaneity, and self-restraint. Differentiated individuals are able to distinguish between their feelings and thoughts and exert control over their reactions (Kerr & Bowen, 1988). Undifferentiated individuals, in contrast, tend to be reactive and impulsive in the face of anxiety-related pressures, exhibiting either excessive degrees of submissiveness or defiance.

When anxiety increases, family members—differentiated or not—are naturally less capable of tolerating one another, experience their differences as either deeper and/or more polarized, and feel an increased need for either closeness or distance from the people around them (Guerin, Fogarty, Fay, & Kautto, 1996). When these tensions go beyond a certain threshold, and dialogue or exchange of support to resolve interpersonal differences or cope with specific difficulties (e.g., a disability) is not possible, one or two members of a family dyad (e.g., husband and wife) tend to seek sympathy in an alliance with a third party (e.g., with one of their children). This occurs as a means to distribute the tension among three rather than two relationships and, thus, to manage the increased emotionality and to somehow resolve the issue. The addition of a third party to decrease the tension and anxiety in a dyad or twosome was coined by Bowen (1976) as a *triangle*.

Triangles are more than a relationship among three people; they are sets of relationships that, inextricably, influence one another. For example, consider a husband who is experiencing caregiver burnout because he is assuming most of the responsibility for the care of his spouse, who lives with a disability. The husband may distance himself from his wife and turn to his son to find not only support and help with caregiver chores but also a space to vent his reactions about the increasing demands posed by his wife. This new alliance around caregiver responsibilities between husband and son will impact the husband–wife relationship as well as the father–son and mother–son relationships. If the relationship between husband and son is helpful in reducing the husband's burnout and in promoting dialogue between husband and wife, then this triangle is considered temporary and resolved. However, if the father–son relationship reduces the likelihood that the husband will invest his energy in resolving issues and rebuilding his connection with his wife, then the triangle has become habitual and fixed and, therefore, detrimental to the health of the marriage.

## Change Process and the Role of the Rehabilitation Health Professional

From a Bowenian perspective, family problems arise when its members are undifferentiated; therefore, therapy focuses on helping individual family members—in the context of family sessions—to overcome unresolved emotional attachments transmitted from one generation to the next and, in turn, to attain a balanced sense of both differentiation from and belonging to the family (Bitter & Corey, 1996). Specifically, the goal of therapy is twofold. On the one hand, this approach attempts to assist family members in gaining awareness about the role they play in the family dynamics, an ability referred to as *self-focus*. On the other hand, a Bowenian therapist's role is to help family members to distinguish their thoughts from their feelings and to reduce their anxiety. Anxiety is perceived as a roadblock to healthy family functioning and family members' self-individuation.

Applied to rehabilitation, this approach invites professionals to take an active stance in helping families to understand the mechanisms by which the individual with a disability influences her or his constellation of family relationships and how each of these intergenerational relationships reciprocally influences the individual's behaviors. Moreover, a rehabilitation health professional working from this approach would use her or his skills to reduce anxiety among family members. A reduction in anxiety decreases blaming behaviors and, subsequently, triangulation patterns, a quagmire in which many persons with disabilities may find themselves. In such cases, the goal is to detriangulate the individual (e.g., deconstruct the cross-generational alliance between the father and the son in the previous example) such that she or he does not find herself or himself in the middle of a subsystem she or he does not belong to, which could negatively impact family dynamics and the care received by the person with a disability.

In order to increase self-awareness, reduce anxiety, and assist families in the detriangulation process, Bowenian therapists take an active and neutral role in sessions, while attending to two elements: *process* (i.e., reactivity patterns) and *structure* (i.e., web of triangles within the family). This is accomplished by the use of *process questions*, a cornerstone of Bowen's work, which are intended to promote thinking and reduce emotional reactivity. In particular, through these questions, family members are prompted to talk not only about their responses to others within the family but also about their involvement in these interactions. This process enables them to assume responsibility for their behaviors. It is important to note that therapists need to avoid taking sides to reduce risk of triangulation.

### Strategic Family Therapy

In the mid-1970s and 80s, family systems were dominated by a model of therapy known for its potential to render considerable changes in family functioning, in spite of the resistances and lack of cooperation of the family members involved in treatment. Bringing honor to its name, *strategic family therapy* (Haley, 1991) became famous for the use of interventions that were considered planned or tactical on the part of the therapist. These interventions grew out of the work of Gregory Bateson, Milton Erickson, and Jay Haley at the Mental Research Institute

(MRI) in Palo Alto, California. These three researchers, each coming from a different field—anthropology, psychiatry, and communications, respectively—were interested in decoding the meaning of communication patterns among families of individuals with schizophrenia. In studying this communication phenomenon, they developed a new and influential form of family therapy, which introduces principles of *communication* to the combined application of cybernetics and systems theory (Nichols & Schwartz, 2007).

According to communication experts, all behavior, even if it is unintentional, unconscious, or unsuccessful, plays an expressive function in human interactions (Watzlawick, Beavin, & Jackson, 1967). Moreover, messages have report and command functions; the *report* contains explicit information or content, whereas the *command* is a statement with regard to the nature of the relationship between the sender and the receiver (Haley, 1991). Commands can be overt (i.e., stated) or implicit (i.e., not stated); the latter becomes the blueprint of familial interactions. In other words, implicit commands transform into regular communicative transactions or *rules* (or frames) among family members. Strategic family therapists emphasize that the term "rule" is used to denote the "regularity" of family interactions, as they conceived these interactions to be chains of regular communicative transactions linked together in a circular way by a stimulus and a response; these chains of transactions constitute the communication version of *feedback loops* (explained earlier from a cybernetic perspective in the Basic Principles section), which serve to maintain the status quo in the family (Nichols & Schwartz, 2007). Thus, supporters of this approach focus on *circular causality* to explain family problems, shying away from any attempt to identify underlying motives.

Strategic family therapists make a distinction between family impasses and problems; whereas the first are experienced and managed regularly and successfully by families, problems are difficulties that the family fails to handle in a healthy way. They explain that an impasse becomes a problem because family members react to it in usual and rigid ways (i.e., responding to negative feedback loops), as determined by the unspoken rules that govern the family, rather than use new and more adaptive transactions (responding to positive feedback loops). As a result, the family engages in a vicious cycle, which serves to maintain its homeostasis, but hinders its ability to accommodate to the changes that are needed to handle and overcome the problem.

As an example, let us think of a family system comprising a preteen daughter and a father who began drinking in excess after his now ex-wife cheated on him. The daughter and father's morning routine or household rule involves an alarm clock waking up the father who, in turn, awakens his daughter. However, when the daughter notices that her father is late coming home, she knows that he is likely to be out drinking, which means that she is now on her own to wake up the next morning and might not be on time for school. This is, too, in a dysfunctional way, a stable rule in this family. If the preteen decides that she wants to start using her own alarm clock, she is introducing new information to the system and attempting to change a rule (i.e., positive feedback loop). If the parent agrees to the change, then the family has adapted well to this transition (i.e., impasse). However, when the father perceives his daughter's request for independence as a threat, interpreting her behavior as a form of rejection toward him, it may trigger emotional pain related to his ex-wife's infidelity (i.e., negative feedback loop). Consequently, he may deny her access to an alarm clock, because he wants to preserve the old and familiar morning routine in the family, possibly to his daughter's detriment. Feeling threatened, the father's drinking problem may escalate, and his daughter may continue arriving to school late, which in turn may increase her frustration toward her father and desire to be independent from him. This collection of transactions perpetuates the family's problems.

Cyclical problems are, according to the systemic theory developers from the MRI, "resistant" to change because family interactions follow seemingly intractable governing rules. Notwithstanding, they conceived change as possible and made an important distinction between temporary and lasting change. From their viewpoint, changes in patterns of family interaction are spearheaded by either alterations in communicative transactions (i.e., behaviors) or rules. A behavioral change that occurs within the existing rules of the family is known as *first-order change* (Nichols & Schwartz, 2007). In the current example, a first-order change would be observed when the daughter of the excessively drinking father decides, herself, to introduce an uncle as a buffer and invite him for dinner, preventing the father from drinking. This type of change tends to be transitory, because behaviors alone are not strong enough to challenge the implicit rules of the family, the role of which is to preserve the status quo. Although the father may feel uncomfortable drinking in front of his brother, he may still be focused on his next opportunity to drink excessively. As such, if the uncle is removed from the equation, then the father is most likely to return to his old drinking pattern. In contrast, *second-order change* occurs when rules are modified (Nichols & Schwartz, 2007), usually by someone outside the system, ideally by a counselor; in this case, one may see long-lasting changes given that the system has modified its rules, allowing new transactions to take place.

### Change Process and the Role of the Rehabilitation Health Professional

Strategic family therapy encompasses a broad range of interventions, given that three distinct models—all considered strategic—emerged from the MRI. These include the MRI's brief therapy model (Watzlawick, Weakland, & Fisch, 1974), Hayley and Madanes's strategic therapy (Haley, 1991; Madanes, 1984), and the Milan systemic model (Selvini Palazzoli, Boscolo, Cecchin, & Prata, 1978). In this section, we describe interventions that are either common to the three models or archetypal of this approach.

Overall, strategic family approaches to therapy are minimalistic, behavioral, and deliberate. Family therapists, who identify themselves as strategic, focus on resolving the presenting problem that brought the family into therapy. They move away from intrapsychic explanations or goals defined by standards of normality within the context of the family (Fisch, 1978; Selvini Palazzoli, Boscolo, Cecchin, & Prata, 1980). Their aim is to problem solve and arrive at tangible changes, seeing themselves as responsible for this process of change and its outcome. Because they are convinced that the responsibility for what happens in therapy rests on the therapists themselves, they intentionally use interventions that mobilize members of the family toward change, with or without their collaboration (Haley, 1963).

Examples of these interventions are the prescriptions of ordeals and paradoxical injunctions. *Ordeals* are directives through which the therapist attempts to outweigh the consequences of having a symptom in an effort to make it disappear (e.g., ask a man who experiences insomnia to wake up at specific times through the night to complete bothersome tasks; Haley, 1984). *Paradoxical injunctions* are a similar technique used to prescribe a symptom in order to make voluntary a behavior that is claimed to be involuntary (e.g., instruct an adolescent with anger management problems to act aggressively in the absence of a specific stimulus; Haley, 1993). As a result of an "ordeal" or "paradox," individuals and family members discover that they have control over the so-called symptom after all. The effectiveness of these seemingly counterintuitive interventions contributed to the prominent place that strategic family therapy occupied in the field; eventually however, the deliberate nature of this approach was criticized and considered manipulated.

From a strategic family therapy perspective, the therapist's role is to assist families in adapting effectively to changing circumstances, which could be accomplished, broadly speaking, by improving their communication patterns. To be more specific, they attempt to "first, identify the positive feedback loops that maintain problems; second, determine the rules (or frames) that support those interactions; and third, find a way to change the rules" (Nichols & Schwartz, 2007, p. 153). Thus, strategic family therapists challenge the existing homeostasis and operate outside of the comfort zone of the family's rules. In the example used in this section, a therapist would attempt to help the preteen daughter and her father with alcohol problems by finding ways to change two specific implicit messages or frames that keep them stuck in a vicious cycle: (a) the daughter's assumption that her father does not want her to arrive on time at school and be more independent and (b) the father's interpretations of her daughter's behavior as rejecting.

Applicable to this case is a well-known and effective technique used by strategic family therapists to modify rules, known as reframing. *Reframing* is the process by which family members modify their implicit interpretations about their family relationships, turning a negative assumption into a positive one. In the example, the therapist would help the daughter understand that her father wants to be close to her and fears their separation and would assist the father in reinterpreting his daughter's request as a desire to do better in school. Notice that reframing is a cognitive process; however, it is brought to the family session to promote a behavioral change.

### Structural Family Therapy

Salvador Minuchin, a child psychiatrist from Argentina, pioneered the development of what is known as *structural family therapy*, one of the most widely practiced models of its kind since the 1970s. Minuchin built his theory on the basis of his formal psychoanalytic training in interpersonal psychiatry and, notably, his collaboration with several colleagues at the Philadelphia Child Guidance Center. With them, Minuchin adopted a hands-on approach, providing services to families and inventing a set of theoretical principles and therapeutic strategies as they moved along (Nichols & Schwartz, 2007). These principles and strategies provide a framework to systematically identify, chart, and understand the meaning of repetitive patterns or sequences of transactions among members or subsets of family members, which, in Minuchin's terms, constitute the *structure* of a family (in a functional sense). According to Minuchin and colleagues, the structure or overall organization of the family can be understood by three interconnected concepts: subsystems, boundaries, and hierarchical relationships (Minuchin, 1974; Minuchin & Fishman, 1981).

*Subsystems* are organized coalitions of two or more family members that differentiate themselves from the larger system on the basis of generation, gender, and/or function. For example, parents form the "parental subsystem," two or more children form the "sibling subsystem," and an alliance between a parent and a child form a "parent–child subsystem or cross-generational coalition." Subsystems are delineated and protected by interpersonal *boundaries*, that is, invisible limits or barriers that define who is inside or outside of a subsystem. Boundaries fall on a continuum from rigid to diffuse. Rigid boundaries are impermeable, limiting subsystems or individuals from interacting with other subsystems within or outside the family. Although rigid boundaries may promote autonomy, they can also lead to *disengagement*, or emotional cutoffs, unsupportive transactions, or isolation. At the other end of the continuum, diffuse boundaries promote closeness among family members and subsystems, with the advantage of offering a great deal of affect, support, and accommodation to others' needs; however, this type of boundary is blurry and can, therefore, lead to *enmeshment* or dependency and intrusive relationships, as well as a lack of relationship-building competencies (Nichols & Schwartz, 2007). In between these two forms of boundaries, there are clear and consistent boundaries (i.e., healthy boundaries), which consist of a blend of rigid and diffuse demarcations. This blend allows family members to strive for a balance between a sense of personal identity and a sense of belonging to their families (Bitter & Corey, 1996). Problematic or healthy boundaries can be evaluated against the extent to which diffusion or rigidity is supporting the well-being of all family members.

Interactions across subsystems are governed by *rules*, which can be either implicit (i.e., unspoken) or explicit (Minuchin, 1985). Rules are formed on the basis of established expectations regarding the behavior and roles of each family member and the patterns of interactions among them. For example, a morning routine that involves an alarm clock waking up a parent who, in turn, awakens her child to get ready for school is a simple, explicit, and stable rule or routine, which assists the parent in playing her or his role. Rules are intended to maintain the status quo and reinforce a family's structure. In this way, sequences of behaviors tend to become self-perpetuating and, therefore, difficult to change on their own (Nichols & Schwartz, 2007). From a structural family therapy perspective, families and their subsystems are also organized in a *hierarchical* manner. For instance, parents are expected to have authority over their children, and, thus, their role is to teach their children to obey rules. Parents are also expected to have complementary or reciprocal roles. For example, when one parent becomes overwhelmed with childrearing responsibilities or the care of a person with a disability and the other responds with support, the behavior of the latter contributes to the formation of a united parental coalition, which facilitates healthy patterns of family functioning.

Unhealthy family functioning occurs when the patterns of transactions among family members (i.e., its structure) are so rigidly organized that they do not allow its members, and the family as a whole, to accommodate to expected life cycle changes (e.g., a son's transition into adolescence), conflicts (e.g., spousal discrepancies regarding financial decisions), or unforeseen events (e.g., a mother being diagnosed with a serious medical condition). For example, let us think of a mother who was recently diagnosed with multiple sclerosis. She lacks the support of her husband, who is overly occupied with his work, but has a close relationship with their only child, a 9-year-old boy. Feeling unable to cope with the stress of her recent diagnosis, the mother "recruits" her child to behave more like a spouse than a child and obtain from him the support that she needs. In this case, the boy has crossed the boundary from the child subsystem into the parental or spousal subsystem. As a result of this cross-generational coalition, a structural family counselor would expect to see deterioration in the boy's behavior either at home or at school.

Healthy families and communities typically make smooth transitions in the face of change (Nichols & Schwartz, 2007). For example, in some families, the introduction of a child with a learning disability may strengthen family ties by (a) forcing the parents to join efforts in assisting their child to do her or his homework (i.e., strengthen the parental subsystem); (b) providing scaffolding to facilitate learning, but not micromanaging the child's tasks (i.e., adopting healthy boundaries that provide support but are not overly intrusive); (c) enforcing a consistent work/homework schedule (i.e., develop rules that encourage positive behavior); and (d) requesting the support of a school counselor to guide them in the process of managing the child's disability (i.e., exchange information with the environment and adjust to change). However, families are often confronted with stressors that are beyond their resources, which creates a crisis (e.g., the parents are unable to work together as a team to help the child with a disability). In response to a crisis, some families seek professional help (i.e., couples therapy in the current example), which could help mobilize the family in a positive direction. In contrast, other systems recoil, isolate, and fail to adjust, resulting in unhealthy functioning and maintaining the status quo.

### Change Process and the Role of the Rehabilitation Health Professional

Therapists working from the structural perspective attempt to restructure the patterns of family interaction by *strengthening family rules*, *amending boundaries*, and *rearranging subsystems*. Through these means, structural family counselors aim to restore a healthy hierarchical order within the family. Take the earlier example of a mother and wife who has been diagnosed with multiple sclerosis. In this case, the aim of therapy would be twofold: (a) to increase affective exchanges between the mother and her spouse, which is achieved, for example, by increasing positive communication and quality time spent with each other (i.e., loosening the boundaries between them), thus strengthening the spousal and parental subsystem and (b) to discourage the mother from obtaining support from her son rather than from her husband, thereby disintegrating the parent–child coalition and liberating the child from adultlike responsibilities. By changing the structure of the family, the counselor would expect an improvement in the 9-year-old boy.

To reach these goals and be able to reorganize the structure of the family, structural family therapists take a series of steps. First, they work on building a solid working alliance with each member of the family by expressing empathy and acceptance, which reduces anxiety and lowers defensiveness. This first process is known as *joining* and is followed by the therapist's efforts to adjust her or his style to that of the family or, in other words, *accommodating* to the patterns of familial interaction. Taking these two steps ensures that the therapist can have enough leverage to initiate restructuring maneuvers (Nichols & Schwartz, 2007).

A hallmark of structural family therapy is the use of *enactments* during sessions. Enactments are transactions among family members that are intentionally prompted by the therapist in order to observe in the here and now, what the family subsystems, rules, and boundaries are. These enactments are supposed to be representative of how family members relate to each other outside therapy, providing the therapist an opportunity not only to observe but also to reshape transactions as they are happening. Once a therapist has mapped out the entire family system and its connections to systems outside of the family, then she or he can begin to divide it by sensible subsystems as well as examine problematic coalitions and disconnections among members of the systems.

Structural family therapy has been criticized for being grounded on an outdated, mid-20th century worldview of a nuclear family, which assumed that a heterosexual married couple in charge of their children was the norm. In today's modern world, complex configurations of families are fully recognized, which include same-sex couples; step, foster, and adoptive parents; single parents who are alone, as well as single or married parents who are part of a multigenerational family household. Furthermore, families live in larger and culturally heterogeneous social contexts, with both deep and shallow connections with others outside of the family. In spite of the criticisms, the universal appeal of structural family therapy is its generalizability across models. Further, structural family therapy is considered an influential framework because a strong database of both theory and empirical research has emerged to fully support its constituent parts and applicability.

### Humanistic and Experiential Family Therapy

Intrigued by the expressive nature of human interactions, the notion of personal freedom, and the immediacy of experience, Carl Whitaker and Virginia

Satir developed a therapeutic model that, under the umbrella of family therapy, mimicked Carl Rogers's individual humanistic psychology, while drawing complementary techniques from gestalt psychology, art therapy, and psychodrama. Born in the 1960s, this approach highlights the importance of emotional expressiveness in regulating healthy psychological functioning. In congruency with the humanistic and experiential tradition, proponents of this type of family therapy argue that individuals have an innate tendency to self-actualize, as long as they are allowed to experience life fully and express a wide range of emotions (Nichols & Schwartz, 2007). Accordingly, healthy families are secure enough to be supportive and validating of their members' affective experiences. In contrast, unhealthy families tend to be frightened; specifically, as Satir explains, members of families functioning in an unhealthy manner communicate in inauthentic ways (e.g., blaming, placating, being irrelevant, and being super-unreasonable/congruent with oneself), because they experience low levels of self-esteem (Satir, 1972; Satir, Stachowiak, & Taschman, 1975). As a result, unhealthy families exert control over their members' behaviors by limiting the expression of affect and impulses, which leads to defensiveness as well as repression and avoidance of feelings.

### Change Process and the Role of the Rehabilitation Health Professional

Within this framework, the goal of therapy is to expand the ability of each member of the family to be in touch with his or her emotions and desires. For Whitaker, the role of the therapist is to facilitate this process while building cohesion among family members; for Satir, this is attained through improving communication. Both agreed that unhealthy families are paralyzed by their internal conflicts, which manifest in a cold and ritualistic environment, in which each of its members is incapable of mutual appreciation and, therefore, all feel lonely and preoccupied with extrafamilial issues (Satir, 1972; Whitaker & Keith, 1981). Thus, in this context, therapy aims to develop a warm and nurturing experience, during which family members can relax and interact, be in touch with deeper layers of emotions, communicate these emotions in sessions, and genuinely connect with each other. This is attained through *existential encounters*, a process by which the therapist is expected to fully engage in a reciprocal exchange of emotions with the family, "sharing his [her] embarrassments, confusions and helplessness" (Kempler, 1968, p. 97). To do so, existential family theorists highlight the need for the therapist to be spontaneous, flexible, and caring. Ultimately, through these means, family therapists assist families in being less defensive and more flexible, allowing each of its members to define her or his self-fulfilling role within the family and, concomitantly, feeling more independent and intimate in their familial relationships (Napier & Whitaker, 1978).

For family therapists working from this perspective, *individual self-expression* is a prerequisite to improving family functioning. Thus, in the case of a young adult male who has undergone a foot amputation, for instance, a rehabilitation health professional would encourage him to explore and articulate his feelings, while assisting his family members in engaging in a similar exercise. The aim of this exercise would be to let each family member experience what the foot amputation means to him or her, respecting personal differences and highlighting common reactions and feelings. This dual process would promote personal growth, family closeness, and the identification of appropriate ways of exchanging support with the person who lost his foot.

The humanistic and experiential approach embodies a tension between individuality and wholeness, a trait that, according to critics, disqualified this approach from being a systemic model. Indeed, to a great extent, the appeal of this approach as a branch of family therapy grew from the charisma of its founders—Whitaker, known for his unconventionality and boldness, and Satir, for her warmth and nurturing character. Not surprisingly, after their deaths, their model lost popularity (Nichols & Schwartz, 2007). Recently, however, two new humanistic and experiential approaches—emotionally focused couples therapy (Greenberg & Johnson, 1988; Johnson, Hunsley, Greenberg, & Schindler, 1999) and the internal family systems model (Schwartz, 1995)—have gained increased attention and acceptance because of efforts to sophisticatedly integrate a focus on individual experiences with the tenets of family systems theory.

Influenced by John Bowlby (1969), *emotionally focused couples therapists* posit that cyclic conflicts between partners often emerge as a result of insecure attachment issues of each or one of the partners. To overcome these issues, therapists working from this perspective take on two main tasks. First, they assist each partner in understanding their individual unresolved relationship longings. Then, therapists help them process how their defenses play out as anger or withdrawal in the relationship, typically eliciting the opposite of what they really want from the other person, that is, closeness and affirmation. Once this is accomplished and partners are able to be in touch and communicate their vulnerabilities (i.e., fear, loneliness, and anxiety), new and more compassionate ways of relating can come to light (Greenberg, James, & Conry, 1988).

The *internal family systems model* argues that family problems can be understood and resolved by helping each of its members identify her or his own inner conflicts, which transcend into problematic family interactions. A key intervention used by internal family therapists is to help each family member recognize how a part or subpersonality of her or him triggers or reacts negatively to the parts or subpersonalities of other members. Reframing conflicts as rooted in parts of one, rather than in the person as a whole, lessens defenses, reduces polarization, and emphasizes the existence of healthier aspects of the whole. It is on the basis of these healthier elements that family members can reconnect and defeat familial impasses. Similar to all forms of existential–humanistic family therapy, this approach rests on the premise that every individual, at her or his core, is healthy and has a natural tendency to self-actualize (Schwartz, 1995).

## CONTEMPORARY FAMILY SYSTEMS THEORIES

In recent decades, many of the 20th-century family therapy theories have been the subject of criticism for three main reasons: First, these theories were overly preoccupied with issues associated with "prototypical families." As such, traditional system theories (a) focused on heterosexual relationships only, (b) dichotomized rigid male–female roles, (c) addressed White middle-class issues, and (d) were grounded in Western culture. As a result, they were not relevant for families from culturally diverse groups, including those with disabilities. Second, they ignored the historical, social, political, and economic inequities in which families are embedded and the influence of these larger systems on family dynamics. Third, they engaged families in therapeutic relationships that were hierarchical in nature, with a clear power differential between the clinician and each of the members of the family (Silverstein & Goodrich, 2003).

In the 21st century, however, feminist and multicultural theories and models not only challenged traditional approaches but also opened the door for a healthy focus on how to work with more culturally diverse families, including families who have members with disabilities. Specifically, systemic theories went through a transformative process, with boundaries across systemic models becoming blurred, giving away to a technical, but also theoretical, eclecticism. This change allowed family therapists to tailor their approaches to satisfy the unique needs of families from different cultural backgrounds. Moreover, with the end of the one-size-fits-all approach that characterized family therapies in the 20th century came an important power dynamic transformation, which eliminated the preexisting hierarchy between the therapist and the family, converting the therapist into a collaborator, whose role was not to "fix," but rather to "partner" with the family in strengthening its own resources (Nichols & Schwartz, 2007). In the context of these conversions, several new and influential approaches to family therapy, known as the family therapies of the 21st century, were born, including the feminist family therapy, narrative and constructivist family therapy, and solution-focused family therapy.

### Feminist Family Therapy

Born in the 1960s with the emergence of the feminist movement, this approach not only unmasks deeply rooted patriarchal values embedded in traditional forms of family therapy but also challenges some of the very principles in which systemic theories were grounded (see Hare-Mustin, 1978). Specifically, feminist family therapy challenges the cybernetic notion that unhealthy functioning mainly arises from flawed family interactions, arguing that this stance ignored the impact of contextual factors, that is, of the social, economic, and political inequalities negatively influencing a family constellation (Avis, 1988). In addition, they criticize the cybernetic characterization of a family as a system in which individual behaviors are ruled by repetitious feedback loops, positing that family members under difficult circumstances may be unable to exert enough personal control to promote change even if they wanted to and, therefore, cannot be perceived as sharing equal responsibility for any problem. Feminist theorists claim that traditional system theorists presented "a hypersophisticated version of blaming the victim and rationalizing the status quo" (Goldner, 1985, p. 33), which has detrimental implications for women, who, even today, experience high rates of abuse (i.e., rape, incest, and battering) within their families and are blamed for provoking it (James & MacKinnon, 1990).

As a value-driven rather than technique-focused approach (Friar Williams, 1977), feminist family therapy seeks to empower women and validate their experiences by dismantling the biases and discriminatory practices that—blatantly or subtly—keep women oppressed within their families and society and, it is important to note, within the family therapy session. Toward this end, the founders of this approach—Peggy Papp, Olga Silverstein, Marianne Walters, and Betty Carter—proposed the adoption of a therapeutic model that highlights the existence of pervasive and unspoken patriarchal norms, which afford men privileges at home, at work, and in society that women do not have. They also challenged the pathologizing views of the "prototypical problematic family," in which the mother is overinvolved and neurotic, the father is disengaged but psychologically sound, and the child is symptomatic.

Family constellations like this one may be seen frequently by rehabilitation health professionals who work with children with learning and other disabilities. In a traditionally organized family of a child with a learning disability, the mother tends to be in charge of all treatment-related matters and may experience a sense of guilt for her child's problems, whereas the father is likely to be resistant to meet with his child's therapist, arguing that his involvement in person is unnecessary and noting that he is already paying for the medical bills. Feminists argue that the roles portrayed in the prototypical problematic family could not be accounted for by flaws and strengths inherent to being a female and male, respectively; instead, they contextualize these patterns as the by-product of historical and sociopolitical processes by which qualities traditionally associated with males became desirable and females traits, unfavorable.

### Change Process and the Role of the Rehabilitation Health Professional

Feminist family therapists use a myriad of psychological theories in guiding their work. As a consequence, it is difficult to outline a change process and a set of psychotherapeutic interventions that are exclusive to this worldview. Nonetheless, feminist family therapists share common goals, grounded in the philosophy that all genders (i.e., male, female, transgender) deserve equal political power within and outside the therapist's office. This worldview influences the type of therapeutic milieu and collaborative role that characterizes their work (Bitter & Corey, 1996).

First and foremost, they strive to assist the family, the parental couple in particular, in developing an egalitarian relationship, in which the woman's voice and perspective are valued. This overarching goal is attained through problem conceptualizations and interventions constructed through a sociopolitical and cultural lens. These underscore women's oppression in the context of each of the patriarchal systems within which the family is embedded, including the nuclear family of origin, the extended family, and the society at large. To this end, feminist family therapists invite family members to understand how the norms, rules, and boundaries of their family are influenced by patriarchal norms. Moreover, they highlight the differential impact of life events, such as divorce, on men and women. Further, they challenge gender stereotypes and prompt members to adopt a gender-neutral attitude toward their roles and responsibilities within the family.

In the previous case of a child with a learning disability, a feminist-oriented family therapist would, for instance, attempt to engage the father in treatment by pointing out concrete examples as to how the child might benefit from his participation in the rehabilitation process. Further, a therapist working from this approach would emphasize the equal value of what the mother (e.g., her time and attention to the child's issues) and the father (e.g., economic input) are contributing to the care of their child and contextualize these differences as rooted in sociopolitical and economic realities.

### Narrative and Constructivist Family Therapy

Although feminist family therapy grew out of the idea that gender injustice was unacceptable, narrative as well as constructivist family therapy emerged in response to the notion that therapists' objectivity was unattainable. In the 1980s and 1990s, a group of psychologists led by Harlene Anderson, Harry Goolishian, and Lynn Hoffman, realized that understanding the meaning that each family member attributed to familial events and problems rendered more benefits than focusing on deciphering the intricacies of patterns of family interaction. They recognized that human experiences are always ambiguous and that the quality or significance of these experiences is relative to the interpretation given by the person or family who experienced them—and not to the observer. This recognition, spawned by the introduction of *hermeneutics* (i.e., theory of interpretation of biblical texts derived from the Greek word for interpretation), led family therapists using this new worldview to identify themselves as facilitators of a process by which family members explore, organize, and construct narratives that help to interpret and resolve family issues.

Take the case of a family that is dealing with end-of-life decisions, given that the father, until recently, the breadwinner, presents with metastasized lung cancer with a poor prognosis (e.g., no more than 2 months of life). In a situation like this, a constructivist family therapist would be cautious about developing a conceptualization of the family problems without the input of each member. In fact, this type of therapist would rely on the explanation and analysis, that is, the narrative, provided by each of the parts involved and the family as a whole. As exemplified, this change in focus, from family theory to family narrative, is also accompanied by the democratization of the therapeutic relationship (Nichols & Schwartz, 2007) whereby family members, not the therapists, are now the experts.

### Change Process and the Role of the Rehabilitation Health Professional

This interpretive and collaborative approach is centered on the construction of meaning and a stance of *not knowing* on the part of the therapist (Anderson, 1993).

As such, constructivist therapists are asked to become assiduous nonjudgmental listeners, who do not keep any information from the recipients of their services. Even clinicians who observe the session from a one-way mirror are invited to join the dialogue and share their impressions with the therapist and the family (Anderson, 1991). The coconstruction of meaning is accomplished with the use of *questions about family relationships*, which prompt each member to share her or his views about the family problems and their unique experiences. This emphasis on questioning is intended to empower and give a voice to each family member in the presence of others and provide the means to explore new possibilities and solutions for the family (Bitter & Corey, 1996). Thus, a constructivist therapist working with a family that is expecting the death of one of its members would ask each of them to share her or his experience of the impending loss of the father (as in the previous example). The therapist's goal would be to engage the family in a conversation that will allow each family member to see her or his situation in a new light (e.g., reframe the father's death as the end of his suffering) and consider new answers to their problems (e.g., identify appropriate ways to support each other during this difficult time). Even though therapists inquire about the past and make process comments, their role is to facilitate a dialogue focused on the present and, particularly, the future.

### Solution-Focused Family Therapy

Solution-focused family therapy emerged in the late 1990s in response to the postmodern revolution and the constrictions of managed-care budgets. As is implicit in its name, this approach aims at resolving a very specific problem with a pragmatic and targeted plan. The founders, Steve Shazer and his colleagues, argued that talking about solutions rather than problems helps families to switch their attention from negative issues to positive alternatives, which in and of itself, helps in the elimination of difficulties. From this perspective, the etiology of family problems is considered irrelevant, and, thus, neither explored nor explained. Further, solution-focused family therapists work under the premise that each family already possesses all the resources that are needed to resolve the problem.

#### Change Process and the Role of the Rehabilitation Health Professional

Family therapists using this approach conceive their role as that of a facilitator who engages the family in two very specific processes. First, they assist the family in identifying the problem. They are interested neither in reorganizing the family structure nor in contextualizing their issues, given a particular agenda. Their aim is to assist family members in understanding what they want to change and in choosing a goal that meets certain conditions. Specifically, solution-focused therapists strive to help families in working on a goal that is concrete, realistic, and achievable in a specific time frame. Given this set of conditions, these goals are typically modest. For instance, a solution-focused family therapist may assist a couple that is experiencing marital problems in mapping out a 6-month strategy to support their 11-year-old boy, who has been diagnosed with leukemia and needs chemotherapy. Rather than addressing long-lived marriage difficulties and an impending divorce, the couple makes, with the assistance of their therapist, a targeted decision to work together on a short-term basis to facilitate their child's treatment and rehabilitation.

In addition to centering their work on a specific issue, solution-focused family therapists promote change by helping family members to acknowledge and use the skills and resources that they already have and activate those abilities that are dormant. In the case just described, for example, the therapist would ask the couple to identify areas in which they effectively work as a team. By doing so, therapists help the family in reframing their reality, from one that is negative and deficiency focused to one that is optimistic and strength based. Proponents of this approach argue that this change in language is sufficient to trigger positive changes and figure out solutions.

### Integrated Approach to Family Systems: A Social–Ecological Model for Rehabilitation Health Professionals

Family therapy pioneers like Bowen (1978) and Minuchin (e.g., Minuchin, Rosman, & Baker, 1978) argued for the importance of addressing physical health-related problems and needs within the family system. Nonetheless, most of the traditional family system theories have focused primarily on mental health and psychosocial dynamics among family members (Pisani & McDaniel, 2005). In contrast, modern approaches to family therapy have addressed disability or chronic illness, as well as other specific clinical contexts; however, they have attended to these issues from a pragmatic stance, giving little attention to broad schemes or theories explaining how families function and change, given the presence of a disability or chronic illness in the family (Lebow, 2005). Thus, we propose a *social–ecological* model for rehabilitation health professionals that integrates the philosophy of the medical family therapy model (McDaniel, Hepworth, & Doherty, 1992) with principles from ecologically based family therapy (Lindblad-Goldberg & Northey, 2013; Szapocznik & Williams, 2000). Our aim in integrating these two complementary approaches is to provide a "meta-framework" that incorporates the fundamental concepts of traditional and modern family systems models, while also being useful and specific to the roles of rehabilitation health professionals.

A *social–ecological* model for rehabilitation is defined as the process by which rehabilitation health professionals attend to each and every relationship in which a person with a disability is immersed that affects her or his course of treatment. This approach conceptualizes rehabilitation care as intervening, to the extent possible, in the different subsystems in which a person with a disability might navigate, beyond her or his family, to include the team of rehabilitation health professionals and members of the informal social support system that interact with her or him (see Figure 14.1). Moreover, it highlights the need to attend to the influence of the larger health care system and the culture and society of a person with a disability.

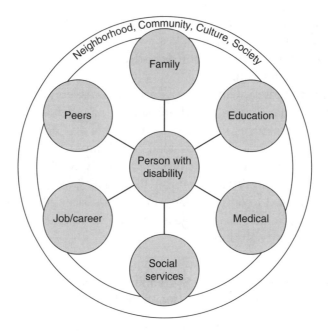

**FIGURE 14.1** Social ecology of persons with disabilities.

This model posits that all of these subsystems are important because they exert direct and indirect influences on the person's rehabilitation process. In fact, from this perspective, a person with a disability is a microsystem member embedded in each of these subsystems (Bronfenbrenner, 1989a). Moreover, the adoption of a social–ecological approach allows rehabilitation health professionals to establish pragmatic goals that are related to the management of the health impairment through the use or, in systemic terms, activation of the social network and family surrounding the person with the disability. Further, the multicontextuality of the social–ecological approach is consistent with most multicultural theories, which highlight the importance of considering an individual's identity across intersecting cultural variables (Ancis & Ladany, 2001) and, thus, with the postmodern forms of family therapy (i.e., family therapy of the 21st century), which were described earlier.

*Medical family therapy* is a relatively new and practical approach that is rooted in general systems theory (von Bertalanffy, 1950) and combines tenets from the biopsychosocial model of health (Engel, 1977) with family systems theory (Bowen, 1978). This form of family therapy attends to the bidirectional relations among health, disability, and illness and the personal dynamics of the individual with a disability, within the context of a family and the broader health care system (McDaniel & Pisani, 2012; Pisani & McDaniel, 2005). Medical family therapy emerged a few decades ago as a practical option that recognized the potential benefits of using primary health care centers to address the mental health needs of individuals and families whose mental health otherwise would be left untreated (Pisani & McDaniel, 2005). This and comparable approaches are likely to gain increased attention with the advent of integrated health care, expanding the roles of rehabilitation health professionals in dealing with the needs of individuals with disabilities and their families.

Similarly, *ecologically based family therapy* goes beyond conceptualizing the family as the locus of attention, to consider all other layers of the environment (Engel, 1977). In this way, the ecological approach to family therapy blends the general systems theory (von Bertalanffy, 1969) with Bronfenbrenner's (1989b) work on social ecology, allowing therapists to conceptualize an individual's behaviors and attitudes toward a disability as the by-product of her or his personal biology and familial and societal influences (e.g., political, economic, and cultural; Okun, 2002), and to intervene at multiple levels of the ecosystem.

Common to both models are three central ideas. First, the experience of individuals with disabilities (a part in the system) can only be understood once there is an understanding of how family members and health care providers (the system as a whole; Figure 14.1) operate together (Brown & Christensen, 1999). Second, although the family of a person with a disability is a system in and of itself, it is also a subsystem within the larger community of formal and informal social support providers, resulting in reciprocal influences (i.e., circular causality) within and among subsystems and systems (Brown & Christensen, 1999; Figure 14.2). Further, systems tend to operate in such ways as to maintain their homeostasis or status quo. This applies to the team of rehabilitation health professionals as well who, as a group, form a subsystem within the ecosystem of the individual with a disability and her or his relatives and the larger rehabilitation organizations.

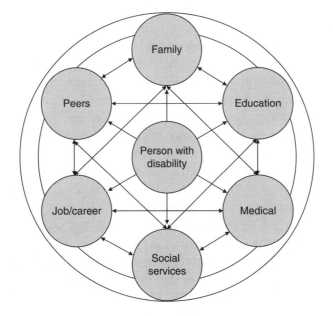

**FIGURE 14.2** Connections between systems in the social ecology of persons with disabilities.

To maintain a homeostatic state, each member of the system plays a particular role (e.g., grandfather) or function (e.g., rehabilitation health professional) and follows rules that are intrinsic to that particular system. For example, consider the case of a grandfather who is the primary caretaker of a boy with cerebral palsy and in charge of taking his grandson to his regular appointments with an occupational therapist. The occupational therapist assists the boy in learning how to work independently at school and interacts frequently not only with the boy but also with the grandfather and other professionals who coordinate the boy's rehabilitation process. The boy and the grandfather have made an implicit contract about their caregiving relationship and how they go about getting ready for his weekly appointments with the occupational therapist. This contract, defined by a series of system rules, delineates boundaries among members of the system (e.g., grandparental or caretaking subsystem in this case) and, as a whole, these unspoken roles, rules, and boundaries constitute a structure, which shapes the interactions among all members of the system (Nichols & Schwartz, 2004). In the current example, the boy complies with treatment as long as his grandfather provides transportation and stays with him during sessions; otherwise, he stays quiet and curses at his therapist. As stipulated by systems theorists, these symptoms (i.e., the uncooperative behavior) serve to maintain the equilibrium of the system's structure. The boy misbehaves to ensure closeness to his grandfather, which helps him cope with the grief of recently losing his father; concomitantly, the grandfather tolerates the boy's behavior because he feels loved and valued, an experience that had become foreign to him after he retired and became a widower.

### Change Process and the Role of the Rehabilitation Health Professional

In the context of the proposed integrative approach, the primary goal of therapy is to improve the quality of the interpersonal relationships of the person with a disability and her or his connections with the different subsystems of the environment, including health care providers. Specifically, from a medical family therapy perspective, the overarching goal is to assist the individual with a disability in attaining a balance between agency and communion (Bakan, 1969; Pisani & McDaniel, 2005). *Agency* refers to the notion that the individual, in spite of her or his disability, is able to make choices regarding health management, which makes her or him feel empowered, and, to the extent possible (depending on the severity of the disability and the influence of sociopolitical and economic factors), in charge of her or his situation. Proponents of this approach argue that an individual's autonomy needs to be accompanied by a sense of emotional and spiritual belonging, or *communion*, with her or his social network of family, friends, and the health care system. Empirical studies suggest that an imbalance between agency and communion is associated with poor health outcomes through the facilitation of isolation or dependence (Helgeson, 1994).

The notion of communion expands the role of the rehabilitation health professional from that of a facilitator of change within the family to that of a facilitator of negotiations between the family and systems outside of the family (Liddle,

Rodriguez, Dakof, Kanzki, & Marvel, 2005). In this sense, this approach allows rehabilitation health professionals to become *agents of social change*, a particularly useful stance when working with socially discriminated or stigmatized groups, such as persons with a disability.

To be effective, such an approach must conceptualize the overall functioning of the person with a disability as influenced by society's power dynamics and dependent on her or his connections with the different subsystems (e.g., family, school, peer group, and culture) in the environment, which could be either weak or strong, depending on the quality of the relationships. Strong and affirming connections have been found to be directly correlated with positive health outcomes, such as quality of life (Szapocznik & Williams, 2000). As such, for successful rehabilitation to occur, it is not sufficient to promote strong family ties; rather, there must be strong ties among family members and each of the other social– ecological systems (e.g., team of rehabilitation health professionals) linked, in a constructive way, to the person with a disability. Likewise, rehabilitation counselors need to discourage connections with subsystems that have a negative or detrimental effect on the person with a disability (e.g., friends who are hold biases against disability-related issues and engage in bullying behaviors). For example, boundary-shifting strategies such as "those intended to enlarge positive informal social support networks and linkages with formal service delivery…and those intended to disconnect…[the affected individuals] from damaging relationships" (Szapocznik et al., 2004, p. 291) constitute a useful strategy to strengthen quality connections.

Another strategy that could be effective in promoting salutary connections with informal social networks and communities is the creation or identification of opportunities for the person with a disability to provide support to others in need. Research studies show that the provision of social support (i.e., offer of support "to" others) is associated with decreased psychological distress, whereas the opposite occurs with the receipt of social support (i.e., receipt of social support "from" others) among aging and other populations (Cruza-Guet, Spokane, Caskie, Brown, & Szapocznik, 2008). Further, we suggest the inclusion of peer specialists in the health rehabilitation team of professionals. In this case, a peer specialist would be an individual who lives with a disability, has achieved a healthy balance between agency and communion, and has received the training necessary to appropriately use her or his own history to instill hope in other persons with disabilities and coach them in the process of learning to be more independent and, at the same time, socially connected with individuals and communities (Davidson, Chinman, Sells, & Rowe, 2006). It is in the context of these layered relationships that coordinated efforts can be effectively used to assist the person with a disability in managing his or her health impairment.

Another important component of the proposed integrative approach is the adoption of the concept of second-order cybernetics (Keeny, as cited in Inman, Rawls, Meza, & Brown, 2002). From a second-order cybernetic perspective, the therapist is not a mere observer of what occurs in sessions, but is rather a coproducer of bidirectional changes (Inman et al., 2002). This position attempts to eliminate the potentially harmful effects of a hierarchy of power within the therapeutic relationship. As stated by Inman et al. (2002, p. 155), "Such a [hierarchical] relationship or environment may mimic the challenges of unequal power differentials faced by persons of color [and, in this case, those with a disability] on a daily basis, thus failing to foster a culturally supportive atmosphere needed to work successfully with such populations."

Indeed, effective family systems counseling within the rehabilitation context must consider sociocultural issues, especially the extent to which power and privilege are addressed. Age, gender, race, ethnicity, sexual orientation, and social class, for example, have socially constructed meanings for individuals, groups, and societies, which are played out in family and therapeutic relationships. These culture-related variables must be considered within the context of families who have a member with a disability; specifically, these factors may inform the meaning of disability and health for the family, how the family views help seeking; their experiences with prejudice, discrimination, and marginalization; and the overall salience of disability and other cultural factors for the individual and the family. Thus, it is recommended that rehabilitation health professionals make a concerted effort to engage the person with a disability, her or his family, and careproviders in an open dialogue as to how their cultural identities influence the rehabilitation process. Further, the person with a disability and her or his family may need support in addressing these culture-related issues (e.g., lack of access to insurance as a spouse in a gay relationship) and in taking advantage of their resources and existing strengths to counter societal attitudes, stigma, and other microaggressions (i.e., daily, seemingly insignificant assaults on individuals based on their outward presentation).

## LIMITATIONS

In this chapter, traditional and contemporary family systems theories have been described, and an integrated model has been proposed for potential application by rehabilitation health professionals. In this section, the limitations of family systems therapy in general, and the limitations of this approach in addressing disability-related issues, in particular, are discussed. Although it is argued that a social–ecological model, in the context of integrated health care, is the next wave in family therapy, it is also recognized that several limitations must be taken into account if this model is to be viable.

First, at the theoretical level, there remains a need to hold any and all family therapy applications to rehabilitation practice to the light of a feminist and multicultural critique. Each model must answer the same questions that Ault-Riche (1986, as cited in Silverstein, 2003, p. 21) raised in her assessment of traditional family therapy models: "Is the nuclear family idealized? Is the interplay between family life and the larger society acknowledged? Are the unequal power relations between husbands and wives recognized?" The failure of traditional family systems theories to address the marginalization of women, nonconventional families, people of color, gays, individuals with disabilities, and persons from non-Western cultures was precisely the impetus for the development of the 21st-century family system therapies.

These therapies and this proposed model acknowledge the presence of power differentials between a family of a person with a disability and the systems in which this family is embedded. However, most postmodern approaches to family therapy, as well as the model that we put forward, could be strengthened by more clearly articulating and attending to the role of power with respect to every aspect of a person's life and, in this case, with respect to the type of disability. Some types of disabilities, for instance, are more accepted and less stigmatized by the dominant culture than others (e.g., dyslexia versus an AIDS-related chronic disability), which impacts family functioning and the interactions among family members and service providers differentially.

From a clinical research perspective, an important limitation, also related to a power differential, is embedded in the "top-down" approach that has characterized the construction process of all forms of family therapy. Unfortunately, service recipients and communities, including persons with a disability and their families, are not driving the assumptions and practices of these models; rather, practitioners and researchers develop and test them on other populations and then transport the tested models to communities, which lack a voice on its creation and implementation. This is also the case of the model proposed here. As such, family systems model development may use community-based participatory research methodology, which asserts that research is initiated as much by the affected communities as it is by researchers. In rehabilitation, such an approach would involve persons with disabilities in articulating their needs, leading to a community-driven needs assessment, and then to an invitation to collaborate with researchers on codeveloping a family systems intervention model that meets their expressed needs.

Another limitation of all family systems approaches has been their focus on and application to families of individuals living with identified psychiatric diagnoses as defined by the *Diagnostic and Statistical Manual of Mental Disorders* (5th ed., *DSM-5*; American Psychiatric Association, 2013). Family therapy research that considers contemporary models of health and disability (e.g., World Health Organization [WHO] *International Classification of Functioning, Disability and Health*; WHO, 2001) and includes conditions beyond those falling in the *DSM* diagnostic system has not received enough attention. Although "diagnosis" is de-emphasized in family systems work, much of the research and application of these models have been described within the context of families managing psychiatric symptoms or diagnoses.

A final limitation of family systems theories is the inherent difficulties in conducting outcomes research given the interdependent nature of systems. Family systems researchers need to design studies that seek to determine how systemic approaches influence such outcomes as quality of life, pain reduction, and employment and how these outcomes are related to the multiple connections between and among the systems to which the person with a disability is a member. From here, researchers can develop useful systemic or social–ecological interventions that are best suited to improve the quality of life of the person with a disability as well as each of the family members involved in her or his life.

## IMPLICATIONS FOR TRAINING AND PRACTICE

Contemporary models of health and disability emphasize the importance of the interaction between individuals with a disability and the context in which they exist (WHO, 2001). This approach has long been underscored as a driving philosophy in rehabilitation health professions (e.g., Wright, 1983; Lewin, 1935). Nonetheless, addressing the family system of those living with a disability has remained a challenge in many rehabilitation training and practice contexts. This is due, in part, to training accreditation standards and counselor licensure laws that place less emphasis on family systems as well as to employment contexts and lack of resources, which limit the extent to which a rehabilitation health professional can do family systems work. For example, although the accreditation agency for rehabilitation counselor training programs, Council on Rehabilitation Education (CORE, 2012), identifies knowledge domains and learning outcomes related to family systems, these training standards are minimal with respect to CORE's overarching emphasis on training related to individual functioning. In fact, the majority of rehabilitation counseling training programs do not require a full course in family systems; instead, they infuse these principles into some rehabilitation courses or offer students the option of taking a family systems elective course.

Notably, the new clinical rehabilitation counseling program standards, implemented jointly by CORE (2013) and the Council for Accreditation of Counseling and Related Educational Programs (CACREP), minimally addresses family systems, noting it only twice in the standards. Specifically, the standards state that students must "recognize the importance of family, social networks, and community in the provision of services for and treatment of people with disabilities" in the Counseling, Prevention, and Intervention Domain, and must "know the effect of co-occurring disabilities on the client and family" in the Assessment and Diagnosis Domain (CORE, 2013). The inclusion of these statements is a step in the right direction; however, these standards are inadequate in meeting the family systems training needs of rehabilitation counselors.

State counselor licensure laws may also contribute to structural training and practice barriers toward learning and implementing a family systems approach within rehabilitation. Many counselor licensure laws (e.g., licensed professional counselor [LPC], licensed professional clinical counselor [LPCC], and licensed mental health counselor [LMHC]) across the United States do not require coursework in family systems. Oftentimes, family systems coursework and training is included only in marriage, couple and family (MCF) counseling training programs and required for their respective licenses. CACREP (2009), for instance, includes a training program in MCF counseling; yet, this is a separate and distinct training program from rehabilitation counseling. Those university programs that offer both counseling specialties (i.e., MCF and rehabilitation counseling) are more likely to afford rehabilitation students the opportunity to be trained in family systems, with additional time and resources required. Unfortunately, this is not the case in many programs. Nonetheless, we are optimistic about the ability of counseling training programs in addressing this need for change.

Current counseling curricula reflect the barriers imposed by accreditation and licensure standards with respect to family systems training. Specifically, the majority of CORE- and CACREP-accredited counseling curricula center on constructs and techniques oriented toward individual functioning, relegating systems theories to a specific family systems course, despite recognition of the importance of the person–environment interaction. In a similar vein, required coursework related to abnormal psychology or psychological diagnoses is typically deeply entrenched in the medical model approach, using the *DSM-5* as a framework for understanding mental illness, without consideration of the role that contextual issues play in the generation of psychopathology.

In response to these systemic, programmatic, and curricular barriers to family systems training, it is suggested that a systemic or, even better, an ecological, approach be incorporated into all counseling courses. The infusion of a social–ecological worldview will allow rehabilitation counseling students the opportunity to gain a different and richer (i.e., contextual, feministic, and multicultural) perspective on mental health functioning and diagnosis, which would offer them a broader range of counseling interventions to choose from in order to best address the multiple needs of individuals with disabilities and their families. Indeed, viewing an individual's functioning from a social–ecological perspective is a paradigmatic shift, a shift that is difficult to make in practice, given the deeply ingrained focus on individual functioning in counselor training programs, accreditation standards and, not coincidentally, the broader individualist values of our society as a whole.

Consistent with larger and in-progress health care changes and paradigmatic shifts (i.e., implementation of fully integrated forms care), which reflect biopsychosocial and ecological conceptualizations of health and illness, not only students but also practicing rehabilitation health professionals need to transition into a systemic or ecological mode of care in order to meet the needs of their service recipients (Rivera, 2012). Currently, traditional public VR settings as well as allied rehabilitation facilities are often ill-equipped to address or provide family systems interventions. Most public VR agencies, for instance, do not have an official service or payment structure designated for the provision of family counseling or support, even though they acknowledge that family functioning does impact rehabilitation outcomes. In addition, VR counselors typically view working with families as beyond the scope of their training and competencies; this view contradicts the fact that rehabilitation counselors do report that working with families is part of their job. In fact, many counselors believe that in order to use any family therapy techniques, one must become a family therapist (Zingaro, 1983).

Despite these challenges, VR counselors and rehabilitation health professionals must address family and larger systemic issues as they relate to their service recipients, given the impact of family functioning and context on rehabilitation. As such, it is suggested that VR agencies and allied rehabilitation settings pursue organization shifts that incorporate the role of the family and the larger system in the rehabilitation process. In addition, the advancement of national health policies is encouraged regarding family systems practice and research for persons with disabilities. Ideally, the inclusion of services to families within the rehabilitation context should become a "standard of care."

Specifically, the integrative approach proposed at the end of this chapter (i.e., the social–ecological model for rehabilitation health professionals) would appear helpful. This approach synthesizes the core concepts of traditional and modern forms of family system therapy, adopting principles from a medical (McDaniel et al., 1992) and ecologically based perspective (Lindblad-Goldberg & Northey, 2013; Szapocznik & Williams, 2000) to offer a meta-framework specific to the needs of rehabilitation health professionals. This model is consistent with the underlying philosophy of rehabilitation and contemporary conceptualizations of disability and health (e.g., the definition established by the WHO's *International Classification of Functioning*; WHO, 2001), which consider disability to be a biopsychosocial phenomenon, that is, a function of the interaction between the person and her or his environment.

Further, this approach is consistent with up-to-date family-centered care policies established by the WHO (WHO, 2007) and The Joint Commission (2010). Together, ecologically and medical-based family therapy provide the means to focus on layered levels of relationships, ranging from those between the person with a disability and her or his rehabilitation therapist to those between the individual and her or his familial and larger social context, thereby facilitating the application of this integrative framework to individuals from a wide range of cultural backgrounds.

## CASE STUDY

John is a 45-year-old, heterosexual, African American male, who was diagnosed with type I, insulin-dependent diabetes mellitus at age 14. He currently lives with his father, who is in his 70s and retired. John's mother, also in her 70s, is alive and lives alone. His parents have been separated for about 30 years. John is the youngest of three children; he has one older sister who lives independently and far from John and another sister who lives abroad. John is married, but separated from his wife, who is also African American.

After John was diagnosed with diabetes, his two older sisters took on the role of haranguing him about taking his insulin and following an appropriate diet. His mother, however, felt that his sisters were too harsh;

*(continued)*

*(continued)*

in response, she provided John with daily reminders and brought his insulin and glucose meter to school and to his room or to any other place and at any time in which he needed to monitor his blood sugar. Despite her efforts, John would forget to give himself insulin injections on schedule and neglected to have emergency food available. John's father worried, but he did not get involved in the care of his son. Instead, he would provide support through criticism of his son's neglectful habits and would blame the mother for spoiling him.

John married his childhood sweetheart at age 18, at a time when he did not present with major complications from diabetes. During his marriage, John's wife attempted to assist him in managing his condition, but tended to be overbearing. John experienced his wife as controlling and felt that she was trying to force him to manage his diabetes. Thus, he did not consider her efforts credible. Throughout his marriage, John maintained regular contact with his sisters, whom he experienced as engaging in their usual "big sister" behaviors by telling him that they had a better understanding of his diabetic condition than he. This was worsened by the fact that one of his sisters was in the health care industry.

Meanwhile, John's mother and father continued to have a different style of handling John's medical situation; his mother would volunteer to send him reminders about when to take his insulin or about doctor's appointments, and his father would tell his daughters about John's inability to care for his health. Over time, John's wife became dissatisfied in the marriage. By age 30, he was told to "move out." However, they never divorced. John then moved in with his father. It was at that point that his health quickly deteriorated. On two occasions, for example, he experienced diabetic ketoacidosis, resulting in hospitalization. Around age 35, his sight began to worsen and, by the age of 40, John was diagnosed as legally blind.

Vocationally, John was trained as a physical therapist, requiring a bachelor's degree. He worked full time until he became visually impaired at age 35. Since that time, he has relied on Social Security disability payments and financial support from his parents to cover expenses. John does not consider himself employable, and his family does not encourage him to seek any job opportunities. From a social standpoint, John is highly isolated. His mother and father are his main sources of social connection and support. Approximately every few months, John's high school and college friends drop by. In spite of his visual impairments, he manages to be relatively active on Facebook, which permits some social interaction beyond his home.

## CONCLUSIONS

In conclusion, family systems therapy, in all of its forms, is a useful and much-needed tool for rehabilitation health professionals who are addressing the complex needs of individuals with disabilities and their families. Persons with disabilities exist within multiple systems, which interact to influence their level of disability. As such, rehabilitation health professionals need to broaden their therapeutic lens to include an integrative or systemic approach toward treatment and intervention that considers the individual, family, and the larger context in which individuals with disability navigate. Although specialized training in family systems theory is ideal, the concepts and models included in this chapter, and exemplified with rehabilitation-related cases, offer rehabilitation health professionals a starting point to understand and successfully begin to manage disability-related issues from a systemic and ecologically based perspective.

## CASE STUDY DISCUSSION EXERCISES

Based on the integrative model presented in this chapter, answer the following questions.

1. How did family interactions change as he grew up, but continue to support John's poor management of his diabetic condition?
2. What family patterns were repeated in John's marriage?
3. How does it benefit each family member to continue to support John's poor management of his diabetic condition?
4. John expresses a wish to be independent because he knows his parents will eventually die and they do not have a large fortune that he will inherit. How would you change the family's story about John and about each family member's role in John's new narrative?
5. What role does the African American culture, the individual's gender, and his social class play in how you understand John and in how you will approach this with John?

## CHAPTER DISCUSSION EXERCISES

1. How does family systems therapy differ from the individual therapies/counseling you are familiar with? Identify at least five differences as applied to disability-related issues.
2. Identify three common threads in traditional family therapies and compare and contrast them with three common threads in contemporary family therapies.
3. Discuss how traditional and contemporary family therapies differ from the social–ecological model proposed in this chapter.
4. Choose two different family system models described in this chapter (e.g., one that you agree with and another one you disagree with). Explain why you chose them. What are the similarities and differences between the two models?
5. Think about all the therapy models you read about in this chapter. Which of them best resonates with your theory or approach to counseling as applied to the rehabilitation field? Explain why.

6. Identify and discuss at least two ways in which the following models are limited in addressing the needs of families of a person with a disability and indicate the reasons:
   Traditional systemic family therapies
   Modern systemic therapy
   Social–ecological therapy
7. In your role as a rehabilitation health professional, what would you do differently after reading this chapter; in other words, how will the knowledge that you attained on family systems theories and a social–ecological approach influence:
   Your case conceptualizations?
   Your counseling interventions?
   Your attitudes regarding current training and practice issues related to the inclusion and application of family systems theory in rehabilitation?

## REFERENCES

Accordino, M. (1999). Implications of disability for the family: Implementing behavioral family therapy in rehabilitation education. *Rehabilitation Education, 13*, 287–293.

American Psychiatric Association. (2013). *Diagnostic and statistical manual of mental disorders* (5th ed.). Washington, DC: Author.

Ancis, J. R., & Ladany, N. (2001). A multicultural framework for counselor supervision. In L. J. Bradley & N. Ladany (Eds.), *Counselor supervision: Principles, process, and practice* (pp. 63–90). New York, NY: Brunner-Routledge.

Anderson, H. (1991). *The reflecting team.* New York, NY: Norton.

Anderson, H. (1993). On a roller coaster: A collaborative language systems approach to therapy. In S. Friedman (Ed.), *The new language of change.* New York, NY: Guilford.

Avis, J. M. (1988). Deepening awareness: A private study guide to feminism and family therapy. In L. Braverman (Ed.), *Women, feminism, and family therapy.* New York, NY: Haworth Press.

Bakan, D. (1969). *The dual reality of human existence.* Chicago, IL: Rand McNally.

Becerra, M. D., & Michael-Makri, S. (2012). Applying structural family therapy with a Mexican-American family with children with disabilities: A case study of a single-parent mother. *Journal of Applied Rehabilitation Counseling, 43*, 17–24.

Bitter, J. R., & Corey, G. (1996). Family systems therapy. In G. Corey (Ed.), *The theory and practice of counseling and psychotherapy* (5th ed., pp. 365–443). Pacific Grove, CA: Brooks/Cole.

Bowen, M. (1966). The use of family theory in clinical practice. *Comprehensive Psychiatry, 7*, 345–374.

Bowen, M. (1976). Theory in the practice of psychotherapy. In P. J. Guerin, Jr. (Ed.), *Family therapy: Theory and practice* (pp. 42–90). New York, NY: Gardner Press.

Bowen, M. (1978). *Family therapy in clinical practice.* New York, NY: Aronson.

Bowlby, J. (1969). *Attachment and loss: Attachment* (Vol. 1). New York, NY: Basic Books.

Bronfenbrenner, U. (1989a). The ecology of the family as a context for human development: Research perspectives. *Developmental Psychology, 22*, 723–742.

Bronfenbrenner, U. (1989b). Ecological systems theory. *Annals of Child Development, 6*, 187–249.

Brown, J. H., & Christensen, D. N. (1999). *Family therapy: Theory and practice.* Pacific Grove, CA: Brooks/Cole.

Chenail, R. J., Levinson, K., & Muchnick, R. (1992). Family systems rehabilitation. *American Journal of Family Therapy, 20*, 157–167.

Cottone, R. R, Handelsman, M. M., & Walters, N. (1986). Understanding the influence of family systems on the rehabilitation process. *Journal of Applied Rehabilitation Counseling, 17,* 37–40.

Council for Accreditation of Counseling and Related Educational Programs (CACREP). (2009). *2009 CACREP accreditation manual.* Alexandria, VA: Author.

Council on Rehabilitation Education (CORE). (2012). *Accreditation manual for rehabilitation counselor education programs.* Rolling Meadows, IL: Author.

Council on Rehabilitation Education (CORE). (2013). *Clinical rehabilitation counseling.* Rolling Meadows, IL: Author. Retrieved from http://www.core-rehab.org/Files/Doc/PDF/Clinical%20Rehabilitation%20Counseling%20Standards.%20FINAL.pdf

Cruza-Guet, M. C., Spokane, A. R., Caskie, G. I. L., Brown, S., & Szapocznik, J. (2008). The relationship between social support and psychological distress among Hispanic elders in Miami, FL. *Journal of Counseling Psychology, 55,* 427–441.

Davidson, L., Chinman, M., Sells, D., & Rowe, M. (2006). Peer support among adults with serious mental Illness: A report from the field. *Schizophrenia Bulletin, 32,* 443–450.

Davidson, M. (1983). *Uncommon sense: The life and thought of Ludwig von Bertalanffy.* Los Angeles, CA: J. P. Tarcher.

Dew, D., Phillips, B., & Reiss, D. (1989). Assessment and early planning with the family in vocational rehabilitation. *Journal of Rehabilitation, 55,* 41–44.

Engel, G. L. (1977). The need for a new medical model: A challenge for biomedicine. *Science, 196,* 129–136.

Fisch, R. (1978). Review of problem-solving therapy by Jay Haley. *Family Process, 17,* 107–110.

Fohs, M. W. (1991). Family systems assessment: Intervention with individuals having a chronic disability. *Career Development Quarterly, 39,* 304–312.

Foley, V. (1984). Family therapy. In R. J. Corsini (Ed.), *Encyclopedia of psychology.* New York, NY: Wiley.

Friar Williams, E. (1977). *Notes of a feminist therapist.* New York, NY: Dell.

Gilbride, D. D. (1993). Parental attitudes toward their children with a disability: Implications for rehabilitation counselors. *Rehabilitation Counseling Bulletin, 36,* 139–150.

Goldner, V. (1985). Feminism and family therapy. *Family Process, 27,* 17–33.

Greenberg, L. S., James, P., & Conry, R. (1988). Perceived chance processes in emotionally focused couples therapy. *Journal of Family Psychology, 1,* 1–12.

Greenberg, L. S., & Johnson, S. M. (1988). *Emotionally focused therapy for couples.* New York, NY: Guilford.

Guerin, P. J., Fogarty, T. F., Fay, L. F., & Kautto, J. G. (1996). *Working with relationship triangles: The one-two-three of psychotherapy.* New York, NY: Guilford.

Haley, J. (1963). *Strategies of psychotherapy.* New York, NY: Grune & Stratton.

Haley, J. (1984). *Ordeal therapy: Unusual ways to change behavior.* New York, NY: Jossey-Boss.

Haley, J. (1991). *Problem-solving therapy.* New York, NY: Wiley.

Haley, J. (1993). *Uncommon therapy: The psychiatric techniques of Milton H. Erikson, M.D.* New York, NY: Norton.

Hare-Mustin, R. T. (1978). A feminist approach to family therapy. *Family Process, 17,* 181–194.

Helgeson, V. (1994). Relation of agency and communion to well being. Evidence and potential explanations. *Psychological Bulletin, 116,* 412–428.

Herbert, J. T. (1989). Assessing the need for family therapy: A primer for rehabilitation counselors. *Journal of Rehabilitation, 55,* 45–51.

Inman, A. G., Rawls, K. N., Meza, M. M., & Brown, A. L. (2002). An integrative approach to assessment and intervention with adolescents of color. In F. W. Kaslow, R. F. Massey, & S. D. Massey (Eds.), *Comprehensive handbook of psychotherapy* (Vol. 3, pp. 3–33). New York, NY: Wiley.

Jackson, D. D. (1959). Family interaction, family homeostasis, and some implications for con-joint family therapy. In J. Masserman (Ed.), *Individual and family dynamics*. New York, NY: Grune & Stratton.

James, K., & MacKinnon, L. (1990). The "incestuous family" revisited: A critical analysis of family therapy myths. *Journal of Marital and Family Therapy, 16*, 71–88.

Johnson, S. M., Hunsley, J., Greenberg, L., & Schindler, D. (1999). Emotionally focused couples therapy: Status and challenges. *Clinical Psychology: Science and Practice, 6*, 67–69.

Kempler, W. (1968). Experiential psychotherapy with families. *Family Process, 7*, 88–89.

Kerr, M., & Bowen, M. (1988). *Family evaluation*. New York, NY: Norton.

Lebow, J. L. (2005). Family therapy in the 21st century. In J. Lebow (Ed.), *Handbook of clinical family therapy* (pp. 1–16). Hoboken, NJ: Wiley.

Lewin, K. (1935). *A dynamic theory of personality*. New York, NY: McGraw-Hill.

Liddle, H. A., Rodriguez, R. A., Dakof, G. A., Kanzki, E., & Marvel, F. A. (2005). Multidimensional family therapy: A science-based treatment for adolescent drug abuse. In J. Lebow (Ed.), *Handbook of clinical family therapy* (pp. 128–163). New York, NY: Wiley.

Lindblad-Goldberg, M., & Northey, W. (2013). Ecosystemic structural family therapy: Theoretical and clinical foundations. *Contemporary Family Therapy, 35*, 147–160.

Lynch, R. T., & Morley, K. L. (1995). Adaptation to pediatric physical disability within the fam-ily system: A conceptual model for counseling families. *Family Journal: Counseling and Therapy for Couples and Families, 3*, 207–217.

Madanes, C. (1984). *Behind the one-way mirror*. San Francisco, CA: Jossey-Bass.

Marshall, K., & Ferris, K. (2012). Utilizing behavioral family therapy (BFT) to help support the system around a person with intellectual disability and complex mental health needs: A case study. *Journal of Intellectual Disabilities, 16*, 109–118.

McDaniel, S., Hepworth, J., & Doherty, W. (1992). *Medical family therapy: A biopsychosocial approach to families with health problems*. New York, NY: Basic Books.

McDaniel, S. H., & Pisani, A. R. (2012). Family dynamics and caregiving for an individual with disabilities. In R. Talley, R. McCorkle, & B. Walter (Eds.), *Caregiving and disability* (pp. 11–28). Oxford, UK: Oxford University Press.

McGoldrick, M., & Gerson, R. (1985). *Genograms in family assessment*. New York, NY: Norton.

Minuchin, P. (1985). Families and individual development: Provocations from the field of family Therapy. *Child Development, 56*, 289–302.

Minuchin, S. (1974). *Families and family therapy*. Cambridge, MA: Harvard University Press.

Minuchin, S., & Fishman, H. C. (1981). *Family therapy techniques*. Cambridge, MA: Harvard University Press.

Minuchin, S., Rosman, B. L., & Baker, L. (1978). *Psychosomatic families: Anorexia nervosa in context*. Cambridge, MA: Harvard University Press.

Napier, A. Y., & Whitaker, C. A. (1978). *The family crucible*. New York, NY: Harper & Row.

Nichols, P., & Schwartz, R. C. (2004). *Family therapy: Concepts and methods*. Boston, MA: Pearson/Allyn & Bacon.

Nichols, P., & Schwartz, R. C. (2007). *The essentials of family therapy*. Boston, MA: Pearson/Allyn & Bacon.

Okun, B. F. (2002). *Effective helping: Interviewing and counseling techniques*. Pacific Grove, CA: Brooks/Cole.

Pisani, A. R., & McDaniel, S. H. (2005). An integrative approach to health and illness in family therapy. In J. LeBow (Ed.), *Handbook of clinical family therapy* (pp. 569–590). New York, NY: Wiley.

Pitschel-Walz, G., Leucht, S., Bauml, J., Kissling, W., & Engel, R. R. (2001). The effects of fam-ily interventions on relapse and rehospitalization in schizophrenia: A meta-analysis. *Schizophrenia Bullletin, 27*, 73–92.

Power, P. W., & Dell Orto, A. E. (1986). Families, illness and disability: The roles of the rehabilitation counselor. *Journal of Applied Rehabilitation Counseling, 17,* 41–44.

Power, P. W., & Dell Orto, A. E. (2004). *Families living with chronic illness and disability: Interventions, challenges, and opportunities.* New York, NY: Springer Publishing Company.

Reagles, S. (1982). The impact of disability: A family crisis. *Journal of Applied Rehabilitation Counseling, 13,* 25–29.

Rivera, P. A. (2012). Families in rehabilitation. In P. Kennedy (Ed.), *The Oxford handbook of rehabilitation psychology* (pp. 160–170). New York, NY: Oxford University Press.

Rolland, J. S. (1999). Parental illness and disability: A family systems framework. *Association for Family Therapy, 21,* 242–266.

Satir, V., Stachowiak, J., & Taschman, H. A. (1975). *Helping families to change.* New York, NY: Jason Aronson.

Satir, V. M. (1972). *Peoplemaking.* Palo Alto, CA: Science & Behavior Books.

Schwartz, R. (1995). *Internal family systems therapy.* New York, NY: Guilford.

Selvini Palazzoli, M., Boscolo, L., Cecchin, G., & Prata, G. (1978). *Paradox and counterparadox.* New York, NY: Aronson.

Selvini Palazzoli, M., Boscolo, L., Cecchin, G., & Prata, G. (1980). Hypothesizing–circularity–neutrality: Three guidelines for the conductor of the session. *Family Process, 19,* 3–12.

Silverstein, L. (2003). Classic texts and early critiques. In L. B. Silverstein & T. J. Goodrich (Eds.), *Feminist family therapy: Empowerment in social context* (pp. 17–35). Washington, DC: American Psychological Association.

Silverstein, L. B., & Goodrich, T. J. (Eds.) (2003). *Feminist family therapy: Empowerment in social context.* Washington, DC: American Psychological Association.

Stavros, M. K. (1991). Family systems approach to sexual dysfunction in neurologic disability. *Sexuality and Disability, 9,* 69–85.

Substance Abuse and Mental Health Services Administration (SAMHSA). (2004). *Substance abuse treatment and family therapy. Treatment Improvement Protocol (TIP) Series No. 39.* Retrieved from http://www.ncbi.nlm.nih.gov/books/NBK64269/

Sutton, J. (1985). The need for family involvement in client rehabilitation. *Journal of Applied Rehabilitation Counseling, 16,* 42–45.

Szapocznik, J., Feaster, D., Mitrani, V. B., Prado, G., Smith, W., Robinson-Batista, C., . . . Robbins, M. S., (2004). Structural ecosystems therapy for HIV-seropositive African-American women: Effects on psychological distress, family hassles, and family support. *Journal of Consulting and Clinical Psychology, 72,* 288–303.

Szapocznik, J., & Williams, R. A. (2000). Brief strategic family therapy: 25 years of interplay among theory, research, and practice in adolescent behavior problems and drug abuse. *Clinical Child and Family Psychology Review, 3,* 117–135.

The Joint Commission. (2010). *Advancing effective communication, cultural competence, and patient- and family-centered care: A roadmap for hospitals.* Oakbrook Terrace, IL: The Joint Commission Resources.

Vogel, E. F., & Bell, N. W. (1960). The emotionally disturbed child as a family scapegoat. In N. W. Bell & E. F. Vogel (Eds.), *A modern introduction to the family* (pp. 382–397). Glencoe, IL: Free Press.

von Bertalanffy, L. (1950). An outline of general system theory. *British Journal of the Philosophy of Science, 1,* 134–165.

von Bertalanffy, L. (1969). *General systems theory.* New York, NY: George Braziller.

Watzlawick, P., Beavin, J., & Jackson, D. (1967). *Pragmatics of human communication.* New York, NY: Norton.

Watzlawick, P., Weakland, J., & Fisch, R. (1974). *Change: Principles of problem formation and problem resolution.* New York, NY: Norton.

Webb-Woodward, L., & Woodward, B. (1982). A case of the blind leading the "blind": Reframing a physical handicap as competence. *Family Process, 21,* 291–294.

Whitaker, C. A., & Keith, D. V. (1981). Symbolic-experiential family therapy. In A. Gurman & D. P. Kniskern (Eds.), *Handbook of family therapy.* New York, NY: Brunner/Mazel.

Woody, R. H. (1993). Americans with Disabilities Act: Implications for family therapy. *American Journal of Family Therapy, 21,* 71–78.

World Health Organization (WHO). (2001). *International classification of functioning, disability and health (ICF).* Geneva, Switzerland: Author.

World Health Organization (WHO). (2007). *Regional committee resolution. People at the centre of care initiative.* Manila, Philippines: WHO Western Pacific Region.

Wright, B. (1983). *Physical disability: A psychosocial approach.* New York, NY: Harper & Row.

Zarski, J. J., Hall, D. E., & DePompei, R. (1987). Closed head injury patients: A family therapy approach to the rehabilitation process. *American Journal of Family Therapy, 15,* 62–68.

Zingaro, J. C. (1983). A family systems approach for the career counselor. *Personnel and Guidance Journal, 62,* 24–27.

# Career and Vocational Counseling

*David R. Strauser, Timothy N. Tansey, and Deirdre O'Sullivan*

## LEARNING OBJECTIVES

The goal of this chapter is to introduce the concept of work as a therapeutic intervention and provide an overview of a theoretical framework for the vocational readiness of individuals with disabilities to engage in work. On completing the chapter, readers will be able to:

1. Describe the importance of work for individuals in meeting human needs.
2. Describe how work centrality is the foundation for career and vocational development.
3. Name and identify the six statuses of the INCOME framework, and explain why statuses, instead of stages, are more appropriate for working with individuals with disabilities.
4. Identify career and vocational interventions commonly used in the rehabilitation counseling process.

## HISTORY

### Importance of Work in Rehabilitation

Historically, one of the primary areas of focus for rehabilitation counseling has been the facilitation of career development, employment, and work adjustment for individuals with disabilities and chronic health conditions (Patterson, Szymanski, & Parker, 2005; Wright, 1980). This vocational focus is important because work has been, and will continue to be, viewed as the primary organizing structure of life. In addition, the significance of work in the lives of individuals with chronic health conditions and disabilities has been significantly altered over the past 50 years and continues to evolve (Maytal & Peteet, 2009; Strauser,

2014). As a result, the underlying philosophy of rehabilitation counseling is that work is a fundamental and central component of people's lives and is the primary means by which individuals define themselves in society (Blustein, 2008; Gottfredson, 2002; Super, 1969; Szymanski & Hershenson, 2005). Understanding the complex interaction among work, society, and the individual is essential for rehabilitation counselors so that they can provide appropriate and efficacious vocational services to facilitate and maximize the career development, employment, and overall work adjustment of individuals with chronic health conditions and disabilities. Rehabilitation counselors contemplate this complex interaction among work, society, and the individual through the theoretically grounded construct of work centrality. Work centrality is the acknowledgment that work is central to all societies and an identifying characteristic in individuals' lives.

Complementing the core principle of work centrality, rehabilitation counseling is also guided by the principles of positive behavioral change, maximizing independence, and valuing the client–counselor relationship. The interaction of these core principles is key in facilitating positive career development, vocational behavior, and employment for individuals with disabilities. In rehabilitation counseling, the focus on maximizing the individual's functioning in the environment of his or her choice is based on the related constructs of independence and choice. Individuals with disabilities must have the desire to bring about change and be empowered to be change agents in their own lives. As a result, the approaches to facilitating career development and employment should focus on the individual being engaged, empowered, and goal directed. However, the focus on empowerment of the individual does not suggest that the rehabilitation counselor plays a passive role in the career counseling process. Rather, the counselor is a facilitator of change and ideally empowers the individual to identify and make choices that facilitate personal development. The counseling relationship between the rehabilitation counselor and the individual with the disability is the fundamental tool that rehabilitation counselors have in their tool kit to bring about effective and positive behavioral change.

Research in the area of disability and vocational rehabilitation has provided significant support for the impact of a strong working alliance on facilitating effective rehabilitation outcomes (Lustig, Strauser, Weems, Donnell, & Smith, 2003). Therefore, building and continually nurturing a strong working alliance is a key focus in facilitating effective career development and maximizing employment opportunities for individuals with disabilities. As discussed in the broader counseling literature, approaches that focus on evidence-based practice, such as motivational interviewing (see Chapter 12 in this volume), would appear to be optimal and have merit in maximizing client involvement while providing the necessary level of complementary direction to facilitate appropriate career choice and increased vocational behavior.

Change, independence, evidence-based practice, and working alliance are central to facilitating career development and vocational behavior. These concepts and constructs are covered in other chapters of this book and the broader counseling literature as a whole, and as such, are not described in detail in this chapter. Rather, this chapter addresses career and vocational counseling of persons with disabilities and provides information on evidence-based vocational interventions associated with supporting efforts to enter the workforce.

## CENTRALITY OF WORK

Work has been, and will continue to be, central to all human societies. Work is related to physical and mental health because it increases the probability of societal advancement, access to social support systems, and opportunities for self-expression and self-determination (Blustein, 2008; Neff, 1985). At the basic level, the activity of work itself is healthy and can be therapeutic. However, for individuals with disabilities, work may be particularly beneficial because people with disabilities experience greater social isolation, stigma, and financial burdens as compared to people without disabilities (Blustein, 2008; Strauser, O'Sullivan, & Wong, 2010). Besides the commonly experienced negative financial impact following a chronic illness or disability, people with disabilities often become isolated and experience a decrease in self-esteem related to their diagnosis, disability, or chronic health condition. The work environment can offset this experience by providing opportunities for income, social interaction, support, and health and retirement benefits. According to Neff (1985), most workplaces provide social environments that require a person to interact with others, perform rituals and customs that are meaningful, and provide opportunities for growth. These are the activities that sustain physical and mental health (Blustein, 2006, 2008).

Despite the many physical and psychological health benefits associated with work, work can become hazardous or harmful and negatively affect individuals. Specifically, an incongruent person–environment fit can lead to higher levels of depression and stress (Neff, 1985; O'Sullivan & Strauser, 2010). An incongruent fit is one in which the individual's personal work style, personality, and value system do not fit well or are incongruent with the work environment (Hershenson, 1981; Holland, 1985; Neff, 1985). Service sector positions—common employment sites for individuals with disabilities—and work environments that are noisy, dirty, require long hours, and with extreme weather conditions will also likely lead to increased stress levels (Szymanski & Parker, 2010). Job role ambiguity, lack of control or input, lack of support in high-responsibility jobs, and very low pay are factors that contribute to the reduction of individuals' mental health status (Neff, 1985; Strauser et al., 2010).

Work stress has been a topic of considerable concern for both psychology and business and has a significant, negative impact on the overall work environment (Baron & Greenberg, 1990; Kahn & Byosiere, 1990; Quick, Quick, Nelsom, & Hurrell, 1997; Szymanski & Parker, 2010). For individuals with disabilities, the relationship between the individual's job and work stress is complex (Tansey, Mizelle, Ferrin, Tschopp, & Mizelle, 2004), with the presence of a disability or chronic health condition further complicating the individual's ability to manage stress in the workplace. Managing work stress for individuals with disabilities is an important factor for rehabilitation counselors to consider in the career development and job-placement process.

Because of its centrality across the life span and subsequent impact on well-being, an understanding of how people must adapt to work after any life-changing event or congenital illness is an important consideration for rehabilitation counselors and should be a major topic of rehabilitation counseling research. Beyond the financial incentives associated with work, employment can improve self-esteem and mental health (Blustein, 2008). As a result, employment can lead to improvements in physical and psychological health. First, employment means income and a social role, both of which lead to improvements in social status (Wolfensberger, 2002). It can result in improved access to better housing, health care, nutrition, neighborhoods, and school districts, as well as reduced-crime communities and better family relationships (Blustein, 2008; Bond et al., 2001; Larson et al., 2007).

Conversely, a study based in urban Chicago found that loss of employment empirically connected to a lower quality of life, including increased drug use, violence, and crime (Wilson, 1996). This same study found that employment status is more important than poverty in predicting family discord, violence in neighborhoods, and low-functioning school systems. In addition, families that function in communities with high employment and are poor experience fewer problems than families that function in communities with high unemployment and high poverty.

From an individual perspective, the loss of employment is linked to higher rates of anxiety, depression, and substance abuse (Blustein, 2008) and has been linked to decreased levels of well-being and health status. Health status and general well-being have been found not to rebound to levels prior to loss of employment despite eventual reemployment (Blustein, 2008; Blustein, Kenna, Gill, & DeVoy, 2008). This finding points to the lasting negative physical and psychological impacts of unemployment, even after returning to work.

## WORK AND HUMAN NEEDS

Due to the centrality of work and its positive effect on physical and psychological health, work has been identified as a foundation for meeting human needs. According to Blustein (2006, 2008) and Blustein et al. (2008), work provides a means by which individuals can fulfill the following three basic human needs: (a) survival and power, (b) social connection, and (c) self-determination and well-being. Understanding from the perspective of the individual with disability how his or her educational experiences, conceptualization of work, work experience, familial and cultural background, and disability-related factors impact these three basic human needs is important when providing vocational rehabilitation services to individuals with disabilities.

Understanding the impact of work on these three fundamental human needs also highlights the complex ways in which working functions in the human experience and the need for multidimensional outcomes in measuring the effectiveness of rehabilitation counseling interventions. The traditional vocational rehabilitation outcomes of *employed* versus *unemployed* are not sufficient to cover the multidimensional impact of work in the lives of individuals with disabilities. Being employed only acknowledges that the person is working and provides no information about the quality of employment, how integrated the individual is in the social environment, and the autonomy with which the individual is functioning. Therefore, it is important to analyze how work impacts the individuals' ability to meet their needs. According to Blustein (2008), work can provide for human survival, power, social connection, and self-determination.

### Basic Need of Survival and Power

Work provides a means for individuals with disabilities to survive and derive power (Blustein, 2006; Blustein et al., 2008). The term *survival* in the modern labor market can be equated with the individual's ability to meet his or her basic needs. Ideally, employment can provide individuals with disabilities with sufficient income and benefits to meet their most basic needs. However, research has found that (a) individuals with disabilities are employed at a much lower rate than their counterparts without disabilities; (b) are likely employed in positions with no real career path and few, if any, benefits; (c) are underemployed; and (d) when employed, occupy low-paying positions (Lustig & Strauser, 2007). In addition, people with disabilities, especially women with disabilities who are unemployed, are more likely to experience significant stress in obtaining appropriate housing and food.

A reciprocal relationship exists between disability and poverty, and this relationship is exacerbated by high rates of unemployment and underemployment for individuals with disabilities (Edgell, 2006; Lustig & Strauser, 2007). Globalization and the changing labor market have made it more difficult for individuals with disabilities to escape poverty (Szymanski & Parker, 2010). As a result, many individuals with disabilities are unable to meet their most basic human needs independently, often creating a state of dependence with no real promise for achieving higher states of vocational or career functioning.

The human need for the acquisition of psychological, economic, and social power is closely tied to meeting basic needs (Blustein, 2006). For individuals with disabilities, working should provide material and social resources that increase an individual's agency within society. In essence, work should give an individual purpose and relevance within the broader contextual environment. Individuals who are working assume an increased social role that ultimately increases their ability to derive psychological, social, and economic power (Wolfensberger, 2002). However, structural and cultural barriers limit the access of individuals with disabilities to high-status employment, which restricts them to low-status occupational and social roles and, ultimately, contributes to a state of disempowerment (Szymanski & Parker, 2010). Occupying these disempowered and low-status roles perpetuates dependence on others (individuals, institutions, and programs) and does not fulfill the individual's personal needs (Strauser, 2014).

Rehabilitation counselors need to be aware that the individuals with whom they work have an inherent need for survival and power and that work is critical to meeting these individual needs. Vocational and career counseling should be directed toward increasing career and employment opportunities to maximize individuals' abilities to sustain themselves and increase their power by obtaining positions that have increased social value. Table 15.1 provides a list of potential outcomes that can measure an individual's ability to meet the needs for survival and power.

### Basic Need for Social Connection

Individuals are social beings who have a strong need to be connected with broader society and to develop meaningful interpersonal relationships (Blustein, 2006; Bowlby, 1982). Participation in work-related activities provides an opportunity for individuals with disabilities to connect with other individuals and the social and cultural environments of those individuals (Blustein, 2008). Ideally, work facilitates individual opportunities to develop positive relationships that

**TABLE 15.1  Needs, Constructs, and Specific Outcome Domains Related to Rehabilitation Counseling Outcomes**

| NEED | OUTCOME CONSTRUCTS | SPECIFIC OUTCOME DOMAINS |
|---|---|---|
| Survival and power | Compensation | Salary<br>Benefits<br>Pay incentives<br>Indirect compensation |
| | Employee development | Internal development<br>External development |
| | Perceived occupational status | Low-status positions<br>High-status positions |
| Social connection | General integration | Conformity<br>Acceptance<br>Orientation |
| | Social support | Close interpersonal relationships<br>Diffuse relationships |
| | Leisure | Leisure activities<br>Recreational activities |
| | Independent living | Individual's living situation |
| Self-determination and well-being | Well-being | Quality of life<br>Satisfaction with life<br>Physical health status<br>Psychological health status |
| | Self-determination | Autonomy<br>Relatedness<br>Capacity<br>Values and goals |

supply the support needed to manage work-related stress and foster identity development (Blustein, 1994; Schein, 1990). In contrast, individuals who experience negative work environments, where they feel isolated, disconnected, and under stress, will potentially experience a decrease in job performance and work adjustment, which will most likely contribute to decreased well-being (Tansey et al., 2004). Finally, working provides a mechanism for individuals with disabilities to develop a sense of connection with their broader social world through contributing to the larger economic structure of society (Blustein, 2006). Earning a paycheck and contributing to society's well-being by paying fair and reasonable taxes is a valued social role (Strauser, 2014).

Rehabilitation counselors, while focused on assisting individuals with disabilities to obtain employment, should also consider how employment can increase individuals' levels of social integration. Many times in rehabilitation counseling, the focus of work and socialization are directed at enhancing the person's socialization on the job and with coworkers. However, Blustein (2008) highlights that the social impact and benefits of work are not limited to the work environment but also include the broader community. As a result, rehabilitation counselors need to ensure that their efforts regarding socialization include not only the work environment but also how work can be leveraged to increase individuals' overall level of social integration in roles and communities that individuals desire to occupy and in which they wish to participate. Potential outcomes for measuring an individual's level of social connection are highlighted in Table 15.1.

### Basic Need for Self-Determination and Well-Being

Individuals are driven to search for environments that promote self-determination, self-expression, and well-being. Rehabilitation counselors fill a critical role in conceptualizing and facilitating work environments that promote physical and psychological well-being for people with disabilities and chronic health conditions. Placing people with disabilities in work environments that are safe, incorporate appropriate workplace accommodations, such as flexibility and remote site access, and the adaptation of environments and tasks to avoid exacerbation of symptoms, are examples of the types of effective services provided through vocational rehabilitation. Although all of these elements are necessary for well-being, they are not sufficient.

Ideally, individuals work in environments that provide them with opportunities to exercise self-determination and self-expression, while also promoting individual well-being by participating in work that is consistent with their skills and interests. However, very few individuals with disabilities have the opportunity to participate in work-related activities that correspond to their personal skills and interests, and they often pursue employment primarily for extrinsic reasons, such as income (Blustein, 2008). Research has suggested that it is possible to increase self-determination and well-being related to work by promoting *autonomy, relatedness*, and *competence* through work that is initially pursued for extrinsic reasons (Ryan & Deci, 2000). Blustein (2008) also suggested that when an individual's personal values and goals coincide with those of the work organization and when the work environment provides individuals with resources and supports that foster successful work experiences, the sense of well-being increases.

It is important to note that the promotion of autonomy, relatedness, and competence may not transform a job with low pay, high stress, and an overall poor work environment into a positive and rewarding work experience. Rather, for individuals with disabilities who are not employed in settings that are consistent with their interests and abilities, rehabilitation counselors can address these constructs of *autonomy*, *relatedness*, and *competence* to promote a better work experience. The provision of vocational counseling should include a careful analysis of how individuals with disabilities derive meaning from their work. Understanding how meaning is derived can provide rehabilitation counselors with the knowledge to enhance the employment conditions that frame the experience of most people with disabilities, who may need to accept employment options that have low pay, no benefits, and limited opportunities for advancement so that they can support themselves and their families (Blustein, 2008). Potential outcomes for measuring self-determination and well-being are highlighted in Table 15.1.

## INCOME FRAMEWORK

With work being central to the lives of individuals, providing effective counseling services that are directed at maximizing educational development and labor market participation is critically important. In providing career and vocational counseling services to individuals with disabilities, rehabilitation counselors employ many of the same counseling techniques found to be effective in facilitating growth and adjustment in other major life areas. Those specific techniques are covered in other chapters in this book and can be readily applied to career and vocational issues.

Unique to career and vocational counseling with people with disabilities, research has found that there are three factors that may limit or impede the career development process (Strauser, 2014). First, many individuals with disabilities experience significant limitations in early career exploration experiences. As a result, they tend to exhibit a reduced knowledge of how to apply their personal skills to meet educational and labor market demands. Second, individuals with disabilities have limited opportunities to develop effective career decision-making skills. Processing personal and contextual information related to education and work, in order to make an effective decision, takes practice and can create significant stress if the individual is unsure or lacks the self-efficacy related to making effective decisions. Due to a lack of experience in making decisions and increased stress, many individuals with disabilities do not necessarily make the best career choices. This in turn can create additional stress and further decrease self-efficacy. Finally, many individual with disabilities develop a negative self-concept stemming from experiencing negative societal attitudes, perceived inability to work, and an overall lack of expectations (Conte, 1983; Curnow, 1989). To address the needs of individuals with disabilities as they seek employment, rehabilitation counselors should implement a framework to guide vocational rehabilitation services to individuals with disabilities (Beveridge, Heller Craddock, Liesener, Stapleton, & Hershenson, 2002).

The INCOME framework is an inclusive framework that can assist rehabilitation counselors in tracking and facilitating the career development and vocational behavior of persons with disabilities (Beveridge et al., 2002). The INCOME framework consists of six statuses through which individuals with disabilities can move: Imagining, iNforming, Choosing, Obtaining, Maintaining, and Exiting (Beveridge et al., 2002). The construction of the INCOME framework was based on career development theories that sought to be applicable to persons with disabilities (Danley & Anthony, 1987; Dawis & Lofquist, 1984; Hershenson, 1996a, 1996b; Super, 1957, 1990), along with other theories that are intended to be applicable to diverse groups (Bandura, 1986, 1997; Hackett & Betz, 1995; Lent, Brown, & Hackett, 2002; Maslow, 1987; Mitchell & Krumboltz, 1996).

Several important factors should be considered when examining the INCOME framework. First, the INCOME framework uses the concept of career statuses as opposed to stages to address the heterogeneity of individuals with disabilities. Statuses are flexible, allowing the individual to occupy more than one status at a time. Further, statuses are not bounded by order or sequential progression, and statuses allow individuals the freedom to skip and revisit as needed (Helms, 1995), thus eliminating the sequential progression, hierarchic integration, and stage-resolution sequencing that limit application to the unique needs and development of individuals with disabilities (Beveridge et al., 2002; Kohlberg, 1968). Second, in each of the six statuses, one must consider the interaction of three factors: the individual, the environment, and the general culture and subcultures within which the other two factors are located (Vondracek, Lerner, & Schulenberg, 1986). Finally, the application of the INCOME framework recognizes that the age of onset and the progressive nature of certain disabilities are factors that impact career development and vocational behavior and, within each status, three distinct subgroups of individuals with disabilities are recognized as having their own unique needs: precareer-onset disabilities, mid career-onset disabilities, and episodic disabilities.

## THE SIX STATUSES OF THE INCOME FRAMEWORK

### Imagining

In the imagining status, the individual develops an awareness that work, job, or careers exist; or that occupations or jobs exist of which he or she was were not previously aware. The imagining status has the following three substatuses: (a) awareness (realizing that there is such a thing as work and that there are occupations that have direct significance to oneself), (b) fantasy (playing doctor or police officer as a child or having adult fantasies or daydreams about being in a different occupation or job), and (c) reality-based imagining (restraining one's imagination to occupations or jobs that are believed to be possible, given one's capacities, resources, and opportunity structure). In early childhood, children become aware and begin to learn about the world of work from their families. As they get older, media, school, and people in their immediate environment continue to form their awareness of work. Children learn through observation that people engage in certain activities to make money, buy things, and define themselves. Through social learning, children observe the reactions of people in their environment, and based on these observations, they develop their own attitudes about work and careers. Imagining continues into adulthood and can be present at any point in one's career. Fantasies and daydreams, in addition to creating awareness of options that was not previously present, can occur with adolescents and adults. Those engaged in imagining as children and adults derive meaning and consider their values regarding their conceptualization of work and careers.

## iNforming

In the iNforming status, the individual obtains information about himself or herself, the world of work, opportunities that exist within the environment, and his or her cultural context. This status includes (a) the individual developing work competencies (work habits, interpersonal skills); (b) acquiring information about himself or herself and the world of work (provided by feedback received from the environment); and (c) developing an awareness of cultural supports and barriers that exist in the environment. From the feedback one receives (e.g., from parents, peers, and school), individuals form beliefs about their abilities, existing opportunities, and cultural supports and barriers, which influence career-related self-efficacy and outcome expectations. Therefore, career self-efficacy is determined by the complex interactions of individual, environmental, and cultural characteristics. If the individuals believe that they are not good at math, then they will not pursue careers in engineering, even if this career matches their interests and values. Thus, the environmental feedback one receives will exert a strong influence on one's career path.

## Choosing

Choosing is the status in which individuals integrate information about themselves and the world of work and choose occupations, jobs, or educational programs from those they know at the time the choice is made. Basically, the individual is integrating the information from the previous statuses (imagining and iNforming) and selects from among known occupations. Occupational choice has multiple factors that interact during this status that mark (affect) the final decision or the direction of career development. Individuals, when choosing an occupation, analyze the fit between the environment and their personality types, personal needs, and values in relation to the perceived benefits of the job, their decision-making style, and chance. That is, their occupational choice is predicted by the information possessed by the individual and the interaction among these factors.

The information obtained by the individual during the previous statuses influences this choice. The information that the individual has developed regarding himself or herself and the world of work is filtered by the career self-efficacy and outcome expectations, thus influencing the individual's choice. Motivation for choosing is greatly impacted by the extent to which the individual's basic needs (food and shelter) are met. If these needs are not adequately met, an individual will not be motivated to satisfy other needs or to make occupational choices. It should be noted that although the choosing status normally takes a logical decision-making approach, not all individuals make decisions in this way. Therefore, rehabilitation counselors must be aware that family can be a critical factor for some individuals in choosing, whereas others may rely on chance, intuition, or impulse to guide their decision making.

## Obtaining

The career choice made in the choosing status remains merely a decision until the person obtains a job. In this status, ideally, individuals seek and obtain jobs of their choice. The obtaining status can include job finding, networking, résumé preparation, job-interviewing skills training, and all things that make up preparing for and implementing a job search. The broader environment is a major factor in the outcome in this status. The economy has a major impact on the availability of jobs. In addition, this status is influenced by the person's family, culture, and society. A person's involvement in the job market can be influenced greatly by the individual's family situation as it relates to employment; cultural attitudes that may clash with work attitudes and behaviors; and societal attitudes, such as prejudice against people with disabilities.

## Maintaining

This status involves the process of adapting to, performing in, and sustaining a career (position or job). In this status, the work environment and the cultural context can either enhance or block successful outcomes. The individual's ability to maintain a job and perform the job successfully is dependent on the correspondence between the individual and the work environment. The reality is that work environments may require unanticipated adaptations and, in order to keep a job, the individual must adjust to the work demands, and the work environment must adjust to the individual. The individual must develop a plan and take into account issues, such as transportation, time management, and medication management, as well as the management of day-to-day challenges likely to create stress for the individual.

## Exiting

The sixth and final component of the INCOME framework involves the process of thinking about leaving or actually leaving one's current vocational situation. Exiting is not the final step in the INCOME model. An individual may be in the exiting status several times over the course of a career. Every time exiting or the desire to exit occurs, the individual may need to revisit previous statuses. Exiting encompasses not only getting terminated or retiring, but also being promoted to a different position or departing voluntarily from a current position in order to enter a new work setting or even a nonwork experience. Factors that might result in an involuntary exiting status can include poor job performance, employer downsizing, or even disability or medically related issues. Voluntarily exiting a position could be due to factors such as a lack of job satisfaction, lack of opportunities for advancement, or lack of important supportive conditions in the workplace. These factors are dynamic and change throughout the individual's career and are influenced by environmental, psychological, social, and economic forces.

Individuals ought to be taught ways to negotiate these statuses so that they can engage in the process independently and successfully without having to reenter the counseling process. Through advocacy, the counselor assists the individual in achieving goals through participating in the individual's environments. The counseling session provides a natural forum for integrating advocacy into practice and training, thus leading to empowerment. As a result of this empowerment, the individual is able to cope with problems and concerns, resulting in a sense of self-efficacy, thus equipping the individual to handle similar problems in the future. A general overview of each status is presented in Table 15.2.

## INTERVENTIONS

There is a variety of career and vocational counseling interventions that rehabilitation counselors can use when working with individuals with disabilities. Incorporating techniques, such as motivational interviewing and the building of the working alliance, individuals may be encouraged to continue to participate in career and vocational services with their counselors. In selecting appropriate career interventions while counseling individuals with disabilities, it is important to acknowledge the following circumstances surrounding disability: (a) No two individuals react to the same types and degrees of functional impairment in the same way, as each brings his or her own personality characteristics, life experiences, and resources (Brodwin, Parker, & DeLaGarza, 1996); (b) it is necessary to select interventions that are developmentally appropriate and in alignment with the individual's cognitive ability and current emotional readiness; and (c) age of disability onset is an important factor that impacts individual career development. Additionally, the following considerations regarding type and intensity of career interventions for persons with disabilities at the individual level should be considered: (a) Selected approaches should always remain consistent with the applicable code of ethics; (b) counseling should help the individual to develop skills for coping with anticipated or future changes in the current place of employment or changes in the overall labor market; and (c) interventions should not disrupt the current work environments of the individual (Enright, Conyers, & Szymanski, 1996).

### Individual and Group Career Counseling

Individual career counseling is a largely verbal process in which the counselor and client are engaged in a dynamic interaction, and the counselor employs a repertoire of diverse behaviors to help bring about self-understanding and action in the form of "good" decision making on the part of the individual, who has responsibility for his or her own actions (Herr & Cramer, 1996). Recent research

**TABLE 15.2 The INCOME Framework**

| STATUS | DEFINITIONS | CONTENT | ADDITIONAL CONSIDERATIONS |
|---|---|---|---|
| Imagining | Developing awareness that careers exist or that occupations one is not aware of exist | Consists of three substatuses: awareness, fantasy, and reality-based imagining | Those who occupy this status derive meaning and consider their values regarding their conceptualization of work and careers |
| iNforming | One obtains information about the self, the world of work, opportunities that exist within the environment, and one's cultural context | Developing work habits; gaining information about oneself and the world of work based on feedback; and developing an awareness of cultural supports and barriers that exist in the environment | The environmental feedback one receives will serve as a strong indicator of one's career path |
| Choosing | One integrates the information from the previous statuses and selects from among the known occupations | Analyzing the fit between the environment and personality type, the fit between job benefits and personal needs and values, decision-making style, and chance | Motivation can be impacted by lack of basic necessities (food and shelter) and decision making impacted by family, chance, intuition, or impulse |
| Obtaining | One seeks and obtains a job ideally of his or her choice | All things that make up preparing for and implementing a job search (job finding, résumé preparation, etc.) | The career choice made in the choosing status remains a decision until the person obtains a job |
| Maintaining | Involves the process of adapting to, performing in, and sustaining a career (position, job) | Maintenance and performance are dependent on the correspondence between the individual and the work environment | The individual must adjust to the work demands as well as the work environment must adjust to the individual |
| Exiting | Involves the process of thinking about leaving or actually leaving one's current vocational situation | Getting fired, retiring, being promoted to a different position, or departing voluntarily to enter a new work setting or even nonwork experience | In this status, several times over the course of the career and every time exiting or the desire to exit occurs, the individual may need to revisit previous statuses |

regarding the vocational behavior of individuals receiving vocational rehabilitation services has indicated that the core elements of the working alliance are especially powerful facilitators of change when providing individual career counseling services (Strauser, Lustig, & Donnell, 2004). The working alliance is a transtheoretical process that consists of the following three elements: (a) bonds, (b) goals, and (c) tasks (Strauser et al., 2004). Individuals who reported a stronger working alliance with their vocational rehabilitation counselors reported more satisfaction with their rehabilitation services and improved vocational outcomes (Lustig et al., 2003). Research has also suggested that individuals receiving vocational services report that they would have liked to receive more vocational counseling and that they desired a strong working relationship with their rehabilitation counselors (Lustig et al., 2003). Group counseling is beneficial when facilitating career exploration, using visual imagery, developing locally relevant occupational information, teaching career decision making, and teaching job-interviewing skills (Pope, 1999).

## Jobsite Accommodation

The Americans with Disabilities Act of 1990 and its subsequent amendments mandate that employers must make reasonable accommodations to the known physical and mental limitations of a qualified applicant or employee with disability. Rehabilitation counselors involved in the accommodation process can work with other rehabilitation professionals to determine the types of workplace accommodations that may be needed to facilitate competitive employment. According to the INCOME framework, a client in the maintaining status may benefit from jobsite accommodation in order to adjust to work demands and the work environment and maintain the job.

## Job Development and Placement

Job development and placement interventions help clients with disabilities connect with the jobs that are consistent with their knowledge, skills, abilities, interests, and needs. Rehabilitation counselors can assist with revising a résumé, preparing the individual for a job interview, finding job leads, assisting with the submission of a job application, setting up and attending interviews, and providing the assistance and support needed to help the individual attain the desired employment outcome. In accordance with the INCOME framework, a client in the choosing and obtaining statuses may benefit from job development and placement services.

## Supported Employment

According to the Rehabilitation Act Amendments of 1998, supported employment is a program to assist people with the most significant disabilities to become, and remain, successfully and competitively employed in integrated workplace settings. Supported employment is targeted at individuals with the most significant disabilities, for whom competitive employment traditionally has not occurred or for whom competitive employment has been interrupted or intermittent because of a disability. Supported employment usually provides assistance, such as job coaches, transportation, assistive technology, specialized job training, and individually tailored supervision.

Typically, supported employment is a way to move people from dependence on a traditional service delivery system to independence via competitive employment (Wehman, 1996). There are several features of supported employment programs that differ from traditional job placement services. First, supported employment programs seek to identify jobs that provide wages above the minimum wage, with fringe benefits and with career trajectories. Second, supported employment programs focus on providing ongoing support required to get and keep a job rather than on getting a person job-ready for future employment. Third, supported employment programs emphasize creating opportunities to work rather than simply providing services to develop job skills for people with disabilities. Fourth, supported employment programs encourage full participation. Thus, all people, regardless of the degree of their disability, have the capacity to undertake supported employment, if appropriate support services can be provided. Fifth, supported employment programs promote social integration in which people with disabilities are encouraged to interact with coworkers, supervisors, and others at work, during lunchtimes or breaks, and during nonwork hours. Finally, supported employment programs promote flexibility in which people with disabilities are provided with various work options consistent with the wide range of job opportunities available in the community.

### Vocational Evaluation

Vocational evaluation is a comprehensive and systematic process in which rehabilitation counselors and clients work together to assess and identify client vocational interests, abilities, aptitudes, work values, functional limitations, and barriers to employment. The main function of vocational evaluation services provided by rehabilitation counselors is to identify the client's relative strengths and weaknesses relative to the rehabilitation goal and employment outcome. According to the INCOME framework, clients in the iNforming status may benefit from a vocational evaluation, in which clients acquire information about themselves, the world of work, and potential supports and barriers.

### Situational Assessment

Situational assessment is a valuable tool for rehabilitation counselors when assisting clients in making choices about the types of jobs and work environments that would be of interest. A situational assessment is an assessment that is commonly conducted in actual employment and community settings, for people with disabilities to explore their interests, assess current skill level, and provide training (Fraser & Johnson, 2010). Situational assessment allows for information to be generated quickly concerning employment options that are worth pursuing further and avoiding client time and effort wasted on inappropriate job searches. In addition, many situational assessments can provide a transition to actual paid employment. Situational assessments can also assist rehabilitation counselors and individuals with disabilities in determining potential accommodations that will be necessary for successful competitive employment. The client in the choosing and obtaining statuses may benefit from situational assessments. Rehabilitation counselors can assist clients in the choosing status make career choices by understanding the fit between the individual and the work environment. Rehabilitation counselors working together with the client in the obtaining status can identify barriers to obtaining employment.

## Benefits Counseling

Obtaining and maintaining competitive employment may have a significant impact on the benefits that individuals with disabilities receive. The provision of benefits counseling focuses on reviewing with the individual and rehabilitation counselor the effects of employment on exiting benefits, if this is a concern for the individual with a disability. The goal of benefits counseling is to develop a plan for achieving self-sufficiency or a work-related expense plan so that the individual can maximize workplace participation while retaining important benefits (Fraser & Johnson, 2010).

## Assistive Technology

Assistive technology is a class of interventions in which people with disabilities use technology to facilitate the performance of functional tasks (Kirsch & Scherer, 2010). Assistive technology includes not only mobility devices, such as walkers and wheelchairs, but also computerized devices, software, and peripherals that assist people with disabilities in assessing computers or other information technologies. Various service delivery models regarding the application of assistive technology for people with disabilities have been developed in state vocational rehabilitation agencies. Some of these services are provided by a vendor who is a rehabilitation counselor, who has special responsibility to provide assistive technology services or, perhaps, a health care provider specializing in assistive technology, such as an occupational therapist. Evidence has shown that assistive technology can also be used to enhance employment opportunities for people with disabilities (Noll, Owens, Smith, & Schwanke, 2006). Thus, it is important that rehabilitation counselors be knowledgeable and competent in assistive technology services. Rehabilitation counselors should identify the need for assistive technology services or devices for people with disabilities, provide information regarding assistive technology to them, and coordinate assistive technology services.

## CONCLUSIONS

Providing career and vocational counseling services to individuals with disabilities is a complex and dynamic process that is developmental in nature, involves the person interacting with the environment, and is moderated by social cognitive factors. This chapter provided an overview of important information related to understanding career and vocational behavior, a framework for conceptualizing counseling interventions, and an overview of commonly used career counseling techniques in rehabilitation settings. In discussing the centrality of work and the ways in which work is critical in meeting human needs, rehabilitation counselors gain an understanding that work plays an important role in the individual's mental health and social integration. The INCOME framework was introduced as a method for conceptualizing and strategizing the provision of rehabilitation services. Finally, various interventions were described that can be used by rehabilitation counselors in facilitating positive employment outcomes.

Overall, there is still significant need to conduct research in an effort to gain a better understanding of the individual and contextual factors that impact the career development and employment of individuals with disabilities. An area of critical need is studies that evaluate the impact of career counseling and vocational interventions for individuals with a range of disabilities, not just severe psychiatric or developmental disabilities. To date, most of the research in this area has focused on supported employment and related interventions. Although these types of interventions appear to be very robust for those with severe disabilities, little, if any, research has been done to examine the development and efficacy of interventions directed at those without severe disabilities. Expanding this research focus would seem to be a high priority over the next 10 to 15 years.

## DISCUSSION EXERCISES

1. The chapter provides an overview of the concept of work being central to the human experience and describes both the potential positive and negative psychosocial outcomes associated with work. In thinking of the potential benefits and concerns related to work, what are psychosocial implications of unemployment for individuals with disabilities?

2. In thinking of the basic human need of social connection described in the chapter, the focus of vocational and career counseling may need to include working with individuals with disabilities on how to disclose their disabilities to employers and coworkers. What are the potential risks and benefits associated with disclosure with regard to promoting social connectivity?

3. In considering the imagining status of the INCOME framework, what effect, if any, would the onset of a disability later in life have on the awareness, fantasy, and reality-based imagining of an individual? What effect, if any, might a congenital disability or a disability acquired early in life have on the individual?

4. Maintaining is the focus on adapting to changes in the work environment. However, disabilities that are chronic and/or progressive in nature also require individuals to adapt to variations in their functional abilities. What supports or interventions, either short or long term, might be useful in assisting individuals with chronic and/or progressive disabilities to maintain employment?

## REFERENCES

Baron, R. A., & Greenberg, J. (1990). *Behavior in organizations: Understanding and managing the human side of work.* Boston, MA: Allyn & Bacon.

Beveridge, S., Heller Craddock, S., Liesener, J., Stapleton, M., & Hershenson, D. (2002). INCOME: A framework for conceptualizing the career development of persons with disabilities. *Rehabilitation Counseling Bulletin, 45,* 195–206.

Blustein, D. L. (1994). "Who am I?": The question of self and identity in career development. In M. L. Savickas & R. W. Lent (Eds.), *Convergence in career development theories: Implications for science and practice* (pp. 139–154). Palo Alto, CA: Consulting Psychologists Press.

Blustein, D. L. (2006). *The psychology of working: A new perspective for career development, counseling, and public policy.* Mahwah, NJ: Erlbaum.

Blustein, D. L. (2008). The role of work in psychological health and well-being. *American Psychologist, 63,* 228–240.

Blustein, D. L., Kenna, A. C., Gill, N., & DeVoy, J. E. (2008). The psychology of working: A new framework for counseling practice and public policy. *Career Development Quarterly, 56,* 294–308.

Bond, G. R., Resnick, S. G., Drake, R. E., Xie, H., McHugo, G. J., & Bebout, R. R. (2001). Does competitive employment improve nonvocational outcomes for people with severe mental illness? *Journal of Consulting and Clinical Psychology, 69,* 489–501.

Bowlby, J. (1982). Attachment and loss: Retrospect and prospect. *American Journal of Orthopsychiatry, 52,* 664–678.

Brodwin, M., Parker, R. M., & DeLaGarza, D. (1996). Disability and accommodation. In E. M. Szymanski & R. M. Parker (Eds.), *Work and disability: Issues and strategies in career development and job placement* (pp. 165–208). Austin, TX: Pro-Ed.

Conte, L. E. (1983). Vocational development theories and disabled persons. *Rehabilitation Counseling Bulletin, 26,* 316–328.

Curnow, T. C. (1989). Vocational development of persons with disabilities. *Career Development Quarterly, 37,* 269–278.

Danley, K. S., & Anthony, W. A. (1987). The choose-get-keep model: Serving severely psychiatrically disabled people. *American Rehabilitation, 13*(4), 6–9, 27–29.

Dawis, R. V., & Lofquist, L. H. (1984). *A psychological theory of work adjustment: An individual differences model and its application.* Minneapolis, MN: University of Minnesota.

Edgell, P. (2006). *Religion and family in a changing society.* Princeton, NJ: Princeton University Press.

Enright, M., Conyers, L. M., & Szymanski, E. (1996). Career and career related educational conerns of college students with disabilities. *Journal of Counseling and Development, 75,* 103–114.

Fraser, R. T., & Johnson, K. (2010). Vocational rehabilitation. In R. G. Frank, M. Rosenthal, & B. Caplan (Eds.), *Handbook of rehabilitation psychology* (pp. 357–363). Washington, DC: American Psychological Association.

Gottfredson, L. (2002). Gottfredson's theory of circumscription, compromise, and self-creation. In D. Brown & Associates (Eds.), *Career choice and development* (pp. 85–148). San Francisco, CA: Jossey-Bass.

Hackett, G., & Betz, N. E. (1995). Self-efficacy and career choice. In J. Maddux (Ed.), *Self-efficacy, adaptation, and adjustment: Theory, research, and application* (pp. 249–280). New York, NY: Plenum.

Helms, J. E. (1995). An update of Helms's white and people of color racial identity models. In J. G. Ponterotto, J. M. Casas, L. A. Suzuki, & C. M. Alexander (Eds.), *Handbook of multicultural counseling* (pp. 181–198). Thousand Oaks, CA: Sage.

Herr, E. L., & Cramer, S. H. (1996). *Career guidance and counseling through the life span: Systematic approaches* (5th ed.). New York, NY: HarperCollins.

Hershenson, D. B. (1981). Work adjustment, disability, and the three R's of vocational rehabilitation: A conceptual model. *Rehabilitation Counseling Bulletin, 25,* 91–97.

Hershenson, D. B. (1996a). A systems reformulation of a developmental model of work adjustment. *Rehabilitation Counseling Bulletin, 40,* 2–10.

Hershenson, D. B. (1996b). Work adjustment: A neglected area in career development. *Journal of Counseling and Development, 74,* 442–446.

Holland, J. L. (1985). *The self-directed search professional manual*. Odessa, FL: Psychological Assessment Resources.

Kahn, R. L., & Byosiere, P. (1990). Stress in organizations. In M. Dunnette (Ed.), *Handbook of industrial and organizational psychology* (2nd ed., Vol. 3, pp. 571–650). Chicago, IL: Rand McNally.

Kirsch, N. L., & Scherer, M. J. (2010). Assistive technology for cognition and behavior. In R. G. Frank, M. Rosenthal, & B. Caplan (Eds.), *Handbook of rehabilitation psychology* (pp. 273–284). Washington, DC: American Psychological Association.

Kohlberg, L. (1968). Early education: A cognitive-development approach. *Child Development, 39*, 1013–1062.

Larson, J. E., Barr, L. K., Corrigan, P. W., Kuwabara, S. A., Boyle, M. G., & Glenn, T. L. (2007). Perspectives on benefits and costs of work from individuals with psychiatric disabilities. *Journal of Vocational Rehabilitation, 26*, 71–77.

Lent, R. W., Brown, S. D., & Hackett, G. (2002). Social cognitive career theory. In D. Brown & Associates (Eds.), *Career choice and development* (4th ed., pp. 255–311). San Francisco, CA: Jossey-Bass.

Lustig, D. C., & Strauser, D. R. (2007). Causal relationships between poverty and disability. *Rehabilitation Counseling Bulletin, 50*, 194–202.

Lustig, D. C., Strauser, D. R., Weems, G. H., Donnell, C., & Smith, L. D. (2003). Traumatic brain injury and rehabilitation outcomes: Does working alliance make a difference? *Journal of Applied Rehabilitation Counseling, 34*(4), 30–37.

Maslow, A. H. (1987). *Motivation and personality* (3rd ed.). New York, NY: Harper & Row.

Maytal, G., & Peteet, J. (2009). The meaning of work. In M. Feuerstein (Ed.), *Work and cancer survivors* (pp. 105–119). New York, NY: Springer Publishing Company.

Mitchell, L. K., & Krumboltz, J. D. (1996). Learning theory of career choice and counseling. In D. Brown, L. Brooks, & Associates (Eds.), *Career choice and development* (pp. 233–276). San Francisco, CA: Jossey-Bass.

Neff, W. S. (1985). *Work and human behavior*. New York, NY: Aldine.

Noll, A., Owens, L., Smith, R. O., & Schwanke, T. (2006). Survey of state vocational rehabilitation counselor roles and competencies in assistive technology. *Work: A Journal of Prevention, Assessment and Rehabilitation, 27*, 413–419.

O'Sullivan, D., & Strauser, D. (2010). Validation of the developmental work personality model and scale. *Rehabilitation Counseling Bulletin, 54*, 46–56.

Patterson, J. B., Szymanski, E. M., & Parker, R. M. (2005). Rehabilitation counseling: The profession. In R. M. Parker, E. M. Szymanski, & J. B. Patterson (Eds.), *Rehabilitation counseling: Basics and beyond* (pp. 1–25). Austin, TX: Pro-Ed.

Pope, M. (1999). Applications of group career counseling techniques in Asian cultures. *Journal of Multicultural Counseling and Development, 27*, 18–31.

Quick, J. C., Quick, J. D., Nelsom, D. L., & Hurrell, J. J., Jr. (1997). *Preventative stress management in organizations*. Washington, DC: American Psychological Association.

Ryan, R. M., & Deci, E. L. (2000). Self-determination theory and the facilitation of intrinsic motivation, social development, and well-being. *American Psychologist, 55*, 68–78.

Schein, E. (1990). Organizational culture. *American Psychologist, 45*, 109–119.

Strauser, D. R. (2014). Introduction to the centrality of work for individuals with disabilities. In D. Strauser (Ed.), *Career development, employment, and disability in rehabilitation* (pp. 1–10). New York, NY: Springer Publishing Company.

Strauser, D. R., Lustig, D. C., & Donnell, C. (2004). The impact of the working alliance on therapeutic outcomes for individuals with mental retardation. *Rehabilitation Counseling Bulletin, 47*, 215–223.

Strauser, D. R., O'Sullivan, D., & Wong, A. W. K. (2010). The relationship between contextual work behaviors self-efficacy and work personality: An exploratory analysis. *Disability and Rehabilitation, 32*, 1999–2008.

Super, D. E. (1957). *The psychology of careers.* New York, NY: Harper & Row.

Super, D. E. (1969). The development of vocational potential. In D. Malikin & H. Rusalem (Eds.), *Vocational rehabilitation of the disabled: An overview* (pp. 75–90). New York, NY: New York University Press.

Super, D. E. (1990). A life-span, life-space approach to career development. In D. Brown, L. Brooks, & Associates (Eds.), *Career choice and development* (2nd ed., pp. 197–261). San Francisco, CA: Jossey-Bass.

Szymanski, E. M., & Hershenson, D. B. (2005). An ecological approach to vocational behavior and career development of people with disabilities. In R. M. Parker, E. M. Szymanski, & J. B. Patterson (Eds.), *Rehabilitation counseling: Basics and beyond* (pp. 225–280). Austin, TX: Pro-Ed.

Szymanski, E. M., & Parker, R. M. (2010). Work and disability: Basic concepts. In E. M. Szymanski & R. M. Parker (Eds.), *Work and disability: Contexts, issues, and strategies for enhancing employment outcomes for people wtih disabilities* (pp. 1–15). Austin, TX: Pro-Ed.

Tansey, T. N., Mizelle, N., Ferrin, J. M., Tschopp, M. K., & Frain, M. (2004). Work-related stress in persons with disabilities: Applying the demand/control model. *Journal of Rehabilitation, 70*(3), 34–41.

Vondracek, E. W., Lerner, R. M., & Schulenberg, J. E. (1986). *Career development: A life-span developmental approach.* Hillsdale, NJ: Erlbaum.

Wehman, P. (1996). Supported employment: Inclusion for all in the workplace. In W. Stainback & S. Stainback (Eds.), *Controversial issues confronting special education: Divergent perspectives* (pp. 293–304). Boston, MA: Allyn & Bacon.

Wilson, W. J. (1996). *When work disappears. The world of the new urban poor.* New York, NY: Alfred A. Knopf.

Wolfensberger, W. (2002). Social role valorization and, or versus, "empowerment." *Mental Retardation, 40*(3), 252–258.

Wright, G. N. (1980). *Total rehabilitation.* Boston, MA: Little, Brown.

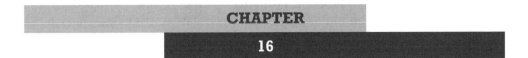

# CHAPTER 16

# Substance Use Disorders, Disability, and Counseling Interventions

*Elizabeth da Silva Cardoso, Arnold Wolf, Susan Miller Smedema, Jessica Brooks, and Michele Mahr*

## LEARNING OBJECTIVES

The goals of this chapter are to define the primary concepts related to substance use disorders; to explain the major models of substance use disorders, as well as related intervention strategies; to review empirical evidence for treatment modalities for various substance use disorders; to outline the primary methods for assessment of substance use disorders and readiness for change; to describe types of substance abuse treatment programs; and to discuss issues related to substance use disorders and disability. After reading the chapter, the reader should be able to:

1. Describe the *Diagnostic and Statistical Manual of Mental Disorders* (5th ed., *DSM-5;* American Psychiatric Association, 2013) criteria for substance use disorders.
2. Distinguish among the major models of substance use disorders.
3. Describe a variety of intervention strategies related to each substance abuse model.
4. Choose appropriate techniques to assess clients with substance use disorders.
5. Demonstrate awareness of issues related to co-occurring substance use disorders and disability.

## SUBSTANCE USE DISORDERS AND DISABILITY

Persons with disabilities are at a much higher risk for substance use disorders than their peers without disabilities. According to the Substance Abuse and Mental Health Services Administration (SAMHSA; 2002), rates of substance use disorders in persons with traumatic brain injuries (TBIs), spinal cord injuries (SCIs), and mental illness in the United States approach or exceed 50%, as compared to 10% for the general population. Individuals with other disabilities, such as deafness, arthritis, and multiple sclerosis, have a risk for substance use disorders that is at least double the rate of the general population. Disability characteristics, such as pain and other medical issues that may lead to misuse of prescription medication and/or self-medication with nonprescription substances, a lack of timely identification of potential problems, and a lack of accessible and appropriate prevention and treatment services are all potential contributing factors to this increased risk.

According to the 2011 National Surveys on Drug Use and Health Services, an estimated 20.6 million Americans, ages 12 and older, were classified as having either a substance abuse or substance dependence disorder based on the *Diagnostic and Statistical Manual of Mental Disorders* (4th ed., *DSM-IV*; American Psychiatric Association, 1994) criteria (SAMHSA, 2012). Nearly 4.7 million individuals have a co-occurring disability and substance abuse problem (SAMHSA, 2002). Substance abuse can lead to significant adverse life events, such as absence from work or school or conflicts at home (SAMHSA, 2002), as well as violence, injury, and death (Clarke & Myers, 2012; World Health Organization [WHO], 2008). Often, an individual's disability itself occurs as a result of an injury acquired while the person was abusing substances (Corrigan, 1995; Radnitz & Tirch, 1995). Substance abuse expenditures related to health care, crime, and work productivity cost the United States more than $428 billion annually, according to the National Institute on Drug Abuse (NIDA, 2012). Health care costs related to substance abuse alone reach approximately $41 billion each year.

The wide-reaching costs of substance use disorders, both in the general population and among people with coexisting disabilities, have significant negative effects on individuals and families. Unfortunately, research shows that most individuals with substance use disorders do not seek treatment (Cohen, Feinn, Arias, & Kranzler, 2007; McCabe, Cranford, & West, 2008). For example, Cohen and colleagues (2007) found that the primary reason individuals do not participate in alcohol abuse treatment was that they believed that they could handle the problem themselves. In addition, programmatic and structural barriers often prevent persons with disabilities from participating in treatment (Sales, 2000). As shown by the high prevalence rates and minimal participation in treatment, substance use disorders are a very difficult problem, with consequences for both the individual and society. This draws attention to the need for effective and accessible substance abuse interventions in rehabilitation settings.

## MAJOR CONCEPTS

Various interrelated terms are frequently used within the literature on substance use disorders. Terms such as *substance* and *drug* describe psychoactive chemicals that create euphoric effects by altering the thoughts, perceptions, emotions, or behavior of the user. The intrinsically rewarding properties of these drugs increase the likelihood of maintained use and the onset of substance use disorders.

Terms including *abuse, dependence,* and *addiction* are often used to describe maladaptive drug use that leads to negative life consequences. Individuals who have problems with use are described as using a drug in an excessive and inappropriate manner despite consequences, whereas individuals who are dependent on drugs tend to compulsively use more and more substances regardless of consequences to daily functioning (Cardoso, Wolf, & West, 2009). Individuals who are dependent on substances need to use increasing amounts over time in order to gain the same desired effects, as a result of drug *tolerance.* Tolerance may also result in a withdrawal syndrome when drug intake is reduced, and the level of drug in the user's system drops below the level to which the body has become accustomed. The effects of tolerance can vary across drugs, but all psychoactive drugs are capable of generating a strong psychological dependence that results in a chronic desire to use.

The revised chapter on substance use disorders in the *DSM-5* includes major changes to the grouping of disorders. Unlike the *DSM-IV*, the *DSM-5* does not separate substance abuse and substance dependence as two disorders. Instead, the *DSM-5* combines the *DSM-IV* categories of substance abuse and substance dependence into the category of substance use disorders. The *DSM-5* substance use disorder criteria are nearly identical to the *DSM-IV* substance abuse and dependence criteria, with the exception that the *DSM-IV* criterion of recurrent legal problems has been removed from *DSM-5*, and a new criterion, craving or a strong desire or urge to use a substance, has been added. The threshold for diagnosis in the *DSM-5* is set at two or more criteria, in contrast to a threshold of one or more criteria for a diagnosis of *DSM-IV* substance abuse and three or more for *DSM-IV* substance dependence. The severity of the *DSM-5* substance use disorders is measured on a continuum based on the number of criteria endorsed: two to three criteria indicate a mild disorder; four to five criteria, a moderate disorder; and six or more, a severe disorder. Each substance, other than caffeine, is labeled as a separate disorder (e.g., alcohol use disorder, stimulant use disorder) based on the same overarching diagnostic criteria.

## MODELS OF SUBSTANCE USE DISORDERS, RELATED COUNSELING INTERVENTIONS, AND RESEARCH SUPPORT

Many models have been developed to conceptualize substance use disorders and describe potential treatment options for individuals dealing with substance abuse. Rehabilitation professionals can use these models to identify counseling interventions that may be effective in treating their clients with substance use disorders. Similarly, significant research in the area of substance use disorders has attempted to identify the most efficacious treatment modalities for individuals with substance use disorders. The application of counseling techniques based on empirical evidence can improve client outcomes as well as efficiency in resource utilization.

When developing treatment plans for clients, rehabilitation professionals should keep in mind the 13 principles of effective substance abuse treatment, as identified by NIDA (2012, pp. 2–5):

1. Addiction is a complex but treatable disease that affects brain function and behavior.
2. No single treatment is appropriate for everyone.
3. Treatment needs to be readily available.
4. Effective treatment attends to multiple needs of the individual, not just his or her drug abuse.
5. Remaining in treatment for an adequate period of time is critical.
6. Behavioral therapies—including individual, family, or group counseling—are the most commonly used forms of drug abuse treatment.
7. Medications are an important element of treatment for many patients, especially when combined with counseling and other behavioral therapies.
8. An individual's treatment and services plan must be assessed continually and modified as necessary to ensure that it meets his or her changing needs.
9. Many drug-addicted individuals also have other mental disorders.
10. Medically assisted detoxification is only the first stage of addiction treatment and by itself does little to change long-term drug abuse.
11. Treatment does not need to be voluntary to be effective.
12. Drug use during treatment must be monitored continuously, as lapses during treatment do occur.
13. Treatment programs should test patients for the presence of HIV/AIDS, hepatitis B and C, tuberculosis, and other infectious diseases as well as provide targeted risk-reduction counseling, linking patients to treatment if necessary.

Pearson and colleagues (2012) recently published meta-analyses for 7 of the 13 treatment principles, as part of NIDA's Evidence-Based Principles of Treatment project. Using the results from randomized controlled trials, cohort studies, quasiexperimental studies, and previous meta-analyses, the authors found empirical support for five of the principles: matching treatment to the client's needs ($g = .24$), attending to the multiple needs of clients ($r = .16$), behavioral counseling interventions ($g = .11–.36$), treatment plan reassessment ($g = .25$), and counseling to reduce the risk of HIV ($g = .19$). Two of the principles, remaining in treatment for an adequate period ($r = .02–.14$) and frequency of testing for drug use ($r = .06$), were not supported. The authors suggested that the unsupported principles may be stated too generally, or that unmeasured moderator variables may be confounding the results. This evidence provides general support for the use of NIDA's principles of effective substance abuse treatment in the development of client treatment plans.

## Disease Model

Many traditional substance abuse treatment models are based on the disease model (Stevens & Smith, 2001), which describes drug addiction as an incurable, relapsing, and possibly fatal chronic brain disease (Johnson, 1980; Milam & Ketcham, 1981; Talbott, 1989). Research indicates addiction can produce long-lasting changes in brain structure and function that can lead to harmful and drug-seeking behaviors (NIDA, 2010). Disease model theorists use behavioral interventions that are centered on treating substance use problems using specific techniques and procedures (Chiauzzi, 1991). Although relapse can occur frequently, every substance abuse client is encouraged to completely abstain from using psychoactive substances (Marlatt & Gordon, 1985). According to this model, once an individual has confronted any denial of chronic problems and ceased substance use, he or she is labeled as being in recovery, but is never cured of the disease (Doweiko, 2002).

Current medical and biological research is exploring the relationship among genetics, proteins, and enzymes with the intent of finding body markers that lead to substance use disorders. The hope is to be able to counter their effects, thus preventing substance use disorders from developing in the first place. For example, Kathiramalainathan et al. (2000) found that certain metabolites significantly contribute to the increased liability of codeine abuse. Another study found that a relationship exists between neuropeptides and alcohol dependence (Lappalainen et al., 2002). Nestler (2001) argued that the current method of diagnosing substance abuse is subjective, whereas "genomics" or the identification of genes that increase risk for addiction, is far more objective. Once genes that contribute to rewards, such as feeling euphoric, are identified, biochemical treatments can then be developed to offset the genetic risk factor. Psychopharmacological approaches to treatment consist of medications that might be related to genetics or other biochemical body reactions. These medications, coupled with psychosocial treatment approaches, may be able to help individuals maintain abstinence more easily.

Three medications, in particular, work in conjunction with psychosocial interventions and counseling and may allow individuals to remain drug free for longer periods of time. A medication called disulfiram (brand name Antabuse) uses a fear–avoidance approach, since an individual who ingests disulfiram and then drinks alcohol will have a physical reaction to the combined chemicals, resulting in physical discomfort which, in turn, leads to avoidance of future alcohol ingestion (Jørgensen, Pedersen, & Tønnesen, 2011). Research on the efficacy of disulfiram has been mixed. For example, a recent meta-analysis conducted by Jørgensen et al. showed a nonsignificant effect of disulfiram on abstinence versus placebo over 12 months (odds ratio [OR] = 1.48). The same meta-analysis found that, compared with other or no treatment, disulfiram was more effective at promoting abstinence (OR = 1.59). Despite the mixed results, disulfiram can be used as part of a total treatment package, including support and counseling (Laaksonen, Koski-Jännes, Salaspuro, Ahtinen, & Alho, 2008)

Naltrexone is an opioid blocker that reduces levels of dopamine, the major reward neurotransmitter in the human brain and, thus, reduces alcohol intake, because there is far less "reward" for alcohol consumption (Gonzales & Weiss, 1998). Research indicates that naltrexone reduces the rate of relapse of heavy drinking and increases the number of days that the person remains abstinent by reducing alcohol cravings (Mann, Lehert & Morgan, 2004). This is further supported by a recent meta-analysis conducted by Del Re, Maisel, Blodgett, and Finney (2013), which found a statistically significant effect for naltrexone versus placebo for percentage of days abstinent ($g = .143$) and for relapse to heavy drinking ($g = .247$), providing support for the use of naltrexone in substance abuse treatment.

A third medication, acamprosate, reduces alcohol use by modulating brain functions related to withdrawal symptoms (Mann, Kiefer, Spanagel, & Littleton, 2008; Wright & Myrick, 2006). Acamprosate may be more effective for persons with an abstinence goal rather than preventing excessive drinking in nonabstinent patients (Mason, Goodman, Chabac, & Lehert, 2006; Rosner, Leucht, Lehert, & Soyka, 2008). A meta-analysis by Maisel, Blodgett, Wilbourne, Humphreys, and Finney (2013) found acamprosate to have a significantly larger effect size than naltrexone on the maintenance of abstinence ($g = .359$ vs. $g = .116$) and naltrexone to have a larger effect size than acamprosate on the reduction of heavy drinking and cravings ($g = .180$ vs. $g = .041$), results that can inform rehabilitation counselors as to the most appropriate way that each medication may be used.

It is outside the scope of this chapter to provide comprehensive information regarding psychopharmacological therapy in persons with substance use problems. The information on psychopharmacological agents provided in this section includes examples of medical treatment currently available to clients with substance use disorders, via a physician. It is important that rehabilitation professionals develop a generic understanding of such medications and defer to medical personnel concerning use, symptoms, side effects, and potential medical problems that may occur with use of any of the identified medications. In addition, it is imperative that rehabilitation professionals make sure that persons seeking treatment are under appropriate medical care at all times when using such medications. Rehabilitation professionals should also make recommendations on the type of supportive, nonmedical treatment approaches, such as relapse prevention (RP) or behavioral therapy, that can accompany medical treatment.

## Biopsychosocial Model

A more holistic approach to understanding substance use disorders is the biopsychosocial model (Donovan & Marlatt, 1988; Zucker & Gomberg, 1986). The biopsychosocial model describes numerous biological, psychological, and social factors that can interact and individually influence the development of addiction (Tarter, 1988). Biological factors may include genetic predispositions (physiological, psychological, or social vulnerabilities) to addictive disorders (Babor, 1993). Psychological factors refer to emotional states, positive or negative, that increase the likelihood of substance use disorders (Marlatt & Gordon, 1985); for instance, a substance user who is angry or sad may be inclined to take drugs in an attempt to improve mood and reduce stress. Social factors can be described as environmental milieus that expose a person to substance use; for example, individuals with close friends or family who routinely visit bar establishments may feel compelled to use alcohol. Risk for addiction may be compounded when individuals are from cultural backgrounds where substance abuse is the norm, reflecting the acquisition of both inherited traits and social pressures. Every individual is predisposed to several of the aforementioned risk factors, as well as protective factors related to addiction, and a person may develop an addiction if unable to manage risks, despite whatever protective factors may be present (Wesson, Havassy, & Smith, 1986).

A comprehensive assessment using the biopsychosocial framework can help to determine appropriate treatment choices. A biopsychosocial assessment can bring to light risk and protective factors related to addiction. Counselors often take a combination approach to treatment, focusing on psychopharmacological therapy, along with psychosocial treatments, many derived from cognitive behavioral therapy (CBT; see Chapter 5 in this volume), including cognitive remediation, skills building, and lifestyle modification. Cognitive remediation may include increasing knowledge and confidence, positive affirmations, distraction devices, and other cognitive coping techniques. Skills building can involve role-playing, self-observation, and relapse rehearsal, whereas lifestyle modification often incorporates physical activity, relaxation practices, and time management strategies into habitual routines. Therefore, counselors can implement a variety of biopsychosocial interventions that aim to modify and improve beliefs and coping behaviors related to substance abuse.

### Relapse Prevention Model

The RP (relapse prevention) model describes the process of relapse as a natural occurrence starting with immediate exposure to a high-risk situation, such as negative social contexts or emotional states (Brownell, Marlatt, Lichtenstein, & Wilson, 1986; Marlatt & Gordon, 1985). This model suggests that both immediate determinants and covert antecedents (e.g., cravings) can contribute to the likelihood of relapse. A primary goal of RP intervention strategies is to teach clients to see the "big picture" view of relapse (Larimer, Palmer, & Marlatt, 1999). This allows clients to determine and plan for potential obstacles and challenges related to the recovery process. This can also help individuals to start recognizing coping skills, which will increase their confidence to quit substances. Other CBT intervention strategies used may include enhancing self-efficacy, restructuring beliefs about relapse, balancing lifestyle factors, creating stimulus control techniques, and developing relapse road maps. Efficacy enhancement strategies involve facilitating a collaborative therapeutic alliance, realistic goal setting, skill acquisition, and performance feedback. Restructuring cognitions can assist clients with understanding that lapses are a part of the learning process of recovery, not a failure. Clients can find lifestyle balance by practicing relaxation, learning stress and time management, and finding healthy alternative activities. Stimulus control techniques encourage clients to remove items or materials (e.g., a corkscrew) that increase urges or impulses to abuse drugs. Finally, relapse road maps offer clients the opportunity to identify and consider various coping responses (and related consequences) to high-risk situations.

RP interventions have been found to be more effective than no treatment and at least equal to other substance abuse treatments in improving drug use outcomes (Witkiewitz & Marlatt, 2004). Irvin, Bowers, Dunn, and Wang (1999) conducted a meta-analysis, using 26 published and unpublished RP outcome studies, and found an overall small effect size ($r = .14$). However, RP was found to be most effective when applied to individuals experiencing problems with alcohol ($r = .37$) or multiple substances ($r = .27$) and when combined with prescription medication ($r = .48$). In addition, RP interventions were found to have a large effect on psychosocial adjustment in clients with substance use disorders ($r = .48$). Overall, the research demonstrates that RP is an effective counseling intervention for improving psychosocial adjustment as well as decreasing substance abuse, especially for individuals with alcohol abuse problems.

In addition, other CBT interventions that are common within the RP framework have been supported by research. Magill and Ray (2009) conducted a meta-analysis of 53 controlled trials of CBT in adults with alcohol and illicit drug use disorders. The results indicated a small but statistically significant treatment effect ($g = .154$). Studies that included follow-ups showed a somewhat diminished effect at 6 to 9 months ($g = .115$) and 12 months ($g = .96$). CBT had the largest effect size in studies on marijuana use ($g = .513$) as well as in studies with a control group ($g = .796$). These results indicate that CBT may be an effective treatment modality for individuals with substance use disorders, particularly marijuana use.

### Learned/Maladaptive Behavior Model

The learned/maladaptive behavior model for substance abuse treatment applies concepts from social learning theory (Bandura, 1977) to the understanding of substance use disorders. Social learning theorists suggest that an addiction may develop as a consequence of faulty learning. Substance abusers may come to believe that substance use is pleasurable and reduces tension, thereby reinforcing drug-seeking behavior (Conger, 1956). Additionally, different social contextual factors may be associated with substance use, which can provide a source of external stimuli; for example, substance abusers may find holiday parties to be a trigger when social drinking is expected. A learned/maladaptive behavioral model focuses on evaluating the perceived costs and benefits of substance use in order to counterbalance various reinforcers (Fingarette, 1991).

Treatment strategies also reinforce new behavioral skills in order to prevent relapse and unlearn maladaptive habits. Specific reinforcement techniques can be used to provide rewards or incentives conditional on a target response, such as a negative toxicology screen (Higgins, Heil, & Lussier, 2004). These reward systems are described as contingency management (CM) interventions (Prendergast et al., 2006). Clinicians may use a number of CM procedures, but one commonly used approach provides clients with vouchers that, once earned, may be exchanged for goods or services that are compatible with a substance-free lifestyle.

Research has shown strong support for CM as an effective method for reinforcing abstinence from substance use disorders. A literature review by Higgins et al. (2004) found that 85% of 55 outcome studies reported that CM interventions significantly and positively influenced substance abuse behavior. Furthermore, Prendergast et al. (2006) conducted a meta-analysis using 47 experimental and quasiexperimental CM studies and found a medium effect size ($d = .42$). A moderator analysis revealed that CM was more useful in treating opiate ($d = .65$) and cocaine use ($d = .66$) compared to treatment for multiple drugs ($d = .42$).

A meta-analysis of 34 randomized controlled trials conducted by Dutra et al. (2008) compared various psychosocial interventions used to treat clients with substance use disorders. The findings indicated that the overall effect size across all substances was moderate ($d = .45$). Substance abuse treatments incorporating both CBT and CM had the highest effect sizes ($d = 1.02$), although this finding included results only from two studies. CM interventions alone produced medium effect sizes ($d = .58$), whereas CBT ($d = .28$) and RP ($d = .32$) revealed small effect sizes. The most efficacious treatments were for cannabis use ($d = .81$), and the least efficacious were for polysubstance use ($d = .24$). Overall, these empirical findings provided the strongest evidence for CM interventions.

### Stages of Change Model

The broader research literature suggests that people change problem behaviors along a stage continuum (e.g., DiClemente & Prochaska, 1982; Marlatt & Gordon, 1985; Norcross, Krebs, & Prochaska, 2011; Rosen & Shipley, 1983). Prochaska and DiClemente (1982) have done the most work in this area and refer to their theoretical model as the stages of change or transtheoretical model (DiClemente, 1991; Prochaska, DiClemente, & Norcross, 1992). The stages of change model proposes that behavioral change is a gradual process involving stages that are not necessarily linear or orderly (Lynch & Chiu, 2009). Prochaska and colleagues (1992) identified five progressive stages of behavioral change in counseling: precontemplation, contemplation, preparation, action, and maintenance. Various behavioral change theories can be used at each of the five stages to provide tailored counseling interventions to people with substance use problems.

Precontemplation is typically the initial phase of the stages of change model (Prochaska et al., 1992). Individuals in the precontemplation stage can be described as being unmotivated to change their substance abuse behaviors in the near future. When confronted regarding substance use and related problems, these individuals may be in denial, frustrated, or attribute blame to other people or to the environment (Norcross et al., 2011). Significant others or health care providers may be aware of substance use problems and encourage the individual to enter treatment. Appropriate counseling strategies for individuals at this stage may include promoting responsibility and awareness of substance use problems. Specific counseling interventions that may be used by rehabilitation counselors include substance abuse education, dramatic relief, and environmental reevaluation. Substance abuse education aims to increase the knowledge of the biopsychological effects of substance abuse. Dramatic relief interventions encourage the communication of feelings, thoughts, and possible solutions related to substance abuse. Environmental reevaluation cultivates the individual's consciousness of the effects of substance abuse on others. Insight-oriented therapies (e.g., person-centered therapy) are often used at this stage in order to help facilitate cognitive processes of the contemplation stage.

Contemplation is the stage during which a person may begin to think about seeking solutions for substance use problems (Norcross et al., 2011). Individuals may start to find discrepancies in their day-to-day behaviors or goals, which may lead them to consider resolving such issues. Although individuals begin to contemplate changing unhealthy behaviors, they have not committed to a plan of action in this stage and may still be weighing the pros and cons of abstinence. They also may not know how or what to change regarding their problems and, as a result, they may remain stagnant in this phase for a long period of time (Lynch & Chiu, 2009). The major therapeutic activities during the contemplation stage are aimed at enhancing commitment to change. The counselor should plan to help clients achieve what they identify as important (e.g., solving a crisis, identifying community resources; Drake & Noordsy, 1994). Additionally, counseling interventions can emphasize restructuring perceptions about substance abuse and increasing sensitivity to contexts that promote substance abuse.

In addition, during the contemplation stage, Miller and Rollnick (1991) suggest the use of motivational interviewing (MI; see Chapter 12 in this volume), which focuses on developing and resolving cognitive dissonance regarding substance use. MI techniques can be used to explore residual ambivalence and enhance motivation to prepare for change through such techniques as expressing empathy, rolling with resistance, developing discrepancy, and cultivating self-efficacy (Miller & Rollnick, 2002). Numerous meta-analyses have provided substantial evidence for the effectiveness of MI strategies for people with substance use problems (Burke, Arkowitz, & Menchola, 2003; Hettema, Steele, & Miller, 2005; Lundahl, Kunz, Brownell, Tollefson, & Burke, 2010; Vasilaki, Hosier, & Cox, 2006) that are commonly used in order to help clients progress through the stages of change. The collective meta-analytic findings suggest that MI is more useful than no substance abuse treatment and is at least equal in effectiveness to other psychosocial interventions. It also produces comparable results in shorter treatment periods. MI, as well as other counseling strategies used in the contemplation stage, can be used to augment the client's self-efficacy and readiness to move to the preparation stage.

The preparation stage occurs when individuals are actively searching for additional information and guidance on substance use problems (Prochaska et al., 1992). In this stage, individuals begin planning to change problematic behaviors and may even start reducing substance consumption. The main goal of counseling at this stage is obtaining a sense of "self-liberation," which is described as the confidence in one's ability to change (DiClemente, 1991). Clients are encouraged to remove or reduce barriers that may hinder abstinence (e.g., cognitions, habits, friends, or living situations; Drake & Noordsy, 1994). Psychoeducation is used to determine abstinence reinforcers in the client's life. Behavioral or vocational skills training is often encouraged during the preparation stage. These psychosocial approaches are used to augment the client's self-efficacy and readiness to move to the action stage.

Action is the stage during which an individual quits substance abuse behavior, often combined with substituting a new healthy behavior (Norcross et al., 2011). The primary goal of counseling during the action stage is to help individuals increase alternative non–substance abuse activities. The action stage requires significant effort to successfully maintain healthy behaviors for a longer period of time. Thus, it is important for counselors to teach clients with substance use problems a variety of CBT strategies for personal and environmental management. Clients should also be encouraged to seek out support from significant, non–substance-abusing others in order to lower the chances of relapse. Other community supports should be identified and provided as needed (Drake & Noordsy, 1994). Follow-up counseling interventions can be planned with multiple options (individual, group, or family), depending on the client preference and areas of concern.

Maintenance is the final stage that occurs after individuals sustain gains accomplished during the action stage of change (Norcross et al., 2011). Abstinence for a period of 6 months to 3 years meets the criteria of the maintenance stage of recovery (Lam et al., 1996). However, this stage may not be permanent, and individuals may regress to earlier stages of change. Therefore, counseling interventions should focus on self-management skills and RP plans (Marlatt & Gordon, 1985). Key components of such interventions include the recognition and avoidance of high-risk situations and the development of techniques for handling the thoughts and emotions that may lead to relapse. Counseling methods can also emphasize behavioral changes, such as improving social relationships, attending self-help groups, and continuing education or vocational training (Drake & Noordsy, 1994). Throughout the maintenance process, counselors should continue to provide support, monitoring, and skills training to expand the client's potential.

The stages of change model appears to hold much promise as a conceptual system for substance abuse treatment (Cardoso, Chan, Berven, & Thomas, 2003; Lam et al., 1996). The model can help to explain the underlying processes behind coping, recovery, and relapse in substance abuse treatment (Nelson, 1986). The theoretical concepts can also offer a standard language to multidisciplinary teams working with individuals with substance use problems, thereby improving communication among rehabilitation professionals (Prochaska et al., 1992).

Empirical evidence supports the use of the stages of change model in substance abuse treatment. Norcross et al. (2011) conducted a meta-analysis of 39 experimental studies to investigate the impact of pretreatment stage of change on outcomes in people with substance use disorders and other disabilities. Their results indicated a medium effect size for stage of change ($d = .46$), indicating that the stages of change model appears to be a useful framework for assessing and predicting substance abuse treatment outcomes. Overall, the accurate evaluation of readiness to change may have the potential to foster individualized and effective substance abuse treatment programs (Jacobson & Christensen, 1996).

## ASSESSMENT OF SUBSTANCE ABUSE

Assessment of substance use issues is critical to successful treatment outcomes. Assessment should address the extent of substance use, in terms of both the amounts and types of substance consumption and the impact on the individual's daily life as well as the individual's readiness for change.

### Clinical Signs

The clinical signs of substance abuse-related symptoms may include observable features, such as slurred speech, bloodshot eyes, impaired coordination, altered mood state, memory problems, unexplained injuries, and the smell of psychoactive substances. Behavioral issues, including challenges with keeping appointments; employment difficulties; financial or legal problems; family or friend conflict; changes in leisure activities; and the misplacing of valuable items may also be indicative of addiction problems. When substance abuse is suspected, counselors should query about substance use history, family history, lifestyle, employment history, legal problems, and health problems.

### Medical Examinations

In addition to clinical interviews with substance abuse clients, medical examinations using a blood analysis can determine signs of recent substance use. Other laboratory examinations include a urinalysis that can indicate alcohol and other drugs in the body, or a breath analysis that can detect alcohol use within the previous 24 hours. Physical symptoms secondary to substance abuse may include varied medical conditions, such as gastrointestinal disturbances, hypertension, heart disease, liver disease, and neurological changes (Falvo, 1999).

### General Psychometric Instruments

#### Substance Abuse Subtle Screening Inventory

The Substance Abuse Subtle Screening Inventory (SASSI) identifies general substance abuse problems (Benshoff & Janikowski, 1999) and was developed to decrease response bias and to guard against faking (Miller, 1985). The SASSI consists of two components, the SASSI Subtle Items and Face Valid Items for alcohol and other drugs. The 67 Subtle Items of the SASSI pose true–false questions that appear to be unrelated to substance use or abuse. The Face Valid Items contain 12 alcohol-related and 14 other drug-related items, rated on a 4-point scale that asks directly about chemical use (e.g., "How often have you had more to drink than you intended to?"). The score is the sum of the responses over all items, with higher scores indicating a greater extent of usage. This instrument has established norms for adult men and women, as well as adolescents (Cardoso et al., 2009).

## The Michigan Alcoholism Screening Test

The Michigan Alcoholism Screening Test (MAST; Selzer, 1971) is one of the most popular screening devices to detect alcohol use. It includes 25 "yes/no" questions (e.g., "Can you stop drinking without difficulty after one or two drinks?"), focusing on areas such as physical symptoms associated with alcohol dependence, marital problems resulting from drinking, hospitalization related to drinking, legal problems, and psychological problems. For each "yes" response, a numerical value ranging from 0 to 5 is assigned, depending on the severity of the problem. Ingraham, Kaplan, and Chan (1992) suggested the use of a cutoff score of 4 and below as indicative of no problems, a score of 5 to 7 as a potential problem, and a score of 8 or higher as indicating alcoholism. Internal consistency reliability estimates have been found to range from .83 to .95 (Hedlund & Vieweg, 1984).

## CAGE Self-Report Screen

Another commonly used and easily interpreted instrument for assessing alcohol use is the CAGE questionnaire (Ewing & Rouse, 1970). The CAGE is a very brief self-report screen, and it takes its name from the four questions asked of clients about alcohol use: "Have you ever felt the need to Cut down?"; "Do you feel Annoyed by people complaining about your drinking?"; "Do you ever feel Guilty about your drinking?"; and "Do you ever drink an Eye-opener in the morning to relieve the shakes?" Two or more affirmative responses to the four items indicate a potential drinking problem. A cutoff score of 2 or more has been found to identify correctly 75% of a group of people with a diagnosis of alcoholism (Mayfield, McLeod, & Hall, 1974). Internal consistency reliability estimates have been found to range from .65 to .89 for the array of responses (Mayfield et al., 1974).

## Psychometric Instruments Focused on Readiness for Change

### Stages of Change Readiness and Treatment Eagerness Scale

The Stages of Change Readiness and Treatment Eagerness Scale (SOCRATES) was developed to assess willingness or readiness to change in substance abuse clients (Miller & Tonigan, 1996). There are two types of SOCRATES self-report questionnaires; one is used to measure drinking and the other to measure drug use. Both short questionnaires include a total of 19 items that partition readiness to change into three main scales: Recognition (e.g., "I really want to make changes in my drinking"), Ambivalence (e.g., "Sometimes I wonder if I'm an alcoholic"), and Taking Steps (e.g., "I have already started making some changes in my drinking"). The items are scored on a 5-point scale and are summed to determine scores for each of the scales. Internal consistency reliability estimates for the three subscales have been found to range from .60 to .96 (Miller & Tonigan, 1996).

## Stages of Change Scale–Substance Abuse

The Stages of Change Scale–Substance Abuse (SCS-SA) was developed to operationalize the stage of change process for people with substance abuse problems (Cardoso et al., 2003). It is composed of 37 items, each rated using a 5-point scale, with four subscales: (a) Precontemplation (e.g., "I may have some alcohol or other drug problems, but there is no reason to change them"), (b) Determination (e.g., "I am preparing myself to change my problem by listening to other people discuss how they stay clean"), (c) Participation (e.g., "I am working on my alcohol and other drug abuse problem, which has been bothering me"), and (d) Relapse (e.g., "I had begun to make changes about my alcohol or other drug problem, but recently I started using drugs again"). Item ratings are summed to determine scores for each scale. Internal consistency reliability estimates for the four scales have been found to range from .73 to .93 (Cardoso et al., 2003).

## Task-Specific Self-Efficacy Scale for People With Substance Abuse Problems

The Task-Specific Self-Efficacy Scale for People with Substance Abuse Problems (TSSES-SA) was adapted from the Task-Specific Self-Efficacy Scale for People with Mental Illness (TSSE-PMI; Chou, Cardoso, Chan, Tsang, & Wu, 2007) in order to operationalize task-specific self-efficacy for people with substance abuse problems. Prochaska and DiClemente (1982) indicated that different task-specific coping skills are significant to different stages of change. The TSSES-SA is composed of 23 items with three subscales: (a) Work-Related Skills, with eight items measuring skills and behaviors that are important to obtaining and maintaining employment (e.g., "I am capable of interviewing for a job"); (b) Help-Seeking Skills, with nine items measuring ability to seek help when having difficulties in daily life (e.g., "I am able to ask for help when I feel sad or when I cannot think clearly"); and (c) Risk-Avoidance Skills, with six items measuring the ability to avoid high-risk situations leading to alcohol and other drug abuse (e.g., "I am able to avoid feeling upset"). The items are each rated on a 6-point scale and summed to determine scores on each subscale. The internal consistency reliability estimates for the four subscales have been found to range from .86 to .92 (Chou et al., 2007).

## TYPES OF SUBSTANCE ABUSE TREATMENT PROGRAMS

Treatment for substance use disorders can take place within a variety of different settings, ranging in intensity from highly structured inpatient treatment programs to self-help groups, such as Alcoholics Anonymous (AA). Rehabilitation counselors and other rehabilitation professionals, in conjunction with the client and any involved third party (e.g. drug court), should determine the most appropriate treatment setting for the client, given his or her individual situation.

### Long-Term Residential Treatment Programs

Long-term residential programs provide 24/7 care in nonhospital settings (NIDA, 2009). They are predominantly therapeutic communities with lengths of stay from 6 to 12 months. These communities provide structured and unstructured treatment programs intended to influence residents' attitudes and behaviors related to drug use (NIDA, 2002). Community is considered the primary agent of change, with residents, rehabilitation professionals, and other community members all considered to be active components of treatment. The philosophy of therapeutic communities is based on a social learning approach to drug prevention that emphasizes client responsibility, behavioral skills training, role modeling, and community building (Wexler, Magura, Beardsley, & Josepher, 1994). Examples of skills training used in such programs focus on overcoming social anxieties, anger management, employment training, and learning other healthy ways of living (Egelko & Galanter, 1993). Therapeutic communities can be modified to accommodate people with disabilities, women, and criminal offenders (NIDA, 2002).

### Short-Term Residential Treatment Programs

Short-term residential programs provide brief, intensive therapy housed within a medical center with nursing care and physician supervision. The treatment programs are conducted in inpatient settings to prevent substance use and separate the client from various contextual factors that may trigger relapse. The conventional length of stay in inpatient treatment is 28 days, but treatment periods may vary based on client needs. This type of treatment is considered group intensive, and it often follows an AA 12-step orientation to recovery (Budziack, 1993). Each day of treatment is highly structured and programmed with sets of predetermined group activities. After short-term treatment stays, individuals are encouraged to enter halfway houses, outpatient treatment, or other aftercare programs to prevent relapse.

### Halfway Houses

Halfway houses are transitional community living settings for individuals in recovery. Halfway houses are designed to integrate clients back into the community via regular monitoring and require specific preconditions for restoration. Many individuals stay in halfway houses after inpatient treatment, prison, homelessness, or as a result of court orders. Halfway houses can include highly structured or minimally structured treatment programs (Pekarik & Zimmer, 1992). Often programs require drug-screening tests, as the houses are not equipped to provide medical treatment for withdrawal symptoms.

### Outpatient Treatment Programs

Outpatient programs vary in intensity and frequency of treatment services (NIDA, 2009). Low-intensity programs may only offer drug education; however, intensive outpatient treatment programs typically involve several hours of treatment activities per day for most days of the week for multiple weeks. These intensive outpatient programs usually use condensed versions of the group treatment schedules followed in inpatient programs. Intensive outpatient programs are less expensive than their inpatient counterparts, less intrusive, and less stigmatizing to individuals participating in the treatment. Intensive programs often rely on legal, employment, or family-based pressures to compel the individual to participate, and many programs require daily drug testing as a condition for treatment.

## Self-Help Groups

Self-help groups are often identified as adjuncts to formal substance abuse treatment. The first self-help groups were founded by AA in the 1950s. The primary purpose of AA is to help alcoholics achieve and maintain sobriety (Doweiko, 2002). The group meetings follow the 12-step principles of recovery. The 12-step self-help programs are strongly influenced by the disease model, and these programs believe that substance abusers must first admit that they are powerless to addiction prior to moving forward with treatment (Doweiko, 2002). After completing the first step, the individual progresses through the other steps until reaching Step 12, where the person acknowledges a spiritual awakening as a result of the process and shares the message with other group members. The success of AA has spawned other self-help groups based on the 12-step principles, including Narcotics Anonymous, Cocaine Anonymous, and Rational Recovery.

## Programs for Families

To help family members of a client with a substance use disorder, treatment providers should offer family services or refer the family to Al-Anon or other substance abuse family groups offering support and education. Programs for families are available to help family members articulate family problems and strengths in order to promote action to support the addicted family member. Family treatment can be conceptualized as a five-step process: (a) identify family problems, (b) separate facts from opinions, (c) identify facts related to addiction, (d) identify feelings associated with these facts, and (e) identify family strengths (Schlesinger & Horberg, 1993). Through the group process, family meetings can provide an outlet of mutual understanding and support.

## ISSUES RELATED TO SUBSTANCE USE DISORDERS AND DISABILITY

As already indicated, people with disabilities have higher rates of substance use disorders as compared to the general public, and the mere presence of disability appears to substantially increase the risk of acquiring a substance use disorder (Brucker, 2007). There may be a variety of reasons why individuals with disabilities are more likely to abuse drugs, ranging from difficulties in living with a label of disability and related stresses to limited availability of substance abuse treatment (Greer, 1986; Moore, 2001; Ogborne & Smart, 1995; Rehabilitation Research and Training Center on Drugs and Disability [RRTCDD], 1996). Several studies indicate that individuals with co-occurring substance use disorders also experience heightened problems with employment, education, and social functioning (e.g., Corrigan, 1995; Hollar, McAweeney, & Moore, 2008). Three types of disabilities have the highest prevalence rates of coexisting substance abuse: mental illness, brain injury, and SCI.

The vast majority of the disability research has focused attention on the intersection of mental illness and substance use disorder (Brucker, 2007). Studies have reported that about 40% of all individuals with psychiatric disorders have a coexisting substance use disorder (Chronister et al., 2008). The increased attention to the size of this "dual diagnosis" population has also led many programs to develop support services to address the particular needs of this group (Slayter, 2010). Unfortunately, there may be problems with detecting substance abuse problems for people with severe mental illness, because drug intoxication may resemble psychiatric symptoms or medication side effects (e.g., slurred speech, staggering gait, tremors; RRTCDD, 1996). Severe and persistent mental illnesses also share insidious features with substance use disorders, such as chronicity and frequent relapse. Consequently, individuals with both diagnoses are considered to be more difficult to treat than people with single disorders (Kelley & Benshoff, 1997). Clients with dual diagnoses are best treated with a combination of counseling, psychopharmacology, education, vocational supports, and psychosocial interventions that attend to symptoms of both mental illness and substance abuse.

Meta-analytic research has addressed treatment in persons with co-occurring mental illnesses and substance use disorders. Dumaine (2003) conducted a meta-analysis of 15 studies related to interventions used to treat individuals with dual diagnoses. The results indicated that there were no statistically significant relationships between outcomes and practitioner training ($r = .37$), practitioner-to-client ratio ($r = .10$), restrictiveness of treatment ($r = -.23$), and length of treatment ($r = .35$). The results showed that the overall average effect size was low ($r = .22$), ranging from $r = .00$ to $r = .50$. The largest effect size ($r = .35$) came from intensive case management with no specialized outpatient psychoeducational groups. The next largest effect size ($r = .25$) came from standard aftercare with specialized outpatient psychoeducational groups. Inpatient treatment had the lowest effect size ($r = .13$), indicating that outpatient treatment, and particularly intensive case management, is associated with the most positive client outcomes.

The rate of substance abuse problems among persons with brain injuries is also known to be high, between 25% and 50% (Chan et al., 1995). The majority of the time, the substance abuse predates the injury, with approximately 60% of TBI cases acquired while the individual is intoxicated (Corrigan, 1995; Radnitz & Tirch, 1995). These clients often struggle with the treatment and vocational rehabilitation process; a past substance history alone has been adversely linked to future life satisfaction and productivity outcomes (Bogner, Corrigan, Mysiw, Clinchot, & Fugate, 2001). Chan et al. (1995) recommended assessing substance abuse history at the beginning of treatment in order to identify potential problems. For those with a history of substance abuse, drug treatment services should be integrated with brain rehabilitation programs in order to optimize success. In particular, structured behavioral interventions can be used to treat substance use problems, as they allow for tasks and strategies to be readily learned.

Motivation enhancement and coping skills training may also augment rehabilitation outcomes in persons with brain injuries and substance use disorders (Langley, 1991). In addition, family and client support groups can be provided as auxiliary services.

Clients with SCIs also often have preinjury substance use disorders, with estimates varying from 25% to 75% (Corrigan, 1995; Heinemann, 1986; Heinemann, Doll, & Schnoll, 1989; West, Graham, & Cifu, 2009). Heinemann and colleagues (1989) suggested that an efficacious substance abuse treatment program for individuals with SCI should include assessment, postinjury education, and coping skills training. Rehabilitation providers should also review the preinjury use of substances and past social activities with clients, as past behaviors may predict future life patterns and habits. Many individuals with SCIs and other mobility disabilities may have secondary health conditions (e.g., spasticity) that require prescription medications. Rehabilitation teams should inform clients that the use of substances in combination with prescription medication can alter treatment effects (e.g., lower seizure thresholds) and may have potentially negative consequences.

Despite the high comorbidity of disability with substance abuse, people with disabilities often have persistent challenges in accessing the substance abuse treatment system (Benshoff & Janikowski, 1999; Moore & Li, 1994). Few substance abuse treatment programs are designed with individuals with disabilities in mind (Tyas & Rush, 1993). Consequently, people with disabilities report frequent substance abuse service denials, in addition to programmatic, structural, or logistical barriers (Sales, 2000). A study using a nationally representative sample of 431 substance abuse treatment facilities in the United States found that only 5% of clients served had a disability (West, Graham, & Cifu, 2009). Hence, there is a crucial need for rehabilitation professionals to assist clients with removing or maneuvering barriers to effective substance abuse treatment.

Ebener and Smedema (2011) have proposed a framework for understanding both recovery from substance use disorders and adaptation to disability. Ebener and Smedema (2011) stated that the relationship between recovery from substance abuse and adaptation to disability is complex and not well understood. However, levels of both recovery and adaptation to disability can fall on a continuum, and an improvement in overall quality of life is the overall goal of counseling for both. Common variables, including health status, life satisfaction, spirituality, and community involvement are variables that relate to quality of life, adaptation to disability, and recovery (Betty Ford Institute Consensus Panel, 2007; Bishop, 2005; Livneh, 2001). These factors may present a starting point for the exploration of the complex relationship between adaptation to disability and recovery by rehabilitation professionals.

## CONCLUSIONS

It is important for rehabilitation counselors and other rehabilitation professionals to be aware of issues related to substance use disorders in persons with disabilities. Persons with disabilities experience problems with substance use at much higher rates than members of the general public (SAMHSA, 2002). As such, rehabilitation professionals will come into contact with many clients struggling with issues related to both substance use and adjustment to disability. Counselors must become knowledgeable of and competent in providing evidence-based assessment and treatment for substance use disorders. With such proficiency, counselors can assist clients to meet their sobriety goals and positively impact their overall quality of life.

## DISCUSSION EXERCISES

1. What are your thoughts on the changes to the *DSM-5* criteria related to substance use disorders? Do you feel the changes are appropriate, or do you prefer the old classification system? Why?
2. Which conceptual model of substance use disorders would you be most likely to implement with your clients with disabilities? Why?
3. What counseling techniques might be most effective at simultaneously addressing both adaptation to disability and substance use problems?
4. What unique characteristics might persons with disabilities possess that make substance abuse particularly important to address?
5. What issues might you need to consider when using the substance abuse assessment techniques discussed in this chapter for persons with disabilities?

## REFERENCES

American Psychiatric Association (APA). (1994). *Diagnostic and statistical manual of mental disorders* (4th ed.). Washington, DC: Author.

American Psychiatric Association (APA). (2013). *Highlights of changes from DSM-IV-TR to DSM-5*. Arlington, VA: Author. Retrieved from http://www.psychiatry.org/File%20Library/Practice/DSM/DSM-5/Changes-from-DSM-IV-TR--to-DSM-5.pdf

Babor, T. F. (1993). Megatrends and dead ends: Alcohol research in global perspective. *Alcohol Health & Research World, 17*(3), 177–186.

Bandura, A. (1977). Self-efficacy: Toward a unifying theory of behavior change. *Psychological Review, 84*, 191–215.

Benshoff, J. J., & Janikowski, T. P. (1999). *The rehabilitation model of substance abuse counseling*. Pacific Grove, CA: Wadsworth.

Betty Ford Institute Consensus Panel. (2007). What is recovery? A working definition from the Betty Ford Institute. *Journal of Substance Abuse Treatment, 33*, 221–228.

Bishop, M. (2005). Quality of life and psychosocial adaptation to chronic illness and disability: Preliminary analysis of a conceptual and theoretical synthesis. *Rehabilitation Counseling Bulletin, 48*, 219–231.

Bogner, J. A., Corrigan, J. D., Mysiw, W. J., Clinchot, D., & Fugate, L. (2001). A comparison of substance abuse and violence in the prediction of long-term rehabilitation outcomes after traumatic brain injury. *Archives of Physical Medicine and Rehabilitation, 82*, 571–577.

Brownell, K. D., Marlatt, G. A., Lichtenstein, E., & Wilson, G. T. (1986). Understanding and preventing relapse. *American Psychologist, 41*, 765–782.

Brucker, D. (2007). Estimating the prevalence of substance use, abuse, and dependence among Social Security disability benefit recipients. *Journal of Disability Policy Studies, 18*, 148–159.

Budziack, T. J. (1993). Evaluating treatment services. In A. W. Heinemann (Ed.), *Substance abuse and physical disability* (pp. 239–255). Binghamton, NY: Haworth.

Burke, B. L., Arkowitz, H., & Menchola, M. (2003). The efficacy of motivational interviewing: A meta-analysis of controlled clinical trials. *Journal of Consulting and Clinical Psychology, 71*, 843–860.

Cardoso, E., Chan, F., Berven, N. L., & Thomas, K. R. (2003). Readiness for change among patients with substance abuse problems in therapeutic community settings. *Rehabilitation Counseling Bulletin, 47*, 34–43.

Cardoso, E., Wolf, A. W., & West, S. L. (2009). Substance abuse: Models, assessment, and interventions. In F. Chan, E. D. Cardoso, & J. A. Chronister (Eds.), *Understanding psychosocial adjustment to chronic illness and disability: A handbook for evidence-based practitioners in rehabilitation* (pp. 399–442). New York, NY: Springer Publishing Company.

Chan, F., Cunningham, J., Kwok, L., Dunlap, L., Kobayashi, R., & Tanquery, M. (1995). *Solving the vocational assessment puzzle: Pieces to meet the challenge with people having traumatic brain injury* [Computer software]. Chicago, IL: Rehabilitation Institute of Chicago.

Chiauzzi, E. J. (1991). *Preventing relapse in the addictions. A biopsychosocial approach.* New York, NY: Pergamon.

Chou, C. C., Cardoso, E. D. S., Chan, F., Tsang, H. W., & Wu, M. (2007). Development and psychometric validation of the task-specific self-efficacy scale for Chinese people with mental illness. *International Journal of Rehabilitation Research, 30*, 261–271.

Chronister, J., Chou, C. C., da Silva Cardoso, E., Sasson, J., Chan, F., & Tan, S. Y. (2008). Vocational services as intervention for substance abuse rehabilitation: Implications for addiction studies education. *Journal of Teaching in the Addictions, 7*, 31–56.

Clarke, P. B., & Myers, J. E. (2012). Developmental counseling and therapy: A promising intervention for preventing relapse with substance-abusing clients. *Journal of Mental Health Counseling, 34*, 308–321.

Cohen, E., Feinn, R., Arias, A., & Kranzler, H. R. (2007). Alcohol treatment utilization: Findings from the National Epidemiologic Survey on Alcohol and Related Conditions. *Drug and Alcohol Dependence, 86*, 214–221.

Conger, J. J. (1956). Alcoholism: Theory, problem, and challenge. Reinforcement theory and the dynamics of alcoholism. *Quarterly Journal of Studies on Alcohol, 13*, 296–305.

Corrigan, J. D. (1995). Substance abuse as a mediating factor in outcome from traumatic brain injury. *Archives of Physical Medicine and Rehabilitation, 76*, 302–309.

Del Re, A. C., Maisel, N., Blodgett, J., & Finney, J. (2013). The declining efficacy of naltrexone pharmacotherapy for alcohol use disorders over time: A multivariate meta-analysis. *Alcoholism: Clinical and Experimental Research, 6*, 1064–1068.

DiClemente, C. C. (1991). Motivational interviewing and stages of change. In W. R. Miller & S. Rollnick (Eds.), *Motivational interviewing: Preparing people for change* (pp. 191–202). New York, NY: Guilford.

DiClemente, C. C., & Prochaska, J. O. (1982). Self-change and therapy change of smoking behavior: A comparison of processes of change in cessation and maintenance. *Addictive Behaviors, 7*, 133–142.

Donovan, D. M., & Marlatt, G. A. (Eds.). (1988). *Assessment of addictive behaviors.* New York, NY: Guilford.

Doweiko, H. E. (2002). *Concepts of chemical dependency* (5th ed.). Pacific Grove, CA: Brooks/Cole.

Drake, R. E., & Noordsy, D. L. (1994). Case management for people with coexisting severe mental disorder and substance use disorder. *Psychiatric Annals, 24*, 427–431.

Dumaine, M. L. (2003). Meta-analysis of interventions with co-occurring disorders of severe mental illness and substance abuse: Implications for social work practice. *Research on Social Work Practice, 13,* 142–165.

Dutra, L., Stathopoulou, G., Basden, S., Leyro, T., Powers, M., & Otto, M. (2008). A meta-analytic review of psychosocial interventions for substance use disorders. *American Journal of Psychiatry, 165,* 179–187.

Ebener, D. J., & Smedema, S. M. (2011). Physical disability and substance use disorders: A convergence of adaptation and recovery. *Rehabilitation Counseling Bulletin, 54,* 131–141.

Egelko, S., & Galanter, M. (1993). Introducing cognitive-behavioral training into a self-help drug treatment program. *Psychotherapy, 30,* 214–221.

Ewing, J. A., & Rouse, B. A. (1970, February). Identifying the hidden alcoholic. In *29th International Congress on Alcohol and Drug Dependence* (Vol. 3), Sydney, Australia.

Falvo, D. (1999). *Medical and psychosocial aspects of chronic illness and disability* (2nd ed.). Gaithersburg, MD: Aspen.

Fingarette, H. (1991). Alcoholism: The mythical disease. In D. J. Pittman & H. R. White (Eds.), *Society, culture, and drinking patterns reexamined. Alcohol, Culture, and Social Control Monograph Series* (pp. 417–438). New Brunswick, NJ: Rutgers Center on Alcohol Studies.

Gonzales, R., & Weiss, F. (1998). Suppression of ethanol-reinforced behavior by naltrexone is associated with attenuation of the ethanol-induced increase in dialysate dopamine levels in the nucleus accumbens. *Journal of Neurosciences, 18,* 1663–1671.

Greer, B. G. (1986). Substance abuse among people with disabilities: A problem of too much accessibility. *Journal of Rehabilitation, 52,* 34–38.

Hedlund, J. L., & Vieweg, B. W. (1984). The Michigan Alcoholism Screening Test (MAST): A comprehensive review. *Journal of Operational Psychiatry, 15,* 55–64.

Heinemann, A. W. (1986). Substance abuse and disability: An update. *Rehabilitation Report, 2*(6&7), 3–5.

Heinemann, A. W., Doll, M., & Schnoll, S. (1989). Treatment of alcohol abuse in persons with recent spinal cord injuries. *Alcohol Health and Research World, 13,* 110–117.

Hettema, J., Steele, J., & Miller, W. R. (2005). Motivational interviewing. *Annual Review of Clinical Psychology, 1,* 91–111.

Higgins, S. T., Heil, S. H., & Lussier, J. P. (2004). Clinical implications of reinforcement as a determinant of substance use disorders. *Annual Review of Psychology, 55,* 431–461.

Hollar, D., McAweeney, M. J., & Moore, D. (2008). The relationship between substance use disorders and unsuccessful case closures in vocational rehabilitation agencies. *Special Issue: Vocational Rehabilitation & Substance Use Disorders, 39*(2), 25–29.

Ingraham, K., Kaplan, S., & Chan, F. (1992). Rehabilitation counselors' awareness of client alcohol abuse patterns. *Journal of Applied Rehabilitation Counseling, 23,* 18–22.

Irvin, J. E., Bowers, C. A., Dunn, M. E., & Wang, M. C. (1999). Efficacy of relapse prevention: A meta-analytic review. *Journal of Consulting and Clinical Psychology, 67,* 563–570.

Jacobson, N. S., & Christensen, A. (1996). Studying the effectiveness of psychotherapy: How well can clinical trials do the job? *American Psychologist, 51,* 1031–1039.

Johnson, V. E. (1980). *I'll quit tomorrow.* San Francisco, CA: Harper & Row.

Jørgensen, C. H., Pedersen, B., & Tønnesen, H. (2011). The efficacy of disulfiram for the treatment of alcohol use disorder. *Alcoholism: Clinical and Experimental Research, 35,* 1749–1758.

Kathiramalainathan, K., Kaplan, H., Romach, M., Busto, U., Li, N., Sawe, J, . . . Sellers, E. (2000). Inhibition of cytochrome P450 2D6 modifies codeine abuse liability. *Journal of Clinical Psychopharmacology, 20,* 435–444.

Kelley, S. D. M., & Benshoff, J. J. (1997). Dual diagnosis of mental illness and substance abuse: Contemporary challenges for rehabilitation. *Journal of Applied Rehabilitation Counseling, 28,* 43–50.

Laaksonen, E., Koski-Jännes, A., Salaspuro, M., Ahtinen, H., & Alho, H. (2008). A randomized, multicentre, open-label, comparative trial of disulfiram, naltrexone and acamprosate in the treatment of alcohol dependence. *Alcohol and Alcoholism, 43,* 53–61.

Lam, C. S., Hilburger, J., Kornbleuth, M., Jenkins, J., Brown, D., & Racenstein, J. M. (1996). A treatment matching model for substance abuse rehabilitation clients. *Rehabilitation Counseling Bulletin, 39,* 202–216.

Langley, M. J. (1991). Preventing post-injury alcohol-related problems: A behavioral approach. In B. T. McMahon & L. R. Shaw (Eds.), *Work worth doing: Advances in brain injury rehabilitation* (pp. 251–275). Orlando, FL: Deutsch.

Lappalainen, J., Kranzler, H. R., Malison, R., Price, L. H., Van Dyck, C., Rosenheck, R. A., . . . Gelernter, J. (2002). A functional neuropeptide Y Leu7Pro polymorphism associated with alcohol dependence in a large population sample from the United States. *Archives of General Psychiatry, 59,* 825–831.

Larimer, M. E., Palmer, R. S., & Marlatt, G.A. (1999). Relapse prevention: An overview of Marlatt's cognitive-behavioral model. *Alcohol Research and Health, 23,* 151–160.

Livneh, H. (2001). Psychosocial adaptation to chronic illness and disability: A conceptual framework. *Rehabilitation Counseling Bulletin, 44,* 151–160.

Lundahl, B. W., Kunz, C., Brownell, C., Tollefson, D., & Burke, B. L. (2010). A meta-analysis of motivational interviewing: Twenty-five years of empirical studies. *Research on Social Work Practice, 20,* 137–160.

Lynch, R. T., & Chiu, C. Y. (2009). Wellness and promotion of health in chronic illness and disability: Theoretical and practical models for assessment and intervention. In F. Chan, E. D. Cardoso, & J. A. Chronister (Eds.). *Understanding psychosocial adjustment to chronic illness and disability: A handbook for evidence-based practitioners in rehabilitation* (pp. 277–306). New York, NY: Springer Publishing Company.

Magill, M., & Ray, L. A. (2009). Cognitive-behavioral treatment with adult alcohol and illicit drug users: A meta-analysis of randomized controlled trials. *Journal of Studies on Alcohol and Drugs, 70,* 516–527.

Maisel, N. C., Blodgett, J. C., Wilbourne, P. L., Humphreys, K., & Finney, J. W. (2013). Meta-analysis of naltrexone and acamprosate for treating alcohol use disorders: When are these medications most helpful? *Addiction, 108,* 275–293.

Mann, K., Kiefer, F., Spanagel, R., & Littleton, J. (2008). Acamprosate: Recent findings and future research directions. *Alcoholism: Clinical and Experimental Research, 32,* 1105–1110.

Mann, K., Lehert, P., & Morgan, M. Y. (2004). The efficacy of acamprosate in the maintenance of abstinence in alcohol-dependent individuals: Results of a meta-analysis. *Alcoholism: Clinical and Experimental Research, 28,* 51–63.

Marlatt, G. A., & Gordon, J. R. (1985). *Relapse prevention.* New York, NY: Guilford.

Mason, B. J., Goodman, A. M., Chabac, S., & Lehert, P. (2006). Effect of oral acamprosate on abstinence in patients with alcohol dependence in a double-blind, placebo-controlled trial: The role of patient motivation. *Journal of Psychiatric Research, 40,* 383–393.

Mayfield, D., McLeod, G., & Hall, P. (1974). The CAGE questionnaire: Validation of a new alcoholism screening instrument. *American Journal of Psychiatry, 131,* 1121–1123.

McCabe, S. E., Cranford, J. A., & West, B. T. (2008). Trends in prescription drug abuse and dependence, co-occurrence with other substance use disorders, and treatment utilization: Results from two national surveys. *Addictive Behaviors, 33,* 1297–1305.

Milam, J. R., & Ketcham, K. (1981). *Under the influence: A guide to the myths and realities of alcoholism.* Seattle, WA: Bantam Books.

Miller, G. A. (1985). *The Substance Abuse Subtle Screening Inventory manual.* Bloomington, IN: Addiction Research & Consultation.

Miller, W. R., & Rollnick, S. (1991). *Motivational interviewing.* New York, NY: Guilford.

Miller, W. R., & Rollnick, S. (2002). *Motivational interviewing: Preparing people for change.* New York, NY: Guilford Press.

Miller, W. R., & Tonigan, J. S. (1996). Assessing drinkers' motivation for change: The Stages of Change Readiness and Treatment Eagerness Scale (SOCRATES). *Psychology of Addictive Behaviors, 10,* 81–89.

Moore, D., & Li, L. (1994). Substance use among rehabilitation consumers of vocational rehabilitation services. *Journal of Rehabilitation, 60,* 48–53.

Moore, L. L. D. (2001). Disability and illicit drug use: An application of labeling theory. *Deviant Behavior, 22,* 1–21.

National Institute on Drug Abuse (NIDA). (2002). *What is a therapeutic community?* Retrieved from http://www.drugabuse.gov/publications/research-reports/therapeutic-community/what-therapeutic-community

National Institute on Drug Abuse (NIDA). (2009). *Principles of drug addiction treatment: A research-based guide* (3rd ed., NIH Publication No. 12-4180). Retrieved from http://www.drugabuse.gov/publications/principles-drug-addiction-treatment

National Institute on Drug Abuse (NIDA). (2010). *Drugs, brains, and behavior: The science of addiction* (NIH Publication No. 10-5605). Retrieved from http://www.drugabuse.gov/publications/science-addiction

National Institute on Drug Abuse (NIDA). (2012). *Trends & statistics.* Retrieved from http://www.drugabuse.gov/related-topics/trends-statistics#costs

Nelson, S. J. (1986). Alcohol and other drugs: Facing reality and cynicism. *Journal of Counseling and Development, 65,* 4–5.

Nestler, E. (2001). Psychogenomics: Opportunities for understanding addiction. *Journal of Neuroscience, 21,* 8324–8327.

Norcross, J. C., Krebs, P. M., & Prochaska, J. O. (2011). Stages of change. *Journal of Clinical Psychology, 67,* 143–154.

Ogborne, A. C., & Smart, R. G. (1995). People with physical disabilities admitted to a residential addiction treatment program. *American Journal of Drug and Alcohol Abuse, 21,* 137–145.

Pearson, F. S., Prendergast, M., Podus, D., Vazan, P., Greenwell, L., & Hamilton, Z. (2012). Meta-analyses of seven of NIDA's principles of drug addiction treatment. *Journal of Substance Abuse Treatment, 43,* 1–11.

Pekarik, G., & Zimmer, L. (1992). Relation of client variables to continuance in five types of alcohol treatment settings. *Addictive Behaviors, 17,* 105–115.

Prendergast, M., Podus, D., Finney, J., Greenwell, L., & Roll, J. (2006). Contingency management for treatment of substance use disorders: A meta-analysis. *Addiction, 101,* 1546–1560.

Prochaska, J. O., & DiClemente, C. C. (1982). Transtheoretical therapy: Toward a more integrative model of change. *Psychotherapy: Theory, Research and Practice, 20,* 161–173.

Prochaska, J. O., DiClemente, C. C., & Norcross, J. C. (1992). In search of how people change: Applications to addictive behaviors. *American Psychologist, 47,* 1102–1114.

Radnitz, C. L., & Tirch, D. (1995). Substance misuse in individuals with spinal cord injury. *Substance Use and Misuse, 30,* 1117–1140.

Rehabilitation Research and Training Center on Drugs and Disability (RRTCDD). (1996). *Substance abuse, disability and vocational rehabilitation.* Dayton, OH: SARDI/Wright State University/New York University.

Rosen, T. J., & Shipley, R. H. (1983). A stage analysis of self-initiated smoking reductions. *Addictive Behaviors, 8,* 263–272.

Rosner, S., Leucht, S., Lehert, P., & Soyka, M. (2008). Acamprosate supports abstinence, naltrexone prevents excessive drinking: Evidence from a meta-analysis with unreported outcomes. *Journal of Psychopharmacology, 22,* 11–23.

Sales, A. (2000). Substance abuse and counseling. In A. Sales (Ed.), *Substance abuse and counseling* (pp. 1–19). Greensboro, NC: CAPS.

Schlesinger, S. E., & Horberg, L. K. (1993). Comprehensive treatment of addictive families. In A. W. Heinemann (Ed.), *Substance abuse and physical disability* (pp. 217–237). Binghamton, NY: Haworth.

Selzer, M. L. (1971). The Michigan Alcoholism Screening Test: The quest for a new diagnostic instrument. *American Journal of Psychiatry, 127*, 1653–1658.

Slayter, E. M. (2010). Disparities in access to substance abuse treatment among people with intellectual disabilities and serious mental illness. *Health & Social Work, 35*, 49–59.

Stevens, P., & Smith, R. L. (2001). *Substance abuse counseling: Theory and practice.* Upper Saddle River, NJ: Prentice Hall.

Substance Abuse and Mental Health Services Administration (SAMHSA). (2002). *Results from the 2002 National Survey on Drug Use and Health: Summary of national findings.* Retrieved from http://www.samhsa.gov/data/nhsda/2k2nsduh/results/2k2Results.htm

Substance Abuse and Mental Health Services Administration (SAMHSA). (2012). *Results from the 2011 National Survey on Drug Use and Health: Summary of national findings.* Retrieved from http://www.samhsa.gov/data/NSDUH/2k11Results/NSDUHresults2011.htm

Talbott, G. D. (1989). Alcoholism should be treated as a disease. In B. Leone (Ed.), *Chemical dependency: Opposing viewpoints.* San Diego, CA: Greenhaven.

Tarter, R. E. (1988). Are there inherited behavioral traits that predispose to substance abuse? *Journal of Consulting and Clinical Psychology, 56*, 189–196.

Tyas, S., & Rush, B. (1993). The treatment of disabled persons with alcohol and drug problems: Results of a survey of addiction services. *Journal of Studies on Alcohol and Drugs, 54*, 275–282.

Vasilaki, E. I., Hosier, S. G., & Cox, W. M. (2006). The efficacy of motivational interviewing as a brief intervention for excessive drinking: A meta-analytic review. *Alcohol and Alcoholism, 41*, 328–335.

Wesson, D. R., Havassy, B. E., & Smith, D. E. (1986). Theories of relapse and recovery and their implications for drug abuse treatment. *Relapse and Recovery in Drug Abuse, 72*, 5–19.

West, S. L., Graham, C. W., & Cifu, D. X. (2009). Rates of alcohol/other drug treatment denials to persons with physical disabilities: Accessibility concerns. *Alcoholism Treatment Quarterly, 27*, 305–316.

Wexler, H. K., Magura, S., Beardsley, M. M., & Josepher, H. (1994). An AIDS education and relapse prevention model for high-risk parolees. *Journal of the Addictions, 29*, 361–386.

Witkiewitz, K., & Marlatt, G. A. (2004). Relapse prevention for alcohol and drug problems: That was Zen, this is Tao. *American Psychologist, 59*, 224.

World Health Organization (WHO). (2008). *mhGAP: Mental Health Gap Action Programme: Scaling up care for mental, neurological and substance use disorders.* Geneva, Switzerland: Author.

Wright, T., & Myrick, H. (2006). Acamprosate: A new tool in the battle against alcohol dependence. *Neuropsychiatric Disability Treatment, 2*, 445–453.

Zucker, R. A., & Gomberg, E. S. (1986). Etiology of alcoholism reconsidered: The case for a biopsychosocial process. *American Psychologist, 41*, 783–793.

# Counseling People With Physical Disabilities

*Erin Martz*

*If a meaning is to be assigned to* life after trauma…
*the meaning of the future could be as important as that of the past…*
*rehabilitation [is] in line with this concept of* healing forward.
—*Shalev, 1997, p. 421, emphasis added*

## LEARNING OBJECTIVES

The aims of this chapter are to provide an overview of stress, trauma, coping, and adaptation theories and how they apply to the onset of chronic illnesses and physical disabilities, in addition to summarizing counseling interventions that can be used to facilitate coping with chronic illness and disability (CID). Learning objectives are the following:

1. Understand theories on stress, trauma, and coping as applied to CID.
2. Understand negative affectivity (e.g., depression, anxiety, and posttraumatic stress disorder [PTSD]) in the context of CID.
3. Understand positive affectivity (e.g., posttraumatic growth and adaptation) in the context of CID.
4. Identify several counseling interventions that may facilitate coping with CID.

## STRESS AND COPING RESPONSES TO THE ONSET OF CID

For many people, the onset of a CID can be extremely stressful, even traumatic. The physical effects of an accident or disease process may remain for a lifetime and require continuous attention and self-management. Multiple sources of stress can arise from the onset of CID, from change in mobility and physical or mental functioning to job loss or rejection from others due to the CID. The onset of CID creates a unique type of stressor or trauma because "the primary source of psychological stress lies within and not outside the person's body boundaries" (Lipowski, 1970, p. 92). Although psychosocial reactions to major changes in one's life are expected and common, stress and trauma triggered by the onset of CID may become problematic or even unhealthy if continuing over a long term.

After CID onset, a range of psychological responses may occur to propel individuals back to psychological homeostasis. The shorter term responses are called coping strategies or mechanisms. Longer term reactions may be grouped under the terms *negative affectivity* (e.g., depression, anxiety, and PTSD) and *positive affectivity* (e.g., posttraumatic growth, adaptation). An integrated view of psychosocial responses after the onset of disability includes concepts at both ends of the affective response continuum, in order to capture the massive psychosocial adjustment that is often needed after the onset of CID. The present chapter provides an overview of stress and trauma reactions to CID, followed by an overview on coping responses to CID. Those sections are followed by brief overviews on negative affectivity and positive affectivity, ending with a section on counseling interventions specific to the promotion of coping with CID, a case study, and discussion questions.

### Stress or Trauma After Disability Onset

Stress is typically viewed as a negative experience that disrupts an individual's psychosocial equilibrium. Hans Selye (1956, 1982), one of the leaders in stress research during the 1950s and 1960s, defined stress as "the non-specific (that is, common) result of any demand upon the body, be the effect mental or somatic" (Selye, 1982, p. 7). A few decades later, two leading stress researchers, Lazarus and Folkman (1984, p. 19) defined stress as "a particular relationship between the person and the environment that is appraised by the person as taxing or exceeding his or her resources and endangering his or her well-being." This definition of stress has been adopted by many researchers as a cornerstone for understanding stress and coping.

Lazarus and Folkman's theory on stress and coping asserted that stress is determined by an individual's subjective perception of the stressful situation, instead of the objective characterizations of the situation itself, and by the ability of the individual to cope with the perceived stress. Thus, according to Lazarus and his colleagues (Folkman & Moskowitz, 2004; Lazarus, 1966; Lazarus & Folkman, 1984; Lazarus & Launier, 1978), stress is a set of interacting personal and environmental characteristics and processes. This relational definition of stress by Lazarus and colleagues added both cognitive appraisal and coping processes as influencing the relationship among the person, the environment (i.e., the person–environment fit), and psychosocial outcomes after stressful events.

Trauma can be defined as a sudden and severe event that triggers multidimensional responses in individuals, including physiological, psychological, social, and existential reactions (Shalev, Galai, & Eth, 1993). Freud (1920–1922) defined trauma as a period of time when external stimuli are powerful enough to break through the individual's protective shield that defends against stimuli, thus triggering every possible defensive measure. In Freud's view, a "stimulus barrier" decreases sensory input, whereas defense mechanisms act as control devices to maintain psychological homeostasis. Traumatization occurs when these controls fail, due to the experience of powerful events (Horowitz, 1983). Psychological energy is needed to master the stimuli that have "broken in" and to bind them psychologically, so that they can be disposed of, but this requires a focus of psychic energy that reduces or paralyzes other aspects of psychic functioning (Freud, 1920–1922).

Terr (1991) used the term *crossover* trauma, such as a CID, to describe a one-time event with long-term, continuous consequences that may elicit a complex set of traumatic reactions. Green (1993) noted that more severe psychological effects may occur as an additive consequence of experiencing multiple traumatic events. This suggests that dual potential triggers for traumatic reactions may be created when an individual experiences a traumatic event involving bodily harm and the consequential injury leads to a disability. Radnitz et al. (1995) suggested a term of "double post-traumatic stress disorder (double PTSD)" to denote how the trauma of the onset of CID can be compounded by other traumas, such as the trauma of war. Other researchers have noted that when evidence of a traumatic event is still present, such as a physical CID, it may serve as a visual or proprioceptive cue to the traumatic event that caused the CID (Blanchard & Hickling, 1997; DuHamel et al., 2001; Miller, 1998). Hence, an injury or CID may act as a continuous reminder of trauma that can trigger anxiety for certain individuals.

## Coping With CID

Coping is a psychological response in circumstances that are new, require special efforts, or are unusually taxing (Costa, Somerfield, & McCrae, 1996; Lazarus & Folkman, 1984). Coping strategies include cognitive, affective, and behavioral attempts to master events that are overwhelming to an individual or that an individual has not experienced previously and, thus, does not have automatic responses to (Inglehart, 1991; Lazarus & Folkman, 1984; Livneh, 2000). Wright (1960, 1983) described a "coping versus succumbing" framework in the context of CID. According to Wright, the coping perspective emphasizes the positive aspects, qualities, and abilities that are inherent in an individual, whereas the succumbing perspective focuses on the impairment, pathology, or insufficiency in an individual's mind or body.

In their transactional theory of coping, Lazarus and Folkman (1984, p. 141) defined coping as the "constantly changing cognitive and behavioral efforts to manage specific external and/or internal demands that are appraised as taxing or exceeding the resources of the person." In defining coping in this way, Lazarus and Folkman argued that coping is process oriented, rather than trait based and involves attempts to master the environment and one's responses to stress. Lazarus and his colleagues typically categorized coping strategies as either problem-solving or emotion-focused. Problem-solving coping strategies are "action-centered coping" and emotion-focused coping strategies "change only the way in which the relationship is *attended to...or interpreted*" (Lazarus, 1991, p. 112).

Moos and colleagues (Holahan, Moos, & Schaefer, 1996; Moos & Schaefer, 1984, 1986) offered another comprehensive definition of coping. They viewed coping as "a stabilizing factor that can help individuals maintain psychosocial adaptation during stressful periods. Coping encompasses cognitive and behavioral efforts to reduce or eliminate stressful conditions and associated emotional distress" (Holahan et al., 1996, p. 25).

Psychological research was dominated for decades by a focus on defense mechanisms, as defined and explained by Sigmund Freud and his daughter Anna. Yet, research on coping evolved out of the interest in the ways in which individuals successfully deal with stress and life difficulties, using conscious choices and particular strategies within an individual's volitional control. Hence, coping research was a stark contrast to the Freudian depiction of psychological drives being primarily unconscious and, thus, out of direct control of the individual. Haan (1977) argued for an integrative perspective by her tripartite model of coping, defense mechanisms, and fragmentation. Radnitz and Tiersky (2007) provided an excellent and comprehensive review of the differences between defense mechanisms and coping strategies.

There have been many discussions about how to categorize coping strategies. Lazarus and Folkman (1984) grouped them into two overarching functional categories, problem-focused and emotion-focused coping, whereas others have added a third category of avoidance coping (e.g., Billings & Moos, 1981). Yet, other theorists and researchers proposed alternative categorizations that included an additional category of social support or that involved a different approach for categorizing coping strategies. For example, Krohne (1996) proposed a hierarchical framework consisting of three levels of coping: (a) coping strategies that involve a higher versus lower level of abstraction (e.g., engagement versus disengagement coping), (b) coping strategies that consist of conceptually coherent groups of coping reactions (e.g., denial, confrontation, distancing, seeking social support), and (c) coping strategies that focus on coping strategies that are anchored on coping behaviors (e.g., specific items on coping measures). Chronister and Chan (2007) and Livneh and Martz (2007) have provided further details on categories of coping and overviews of coping with CID research.

Problem-focused coping strategies are typically viewed as being directed at modifying the problem that lies at the root of the distress. In contrast, emotion-focused coping strategies focus on regulating or altering one's emotions. Emotion-focused coping also involves changing one's perspective or "appraisal" about the meaning of a situation. Avoidance coping seeks to ignore or downplay the stressor. It is important to note that using emotion-focused or avoidance coping strategies should not be necessarily viewed as "negative" or "nonadaptive" because, in some circumstances, when individuals are unable to change or eliminate a problem, emotion-focused or avoidance coping could be beneficial by helping to maintain emotional balance or regulation (Aldwin, 1994; Mattlin, Wethington, & Kessler, 1990; Suls & Fletcher, 1985; Taylor, 1999; Zeidner & Saklofske, 1996).

Folkman and Moskowitz (2004) noted that, in a majority of studies, emotion-focused coping strategies are helpful in the short term but, in the long term, these types of strategies are associated with greater distress. In general, research indicates that problem-focused or active forms of coping are typically more adaptive than emotion-focused coping strategies (Folkman & Moskowitz, 2004). The Suls and Fletcher (1985) meta-analysis of coping research indicated that nonavoidant or "attention" coping strategies, including problem-solving coping, are related to better long-term outcomes over time, although avoidant coping can sometimes be effective in the short term (e.g., to reduce stress). It is important to note that coping with stressors, such as those related to CID, involves the use of fluctuating and fluid strategies in order to meet changing demands and contexts and to facilitate adaptation to disability (Livneh & Antonak, 2005). Individuals may simultaneously use multiple types of coping to manage stress and anxiety (Lawrence & Fauerbach, 2003).

Psychosocial adaptation to CID, which is discussed in more detail in a later section of this chapter, should be distinguished from the construct of coping. One difference is the temporal element, that is, psychosocial adaptation to CID can be viewed as a longer term outcome that reflects psychological equilibrium, reintegration, and a reassertion of a positive self-concept (Livneh, 2001; Livneh & Antonak, 1990, 1991, 1994, 1997; Shontz, 1975). In contrast, coping strategies can be described as the more immediate set of psychological defense strategies in response to CID (Bracken & Shepard, 1980; Livneh & Martz, 2007). Both coping and adaptation can be defined in tripartite terms of cognitive, affective, and behavioral aspects.

Research on coping with a CID has been expanding at a rapid rate (see Martz & Livneh, 2007; Zeidner & Endler, 1996). Because coping strategies are the more immediate responses to stress and trauma, it is important for rehabilitation counselors and other rehabilitation health professionals to be cognizant of coping processes related to CID.

## NEGATIVE AFFECTIVITY

The stress and trauma related to the onset of CID may cause a range of psychological reactions that may become problematic and unhealthy and, thus, may require interventions. These reactions are grouped under the term *negative affectivity* and may include reactions such as depression, anxiety, and PTSD. Sometimes an individual may experience multiple psychological reactions in the negative affectivity cluster. For example, Ladwig et al. (1999) found that individuals with PTSD who were in cardiac arrest experienced anxiety and depression to a significantly higher degree than individuals in cardiac arrest who did not have PTSD.

### Disability-Related Depression

Depression can be described as "a reactive response of bereavement for the lost body part or function, or of impending death and suffering" (Livneh & Antonak, 1997, p. 21) and can include affective responses, such as helplessness, hopelessness, despair, isolation, self-depreciation, and distress. Dunn (1975) included feelings of worthlessness, sadness, and loss of purpose after CID onset. In addition to the aforementioned symptoms of depression, Judd, Burrows, and Brown (1986) listed loss of pleasure in almost all activities or hobbies, sleep disturbances, slowed movements or agitation, loss of energy, fatigue, excessive guilt, poor concentration, slowed thinking, recurrent thoughts of death, or suicidal attempts.

Research suggests that depression often occurs after the onset of an impairment or disability. In a longitudinal analysis of 730 individuals with physical disabilities, Turner and Noh (1988) found that 35% experienced depression at initial assessment, as measured by the Center for Epidemiological Studies Depression Scale (CED-S). Four years later, 37% of these individuals had clinically significant depression, in contrast to 12% of a comparison group with no disabilities; thus, the number of individuals with physical disabilities who experienced depression was three times higher than those in the comparison group.

### Disability-Related Anxiety

Anxiety, as a response to CID onset, is a reaction that involves panic, confused thinking, cognitive flooding, physiological responses, and purposeless overactivity (Livneh & Antonak, 1997). Summerfeldt and Endler (1996) proposed that disability-related anxiety can be adaptive in helping individuals to meet challenges and avoid harm. Yet, anxiety also can be psychologically challenging when, for example, recurring fears are experienced about the outcome of a disease and whether it will be possible to cope.

Lilliston (1985, p. 9) explained that anxiety may be experienced by individuals with CID because their trust has been shattered, and "it is frightening and stressful to learn that one has misperceived the world" as a safe and/or just place. Verwoerdt (1966) contrasted depression with anxiety, depicting depression as an energy-saving activity and anxiety as an energy-consuming activity. To Verwoerdt, anxiety signals a threat of loss of an essential object, whereas depression signifies that the object has been lost and, consequently, that it is useless to expend any more energy.

### Posttraumatic Stress Disorder

Posttraumatic stress reactions, which may be diagnosed as PTSD, represent one cluster of many types of possible psychological reactions following a traumatic event, such as the onset of CID. PTSD is a cluster of cognitive, emotional, and physiological responses that continues for at least 1 month after a traumatic event, and these symptoms are grouped into three symptom clusters of Avoidance, Intrusion, and Hyperarousal, according to the American Psychiatric Association (APA, 2013) *Diagnostic and Statistical Manual of Mental Disorders* (5th ed., *DSM-5*). Freud's concept of "traumatic neurosis" was used as the basis of the PTSD diagnosis. He defined traumatic neurosis as a result of an external trauma that breaks through the individual's protective psychic shield and causes harm (Martz & Lindy, 2010).

Some researchers view PTSD not as a disorder, but as a condition in response to extreme stress. For example, Lifton (1988, p. 9) depicted PTSD as "a normal adaptive process of reaction to an abnormal situation" and as a "normal reaction to extreme stress" (Lifton, 1993, p. 12). Other researchers also view PTSD as part of a process of adaptation to trauma (Horowitz, 1976, 1983, 1986, 1997; McFarlane, 2000; O'Brien, 1998; Van der Kolk et al., 1996; Yehuda & McFarlane, 1995). Though many researchers continue to debate whether PTSD should be viewed as a mental disorder or as an adaptive reaction to trauma, Wilson (1995, p. 19) noted that "the psychopathology of traumatic reactions is discerned when the presence of the symptoms persists and exerts an adverse effect on adaptive functioning." Thus, although PTSD may be an adaptive response to extreme stress, it still, by definition, has significant impact on adaptive functioning. Empirical research on PTSD in the context of CID is growing (e.g., Alter et al., 1996; Blanchard & Hickling, 1997; Lawrence & Fauerbach, 2003; Martz, 2004, 2005; Martz, Bodner, & Livneh, 2010). Martz and Cook (2001) found several CIDs to be risk factors for PTSD.

DuHamel et al. (2001, p. 109) noted, "[P]hysical limitations serve as a cue of cancer that activates trauma-related symptomatology such as intrusive thoughts about cancer and its treatment." Their view reflects that individuals can experience intrusive memories about the traumatic event that caused the CID, and the existence of a CID can also continue to remind them about the CID-related treatment and its future effects. Indeed Brewin, Watson, McCarthy, Hyman, and Dayson (1998) found that a large portion of the intrusive memories experienced by individuals with cancer revolved around illness, injury, and death. Individuals with CID may also experience secondary medical problems that can be life-threatening, which may be traumatic and, hence, another source of PTSD.

## POSITIVE AFFECTIVITY

A second category of responses to CID can be grouped under the term *positive affectivity*. This can include adaptation to disability, which is called *acceptance* or *adjustment* by some researchers and scholars, and has also been called *posttraumatic growth*.

### Adaptation to Disability

Costa et al. (1996, p. 45) declared that the term *adaptation* is so broad that "it covers virtually the whole of psychology (if not biology)." Psychology is permeated with concepts on adaptation, in the view that almost every type of psychotherapy is geared to helping individuals modify their patterns of adjustment to facilitate long-term well-being (Summerfeldt & Endler, 1996). Adaptation to the "crisis" of disability implies change (Shontz, 1965). Four value changes were posited as inherent in the process of acceptance of or adaptation to disability, according to Dembo, Leviton, and Wright (1956) and Wright (1960, 1983): enlarging one's scope of values, limiting the spread of the effects of a disability, emphasizing one's assets instead of comparing oneself to others, and subordinating one's physical aspects over other parts of oneself.

Generally speaking, adaptation is a mastery construct that can include both psychological and physical mastery. Some research on adaptation makes a distinction between mastery of self and mastery of the environment, whereas most CID-related theories merge the two, combining physical and environmental factors with psychological factors—hence the term *psychosocial adaptation*. Consideration of multilevel factors is needed, as the process of adapting to a CID often requires restoration or enhancement of remaining physical and psychological abilities, as well as adjustment to attitudinal and physical barriers in the environment.

A number of empirically based and clinically based theories on adaptation to CID exist, reflecting a wide spectrum of views (for summaries, see Livneh & Antonak, 1997; Livneh & Martz, 2012). According to Livneh and Parker (2005), some models propose that reactions to CID follow a general sequence of psychological experiences or reactions, which are also termed *stages* or *phases* (e.g., Dunn, 1975; Falek & Britton, 1974; Hohmann, 1975; Krueger, 1984; Shontz, 1965). Some propose *pendular models* of psychosocial adaptation to CID, in which there are alterations between an old and the new identity of oneself with a CID (e.g., Charmaz, 1983, 1993, 1995; Kendall & Buys, 1998; Shontz, 1975; Stroebe & Schut, 1999; Yoshida, 1993). More complex models of adaptation include Moos and Holahan's (2007) biopsychosocial model, which includes three components or panels (e.g., personal resources and characteristics, health-related factors, and an individual's social–physical environment; cognitive appraisal, adaptive tasks, and coping skills; and health-related outcomes). Other multidimensional models on the psychosocial reactions to disability include Devins's illness intrusiveness model (Devins & Binik, 1996; Devins, Edworthy, Guthrie, & Martin, 1992; Devins, Seland, Klein, Edworthy, & Saary, 1993) and Bishop's disability centrality model (Bishop, 2005a, 2005b; Bishop, Smedema, & Lee, 2009).

One empirically based multidimensional model defines psychosocial adaptation as a dynamic, continuously evolving process that involves an integration of intra-personal, interpersonal, and environmental elements (Antonak & Livneh, 1991; Livneh, 2001; Livneh & Antonak, 1990, 1991, 1994, 1997). This particular model of psychosocial adaptation to disability suggests that the process of adaptation includes eight particular reactions to the onset of CID, namely, shock, anxiety, denial, depression, internalized anger, externalized anger, acknowledgment, and adjustment. The acknowledgment reaction of CID is defined as a cognitive acceptance of disability, whereas adjustment reaction is defined as an emotional and behavior acceptance and integration of CID into one's life. Livneh (2001) elaborated on the view that the process of adaptation consisted of three main components, namely, antecedents (e.g., CID-triggering events and contextual variables), processes (e.g., unfolding psychosocial reactions and contextual influences), and psychosocial outcomes of adaptation (e.g., intrapersonal functioning, interpersonal functioning, and extrapersonal functioning).

### Posttraumatic Growth and Disability

Posttraumatic growth is a second indicator of positive affectivity. Tedeschi and Calhoun (1995, 1996, 1998, 2004) have been leaders in the investigation of the idea that individuals can experience posttraumatic growth after traumatic events. Tedeschi and Calhoun (1996) reviewed literature on this topic and created an instrument called the Posttraumatic Growth Inventory. They proposed that positive events after trauma may occur in three areas: (a) alterations in self-perception, such as emotional growth and a new sense of strength; (b) changes in relationships with others, such as a greater appreciation of and sensitivity to one's relationships, an awareness of how quickly those relationships can be lost, a greater emotional expressiveness, and learning how to develop more positive intimate relationships with others; and (c) changes in the philosophy about life and in some of the assumptions about life, such as a greater appreciation and enjoyment of life, living a more fulfilling and meaningful life, and developing a heightened spirituality.

Tedeschi and Calhoun (2004) emphasized that the process of posttraumatic growth does not necessarily decrease emotional distress, because it may involve an existential struggle that survivors may need to undergo in order to rebuild their worldviews. In other words, "For most trauma survivors, posttraumatic growth and distress will coexist, and the growth emerges from the struggle with coping, not from the trauma itself" (Tedeschi & Calhoun, 2004, p. 2).

Research is growing in the area of posttraumatic growth and CID (e.g., Chun & Lee, 2008; Manne, Ostroff, Winkel, Grana, & Fox, 2005). Joseph and Linley (2008, p. 341) called the research on posttraumatic growth a "paradigm shift" and stated that "we do not see posttraumatic stress and growth as an either-or dichotomy, but rather as a more integrative way of understanding the variety of processes and outcomes that may ensue following trauma." This reflects the view proposed in this chapter and elsewhere that an integrative approach that includes both positive and negative affectivity should be used when conducting empirical research related to CID.

## COUNSELING INTERVENTIONS TO PROMOTE COPING

Numerous authors (e.g., Chan, Cardoso, & Chronister, 2009; Livneh, 2001; Livneh & Antonak, 1997, 2005) have provided overviews and analyses of a range of theoretical approaches and therapeutic interventions that can be used specifically for facilitating adaptation to CID. Other chapters in the present volume also explore a variety of counseling approaches. Thus, the following section is delimited to counseling interventions that may be specifically targeted at coping with CID.

Most modern-day counseling and psychotherapy approaches tend to be weighted to brief and time-limited, highly structured, evidence-based protocols. Thus, practitioners need flexible, psychotherapeutic toolboxes to help facilitate the functioning of a client as quickly as possible. A range of psychotherapeutic interventions can be used to facilitate various coping skills and components. For example, person-centered or gestalt therapy can target emotion-focused coping by providing interpersonal support, validation of feelings, and encouragement to maintain hope. Cognitive behavioral therapy (CBT) interventions are available that target skills to promote active coping strategies or problem-focused coping, and that include such techniques as modeling, exposure to feared stimuli, changing irrational beliefs, altering information-gathering cognitive processes, and role-playing (Radnitz, 2000). In addition, CBT can bolster emotion-focused coping by teaching stress management skills (e.g., relaxation, meditation).

One of the major treatment issues related to coping with CID onset is the stress and trauma that may be triggered by the onset of CID, which can dominate the attention, and even become the identity, of a person with CID. In gestalt therapy terms, the CID becomes the "foreground" in a person's life; therapy can help a person shift the CID presence to the "background" of the mental gestalt or outlook (Degeneffe & Lynch, 2004). This kind of therapy can facilitate adaptive coping by reducing the mental energy invested in thinking about CID.

Coping interventions may be viewed as a CBT approach to CID, but note that coping interventions will specifically target coping strategies and will attempt to bolster adaptive coping strategies. Coping interventions involve teaching coping skills to manage stress and helping clients examine the cognitive, emotional, and behavioral choices that they typically use to manage stress in their lives. Two specific coping interventions seem to be worthy of additional attention, coping effectiveness training (CET) and cognitive coping therapy (CCT).

### Coping Effectiveness Training

Chesney and Folkman (1994) developed CET, grounded in the Lazarus and Folkman (1984) theory of stress and coping. Chesney, Folkman, and Chambers (1996) described the CET intervention as teaching a framework for choosing among coping strategies and fitting the coping strategy to the changeability of an event, in order to promote adaptive coping and reduce distress. They noted that most stress management programs (including CBT) only provide *general* information about how to apply the cognitive skills that are taught. CET specifically targets the coping strategies that individuals choose to deal with stressors. The components of the original CET groups (Center for AIDS Prevention Studies, 1997; Chesney & Folkman, 1994; Chesney et al., 1996) focused on teaching individuals about stress and coping, problem solving, the differences between adaptive and nonadaptive coping (i.e., how to match that type of coping strategy with the type of stressor), and how to use social support as a form of coping.

What makes CET a unique psychotherapeutic intervention is the teaching of a metastrategy to help individuals choose the most appropriate type of coping for a particular type of stressor. A CET intervention combines stress management techniques with the addition of "a meta-strategy for choosing among coping strategies to maximize effectiveness in managing stressful situations and reducing stress. The meta-strategy converts the major tenets of stress and coping theory into action" (Chesney & Folkman, 1994, p. 173). Hence, CET focuses on helping individuals choose the most appropriate type of coping for a particular type of stressor, which is one of the main reasons why CET is distinct from general CBT interventions.

Kennedy (2008) developed a CET manual tailored to individuals coping with a spinal cord injury. CET workbooks are provided to participants by both the Chesney and Kennedy protocols, using homework to help reinforce the concepts taught during CET.

Research has demonstrated the efficacy of CET in reducing a range of negative affective states, such as distress, depression, and anxiety (Chesney et al., 1996; Chesney, Chambers, Taylor, Johnson, & Folkman, 2003; Duchnick, Letsch, & Curtiss, 2009; Kennedy, Duff, Evans, & Beedie, 2003; King & Kennedy, 1999). These findings support the success of CET in helping individuals with CIDs to learn how to choose coping skills that are associated with improved psychological well-being.

In summary, CET can help individuals with CID to learn how to cope better with the stress created by the onset of CID and the stress related to self-managing a CID. CET can also teach individuals how to discern the types of coping strategies that can be used with the types of stressors, unchangeable or changeable, in the sense of "fitting" the coping strategies with the stressor. This perspective may help individuals realize that, although some aspects of their lives are unchangeable due to CID issues, they can use a variety of coping strategies to modify the stressors that *are* changeable in their lives.

## Cognitive Coping Therapy

Sharoff (2004) proposed a CCT, which is based on the CBT principle of not taking thoughts as facts but, rather, viewing thoughts as hypotheses that need to be tested for validity. Sharoff's CCT is based on a holistic model that uses cognitive, emotional, perceptual, physical, and behavioral abilities. Sharoff proposed that there is no such thing as a "bad" coping skill, because a skill is only part of a particular strategy; rather, what matters most is how, when, and where it is used. Sharoff asserted that even nonadaptive strategies, psychopathology, and psychological symptoms include invaluable, viable skills that can aid adaptation, thus requiring a focus on finding the positive within individual reactions that are perceived as negative.

Sharoff (2004) created both a book and manual that include a number of exercises to help promote adaptive coping strategies among individuals with a wide range of CIDs. Although the therapeutic techniques that he proposed have not yet been empirically examined, many can be used to promote coping with CID, such as self-instruction training (i.e., setting up a self-dialogue to help when situations trigger suffering or hatred of one's illness); using predetermined imagery; enacting a role model (i.e., a person is asked to notice those who handle their medical problems well, to analyze what they are doing, and then use them as role models for a period of time); anchoring (i.e., a person is asked to think about a time when the person was able to deal with the suffering and then anchor that memory by touching a certain part of the body); value clarification (i.e., to help reorder actions based on a person's "old self" and the values that must be put aside based on the CID existence); acceptance training (i.e., recognizing that certain actions can no longer be done and that actions should fit within one's CID-related limitations); limit setting (i.e., communication training on assertiveness and conflict resolution because the individual with a CID has a "gatekeeper" function about what activities and actions the individual can or cannot do, given the CID-related limitations); frustration management (i.e., building frustration tolerance by cognitive restructuring, cognitive rehearsal, self-monitoring, relaxation training, symbolic gesturing, and imagery usage); frustration accommodation (i.e., developing flexibility around limitations imposed by CID); area thinking (i.e., selecting realistic goals that are within the area of the individual's control); and blending one's old and new identities (i.e., new identity after the onset of CID).

## CASE STUDY

Phil is a 51-year-old, self-employed farmer with an eighth-grade education. While mowing grass on a slope, his tractor hit a hole and threw him onto the ground. Subsequently, his tractor ran over his right leg. Due to massive trauma and the severity of the injury, his leg had to be amputated.

In general, Phil does not believe in following directions; in other words, he thinks "rules are made to be broken." As a result, he did not follow basic safety precautions when he was mowing. He received a prosthetic leg, which would enable him to walk around slowly. But he experienced considerable depression after his injury and was not motivated to learn how to walk with the artificial limb. Further, he refused the offers of help to make accommodations in his house or farm equipment.

Phil also has high blood pressure, for which he refuses to take medication. He served in the Vietnam War and still experiences nights of sleeplessness, due to intrusive images related to his war experiences. His wife divorced him 10 years prior to the accident, claiming that he was too irritable and angry to live with anymore. He claims that he does not drink too much alcohol, but "only a six-pack a night so I can sleep." His wife accused him of being addicted to alcohol when she divorced him.

Although multiple approaches and techniques could be used with Phil in counseling sessions, rehabilitation professionals could identify the following issues as possible areas for intervention: (a) Phil's worldview of not wanting to follow rules (i.e., Which rules does he follow? How does he choose what rules to follow?); (b) the numerous sources of stress and trauma in his life (i.e., health, social and intimacy issues, financial issues); (c) some of his symptoms (i.e., intrusions, sleeplessness, irritability, and anger possibly related to wartime experiences), which suggest the need to assess for PTSD; (d) the possibility that his PTSD may interact with his psychological reactions to his amputation, hence making the psychological picture more complicated; (e) his depression, which may have been triggered by his amputation, although other factors in his life may be influencing his

*(continued)*

*(continued)*

> depression levels (e.g., divorce); (f) Phil may also be experiencing denial, in view of his refusal to allow accommodations in his home or farm equipment as well as his refusal to take medication for his blood pressure; and (g) Phil should be assessed for alcoholism, which can be one way that he is attempting to cope with his problems, or it could be a habit that contributed to his farm accident. Other issues that could be the focus of clinical attention include lack of motivation to walk again, his current unemployment, and lack of self-management skills for his high blood pressure. Proactive coping skills could be taught to help him take charge of some of the issues that he has control over in his life. This may help to reduce his use of nonadaptive coping skills, such as heavy use of alcohol.

## CONCLUSIONS

Mastery over psychological stress and trauma related to the onset of a CID is evident when individuals have authority over the memory processes, can choose whether or not to think about the trauma, and are no longer overwhelmed by the "terrible immediacy and fierce intensity" of traumatic memories (Harvey, 1996, p. 12). Further indications that individuals are adapting to or healing from psychological stress and trauma related to CID include a restoration of self-esteem and self-caring behaviors and the pursuit of a self-fulfilling life (Livneh, 2001; Livneh & Antonak, 1997).

Counselors, therapists, and rehabilitation professionals can provide interventions that specifically target coping skills for individuals with CID and thus may help them better self-manage their psychosocial reactions to their CID. Increasing adaptive coping skills may also reduce the negative emotions and cognitions triggered by the continuous presence of a CID. Although the onset of a CID may be life changing, stressful, negative, and traumatic, coping skills training and interventions can help to facilitate individuals' return to psychological homeostasis and to enhance their positive affectivity.

## DISCUSSION EXERCISES

1. Why is it important to understand theories on stress and trauma as applied to chronic illness and disability?
2. Why is it important to understand both negative and positive affectivity in the context of CID?
3. Which aspects of positive affectivity, CID-related posttraumatic growth or adaptation, have received more research attention?
4. Which coping intervention has the most professional appeal to you?
5. What are two of the primary coping mechanisms that you use to handle your own stressful experiences?

# REFERENCES

Aldwin, C. M. (1994). *Stress, coping, and development: An integrative perspective.* New York, NY: Guilford.

Alter, C. L., Pelcovitz, D., Axelrod, A., Goldenberg, B., Harris, H., Meyers, B., . . . Kaplan, S. (1996). Identification of PTSD in cancer survivors. *Psychosomatics, 37,* 137–143.

American Psychiatric Association. (2013). *Diagnostic and statistical manual of mental disorders* (5th ed.). Washington, DC: Author.

Antonak, R. F., & Livneh, H. (1991). A hierarchy of reactions to disability. *International Journal of Rehabilitation Research, 14,* 13–24.

Billings, A., & Moos, R. (1981). The role of coping responses and social resources in attenuating the stress of life events. *Journal of Behavioral Medicine, 4,* 139–157.

Bishop, M. (2005a). Quality of life and psychosocial adaptation to chronic illness and acquired disability: A conceptual and theoretical synthesis. *Journal of Rehabilitation, 71*(2), 5–14.

Bishop, M. (2005b). Quality of life and psychosocial adaptation to chronic illness and disability: Preliminary analysis of a conceptual and theoretical synthesis. *Rehabilitation Counseling Bulletin, 48,* 219–231.

Bishop, M., Smedema, S., & Lee, E. (2009). Quality of life and psychosocial adaptation to chronic illness and disability. In F. Chan, E. Cardoso, & J. A. Chronister (Eds.), *Understanding psychosocial adjustment to chronic illness and disability: A handbook for evidence-based practitioners in rehabilitation* (pp. 521–550). New York, NY: Springer Publishing Company.

Blanchard, E. B., & Hickling, E. J. (1997). *After the crash: Assessment and treatment of motor vehicle accident survivors.* Washington, DC: American Psychological Association.

Bracken, M. B., & Shepard, M. J. (1980). Coping and adaptation following acute spinal cord injury: A theoretical analysis. *Paraplegia, 18,* 74–85.

Brewin, C. R., Watson, M., McCarthy, S., Hyman, P., & Dayson, D. (1998). Intrusive memories and depression in cancer patients. *Behavior Research and Therapy, 36,* 1131–1142.

Center for AIDS Prevention Studies. (1997). *Coping effectiveness training: Facilitator's manual.* Retrieved November 4, 2012, from http://caps.ucsf.edu/uploads/projects/CHANGES/pdf/CET%20Facilitator's%20Manual.pdf

Chan, F., Cardoso, E., & Chronister, J. A. (Eds.). (2009). *Understanding psychosocial adjustment to chronic illness and disability: A handbook for evidence-based practitioners in rehabilitation.* New York, NY: Springer Publishing Company.

Charmaz, K. (1983). Loss of self: A fundamental form of suffering in the chronically ill. *Sociology of Health and Illness, 5,* 168–195.

Charmaz, K. (1993). *Good days, bad days: The self in chronic illness and time*: New Brunswick, NJ: Rutgers University Press.

Charmaz, K. (1995). The body, identity, and self: Adapting to impairment. *Sociological Quarterly, 36,* 657–680.

Chesney, M., & Folkman, S. (1994). Psychological impact of HIV disease and implications for intervention. *Psychiatric Clinics of North America, 17,* 163–182.

Chesney, M., Folkman, S., & Chambers, D. (1996). Coping effectiveness training for men living with HIV: Preliminary findings. *International Journal of STD & AIDS, 7*(Suppl. 2), 75–82.

Chesney, M. A., Chambers, D. B., Taylor, J. M., Johnson, L. M., & Folkman, S. (2003). Coping effectiveness training for men living with HIV: Results from a randomized clinical trial testing a group-based intervention. *Psychosomatic Medicine, 65,* 1038–1046.

Chronister, J., & Chan, F. (2007). Hierarchical coping: A conceptual framework for understanding coping within the context of chronic illness and disability. In E. Martz & H. Livneh (Eds.), *Coping with chronic illness and disability: Theoretical, empirical, and clinical aspects* (pp. 49–71). New York, NY: Springer Publishing Company.

Chun, S., & Lee, Y. (2008). The experience of posttraumatic growth for people with spinal cord injury. *Qualitative Health Research, 18*, 877–890.

Costa, P. T., Somerfield, M. R., & McCrae, R. R. (1996). Personality and coping: A reconceptualization. In M. Zeidner & N. S. Endler (Eds.), *Handbook of coping: Theory, research, applications* (pp. 44–61). New York, NY: Wiley.

Degeneffe, C. E., & Lynch, R. T. (2004). Gestalt therapy. In F. Chan, N. L. Berven, & K. R. Thomas (Eds.), *Counseling theories and techniques for rehabilitation health professionals* (pp. 98–117). New York, NY: Springer Publishing Company.

Dembo, T., Leviton, G. L., & Wright, B. A. (1956). Adjustment to misfortune: A problem of social-psychological rehabilitation. *Artificial Limbs, 3*, 4–62.

Devins, G., & Binik, Y. (1996). Facilitating coping with chronic physical illness. In M. Zeidner & N. S. Endler (Eds.), *Handbook of coping: Theory, research, applications* (pp. 640–696). New York, NY: Wiley.

Devins, G., Edworthy, S., Guthrie, N., & Martin, L. (1992). Illness intrusiveness in rheumatoid arthritis: Differential impact on depressive symptoms over the adult lifespan. *Journal of Rheumatology, 19*, 709–715.

Devins, G., Seland, T., Klein, G., Edworthy, S., & Saary, M. (1993). Stability and determinants of psychosocial well-being in multiple sclerosis. *Rehabilitation Psychology, 38*, 11–26.

Duchnick, J. J., Letsch, E. A., & Curtiss, G. (2009). Coping effectiveness training during acute rehabilitation of spinal cord injury/dysfunction: A randomized clinical trial. *Rehabilitation Psychology, 54*, 123–132.

DuHamel, K. M., Smith, M. Y., Vickberg, S. M., Papadopoulos, E., Ostroff, J., Winkel, G., . . . Redd, W. H. (2001). Trauma symptoms in bone marrow transplant survivors: The role of nonmedical life events. *Journal of Traumatic Stress, 14*, 95–113.

Dunn, M. K. (1975). Psychological intervention in a spinal cord injury center: An introduction. *Rehabilitation Psychology, 22*, 165–178.

Falek, A., & Britton, S. (1974). Phases in coping: The hypothesis and its implications. *Social Biology, 21*, 1–7.

Folkman, S., & Moskowitz, J. (2004). Coping: Pitfalls and promise. *Annual Review of Psychology, 55*, 745–774.

Freud, S. (1920–1922). Beyond the pleasure principle. In J. Strachey (Ed. and Trans.), *The standard edition of the complete psychological works of Sigmund Freud* (Vol. 18). London, UK: Hogarth Press.

Green, B. L. (1993). Identifying survivors at risk: Trauma and stressors across events. In J. P. Wilson & B. Raphael (Eds.), *International handbook of traumatic stress syndromes* (pp. 135–144). New York, NY: Plenum Press.

Haan, N. (1977). *Coping and defending: Processes of self-environment organization*. New York, NY: Academic Press.

Harvey, M. (1996). An ecological view of psychological trauma and trauma recovery. *Journal of Traumatic Stress, 9*, 3–23.

Hohmann, G. W. (1975). Psychological aspects of treatment and rehabilitation of the spinal cord injured person. *Clinical Orthopaedics and Related Research, 112*, 81–88.

Holahan, C. J., Moos, R. H., & Schaefer, J. A. (1996). Coping, stress, resistance, and growth: Conceptualizing adaptive functioning. In M. Zeidner & N. Endler (Eds.), *Handbook of coping: Theory, research, and application* (pp. 24–43). New York, NY: Wiley.

Horowitz, M. (1976). *Stress response syndromes*. New York, NY: Jason Aronson.

Horowitz, M. J. (1983). Psychological response to serious life events. In S. Breznitz (Ed.), *The denial of stress* (pp. 129–159). New York, NY: International Universities Press.

Horowitz, M. J. (1986). *Stress response syndromes* (2nd ed.). New York, NY: Jason Aronson.

Horowitz, M. J. (1997). *Stress response syndromes: PTSD, grief, and adjustment disorders* (3rd ed.). New York, NY: Jason Aronson.

Inglehart, M. R. (1991). *Reactions to critical life events: A social psychological analysis.* New York, NY: Praeger.

Joseph, S. E., & Linley, P. A. (Eds.). (2008). Reflections on theory and practice in trauma, recovery, and growth: A paradigm shift for the field of traumatic stress. In S. E. Joseph & P. A. Linley (Eds.), *Trauma, recovery, and growth: Positive psychological perspectives* (pp. 339–356). Hoboken, NJ: Wiley.

Judd, F. K., Burrows, G. D., & Brown, D. J. (1986). Depression following acute spinal cord injury. *Paraplegia, 24,* 358–363.

Kendall, E., & Buys, N. (1998). An integrated model of psychosocial adjustment following acquired disability. *Journal of Rehabilitation, 64*(3), 16–20.

Kennedy, P. (2008). *Coping effectively with spinal cord injury: A group program therapist's guide.* New York, NY: Oxford University Press.

Kennedy, P., Duff, J., Evans, M., & Beedie, A. (2003). Coping effectiveness training reduces depression and anxiety following traumatic spinal cord injuries. *British Journal of Clinical Psychology, 42,* 41–52.

King, C., & Kennedy, P. (1999). Coping effectiveness training for people with spinal cord injury: Preliminary results of a controlled trial. *British Journal of Clinical Psychology, 38,* 5–14.

Krohne, H. W. (1996). Individual differences in coping. In M. Zeidner & N. S. Endler (Eds.), *Handbook of coping: Theory, research, applications* (pp. 381–409). New York, NY: Wiley.

Krueger, D. W. (1984). Psychological rehabilitation of physical trauma and disability. In D. W. Krueger (Ed.), *Rehabilitation psychology: A comprehensive textbook* (pp. 3–14). Rockville, MD: Aspen.

Ladwig, K., Schoefinius, A., Dammann, G., Danner, R., Gurtler, R., & Hermann, R. (1999). Long-acting psychotraumatic properties of a cardiac arrest experience. *American Journal of Psychiatry, 156,* 912–919.

Lawrence, J. W., & Fauerbach, J. A. (2003). Personality, coping, chronic stress, social support and PTSD symptoms: A path analysis. *Journal of Burn Care and Rehabilitation, 24,* 63–72.

Lazarus, R. (1966). *Psychological stress and the coping process.* New York, NY: McGraw-Hill.

Lazarus, R. S. (1991). *Emotion and adaptation.* New York, NY: Oxford University Press.

Lazarus, R. S., & Folkman, S. (1984). *Stress, appraisal, and coping.* New York, NY: Springer Publishing Company.

Lazarus, R. S., & Launier, R. (1978). Stress-related transactions between person and environment. In L. A. Pervin & M. Lewis (Eds.), *Perspectives in interactional psychology* (pp. 287–327). New York, NY: Plenum.

Lifton, R. J. (1988). Understanding the traumatized self: Imagery, symbolization, and transformation. In J. P. Wilson, Z. Harel, & B. Kahana (Eds.), *Human adaptation to extreme stress: From the Holocaust to Vietnam* (pp. 7–31). New York, NY: Plenum.

Lifton, R. J. (1993). From Hiroshima to the Nazi doctors: The evolution of psychoformative approaches to understanding traumatic stress syndromes. In J. P. Wilson & B. Raphael (Eds.), *International handbook of traumatic stress syndromes* (pp. 11–23). New York, NY: Plenum.

Lilliston, B. A. (1985). Psychosocial responses to traumatic physical disability. *Social Work in Health Care, 10,* 1–13.

Lipowski, Z. J. (1970). Physical illness, the individual, and the coping process. *Psychiatry in Medicine, 1,* 91–102.

Livneh, H. (2000). Psychosocial adaptation to spinal cord injury: The role of coping strategies. *Journal of Applied Rehabilitation Counseling, 31*(2), 3–10.

Livneh, H. (2001). Psychosocial adaptation to chronic illness and disability. *Rehabilitation Counseling Bulletin, 44,* 151–160.

Livneh, H., & Antonak, R. F. (1990). Reactions to disability: An empirical investigation of their nature and structure. *Journal of Applied Rehabilitation Counseling, 21*(4), 13–21.

Livneh, H., & Antonak, R. F. (1991). Temporal structure of adaptation to disability. *Rehabilitation Counseling Bulletin, 34*, 298–318.

Livneh, H., & Antonak, R. F. (1994). Psychosocial reactions to disability: A review and critique of the literature. *Critical Reviews in Physical and Rehabilitation Medicine, 6*, 1–100.

Livneh, H., & Antonak, R. F. (1997). *Psychosocial adaptation to chronic illness and disability.* Gaithersburg, MD: Aspen.

Livneh, H., & Antonak, R. F. (2005). Psychosocial adaptation to chronic illness and disability: A primer for counselors. *Journal of Counseling & Development, 83*, 12–20.

Livneh, H., & Martz, E. (2007). An introduction to coping theory and research. In E. Martz & H. Livneh (Eds.), *Coping with chronic illness and disability: Theoretical, empirical, and clinical aspects* (pp. 3–28). New York, NY: Springer Publishing Company.

Livneh, H., & Martz, E. (2012). Adjustment to chronic illness and disabilities: Theoretical perspectives, empirical findings, and unresolved issues. In P. Kennedy (Ed.), *Oxford handbook of rehabilitation psychology* (pp. 47-87). New York, NY: Oxford University Press.

Livneh, H., & Parker, R. M. (2005). Psychological adaptation to disability: Perspectives from chaos and complexity theory. *Rehabilitation Counseling Bulletin, 49*, 17–28.

Manne, S. L., Ostroff, J., Winkel, G., Grana, G., & Fox, K. (2005). Partner unsupportive responses, avoidant coping, and distress among women with early stage breast cancer: Patient and partner perspectives. *Health Psychology, 24*, 635–641.

Martz, E. (2004). Do posttraumatic stress symptoms predict reactions of adaptation to disability after a sudden-onset spinal cord injury? *International Journal of Rehabilitation Research, 27*, 185–194.

Martz, E. (2005). Associations of posttraumatic stress levels with demographic, disability-related, and trauma-related variables among individuals with spinal cord injuries. *Rehabilitation Psychology, 50*, 149–157.

Martz, E., Bodner, T., & Livneh, H. (2010). Social support and coping as moderators of perceived disability and posttraumatic stress levels among Vietnam theater veterans. *Health, 2*, 332–341.

Martz, E., & Cook, D. (2001). Physical impairments as risk factors for posttraumatic stress disorder. *Rehabilitation Counseling Bulletin, 44*, 217–221.

Martz, E., & Lindy, J. (2010). Exploring the trauma membrane concept. In E. Martz (Ed.), *Trauma rehabilitation after war and conflict: Community and individual perspectives* (pp. 27–54). New York, NY: Springer Publishing Company.

Martz, E., & Livneh, H. (Eds.). (2007). *Coping with chronic illness and disability: Theoretical, empirical, and clinical aspects.* New York, NY: Springer Publishing Company.

Mattlin, J. A., Wethington, E., & Kessler, R. C. (1990). Situational determinants of coping and coping effectiveness. *Journal of Health and Social Behavior, 31*, 103–122.

McFarlane, A. C. (2000). Posttraumatic stress disorder: A model of the longitudinal course and the role of risk factors. *Journal of Clinical Psychiatry, 61*(Suppl. 5), 15–23.

Miller, L. (1998). *Shocks to the system: Psychotherapy of traumatic disability syndromes.* New York, NY: Norton.

Moos, R., & Holahan, C. (2007). Adaptive tasks and methods of coping with illness and disability. In E. Martz & H. Livneh (Eds.), *Coping with chronic illness and disability: Theoretical, empirical, and clinical aspects* (pp. 107–126). New York, NY: Springer Publishing Company.

Moos, R. H., & Schaefer, J. A. (1984). The crisis of physical illness. In R. H. Moos (Ed.), *Coping with physical illness. Volume 2: New perspectives* (pp. 3–31). New York, NY: Plenum.

Moos, R. H., & Schaefer, J. A. (1986). Overview and perspective. In R. H. Moos (Ed.), *Coping with life crises: An integrated approach* (pp. 3–28). New York, NY: Plenum.

O'Brien, L. S. (1998). *Traumatic events and mental health.* Cambridge, UK: Cambridge University Press.

Radnitz, C. L. (Ed.). (2000). *Cognitive behavioral therapy for persons with disabilities*. New York, NY: Jason Aronson.

Radnitz, C. L., Schlein, I. S., Walczak, S., Broderick, C. P., Binks, M., Tirch, D. D., . . . Green, L. (1995). The prevalence of posttraumatic stress disorder in veterans with spinal cord injury. *SCI Psychosocial Process, 8*, 145–149.

Radnitz, C. L., & Tiersky, L. (2007). Psychodynamic and cognitive theories of coping. In E. Martz & H. Livneh (Eds.), *Coping with chronic illness and disability: Theoretical, empirical, and clinical aspects* (pp. 29–48). New York, NY: Springer Publishing Company.

Selye, H. (1956). *The stress of life*. New York, NY: McGraw-Hill.

Selye, H. (1982). History and present status of the stress concept. In L. Goldberger & S. Bernitz (Eds.), *Handbook of stress: Theoretical and clinical aspects*. New York, NY: Free Press.

Shalev, A. Y. (1997). Discussion: Treatment of prolonged posttraumatic stress disorder— Learning from experience. *Journal of Traumatic Stress, 10*, 415–423.

Shalev, A. Y., Galai, T., & Eth, S. (1993). Levels of trauma: Multidimensional approach to the psychotherapy of PTSD. *Psychiatry, 56*, 166–177.

Sharoff, K. (2004). *Coping skills therapy for managing chronic and terminal illness*. New York, NY: Springer Publishing Company.

Shontz, F. C. (1965). Reactions to crisis. *Volta Review, 67*, 364–370.

Shontz, F. C. (1975). *The psychological aspects of physical illness and disability*. New York, NY: Macmillan.

Stroebe, M., & Schut, H. (1999). The dual process model of coping with bereavement: Rationale and description. *Death Studies, 23*, 197–224.

Suls, J., & Fletcher, B. (1985). The relative efficacy of avoidant and nonavoidant coping strategies: A meta-analysis. *Health Psychology, 4*, 249–288.

Summerfeldt, L. J., & Endler, N. S. (1996). Coping with emotion and psychopathology. In M. Zeidner & N. S. Endler (Eds.), *Handbook of coping: Theory, research, applications* (pp. 602–639). New York, NY: Wiley.

Taylor, S. E. (1999). *Health psychology* (4th ed.). New York, NY: McGraw-Hill.

Tedeschi, R. G., & Calhoun, L. G. (1995). *Trauma and transformation: Growing in the aftermath of suffering*. Thousand Oaks, CA: Sage.

Tedeschi, R. G., & Calhoun, L. G. (1996). The Posttraumatic Growth Inventory: Measuring the positive legacy of trauma. *Journal of Traumatic Stress, 9*, 455–471.

Tedeschi, R. G., & Calhoun, L. G. (Eds.). (1998). *Posttraumatic growth: Positive changes in the aftermath of crisis*. Mahwah, NJ: Erlbaum.

Tedeschi, R. G., & Calhoun, L. G. (2004). Posttraumatic growth: A new perspective on psychotraumatology. *Psychiatric Times, 21*(4), 1–2.

Terr, L. C. (1991). Childhood traumas: An outline and overview. *American Journal of Psychiatry, 148*, 10–20.

Turner, R. J., & Noh, S. (1988). Physical disability and depression: A longitudinal analysis. *Journal of Health and Social Behavior, 29*, 23–37.

Van der Kolk, B. A., Pelcovitz, D., Roth, S., Mandel, F., McFarlane, A., & Herman, J. L. (1996). Dissociation, somatization, and affect dysregulation: The complexity of adaptation to trauma. *American Journal of Psychiatry, 153*, 83–93.

Verwoerdt, A. (1966). *Communication with the fatally ill*. Springfield, IL: Charles C Thomas.

Wilson, J. P. (1995). The historical evolution of PTSD diagnostic criteria: From Freud to DSM-IV. In G. S. Everly, Jr., & J. M. Lating (Eds.), *Psychotraumatology: Key papers and core concepts in post-traumatic stress* (pp. 9–26). New York, NY: Plenum.

Wright, B. A. (1960). *Physical disability: A psychological approach*. New York, NY: Harper & Row.

Wright, B. A. (1983). *Physical disability: A psychosocial approach* (2nd ed.). New York, NY: Harper & Row.

Yehuda, R., & McFarlane, A. C. (1995). Conflict between current knowledge about posttraumatic stress disorder and its original conceptual basis. *American Journal of Psychiatry, 152,* 1705–1713.

Yoshida, K. (1993). Reshaping of self: A pendular reconstruction of self and identity among adults with traumatic spinal cord injury. *Sociology of Health and Illness, 15,* 217–245.

Zeidner, M., & Endler, N. S. (1996). *Handbook of coping: Theory, research, applications.* New York, NY: Wiley.

Zeidner, M., & Saklofske, D. (1996). Adaptive and maladaptive coping. In M. Zeidner & N. S. Endler (Eds.), *Handbook of coping: Theory, research, applications* (pp. 505–531). New York, NY: Wiley.

# Counseling Interventions for People With Psychiatric Disabilities

*Patrick Corrigan and Nev Jones*

## LEARNING OBJECTIVES

The goals of this chapter are to provide an overview of some of the major psychosocial barriers faced by individuals with psychiatric disabilities, to describe strengths-based psychiatric rehabilitation counseling as a foundation for promoting and supporting client recovery, and to emphasize the importance of evidence-based practices (EBPs) and review core EBPs in psychiatric rehabilitation. As learning objectives, the reader should be able to:

1. Describe major psychosocial barriers to recovery for individuals with psychiatric disabilities.
2. Explain the importance of strengths-based counseling.
3. Discuss the reasons why EBPs are of central importance in psychiatric rehabilitation.
4. List the current EBPs in psychiatric rehabilitation and the nature of the evidence supporting them.

## THE CHALLENGES OF PSYCHIATRIC DISABILITIES

People with serious mental illnesses have a variety of concerns, which may need to be considered when providing meaningful and effective counseling services. Counseling is construed, perhaps a bit more broadly here, as challenging some notions and expanding on others. Good counseling services are generally directed by the person's goals in his or her community over time. Services rarely reflect one-on-one 50-minute counseling sessions with hierarchical relationships in an office setting. Effective programs are almost always conducted in the community, sometimes by peers.

## Diagnoses

People with psychiatric disabilities are typically defined by a diagnosis of serious mental illness, as specified in the *Diagnostic and Statistical Manual of Mental Disorders* (5th ed., *DSM-5*; American Psychiatric Association, 2013). Although *DSM-5* includes a broad range of conditions, those typically associated with psychiatric disabilities are in Axis I, which includes all psychiatric diagnostic categories, except personality disorders and mental retardation (intellectual disabilities); Axis II, excluding those on the developmental spectrum, including autism and mental retardation; and syndromes not associated with traumatic brain injury, delirium, or dementia. People with sole diagnoses of substance use disorders also are not typically grouped among those with psychiatric diagnoses. Psychiatric rehabilitation professionals recognize the challenges of dual diagnoses, which typically include one of the Axis I or Axis II disorders, in combination with a substance use disorder and/or developmental disability.

Specific diagnoses are defined by a profile of symptoms or behaviors, which have been organized into five groups (Corrigan, Mueser, Bond, Drake, & Solomon, 2008): (a) *affect*, characterized by marked and lengthy manifestations of normal emotions, including distressing experiences of sadness, anxiety, anger, or euphoria; (b) *perception and cognition*, characterized by distortions in one's ability to make sense of the world, at the most extreme appearing as hallucinations, delusions, or formal thought disorder; (c) *motivation and activity*, appearing as inappropriate behaviors because of disinhibitions and expansiveness or absence of behaviors that occurs because of withdrawal or lethargy; (d) *interpersonal functioning*, characterized by inappropriate (social or sexually awkward) or asocial (total disinterest in others) actions; and (e) *suicide and dangerousness*, characterized by decisions to hurt self or others.

Severity of mental illness is reflected by disability, which refers to the extent that symptoms interfere with achieving personal goals in such social spheres as education and work, independent living, and interpersonal relationships. Although some diagnoses are more typically associated with disability, including schizophrenia and bipolar disorder, severity is defined solely by the inability to achieve significant life goals. Hence, a person with an anxiety disorder might be included in the category of people with psychiatric disabilities if he or she is unable to find and maintain a personally meaningful job because of anxiety.

Epidemiologists and psychiatrists attempt to make sense of a person's future via prognosis; the prediction of the course of various mental illnesses in general as well as a specific individual's own journey (e.g., "Will Fred be able to get a job given his symptoms?"). Schizophrenia is traditionally portrayed as having the worst prognosis; Kraepelin's (1971) definition described schizophrenia as a *precocious dementia*, and this description influenced psychiatric practice for many years. People with schizophrenia were expected to inevitably require custodial care, which undermined most plans for a vocation and independent living. Long-term follow-up research, however, which has resoundingly failed to support this pessimistic outlook, based on following people diagnosed with schizophrenia for 20 to 30 years. If Kraepelin were correct, most should be found on the back wards of hospitals, incapable of even the activities of daily living. Research, however, shows the opposite, with as many as 75% of people with diagnoses of schizophrenia achieving work and independent living goals comparable to the rates of their peers (Emsley, Chiliza, Asmal, & Lehloenya, 2011). The vast majority of the remaining 25% are able to live quality lives when intensive rehabilitation and counseling services are available (Liberman, 2002).

As a result of this type of longitudinal research, experts have recently called into question the utility of prognosis in clinical practice (Corrigan, 2013). Rather than providing information that might impact an intervention plan, negative prognoses undermine the person's pursuit of meaningful goals. People with schizophrenia should be encouraged to understand and pursue their goals, no matter how grand, rather than being haunted by the specter of Emil Kraepelin and doubting their possibilities.

### The Hurdles of Stigma and Other Disadvantages

Life goals of people with serious mental illnesses are threatened by the stigma of mental illness (Corrigan, 2005; Hinshaw, 2006; Thornicroft, Leff, Warner, Sartorius, & Schulze, 2006). Two types of stigma are especially troublesome barriers to the pursuit of personal goals. *Public* stigma occurs when others generally endorse stereotypes about mental illness that lead to discrimination. Of the many stereotypes, the most problematic are the ideas of dangerousness (i.e., people with mental illness should be avoided because they are unpredictably violent) and incompetence (i.e., people with mental illness are unable to do anything but the most meager of jobs and cannot live independently). As a result of these stereotypes, employers may be less likely to hire people with mental illness, and landlords may be less likely to rent to them. *Self*-stigma occurs when people with mental illness agree with the stereotypes and apply them to themselves (i.e., "I have a mental illness and so I must be incompetent"). Self-stigma leads to diminished self-esteem and self-efficacy and what has been called the "why try" effect (e.g., "Why try to get a job? Someone like me is not worthy of it"; Corrigan, Larson, & Rusch, 2009).

Erasing the stigma of mental illness has become a priority for advocates. Education (contrasting the myths with the facts about mental illness) and contact (facilitating interactions between people with lived experience and target groups such as landlords, employers, or police officers) are widely used to decrease the impact of public stigma on people with serious mental illness. Findings from a recent meta-analysis show that both lead to significant change, though the impact of contact seems to be twice that of education, in addition to maintaining positive effects better over time (Corrigan, Morris, Michaels, Rafacz, & Rusch, 2012). In terms of self-stigma, psychoeducational groups (i.e., teaching participants about the wrongs of stereotypes), cognitive behavioral therapy (i.e., helping participants learn to challenge stereotypes as irrational beliefs), and strategic disclosure (i.e., weighing the costs and benefits of strategically coming out with one's past experiences) have been used to counter the impact of self-stigma, though research on their relative value is lacking (Corrigan & Rao, 2012).

Additional determinants of social disadvantage often negatively affect people with psychiatric disabilities, in some ways more than the disabilities themselves (Draine, Salzer, Culhane, & Hadley, 2002). One is *poverty and unemployment,* as people with psychiatric disabilities often have prolonged periods of unemployment making workforce reentry problematic (Nordt, Müller, Rössler, & Lauber, 2007), and they are three times more likely to be members of a family living in poverty (Vick, Jones, & Mitra, 2012). Another factor is **homelessness**, as adults with serious mental illness have a greater risk for homelessness, which compounds morbidity and mortality (Martens, 2001). A third factor is more likely involvement in the **criminal justice system**, which limits health care access (Constantine et al., 2010), and people with mental illness are also at significant risk to be victims of crime (Maniglio, 2009). Yet another factor is **substance abuse**, as people with mental illness are at a significantly greater risk of substance abuse, which is associated with markedly increased physical illness (Carrà & Johnson, 2009).

**Ethnic disparities** further exacerbate disability and the system of care. Compared to Caucasians, twice as many African Americans and Latinos are below the poverty level (DeNavas-Walt, Proctor, & Smith, 2012). African Americans are three times more likely to experience homelessness, and Latinos make up 15.7% of the people who are homeless (U.S. Department of Housing and Urban Development, 2010). People of color with mental illness are more likely to be involved with the criminal justice system (Warf, Clark, Herz, & Rabinovitz, 2009) and to be victims of or generally more exposed to crime (Biafora & Warheit, 2007). Disparities also lead to barriers in health care for people of color, with both mental and primary care services less available to people of color because of poverty (Lanouette, Folsom, Sciolla, & Jeste, 2009). People from ethnic minority groups are less likely to be insured than others (Lee, O'Neill, Park, Scully, & Shenassa, 2012), and services provided by the government safety net are sometimes lacking (Rosenbaum, Markus, & Darnell, 2000).

Accentuating implications of stigma and other social disadvantages recapitulates a central theme to rehabilitation professionals. Given the challenges faced by individuals with mental illness, treatment focusing on symptoms and dysfunctions alone is not sufficient to facilitate rehabilitation goals. Impacting the social system in which the person lives is equally important. People need personal power over their lives to fight the egregious effects of prejudice, and they need good jobs and, sometimes, the education and training necessary to obtain those jobs to move out of poverty.

## PRINCIPLES OF COUNSELING

Counseling approaches for people with serious mental illness have evolved substantially over the past 20 years. Prior focus of medical models led providers to pessimistic prognoses, a view transmitted to people with lived experience and their families, which robbed them of the sense of future and opportunity central to the pursuit of personal goals and a quality of life. The consumer movement,

**TABLE 18.1  Principles and Practices That Define Effective Counseling Approaches for People With Psychiatric Disability**

| PRINCIPLES | PRACTICES |
|---|---|
| Recovery: People with serious mental illness are able to achieve personal goals and a sense of well-being despite significant symptoms and disabilities | Supported employment and education: Directly placing clients in employment or school settings and providing them with the supports necessary to succeed |
| | Community support and supported housing: Providing supports in the community that allow clients to live independently |
| | Wellness management and recovery: Psychoeducation and skills training program aimed at promoting self-management of symptoms as well as goal setting and achievement |
| Self-determination: People should have total control over life goals and all interventions meant to achieve them | Family services: Involving family members in treatment and/or providing services that help clients manage their own parenting or caregiver responsibilities |
| | Strategic medication management: Supporting clients to understand treatment effects and make thoughtful decisions about medication use |
| | Peer support: Services, initiatives, or groups led by and for individuals with psychiatric disabilities |
| Strengths: A disease focus describes the person as flawed, ignoring her or his many capabilities; a strengths focus helps the person regain his or her sense of ability | Integrated health care: Services and supports that aim to integrate and coordinate physical and mental health needs and problems |
| | Faith-based services: Mental health services and programs that are located and grounded in religious faiths or institutions |

a spontaneously evolving grassroots collection of people with serious mental illness, realized the pernicious state of affairs more than 50 years ago and demanded a service system reflecting hope and recovery rather than failure and shame (Ralph & Corrigan, 2005). The resulting principles are the foundation of counseling strategies for people with psychiatric disability: recovery, self-determination, and strengths, which are listed in Table 18.1 and reviewed here.

## Recovery

Recovery has evolved into two related perspectives. The first reflects a medical perspective, namely, people with the most severe of psychiatric disabilities can overcome their symptoms and disabilities to achieve life goals, typically with effective medication and psychiatric rehabilitation. Researchers define criteria that putatively reflect recovery, such as significant change in symptoms from baseline and achieving some standard of employment and independent living (Liberman & Kopelwicz, 2005). Despite the optimism of this perspective, recovery, as an achievable goal, misses its important processes. This is an alternative view developed mostly by the consumer community, which recognizes that personal well-being and quality of life can be achieved *separate* from one's symptoms and disabilities (Ralph & Corrigan, 2005). Recovery is viewed more as a journey, in which all people with psychiatric disability engage in the here and now, rather than after some hurdle is cleared. Central to either view of recovery is the reintroduction of hope into the lives of people with serious mental illness. The reality is that personal goals can be achieved, a quality life enjoyed, and psychological well-being relished.

### Self-Determination

Central to recovery is having personal power over one's life choices and over the rehabilitation plan meant to help individuals achieve their goals. Unfortunately, old models of mental health are replete with examples of the person with mental illness as incapable of making successful choices. In part, this represents benevolence stigma (Watson & Corrigan, 2005), the notion that adults with serious mental illness are fundamentally childlike and hence need a benign authority figure, such as doctor or parent, to make choices for them. Benevolence stigmas often lead to conservative attitudes about a person's goals, for example, "Thelma should not pursue an accounting job because she won't be able to handle it." It also promoted themes of adherence and compliance, suggesting that there are times when a person should be compelled to follow a treatment prescription, regardless of interest. This kind of antiquated notion of compliance leads to multiple harms. Some treatments have very negative side effects; just as an individual might decide to stop a blood pressure medication because of its unintended harm, so might individuals opt out of an antidepressant or antipsychotic medication. Sometimes, a call for compliance asks people to put off goals they wish to pursue now, for example, "Bob, I think you should stay in the halfway house several more months. You're not ready for your own apartment." Cautions like these rob the person of the excitement and spontaneity consistent with the pursuit of personal goals and quality of life.

Modern notions of rehabilitation are fundamentally anchored in self-determination. People are helped to fully understand disabilities *and* possibilities in order to identify current goals and the path to their achievement. Although the perspective of family and friends is important, it is ultimately up to the person with disabilities to decide how other opinions weave into personal plans. Rehabilitation counselors support the dignity of choice and of failure (Corrigan, 2011). Like all people, some options do not work, perhaps leading to a significant sense of loss. This is not indicative of the person's illness, but rather of the kind of rollercoaster that everyone rides in pursuit of well-being. Shared decision making (SDM), problem solving, and relapse prevention are tools that help to promote self-determination.

- SDM helps people make sense of individual options by assisting the person in obtaining information about the extent of an option in order to weigh the costs and benefits of moving forward.

- Problem solving teaches people to break down complex barriers to specific goals into meaningful parts. People learn to define a problem in terms of who, what, when, and where; brainstorm solutions; evaluate relative benefits of each solution; plan its real-world implementation; and assess impact sometime later in order to determine whether the plan should be adapted further.
- Through relapse prevention, people learn that symptoms and disabilities often recur. Hence, they plan during periods of less distress what to do when relapse occurs. They also learn to identify situations in which relapse is more likely to emerge, stressful places, for example, and other triggers that increase setbacks.

Central to all these tools, and to the remaining interventions reviewed in the following text, are the fundamentals of active listening that make up good counseling (see Chapter 11 in this volume). Active listening includes attending skills (a posture of involvement, appropriate eye contact, and nondistracting involvement), following skills (door openers, minimal encouragers, infrequent questions, and attentive silence), and reflecting skills (including those attempting to share emotional and other latent aspects of a message).

## Strengths

People with serious mental illness are not and should not be defined solely by symptoms and disabilities. They have strengths that are equally important for understanding choices as they are superimposed on one's life trajectory. In fact, if disabilities and strengths could be quantified, strengths would clearly outweigh disabilities, given the many accomplishments that people with mental illness achieve daily. This is another paradox with medical models of mental illness; describing people in terms of their limitation yields a disheartening picture that naturally leads to pessimism for all involved. The rehabilitation counselor's task is to help people take stock of individual strengths in order to regain a solid stance to tackle their world.

In making sense of goals, the rehabilitation counselor is boosting a person's optimism. In addition, counselors attempt to help people identify and capitalize on their strengths. Sometimes, the person might need to learn activation skills; for example, one's ability to have a jaunty exchange about sports requires the person to learn how to identify people who might want to share in this kind of intercourse. Sometimes, the person might need "permission," from counselors, family, and friends that enjoying these strengths is okay, for example, "Harold, it's a good thing to be attracted to girls and ask a few out on a date." Sometimes rehabilitation counselors need to help family and friends make sure that they are not discouraging the person from using a strength to pursue a goal. Peer-based interventions discussed in the following text can be especially useful for this purpose.

## EVIDENCE-BASED PRACTICE

A variety of practices has emerged to address the personal goals of people with psychiatric disability. Recently, researchers and advocates have called for this list to be limited to those with some evidence base (Corrigan et al., 2008). In part, this occurred because providers and advocates realized that some approaches, thought to be effective for promoting personal goals, yielded no such benefits and actually led to unintended consequences that worsened the status quo. The exact formula for meeting an evidence-based criterion remains in flux; although randomized clinical trials (RCTs) are the gold standard for good research in many health settings, there are interventions that are not understood well by such approaches (Corrigan & Salzer, 2003). For example, choice and commitment tend to be fundamental to the kind of peer-based interventions described in the following text. RCTs, in which people are assigned to a group by a flip of a coin undermine choice and commitment. As research on rehabilitation approaches matures, investigators look for methods that augment the RCT standard.

One assumption permeates the practices reviewed in the following text; they are place–train interventions (Bond, 1998; Corrigan & McCracken, 2005). More traditional notions of rehabilitation were based on a train–place principle; in other words, train a person to fully manage symptoms and disabilities before placing him or her in a real-world setting where personal goals might be accomplished. For example, a person should show mastery of social and symptom management skills before meeting with a vocational counselor to consider work goals. Unfortunately, these intermediate steps put up unnecessary hurdles to seeking out aspirations important in the here and now. Moreover, skills learned in generic treatment settings may not generalize to real-life settings. Place–train interventions help the person go directly to the setting of immediate interest, such as work, housing, or relationships, and then train or teach the person skills to be successful in that setting. The right-hand side of Table 18.1 summarizes the EBPs reviewed hereafter.

### Supported Employment and Education

Individual placement and support (IPS) is the supported employment approach for people with psychiatric disabilities with, perhaps, the greatest empirical base, and it reflects fundamental principles relevant to both employment and education goals (Bond, Campbell, & Drake, 2012; Drake, Bond, & Becker, 2012). The most recent specifications of IPS include six principles and activities.

1. **Zero exclusion:** All people with psychiatric disabilities who are so inclined should be able to seek out work. No indicators of symptom or dysfunction should preclude receiving supported employment services.
2. **Person preference:** Work goals should be entirely defined by the person and not the availability of specific jobs in a program.
3. **Rapid job search:** No hurdles are placed between people and their work goals. People should begin to seek out jobs in the competitive job market as soon as they are ready, even on day 1 of the program if they like.

4. **Follow-along supports:** IPS includes job coaches who provide support where the person needs it: on the job or another appropriate place in the community. This kind of support is provided as often and as long as the person asks for it.
5. **Integration of mental health and vocational services:** One of the pitfalls of many service systems is separation of psychiatric treatment and vocational programs, which undermines a seamless plan for the whole person. The total panoply of interventions needs to be provided by a single team.
6. **Benefits counseling:** In order to facilitate transition into the competitive employment world, people need to understand how their entitlements might change with work, especially related to income and health benefits.

Research has shown that IPS and similar supported employment programs significantly improve the ability of individuals to obtain and maintain competitive employment (Corrigan et al., 2008). Several concerns, however, have emerged that are the focus of ongoing development. Two are illustrative and reviewed here. First, job tenure of IPS participants seems relatively brief, with the average tenure on longest held jobs of 21.3 weeks. Second, IPS may lead to better jobs, but not necessarily a sense of career and vocation. Adaptations of supported employment include attempts to help the person understand the multiple levels of work decisions related to career.

Supported education has similar aims, namely, helping people reach their educational goals in real-world settings, but supported education has not been developed or tested to the same extent as supported employment and IPS. Several models have been proposed that include both on- and off-campus perspectives (Mowbray, Strauch Brown, Furlong-Norman, & Sullivan Soydan, 2002). Recently, IPS has been adapted to help people with psychiatric disabilities attain educational goals, including rapid search, placement, and ongoing support in community college or other settings that are consistent with a person's desires and goals (Nuechterlein et al., 2008).

### Community Support and Supported Housing

Although community support and supported housing are, in principle, separate rehabilitation domains, in practice they are frequently combined. Among community support models, assertive community treatment (ACT) is one of the most rigorously researched evidence-based interventions in all of psychiatric rehabilitation (Bond, Drake, Mueser, & Latimer, 2001; Dieterich, Irving, Park, & Marshall, 2010). ACT uses multidisciplinary teams to engage people in the community and to provide the resources and supports necessary to manage comorbid medical conditions, avoid hospitalization, manage symptoms, and live independently. Members of ACT teams meet on a regular basis to discuss a person's status and any issues or challenges facing individuals on their caseload. Teams are available 7 days per week, 24 hours per day, and they provide all services, including medical outreach and medication management, in the client's home or community locations of his or her choice. ACT services are designed to be as flexible as possible in order to meet the unique needs of individual clients, needs that might include grocery and clothes shopping, as well as supportive therapy, skills training, and medication management.

Independent living requires not only appropriate case management, but also a physical place to live. Although many different housing models have been used, including a variety of models combined with ACT or less intensive forms of community-based case management, "housing first" has garnered increasing public and empirical support over the past decade (Nelson, 2010). Unlike so-called treatment first models, which require that clients participate in treatment programs, stop using illegal drugs, or live in transitional settings prior to being granted access to independent housing, housing first models stress that housing is a basic and unconditional human right (Tsemberis & Asmussen, 1999). Housing first programs often use federal and state housing vouchers to place people as rapidly as possible in the open-market housing of their choice. Independent housing is virtually always paired with either ACT or less intensive forms of community-based team case management. For clients with alcohol or drug problems, housing first advocates for harm reduction rather than abstinence. Although clients are encouraged to cut back on alcohol and illegal substance use, and are provided help to do so, continued support is never made contingent on abstinence or adherence to substance use treatment programs.

Empirical research on ACT has consistently demonstrated advantages over intensive case management and other comparison interventions, particularly with respect to reducing hospitalizations; at least some of these effects, however, have declined in RCTs carried out over the past decade (Burns et al., 2007). These less dramatic effects may actually be due to the success of ACT; in general, community-based mental health services have moved closer to an ACT model, making extensive use of multidisciplinary teams oriented toward providing intensive, individualized supports (Burns, 2010). For individuals with mental illness and a history of homelessness, Nelson, Aubry, and Lafrance (2007) concluded that the effects of ACT, combined with housing first, were significantly greater than either ACT alone or intensive case management.

## Wellness Management and Recovery

Wellness management and recovery (WMR), which is also referred to as illness management and recovery (IMR), is one of six evidence-based programs developed with support from the Substance Abuse and Mental Health Services Administration (SAMHSA; Mueser et al., 2002). WMR incorporates five empirically supported components of recovery into one comprehensive package: psychoeducation, medication adherence-oriented behavioral intervention, relapse prevention training, social skills training, and symptom self-management (Mueser et al., 2006). WMR can be delivered in either group or individual settings, and emphasizes individual goal setting and the connection among these goals and each of the program's topic areas. The curriculum is divided into 10 modules, usually completed over the course of 6 to 10 months, with a focus on such issues as drug and alcohol use, medication management, and coping with stress. Recent outcomes from RCTs suggest that WMR significantly impacts multiple domains, including quality of life and goal attainment (Hasson-Ohayon, Roe & Kravetz, 2007; Levitt et al., 2009), and these effects are sustained for at least 1 year (Roe, Hasson-Ohayon, Salyers & Kravetz, 2009).

## Family Services

Long subject to discrimination and stigma as the cause of their children's mental illness, family members' involvement is now often seen as a crucial aspect of evidence-based psychiatric rehabilitation (Corrigan et al., 2008). In the wake of deinstitutionalization, an estimated one third to two thirds of individuals with a psychiatric disability have been found to live with family members (Beeler, Rosenthal, & Cohler, 1999), and family are often strongly involved in caregiving, even when not physically living with them. In the context of psychiatric rehabilitation counseling, potentially helpful interventions include direct support and psychoeducation (McFarlane, Dixon, Lukens, & Lucksted, 2007), family involvement in client treatment and rehabilitation planning (Meis et al., 2012), and multifamily or family-to-family mutual support groups (Lucksted et al., 2013). Individuals with psychiatric disabilities may also require specialized supports related to their own role as parents or caregivers of other dependents. In particular, mothers of young children may need additional services aimed at supporting management of both normal difficulties raising children and dealing with a child with a serious mental illness (Lagan, Knights, Barton, & Boyce, 2009).

## Integrated Care for Dual Diagnosis

At least half of the individuals with serious mental illness also report concurrent substance abuse (Kessler et al., 1996). Individuals with a dual diagnosis are at a substantially greater risk of poor outcomes, including homelessness, hospitalization, and incarceration (Najit, Fusar-Poli, & Brambilla, 2011). The importance of identifying a co-occurring substance use disorder, exploring the relationship between client mental illness and substance use, and providing appropriate intervention cannot be overemphasized. Although many specific interventions for dual diagnosis have been developed, including programs focused on abstinence (i.e., the total cessation of substance use) and the principles of harm reduction, basic overarching principles can be specified. Interventions should be well coordinated, use multidisciplinary teams to address comprehensive needs, involve staff with specialized training in addictions, include a variety of more specific approaches that are matched to the needs and stage of the individual, and ensure long-term follow-up and support (Corrigan et al., 2008; Horsfall, Cleary, Hunt, & Walter, 2009). Research suggests that integrated dual diagnosis programs, combined with supported housing and ACT, can have substantial positive effects on hospitalization, incarceration, homelessness, and employment (Tsai, Salyers, Rollins, McKasson, & Litmer, 2009).

## Strategic Medication Management

A large body of evidence affirms the efficacy of psychotropic medications in ame-liorating symptoms during acute exacerbations and in preventing relapse (Davis, Chen, & Glick, 2003). In medical contexts, however, the term *efficacy*, which is indicative of how well a treatment works in a highly controlled clinical trial, must be distinguished from *effectiveness*, which reflects how well a treatment works in real-world settings. In spite of high efficacy, the real-world impact of medications is limited by high discontinuation rates. For example, a major national multisite effectiveness trial of antipsychotics documented a discontinuation rate exceed-ing 70% (Lieberman et al., 2005) and nonadherence outcomes that were attribut-able to significant side effects, sociocultural attitudes toward pharmacological versus psychosocial interventions, and insight into symptoms and their impact, among other factors (Velligan et al., 2009). Strategic medication management in the context of psychiatric rehabilitation thus involves the active negotiation of these complexities, with an emphasis on shared decision making about medica-tions and support for thoughtful self-determination (Corrigan et al., 2008, 2012; Deegan & Drake, 2006).

In practice, SDM involves a fundamental reframing of the practitioner role; instead of serving as an authoritative decision maker who instructs a client on medications to take, practitioners serve as collaborative partners, whose primary role is to provide information, answer questions, and foster an environment of autonomous motivation and choice. In community settings, psychiatric rehabili-tation counselors often work as part of a team, including prescribers; in such con-texts, shared decision making may involve liaising with prescribing clinicians, advocating for clients, and encouraging them to ask questions and raise con-cerns during medication management appointments (Corrigan et al., 2008). The basic concept of "dignity to fail" should be reflected on whenever discussions about medications arise; like all adults, clients ultimately have the right to decide what is in their own best interest and what risks are or are not worth taking. Counselors should keep these principles in mind while continuing to provide nonjudgmental information, resources, and support.

## Peer Support

Since the early years of the consumer movement, advocates have emphasized the fundamental importance of peer support and peer-led services (Chamberlin, 1978). Peer support may take place apart from traditional mental health ser-vices or alongside nonpeer services, and may or may not involve formal train-ing, although training is increasingly common for paid peer specialists (Salzer, Schwenk, & Brusilovskiy, 2010). Peer support initiatives may focus on particular problems, such as self-stigma, trauma, or substance use, or may provide a more general forum for consumers to share a wide range of experiences and insights. A survey undertaken by SAMHSA in 2002 identified approximately 7,500 mental health support groups and consumer-operated services (Goldstrom et al., 2006); this number has likely increased substantially over the past decade. Results from the National Comorbidity Survey suggest that almost 18% of Americans report using a self-help group at least once in their lives (Wang, Berglund, & Kessler, 2001).

Although the evidence base for many specific types of peer support is still emerging, peer support is seen as a fundamentally important supplement to traditional mental health services (President's New Freedom Commission on Mental Health, 2003). Peer support has been repeatedly found to empower consumers and increase hope, outcomes potentially resulting from upward social comparisons, a greater sense of autonomy, and horizontal, reciprocal relationships with peers (Davidson, Bellamy, Guy, & Miller, 2012). Peers are often in a unique position to share insights regarding helpful techniques and strategies for coping with symptoms, navigating the mental health and welfare systems, and combating stigma, among others. Recently, several peer-led support interventions have been investigated in rigorous RCTs, documenting significant positive impacts on such domains as symptomatology, hope, and quality of life (Cook et al., 2012a, 2012b).

In contemporary psychiatric rehabilitation settings, counselors may primarily make referrals to outside peer support groups or may also work as, or directly alongside, peer specialists or peer staff. In some situations, peers may also work as group facilitators at the same agency where they are themselves clients. Although these situations may create unusual dynamics, it is critical that service providers treat nonclient peer support leaders and peer staff the same way they would any other staff member. Counselors should also familiarize themselves with the range of peer support options available in their community in order to make appropriate referrals.

## Integrated Health Care

With the passage of the Patient Protection and Affordable Care Act, growing emphasis has been placed on the integration of physical and mental health care, integration aimed at increasing the efficiency of health systems, and ensuring that health problems are addressed in a timely way (Merrens & Drake, 2013; Shim et al., 2012). Such integration is all the more urgent, given evidence that individuals with serious mental illness die on average 25 years earlier than other Americans (Colton & Manderscheid, 2006). In the context of psychiatric rehabilitation, counselors can help address these issues by including health and wellness programs and interventions, including smoking cessation, in behavioral health settings, making sure that clients are screened for physical medication side effects and facilitating clear communication with primary care and other specialists (Corrigan et al., 2008).

## Faith-Based Services

Faith-based services represent a historically neglected area of mental health research and intervention. With the exception of mutual support groups, such as

Alcoholics Anonymous, mental health professionals and researchers have only recently begun to pay greater attention to, and empirically study, faith-based mental health services as well as collaborations between mental health programs and faith-based community institutions and resources (Koenig, 2005; Singh, Shah, Gupta, Coverdale, & Harris, 2012). For many individuals, faith-based communities are both an enormous source of support and negatively impact discrimination. Rehabilitation counselors need to be aware of the importance of sensitivity to client cultural and faith backgrounds, while also being prepared to proactively reach out to religious and spiritual leaders to address potentially counterproductive attitudes toward mental illness.

## CONCLUSIONS

Much of the evidence base discussed in this chapter has used traditional research teams (i.e., teams composed of trained researchers with no lived experience of serious mental illness). Consumers are typically involved only to the extent that they can provide "data points." Community-based participatory research approaches, in contrast, bring together community members and researchers to set initial research agendas, design interventions, select what outcome measures to use, analyze data, and disseminate project findings (Wallerstein & Duran, 2006). Although researchers bring necessary expertise regarding design, methods, and analytical strategies to the table, community coresearchers contribute an experientially grounded understanding of intervention strengths and weaknesses, feasibility, and relevance to the community (Israel et al., 2010). Moving forward, significant resources will ideally be earmarked for projects and evaluations that employ participatory methods and empower consumers to directly determine what psychiatric rehabilitation interventions are most effective, valuable, and empowering.

## DISCUSSION EXERCISES

1. "Rather than providing information that might impact an intervention plan, negative prognoses undermine the person's pursuit of meaningful goals." What is the true value of this claim in understanding how psychiatric diagnosis and prognosis might negatively impact clients?
2. "Additional determinants of social disadvantage often hound people with psychiatric disabilities, in some ways more than disabilities themselves." Discuss how other determinants of social disadvantage might hurt clients more than their disabilities.
3. Discuss any three different EBPs. How might they be combined to promote recovery?
4. Based on your reading of the chapter, discuss and justify the essential ingredients of high-quality psychiatric rehabilitation counseling.

# REFERENCES

American Psychiatric Association. (2013). *Diagnostic and statistical manual of mental disorders* (5th ed.). Washington, DC: Author.

Beeler, J., Rosenthal, A., & Cohler, B. (1999). Patterns of family caregiving and support provided to older psychiatric patients in long-term care. *Psychiatric Services, 50,* 1222–1224.

Biafora, F., & Warheit, G. (2007). Self-reported violent victimization among young adults in Miami, Florida: Immigration, race/ethnic and gender contrasts. *International Review of Victimology, 14,* 29–55.

Bond, G. (1998). Principles of the individual placement and support model: Empirical support. *Psychiatric Rehabilitation Journal, 22,* 11–23.

Bond, G. R., Campbell, K., & Drake, R. E. (2012). Standardizing measures in four domains of employment outcomes for individual placement and support. *Psychiatric Services, 63,* 751–757.

Bond, G. R., Drake, R. E., Mueser, K. T., & Latimer, E. (2001). Assertive community treatment for people with severe mental illness: Critical ingredients and impact on patients. *Disease Management & Health Outcomes, 9,* 141–159.

Burns, T. (2010). The rise and fall of assertive community treatment? *International Review of Psychiatry, 22,* 130–137.

Burns, T., Catty, J., Dash, M., Roberts, C., Lockwood, A., & Marshall, M. (2007). Use of intensive case management to reduce time in hospital in people with severe mental illness: Systematic review and meta-regression. *British Medical Journal, 335,* 336–340.

Carrà, G., & Johnson, S. (2009). Variations in rates of comorbid substance use in psychosis between mental health settings and geographical areas in the UK. *Social Psychiatry and Psychiatric Epidemiology, 44,* 429–447.

Chamberlin, J. (1978). *On our own: Patient-controlled alternatives to the mental health system.* New York, NY: McGraw-Hill.

Colton, C. W., & Manderscheid, R. W. (2006). Congruencies in increased mortality rates, years of potential life lost, and causes of death among public mental health clients in eight states. *Preventing Chronic Disease, 3*(2), 1–14.

Constantine, R., Andel, R., Petrila, J., Becker, M., Robst, J., Teague, G., & Howe, A. (2010). Characteristics and experiences of adults with a serious mental illness who were involved in the criminal justice system. *Psychiatric Services, 61,* 451–457.

Cook, J. A., Copeland, M. E., Jonikas, J. A., Hamilton, M. M., Razzano, L. A., Grey, D. D., & Boyd, S. (2012a). Results of a randomized controlled trial of mental illness self-management using wellness recovery action planning. *Schizophrenia Bulletin, 38,* 881–891.

Cook, J. A., Steigman, P., Pickett, S., Diehl, S., Fox, A., Shipley, P., . . . Burke-Miller, J. K. (2012b). Randomized controlled trial of peer-led recovery education using Building Recovery of Individual Dreams and Goals through Education and Support (BRIDGES). *Schizophrenia Research, 136,* 36–42.

Corrigan, P. W. (2005). *On the stigma of mental illness: Practical strategies for research and social change.* Washington, DC: American Psychological Association.

Corrigan, P. W. (2011). The dignity to fail. *Psychiatric Services, 62,* 241.

Corrigan, P. W. (2013). The risk of prognostication. *Psychiatric Services, 8,* 719.

Corrigan, P. W., Angell, B., Davidson, L., Marcus, S. C., Salzer, M. S., Kottsieper, P., . . . Stanhope, V. (2012). From adherence to self-determination: Evolution of a treatment paradigm for people with serious mental illnesses. *Psychiatric Services, 63,* 169–173.

Corrigan, P. W., Larson, J. E., & Rusch, N. (2009). Self-stigma and the "why try" effect: Impact on life goals and evidence-based practices. *World Psychiatry, 8,* 75–81.

Corrigan, P. W., & McCracken, S. G. (2005). Place first, then train: An alternative to the medical model of psychiatric rehabilitation. *Social Work, 50,* 31–39.

Corrigan, P. W., Morris, S. B., Michaels, P. J., Rafacz, J. D., & Rüsch, N. (2012). Challenging the public stigma of mental illness: A meta-analysis of outcome studies. *Psychiatric Services, 63*, 963–973.

Corrigan, P. W., Mueser, K. T., Bond, G., Drake, R., & Solomon, P. (2008). *Principles and practice of psychiatric rehabilitation: An empirical approach.* New York, NY: Guilford.

Corrigan, P. W., & Rao, D. (2012). On the self-stigma of mental illness: Stages, disclosure, and strategies for change. *Canadian Journal of Psychiatry, 57*, 464–469.

Corrigan, P. W., & Salzer, M. S. (2003). The conflict between random assignment and treatment preference: Implications for internal validity. *Evaluation and Program Planning, 26*, 109–121.

Davidson, L., Bellamy, C., Guy, K., & Miller, R. (2012). Peer support among persons with severe mental illnesses: A review of evidence and experience. *World Psychiatry, 11*, 123–128.

Davis, J. M., Chen, N., & Glick, I. D. (2003). A meta-analysis of the efficacy of second-generation antipsychotics. *Archives of General Psychiatry, 60*, 553–564.

Deegan, P., & Drake, R. (2006). Shared decision making and medication management in the recovery process. *Psychiatric Services, 57*, 1636–1639.

DeNavas-Walt, C., Proctor, B. P., & Smith, J. C. (2012). *U.S. Census Bureau. Current population reports, income, poverty, and health insurance coverage in the United States: 2010.* Washington, DC: U.S. Census Bureau.

Dieterich, M., Irving, C., Park, B., & Marshall, M. (2010). Intensive case management for severe mental illness. *Cochrane Database of Systematic Reviews*, (10). Retrieved from http://szg.cochrane.org/sites/szg.cochrane.org/files/uploads/Intensive%20case%20 management%20for%20severe%20mental%20illness.pdf

Draine, J., Salzer, M. S., Culhane, D. P., & Hadley, T. R. (2002). Role of social disadvantage in crime, joblessness, and homelessness among persons with serious mental illness. *Psychiatric Services, 53*, 565–573.

Drake, R. E., Bond, G. R., & Becker, D. R. (2012). *Individual placement and support: An evidence-based approach to supported employment.* New York, NY: Oxford University Press.

Emsley, R., Chiliza, B., Asmal, L., & Lehloenya, K. (2011). The concepts of remission and recovery in schizophrenia. *Current Opinion in Psychiatry, 24*, 114–121.

Goldstrom, I. D., Campbell, J., Rogers, J. A., Lambert, D. B., Blacklow, B., Henderson, M. J., & Manderscheid, R. W. (2006). National estimates for mental health mutual support groups, self-help organizations, and consumer-operated services. *Administration and Policy in Mental Health and Mental Health Services Research, 33*, 92–103.

Hasson-Ohayon, I., Roe, D., & Kravetz, S. (2007). A randomized controlled trial of the effectiveness of the illness management and recovery program. *Psychiatric Services, 58*, 1461–1466.

Hinshaw, S. P. (2006). *The mark of shame: Stigma of mental illness and an agenda for change.* New York, NY: Oxford University Press.

Horsfall, J., Cleary, M., Hunt, G. E., & Walter, G. (2009). Psychosocial treatments for people with co-occurring severe mental illnesses and substance use disorders (dual diagnosis): A review of empirical evidence. *Harvard Review of Psychiatry, 17*, 24–34.

Israel, B. A., Coombe, C. M., Cheezum, P. R., Schulz, A. J., McGranagh, R. J., Lichenstein, R., . . . Burris, A. (2010). Community-based participatory research: A capacity-building approach for policy advocacy aimed at eliminating health disparities. *American Journal of Public Health, 100*, 2094–2102.

Kessler, R. C., Nelson, C. B., McGonagle, K. A., Edlund, M. J., Frank, R. G., & Leaf, P. J. (1996). The epidemiology of co-occurring addictive and mental disorders: Implications for prevention and service utilization. *American Journal of Orthopsychiatry, 66*, 17–31.

Koenig, H. G. (2005). *Faith and mental health: Religious resources for healing.* West Conshohocken, PA: Templeton Press.

Kraepelin, E. (1971). *Dementia praecox and paraphrenia.* Malabar, FL: Krieger.

Lagan, M., Knights, K., Barton, J., & Boyce, P. M. (2009). Advocacy for mothers with psychiatric illness: A clinical perspective. *International Journal of Mental Health Nursing, 18*, 53–61.

Lanouette, N. M., Folsom, D. P., Sciolla, A., & Jeste, D. V. (2009). Psychotropic medication nonadherence among United States Latinos: A comprehensive review of the literature. *Psychiatric Services, 60*, 157–174.

Lee, S., O'Neill, A., Park, J., Scully, L., & Shenassa, E. (2012). Health insurance moderates the association between immigrant length of stay and health status. *Journal of Immigrant and Minority Health, 14*, 345–349.

Levitt, A., Mueser, K., DeGenova, J., Lorenzo, J., Bradford-Watt, D., Barbosa, A., . . . Chernick, M. (2009). Randomized controlled trial of illness management and recovery in multiple-unit supportive housing. *Psychiatric Services, 60*, 1629–1636.

Liberman, R. P. (2002). Future directions for research studies and clinical work on recovery from schizophrenia: Questions with some answers. *International Review of Psychiatry, 14*, 337–342.

Liberman, R. P., & Kopelowicz, A. (2005). Recovery from schizophrenia: A concept in search of research. *Psychiatric Services, 56*, 735–742.

Lieberman, J. A., Stroup, T. S., McEvoy, J. P., Swartz, M. S., Rosenheck, R. A., Perkins, D. O., . . . Hsiao, J. K. (2005). Effectiveness of antipsychotic drugs in patients with chronic schizophrenia. *New England Journal of Medicine, 353*, 1209–1223.

Lucksted, A., Medoff, D., Burland, J., Stewart, B., Fang, L. J., Brown, C., . . . Dixon, L. B. (2013). Sustained outcomes of a peer-taught family education program on mental illness. *Acta Psychiatrica Scandinavica, 127*, 279–286.

Maniglio, R. (2009). Severe mental illness and criminal victimization: A systematic review. *Acta Psychiatrica Scandinavica, 119*, 180–191.

Martens, W. H. (2001). A review of physical and mental health in homeless persons. *Public Health Reviews, 29*, 13–33.

McFarlane, W. R., Dixon, L., Lukens, E., & Lucksted, A. (2007). Family psychoeducation and schizophrenia: A review of the literature. *Journal of Marital and Family Therapy, 29*, 223–245.

Meis, L., Griffin, J., Carlyle, M., Greer, N., Jensen, A., MacDonald, R., & Rutks, I. (2012). *Family involved psychosocial treatments for adult mental health conditions: A review of the evidence.* Washington, DC: Department of Veterans Affairs Health Research.

Merrens, M. R., & Drake, R. E. (2013). Health care reform and behavioral health: The journey ahead. *Journal of Dual Diagnosis, 11*, 94–95.

Mowbray, C., Strauch Brown, K., Furlong-Norman, K., & Sullivan Soydan, A. (2002). *Supported education and psychiatric rehabilitation: Models and methods.* Baltimore, MD: International Association of Psychosocial Rehabilitation Services.

Mueser, K. T., Corrigan, P. W., Hilton, D. W., Tanzman, B., Schaub, A., Gingerich, S., . . . Herz, M. I. (2002). Illness management and recovery: A review of the research. *Psychiatric Services, 53*, 1272–1284.

Mueser, K. T., Meyer, P. S., Penn, D. L., Clancy, R., Clancy, D. M., & Salyers, M. P. (2006). The Illness Management and Recovery Program: Rationale, development, and preliminary findings. *Schizophrenia Bulletin, 32*(Suppl. 1), S32–S43.

Najit, P., Fusar-Poli, P., & Brambilla, P. (2011). Co-occurring mental and substance abuse disorders: A review on the potential predictors and clinical outcomes. *Psychiatry Research, 186*, 159–164.

Nelson, G. (2010). Housing for people with serious mental illness: Approaches, evidence, and transformative change. *Journal of Sociology and Social Welfare, 37*, 123–146.

Nelson, G., Aubry, T., & Lafrance, A. (2007). A review of the literature on the effectiveness of housing and support, assertive community treatment, and intensive case management interventions for persons with mental illness who have been homeless. *American Journal of Orthopsychiatry, 77*, 350–361.

Nordt, C., Müller, B., Rössler, W., & Lauber, C. (2007). Predictors and course of vocational status, income, and quality of life in people with severe mental illness: A naturalistic study. *Social Science and Medicine, 65*, 1420–1429.

Nuechterlein, K. H., Subotnik, K. L., Turner, L. R., Ventura, J., Becker, D. R., & Drake, R. E. (2008). Individual placement and support for individuals with recent-onset schizophrenia: Integrating supported education and supported employment. *Psychiatric Rehabilitation Journal, 31*, 340–349.

President's New Freedom Commission on Mental Health. (2003). *Achieving the promise: Transforming mental health care in America.* Rockville, MD: United States Department of Health and Human Services.

Ralph, R. O., & Corrigan, P. W. (2005). *Recovery in mental illness.* Washington, DC: American Psychological Association.

Roe, D., Hasson-Ohayon, I., Salyers, M. P., & Kravetz, S. (2009). A one-year follow-up of illness management and recovery: Participants' accounts of its impact and uniqueness. *Psychiatric Rehabilitation Journal, 32*, 285–291.

Rosenbaum, S., Markus, A., & Darnell, J. (2000). U.S. civil rights policy and access to health care by minority Americans: Implications for a changing health care system. *Medical Care Research and Review, 57*(Suppl. 4), 236–259.

Salzer, M., Schwenk, E., & Brusilovskiy, E. (2010). Certified peer specialist roles and activities: Results from a national survey. *Psychiatric Services, 61*, 520–523.

Shim, R. S., Koplan, C., Langheim, F. J., Manseau, M., Oleskey, C., Powers, R. A., & Compton, M. T. (2012). Health care reform and integrated care: A golden opportunity for preventive psychiatry. *Psychiatric Services, 63*, 1231–1233.

Singh, H., Shah, A. A., Gupta, V., Coverdale, J., & Harris, T. B. (2012). The efficacy of mental health outreach programs to religious settings: A systematic review. *American Journal of Psychiatric Rehabilitation, 15*, 290–298.

Thornicroft, G., Leff, J., Warner, R., Sartorius, N., & Schulze, H. (2006). *Shunned: Discrimination against people with mental illness.* New York, NY: Oxford University Press.

Tsai, J., Salyers, M. P., Rollins, A. L., McKasson, M., & Litmer, M. L. (2009). Integrated dual disorders treatment. *Journal of Community Psychology, 37*, 781–788.

Tsemberis, S., & Asmussen, S. (1999). From streets to homes. *Alcoholism Treatment Quarterly, 17*, 113–131.

U.S. Department of Housing and Urban Development (HUD). (2010). *The 2010 annual homeless assessment report to Congress.* Retrieved from http://www.hudhre.info/documents/2010 HomelessAssessmentReport.pdf

Velligan, D. I., Weiden, P. J., Sajatovic, M., Scott, J., Carpenter, D., Ross, R., & Docherty, J. P. (2009). The Expert Consensus Guideline Series: Adherence problems in patients with serious and persistent mental illness. *Journal of Clinical Psychiatry, 70*, 1–49.

Vick, B., Jones, K., & Mitra, S. (2012). Poverty and severe psychiatric disorder in the U.S.: Evidence from the Medical Expenditure Panel Survey. *Journal of Mental Health Policy and Economics, 15*, 83–96.

Wallerstein, N. B., & Duran, B. (2006). Using community-based participatory research to address health disparities. *Health Promotion Practice, 7*, 312–323.

Wang, P. S., Berglund, P., & Kessler, R. C. (2001). Recent care of common mental disorders in the United States. *Journal of General Internal Medicine, 15*, 284–292.

Warf, C. W., Clark, L. F., Herz, D. C., & Rabinovitz, S. J. (2009). The continuity of care to nowhere: Poverty, child protective services, juvenile justice, homelessness and incarceration: The disproportionate representation of African American children and youth. *International Journal of Child and Adolescent Health, 2*, 48–64.

Watson, A. C., & Corrigan, P. W. (2005). Challenging public stigma: A targeted approach. In P. W. Corrigan (Ed.), *On the stigma of mental illness: Practical strategies for research and social change* (pp. 281–295). Washington, DC: American Psychological Association.

# Multicultural Rehabilitation Counseling: Optimizing Success With Diversity

*Elias Mpofu and Debra A. Harley*

## LEARNING OBJECTIVES

The goals of this chapter are to enhance conceptual clarity in the use of terms descriptive of minority status in clients seeking rehabilitation services, to characterize multicultural counseling as an essential approach to address diversity issues that impact the quality of rehabilitation services, to propose the ways in which rehabilitation professionals may enhance cultural sensitivity in their education and practice, and to address ethical issues in rehabilitation counseling practice for which the use of multicultural counseling approaches would be a solution. After completing the chapter, the reader should be able to:

1. Outline three sociocultural criteria for minority statuses.
2. Explain the relevance of multicultural counseling to rehabilitation counseling practice.
3. Distinguish rehabilitation service qualities for diversity-sensitive counseling.
4. Discuss the ways in which theories of counseling could address cultural differences in rehabilitation service delivery.

## QUALITIES DEFINING MINORITY STATUS

Individuals who are viewed as minorities (e.g., persons of color, persons with disabilities, women, sexual minorities) make up this population, which multiculturalism seeks to include in a sociopolitical and cultural landscape (Balcazar, Suarez-Balcazar, Taylor-Ritzler, & Keys, 2010). Persons with disabilities, who are also members of a racial minority group, must be considered from two perspectives. One is of belonging to a group of people with disabilities, and the other is of belonging to a group designation by race. In essence, they are a minority within a minority (Bryan, 2007). Specific racial minorities, such as African Americans with disabilities, are covered by two sets of legislation, one, as racial minority citizens covered by the Civil Rights Acts of 1965, and, two, as citizens with disabilities, covered by the Rehabilitation Act of 1973 and subsequent amendments, along with the Americans with Disabilities Act (ADA) of 1990. Minority status is one of many human identities in the lived environment. Beyond identity development, many elements shape and influence people's lives, including, but not limited to, positioning, power and privilege, globalization, social class and poverty, religion, and generational variation. Each of these elements is a construct of identity and a source of difference. Multicultural counseling takes into account the worldview of different others from the counselor who addresses their needs for counseling.

Minority status refers to groups that share a history of being denied access to resources and privileges, such as economic opportunities, communicative self-representation, resources and privileges, and preferred lifestyles (Habermas, 1987; Mpofu & Conyers, 2002, 2004; D. L. Smith & Alston, 2010). These effects influence the participation in rehabilitation counseling of clients with minority status.

### Numerical Minority Representation

Persons with disabilities constitute the largest minority group in the United States. There are approximately 56.7 million (18.7%) people in the U.S. civilian noninstitutionalized population with a disability, of whom 38.3 million (12.6%) have a severe disability (Brault, 2012). Persons with disabilities have been called a minority on the basis of their numerical inferiority (Bryan, 2007); however, numbers per se do not define minority status, because persons with numerical superiority can be minorities (e.g., females). Persons with disabilities are minorities because they, like racial, ethnic, and cultural minorities groups in the United States, meet the three criteria for minority status as previously described. Individuals with disabilities are more likely to be unemployed, to experience persistent poverty, and to often rely on various government interventions (e.g., Social Security, Medicare) in order to maintain their participation in the community, and "as a demographic category, disability is an attribute with which individuals may broadly identify, similar to race or gender" (Brault, 2012, p. 1).

Job and employment-related discrimination against persons with disabilities continue regardless of the passage of the ADA (Draper, Reid, & McMahon, 2011). The unemployment rate is particularly high for individuals with certain types of disabilities, such as HIV/AIDS (Jung & Bellini, 2011); psychiatric disorders (An, Roessler, & McMahon, 2011); sensory and communicative disorders; multiple and severe disabilities (Brault, 2012); and also for specific groups of people with disabilities, such as women (D. L. Smith & Alston, 2010), elderly individuals (Redfoot & Houser, 2010), veterans (LePage, Washington, Lewis, Johnson, & Garcia-Rea, 2011), and ex-offenders (Whitfield, 2009). As pointed out by Draper et al., much of the employment discrimination against persons with disabilities is stigma based rather than associated with any meaningful functional differences in worker capability.

## Restrictions on Economic Opportunity

Employment outcomes for persons with disabilities have been persistently more negative than those for people without disabilities, and "there is no evidence that employment outcomes for people with disabilities as a whole have improved since 1990" (Harkin, 2012, p. 6). Individuals from racial minority groups, hereafter referred to as multicultural populations, have a long history of disparities in access to the vocational rehabilitation (VR) system and outcomes of rehabilitation services (Alston & Mngadi, 1992; Atkins, 1988; Atkins & Wright, 1980; Herbert & Martinez, 1992; Wilson, 2002, 2005; Wilson, Harley, McCormick, Jolivette, & Jackson, 2001). According to the National Council on Disability (1992, p. 6):

> The combination of disability and ethnicity, race and/or cultural background often results in a double form of discrimination. Individuals with disabilities who are members of ethnic, racial and/or ethnic cultural groups frequently experience discrimination disproportionately in comparison to their White or European counterparts.

Evidence indicates that minorities were generally underserved by VR and had a higher rate of rejection for rehabilitation services, with poorer outcomes, which resulted in rehabilitation legislation that emphasized a need for VR services to be more inclusive of minorities. The resulting legislation was the reauthorization of the Rehabilitation Act, and new legislative mandates have resulted in the need to make rehabilitation services more available to racial minorities (Rehabilitation Act Amendments, 1992), adding to the significance of diversity issues in rehabilitation counseling. The Rehabilitation Act Amendments (1992, p. 4364) stated:

> Patterns of inequitable treatment of minorities have been documented in all major junctures of the vocational rehabilitation process. As compared to White Americans, a larger percentage of African-American applicants to the vocational rehabilitation system is denied acceptance. Of applicants for service, a larger percentage of African-American cases is closed without being rehabilitated. Minorities are provided less training than their White counterparts. Consistently, less money is spent on minorities than their White counterparts.

Several trends persist for individuals with disabilities: (a) Their comparable employment participation rate is lower than that of any other group tracked by the U.S. Bureau of Labor Statistics; (b) they have been affected more dramatically and have been slower to rebound from losses experienced during recession; (c) they are more often underemployed than people without disabilities; (d) they indicate a high desire to be in the workforce (Schur, Kruse, & Blanck, 2005); (e) they have a poverty rate for working age adults with disabilities that is almost 30% (Disability Statistics & Demographics Rehabilitation Research and Training Center, 2011; Livermore, 2011); (f) they are more likely to be overrepresented in entry-level, low-paying jobs; (g) they have lower access to job networks tied to firms with job openings; (h) they experience more work-related performance pressures; (i) their work contributions and their skill levels are undervalued (Yelin

& Trupin, 2003); and (j) there continues to be a disproportionately lower rate of acceptance and successful closure of VR services for those ethnic minorities with disabilities (Wilson, 2005; Wilson & Senices, 2005). The needs of people with disabilities have been commodified into a profit-making helping industry in which typically developing or nondisabled others are thriving entrepreneur-providers, whereas those with lived disability mostly are clients with severe socioeconomic disadvantage (Mpofu, Thomas, & Thompson, 1998).

## Communicative Self-Representation

Historically, persons with disabilities have been denied the right to communicative self-representation, and there is still a wide use of language that is disrespectful of persons with disabilities by the scientific community, the general public, and the media (e.g., "the disabled," "the mentally handicapped," "the autistic"), in spite of the wishes of persons with disabilities to be referred to in preferred terms with person-first language (e.g., "persons with disabilities"; Bailey, 1992; Bryan, 2007). In addition, terms have been used in an attempt to describe persons with disabilities in benevolent ways, such as people who "suffer from a tragedy," "struggle to become normal again," and "fight to overcome their challenges" (Snow, 2008). In addition, the term *disabled person* places a disability-related difference before "person," which may have the effect of overlooking the numerous ways in which the individual with a disability is like many other nondisabled persons (Wright, 1991). It is important to recognize that a person with a *disability* is not his or her disability. "A disability descriptor is simply a medical diagnosis, which may become a sociopolitical passport to services or legal status" (Snow, 2008, p. 1). The World Health Organization (WHO, 2011) *International Classification of Functioning, Disability and Health* (ICF) specifies the term *disability* as an umbrella term for impairments, activity limitations, and participation restrictions that impact an individual.

The person-first language (e.g., person with a disability), which was first adopted by The Association for Persons with Severe Handicaps (TASH; Bailey, 1992), represents an attempt by a minority group to gain communicative self-representation from nondisabled persons. The effort to eradicate archaic terms and inaccurate descriptors is more than political correctness; it is an act of empowerment and respect. Although progress has been made toward this end, more work is needed in achieving the intended purpose.

Several studies have examined the use of terms to refer to persons with disabilities. For instance, Sandieson (1998) conducted a survey on the terms used to refer to persons with mental retardation by researchers in the area of mental retardation and developmental disabilities over the 10-year period from 1985 to 1995. Sixty-six terms were used to identify persons with mental retardation, 36 (56%) of which were unfriendly to persons with mental retardation (e.g., intellectual deficiency, mentally handicapped, intellectual subnormality). Other research on the terms used to refer to persons with disabilities by the general public and the media shows a higher use of terms unfriendly to persons with disabilities by nondisabled persons (Auslander & Gold, 1999; Wilgosh & Sandulac, 1997). Dajani (2001) found that national media differ in the frequency in which they used person-first language, with Disability News Service using person-first language 89% of the time and the Associated Press, 18% of the time. The media act as mechanisms in the social construction of persons with disabilities (Haller, 1998). Clearly, names that define groups help to determine how group members and agents of group members respond to the group. According to Simpson and Yinger (1972, p. 32), "Words prefigure and control experience to some degree; they are not simply innocent labels."

## Theoretical and Empirical Bases for Cultural Influences

Counseling practices that are respectful of the diverse backgrounds of clients have been called diversity-sensitive counseling, multicultural counseling, or minority counseling (Lee, Blando, Mizelle, & Orozco, 2007). Multiculturalism seeks to promote intercultural dialogue among majority cultures and minority cultures in the belief that such exchanges will result in the enrichment of both majority and minority counselors and clients. In practical terms, multicultural counseling seeks to recognize and use the unique worldviews of clients that are influenced by client background and strives to understand the complex strands of discourse that influence people's lives. The ethical objective is to base treatment decisions on the client's strengths, preferences, and limitations, which is likely to be met when multicultural or diversity-sensitive counseling approaches are used in the provision of rehabilitation counseling services. Multicultural practices are increasingly addressed by rehabilitation professional standards and curricula.

## Multicultural Standards and Curriculum Guidelines

The significance and awareness of multiculturalism in service delivery that is echoed by rehabilitation professionals, along with the availability of legislation supportive of multicultural practices, have yielded corresponding changes by educators and professional organizations to integrate cultural sensitivity into service delivery, rehabilitation education curricula, and the Commission on Rehabilitation Counselor Certification's (CRCC, 2010) *Code of Professional Ethics for Rehabilitation Counselors* (hereafter referred to as the *Code*). The *Code* has infused content on cultural diversity throughout, while maintaining specific standards on diversity. Most notable changes in the *Code* are (a) in the preamble, which states a commitment to "appreciating the diversity of human experience and culture" (p. 103); (b) respecting diversity (Section A.2); (c) developmental and cultural sensitivity (Section A.3.c); (d) respecting client rights (Section B.1.a); (e) relationships with colleagues, employers, and employees (Section E.1.a); (f) proper diagnosis of mental disorders (Section G.3.b); (g) test selection (Section G.5.c); (h) test scoring and interpretation (Section G.7.b); (i) rehabilitation counselor supervision competence (Section H.2.b); (j) responsibilities of rehabilitation counselor educators (Section H.6.b); and (k) cultural diversity competence in rehabilitation counselor education programs and training programs (Section H.8).

The Council on Rehabilitation Education (CORE; 2011) has incorporated a standard on cultural diversity (Standard C.2.3) into rehabilitation counselor education programs. The standard requires the curriculum to address cultural beliefs and values and diversity issues that may affect the rehabilitation process, identify the influences of cultural differences and integrate this knowledge into practice, and articulate an understanding of the role of ethnic/racial and other diversity characteristics. The evolution of the *Code* and standards for curricula accreditation reflects the values of a profession, its current resources, and future prospects for responding to a diverse constituency. The establishing of standards and guidelines for practice in multiculturalism is a step in the right direction, which should predispose a rehabilitation counselor and other professionals to be sensitive to cultural values and perspectives in the counseling process. However, the presence of these standards and guidelines does not mean that the counseling process is totally value-free, unbiased, and objective. Ongoing education and training in multiculturalism are necessary to update, reinforce, and hold accountable a profession and practitioners in a multicultural society.

With the increased attention and awareness that has been given to multiculturalism in the rehabilitation and counseling literature, there is considerably more consistency among rehabilitation (and other helping) professionals in broadly defining the elements of client variables (e.g., race, ethnicity, gender, sexual orientation, age, and disability status) that constitute minority status and diversity, as well as their relationships to one another (Atkinson, 2004; Robinson-Wood, 2009; Sue, 2006; Sue & Sue, 2013). The literature supports an examination of multiculturalism based on the convergence of multiple identities (Robinson-Wood, 2009). In addition, Harley (2009, p. 128) contends that multicultural counseling has contributed to the concept of client empowerment and serves to "deconstruct the persistent features of ism in counseling that structure privilege for the benefit of one group in society to the exclusion and/or devaluation of others." Value orientations underpin the construction of disability and normative responses to disability (Mpofu, Chronister, Johnson & Denham, 2012; Mpofu & Oakland, 2006).

### Cultural Templates for Values

Cultural communities are defined by intersubjectively shared values that preset responses to social phenomena, including disability and culture-related differences (Mpofu, Chronister et al., 2012). Sue and Sue (2013) enumerated the salient intersubjectively shared value systems of several cultural groups, which are informed by and reflect significant aspects of the worldviews in specific cultures. The value of saving face in Far Eastern cultures is a prominent example, but other Asian culture-bound beliefs and values include behaviors that lead to restraint in showing strong feelings, showing loyalty and respect for one's family and elders, and a preference for clearly defined roles of dominance and deference. The worldview of deference to others influences rehabilitation services consultation in which disability is perceived as a family matter rather than an individual matter, and preferred relationships with rehabilitation professionals may be hierarchical, with the rehabilitation professional expected to provide guidance on services.

There are many other examples to illustrate the importance of culture. In Latino cultures, the distinction between "mental" and "physical" health states overlaps, enabling an appreciation of the psycho-physiognomy of health conditions and multimodal treatment approaches. Moreover, Latinos engage in more body contact in greeting others, show a greater orientation toward the family or interdependence than the more individualistic Western culture, which would suggest bringing the role of family or social group to the forefront in rehabilitation counseling interventions with Latinos. American Indians and Alaskan Natives believe in a Supreme Creator who is sacred and central to harmonious relationships with nature and all things so that (dis)ability is an attribute on a continuum of relationship abilities. Thus, wellness is a balance of the mind, body, spirit, and natural environment. Values common among people of African descent include participation of the extended family, and collateral relations are valued highly over individualistic ones (Robinson-Wood, 2009) since individuals are an indelible part of collectives. The Arab family tends to be patriarchal, pyramidcally hierarchal with regard to age, gender, and extended family; communication styles with others external to the family (e.g., professional counselors) may be more scripted to keep "personal" stories from being disclosed outside of the family (Abudabbeh, 2005).

It is important to point out that there is great diversity within cultural groups, and they are not homogeneous. Other factors, such as acculturation level, generational differences, and country of origin, may influence one's worldview and cultural perception. Thus, responding to individuals seeking rehabilitation service solely on the bases of visible characteristics (race, disability type) perpetuates stereotypes that are harmful to the client and significant others (e.g., family, employers).

## SELECTED SOURCES OF MAJORITY BIAS IN REHABILITATION SERVICE DELIVERY

In this section, the implications are considered for counseling of individuals with minority status, as defined by communication style preference differences and also imputed negative sociocultural visibility by socially privileged others, such as professional counselors. Lack of cultural awareness in the provision of rehabilitation services carries the risk of ethnocentrism or the assumption that one's cultural heritage is superior to that of others and so different others must necessarily use the same social framework in their presentation for counseling. Ethnocentric biases in counseling practice are serious failures in ethical practice. If not attended to, these qualities disempower minority status clients in their participation of rehabilitation services. In this section, aspects of multicultural rehabilitation counseling are addressed to empower clients to achieve the goals for which they seek counseling and to assist would-be counselors to practice with cultural sensitivity.

## Communication Style and Language

Communication serves as the basis for effective multicultural counseling. The ability of the client and counselor to send and receive both verbal and nonverbal messages accurately and appropriately is the true measure of communication. Communication styles have a tremendous impact on face-to-face encounters (Sue & Sue, 2013). Communication styles consist of *social rhythms* that underlie all our speech and actions, which are strongly correlated with race, culture, and ethnicity (Garrett & Portman, 2011; Kim, 2011). Unfortunately, as pointed out by Sue and Sue (2013), many counselors and other helping professionals have been reared with a Euro-American middle-class perspective and may assume that certain behaviors or rules of speaking are universal and possess the same meaning. However, communication styles and the use of the English language have sometimes presented barriers to communication between practitioners and clients; the demographics of the United States have shifted dramatically over the last decade, with many clients speaking English as their second language, which may further impede the communication process. Linguistic or language barriers often place culturally diverse clients at a disadvantage (Montgomery, 2005). The cultural upbringing of many ethnic minority clients dictates different patterns of communication that may place them at a disadvantage in counseling.

The language of counseling influences the use of health services by minorities (Altarriba, 2007; Green, 1999). The language that a client uses is an important indicator of his or her worldview and interpretation of health status. According to Green (1999, p. 125), "To really know what and how people experience the things they do, to be truly empathic, we have to focus first on their language because language is our most direct window onto what they know and feel." For instance, a significant problem for psychiatric evaluation of Hispanic clients is language. Even with some fluency in Spanish, evaluators may diagnose Hispanic individuals differently than professionals of the individual's own culture. Often, words may have to be translated, when a counterpart does not exist in Spanish and, an approximation of the word is translated, which may change the meaning. For example, immigrant workers of Mexican origins have no words for *disability*, although they often experience chronic and severe health problems (Schaller, Parker, & Garcia, 1998). The fact that immigrant Mexican workers may not be aware that chronic illness constitutes a disability suggests that they may be less likely to seek rehabilitation services. They are also more likely to prematurely terminate counseling as compared to majority clients.

Similarly, many Native American languages have no terms for *disability*, *mental retardation*, and *handicap*, ostensibly because it is the social roles that a person performs in his or her community that are viewed as defining the person, rather than a disability per se. Perceptions of individuals by minorities in terms of social role functions may contrast with those of rehabilitation professionals, who may focus more on medical categories and the associated clinical picture (e.g., etiology, diagnosis, prognosis). The National Council on Interpreting in Health Care (2005) published national standards for interpreters of health care that address issues of cultural awareness and confidentiality.

The differences in perceptions reflect differences in underlying worldviews and can result in significant misunderstandings between counselors and minority clients with regard to the presenting condition and appropriate methods of rehabilitation. Minority clients may deny certain labels that are ordinarily used by rehabilitation counselors to describe certain disabilities, unless the condition is extreme (Altarriba, 2007). The primary medium by which counselors and helping professionals perform their work is through verbalizations, and because of linguistic bias and monolingualism, the form of communication is English (Sue, 2006). The bilingual background of many minority clients may lead to much misunderstanding. In addition, understanding Black communication styles and patterns is indispensable for counselors working with some African Americans. As stated by Sue, failure to understand imagery, analogies, and nuances of cultural sayings may render the counselor ineffective in establishing relationships and building credibility. As also indicated by Montgomery (2005) and Sue, if bilingual clients are unable to use their native tongue in counseling and, because they may have difficulty using the complexity of English to describe their particular thoughts, feelings, and unique situations, many aspects of their emotional experience may be inaccessible for intervention.

### Effects of Tokenism in Counseling

In any social group, a category of people (e.g., people of color, persons with disabilities, and women) may be underrepresented and, when this discrepancy is extreme (i.e., less than 15% of the group), those individuals are considered to be token representatives of their group (Settles & Buchanan, 2006). According to tokenism theory, tokens are expected to experience a variety of hardships in societal situations, such as feelings of heightened visibility, isolation, and limited opportunities (Stroshine & Brandl, 2011). Minority persons comprise the majority of persons with disabilities (Brault, 2012) and, at the same time, they are less likely to use rehabilitation services or are more likely to be denied services (Balcazar et al., 2010; Rehabilitation Act Amendments, 1992; Wilson, 2005; Wilson et al., 2001).

The relatively small percentage who access rehabilitation services may experience the tokenism effects of *visibility*, *contrast*, *role encapsulation*, and *assimilation* (Mpofu, Crystal, & Feist-Price, 2000; Settles & Buchanan, 2006). *Visibility* refers to those characteristics that mark individuals (e.g., racial minorities) so that they will tend to stand out in the groups in which they are involved. Such individuals tend to be watched more closely by the majority and may experience performance pressures. *Contrast* refers to those who are visibly different from the majority, but whose similarities to the majority tend to minimize any perceived differences. Role encapsulation occurs when members with minority status are treated by members of the majority group in stereotypical ways and in which treatment is also a consequence of minority status. Assimilation effects of tokenism are the pressures that are exerted on minority persons by the majority to adopt the worldviews of the majority. Often, majority group members contrast differences between themselves and token members, creating artificial boundaries between the two groups. As indicated by Settles and Buchanan (2006), these boundaries serve as protection to majority-group members, who are unsure about the attitudes and beliefs of token members, as well as to isolate token members socially.

Possible tokenism effects of majority-oriented rehabilitation services may explain, in part, the lower use of rehabilitation services by racial minorities. For instance, rehabilitation clients who are racial minorities may be more visible among majority rehabilitation clients and counselors. As a result, they may experience greater scrutiny and different treatment from majority clients, which could lead to premature termination of rehabilitation services. Similarly, the underrepresentation of racial minority clients at rehabilitation service centers may add to the chances that minority clients will be seen as different from majority clients, even though they may be presenting with the same concerns. Consequently, minority clients may be at a higher risk of denial of services or unsuccessful case closure.

Visibility and contrast tokenism effects may also explain the reported higher frequency of "unable to locate" closures among racial minority as compared to racial majority rehabilitation clients (Mpofu et al., 2000). Racial minority clients may also avoid rehabilitation service use because they anticipate being treated in stereotypical ways, similar to how the majority group treats them in the wider society. Racial or cultural minorities may also drop out of rehabilitation services because they experience cultural pressures from rehabilitation counselors to assimilate to the majority worldview on disability and treatment or to abandon their perception of disability and preferred ways of coping (Schaller et al., 1998).

### Counseling Theories and Techniques

Consistently, worldview has been the most popular construct in the multicultural counseling literature (Sotnik & Jezewski, 2005). Counseling that takes a multicultural vision into account has evolved through a series of cycles, moving from the White counselor being culturally encapsulated to multicultural competencies that counselors should master and toward a projection of more models of community (Monk, Winslade, & Sinclair, 2008). Monk et al. (2008, p. 315) suggest that the next focus of multicultural counseling is where "communities will develop a social formula as a basis for including immigrant newcomers, recognizing indigenous populations, and providing social inclusion for former slave populations." Edberg (2007), in examination of health behavior, advocates for a focus on the multiplicity of influences on the behavior of individuals, called the ecological model, which is applicable to multicultural counseling in rehabilitation. Under the ecological model, it is assumed that no one factor influences people's behavior; instead, there is a complex interaction between individuals and environment. Edberg identified potential contributors to the behavior of individuals to include (a) individual factors, (b) social/cultural/group factors, (c) socioeconomic and structural factors, (d) political factors, and (e) environmental factors.

The multicultural counseling/therapy (MCT) is the approach that often contrasts markedly with the traditional view of counseling (Sue & Sue, 2013).

There are over 300 approaches to psychological counseling and psychotherapy; however, most can be classified into one of three basic schools of thought: (a) psychodynamic, (b) behavioral, and (c) humanistic (Bryan, 2007). Too often, rehabilitation counselors may incorrectly assume that mainstream counseling theories have universal applicability. Counselors may use terminology that makes it difficult for clients to participate meaningfully in the rehabilitation process (Baron & Byrne, 2008; Schaller et al., 1998) and may perceive their clients in stereotypical ways (Abreu, 2001; Pedersen, 2007a). In addition, rehabilitation agencies and counselors may fail to project a service orientation that is consistent with the requirements of the user community (Schaller et al., 1998).

Most of the mainstream theories of counseling used by rehabilitation (and other) counselors are individualistic in orientation and assume that the core of the problems that the individual is experiencing is essentially personal and intrapsychic. Counselors operating from this premise may regard interventions aimed at changing the individuals' cognitions, behaviors, and emotions toward particular experiences (e.g., an acquired disability) as primary to treatment efforts. Minority clients may have an interpersonal worldview and center their experience of a challenging event (e.g., an acquired disability) on the ways that it affects their cultural role expectations (e.g., for males and females, older and younger persons, firstborns; Schaller et al., 1998). Thus, the experience of disability with racial minorities is more likely to be a family or community issue as compared to European American clients. In turn, mainstream approaches to rehabilitation may be perceived by minority clients as treating persons like nonhistorical and nonsocial units. Such approaches may be viewed as pressuring minorities to adapt to the cultural values of the majority. "The issue of how majority and minority can communicate effectively is a major concern of the helping profession" (Pedersen, 2007a, p. 125).

The use of counseling approaches that foster the notion that psychosocial adjustment will be resolved through insight and self-exploration may not be appropriate for all minorities. Insight-oriented theories assume a wide choice of self-representations and preferred ways of life, which may not be true of minorities due to their historical and ongoing experience of oppression and prejudice by the majority. For example, minority status persons may be relatively less troubled by how they see or feel about themselves than by societywide restrictions on their economic participation, communicative self-representation, and preferred ways of life (Dovidio, Gaertner, & Kawakami, 2003). Insight-oriented interventions also assume that the individual self is the center of a person's subjective well-being, a view that is inconsistent with that of racial or ethnic minorities whose sense of self may be nested in relationships with the social and inanimate metaphysical environment (Landrine, 1992; Robinson-Wood, 2009). Mainstream treatment approaches, with their goal of redefining the self as separate from the community and environment, would be inappropriate for those minority clients who have a relational sense of self.

Self-disclosure, an essential component of mainstream counseling approaches, is incongruent with the views of some minority groups that personal life stories are ultimately the stories of significant others (e.g., family), and should not be told to strangers, including counselors. Thus, expecting minority clients to self-disclose as a way of generating clinical material may be asking them to operate in an unfamiliar mode of selfrepresentation and to violate the integrity of the life stories of the collective of which the client's story is a part. For that reason, some minority clients have been observed to be very tentative in their initial commitment and participation with traditional counseling and to take a longer time to establish a working relationship with a counselor (Brooks, Haskins, & Kehe, 2004). The importance of personal relationship factors, like empathy, genuineness, and warmth, may be perceived by some minority clients as an attempt to substitute facilitative conditions for a true understanding of their situation as oppressed or disadvantaged persons (Green, 1999).

Minority clients may also bring to counseling a personal history of experiencing societal oppression and discrimination, which may predispose them to rejecting counseling services (Sue & Sue, 2013). For instance, mainstream counseling approaches that emphasize changing the individual may be perceived by some minority clients as attempts to blame them for sources of difficulty that are institutionally generated and are part of the oppression of minorities. The higher unemployment rate among persons with disabilities is a case in point. Failure to secure a job placement in rehabilitation service may be perceived by rehabilitation counselors as problems of motivation or lack of skills, when the employment difficulties could be better explained by prejudice against persons with disabilities by employers (Yelin & Trupin, 2003). The problems of securing jobs as part of the rehabilitation process are compounded for persons in multiple minority status (race, gender, and with disability).

Mainstream counseling theories and techniques have both advantages and disadvantages in their application with minority populations. In addition to such advantages and disadvantages, the competency of the counselor must also be considered. According to Bryan (2007), if a counselor or professional helper becomes culturally sensitive, most contemporary therapies can be effective.

## CULTURE-SENSITIVE REHABILITATION INTERVENTION STRATEGIES

There are three issues to which rehabilitation counselors need to attend when working with clients from nonmajority cultures. First is knowledge of the culture(s) with which the client identifies. Although there are many within-group differences in cultures, the client's culture still provides hypotheses to investigate in the process of conceptualizing the client's perceptual world. Second is an awareness of the client's worldview. With an awareness of the counselors' own cultural beliefs and assumptions, and their possible marginalizing effects on clients, counselors ought to listen and ask the client questions that educate them about their client's values and life meanings. Third, counselors need counseling skills that tend to accommodate client differences in terms of values, rate of conversation, style of nonverbal cues, and expectations (Sue & Sue, 2013). Only by reaching out to clients in terms of their worldview can counselors hope to provide culture-sensitive counseling. Although research on the basic issue of helping (counseling) is incomplete, Pedersen (2007b) stresses that available data on microcounseling suggest the following:

1. *Alternative theoretical orientations, such as gestalt, Rogerian, and trait and factor, use very different patterns of helping skills.* Helping needs to consider matching the goals of the client with the goals of the helping intervention. Clients preferring more directive therapies should have access to such therapies and recognition as experienced in their help-seeking to address significant life issues (Mpofu, Madden, et al., 2012). Although matching on the wide range of individual variation that exists in a culture may generally be sought, it is important to remember that individual differences on individual treatment probably will always be necessary. The now-established evidence for solution-focused brief therapies speaks about specific ways in which professional counselors can help resolve with their clients significant issues of clients, while minimizing the risk of imposing a worldview on the clients.

2. *All theoretical orientations seem to have much in common.* A majority of the traditional or classical counseling approaches focus on the individual (while simultaneously generally ignoring societal–cultural issues) and emphasize freeing the individual from polarities, blocks, and mixed messages, so that the client can get "unstuck" and generate new and more creative ways of interacting with his or her world. However, some facilitative conditions for successful counseling (e.g., genuineness, respect and warmth, empathy) appear to have cross-cultural transportability. Professional counselors need to be mindful of how these transcending counseling qualities are expressed both among and within cultural groupings.

Multicultural counseling has had a positive effect on making counselors more introspective about how their values and cultural blind spots may have a negative impact on clients from cultural backgrounds that differ from their own. However, more emphasis is needed on translating multicultural counseling knowledge and awareness into improved services and practices (Gielen, Draguns, & Fish, 2008; Pedersen, 2007a).

## Structuring Service Delivery

Clients want to feel that the person with whom they are sharing their life stories is genuinely interested in their worldview (Ivey & Ivey, 1999; T. B. Smith, Richards, Granley, & Obiakor, 2004). Authenticity with oneself and one's clients may be achieved by directly addressing a potential or real difference between the counselor and client at the beginning or during the course of counseling.

For instance, a counselor and client may have different perceptions of the goals, resources, and procedures in rehabilitation service. In addition, counselors may differ from clients in terms of race, disability status, economic level, and gender. The counselor can minimize the chances of frustration arising from differences in expectations about counseling by negotiating with the client about goals and procedures of counseling service.

Structuring service delivery for clients makes it possible for them to participate in their own rehabilitation by examining the fit between their needs and the resources and procedures of the particular rehabilitation agency. It also facilitates the referral of clients to compatible community resources. Visible differences (e.g., race, disability status, gender) can be addressed by (a) asking the client whether he or she is comfortable working with a counselor who has an apparent difference from the client (racial, disability status, gender, or multiple differences); (b) openly acknowledging to the client the limitations that one may have in terms of experience in the client's world; (c) encouraging the client to inform the counselor whether he or she may be overlooking a significant issue in the client's view of his or her situation; and (d) communicating a genuine willingness to learn from the client.

Confronting differences that may impact the quality of service delivery in such a direct way communicates openness on the part of the counselor and invites the client to share ownership of the processes and outcomes of counseling (Ivey, Gluckstern, & Ivey, 1997; Vaughn, 2004). It may also help reduce any difference-related anxiety that counselor and client may have about unspoken and yet real differences in an experience that has a bearing on client participation. Directly addressing the differences minimizes the chances of stereotyping by both counselor and client and should assist in the forging of a working alliance at an early stage of rehabilitation service when minority clients are most likely to drop out.

### Assessing Client and Counselor Worldviews

The client's worldview may be a critical component of the information-gathering process during the intake interview. Counselors can also use semistructured or qualitative measures to assess client worldview. The qualitative measures would need to be checked for data convergence using multiple informant methods or observational techniques. A number of quantitative measures used to determine one's worldview are also available to counselors (Ibrahim, Roysicar-Sodowsky, & Ohnishi, 2001; Pedersen, 2007b). Counselors can also assess their own worldviews and multicultural competencies (knowledge, awareness, skills) by using existing quantitative measures, such as the Multicultural Counseling Inventory (MCI; Sodowsky, Taffe, Gutkins, & Wise, 1994).

### Employing the Language of Helping

In multilingual settings in which services are being provided to persons with a limited proficiency in English, the services of an interpreter or translator may help reduce some of the miscommunication arising from rehabilitation professionals and minority clients being unfamiliar with each other's languages (Sue, 2006). The interpreters may also help as culture brokers in cases in which communication may be hindered by implicit differences in worldviews or culturally restricted use of terms (National Council on Interpreting in Health Care, 2005).

Some basics in the use of translators apply: (a) facing toward and speaking directly to the client rather than to the translator, (b) keeping the translator fully involved throughout the interview, (c) repeating for confirmation with the client that he or she has been correctly understood, (d) requesting the client to correct any misunderstanding, (e) observing cultural protocols (age, kin, class, gender) about appropriate translators, (e) allowing extra time, and (f) keeping the agenda short and focused. The question of using family members as interpreters needs to be approached judiciously, because they are likely to be involved in the client's presenting situation and may be more helpful as information providers and allies in designing, implementing, and evaluating treatment, as opposed to their role as interpreters. Interpreters need to be trained in their role so that they convey the intended messages rather than personal versions.

Understanding minority clients' referent terms for disabling conditions is important for effective service delivery. Each ethnic minority group's perception of disability and what disability means is a reflection of its culture, religious beliefs, and traditions. In addition, there are intervening factors—such as the influence of the majority culture, the nature of the disabling condition, and the acculturation of the individual and/or family members—that affect the views of any given individual (Bryan, 2007; Leung, 2003). Shweder (1985) discussed the cultural context of language in depictions of illness and pain that may be useful to rehabilitation professionals working with minority populations. He identified five areas of language participation and use that professionals may take into account: common illness states and their descriptions, individual interpretations, community-wide meanings, associated expressive styles, illness power, and social position. For instance, some racial minorities have been reported to present with physical symptoms for what may be emotional problems (Schaller et al., 1998).

Communication with minority clients may be facilitated by counselors compiling terms commonly used by minority clients to describe various disabling conditions and carefully equating them with corresponding terms used by the majority. The culturally grounded functional interpretations that minority clients give to particular conditions of illness may also help rehabilitation professionals in identifying treatment goals with which clients and community identify (e.g., social role perceptions of rehabilitation). In addition to verbal communication, the counselor should be aware of how to interpret the client's body language, gestures, facial expressions, and eye contact. Body language may convey one message, whereas verbal expression may convey another (Harley & Stansbury, 2011). The meaning attached to specific nonverbal gestures is culturally determined and not universal in nature, which suggests that counselors must be concerned with both their own nonverbal messages and those of the client when in a multicultural counseling relationship (Hackney & Cormier, 2013).

## Minimizing Effects of Tokenism

Effects of tokenism on minority clients may be minimized by involving family and significant others in all stages of rehabilitation. For instance, minority clients could be asked whom they would like to be involved in their treatment planning. The nominated persons could then be invited to rehabilitation counseling sessions as often as the client chooses. Involvement of persons with a similar worldview and values to the minority client in rehabilitation service planning and delivery serves several functions: (a) enabling the client to draw on the resources of persons historically involved in his or her situation, (b) minimizing the tokenism effects of feeling isolated as a result of seeking rehabilitation services, and (c) enhancing the chances that salient issues to the client's rehabilitation will be addressed. The locating of rehabilitation services at centers that are accessible to minority clients (e.g., community centers) and including other resources or services relevant to the client's needs may also minimize the effects of tokenism. Carefully planned outreach programs may also be useful in increasing the use of rehabilitation services by minority clients.

Perhaps the most egregious challenge related to tokenism is that it impedes multicultural counseling as a means for advocacy and empowerment that would facilitate systemic changes in the rehabilitation process, thereby diminishing institutional discrimination. Kosciulek (2004) recommends a framework for empowering persons with disabilities in the rehabilitation process that presents the primary model constructs of working alliance, informed choice, self-determination, and empowerment. Harley (2009) suggests that at any point in time an individual can occupy multiple identities, and invoking those multiple identities may serve to further minimize the effects of tokenism because an individual is not boxed into being one-dimensional.

The way in which individuals look at their *positionality* offers a means of minimizing tokenism. Persons with disabilities, women, and those with minority group membership are clearly marginalized in the United States. Mayo (1982) introduced the notion of *positive marginality*, which acknowledges the strengths that lie and grow in the margins of social arrangements. Mayo recognized that people situated at the social margins do not necessarily internalize their exclusion, but instead embrace differences as strengths and sometimes as a source of critique and action (Hall & Fine, 2005). A number of women-of-color scholars, writers, and activists (e.g., Patricia Hill Collins, bell hooks, and Audre Lorde) critiqued *positionalities* and debunked living at the margins of mainstream society as a site of impotence, victimization, or marginality. Persons with disabilities and minority groups already have an established track record of self-advocacy. The focus of rehabilitation counselors is to work with these groups to enhance advocacy skills that will reframe their *positionalities* and tokenism.

## Increasing Disability Consciousness

The construct of disability consciousness has the potential to link group, community, and individual responses to minority statuses among persons with disabilities.

Disability consciousness is a multidimensional construct that refers to collective consciousness by persons with disabilities regarding their minority status or disability identity, as well as disability-friendly environments, and individual disability identity (Barnartt, 1996; Mpofu, 1999; Surbaugh, 2008). Barnartt regarded disability consciousness as a collective awareness among persons with disabilities regarding their minority status and the use of that consciousness as the basis for social movements that seek to advance the interests of persons with disabilities. In this regard, disability consciousness transcends gender, racial, and ethnic differences and may be a factor that rallies persons in the disability community together.

Collective disability consciousness may make it possible for persons with disabilities to form social movements through which they may achieve higher economic participation, gain control over self-definition, and have greater access to a way of life that validates their disability-related experiences. In other words, collective disability consciousness in persons with disabilities may be empowering at a group level and is similar to the Marxist notions of class consciousness. Disability consciousness may also be regarded as a sensitivity of the environment (e.g., community, workplaces) to disability-related differences.

Environments that are supportive of disability-related differences (e.g., positive social attitudes, enabling structures, and resources) may make disability-related differences less salient and may enhance perceived similarities between persons with disabilities and those without. Persons with disabilities in such enabling environments may be less susceptible to economic deprivation, loss of control of self-referential terms, and limitations in the choice of a preferred lifestyle. In other words, having a disability in a disability-enabling environment may not result in disability-related minority status effects, although other minority statuses (e.g., gender) may still apply. According to Dewey (2005), people in general are embedded in an environment and are part of the environment that others experience; therefore, we can engage others in ways that alter the collective experience of the environment to promote sensory aesthetic dimensions to the moral and ethical betterment of all.

Disability identity or consciousness may be positive or negative. Positive disability consciousness may result in proactive actions to restore the economic, self-identity, and cultural integrity of persons with disabilities. For instance, positive disability consciousness may be linked to higher levels of collective disability consciousness in persons with disabilities (Barnartt, 1996). Negative disability consciousness is exemplified by lower involvement in activities that would counter minority status effects in persons with disabilities or denial of their minority status in communities with high levels of prejudice against persons with disabilities. Surbaugh (2008, p. 397) stresses that "multiple points of view characterize disability consciousness, demonstrating reciprocity exists at various levels of experience: consciousness of self, of others, and of the interrelations of the two."

### Teaching Clients About Informed Choice

The language of service delivery is another area in which counselors can demonstrate sensitivity to the needs of minority clients. Minorities with disabilities have been found to be four times as likely as majority clients to be uninformed about disability legislation and their role in the individualized plan of employment (IPE; Smart & Smart, 1997a). Even more significant is the need for rehabilitation counselors to ensure that minority clients have the information that will enable them to make informed decisions. That involves understanding concerns from the client's perspective and sharing information with the client on resources that are likely to be useful in assisting the client in making effective choices and helping the client evaluate the relative merits of each option with regard to the client's values, needs, and preferences. In that connection, some minority clients may expect the rehabilitation counselor to assume a leading role in rehabilitation service delivery because of cultural conditioning.

Only 10% of minorities have been found to be aware of the ADA, in contrast to 40% in the general population (Smart & Smart, 1997b). Thus, minority clients may not be informed regarding their rights and responsibilities under the act. Rehabilitation counselors may fail to mention the ADA and other related legislation to minority clients under the assumption that clients are already aware of the legislation; failure to inform contributes to the mystification of clients regarding the rehabilitation process. Regardless of counselor assumption, the CRCC *Code* (2010) specifies that rehabilitation counselors and clients work jointly in developing plans and regularly review plans to assess continued viability and effectiveness (Section A.1.b) and informed choice/autonomy (Section A.1.d).

A significant component of rehabilitation legislation is informed choice in the provision of rehabilitation services to clients, which includes the collaborative preparation of an IPE by counselor and client. Minority clients may not be aware of the legal requirement of IPEs as part of the rehabilitation process and their role in formulating, implementing, monitoring, and evaluating the IPE. The active participation requirements in formulating the IPE may be incongruent with the worldviews and helpseeking behaviors of some minority clients (e.g., traditionalist Native Americans and Asian Americans) who may prefer to defer to the counselor in treatment decisions. Rehabilitation counselors who assume that minority clients know of their collaborative role in formulating and implementing IPEs could create unintended difficulties for minority clients. Such counselors may also experience higher minority client dropout rates, which could lead them to the erroneous conclusions that minority clients were unmotivated or uncooperative.

### RECONCILING OPPOSING POINTS OF VIEW

The polemics accompanying the debate on multicultural counseling create the impression that there are no elements in mainstream counseling that could be useful to minority counseling or that the two approaches do not overlap at all. It is more realistic to perceive mainstream and minority counseling approaches on a continuum with some aspects of mainstream counseling applicable to working with minority clients and vice versa.

A dichotomous view of counseling approaches (a) fails to recognize that clients in a multicultural society transverse realities in both the minority and mainstream contexts and may have their needs better met by being able to negotiate both contexts; (b) may have the effect of creating high levels of performance anxiety and guilt in majority counselors, which would compromise their ability to meet client needs; (c) creates the unjustified perception in majority counselors that the training they already have is totally irrelevant to serving minorities or cannot be the basis for personal growth and development in multicultural skills; (d) could create bad feelings in some majority counselors who may misperceive diversity-sensitive counseling to be some preferential treatment for minorities; (e) encourage the incorrect belief that counselors from a minority background are necessarily better at working with minority clients than those from a majority background; and (f) lead to the stigmatization of minority counselors as being preoccupied with political, as opposed to counseling, agendas.

In addition, the professional literature that addresses the provision of counseling to specific minority groups tends to be very general, and counselors are thus left with little guidance as to how they can improve in their practice with individual clients (Green, 1999; Monk et al., 2008). There are likely to be large within-group differences in clinically significant variables so that overgeneralizations may have the unfortunate effect of perpetuating stereotypes and useless categorizations, narrowing the perspectives of practitioners (Weinrach & Thomas, 1998). The fact that persons of color vary widely among themselves in terms of acculturation to the majority culture also adds to the complexity of counseling racial minorities. Racial, ethnic, or cultural minorities at different levels of racial/ethnic identity development will vary in their identification with the majority culture and their responsiveness to mainstream methods of counseling.

Moreover, a meta-analysis of 66 studies on the association among racial, ethnic, or cultural minority status and counseling outcomes indicated that clients consistently rated counselor *competence* higher than *racial or ethnic similarity* (Coleman, Wampold, & Casali, 1995). The same meta-analytic study also reported that studies that reported preferences for counselors of a similar race or ethnicity were limited by apparent social desirability effects (e.g., choice limited to race/ethnicity/culture only) and sampling bias (e.g., ethnic minority students at predominantly White universities). Majority and minority counselors were more alike than different in their worldviews (Mahalik, Worthington, & Crump, 1999). This similarity could be explained by counselor socialization during professional training or personality characteristics of persons in the helping professions. To assume that mainstream methods of counseling and majority counselors are inherently unsuited to working with persons of color, on the basis of color alone, smacks of racism (Weinrach & Thomas, 1998) and may hurt the needs of persons of color who may prefer working with counselors from the majority.

## CONCLUSIONS

It is important to address minority status issues in providing rehabilitation services. Among the significant client variables that counselors should consider are minority status, race, ethnicity, gender, disability status, and culture. Persons of minority status share cultural syndromes, which may be influenced by their historical and current oppression by the majority. Persons of minority status may experience denial of economic and sociocultural privileges in a manner that may make their worldviews and health-related experiences quite different from members of the majority. Clearly, a need exists and there is merit in providing culturally distinctive services in a multicultural setting such as the United States (Draguns, 2008).

Addressing diversity issues in rehabilitation service provision is an ethical imperative. What needs to be considered are the ways in which diversity can be achieved without stigmatizing the same clients who are supposed to benefit from services. Both multicultural and mainstream counseling approaches should be held accountable to meet client needs. The ethical objective to base treatment decisions on client strengths, preferences, and limitations is likely to be met when multicultural and mainstream counseling approaches are used in complementary ways. Ethnocentric biases in counseling represent serious ethical failures. Similarly, responding to individuals seeking rehabilitation services solely on the basis of visible characteristics (e.g., race, disability type) perpetuates stereotypes that are harmful to the client and his or her significant others (e.g., family, employers). Client outcomes in rehabilitation are a product of an interaction between rehabilitation service capacity and client participation, and counseling outcomes improve as client participation increases.

## DISCUSSION EXERCISES

1. "Minority status is a socially constructed or negotiated phenomenon." What is the truth of this claim in your understanding of the sociocultural foundations of minority statuses?
2. "All counseling is essentially multicultural." Discuss with reference to practices with which you are familiar.
3. Discuss any three specific ways to enhance cultural sensitivity in the provision of rehabilitation services.
4. How is multicultural or diversity-sensitive counseling an ethical imperative in the provision of rehabilitation counseling services?

## REFERENCES

Abreu, J. M. (2001). Theory and research on stereotypes and perceptual bias: A didactic resource for multicultural counseling trainers. *Counseling Psychologist, 29*, 487–512.

Abudabbeh, N. (2005). Arab families: An overview. In M. McGoldrick, J. Giordano, & N. Garcia-Preto (Eds.), *Ethnicity and family therapy* (pp. 423–436). New York, NY: Guilford.

Alston, R. J., & Mngadi, S. (1992). The interaction between disability status and the African-American experience: Implications for rehabilitation counseling. *Journal of Applied Rehabilitation Counseling, 23*(2), 12–15.

Altarriba, J. (2007). *Encyclopedia of multicultural psychology.* Thousand Oaks, CA: Sage.

An, S., Roessler, R. T., & McMahon, B. T. (2011). Workplace discrimination and Americans with psychiatric disabilities: A comparative study. *Rehabilitation Counseling Bulletin, 55*, 7–19.

Atkins, B. (1988). An asset-oriented approach to cross cultural issues: Blacks in rehabilitation. *Journal of Applied Rehabilitation Counseling, 19*(4), 45–49.

Atkins, B., & Wright, G. (1980). Three views of vocational rehabilitation of blacks: The statement. *Journal of Rehabilitation, 46*, 40–46.

Atkinson, D. R. (2004). *Counseling American minorities* (6th ed.). New York, NY: McGraw-Hill.

Auslander, G. K., & Gold, N. (1999). A comparison of newspaper reports in Canada and Israel. *Social Science and Medicine, 48*, 1395–1405.

Bailey, D. B. (1992). Guidelines for authors. *Journal of Early Intervention, 15*, 118–119.

Balcazar, F. E., Suarez-Balcazar, Y., Taylor-Ritzler, T., & Keys, C. B. (2010). *Race, culture, and disability: Rehabilitation science and practice.* Sudbury, MA: Jones & Bartlett.

Barnartt, S. (1996). Disability culture or disability consciousness? *Journal of Disability Policy Studies, 7*, 1–19.

Baron, R., & Byrne, D. (2008). *Social psychology* (12th ed.). Boston, MA: Allyn & Bacon.

Brault, M. W. (2012). *Americans with disabilities: 2010 household economic studies.* Washington, DC: U.S. Department of Commerce Economics and Statistics Administration, U.S. Census Bureau.

Brooks, L. J., Haskins, D. G., & Kehe, J. V. (2004). Counseling and psychotherapy with African American clients. In T. B. Smith (Ed.), *Practicing multiculturalism: Affirming diversity in counseling and psychology* (pp. 145–166). Boston, MA: Pearson.

Bryan, W. V. (2007). *Multicultural aspects of disabilities: A guide to understanding and assisting minorities in the rehabilitation process.* Springfield, IL: Charles C Thomas.

Coleman, H. L. K., Wampold, B. E., & Casali, S. L. (1995). Ethnic minorities' ratings of ethnically similar and European American counselors: A meta-analysis. *Journal of Counseling Psychology, 42*, 55–64.

Council on Rehabilitation Counselor Certification (CRCC). (2010). *Code of professional ethics for rehabilitation counselors.* Schaumburg, IL: Author.

Council on Rehabilitation Education (CORE). (2011). *Professional standards.* Retrieved from http://www.core-rehab.org

Dajani, K. F. (2001). Other research—What's in a name? Terms used to refer to people with disabilities. *Disability Studies Quarterly, 21*, 196–209.

Dewey, J. (2005). *Art as experience.* New York, NY: Penguin.

Disability Statistics & Demographics Rehabilitation Research and Training Center. (2011). *2011 annual disability statistics compendium.* Durham, NH: Institute on Disability.

Dovidio, J. F., Gaertner, S. L., & Kawakami, K. (2003). Intergroup contact: The past, present and future. *Group Processes and Intergroup Relations, 6*, 5–21.

Draguns, J. G. (2008). What have we learned about the interplay of culture with counseling and psychotherapy? In U. P. Gielen, J. G. Draguns, & J. M. Fish (Eds.), *Principles of multicultural counseling and therapy* (pp. 393–417). New York, NY: Routledge.

Draper, W. R., Reid, C. A., & McMahon, B. T. (2011). Workplace discrimination and the perception of disability. *Rehabilitation Counseling Bulletin, 55*, 29–37.

Edberg, M. (2007). *Essentials of health behavior: Social and behavioral theory in public health.* Sudbury, MA: Jones & Bartlett.

Garrett, M. T., & Portman, T. A. A. (2011). *Counseling native Americans.* Belmont, CA: Cengage.

Gielen, U. P., Draguns, J. G., & Fish, J. M. (2008). Principles of multicultural counseling and therapy: An introduction. In U. P. Gielen, J. G. Draguns, & J. M. Fish (Eds.), *Principles of multicultural counseling and therapy* (pp. 1–34). New York, NY: Routledge.

Green, J. W. (1999). *Cultural awareness in the human services: A multi-ethnic approach* (3rd ed.). Boston, MA: Allyn & Bacon.

Habermas, J. (1987). *The theory of communicative action: Vol. 2, Lifeworld and systems: A critique of functionalist reason.* Boston, MA: Beacon.

Hackney, H. L., & Cormier, S. (2013). *The professional counselor: A process guide to helping* (7th ed.). Boston, MA: Pearson.

Hall, M., & Fine, R. L. (2005). The stories we tell: The lives and friendship of two older black lesbians. *Psychology of Women Quarterly, 29,* 177–187.

Haller, B. (1998). Crawling toward civil rights: News media coverage of disability activism. In Y. R. Kamailpour & T. Carilli (Eds.), *Cultural diversity and the U.S. media* (pp. 89–98). Albany, NY: SUNY Press.

Harkin, T. (2012). *Unfinished business: Making employment of people with disabilities a national priority.* Washington, DC: U.S. Senate Committee on Health, Education, Labor & Pensions.

Harley, D. A. (2009). Multicultural counseling as a process of empowerment. In C. C. Lee, D. A. Burnhill, A. L. Butler, C. P. Hipolito-Delgado, M. Humphrey, O. Munoz, & H. Shin (Eds.), *Elements of culture in counseling* (pp. 127–147). Upper Saddle River, NJ: Pearson.

Harley, D. A., & Stansbury, K. L. (2011). Diversity counseling with African Americans. In E. Mpofu (Ed.), *Counseling people of African ancestry* (pp. 193–208). Cambridge: Cambridge University Press.

Herbert, J. T., & Martinez, M. Y. (1992). Client ethnicity and vocational rehabilitation case service outcomes. *Journal of Job Placement, 8,* 10–16.

Ibrahim, F. A., Roysircar-Sodowsky, G., & Ohnishi, H. (2001). Worldview: Recent developments and needed directions. In J. G. Ponterrotto, J. M. Casas, L. A. Suzuki, & C. M. Alexander (Eds.), *Handbook of multicultural counseling* (3rd ed., pp. 425–456). Thousand Oaks, CA: Sage.

Ivey, A. E., Gluckstern, N. B., & Ivey, M. B. (1997). *Basic influencing skills.* North Amherst, MA: Microtraining Associates.

Ivey, A. E., & Ivey, M. B. (1999). *Intentional interviewing and counseling: Facilitating client development in a multicultural society* (4th ed.). Pacific Grove, CA: Brooks/Cole.

Jung, Y., & Bellini, J. L. (2011). Predictors of employment outcomes for vocational rehabilitation consumers with HIV/AIDS: 2002–2007. *Rehabilitation Counseling Bulletin, 54,* 142–153.

Kim, B. S. K. (2011). *Counseling Asian Americans.* Belmont, CA: Cengage.

Kosciulek, J. F. (2004). Empowering people with disabilities through vocational rehabilitation counseling. *American Rehabilitation, 28,* 40–47.

Landrine, H. (1992). Clinical implications of cultural differences: The referential versus the indexical self. *Clinical Psychology Review, 12,* 401–415.

Lee, W. M. L., Blando, J. A., Mizelle, N. D., & Orozco, G. L. (2007). *Introduction to multicultural counseling for helping professionals.* New York, NY: Routledge.

LePage, J. P., Washington, E. L., Lewis, A. A., Johnson, K. E., & Garcia-Rea, E. A. (2011). Effects of structured vocational services on job-search success in ex-offender veterans with mental illness: 3-month follow-up. *Journal of Rehabilitation Research & Development, 48,* 277–286.

Leung, P. (2003). Multicultural competencies and rehabilitation counseling/psychology. In D. B. Pope-Davis, H. L. K. Coleman, W. M. Liu, & R. L. Toporek (Eds.), *Handbook of multicultural competencies in counseling and psychology* (pp. 439–455). Thousand Oaks, CA: Sage.

Livermore, G. A. (2011). Social security disability beneficiaries with work-related goals and expectations. *United States Social Security Administration Social Security Bulletin, 71*(3), 61–82.

Mahalik, J. R., Worthington, R. L., & Crump, S. (1999). Influence of racial/ethnic membership and "therapist culture" on therapists' worldview. *Journal of Multicultural Counseling and Development, 27*, 2–17.

Mayo, C. (1982). Training for positive marginality. In C. L. Bickman (Ed.), *Applied social psychology annual* (Vol. 3, pp. 57–73). Beverly Hills, CA: Sage.

Monk, G., Winslade, J., & Sinclair, S. (2008). *New horizons in multicultural counseling.* Thousand Oaks, CA: Sage.

Montgomery, M. (2005). Language and multidimensional contextual practice. In K. L. Guadalupe & D. Lum (Eds.), *Multidimensional contextual practice* (pp. 130–145). Belmont, CA: Brooks/Cole.

Mpofu, E. (1999). *Social acceptance of Zimbabwean adolescents with physical disabilities.* Ann Arbor, MI: UMI.

Mpofu, E., Chronister, J., Johnson, E., & Denham, G. (2012). Aspects of culture influencing rehabilitation with persons with disabilities. In P. Kennedy (Ed.), *Handbook of rehabilitation* (pp. 543–553). New York, NY: Cambridge.

Mpofu, E., & Conyers, L. M. (2002). Application of tokenism theory to enhancing quality in rehabilitation services. *Journal of Applied Rehabilitation Counseling, 33*(2), 31–38.

Mpofu, E., & Conyers, L. M. (2004). A representational theory perspective of minority status and people with disabilities: Implications for rehabilitation education and practice. *Rehabilitation Counseling Bulletin, 47*, 142–151.

Mpofu, E., Crystal, R., & Feist-Price, S. (2000). Tokenism in rehabilitation clients: Strategies for quality enhancement in rehabilitation services. *Rehabilitation Education, 14*, 243–256.

Mpofu, E., Madden, R., Athanasou, J. A., Manga, R. Z., Gitchel, W. D., Peterson, D. B., & Chou, C. (2012). Person-centered assessment in rehabilitation and health. In P. J. Toriello, M. Bishop, & P. D. Rumrill (Eds.), *New directions in rehabilitation counseling: Creative responses to professional, clinical, and educational challenges* (pp. 209–235). Linn Creek, MO: Aspen Professional Services.

Mpofu, E., & Oakland, T. (2006). Assessment of value change in adults with acquired disabilities. In M. Hersen (Ed.). *Clinician's handbook of adult behavioral assessment* (pp. 601–630). New York, NY: Elsevier Press.

Mpofu, E., Thomas, K. R., & Thompson, D. (1998). Cultural appropriation and rehabilitation counseling: Implications for rehabilitation education. *Rehabilitation Education, 12*, 205–216.

National Council on Disability. (1992). *Meeting the unique needs of minorities with disabilities.* Washington, DC: Author.

National Council on Interpreting in Health Care. (2005). *National standards of practice for interpreters in health care.* Retrieved from http://www.ncihc.org/ethics-and-standards-of-practice

Pedersen, P. (2007a). Cultured-centered microtraining. In T. Daniels & A. Ivey (Eds.), *Microcounseling: Making skills training work in a multicultural world* (pp. 109–131). Springfield, IL: Charles C Thomas.

Pedersen, P. (2007b). Toward identifying culturally relevant processes and goals for helpers and helpees. In T. Daniels & A. Ivey (Eds.), *Microcounseling: Making skills training work in a multicultural world* (pp. 137–157). Springfield, IL: Charles C Thomas.

Redfoot, D. L., & Houser, A. (2010). *More older people with disabilities living in the community: Trends from the National Long-Term Care Survey, 1984–2004.* Washington, DC: AARP Public Policy Institute.

Rehabilitation Act Amendments of 1992, Pub. L. No. 102-569, 106 Stat. 4344–4488 (1992).

Robinson-Wood, T. L. (2009). *The convergence of race, ethnicity, and gender: Multiple identities in counseling* (3rd ed.). Upper Saddle River, NJ: Prentice Hall.

Sandieson, R. (1998). A survey of terminology that refers to people with mental retardation/developmental disabilities. *Education and Training in Mental Retardation and Developmental Disabilities, 33*, 290–295.

Schaller, J., Parker, R., & Garcia, S. B. (1998). Moving toward culturally competent rehabilitation counseling services: Issues and practices. *Journal of Applied Rehabilitation Counseling, 29,* 40–48.

Schur, L., Kruse, D., & Blanck, P. (2005). Corporate culture and the employment of persons with disabilities. *Behavioral Sciences and the Law, 23,* 3–20.

Settles, I. H., & Buchanan, N. T. (2006). Tokenism/psychology of tokenism. In Y. Jackson (Ed.), *Encyclopedia of multicultural psychology* (pp. 456–457). Thousand Oaks, CA: Sage.

Shweder, R. A. (1985). Menstrual pollution, soul loss, and comparative study of emotions. In A. Kleinman & B. Good (Eds.), *Culture and depression* (pp. 182–215). Berkeley, CA: University of California Press.

Simpson, G. E., & Yinger, M. J. (1972). *Racial and cultural minorities: An analysis of prejudice and discrimination* (4th ed.). New York, NY: Harper & Row.

Smart, J. F., & Smart, D. W. (1997a). Culturally sensitive informed choice in rehabilitation counseling. *Journal of Applied Rehabilitation Counseling, 28,* 32–37.

Smart, J. F., & Smart, D. W. (1997b). The racial/ethnic demography of disability. *Journal of Rehabilitation, 63*(4), 9–15.

Smith, D. L., & Alston, R. (2010). Employment and rehabilitation issues for racially and ethnically diverse women with disabilities. In F. E. Balcazar, Y. Saurez-Balcazar, T. Taylor-Ritzler, & C. B. Keys (Eds.), *Race, culture, and disability: Rehabilitation science and practice* (pp. 159–183). Sudbury, MA: Jones & Bartlett.

Smith, T. B., Richards, P. S., Granley, H. M., & Obiakor, F. (2004). Practicing multiculturalism: An introduction. In T. B. Smith (Ed.), *Practicing multiculturalism: Affirming diversity in counseling and psychology* (pp. 3–16). Boston, MA: Allyn & Bacon.

Snow, K. (2008). *To ensure inclusion, freedom, and respect for all, it's time to embrace people first language.* Retrieved from http://www.disabilityisnatural.com

Sodowsky, G. R., Taffe, R. C., Gutkins, T. B., & Wise, S. L. (1994). Development of the Multicultural Counseling Inventory: A self-report measure of multicultural competencies. *Journal of Counseling Psychology, 41,* 137–148.

Sotnik, P., & Jezewski, M. A. (2005). Culture and the disability services. In J. H. Stone (Ed.), *Culture and disability: Providing culturally competent services* (pp. 15–36). Thousand Oaks, CA: Sage.

Stroshine, M. S., & Brandl, S. G. (2011). Race, gender, and tokenism in policing: An empirical elaboration. *Police Quarterly, 14,* 344–365.

Sue, D. W. (2006). *Multicultural social work practice.* Hoboken, NJ: Wiley.

Sue, D. W., & Sue, D. (2013). *Counseling the culturally different: Theory and practice* (6th ed.). Hoboken, NJ: Wiley.

Surbaugh, M. (2008). Disability consciousness: A prolegomenon. *Philosophy of Education.* Retrieved April 22, 2013, from http://ojs.ed.uiuc.edu/index.php/pes/article/view/1397/147

Vaughn, B. E. (2004). Intercultural communication as contexts for mindful achievement In T. B. Smith (Ed.), *Practicing multiculturalism: Affirming diversity in counseling and psychology* (pp. 57–75). Boston, MA: Pearson.

Weinrach, S. G., & Thomas, K. R. (1998). Diversity-sensitive counseling today: A postmodern clash of values. *Journal of Counseling and Development, 76,* 115–122.

Whitfield, H. W. (2009). Occupations at case closure for vocational rehabilitation applicants with criminal backgrounds. *Rehabilitation Counseling Bulletin, 53,* 56–58.

Wilgosh, L., & Sandulac, C. (1997). Media attention to and treatment of disabilities information. *Developmental Disabilities Bulletin, 25,* 94–103.

Wilson, K. B. (2002). The exploration of vocational rehabilitation acceptance and ethnicity: A national investigation. *Rehabilitation Counseling Bulletin, 45,* 168–176.

Wilson, K. B. (2005). Vocational rehabilitation closure statuses in the United States: Generalizing to the Hispanic/Latino ethnicity. *Journal of Applied Rehabilitation Counseling, 36*(2), 4–11.

Wilson, K. B., Harley, D. A., McCormick, K., Jolivette, K., & Jackson, R. (2001). A literature review of vocational rehabilitation acceptance and explaining bias in the rehabilitation process. *Journal of Rehabilitation, 32,* 24–35.

Wilson, K. B., & Senices, J. (2005). Exploring the vocational rehabilitation acceptance rates of Hispanics and non-Hispanics in the United States. *Journal of Counseling and Development, 83,* 86–96.

World Health Organization (WHO). (2011). *World report on disability.* Geneva, Switzerland: Author.

Wright, B. A. (1991). Labeling: The need for greater person–environment individuation. In C. R. Snyder & D. R. Forsyth (Eds.), *Handbook of social and clinical psychology* (pp. 469–487). Elmsford, NY: Pergamon.

Yelin, E., & Trupin, L. (2003). Disability and the characteristics of employment. *Monthly Labor Review, 126,* 20–31.

# Clinical Supervision

*James T. Herbert and Tierra A. Caldwell*

## LEARNING OBJECTIVES

The goals of this chapter are to define clinical supervision and barriers to supervision in rehabilitation settings, to examine the developmental process in progressing from counselor to supervisor roles, review effective practices in group supervision, discuss multicultural perspectives on supervision, and identify clinical supervision strategies consistent with good ethical practice. As learning objectives, the reader will be able to:

1. Define clinical supervision and its differentiation from administrative supervision and three reasons why clinical supervision is not practiced more widely.
2. Identify behavioral indicators associated with Stages 1, 2, 3, and 4 supervisors, as proposed by Stoltenberg and Delworth (1987).
3. Identify at least three preferred and three ineffective clinical supervisory practices, in addition to one supervision strategy consistent with each of the three counselor development levels, as conceptualized through the integrated development model.
4. Determine who is responsible for initiating discussions regarding diversity within the supervisory relationship.
5. Understand what is meant by "parallel/cross-progressive/cross-regressive" supervision dyads as applied to racial identity and its impact on clinical supervision.

## CLINICAL SUPERVISION

### Clinical Versus Administrative Supervision

Earlier discussions of rehabilitation counselor supervision have delineated differences between administrative and clinical supervision (Herbert, 1997, 2011). In general, administrative supervision seeks to maintain the effectiveness of the organization by following specific policies and procedures that personnel must follow to ensure successful outcomes occur (Herbert & Schultz, 2013). As Campbell (2006, p. 4) notes, "The focus of administrative supervision is on productivity, workload management and accountability, not individuals." In contrast, clinical supervision is concerned with helping counselors improve counseling skills by examining their working relationships with clients and interventions used to promote desired outcomes. It bears noting that the term *clinical* may conjure images associated with a medical model, subservience, pathology, and/or professional detachment (Herbert, 2011); all of which are aspects inconsistent with rehabilitation counseling philosophy, which has historical roots based on empowerment (Emener, 1991). Although this term will be used in this chapter as it is the one designated in the professional literature, the term *clinical supervision* is interchangeable with *counselor supervision*.

Beyond the obvious benefit of enhancing counselor skill levels (e.g., Brislin & Herbert, 2009; Schaefle, Smaby, Maddux, & Cates, 2005; Worthington, 1987), other reported benefits of clinical supervision include contributing to the counselor's overall well-being (Livni, Crowe, & Gonsalvez, 2012), lowering work stress and increasing job satisfaction (Sterner, 2009), and reducing professional burnout (Yagil, 2006). Given these reported benefits, one might expect that clinical supervision, as a research area, would generate a great deal of interest to inform rehabilitation counseling practice. As will become apparent after reading this chapter, there is a great deal more that is not known as compared to what is known pertaining to clinical supervision.

### Clinical Supervision Defined

Clinical supervision involves an evaluative relationship between a supervisor and counselor for the purpose of developing greater competence in the "junior" professional and for monitoring the quality of client services provided by this individual (Bernard & Goodyear, 1998). Accordingly, this relationship assumes that the clinical supervisor functions as a "gatekeeper" to persons wanting to work as professional counselors. Within rehabilitation counseling practice, Stebnicki (1998) suggested that rehabilitation counselor supervision was different from other counseling disciplines because of the variety of supervisory styles and approaches to (a) enhance counselor processing skills as they relate to psychosocial interventions; (b) promote counseling self-efficacy and personal growth among supervisees; and (c) develop supervisee case conceptualization skills, particularly as they relate to disability issues. He contended that psychosocial aspects of chronic illness and disability represent the core of clinical supervision as supervisors assume educator, consultant, and counselor roles.

Building on some of these earlier concepts and, to some extent, expanding on them, clinical or counselor supervision in this chapter is defined by Herbert (2011) as:

> a developmental and supportive relationship that requires the supervisor working in various capacities as consultant, counselor and teacher where the intent is to improve counselor skills and case management decisions so that successful rehabilitation outcomes occur. Using individual, triadic and/or group supervision approaches through direct and indirect observation methods, the supervisor works to promote counselor awareness, knowledge and skills so that effective counseling services are provided consistent with ethical and professional standards.

It is inherent in this definition that clinical supervisors recognize that each counselor comes into the supervision relationship with a unique set of skills, knowledge, and developmental needs based on training, experience, and personal attributes. Recognizing that counselors go through a set of developmental phases (Stoltenberg, McNeill, & Delworth, 1998), supervisors are in a position to assist counselors in developing greater awareness of cognitive and affective factors that impact the client–counselor relationship, support counselor autonomy, and maintain sufficient motivation to continue to grow as professional rehabilitation counselors (Maki & Delworth, 1995). From this perspective, Stoltenberg et al. (1998) suggest that inexperienced counselors have a tendency to focus more on themselves rather than on clients during supervision and, as a result, there is a stronger need for direction from the supervisor while providing ongoing encouragement and structure. Conversely, more experienced and clinically skilled counselors express a greater desire for autonomy and prefer supervisors who focus on promoting greater self-awareness, examine client–counselor dynamics (transference/countertransference), and identify and facilitate professional growth areas unique to each counselor.

Promoting greater awareness regarding intra- and interpersonal aspects within the client–counselor and counselor–supervisor relationships requires active listening. This reflective orientation, as Franklin (2011) contends, involves the supervisor in raising questions regarding the counselor's feelings about the client–counselor session, their meaning in terms of the counselor's life (past events, current experiences), and how this interpretation might influence the counselor's view of the client.

### Barriers to Providing Clinical Supervision

The essential goals of clinical supervision are to protect client welfare and support the professional development of the counselor being supervised (Aasheim, 2012). In order to accomplish these goals, the clinical supervisor must develop a positive and trusting relationship, provide guidance when needed, and adopt a Socratic dialogue to examine topics relevant to counseling goals and interventions consistent with counseling theoretical orientation (Overholser, 2004). Protecting client welfare requires continual monitoring of counselor performance that is typically done through direct (e.g., audio and videotaping and e-supervision) and/or indirect (e.g., case review) methods that occur either after the fact (i.e., delayed) or during live interactions (i.e., observing client–counselor interactions in the field; Herbert, 2004a).

Although close monitoring of counselor–client interactions is something that has been commonly practiced (Herbert, Hemlick, & Ward, 1991; Herbert & Ward, 1989) and, in fact, continues to be a required part of preprofessional training (Council on Rehabilitation Education, 2012), it is often not provided frequently in some agencies and programs, particularly in the public sector (e.g., English, Oberle, & Byrne, 1979; King, 2008; Schultz, Ososkie, Fried, Nelson, & Bardos, 2002). This disconnect between preprofessional and subsequent professional practice seems attributable to (a) a lack of understanding as to its importance to counselor development, (b) the time needed to provide this type of supervision, and (c) skills required to provide clinical supervision (Herbert, 2004b). As noted in several reports (e.g., Herbert, 2004b; Schultz et al., 2002), the overwhelming majority of rehabilitation counseling supervisors have not been indoctrinated in the practice of clinical supervision as counselors. As a result, one would not expect that these supervisors would be sufficiently skilled to provide clinical supervision when they themselves did not receive it as part of their professional training.

Consequently, without any formal training in clinical supervision, uninformed supervisors can operate from several frameworks that include "laissez-faire" (no clinical supervision), "expert" (supervisor assumes role as the "problem solver" to the counselor), "one-size-fits-all" (supervisees get the same type of supervision regardless of individual counselor need and skill level), "buddy" (supervisor seeks more of a friendship and social support in supervisory role), and "doctor" (supervisor responds to counselor as if it were a client–counselor relationship in which the intent is to find out what is "wrong" with the counselor; Campbell, 2006). Each of these perspectives is unproductive and, rather, what is needed is a supportive developmental approach, whereby the supervisor has a clear understanding of supervisory style, theoretical orientation to promote counselor growth, development, and abilities, and the knowledge and skills needed to promote a good working alliance (Herbert & Schultz, 2013). Despite these obstacles, once the counselor and the supervisor understand and agree on the goals of supervision and the tasks involved in achieving these goals and developing a trusting relationship, supervision has the potential to promote successful vocational rehabilitation outcomes for clients of rehabilitation counselors, particularly for counselors just entering the field (McCarthy, 2013).

### Making the Developmental Shift From Counselor to Supervisor

Stoltenberg and Delworth (1987) contend that supervisors go through a four-stage developmental process when making the transition from counselor to supervisor. In Stage 1, the newly promoted supervisor is often overly anxious or naïve regarding the skills needed to supervise effectively. During this initial stage, supervisors may question their value or worth as supervisors. As many supervisors were effective counselors, they may see themselves as being "expert" counselors and, therefore, may be more dogmatic in their approach to help other counselors adopt similar counseling approaches and strategies that have worked for them. Watkins (1993), in articulating a similar developmental model, believed that new supervisors also have a tendency to be preoccupied with administrative tasks to the exclusion of counselor–supervisor process aspects. In Stage 2, the supervisor begins to acknowledge the complexities of work as an effective clinical supervisor and, during this period, the supervisor experiences conflict and role confusion. For Watkins, supervisors in this stage are aware of process issues, but they are infrequently addressed as part of supervision. Though an awareness of supervisory strengths is becoming evident, there is a stronger focus on supervisory inadequacies. Stoltenberg and Delworth (1987) also indicate that supervisor motivation in this stage fluctuates, and if supervisor conflicts and doubts are successfully managed, supervisors move to Stage 3. In this stage, both developmental models indicate that supervisors have a better sense of their relative strengths and areas requiring greater development, in addition to a better understanding of their individual supervisory styles. Finally, in Stage 4, supervisors have even greater interest and commitment to supervision and welcome situations that challenge them as supervisors and provide further opportunities for growth. Watkins indicates that in this final developmental stage, supervisors have well-integrated identities as clinical supervisors and a unique supervisory style that addresses both client needs and those presented by the counselor.

In making the progression through each developmental stage, an important cognitive shift must occur; what Herbert and Schultz (2013) define as the "litmus test" for clinical supervisors. This test requires supervisors to make an important developmental shift and, as Borders (1992, p. 138) describes: "Supervisors who think like supervisors give priority to counselors' learning needs and take primary responsibility for meeting those needs. They ask themselves, 'How can *I* intervene so that this counselor will be more effective with current and future clients?'" This framework indicates that, in essence, rehabilitation counselor supervisors recognize that their "clients" are not persons seeking rehabilitation counseling services but, rather, the counselors they supervise. As noted earlier, although a primary responsibility of clinical supervisors must ultimately be concerned with client welfare, this focus must be addressed from the perspective of the counselor. In other words, discussion about client concerns, barriers that prevent change to achieve counseling goals, or the importance of meaningful events, for instance, must be reframed from what these aspects mean for the counselor.

For example, a counselor may have a great deal of anxiety about a client not being able to find work because of a belief that "employers will simply not hire someone with my disability." The supervisor could devote a great deal of time trying to discern what this statement may mean to the client, examine how this belief was developed, and determine perhaps what needs to be done to challenge this self-defeating belief. These questions would be oriented from a rehabilitation counselor perspective. From a clinical supervision perspective, however, the "client" is not the person seeking rehabilitation services. Rather, the "client" is the counselor being supervised—the person in the room, on the video screen, or on the phone with the supervisor. From this perspective, examination of client information should be addressed in terms of its importance or meaning to the counselor. Using this example, the supervisor may want to explore the counselor's (a) anxieties and/or frustrations about working with this client; (b) beliefs about how to facilitate affective, behavioral, and cognitive change as applied to the expressed problem; (c) counseling theory used in this situation and indications that support its use; (d) perceived messages not being expressed during supervision that may impact the client–counselor relationship; and/or (e) examining the role of self-advocacy applicable to this situation. Any of these avenues may provide a clear path in learning more about what the presenting problem expressed in supervision (client believes because of a given disability he/she will not be hired) means to the counselor and, as a result, the focus is addressed from this perspective.

In making this shift from thinking like a counselor to thinking like a supervisor, Borders (1992) offers several pragmatic suggestions. The supervisor may wish to review the audio- or videotape of the counselor and make notes, as if a meeting with the counselor was to take place. After a brief time (10–15 minutes), the supervisor should record the number of statements attributable to the client and the number attributed to the counselor. This activity will help the supervisor with a reminder that "they will be meeting with the *counselor*, not the client, during the next hour. What are they going to do during the *supervision* session to help the *counselor*?" (Borders 1992, p. 139). Supervisors should also plan for each supervision session by identifying learning goals for each counselor and make a list of strengths and areas needing improvement. This process results in developing an individualized supervision plan for each counselor that also includes documentation of supervisory session notes related to session goals, summary of transpired events, and an evaluation of counselor performance. Borders also recommends that supervisors seek feedback regarding their performance and, in the case of group supervision, one strategy would be to assign individual members within the group a specific role, such as focusing on supervisory nonverbal behavior or helpfulness of feedback provided. By doing so, role assignments provide a context for counselors who participate in other structured group supervision experiences.

## CLINICAL SUPERVISION PRACTICES

As noted earlier, most of what is known about clinical supervision within rehabilitation counseling settings has been limited to the state vocational rehabilitation system and, as a result, an understanding of supervisory behaviors is offered within this context. Structured interviews with rehabilitation counselors and supervisors indicate that effective supervisors are persons who demonstrate sensitivity to counselor needs (e.g., understands counselor developmental level); communicate effectively (e.g., uses constructive criticism, demonstrates counseling skills and techniques); devote specific time and planning for supervision (e.g., schedules individual meeting times and, when necessary, meets with counselors when consultation is warranted); model appropriate ethical behavior (e.g., consults with ethical codes, emphasizes client welfare as first priority); and, when solicited, provide alternatives and suggestions in addressing client problems (Herbert, 2004b). Conversely, ineffective and, in some cases, damaging supervision occurs when supervisors are perceived as disinterested in supervision (e.g., cancel appointments, provide advice about irrelevant matters, provide simplistic solutions to complex problems); demonstrate unprofessional behavior (e.g., appearing aloof, apathetic, or arrogant, gossiping about others, using intimidating or threatening remarks, making sexual advances, and using profanity); and "take over" for the counselor when cocounseling is provided. These ineffective supervisory behaviors may have several negative consequences, including hesitance on the part of counselors to disclose mistakes, which raises doubts regarding one's capabilities and may also contribute to counseling skill regression (Watkins, 1997), work dissatisfaction (Garske, 1995), and staff turnover (Roche, Todd, & O'Connor, 2007). For these reasons alone, it is important that supervisors recognize that negative outcomes can result from poor or nonexistent clinical supervision.

### Importance of Counselor Development Level and Supervisory Roles

Part of the process in developing a productive clinical supervision relationship not only involves demonstrating effective behaviors but also recognizing that supervisory interventions must take into account the developmental level of each counselor. Hatcher and Lassiter (2007) proposed a rudimentary classification scheme to describe novice, intermediate, and advanced counselor levels. The novice counselor is someone with limited understanding and skill related to conceptualizing client problems and interventions needed to address client concerns. The intermediate counselor recognizes possible intervention strategies, but requires supervisory input to refine understanding and counseling technique, whereas the advanced counselor has developed an integrated and well-developed knowledge of counseling practice.

The integrated development model, proposed by Stoltenberg et al. (1998), indicates that developing counselors go through three major stages. Level 1 is applicable to beginning counselors, who often experience high levels of anxiety and doubt regarding skills and, as a result, tend to expend a great deal of energy focusing on their performance and wanting to do things "the right way." Consequently, these counselors often miss the client–counselor process and client dynamics. In this initial stage, counselors are usually highly motivated for clinical supervision because of the desire to improve skills and reduce anxieties that can occur within the client–counselor relationship. Supervisors working with these counselors need then to provide greater structure and support and devote greater attention to tying in counseling theory with counselor behavior and interventions in order to facilitate client change. Supervisors need to conduct direct observations of client–counselor interactions and not rely on a case review method that may not accurately reflect what transpired in the counseling session. In order to normalize the initial adjustment period, these counselors may particularly benefit from group supervision as they may be able to emulate other, more experienced counselors and expand on their skillset. Supervisors also need to pay close attention to client progress to insure that no undue harm is caused nor other ethical considerations compromised.

In Level 2, counselors begin to develop a greater sense of what it means to work as a counselor. They are better able to focus more on the client rather than struggling with internal dialogues about their insecurities as a counselor, which occurred more often at the previous level. As counseling self-efficacy increases, they are less satisfied with simple answers and solutions and recognize the complexities involved in promoting client change. With greater confidence comes a greater desire for autonomy and, as a result, the motivation for clinical supervision fluctuates. Experienced counselors also have greater clarity in their personal counseling theory and, in terms of clinical supervision, can be directed from this framework. The supervisor may adopt more of a consultant role and provide less structure than noted earlier, when the counselor was just starting to develop a professional identity.

Eventually, with greater experience and competence, Level 3 counselors have a strong sense of counseling strengths and areas needing further growth, along with a greater desire for autonomy and openness from the supervisor. Supervising counselors at this level may again involve playing even more of a consultant role, where exchanges are more reciprocal as opposed to using teaching or counseling roles noted for prior levels.

Bernard (1979, 1997) describes three basic roles that clinical supervisors often adopt: consultant, counselor, or teacher. As consultant, the supervisor serves as a resource person to help the counselor conceptualize problems and consider interventions consistent with the counselor's theoretical orientation in order to promote autonomy. A primary role for the clinical supervisor is to generate data about the client and its meaning to the counselor (Fall & Sutton, 2004). When adopting a counselor role within the supervisory relationship, the supervisor examines the intra- and interpersonal reality of the counseling experience as it pertains to the counselor's view of clients receiving services, as well as the ways in which the counselor experiences the supervisory relationship. This framework is intended to clarify the counselor's worldview and how these perceptions impact the client–counselor relationship and, in a parallel manner, the supervisory relationship. Using a teacher role, the clinical supervisor evaluates counselor skill levels and, where needed, trains the counselor to enhance and/ or learn new skills using brainstorming, role-playing, and live demonstration. This role places the supervisor "in charge" and, as such, determines the direction of supervision, with the supervisor functioning as an advisor or expert (Fall & Sutton, 2004). Each of these roles could be used within individual, triadic (one supervisor working with two counselors simultaneously), or group supervision formats. Determining which role to use and why represents a key question that each supervisor must determine before engaging in a particular role (Corey, Haynes, Moulton, & Muratori, 2010).

## Group Supervision

Despite its popularity in general counselor supervision, group supervision has been described as "widely practiced but poorly understood" (Holloway & Johnson, 1985, p. 332). Ten years after this initial assessment, the same conclusion was reiterated (Prieto, 1996) and, from the lack of comparative empirical studies, the same appraisal seems applicable today. What is interesting though is that group supervision remains the most used method in counselor supervision in both preprofessional and professional training (Bernard & Goodyear, 1998; Grigg, 2006). Although popular in the other counseling specialties, its use is almost non-existent in the public vocational rehabilitation system (Herbert & Trusty, 2006).

In the few studies that have compared group and individual supervision formats (e.g., Borders et al., 2012; Gillam & Crutchfield, 2001), the evidence suggests that each approach produces similar outcomes in the facilitation of counselor development and skills. Although group supervision provides exposure to multiple perspectives and opportunities for vicarious learning and for normalizing the supervision experience, it also limits time for feedback for each individual member of the group and introduces trust issues that may occur among members (Ray & Altekruse, 2000). Individual supervision, in contrast, provides greater opportunity for individualized feedback that can increase self-awareness, but also results in the possibility that power concerns between supervisee and supervisor may emerge.

A recent study has shown that group supervisors can range from being very task oriented (e.g., supervisors focus more on case presentation formats with little or no attention given to group dynamics) to very relationship oriented (e.g., supervisors focus more on processes in which where individual members express anxieties and concerns and share feedback with one another; Smith, Riva, & Cornish, 2012). These orientations impact group process and the extent to which group phenomena are addressed. Research by Enyedy et al. (2003) indicates that group supervision is hindered when individual members avoid giving candid feedback to others for fear of causing anxiety or embarrassment or when they experience pressure to conform to group norms that may have been expressed or implied. Accordingly, when these perceptions exist, they may contribute to feelings of being misunderstood or disconnected from other group members and may stymy individual creativity. In order to minimize these possibilities, it has been suggested that individual feedback regarding a counselor's performance be given earlier in group sessions, with the remaining time devoted to encouraging positive and corrective feedback specific to observable counselor behavior (Morran, Stockton, Cline, & Teed, 1998).

When feedback is given, the group supervisor needs to be sensitive to the readiness of each individual group member to receive feedback and should serve as a model to other members as to how feedback should be expressed (Westwood, 1989). When offering feedback, supervisory guidelines generally recommend that the feedback be balanced (providing information regarding positive and improvement areas), consistent, credible (based on observation of client–counselor sessions), and understandable (Heckman-Stone, 2004). Because individual members can interpret feedback from others negatively, resulting in self-defeating thoughts and anxieties, supervisors must distinguish between irrational and realistic self-appraisal. Fitch and Marshall (2002) indicate that beginning counselors are particularly susceptible to criticism and, therefore, group supervisors must be able to differentiate between evaluation anxieties that are irrational and acceptable performance anxiety. When supervisors believe anxiety levels are irrational, the authors recommend that supervisors (a) recognize counselor anxiety and defense mechanism responses, (b) identify cognitive patterns that are seeking approval from others, (c) challenge and dispute irrational beliefs and replace them with more rational thoughts, and (d) encourage supervisees to take behavioral risks that support logical arguments.

## DIVERSITY CONSIDERATIONS IN SUPERVISION

Issues of diversity in age, disability, ethnicity, gender, religious affiliation and spirituality, sexual orientation, and/or socioeconomic status are embedded in every professional and social relationship and, as a result, how we perceive one another will also be manifested within the supervisory relationship (Borders, 2005). In promoting greater multicultural awareness, Hays (2008, p. 31) suggested that counselors conduct a self-inventory by asking the following questions of the particular group(s) being discussed:

- How did I come to this understanding?
- How do I know that this is true?
- Are there alternative explanations or opinions that might be equally valid in this situation?
- How might my view of the client's situation be influenced by my age or generational experiences, my ethnic background, and my socioeconomic status?

Although these questions can be asked introspectively, they could also be addressed within the counselor–supervisor relationship and, as a number of authors have indicated (e.g., Bernard & Goodyear, 2004), it is always the supervisor's responsibility to initiate and address multicultural aspects. Given that the supervisor is in a position to evaluate counselor performance, it introduces a unique power dynamic that must be acknowledged (Borders & Brown, 2005).

It is clear that diversity issues have received increasing attention in the clinical supervision literature, perhaps none more so than race and ethnicity. Chang, Hays, and Shoffner (2004) contend that racial identity or how each of us conceptualize how race consciousness originates, develops, and impacts our lives, as well as the lives of those with whom we interact, plays a critical role in the supervisory relationship.

In order to better understand this role, racial identity development models for White persons (Helms & Carter, 1990) as well as persons of color (Atkinson, Morten, & Sue, 1998) have been used to explain why supervisory conflicts can occur. Chang et al. (2004) contend that when supervisor and counselor share similar racial identity development statuses or a "parallel relationship" where lower evolved identity development exists, neither individual is aware of multicultural concerns. As a result, diversity issues related to race and ethnicity are avoided. In this situation, both supervisor and supervisee are likely to experience anxiety, dislike, and mistrust of one another, because neither can empathize with the other person's racial attitudes. In essence, the perception of being superior while holding others inferior may be expressed in subtle (e.g., arriving late for supervision, missing appointments) or blatant ways (e.g., making insensitive jokes or remarks) to one another.

At the other end of the continuum, where both supervisor and supervisee have more developed racial identities, open and frank discussions regarding racial and cultural issues are more evident. Examination of personal biases is encouraged and supported within the supervisory relationship, and there is clear indication of cultural proficiency (e.g., knowledge of other cultures, avoidance of expressing stereotypical beliefs, inviting conversations regarding race and ethnicity while respecting individual differences). Similarly, in situations in which there is a "cross-progressive" supervisory relationship, indicating that the supervisor has a more evolved racial identity, the importance of racial and cultural issues is recognized. Typically, these discussions are conducted in an open and honest manner, but the extent of counselor growth is often mediated by the racial identity of a counselor.

Chang et al. (2004) believe that supervisors, who are skilled in self-disclosing their cultural heritage, biases, values, and worldviews consistent with their supervisory style, can offer a safe environment for the counselor with a more regressed racial identity, so that greater self-awareness occurs to promote change.

In contrast to this type of supervisory relationship, the final supervisory dyad is the "cross-regressive" in which the counselor is more aware and willing to examine multicultural issues than the supervisor. In this dyad, the supervisor may be unaware of cultural biases and tends to respond to the counselor based on self-perceived stereotypes. This scenario, like the parallel relationship in which both counselor and supervisor have lower developmental awareness of diversity issues, is the most problematic to address because it requires an examination of beliefs and assumptions on the part of the supervisor as well.

In order to enhance multicultural awareness, Chang et al. (2004) recommend that counselors and supervisors assess their respective racial identities using a standardized measure, such as the White Racial Identity Attitude Scale and the People of Color Racial Identity Attitude Scale (Helms & Carter, 1990). After this assessment is completed, a discussion of how these individual stages may interact within the supervisory relationship (i.e., cross-progressive, cross-regressive, and parallel) should take place. The authors recommend open-ended questions, such as "What do you think about your client's race?" "What do you think about my race?" "How do [you] [sic] feel your racial heritage influences your interaction with your client?" [and] "With [me as] your supervisor?" (Chang et al., 2004, p. 133). In order to better understand the individual worldviews that each counselor has regarding diversity issues, Gray and Smith (2009) believe that reflective conversations, using questions such as those mentioned, can address cultural assumptions that are expressed or implied.

Although not as articulated in the clinical supervision literature, there has been some discussion of diversity issues related to disability (Pardeck, 2001) and sexual orientation (Pfohl, 2004). Although there are parallels between racial identity development models and similar models applicable to disability (Mackelprang & Salgiver, 2009) and sexual orientation (Cass, 1979), the importance of either identity can range from having no importance at all to being central to the person. Perhaps what is unique to these identities, as compared to ethnicity and race, is the tendency to underestimate their importance in everyday life, in addition to the lack of preparedness of counselors and supervisors to address them. This lack of preparedness is considered unethical for any supervisor who is also a certified rehabilitation counselor (CRC), as indicated in Section H.2.b of the Commission on Rehabilitation Counselor Certification (CRCC, 2010, p. 20) professional code: "Rehabilitation counselor supervisors are aware of and address the role of cultural diversity in the supervisory relationship."

## SUPERVISION ETHICS

Poor supervision is often more attributable to a failure to provide good supervision than necessarily ineffective supervision and, in these situations, unethical supervision must be addressed (Greer, 2003). Although professional ethical standards pertaining to counselor supervision have been incorporated into standards of practice for counselors by the American Counseling Association (ACA, 2005) as well as by the CRCC (2010) ethical standards for rehabilitation counselors, they do not necessarily provide a clear action plan in resolving common ethical concerns, such as those pertaining to supervisory competence, confidentiality, dual relationships, due process, and informed consent (Blackwell, Strohmer, Belcas, & Burton, 2002; Tarvydas, 1995). In fact, interpretation of these ethical conflicts varies as a function of work setting, as university supervisors differ in their interpretation, as compared to on-site practicum and internship supervisors. For example, a study by Lee and Cashwell (2001) found that university supervisors responded "more conservatively" on ethical dilemmas involving dual relationships, supervisor competence, and informed consent, whereas site supervisors expressed more conservatism on due process. Lee and Cashwell (2001) believe these findings imply that university supervisors should have more consultation with on-site supervisors so that any inconsistency in ethical practices can be addressed.

Sometimes, the issue as to who to consult about ethical dilemmas is problematic, as there are instances when counselors or counselors-in-training may have both an internal (university faculty member) and an external supervisor (practicum or internship on-site member or other contracted supervisor). In each situation, the counselor or counselor-in-training has to consider two types of supervisory power—positional power, which applies to the supervisor who works in the same organizational structure as the supervisee, and expertise power, which applies to the supervisor outside of the organization (Itzhaky, 2001). Positional power posits that a person supervised by an internal supervisor, such as a university faculty member assigned to fieldwork supervision, has more formal authority by nature of having the responsibility for performance evaluations (grading, hiring, promotion). Expert power suggests that persons supervised by an external authority will have less formal authority, but more expertise-related authority (knowledge, skills). In this instance, field site supervisors assigned to practica and/or internship or supervisors contracted by an agency to provide clinical supervision may be persons with perceived expert power.

Research by Itzhaky (2001) suggests that clinical social workers supervised by external supervisors were more likely to receive constructive criticism, engage in more confrontation when needed and justified, and were perceived as having more knowledge and skills in comparison to those supervised by internal supervisors working within the same organizational structure. Thus, ethical concerns may be more likely expressed with supervisors with external authority than with supervisors with more internal authority. In terms of the supervision implications, ethical concerns should be brought to the attention of both supervisors, who should review and consult with one another (Lee & Cashwell, 2001). In addition, further ethics training for external supervisors may be needed and, as a proactive strategy, training supervisees about the nuances involved with clinical supervision could also be included. An example of an earlier didactic course proposed by Herbert and Bieschke (2000) that covered this topic area, as well as others that could be offered to field site supervisors and counselors preparing to work as clinical supervisors, may serve as a useful guide.

Schultz (2011) indicates that one of the best strategies for instilling ethical behavior in counselors is for supervisors to model the behavior that is expected. Beyond serving as a professional role model who engenders ethical behavior, Schultz indicates that supervisors can increase awareness of fundamental ethical principles as part of ongoing supervision. For example, counselors can emulate a stronger ethical identity if supervisors include ethical aspects as part of case study presentations during individual and/or group supervision. With greater discussion of ethical principles and their application to rehabilitation counseling practice, Schultz maintains that counselors will not have to feel timid about raising ethical concerns. One hopes that using these practices will result in counselors having a stronger working knowledge of the six basic principles that guide ethical practice: autonomy (promote the right of self-determinism and freedom of choice), beneficence (do good for others), fidelity (keep promises), justice (treat others fairly), nonmaleficence (do no harm to others), and veracity (be honest and truthful with others; Cottone & Tarvydas, 2007).

In terms of formal procedures to foster ethical practices for group supervision, Smith et al. (2012) recommended that (a) written contracts for group members be developed explaining purpose and procedures used, (b) norms and expectations of all members be discussed and agreed on before beginning (e.g., starting on time, verbalizing expectations during case presentations, and also expressing feelings and reactions to session content), (c) persons familiar with any client being discussed must recuse themselves to maintain client confidentiality, (d) degree and nature of disclosure about each member should be addressed beforehand as well as the ways in which sharing such information may impact individual evaluations, and (e) multiple-role relationships that can develop between group members and agency staff must be addressed in terms of identifying when potential conflicts occur. It is incumbent upon a group supervisor to initiate the discussion of the ground rules and to establish group norms so that any breach of ethical conduct can be minimized. Clarity of explicit description as what constitutes appropriate group norms and structure is something about which both supervisors and supervisees typically have consensual agreement; despite this agreement, in a study of group supervision among doctoral psychology interns and internship directors, over one half of supervisees and supervisors reported never having a written contract regarding group supervision (Smith et al., 2012).

## CURRENT STATUS OF CLINICAL SUPERVISION

Clinical supervision is an important part of developing and enhancing counselor proficiency that begins during preprofessional training and, we hope, continues throughout one's career as a professional rehabilitation counselor. However, rehabilitation counselors and, in particular, their supervisors may have an underappreciation of its value to professional practice. This belief is partially based on conclusions from prior studies already cited that suggest that supervisors (at least those in the state–federal vocational rehabilitation program and the proprietary sector) do not understand its relevance and potential for counselor development (Herbert & Trusty, 2006; King, 2008; Schultz et al., 2002).

Further evidence to support this belief may be extrapolated from a study of 648 randomly selected CRCs who were asked about 81 essential knowledge subdomains required for rehabilitation counseling practice (Leahy, Muenzen, Saunders, & Strauser, 2009). One of these subdomains was applicable to "theories and techniques for providing clinical supervision." Results indicated that CRCs perceived this subdomain somewhere between "minimally important" to "moderately important." In terms of how often this knowledge domain is used, respondents indicated that it was closer to being used "yearly or almost yearly." The relatively lower evaluation of this item should be understood, as the wording was focused on "providing clinical supervision" as opposed to "providing/receiving clinical supervision." Given there are fewer CRCs providing supervision than receiving supervision, this situation may explain the relatively lower ratings for this item than most other knowledge subdomains. However, recent consultation with the lead investigator in this study and data not explicitly presented in a current study of CRCs' perceived importance of job functions related to rehabilitation counseling practice (Leahy, Chan, Sung, & Kim, 2013) indicated that there were no differences in ratings of importance and preparation levels between counselors and supervisors (M. J. Leahy, personal communication, October 31, 2013). In both instances, rehabilitation supervisors ($n = 23$) and rehabilitation counselors ($n = 159$) reported that knowledge pertaining to theories and techniques of clinical supervision was perceived as being between "important" and "very important" to professional practice. In terms of levels of preparation, both groups perceived almost identical levels of preparation, approximating a "moderate" level.

The Leahy et al. studies (2009, 2013), in combination with results from earlier studies, which concluded that clinical supervision is a reactive and infrequent occurrence (English et al., 1979; Herbert & Trusty, 2006; King, 2008; Schultz et al., 2002), suggest that there is a disconnect as students complete their degree programs. Clearly, as counselors-in-training, they are indoctrinated into the clinical supervision process as a function of supervised practicum and internship required in every accredited professional training program. Once they begin their professional careers, however, it seems that counselor supervision is something largely forgotten. If this perception is correct, rehabilitation counselor educators must make greater efforts to instill a sense of lifelong learning in students, with a core commitment to ongoing clinical supervision. This commitment has to be not only for those CRCs interested in counselor licensure who, by state requirement, must document clinical supervision activity (ACA, 2011), but for all rehabilitation counselors. Educators must also assist the many field site supervisors who work as educational partners and play an influential role in the professional development of rehabilitation counselors-in-training in order to further develop their competence as clinical supervisors. In short, clinical supervision needs to be something not only applicable to the initial entry into the profession but continued throughout one's professional career.

## DISCUSSION EXERCISES

1. How has clinical supervision that you have received as part of graduate training or earlier impacted your development as a rehabilitation counselor?
2. What advantages and drawbacks do you perceive between individual and group supervision?
3. How have multicultural aspects been addressed as part of the clinical supervision that you have received thus far in your training? What could be done to further enhance your competence as a multicultural counselor?
4. What are some ethical concerns that you struggle with or anticipate struggling with when you work as a rehabilitation counselor? How might you discuss them in clinical supervision?
5. If you are employed in a setting where little or ineffective clinical supervision is being provided, what could you do to improve this situation?

# REFERENCES

Aasheim, L. (2012). *Practical clinical supervision for counselors: An experiential guide*. New York, NY: Springer Publishing Company.

American Counseling Association (ACA). (2005). *ACA code of ethics*. Alexandria, VA: Author.

American Counseling Association (ACA). (2011). *Who are licensed professional counselors*. Alexandria, VA: Author. Retrieved from http://www.google.com/url?sa=t&rct=j&q=&esrc=s&source=web&cd=6&ved=0CG0QFjAF&url=http%3A%2F%2Fwww.counseling.org%2FPublicPolicy%2FWhoAreLPCs.pdf&ei=0SLaUfCOK5Do0wHluoGwAQ&usg=AFQjCNFpM6XhhHU5OpY1Ta4rpRCDd3ldQQ&bvm=bv.48705608,d.dmQ

Atkinson, D. R., Morten, G., & Sue, D. W. (1998). *Counseling American minorities* (5th ed.). Boston, MA: McGraw-Hill.

Bernard, J. M. (1979). Supervisory training: A discrimination model. *Counselor Education and Supervision, 19*, 60–68.

Bernard, J. M. (1997). The discrimination model. In C. E. Watkins, Jr. (Ed.), *Handbook of psychotherapy supervision* (pp. 310–327). Hoboken, NJ: Wiley.

Bernard, J. M., & Goodyear, R. K. (1998). *Fundamentals of clinical supervision* (2nd ed.). Needham Heights, MA: Allyn & Bacon.

Bernard, J. M., & Goodyear, R. K. (2004). *Fundamentals of clinical supervision* (3rd ed.). Needham Heights, MA: Allyn & Bacon.

Blackwell, T., Strohmer, D. C., Belcas, E. M., & Burton, K. A. (2002). Ethics in rehabilitation counselor supervision. *Rehabilitation Counselor Bulletin, 45*, 240–247.

Borders, L. D. (1992). Learning to think like a supervisor. *Clinical Supervisor, 10*, 135–148.

Borders, L. D. (2005). Snapshot of clinical supervision in counseling and counselor education: A five-year review. *Clinical Supervisor, 24*, 69–113.

Borders, L. D., & Brown, L. L. (2005). *The new handbook of counseling supervision*. Mahwah, NJ: Erlbaum.

Borders, L. D., Welfare, L. E., Greason, P. B., Paladino, D. A., Mobley, A. K., Villalba, J. A., & Wester, K. L. (2012). Individual and triadic and group: Supervisee and supervisor perceptions of each modality. *Counselor Education and Supervision, 51*, 281–295.

Brislin, D. C., & Herbert, J. T. (2009). Clinical supervision for developing counselors. In I. Marini & M. Stebnicki (Eds.), *The professional counselor's desk reference* (pp. 39–48). New York, NY: Springer Publishing Company.

Campbell, J. M. (2006). *Essentials of clinical supervision*. Hoboken, NJ: Wiley.

Cass, V. C. (1979). Homosexual identity formation: A theoretical model. *Journal of Homosexuality, 4*, 219–235.

Chang, C. Y., Hays, D. G., & Shoffner, M. F. (2004). Cross-racial supervision: A developmental approach for white supervisors working with supervisees of color. *Clinical Supervisor, 22*, 121–138.

Commission on Rehabilitation Counselor Certification (CRCC). (2010). *Code of professional ethics for rehabilitation counselors*. Retrieved from http://www.crccertification.com/pages/crc_ccrc_code_of_ethics/10.php

Corey, G., Haynes, R., Moulton, P., & Muratori, M. (2010). *Clinical supervision in the helping professions: A practical guide* (2nd ed.). Alexandria, VA: American Counseling Association.

Cottone, R. R., & Tarvydas, V. M. (2007). *Counseling ethics and decision making* (3rd ed.). Upper Saddle River, NJ: Pearson Prentice Hall.

Council on Rehabilitation Education. (2012). *Accreditation manual for masters level rehabilitation counselor education program*. Schaumburg, IL: Author.

Emener, W. (1991). Empowerment in rehabilitation: An empowerment philosophy for rehabilitation in the 20th century. *Journal of Rehabilitation, 57*, 7–12.

English, W. R., Oberle, J. B., & Byrne, A. R. (1979). Rehabilitation counselor supervision: A national perspective. *Rehabilitation Counseling Bulletin, 22*, 7–123.

Enyedy, K. C., Arcinue, F., Puri, N. N., Carter, J. W., Goodyear, R. K., & Getzelman, M. A. (2003). Hindering phenomena in group supervision: Implications for practice. *Professional Psychology: Research and Practice, 34*, 312–317.

Fall, M., & Sutton, J. M., Jr. (2004). Supervision of entry level licensed counselors. *Clinical Supervisor, 22*, 139–151.

Fitch, T. J., & Marshall, J. L. (2002). Using cognitive interventions with counseling practicum students during group supervision. *Counselor Education and Supervision, 41*, 335–342.

Franklin, L. D. (2011). Reflective supervision for the clinical social worker: Practical applications for the green social worker. *Clinical Supervisor, 30*, 204–214.

Garske, G. G. (1995). Self-reported levels of job satisfaction of vocational rehabilitation professionals: A descriptive study. *Journal of Rehabilitation Administration, 19*, 215–224.

Gillam, S. L., & Crutchfield, L. B. (2001). Collaborative group supervision of practicum students and interns. *Clinical Supervisor, 20*, 49–60.

Gray, S. W., & Smith, M. S. (2009). The influence of diversity in clinical supervision: A framework for reflective conversations and questioning. *Clinical Supervisor, 28*, 155–179.

Greer, J. A. (2003). Where to turn for help. *Clinical Supervisor, 21*, 135–143.

Grigg, G. (2006). Designs and discriminations for clinical group supervision in counseling psychology: An analysis. *Canadian Journal of Counselling, 40*, 110–122.

Hatcher, R., & Lassiter, K. (2007). Initial training in professional psychology: The practicum competencies outline. *Training and Education in Professional Psychology, 1*, 49–63.

Hays, P. A. (2008). *Addressing cultural complexities in practice: Assessment, diagnosis, and therapy* (2nd ed.). Washington, DC: American Psychological Association.

Heckman-Stone, C. (2004). Trainee preferences for feedback and evaluation in clinical supervision. *Clinical Supervisor, 22*, 21–33.

Helms, J. E., & Carter, R. T. (1990). Development of the White racial identity inventory. In J. E. Helms (Ed.), *Black and White racial identity: Theory, research and practice* (pp. 67–80). Westport, CT: Greenwood Press.

Herbert, J. T. (1997). Quality assurance: Administration and supervision. In D. R. Maki & T. F. Riggar (Eds.), *Rehabilitation counseling: Profession and practice* (pp. 246–258). New York, NY: Springer Publishing Company.

Herbert, J. T. (2004a). Clinical supervision in rehabilitation counseling settings. In F. Chan, N. L. Berven, & K. R. Thomas (Eds.), *Counseling theories and techniques for rehabilitation health professionals* (pp. 510–533). New York, NY: Springer Publishing Company.

Herbert, J. T. (2004b). Qualitative analysis of clinical supervision within the public vocational rehabilitation program. *Journal of Rehabilitation Administration, 28*, 51–74.

Herbert, J. T. (2011). Clinical supervision. In D. R. Maki & V. Tarvydas (Eds.), *The professional practice of rehabilitation counseling* (pp. 427–446). New York, NY: Springer Publishing Company.

Herbert, J. T., & Bieschke, K. J. (2000). A didactic course in clinical supervision. *Rehabilitation Education, 14*, 187–198.

Herbert, J. T., Hemlick, L., & Ward, T. J. (1991). Supervisee perception of rehabilitation counseling practica. *Rehabilitation Education, 5*, 121–129.

Herbert, J. T., & Schultz, J. C. (2013). *Training manual for clinical supervision of state vocational rehabilitation supervisors*. Unpublished manuscript, Penn State University, University Park, PA.

Herbert, J. T., & Trusty, J. (2006). Clinical supervision practices and satisfaction within the public vocational rehabilitation program. *Rehabilitation Counseling Bulletin, 49*, 66–80.

Herbert, J. T., & Ward, T. J. (1989). Rehabilitation counselor supervision: A national survey of graduate training practica. *Rehabilitation Education, 3*, 163–175.

Holloway, E. L., & Johnson, R. (1985). Group supervision widely practiced and poorly understood. *Counselor Education and Supervision, 24*, 332–340.

Itzhaky, H. (2001). Factors relating to "interferences" in communication between supervisor and supervisee. *Clinical Supervisor, 20,* 73–85.

King, C. L. (2008). *Rehabilitation counselor supervision in the private sector: An examination of the long term disability system* (Unpublished doctoral dissertation). Boston University, Boston, MA.

Leahy, M. J., Chan, F., Sung, C., & Kim, M. (2013). Empirically derived test specifications for the certified rehabilitation counselor examination. *Rehabilitation Counseling Bulletin, 56,* 199–214.

Leahy, M. J., Muenzen, P., Saunders, J. L., & Strauser, D. (2009). Essential knowledge domains underlying effective rehabilitation counseling practice. *Rehabilitation Counseling Bulletin, 52,* 95–106.

Lee, R. W., & Cashwell, C. S. (2001). Ethical issues in counselor supervision. *Clinical Supervisor, 20,* 91–100.

Livni, D., Crowe, T. P., & Gonsalvez, C. J. (2012). Effects of supervision modality and intensity on alliance and outcomes for the supervisee. *Rehabilitation Psychology, 57,* 178–186.

Mackelprang, R. W., & Salgiver, R. O. (2009). *Disability: A diversity model approach in human service practice* (2nd ed.). Chicago, IL: Lyceum Books.

Maki, D. R., & Delworth, U. (1995). Clinical supervision: A definition and model for the rehabilitation counseling profession. *Rehabilitation Counseling Bulletin, 38,* 282–293.

McCarthy, A. K. (2013). Relationship between supervisory working alliance and client outcomes in state vocational rehabilitation counseling. *Rehabilitation Counseling Bulletin, 57,* 23–30.

Morran, D. K., Stockton, R., Cline, R. J., & Teed, C. (1998). Facilitating feedback exchange in groups: Leader interventions. *Journal of Specialists in Group Work, 23,* 257–258.

Overholser, J. S. (2004). The four pillars of psychotherapy supervision. *Clinical Supervisor, 23,* 1–13.

Pardeck, J. T. (2001). Using the Americans with Disabilities Act (ADA) as a tool for helping social work faculty develop cultural competence in the area of disability. *Clinical Supervisor, 20,* 113–125.

Pfohl, A. H. (2004). The intersection of personal and professional identity. *Clinical Supervisor, 23,* 139–164.

Prieto, L. R. (1996). Group supervision: Still widely practiced but poorly understood. *Counselor Education and Supervision, 35,* 295–307.

Ray, D., & Altekruse, M. (2000). Effectiveness of group supervision versus combined group and individual supervision. *Counselor Education and Supervision, 40,* 19–30.

Roche, A. M., Todd, C. L., & O'Connor, J. (2007). Clinical supervision in the alcohol and other drugs field: An imperative or an option. *Drug and Alcohol Review, 26,* 241–249.

Schaefle, S., Smaby, M. H., Maddux, C. D., & Cates, J. (2005). Counseling skills attainment, retention, and transfer as measured by the skilled counseling scale. *Counselor Education and Supervision, 44,* 281–292.

Schultz, J. C. (2011). Construction and validation of a supervisor principle ethics scale. *Australian Journal of Rehabilitation Counseling, 17*(2), 96–105.

Schultz, J. C., Ososkie, J. N., Fried, J. H., Nelson, R. E., & Bardos, A. N. (2002). Clinical supervision in public rehabilitation counseling settings. *Rehabilitation Counseling Bulletin, 45,* 213–222.

Smith, R. D., Riva, M. T., & Cornish, J. A. E. (2012). The ethical practice of group supervision: A national survey. *Training and Education in Professional Psychology, 6,* 238–248.

Stebnicki, M. A. (1998). Clinical supervision in rehabilitation counseling. *Rehabilitation Education, 12,* 137–159.

Sterner, W. R. (2009). Influence of the supervisory working alliance on supervisee work satisfaction and work-related stress. *Journal of Mental Health Counseling, 31,* 249–263.

Stoltenberg, C., & Delworth, U. (1987). *Supervising counselors and therapists: A developmental approach*. San Francisco, CA: Jossey-Bass.

Stoltenberg, C. D., McNeill, B., & Delworth, U. (1998). *IDM supervision: An integrated developmental model for supervising counselors and therapists*. San Francisco, CA: Jossey-Bass.

Tarvydas, V. M. (1995). Ethics and the practice of rehabilitation counselor supervision. *Rehabilitation Counseling Bulletin, 38*, 294–306.

Watkins, C. E., Jr. (1993). Development of the psychotherapy supervisor: Concepts, assumptions, and hypotheses of the supervisor complexity model. *American Journal of Psychotherapy, 47*, 58–74.

Watkins, C. E., Jr. (1997). The ineffective psychotherapy supervisor: Some reflections about bad behaviors, poor process, and offensive outcomes. *Clinical Supervisor, 16*, 163–180.

Westwood, M. J. (1989). Group supervision for counselors-in-training. *Canadian Journal of Counselling, 23*, 348–353.

Worthington, E. L., Jr. (1987). Changes in supervision as counselors and supervisors gain experience: A review. *Professional Psychology: Research and Practice, 18*, 189–208.

Yagil, D. (2006). The relationship of abusive and supportive workplace supervision to employee burnout and upward influence tactics. *Journal of Emotional Abuse, 6*, 49–65.

# Managing Risk in Professional Practice

*Linda R. Shaw, Abigail Akande, and Jodi Wolff*

## LEARNING OBJECTIVES

The goals of this chapter are to define risk prevention in rehabilitation counseling practice; to identify how professional codes of ethics intersect with the law; to identify action steps that rehabilitation counselors should take when faced with ethical dilemmas; to identify areas of practice, which are "hot spots" for risk-management concerns; to highlight issues related to maintaining and breaching confidentiality; to discuss unique dynamics and liabilities within the counseling relationship; and to identify counselor protections against malpractice. As learning objectives, readers will be able to:

1. Discuss recent trends in rehabilitation counselor liability and risk.
2. Describe the five categories of law relevant to rehabilitation counseling practice and the differences between criminal and civil cases and courts.
3. Articulate the role that consultation plays in risk management.
4. Define what is meant by malpractice and identify four conditions that must exist to prove malpractice in court.
5. Articulate the limitations of confidentiality within the counseling relationship and explain the concept of privileged communication.
6. Discuss variability in mandated reporting laws and how they affect duty to protect.
7. Identify precautionary measures to avoid the blurring of boundaries and/or therapist misconduct in the therapeutic relationship.
8. Understand the role documentation plays in risk management and identify essential components of documentation.

## CREDENTIALING AND RISK MANAGEMENT

As the profession of rehabilitation counseling has evolved, rehabilitation counselors have taken on increasing responsibility and, consequently, have assumed increasing obligations to practice ethically, legally, and professionally. The importance of the roles of the rehabilitation counselor and the special nature of the rehabilitation counseling relationship have increasingly been acknowledged by legal bodies through the inclusion of rehabilitation counselors, as well as other counselors, in licensure and in other functions stipulated by statutory and regulatory bodies (Cottone & Tarvydas, 2003; Tarvydas, Leahy, & Zanskas, 2010). Rehabilitation counselors, as well as other counselors, have fought long and hard to achieve legitimacy through certification and licensure and through recognition by third-party payers as qualified service providers.

Today, rehabilitation counselors in many places possess the legal right to make psychiatric diagnoses, perform evaluations of suicidal intent, initiate involuntary commitments to psychiatric facilities, and engage in a wide range of activities requiring specialized skills and the exercise of sound professional judgment (Backlar & Cutler, 2002). With that hard-won recognition, however, comes increased accountability and liability. Those same statutes and regulations that empower rehabilitation counselors to practice a broad scope of professional activities and to be recognized by third-party payers for the critical services that they provide also stipulate acceptable and nonacceptable behavior. Failure to perform in accordance with legal and professional standards may have serious consequences for all parties involved, including the possibility of punitive and damaging legal and professional consequences for the counselor (Cottone & Tarvydas, 2007; Woody, 2000).

The need for counselors to address risk prevention transcends liability issues, however. When rehabilitation counselors manage risks in their service provision, they manage the risks not only to themselves, in terms of legal liability, but also to their clients. Good risk-management practices decrease the risk of harm and promote the autonomy and well-being of the individuals served by rehabilitation counselors (Cullity, Jackson, & Shaw, 1990; Shaw & Jackson, 1994). The benefits of risk management transcend self-protection and extend to the rehabilitation counselor's clients, specifically referred to in the Commission on Rehabilitation Counselor Certification (CRCC, 2010) *Code of Professional Ethics for Rehabilitation Counselors* as the individuals to whom the rehabilitation counselor has a primary obligation.

Over a decade ago, Vallario and Emener (1991) asserted that rehabilitation counselors need to increase their familiarity with law and legal concepts, citing the potential for malpractice as a major reason. Additionally, numerous experts in both mental health and mental health law have emphasized the need for counselors to become aware of those practices that will mitigate against charges of unethical or illegal practice (Behnke, Winick, & Perez, 2000; Crawford, 1994; Otto, Ogloff, & Small, 1991; Picchioni & Bernstein, 1990; Saunders et al., 2007; Woody, 1988).

## THE LEGAL SYSTEM

Although contact with the legal system may strike fear into the hearts of many counselors, several investigations into the outcomes of such encounters should be reassuring. Otto and Schmidt (1991) maintain that there are few reported court decisions in which clients have claimed successfully that they were harmed by negligently provided counseling or psychotherapy. There is no doubt, however, that knowledge of the legal system and of laws applying to counselors may help mitigate such claims and also may prove helpful, should such claims be filed against them (Corey, Corey, & Callanan, 2011). Behnke et al. (2000) discuss laws within five categories: (a) constitutions, (b) statutes enacted by legislatures, (c) regulations promulgated by boards or agencies, (d) rules of court adopted by the judiciary, and (e) decisions made by the courts.

### Constitutions

Constitutions establish laws affecting the practice of counseling at both the federal and state levels. At both levels, their respective constitutions establish the most important laws. The constitution is often referred to as "supreme" because it establishes the foundation for all other law and is the "touchstone" by which other laws are deemed legitimate or illegitimate.

### Statutes

Statutes enacted by legislatures are written and enacted into law by elected legislatures at both the federal and state levels. At the federal level, the body that creates statutes is the U.S. Congress. At the state level, the elected state legislators create and enact statutes.

### Regulations Promulgated by Boards and Agencies

Regulations promulgated by boards and agencies are not technically laws because they do not emanate from any legislative body. Rather, the legislature delegates boards or commissions to develop regulations. Regulations are rules that interpret statutes and provide greater specificity and definition to the statutes themselves. Regulations do carry the weight of law, however, in that failure to comply with regulations is seen as a failure to comply with the laws from which they originated and which they serve to interpret.

### Rules of Court Adopted by the Judiciary

Rules of court adopted by the judiciary govern the processes and activities of judges and attorneys in judicial proceedings, specifying how things should work. Failure to abide by the rules of court is harmful in that it could result in damaging, or even the dismissal, of legal cases. Understanding rules of court may be very helpful in understanding the legal process, including such concepts as admissibility of evidence, rules of discovery, and other "process" issues.

## Decisions Made by Courts

Decisions made by courts are not technically laws, but because they interpret statutes, regulations, or court rules, they are often collectively referred to as "case law." Such decisions often find their way to the legislature and become integrated into statutes. Even when they do not become statutes, however, case law is legally binding.

Because all states differ in their legal structure, there is no absolute uniform system to which all ascribe. Generally, however, all states have a system that is hierarchical or "tiered." The first level of courts, such as county or circuit courts, try cases initially. The decision of the court may be accepted by both parties and will go no farther within the court system. Decisions made by the lower courts can also be appealed to an appellate court. Finally, the state's supreme court may agree to hear a small minority of cases coming out of the appellate court, with direct relevance to certain criteria established by the state. The federal system is similarly structured, with higher courts able to hear cases decided in the lower courts that have been appealed, with a very small number of cases eventually heard by the U.S. Supreme Court.

All laws may also be classified as either criminal or civil. Criminal law deals with violations of laws promulgated by the state. The state is responsible for charging and prosecuting the case, and a party found to be guilty suffers the punishments stipulated by the state. Such punishments may include loss of liberty, fines, and other penalties. Civil law involves an accusation by one party against another. The trial is an attempt to assign responsibility for harm that has accrued to the wronged party and to provide an appropriate remedy for that harm. Malpractice cases are generally heard in civil court proceedings, and penalties may include both compensatory damages (usually a sum of money that must be paid to compensate the individual for his/her losses) and punitive damages (money paid in order to punish the perpetrator of the harm).

Criminal and civil cases carry a different "standard of proof." Standard of proof is the degree of certainty that must exist in order to prove guilt. In criminal cases, the burden of proof is very high, due to the severity of the potential penalties. Because U.S. society places a high value on personal liberty, the standard is set very high in cases for which a guilty verdict might result in loss of liberty. Consequently, for criminal cases, the state must prove that a defendant is guilty beyond a reasonable doubt. Note that the burden of proof, or the responsibility for proving guilt, rests with the state. Although the accused party usually presents evidence in his or her defense, this is not necessary. Should the state fail to prove guilt beyond reasonable doubt, the defendant could, hypothetically, be found not guilty without presenting any evidence whatsoever. In civil cases, the standard of proof is much lower. In such cases, including most malpractice cases, the standard of proof is referred to as a preponderance of the evidence, meaning that there is more evidence that a party is guilty than not guilty. In civil cases, the burden of proof is on the plaintiff or the party who makes the accusation. Behnke et al. (2000, pp. 58–59) provide a succinct description of the concepts of standard of proof and burden of proof, observing that standard of proof can be thought of as "How high is the hurdle [that has to be jumped to win the case]?" and burden of proof can be thought of as "Which party must jump the hurdle?"

## CODES OF PROFESSIONAL ETHICS

Codes of professional ethics are very relevant to a discussion of legal liability for several reasons. Codes of professional ethics are generally developed by private or professional organizations and reflect the collective opinions of the professionals that the code is intended to govern. They do not carry the weight of law per se, but may be critical in establishing the standard against which a professional who has been charged with negligence or malpractice is judged. For rehabilitation counselors, the *Professional Code of Ethics for Rehabilitation Counselors* (Commission on Rehabilitation Counselor Certification [CRCC], 2010) stipulates the rules for ethical behavior for rehabilitation counselors (www.crccertification. com/filebin/pdf/CRCCodeOfEthics.pdf). Key components of the CRC/CCRC *Code of Ethics* include (a) the counseling relationship; (b) confidentiality, privileged communication, and privacy; (c) advocacy and accessibility; (d) professional responsibility; (e) relationships with other professionals; (f) forensic and indirect services; (f) evaluation, assessment, and interpretation; (g) teaching, supervision, and training; (h) research and publication; (i) technology and distance counseling; (j) business practices; and (k) resolving ethical issues. Other codes of ethics and standards of practice may also help provide greater specificity about some aspect of practice. For example, a rehabilitation counselor engaged in group work might find additional guidance from the Association for Specialists in Group Work (ASGW; Thomas & Pender, 2007) *Best Practice Guidelines*, and all counselors should be familiar with the 2014 American Counseling Association (ACA, 2014) *Code of Ethics*. A listing of websites for codes and standards developed by various associations and groups with relevance to rehabilitation counseling is included in the Appendix.

When states develop regulations, they often look to the professions for guidance about what actions are appropriate or inappropriate, within the context of the activities and responsibilities of an individual engaged in a given profession. Consequently, the boards that develop regulations often use and adapt large portions of the profession's codes of ethics. For licensed professional counselors, the ACA (2014) *Code of Ethics* is most often a basis for licensing regulations.

Ideally, laws at all levels and all relevant codes of ethics would be perfectly in tune with one another. Unfortunately, this is not always the case. Cottone and Tarvydas (2007) stress that counselors may encounter situations requiring them to exercise personal and professional judgments because their legal and professional requirements are inconsistent with one another. Counselors may at times be faced with the choice of acting in a manner that is legal, but not ethical (e.g., complying with a court order to produce information, which a counselor believes will be harmful to a client) or is ethical, but not legal (e.g., uncertainty about complying with a spousal abuse-reporting law out of concern for a client's safety). Such dilemmas are justifiably distressing to counselors and require careful deliberation and action. Recommended actions in this case include the following (Behnke et al., 2000; Cottone & Tarvydas, 2003; Remley, 1996; Rivas-Vasquez, Blais, Gustavo, & Rivas-Vasquez, 2001):

1. Identify the laws, rules, or other forces affecting the counselor's possible actions.
2. Seek legal advice regarding any legal requirements.
3. Seek consultation from supervisors, regulators, professional boards, colleagues, and/or experts, as appropriate.
4. Use appropriate models of ethical decision making to assist in approaching the dilemma in a structured, "clear-headed" manner.
5. Document the process used to reach the decision.

## MALPRACTICE AND NEGLIGENCE

According to Corey et al. (2011, p. 195), malpractice is "the failure to render professional services or to exercise the degree of skill that is ordinarily expected of other professionals in a similar situation." In order to prove malpractice, a preponderance of the evidence presented by the plaintiff must demonstrate that four conditions existed, duty, breach of duty, injury, and causation.

### Duty

For malpractice to occur, it is necessary to demonstrate that a professional relationship was established and that the therapist owed a duty of care to the client.

### Breach of Duty

After the plaintiff proves that a professional relationship did exist, he or she must show that the duty was breached, or that the practitioner failed to provide the appropriate standard of care. The breach of duty may involve either actions taken by the therapist or the failure to take certain precautions.

### Injury

Plaintiffs must prove that they were harmed in some way, either physically or psychologically, and that actual injuries were sustained. Examples of such injuries include wrongful death (suicide), loss (divorce), and pain and suffering.

### Causation

Plaintiffs must demonstrate that a professional's breach of duty was the direct cause of the injury that they suffered. The test in this case lies in proving that the harm would not have occurred if it were not for the practitioner's actions or failure to act.

In establishing the existence of a duty, there are two issues to consider: What is the duty and to whom is the duty owed? The 1976 case, *Tarasoff v. Regents of University of California*, one of the most famous cases in mental health law, directly impacted these two questions and is addressed in some detail later in the chapter.

Proving that breach of duty (sometimes referred to as dereliction of duty) occurred requires the plaintiff to show that the counselor's care was not reasonable. Reasonable care is generally defined as care that is within the standard of practice of an average member of the profession practicing within his or her specialty. Therefore, plaintiffs' attorneys often rely on professional codes and standards, literature from the field, and expert testimony to establish what the standard should have been for reasonable care and to establish that the defendant's care was not reasonable.

It is important to remember that all four criteria must be met in order to establish malpractice. Therefore, even if the duty was clearly established and the defendant clearly breached that duty, malpractice cannot be established unless the breach of duty resulted in some type of injury to the plaintiff and the injury resulted directly from the breach of duty.

## MALPRACTICE "MINEFIELDS"

### Confidentiality and Privilege

Confidentiality is generally considered essential to the counselor–client relationship in that clients need assurance that their sensitive and potentially embarrassing issues will remain with the counselor, with whom they have developed a trusting relationship (Herrick & Brown, 1999; Sperry, 2007). As Shaw and Tarvydas (2001) noted, most clients assume that everything shared with their counselors will remain strictly confidential unless they are explicitly informed otherwise. Consequently, it becomes very important for counselors to become aware of limitations on confidentiality that are externally imposed, by law or by policy.

Most clients will readily understand that some information must be shared with others in order to facilitate treatment. For example, counselors referring clients to physicians for evaluation will want to include any related medical information that they may already have procured, and most clients will readily agree to release the counselor to share such information. Permission should always be obtained in writing and should specify what information is to be released, to whom, and for what purpose. Additionally, the document should specify a time frame for which the permission is granted and provide a place for the client's signature. Many counselors and counseling agencies use preprinted "release of information" forms with blank spaces in which the aforementioned information can be specified.

There are a number of other situations in which information is commonly shared with others. In order to prevent misunderstandings and perceived violations of client trust, it is essential that the counselor review any possible situations in which information or records might be shared with others and secure the client's informed consent. The purpose of informed consent is to protect client autonomy (Miller & Emanuel, 2008). Therefore, it is critical that counselors make every effort to ensure that their clients understand the consenting process, the releasing of information, and any other related areas in which privacy might be breached. Consent forms, release-of-information forms, and other documentation requiring signatures should be written at reading levels that will be comprehensible to clients (Christopher, Foti, Roy-Bujnowski, & Appelbaum, 2007). In addition, forms of this nature should always be explained clearly at the time of signature and available in alternate languages or with translation when necessary.

Fairly routine situations in which consent is sought include clinical supervision; case audits by regulatory bodies; sharing of information among treatment team members; forwarding of reports to third-party payers, such as insurance companies or other funding agencies; and provision of information to parents or guardians when the client is a minor or has a legally appointed guardian (Campbell, 1994; Cobia & Boes, 2000; Cooper, 2000; Guest & Dooley, 1999; Harrison & Hunt, 1999; Plante, 1999; Sullivan, 2002; Tarvydas, 1994). Other possible departures from confidentiality are somewhat less routine, and it is essential that they be discussed and that clients be fully informed about the circumstances in which the counselor might need to violate client confidentiality, so that clients can make fully informed decisions about what to share with the counselor. These less common and more perilous exceptions to confidentiality are discussed in the following text.

### Mandatory Reporting Laws

In most states, there are several types of information that must be reported by counselors. Generally speaking, mandatory reporting laws are designed to protect those members of society who are considered to be particularly vulnerable and unable to protect themselves (Valkyrie, Creamer, & Vaughn, 2008). In these cases, counselors are not allowed the option of independent judgment. If counselors fail to report, they are in violation of state law. The types of information that must be reported vary from state to state. Although the following list is not all inclusive, most states have mandatory laws that require the reporting of at least the following: child abuse, elder abuse, and abuse of individuals with disabilities.

The conditions that must exist before reporting becomes mandatory also vary from state to state. For example, in some states a mere suspicion may be enough to trigger a mandatory report, whereas in others more definitive evidence may be needed. Definitions of abuse, negligence, and abandonment may also vary from state to state, as well as definitions of *child* or other protected classes of people (Renninger, 2002; Small, 2002). Often, counselors who must make mandatory reports are afforded protections against charges of malpractice due to violations of confidentiality; however, such protections may not prevent clients from feeling betrayed when the counselor has failed to warn them that there is some information that they are legally bound to report. Failure to fully inform clients about limitations of confidentiality deprives clients of the right to choose what they may or may not wish to disclose, with full knowledge of the consequences of a particular disclosure.

## Duty to Protect

In all jurisdictions, the law allows counselors to violate confidentiality in situations in which clients are believed to pose a serious risk to themselves or to others. In such situations, the state's obligation to protect others is seen as outweighing the importance of maintaining confidentiality. Several studies have established that most counselors will, over the course of their careers, confront the need to violate confidentiality to protect a client from harming himself or herself (e.g., suicide) or another (e.g., homicide; Weinstein et al., 2000). Counselors in such situations may be faced with the need to take actions that the client will view as harmful, based on uncertain evidence (Jobes & Berman, 1993). The difficulties in predicting dangerousness are well documented (Bednar, Bednar, Lambert, & Waite, 1991; Otto, 1992), and most counselors find that "threats" of suicide or of intentions to harm are rarely, in fact, carried out (Corey et al., 2011). When coupled with the devastating finality of the taking of a life, it is not surprising that suicide emerges as a common issue in many malpractice cases (Baerger, 2001; Szasz, 1986).

Although the law recognizes the difficulties entailed in predicting violent behavior, it also holds counselors accountable for doing so in accordance with the standards established within their professions. Consequently, when a malpractice issue arises in connection with a duty to protect, the key legal issue in establishing negligence often becomes the question as to whether or not the counselor acted reasonably and prudently or in a manner that rises to the standards established within the mental health professions. Courts will examine such evidence as whether the counselor used an accepted procedure for assessing the threat, consulted with others, and took reasonable steps to ensure safety (Fujimura, Weis, & Cochran, 1985; King, 1999; Lewis, 2002; Picchioni & Bernstein, 1990; Pope, 1985; Rivas-Vasquez et al., 2001; Simon, 1999; VandeCreek & Knapp, 2000; Welfel, 1998). In other words, in the absence of the ability to predict dangerousness with a high degree of certainty, the courts are more likely to examine the process used by the counselor to ensure that he or she did at least as well as most counselors would have done in the same situation.

One of the limitations on confidentiality that is, perhaps, the most intimidating and anxiety provoking, is the counselor's responsibility to take steps to prevent harm from coming to the client or to another person or persons when the client has disclosed an intention to commit such an act. The counselor's duty in such a situation was highlighted and expanded, following the outcome of a controversial 1976 malpractice case, *Tarasoff v. Regents of University of California*. In the Tarasoff case, Dr. Lawrence Moore, a psychologist at the University of California–Berkeley Student Health Center, was treating a graduate student named Prosenjit Poddar, who had become obsessed with an undergraduate student, Tatianna Tarasoff. The two students had met each other at a social function for international students and had become friendly. The more serious Poddar became about the relationship, the more distant Tatianna became. Poddar had taped their calls and become consumed with furthering the relationship. Frustrated in his efforts, Poddar reported to Dr. Moore that he intended to kill a girl that he identified only as "Tatianna." Dr. Moore informed Poddar that he would have to report the incident if he persisted in his intention to harm the girl, at which point Poddar discontinued therapy. After consulting with others, Moore wrote a letter to the police department warning them of Poddar's intentions and recommending that Poddar be committed to a psychiatric hospital for observation. The police detained Poddar, but after questioning, they released him. A very short time thereafter, Poddar murdered Tarasoff.

Tarasoff's parents subsequently filed suit against several parties, including Dr. Moore and several colleagues with whom he had consulted, stating that they should have warned Tarasoff that her life was in danger. The defendants in the case argued that Tatianna was not a client and, therefore, the therapists owed her no duty and, consequently, they could not have breached that duty. Additionally, they argued that counselor–client confidentiality prevented the therapist from warning Tarasoff. The court decided otherwise, on several points. First, they determined that a duty may exist when there is a "special relationship" between the parties. The court further decided that, when such a "special relationship" exists, the duty may be extended to a third party where that party is the foreseeable victim of harm perpetrated by the individual with whom the special relationship exists. The court then further defined that duty as "the duty to exercise reasonable care to protect the foreseeable victim of that danger" (Behnke et al., 2000, p. 345).

Behnke et al. (2000) point out that the Tarasoff decision is frequently misinterpreted as a "duty to warn," when in fact it is a "duty to protect." The court also addressed the issue of the therapist's responsibility to explicitly identify the potential victim, noting that although a therapist may not be required to "interrogate his patient to discover the victim's identity…there may be cases in which a moment's reflection will reveal the victim's identity" (Behnke et al., 2000, p. 345). As Behnke et al. observe, this portion of the decision has resulted in many different interpretations regarding the degree to which the therapist must be certain of the identity of the potential victim before a duty to protect exists. Consequently, there is wide variation in state laws regarding this point. Regarding the defense that confidentiality prohibited the therapist from warning Tarasoff, the court clearly stipulated that the privilege of confidentiality is secondary to the therapist's responsibility to prevent foreseeable danger to others.

The negligence case against Dr. Moore was never decided, as the case was settled out of court (i.e., Ms. Tarasoff's family agreed to dismiss the lawsuit in exchange for a financial payment by the defendant). Regardless of the outcome of the civil case, however, the California Supreme Court had adopted the principles regarding duty and the limitations on confidentiality as a rule of law. The case reverberated throughout the mental health community, and one by one, the states adopted "duty" laws, each of which differed somewhat in such issues as the definition of "forseeability," the stipulation of the actions that are required for a therapist to be carrying out his or her "duty" appropriately, and the specificity of the required "threat." The "serious and foreseeable harm" exception is included in the ACA (2014) *Code of Ethics*, as well as those of most other counseling organizations.

Counselors must be aware of the statutes that exist in their specific states regarding "duty" laws. For instance, Barbee, Combs, Eckleberry, and Villalobos (2007) discuss statutes in the state of Texas that are different from the Supreme Court decision in the Tarasoff case, in that no exact directives are specified.

### Privileged Communication

The right of clients to have their communications with their counselors or therapists kept confidential is often referred to as privileged communication or testimonial privilege. The Supreme Court, in its 1996 *Jaffee v. Redmond* decision, expanded confidentiality in therapeutic relationships to include nondoctoral-level therapists. In many states, this right is extended to client–counselor relationships by statute, in recognition of the importance of confidentiality to the trust and freedom to disclose that must occur in therapeutic relationships. As discussed earlier, however, this privilege is not absolute. As mandatory reporting laws and the Tarasoff decision emphasize, the right to confidentiality must be balanced against the right to protect society, particularly individuals who are the most vulnerable. In such cases, the counselor may not be able to protect confidentiality, ethically or legally, and several factors must be considered.

First, it is important to remember that the right to privileged communication is owned by the client, not the counselor. Clients may or may not choose to invoke this right. Should a client choose to waive the right to confidentiality, the counselor may not choose to maintain it. Some examples of occurrences when a client might choose to invoke this right might include situations in which a client shares information about his or her counseling sessions with others, or a client elects to have other parties present at counseling sessions, who then share privileged information with others who were not present (Hendricks et al., 2011).

Second, because there are some situations in which confidentiality cannot be maintained, counselors are obligated to fully inform clients of potential situations in which they may need to break confidentiality. As many researchers have noted, many counselors appear to be somewhat derelict in this responsibility due to concerns about inhibiting client disclosure or other concerns (Berlin, Malin, & Dean, 1991; Shaw, Chan, Lam, & McDougall, 2004; Shaw & Tarvydas, 2001; Steinberg, Levine, & Doueck, 1997; Weinstein et al., 2000; Zellman, 1990).

## Sexual Exploitation

When a counselor enters into a counseling relationship with a client, it is assumed that the counselor's focus should, at all times, be the promotion of the best interests of the client. This value is prominently featured in the counseling codes of ethics and the professional literature (ACA, 2014; CRCC, 2010; Hannold & Young, 2001). This is, in many ways, one of the most unique features of the counseling relationship, in that the relationship is purposely one-sided. The counselor's needs must be deliberately subverted to allow the relationship to focus on client needs. When the relationship between the counselor and client takes on other dimensions (e.g., friend, business partner, or romantic interest), the counselor's needs take on an increased importance in the relationship, too often to the client's detriment.

Nowhere is this seen more graphically than when counselors develop a sexual relationship with a client. Sexual relationships with clients are almost universally viewed as detrimental to the client and to the counseling relationship (Bouhoutsos et al., 1983; Cottone & Tarvydas, 2003; Farnill, 2000; Pope, 1988; Somer, 1999; Somer & Saadon, 1999). Furthermore, they are among the most prevalent and most costly types of malpractice lawsuits brought against mental health professionals (Association of State and Provincial Psychology Boards, 2001; Reaves, 1999). Nevertheless, in a review of surveys on the topic, Fisher (2004) found that 70% to 90% of therapists reported feelings of attraction toward a client at some point in their careers.

Such relationships are exploitive, almost by definition. In order to avoid the ethical and legal devastation of such relationships, to both counselor and client, counselors must be extrasensitive to signs of sexual attraction, both in themselves and in their clients. They must carefully manage their own feelings of attraction toward a client, which are certainly natural and common (Bernsen, Tabachnick, & Pope, 1994; Nickell, Hecker, Ray, & Bercik, 1995; Pope, Kieth-Speigel, & Tabachnick, 2006; Pope, Tabachnick, & Keith-Spiegel, 1987; Stake & Oliver, 1991). However, the counselor should be alerted to his or her feelings about the client and carefully self-monitor his or her own emotions and behavior. Some clients may be particularly vulnerable to therapist misconduct when they have a history of sexual or physical abuse, posttraumatic stress disorder, or promiscuous behavior (Pope, 1988).

Counselors are well advised to take precautionary measures, particularly with "high-risk" clients, both to set an atmosphere of therapeutic work rather than social or personal pleasure and to establish a pattern of prudent behavior in this regard. Simple, yet effective, precautions might include not seeing clients after hours when they are likely to be alone, taping sessions (with client consent), and not attending to clients outside of the usual and customary place where meetings typically occur. Also, the prevalence of such attractions warrants more proactive measures to assist counselors before they find themselves in these types of situations, such as ongoing training, the establishment of safe environments in which they can comfortably talk about such issues, and the conduct of additional research (Pope et al., 2006).

Counselors should address transference issues as they arise, and establish clear boundaries for the relationship. The use of touch between counselor and client may be therapeutic, but also may be misunderstood or misinterpreted, both by the client and later by the court, should a liability situation arise. Counselors who make use of touch in their counseling interactions should do so cautiously and carefully. When uncertain about the nature of a counselor's feelings toward a client, a consultation is strongly advised. The dynamic of culture should also be considered, as individual customs and practices can potentially play a role in how different feelings, such as attraction, respect, or simple gratitude, are expressed (e.g., touch, tone of voice, or eye contact) and received between counselor and client (Harding, 2007; Kleinsmith, De Silva, & Bianchi-Berthouze, 2006; Pentland, 2004).

It is also important to note that in some states, and in many codes of ethics, there is a presumption that the counseling relationship does not automatically end when the counselor and client have discontinued their treatment or service provision relationship. Many statutes and codes of ethics require mental health professionals to refrain from any sexual involvement with former clients for a specified period of time, which varies among statutes and codes. Because the client's vulnerability to exploitation is not likely to automatically disappear upon termination of the counseling relationship, careful consideration prior to initiating such a relationship is recommended, even if legally permissible (Herlihy & Corey, 1997).

### Other Liability Issues

Beyond violations of confidentiality and sexual exploitation, there are many other risk-management issues for counselors. Other issues that frequently give rise to charges of illegal and unethical behavior include inappropriate financial exploitation, failure to report the unethical behavior of others, legal risks associated with supervision and administration, and failure to provide appropriate care, among others (American Psychological Association [APA], 2002; Bednar et al., 1991; Bernstein & Hartsell, 2000; Campbell, 1994; Otto & Schmidt, 1991; Smith, 1996; Vallario & Emener, 1991; Woody, 2000). Although this chapter cannot address all of the issues relevant to each of these topics in detail, there are some general precautions that will help to prevent and to defend against charges of malpractice that apply to all of these areas of potential liability.

### PROTECTIONS AGAINST MALPRACTICE

There is a substantial body of literature within the mental health disciplines that suggests methods and practices that can both prevent and defend against charges of malpractice. The following suggestions are a compilation of recommendations derived from multiple sources (APA, 2002; Bednar et al., 1991; Behnke et al., 2000; Bernstein & Hartsell, 2000; Campbell, 1994; Doverspike, 1999; Montgomery, 1999; Otto & Schmidt, 1991; Smith, 1996; Vallario & Emener, 1991; Woody, 2000)

### Abide by the Law of No Surprises

Behnke et al. (2000) use this term to describe the importance of thoroughly informing one's client *in advance* about all of the potential information necessary for fully informed consent, as well as any other information that the client may need in order to thoroughly understand the counseling experience. Shaw, Chan, Lam, and McDougall (2004) suggest that rehabilitation counselors should engage in a thorough process of written and verbal professional disclosure. Shaw and Tarvydas (2001, p. 40) assert that the disclosure should consist of "all of the pertinent facts and considerations relevant to decisions that need to be made during the provision of services." These include, at a minimum:

1. Information about the procedures and duration of counseling
2. Limitations on confidentiality
3. Client's right to make complaints and/or discontinue services
4. Logistics of counseling (making and canceling appointments, etc.)
5. What to do in an emergency
6. Policies and procedures regarding fees (Tarvydas, 2001, pp. 40–41)

Shaw et al. (2004) listed many other potential items for possible disclosure and stressed the importance of tailoring the professional disclosure process to the setting and clients for which it is intended.

### Know Your Legal and Ethical Responsibilities

Rehabilitation counselors should become thoroughly familiar with the codes of ethics that apply to their profession and to their practice. Additionally, they must become thoroughly familiar with their legally mandated responsibilities and structure their policies, procedures, and practices in such a manner as to facilitate compliance with legal requirements (Hennessey, Rumrill, Roessler, & Cook, 2006). When in doubt, or at any point when a counselor may feel unsure or uncomfortable about potential liability, he or she should not hesitate to consult a lawyer experienced in mental health law for clarification of legal obligations. Counselors concerned with charges of malpractice or unethical behavior should remember that attorneys hired to represent the agencies that employ them may or may not have their personal best interests at heart. At times, the counselor's best interests may conflict with those of the employing organization. Additionally, the CRCC Ethics Committee will address questions of a general nature, submitted in writing, and will issue advisory opinions about any aspect of ethical behavior on the part of rehabilitation counselors.

### Consult

Consultations are invaluable in helping counselors to sort through the complexities of ethical and legal quagmires that can occur in counseling. Often, counselors are too intimately involved to see a situation with complete clarity or may lack information essential to developing the best response to ethical and legal challenges. Consultation allows counselors to "reality test" and to obtain a perspective different from their own. Consultations also serve as a critical element in managing the risks associated with difficult ethical decisions. Because the legal standard is based on the degree to which the profession views an action or care as "reasonable," it is critical for counselors to consult with members of that profession about their beliefs regarding the "reasonableness" of any action.

Consultations demonstrate that counselors understood the seriousness of a given situation, afforded the matter due care and consideration, and reached out to the professional community to help make the best decision possible. Consultation is also a valuable hedge against charges of exploitation, as few counselors who are purposely exploiting their clients would voluntarily bring this to the attention of others within their profession. Supervision, which consists of obtaining guidance from a boss or supervisor, has a similar effect, with the added element of shared liability, because the supervisor is accountable for the work that he or she supervises.

### Document

As mentioned earlier, when defending against charges of malpractice, the process is often considered just as important as the action taken. The counselor's documentation is proof that a careful process of deliberation was followed (Barnett, 1999). Counselors should document the facts surrounding the issue in question; the actions taken to determine the best course of action, including supervision, consultation, and fact-finding; and the results and follow-up activities associated with the incident. Notes should be clear, detailed yet succinct, and dated and signed. The notes should be objective, consisting of direct quotes and statements of fact to the greatest possible extent. Opinions, diagnoses, and hypotheses should be avoided. Cross-outs, erasures, and backdating are viewed as suspect and should always be avoided (Barnett, 1999; Mitchell, 2007).

The dangers of insufficient or poor documentation are summed up in the phrase, "If it isn't documented, it didn't happen." Often, lawsuits occur months or even years after an incident occurred. The court is much more likely to put greater stock in a case note made at the time of the incident than in a counselor's vague recollections years later, after an accusation has been levied. Remley and Herlihy (2001) offer an excellent set of guidelines for self-protective documentation that emphasizes the appropriate timing, content, and disposition of case notes.

### Insure Against Malpractice

Regardless of how careful or knowledgeable counselors may be, they can have legal or ethical complaints filed against them at any time. Sometimes malpractice charges result from misinformation or misunderstanding and are relatively quickly resolved, but they may also result in a lengthy and expensive legal process. Even when the counselor has acted appropriately in every way, a suit can still be filed and the counselor may have to expend considerable time and money, not to mention anxiety, to address the charges.

Counselors should carefully consider whether they have the resources to help themselves through this process. Malpractice insurance is considered essential, by most practicing counselors, to adequate self-protection. The amount and cost of malpractice insurance will vary, depending on the type of practice, volume of clients seen, and the extent to which a counselor is already covered by some type of corporate liability insurance. Most professional associations provide linkages and discounts to insurers who can issue malpractice insurance to practitioners and students completing practicum or internship requirements.

## CONCLUSIONS

As rehabilitation counselors have expanded their visibility, professional presence, and scope of practice, their liability risk has also increased. Counselors should continually educate themselves regarding legal and ethical guidelines and responsibilities. Ethical and legal practice benefits everyone involved in the counseling relationship. Consequently, rehabilitation counselors should continually seek to enhance their understanding of this important aspect of practice.

## DISCUSSION EXERCISES

1. What thoughts and emotions come to mind when you consider risk management within your own practice as a counselor?
2. Can you think of reasons why some counselors might be hesitant to tell a client about the limitations of confidentiality at the beginning of a session? What are the dangers of waiting to disclose limitations on confidentiality?
3. Who do you currently know or know of who could serve as a consultant regarding ethical dilemmas in your field of practice and/or internships? Do you feel comfortable seeking consultation and, if not, why not?
4. Consenting procedures are typically standardized within agencies. Describe the consenting process where you work and how it might be improved to inform clients more effectively.
5. How might client cultural diversity play a role in (a) consenting, (b) privileged communication, and (c) intimacy within the counseling relationship?

## REFERENCES

American Counseling Association (ACA). (2014). *Code of ethics.* Alexandria, VA: Author.

American Psychological Association (APA). (2002). Report of the Ethics Committee. *American Psychologist, 57,* 646–653.

Association of State and Provincial Psychology Boards. (2001). *Ethics, law and avoiding liability in the practice of psychology.* Montgomery, AL: Author.

Backlar, P., & Cutler, D. L. (Eds.). (2002). *Ethics in community mental health care: Commonplace concerns.* New York, NY: Kluwer Academic/Human Sciences Press.

Baerger, D. R. (2001). Risk management with the suicidal patient: Lessons from case law. *Professional Psychology: Research & Practice, 32,* 359–366.

Barbee, P. W., Combs, D. C., Ekleberry, F., & Villalobos, S. (2007). Duty to warn and protect: Not in Texas. *Journal of Professional Counseling: Practice, Theory & Research, 35,* 18–25.

Barnett, J. E. (1999). Recordkeeping: Clinical, ethical, and risk management issues. In L. VandeCreek & T. L. Jackson (Eds.), *Innovations in clinical practice: A source book* (Vol. 17, pp. 237–254). Sarasota, FL: Professional Resource Press.

Bednar, R. L., Bednar, S. C., Lambert, M. J., & Waite, D. R. (1991). *Psychotherapy with high-risk clients: Legal and professional standards.* Pacific Grove, CA: Brooks/Cole.

Behnke, S. H., Winick, B. J., & Perez, A. M. (2000). *The essentials of Florida mental health law.* New York, NY: Norton.

Berlin, F. S., Malin, M., & Dean, S. (1991). Effects of statutes requiring psychiatrists to report suspected sexual abuse of children. *American Journal of Psychiatry, 148,* 449–453.

Bernsen, A., Tabachnick, B. G., & Pope, K. S. (1994). National survey of social workers' sexual attraction to their clients: Results, implications and comparison to psychologists. *Ethics and Behavior, 4,* 369–388.

Bernstein, B. E., & Hartsell, T. L., Jr. (2000). *The portable ethicist for mental health professionals: An A-Z guide to responsible practice.* New York, NY: Wiley.

Bouhoutsos, J., Holroyd, J., Lerman, H., Forer, B., & Greenberg, M. (1983). Sexual intimacy between psychologists and patients. *Professional Psychology, 14,* 185–196.

Campbell, T. W. (1994). Psychotherapy and malpractice exposure. *American Journal of Forensic Psychology, 12,* 4–41.

Christopher, P., Foti, M. E., Roy-Bujnowski, K., & Appelbaum, P. (2007). Consent form readability and educational levels of potential participants in mental health research. *Psychiatric Services, 58,* 227–232.

Cobia, D. C., & Boes, S. R. (2000). Professional disclosure statements and formal plans for supervision: Two strategies for minimizing the risk of ethical conflicts in post-master's supervision. *Journal of Counseling & Development, 78,* 293–296.

Commission on Rehabilitation Counselor Certification (CRCC). (2010). *The CRCC desk reference on professional ethics: A guide for rehabilitation counselors.* Athens, GA: Elliott & Fitzpatrick.

Cooper, C. C. (2000). Ethical issues with managed care: Challenges facing counseling psychology. *Counseling Psychologist, 28,* 179–236.

Corey, G., Corey, M. S., & Callanan, P. (2011). *Issues and ethics in the helping professions* (8th ed.). Pacific Grove, CA: Brooks/Cole.

Cottone, R. R., & Tarvydas, V. M. (2003). *Ethical and professional issues in counseling* (2nd ed.). Upper Saddle River, NJ: Prentice Hall.

Cottone, R. R., & Tarvydas, V. M. (2007). *Counseling ethics and decision making* (3rd ed.). Upper Saddle River, NJ: Merrill/Prentice Hall.

Crawford, R. L. (1994). *Avoiding counselor malpractice.* Alexandria, VA: American Counseling Association.

Cullity, L. P., Jackson, J. D., & Shaw, L. R. (1990). Community skills training. In B. T. McMahon & L.R. Shaw (Eds.), *Work worth doing: Advances in brain injury rehabilitation.* Orlando, FL: PMD Press.

Doverspike, W. F. (1999). Ethical risk management: Protecting your practice. In L. VandeCreek & T. L. Jackson (Eds.), *Innovations in clinical practice: A source book* (Vol. 17, pp. 269–278). Sarasota, FL: Professional Resource Press.

Farnill, D. (2000). Sexual relationships with former patients: Prevalence, harm, and professional issues. *Australian Journal of Clinical and Experimental Hypnosis, 28,* 42–60.

Fisher, C. D. (2004). Ethical issues in therapy. *Ethics and Behavior, 14,* 105–121.

Fujimura, L. E., Weiss, D. M., & Cochran, J. R. (1985). Suicide: Dynamics and implications for counseling. *Journal of Counseling and Development, 63,* 612–615.

Guest, G. L., Jr., & Dooley, K. (1999). Supervisor malpractice: Liability to the supervisee in clinical supervision. *Counselor Education and Supervision, 38,* 269–279.

Hannold, E., & Young, M. E. (2001). Consumer perspectives on the revised Code of Professional Ethics for Rehabilitation Counselors. *Journal of Applied Rehabilitation Counseling, 32*, 5–9.

Harding, D. J. (2007). Cultural context, sexual behavior, and romantic relationships in disadvantaged neighborhoods. *American Sociological Review, 72*, 341–364.

Harrison, L., & Hunt, B. (1999). Adolescent involvement in the medical decision making process. *Journal of Applied Rehabilitation Counseling, 30*, 3–9.

Hendricks, B., Bradley, L. J., Southern, S., Oliver, M., & Birdsall, B. (2011). Ethical code for the International Association of Marriage and Family Counselors. *Family Journal, 19*, 217–224.

Hennessey, M. L., Rumrill, P. D., Roessler, R. T., & Cook, B. G. (2006). Career development needs among college and university students with learning disabilities and attention deficit disorder/attention deficit hyperactivity disorder. *Learning-Disabilities Multidisciplinary Journal, 14*, 57.

Herlihy, B., & Corey, G. (1997). Codes of ethics as catalysts for improving practice. In *Ethics in therapy. The Hatherleigh Guides series* (Vol. 10, pp. 37–56). New York, NY: Hatherleigh.

Herrick, C., & Brown, H. N. (1999). Mental disorders and syndromes found among Asians residing in the United States. *Issues in Mental Health Nursing, 20*, 275–296.

Jaffee v. Redmond, 51 F.3d 1346, 1358, 116 S. Ct. 334 (1996).

Jobes, D. A., & Berman, A. L. (1993). Suicide and malpractice liability: Assessing and revising policies, procedures, and practice in outpatient settings. *Professional Psychology: Research & Practice, 24*, 91–99.

King, A. (1999). Toward a standard of care for treating suicidal outpatients: A survey of social workers' beliefs about appropriate treatment behaviors. *Suicide and Life-Threatening Behavior, 29*, 347–352.

Kleinsmith, A., De Silva, P. R., & Bianchi-Berthouze, N. (2006). Cross-cultural differences in recognizing affect from body posture. *Interacting with Computers, 18*, 1371–1389.

Lewis, B. L. (2002). Second thoughts about documenting the psychological consultation. *Professional Psychology: Research & Practice, 33*, 224–225.

Miller, F. G., & Emanuel, E. J. (2008). Quality-improvement research and informed consent. *New England Journal of Medicine, 358*, 765–767.

Mitchell, R. (2007). *Documentation in counseling records* (3rd ed.). Alexandria, VA: American Counseling Association.

Montgomery, L. M. (1999). Complaints, malpractice, and risk management: Professional issues and personal experiences. *Professional Psychology: Research & Practice, 30*, 402–410.

Nickell, N. J., Hecker, L. L., Ray, R. E., & Bercik, J. (1995). Marriage and family therapists' sexual attraction to clients: An exploratory study. *American Journal of Family Therapy, 23*, 315–327.

Otto, R. (1992). The prediction of dangerous behavior: A review and analysis of "second generation" research. *Forensic Reports, 5*, 103–133.

Otto, R. K., Ogloff, J. R., & Small, M. A. (1991). Confidentiality and informed consent in psychotherapy: Clinicians' knowledge and practices in Florida and Nebraska. *Forensic Reports, 4*, 379–389.

Otto, R. K., & Schmidt, W. C. (1991). Malpractice in verbal psychotherapy: Problems and potential solutions. *Forensic Reports, 4*, 309–336.

Pentland, A. (2004, October). Social dynamics: Signals and behavior. In *International Conference on Developmental Learning* (Vol. 5). San Diego, CA: Salk Institute.

Picchioni, T., & Bernstein, B. (1990). Risk management for mental health counselors. *Texas Association for Counseling and Development Journal, 18*, 3–19.

Plante, T. G. (1999). Ten strategies for psychology trainees and practicing psychologists interested in avoiding ethical and legal perils. *Psychotherapy: Theory, Research, Practice, and Training, 36*, 398–403.

Pope, K. S. (1985). The suicidal client: Guidelines for assessment and treatment. *California State Psychologist, 20,* 3–7.

Pope, K. S. (1988). How clients are harmed by sexual contact with mental health professionals: The syndrome and its prevalence. *Journal of Counseling and Development, 67,* 222–226.

Pope, K. S., Keith-Spiegel, P., & Tabachnick, B. G. (2006). Sexual attraction to clients: The human therapist and the (sometimes) inhuman training system. *American Psychologist, 41,* 147–148.

Pope, K. S., Tabachnick, B. G., & Keith-Spiegel, P. S. (1987). Ethics of practice: The beliefs and behaviors of psychologists as therapists. *American Psychologist, 42,* 993–1006.

Reaves, R. P. (1999). *Avoiding liability in mental health practice.* Montgomery, AL: Association of State and Provincial Psychology Boards.

Remley, T. P., Jr. (1996). Counseling records: Legal and ethical issues. In B. Herlihy & L. Golden (Eds.), *ACA ethical standards casebook* (4th ed., pp. 162–169). Alexandria, VA: American Counseling Association.

Remley, T. P., Jr., & Herlihy, B. (2001). *Ethical, legal, and professional issues in counseling.* Upper Saddle River, NJ: Prentice Hall.

Renninger, S. M. (2002). Psychologists' knowledge, opinions, and decision-making processes regarding child abuse and neglect reporting laws. *Professional Psychology: Research and Practice, 33,* 19–23.

Rivas-Vazquez, R., Blais, M. A., Gustavo, J., & Rivas-Vasquez, A. A. (2001). A brief reminder about documenting the psychological consultation. *Professional Psychology: Research and Practice, 32,* 194–199.

Saunders, J. L., Barros-Bailey, M., Rudman, R., Dew, D. W., & Garcia, J. (2007). Ethical complaints and violations in rehabilitation counseling: An analysis of Commission on Rehabilitation Counselor Certification data. *Rehabilitation Counseling Bulletin, 52,* 7–13.

Shaw, L. R., Chan, F., Lam, C., & McDougall, G. (2004). Professional disclosure practices of rehabilitation counselors. *Rehabilitation Counseling Bulletin, 48,* 38–50.

Shaw, L. R., & Jackson, J. D. (1994). The dilemma of empowerment in brain injury rehabilitation. In B. T. McMahon & R. W. Evans (Eds.), *The shortest distance: The pursuit of independence for persons with acquired brain injury.* Orlando, FL: PMD Press.

Shaw, L. R., & Tarvydas, V. M. (2001). The use of professional disclosure in rehabilitation counseling. *Rehabilitation Counseling Bulletin, 45,* 40–47.

Simon, R. I. (1999). The suicide prevention contract: Clinical, legal, and risk management. *Journal of the American Academy of Psychiatry and the Law, 27,* 445–450.

Small, M. A. (2002). Liability issues in child abuse and neglect reporting statutes. *Professional Psychology: Research and Practice, 33,* 13–18.

Smith, S. R. (1996). Malpractice liability of mental health professionals and institutions. In B. D. Sales & D. W. Shuman (Eds.), *Law, mental health, and mental disorder* (pp. 76–98). Pacific Grove, CA: Brooks/Cole.

Somer, E. (1999). Therapist-client sex: Clients' retrospective reports. *Professional Psychology: Research and Practice, 30,* 504–509.

Somer, E., & Saadon, M. (1999). Therapist-client sex: Clients' retrospective reports. *Professional Psychology: Research and Practice, 30,* 504–509.

Sperry, L. (2007). *The ethical and professional practice of counseling and psychotherapy.* Boston, MA: Pearson.

Stake, J. E., & Oliver, J. (1991). Sexual contact and touching between therapist and client: A survey of psychologists' attitudes and behavior. *Professional Psychology: Research and Practice, 22,* 297–307.

Steinberg, K. L., Levine, M., & Doueck, H. J. (1997). Effects of legally mandated child abuse reports on the therapeutic relationship: A survey of psychotherapists. *American Journal of Orthopsychiatry, 38,* 112–122.

Sullivan, J. R. (2002). Factors contributing to breaking confidentiality with adolescent clients: A survey of pediatric psychologists. *Professional Psychology: Research and Practice, 33,* 396–401.

Szasz, T. (1986). The case against suicide prevention. *American Psychologist, 41,* 806–812.

Tarasoff v. Regents of University of California, 529 P.2d 553, 118 Cal. Rptr. 129 (1974), *vacated,* 17 Cal. 3d 425, 551 P.2d 334, 131 Cal. Rptr. 14 (1976).

Tarvydas, V. M. (1994). Ethics and the practice of rehabilitation counselor supervision. *Rehabilitation Counseling Bulletin, 38,* 294–306.

Tarvydas, V., Leahy, M. J., & Zanskas, S. A. (2010). Judgment deferred: Reappraisal of rehabilitation counseling movement toward licensure parity. *Rehabilitation Counseling Bulletin, 52,* 85–94.

Thomas, R. G., & Pender, D. A. (2007). Association for Specialists in Group Work: Best practice guidelines 2007 revisions. *Journal for Specialists in Group Work, 33,* 111–117.

Valkyrie, K. T., Creamer, D. A., & Vaughn, L. (2008). Mandatory reporting and school counselors: Reporting laws, obstacles, and solutions. *Alabama Counseling Association Journal, 34*(1), 18–33.

Vallario, J. P., & Emener, W. G. (1991). Rehabilitation counseling and the law: Critical considerations of confidentiality and privilege, malpractice, and forensics. *Journal of Applied Rehabilitation Counseling, 22,* 7–14.

VandeCreek, L., & Knapp, S. (2000). Risk management and life-threatening patient behaviors. *Journal of Clinical Psychology, 56,* 1335–1351.

Weinstein, B., Levine, M., Kogan, N., Harkavy-Friedman, J., & Miller, J. M. (2000). Mental health professionals' experiences reporting suspected child abuse and maltreatment. *Child Abuse and Neglect, 24,* 1317–1328.

Welfel, E. R. (1998). *Ethics in counseling and psychotherapy: Standards, research, and emerging issues.* Pacific Grove, CA: Brooks/Cole.

Woody, R. H. (1988). *Fifty ways to avoid malpractice: A guidebook for mental health professionals.* Sarasota, FL: Professional Resource Exchange.

Woody, R. H. (2000). Professional ethics, regulatory licensing, and malpractice complaints. In F. W. Kaslow (Ed.), *Handbook of couple and family forensics: A sourcebook for mental health and legal professionals.* New York, NY: Wiley.

Zellman, G. L. (1990). Child abuse reporting and failure to report among mandated reporters: Prevalence, incidence and reasons. *Journal of Interpersonal Violence, 5,* 3–22.

# Appendix

American Academy of Forensic Psychology: Specialty Guidelines

American Academy of Psychiatry & Law: Ethical Guidelines for the Practice of Forensic Psychiatry

American Association for Marriage and Family Therapy: Code of Ethics

American Association of Christian Counselors: Code of Ethics

American Association of Pastoral Counselors: Code of Ethics

American Association of Sexuality Educators Counselors and Therapists: Code of Ethics

American Board of Examiners in Clinical Social Work: Code of Ethics

American College Personnel Association: Statement of Ethical Principles and Standards

American Counseling Association: Code of Ethics and Standards of Practice

American Group Therapy Association: Guidelines for Ethics

American Medical Association: Principles of Medical Ethics

American Psychiatric Association: The Principles of Medical Ethics with Annotations Especially Applicable to Psychiatry

American Psychoanalytic Association: Principles and Standards of Ethics for Psychoanalysts

American Psychological Association: Ethical Principles of Psychologists and Code of Conduct

American Society of Clinical Hypnosis: Code of Ethics

Association for Addiction Professionals: Ethical Standards

Association for Assessment in Counseling: Multicultural Assessment Standards

Association for Family Therapy & Systematic Practice in the U.K.:
Code of Ethics & Practice

Association for the Treatment of Sexual Abusers: Professional Code of Ethics

Association of Marital & Family Therapy: Model Code of Ethics for Marriage &
Family Therapists

Australian Association of Social Workers: Code of Ethics

Australian Psychological Society: Code of Ethics

British Columbia Association of Clinical Counselors: Code of Ethical Conduct

British Psychological Society: Code of Conduct, Ethical Principles & Guidelines

California Association of Marriage and Family Therapists: Ethical Standards

Canadian Psychological Association: Canadian Code of Ethics for Psychologists

Canadian Traumatic Stress Network: Ethical Principles

Christian Association for Psychological Studies: Ethical Guidelines

Clinical Social Work Federation: Code of Ethics

Commission on Rehabilitation Counselor Certification: Code of Professional
Ethics

European Association for Body Psychotherapy: Ethical Guidelines & Code

Feminist Therapy Institute: Code of Ethics

International Society of Mental Health Online: Suggested Principles for the
Online Provision of Mental Health Services

Irish Association for Counselling & Therapy: Code of Ethics & Practice

Joint Committee on Testing Practices: Code of Fair Testing Practices in Education

Mental Health Patient's Bill of Rights

National Academies of Practice

National Association of Alcoholism and Drug Abuse Counselors:
Ethical Standards

National Association of School Counselors: Professional Conduct Manual—
Principles for Professional Ethics

National Association of School Psychologists: Principles for Professional Ethics

National Association of Social Workers: Code of Ethics

National Board for Certified Counselors: Code of Ethics

National Career Development Association: Ethical Standards

National Council for Hypnotherapy: Code of Ethics & Conduct

Spiritual Directors International: Guidelines for Ethical Conduct

*Source*: www.kspope.com/ethicscodes.html

# Index